CONGRESS VOLUME

CAMBRIDGE 1995

SUPPLEMENTS

TO

VETUS TESTAMENTUM

VOLUME LXVI

CONGRESS VOLUME

CAMBRIDGE
1995

EDITED BY

J.A. EMERTON

BRILL
LEIDEN · NEW YORK · KÖLN
1997

This book is printed on acid-free paper.

Library of Congress Cataloging-in-Publication Data

Congress volume : Cambridge, 1995 / edited by John A. Emerton.
p. cm. — (Supplements to Vetus Testamentum, ISSN 0083–5889 ; v. 66)
English, French, and German.
Papers given by invitation at the Congress of the International Organization for the Study of the Old Testament, held July 1995 at Cambridge (England).
ISBN 9004106871 (cloth : alk. paper)
1. Bible. O.T.—Criticism, interpretation, etc.—Congresses. I. Emerton, John Adney. II. International Organization for the Study of the Old Testament. Congress (15th : 1995 : Cambridge (England). III. Series.
BS410.V452 vol. 66
[BS1171.2]
221.6—dc21 96–46665
CIP

Die Deutsche Bibliothek – CIP-Einheitsaufnahme

[Vetus testamentum / Supplements]
Supplements to Vetus testamentum. - Leiden ; New York ; Köln : Brill.
Früher Schriftenreihe
Reihe Supplements zu: Vetus Testamentum
ISSN 0083-5889
NE: HST
Vol. 66. International Organization for the Study of the Old Testament: Congress volume .../[International Organization for the Study of the Old Testament].
1995. Cambridge 1995. - 1996

International Organization for the Study of the Old Testament:
Congress volume.../ [International Organization for the Study of the Old Testament]. - Leiden ; New York Köln : Brill.
(Supplements to Vetus testamentum ; ...)
NE: Congress volume ...
1995. Cambridge 1995 / ed. by John A. Emerton. - 1996
(Supplements to Vetus Testamentum ; Vol. 66)
ISBN 90-04-10687-1
NE: Emerton, John A. (Hrsg.)

ISSN 0083-5889
ISBN 90 04 10687 1

PRINTED IN THE NETHERLANDS

CONTENTS

PREFACE

The Fifteenth Congress of the International Organization for the Study of the Old Testament was held in Cambridge 15–21 July 1995. All who attended are grateful to Dr G.I. Davies, the Secretary of the Congress, for the efficient way in which everything was organized. We are also grateful to the University of Cambridge, especially the Faculty Boards of Divinity and Oriental Studies, for their support for the Congress, and to St John's College for its financial and other help. I shall always remember the banquet in my own College hall on the last evening of the Congress when the College kitchen served an excellent dinner and the Gentlemen of St John's sang to us after the meal.

In editing this volume I am grateful to Mr Jaap Oppedijk, who did preliminary work on the typescripts and on the proofs, and to Mr L.K. Tiffany, the Librarian of the Computer Laboratory of Cambridge University, for help in verifying some bibliographical references.

J.A. Emerton

COMPARATIVE SEMITIC PHILOLOGY AND HEBREW LEXICOGRAPHY[1]

by

J.A. EMERTON
Cambridge

Controversy is not something new to the study of the Classical Hebrew language or the translation and exegesis of the Old Testament. It would be difficult to find any subject in those areas of study that has not been a matter of dispute. In this article, however, I shall focus attention on just one subject that is a matter of controversy at the present time: the use of Semitic languages other than Hebrew in Classical Hebrew lexicography.

It has long been customary in lexicons of Biblical Hebrew to compare cognates in other Semitic languages. The practice is continued in such important works as the *Hebräisches und aramäisches Lexikon zum Alten Testament*, begun by Walter Baumgartner and completed under the editorship of J.J. Stamm. It is also found in the current edition by Herbert Donner of the lexicon begun long ago by Wilhelm Gesenius. Yet this familiar aspect of Classical Hebrew dictionaries has recently been challenged—challenged by omission and also by explicit argument.

The Spanish dictionary of Biblical Hebrew, edited by Luis Alonso Schökel, which started to appear in 1990, does not record cognates. Nor does the *Dictionary of Classical Hebrew*, edited by David Clines in Sheffield, of which the first two volumes have been published. In his introduction to volume 1, Clines has given reasons why comparative material has not been included. This is plainly a live issue in current Classical Hebrew lexicography.

Readers will, I hope, bear with me when I mention that there is a personal aspect to this controversy as far as I am concerned—personal and, indeed, autobiographical. I was a pupil of G.R. Driver—later Sir

---

[1] This expanded version of the Presidential address at the Congress also served as the basis of a lecture to the Israel Academy of Sciences and Humanities on 3 June 1996.

Godfrey Driver—the Professor of Semitic Philology at Oxford University. In my first term at Oxford, I heard him read a fascinating paper about new ideas for the translation of the Hebrew Bible, new ideas that were later to appear in the *New English Bible*. Three years later, I started to read for the Final Honour School of Oriental Studies, and I was delighted to sit at Driver's feet, excited by every lecture of his that I heard.

Driver often pointed out that the number of words attested in the Hebrew Bible is not large enough to include all the words that must have been in use in ancient Israel. That is obviously true. He also pointed out that there are a number of rare words, even *hapax legomena*, which may have been in common use at the time. He maintained that a valuable clue to their meaning was to be found in other Semitic languages. Further, some passages in the Hebrew Bible that had been thought to be textually corrupt might be explained with the help of the same method.

This approach to Hebrew lexicography was, of course, not new. It had its origin partly in the work of medieval Jewish scholars, who spoke Arabic in everyday life and used it to explain the meanings of some Hebrew words. In later centuries, scholars made comparable suggestions along comparable lines. In the 18th century, for example, J.D. Michaelis in Göttingen made many suggestions about Hebrew lexicography in the light of the Semitic languages known to him. Some of the results appear in his translation of the Bible into German. In the following century, Wilhelm Gesenius made use of cognate languages in his substantial contributions to Hebrew lexicography.

At this point it is necessary to make a distinction between two uses of cognate languages which, however, overlap at times. We must think, not only of the use of cognate languages to discover supposed lost meanings of words, but also of their use in giving an account of the etymology of words of known meaning. It is, of course, common for scholarly dictionaries to say something about the etymology of the words that they record.[2]

To return to the subject of my student days at Oxford, Driver was not the only person to make use of other Semitic languages in his study of Hebrew. Another of my teachers was Chaim Rabin, whose illness and recent death are a source of sadness to all who knew him.

---

[2] Barr ("Hebrew Lexicography", p. 112) has pointed out that the word "etymology" is used in several different senses, but it seems unnecessary to go into details for the present purpose.

While his main teaching duty in Oxford was to lecture on Mishnaic and Medieval Hebrew, he frequently spoke and wrote about Classical Hebrew in the light of possible cognates.

But there was another side to the picture. The Regius Professor of Hebrew at Oxford was Herbert Danby, and to him I also owe much. His approach was strikingly different. His way of dealing with the Hebrew Bible was to seek to make sense of the text on the basis of well-attested and generally-accepted meanings. On one occasion, he asked me to translate a verse of Hebrew, and he seemed impatient when I rashly ventured to say that I understood that a meaning for a particular word had been suggested other than the usual meaning. His exegesis was based on a careful grammatical study of the text; and it was informed by the writings of medieval Jewish commentators, though I do not recall his ever mentioning the views of those who explained Hebrew words by comparing them with Arabic.

I may have over-simplified Danby's position, but I do not think I have misrepresented the approach shown in his lectures. At the time, I tended to regard Danby's teaching as unimaginative. It was only later, when I too had to teach, that I learned its quality and sought to benefit from it in my own preparation of lectures.

These two approaches to the Hebrew text have confronted each other in my mind ever since. My teachers at Oxford were not alone in their use of cognate languages. One thinks, for example, of W.F. Albright and his pupils—not least of Mitchell Dahood, who became a friend but with whom I often found it impossible to agree. Dahood's application of the comparative method was radical, and it seemed to me that it was undisciplined and often lacking in self-criticism. It is interesting that Driver, who made such extensive use of comparison with other Semitic languages when discussing the Hebrew text, was sharply critical of the way in which Dahood worked.[3]

In 1960, I was invited to join the committee responsible for translating the Hebrew text of the Old Testament for the *New English Bible*, and Driver was the chairman. It was a demanding and stimulating experience for me. There is no better way of facing the problems of the Hebrew Bible than having to express its meaning in one's own language, and to do so in the company of scholars with varying views. An awareness of one's own fallibility and a willingness to learn some lessons in humility were both needed. Driver had the ability

[3] See, for example, his review in *JSS* 10 (1965), pp. 112–17, of Dahood, *Proverbs and Northwest Semitic Philology* (Rome, 1963).

to take a fresh look at familiar passages, and to ask fundamental questions about their meaning. Sometimes, however, the solutions that he proposed to problems did not seem to me to be sufficiently well founded. Such solutions usually involved comparison with cognate languages. Perhaps it was, partly at least, the Danby side of my training that encouraged such scepticism in me.

When James Barr invited me to read the typescript of his then forthcoming book, *Comparative Philology and the Text of the Old Testament*, I found myself in agreement with a large part of the contents. Although others had criticized aspects of the use of cognate languages in Hebrew lexicography, Barr was the first to tackle the problem systematically and on a large scale. His book did not argue that comparison with other Semitic languages had no value, but he drew attention to many examples of unsatisfactory argument and method. The general impression gained by many readers is that the method involves so many difficulties that it should be used only sparingly, and that perhaps it would be wiser not to use it at all. Such a conclusion goes beyond what Barr says, but it is not difficult to understand the reaction against the kind of work done by Driver and others.

I

What are the principal objections that have been raised, if not against the method as such, at least against many examples of its use? The fundamental difficulty is that many precautions have to be taken, and much that is hypothetical has sometimes to be postulated, and so it is difficult to claim probability for many of the results. It is impossible in this one article to go into many details. All I can do is to list and illustrate some of the principal considerations.

(1) *The consonants in alleged cognates need to conform to the normal rules of interchange among the Semitic languages.*

For example, one cannot rely on Alfred Guillaume's suggested additions to the generally-accepted list. According to Guillaume, the "underlying principle" on which his suggestions are based is that if certain consonants are known to be "interchangeable in Arabic, it is reasonable to infer that the same changes can legitimately be used to provide a parallel from Arabic to a word in Hebrew which stands devoid of support from the sister tongue" (1961, p. 4).

Some of Guillaume's examples are more plausible than others, but we should not accept his thesis about a regular interchange. For instance, he argues (1962, p. 14) that Hebrew *ḥākâ*, which is used in the *piʿel* to mean "to wait, await", corresponds to Arabic *ḥaja*, "He remained, stopped in a place". Whether or not he is right in relating the two verbs to each other (and I offer no judgement on this question), the Arabic consonant *jim* corresponds to Hebrew *gimel*, and *gimel* is the voiced counterpart of unvoiced *kaph*. It is thus conceivable that the Arabic and Hebrew verbs are related, but it would be an oversimplification to say that Arabic *jim* and Hebrew *kaph* are interchangeable. Guillaume adds nothing to his case by appealing to what appears to be a dialectal Yemenite pronunciation of a sound "between *k* and *j*". A dialectal variant in the Yemenite pronunciation of Arabic is scarcely a firm foundation for a regular comparison with Hebrew.

Other examples in Guillaume's list are less plausible. In proposing some of them, he fails to do justice to the fact that a consonant in one Semitic language that corresponds to a consonant in another Semitic language is normally articulated in the same part of the mouth. It is therefore implausible to suggest, for example, that, because Hebrew *nāšak* and Arabic *nasafa* both mean "to bite", the Hebrew palatal consonant *k* can interchange with the labio-dental *f* in Arabic (1965, p. 10). Guillaume also notes that Hebrew uses *šātâ* in the *qal* to mean "to drink", but that for the causative meaning it uses *hišqâ*, the *hiphʿil* of a root cognate with Arabic *saqa*(*y*). But this is scarcely evidence that, as Guillaume puts it, "In reality *šqh* and *šth* are one and the same verb in origin" (1965, p. 14), Correspondence between the palatal *q* and the dental *t* is scarcely probable.

It is a commonplace that the whole range of Arabic literature attests an enormous vocabulary of varied origins, and the fact that Arabic synonyms exist does not necessarily testify that two words with the same meaning and two consonants in common are related or "one and the same . . . in origin", and that the third consonant in one of the words is interchangeable with the third consonant in the other. Scholars must work only with the regular correspondences.

(2) *Attempts to determine hitherto unknown meanings of words often tend to increase the number of homonyms or, at least, homographs.* There certainly are homonymous roots in Hebrew, but to postulate too many can involve implausibility. See Barr 1968, pp. 145–55.

(3) *The meaning in a cognate language must be adequately attested before it is used to explain Hebrew.*

Two good examples are provided by Barr's discussion of theories advanced by Dahood. The first is the verb *šbm* which occurs in Ugaritic in *CTA* 3 III 37 (= *KTU* 1.3 III 40) and was thought by Virolleaud (pp. 50, 53) to mean "to muzzle" because of the verb *šabama* in Arabic. On the basis of this alleged meaning in Ugaritic, Dahood postulated the existence of a Hebrew verb *šābam*, "to muzzle". He found it in Ps. lxviii 23 by emending the text. Where the MT has *ʾāšîb mimmᵉṣūlôt yām*, he read *ʾešbōm mᵉṣūlôt yām*, "I muzzled the Deep Sea" (*Psalms II*, pp. 131, 145; cp. *JBL* 80, pp. 270–1; *Biblica* 42, p. 385). Even apart from the fact that it is hazardous to emend the text to produce a *hapax legomenon*, Barr has shown that the meaning of the Arabic verb is scarcely appropriate to the muzzling of a monster (*JSS* 18, pp. 17–39).

The second example is Dahood's argument that, in some verses where the MT has *māgēn*, we should read **māgān* and translate the word "suzerain" or "sovereign". He argues that the meaning "shield" does not always fit the context. He compares the use of *mgn* in Ugaritic and the Hebrew verb *mgn*, which means "to give" in the *piʿel*, and also compares a Punic noun. On the basis of the verb he postulates a noun meaning "benefactor", from which the meaning "suzerain" developed. The alleged semantic development is illustrated by him from Luke xxii 25, where it is said that kings are called benefactors (*Biblica* 45, p. 129; *Psalms I*, p. 17). Dahood vocalizes the word as either a participle, *mōgēn*, or a noun, *māgān* or *māgōn* (*Biblica* 45, pp. 129, 282). He translates the word as "King" in Ps. lxxxiv 23, because the king was the "bestower of gifts" (*Mélanges . . . Tisserant*, p. 94). Later, however, he seems to have preferred "suzerain". Dahood's theory is dependent on an article by Maurin on "Himilcon le Magonide" in a work that Dahood reviewed in 1964 (p. 129). According to Dahood, there was a Punic noun *māgōn*, which was used of Carthaginian generals, of whom the Latin words *imperator* and *dux* were also used. In *Psalms I*, p. XXXVII, he refers to "the Punic name for 'emperor' *māgōn*".

Barr, however, has shown that Dahood's statements misrepresent what Maurin says, and that "everything said [by Dahood] about Punic *magon* is wrong" (1974, p. 47). It may be added that, even apart from Barr's demonstration of the irrelevance of the Punic evidence, the connection made by Dahood between a supposed noun meaning "benefactor" and the meaning "suzerain" is questionable. Suzerains doubtless claimed to be benefactors, but that does not prove that a noun meaning "benefactor" can be translated "suzerain".

Another example of a misunderstanding of a cognate root is to be found in D. Winton Thomas's use of an Arabic verb to explain the Hebrew verb *yādaʿ* in some places where the meaning "to know" does not fit the context (see Emerton 1970, and 1991, pp. 145–63). Thomas's theory is based on the Arabic verb *waduʿa*, "to have rest, be still, be quiet". On this foundation he built an extensive theory, but William Johnstone has shown that the theory rests on a misunderstanding of the Arabic. I have myself drawn attention to other weaknesses in Thomas's theory (1991, pp. 145–63).

Finally, the use of Arabic lexicons to shed light on the meanings of Hebrew words requires special care. Kopf discusses the problems and the need for caution.

(4) *A meaning found in a particular Semitic language was not necessarily shared by a word with the same consonants in another Semitic language.*

There is scarcely any need to illustrate this fact. Mention may, however, be made of the example considered in the previous paragraph. Hebrew verbs beginning with *y* often have Arabic cognates beginning with *w*, but the alleged relationship of Hebrew *yādaʿ* to Arabic *waduʿa* now seems improbable.

(5) *The question arises how close the relevant cognate language is to Hebrew, and whether the answer affects the plausibility of the theory.*

For example, is a supposed cognate found only in Ethiopic as plausible as one found in several North-West Semitic languages (cp. Barr 1968, pp. 111–14, 156–87)?

(6) *The ancient versions must be used with caution if it is claimed that they support a philological theory.*

It must, for example, be asked whether a particular translation testifies to the existence of a meaning of a word other than the usual one, or whether it can reasonably be explained as an attempt to render the word understood in its usual sense, or, indeed, whether the translation is based on the same consonantal text as that of the Massoretes.

D.W. Thomas's treatment of *yādaʿ* offers a relevant example. He noted a difficulty in making sense of *nôdaʿ*, the *niphʿal* of the verb, in 1 Sam. vi 3, and he drew attention to the fact that the LXX understands the Hebrew in terms of expiation, and the Targum in terms of relief coming to the Philistines. He therefore argued that *nôdaʿ* here denotes giving rest and corresponds to a meaning attested in a supposed Arabic cognate (1960, p. 52). He did not know—and cannot be blamed for not knowing—that a manuscript from Qumran, 4QSam[a], has a different reading from the MT. It has the *nipḥʿal* of *kpr*, "to expiate". It is probable that the LXX, though not the Targum, was based on this reading (cp. Emerton, 1991, pp. 147–8).[4]

(7) *It must be asked whether the alleged new meaning fits only one passage, or whether it enables us to make better sense of several.*

The more passages that can be better explained by a suggestion, the more likely the suggestion is to be correct. The corollary is obvious.

(8) *There is the important question whether the postulated meaning makes better sense of a passage than an interpretation based on the usual meaning.*

The failure to consider that question is illustrated by Dahood's theory that the words *šām yāšabnû gam-bākînû* in Ps. cxxxvii 1 are to be translated "there we sat; loudly we wept" (*Psalms III*, p. 268). There is a Ugaritic word spelled *gm* which is probably to be translated "aloud", to judge by the contexts in which it is used and by the fact that it seems to be a form of a noun *g* meaning "voice". But the normal meaning of the Hebrew particle *gam* makes good sense in Ps. cxxxvii, and there is no need to postulate another meaning. Dahood claims to find other examples of *gam* in the sense that he ascribes to it here, but they too seem unnecessary. In any case, neither in his comments on this verse on pp. 269–70 nor in his discussion of Ps. li 7 (*Psalms II*, p. 14), where he claims to offer a "full discussion", does he give a reason why the usual meaning of *gam* is unsuitable. Further, although the Ugaritic noun *g* seems to mean "voice", no such noun is attested in Hebrew.

More could doubtless be said about the problems involved in the use of cognate languages to rediscover supposedly lost meanings in Hebrew, and about the precautions needed in their employment. But what I have written may serve as a sufficiently long list of difficulties.

---

[4] I thought in 1991 that the Targum might be based on the same reading as the LXX, but, as Professor R.P. Gordon has rightly pointed out to me, it is improbable that the Targum would have translated the *nipḥʿal* of *kpr* in such a way.

II

It is appropriate at this point to consider the arguments advanced by two people associated with *The Dictionary of Classical Hebrew*, which, as was noted above, does not list cognates to Hebrew words in other Semitic languages.

In a volume of essays on the work of William Robertson Smith, J.F. Elwolde, the Executive Editor of the *Dictionary*, discusses the use of Arabic in Hebrew lexicography. He maintains that the "use of Arabic or other comparative languages in Hebrew lexicography *should* be disappearing, indeed should have disappeared at least 30 years ago", and that the publication of two lexicons that do contain comparative material—the eighteenth edition of Gesenius and the English translation of Baumgartner—"will mark nothing more than the last gasps of a too-long established and theoretically quite unsustainable aberration in the development of Hebrew studies" (p. 373). Elwolde is plainly uncompromising in the expression of his views.

The reasons for his opinion are set out on pp. 369–72 with special reference to the eighteenth edition of Gesenius. Elwolde considers four conceivable reasons for citing cognates in a lexicon, and he dismisses them all.

The first is "grounds of pedagogy" (p. 371), to which a long paragraph on pp. 369–70 is devoted. Elwolde begins with a quotation from the eighteenth edition of Gesenius, p. ix, to the effect that etymological references are of little use to beginners, "für den fortgeschrittenen Benutzer aber sind sie hilfreich, wenn nicht unentbehrlich". Elwolde asks who these more advanced users are, and also whether their needs, or "the intrinsic value of the comparative information" is of "such importance as to override the importance of other—non-etymological—information, which, presumably, has had to be sacrificed in order to make room for the lengthy etymological sections of *Gesenius 18* in particular". He then asks if we are to infer that a reader who has once mastered Hebrew would be expected to learn related languages "using Hebrew as a kind of step-up to the other language". This "educationally rather dubious approach" is ascribed "to some extent" to Eduard König and BDB. He finds this "inconsistent" with the failure in the new Gesenius to record the evidence of inscriptions and the Qumran scrolls. He also rejects the possibility that the etymological information "is intended for mature scholars of comparative Semitics, who might be able to use material from biblical Hebrew to elucidate difficult data from their other specialist languages". If it were so, then "*Gesenius 18* would no longer really be a dictionary of Hebrew but of Semitic languages in general, albeit with a particular emphasis on Hebrew". Not "all dictionaries of other Semitic languages systematically include Hebrew cognates, so why should dictionaries of Hebrew be especially privileged—or humbled—in this way?"

The second conceivable reason for recording cognates concerns "comparative lexicology or historical linguistics", and it is rejected because it fails to record such important information as "the relative ages of the forms cited" and whether a word cited in one language was borrowed from another "or 'inherited' from Hebrew's immediate Semitic ancestor" (pp. 370–1). The third conceivable reason—that the use of comparative material may "tell readers something about the *meaning* of the Hebrew word"—is also questioned, as is "a view that equates meaning with etymology" (p. 371). Finally, Elwolde does not believe that the provision of etymological information should be continued merely for the sake of tradition.

There are a number of details in Elwolde's argument that are open to question. For example, the preface to BDB, p. vi, refers to the fact that C. Siegfried and B. Stade have excluded "the etymological feature almost entirely from their lexicon" and says that this "method deprives the student of all knowledge as to the extra-Biblical history and relationship of his words, and of the stimulus to study the cognate languages . . ." The authors of BDB thus believe that it is beneficial for a student to study the cognate languages, but nothing is said about "using knowledge of Hebrew as a kind of step-up to the other language". Further, it is possible to acknowledge the value of "non-etymological" information—and, indeed, to recognize the fresh contribution to Hebrew lexicography made by the Sheffield *Dictionary*—but one may doubt Elwolde's presumption that it has been "sacrificed" in the new Gesenius to make room for references to the cognate languages. If (unlike Elwolde) one believes that knowledge of cognates is helpful in Hebrew lexicography, one will want it to be included and not itself "sacrificed" on behalf of something else. Is it not possible to find a place for both etymological and non-etymological information? Elwolde also notes a current "shift away from comparativism . . . in the move away from text-criticism and philology to a new emphasis on the Bible as a literary document—or series of documents—to be valued and analysed in its own right" (p. 372). It is not clear why he appears to regard this trend in scholarship as an argument against the use of comparative evidence in Hebrew lexicography. Current fashions (which are not shared by all scholars) are not evidence. Similarly, they are not evidence against textual criticism. If there is reason to suspect the Hebrew text, does Elwolde think that a scholar should abstain from textual criticism?

It is, however, probably best to focus attention on what appears to be the heart of Elwolde's argument, namely, the belief that comparison with other Semitic languages does not have a valuable contribution to make to Hebrew lexicography. It will be argued below that it does have such a contribution, as may be seen, for example, in the study of the verb *rḥp* or *štʿ*, or in the belief that *nepeš* sometimes denotes the throat.

A more moderate and restrained view is expressed by D.J.A. Clines, the Editor of *The Dictionary of Classical Hebrew*. He discusses the use of cognate languages in the introduction to volume I, where he does not deny all value to its contribution to Hebrew lexicography. Indeed, he writes on p. 25 that philology—which appears to include "an historical enquiry after meanings and historical developments"—"remains an important and productive area of research". On the other hand, p. 17 says that the presence of such information "in a Hebrew dictionary is highly problematic". He gives reasons for omitting comparative information from a Hebrew lexicon:

> ... it is difficult to see what purpose it [i.e. information about cognates] serves. Theoretically speaking, that is, data about the meaning of words ... are strictly irrelevant to the Hebrew language; and, practically speaking, ... the significance of the cognates has been systematically misunderstood by many users of the traditional dictionaries. It is often said, for example, that the function of noting the cognates is to indicate how it is that we know the meaning of the Hebrew word to be such and such; but this is incorrect, since there is usually a quite complex set of evidences for such matters ... and there is no reason to privilege the particular type of evidence, problematic as it is, that is provided by the cognate languages [pp. 17–18].

Clines's reasons are thus clearly set out. Even on his own principles, however, there is at least one problem. Volume I lists, for example, three roots *ʾbl*, but for II and III merely refers to parts of the entry for *ʾbl* I. Yet the reader is given no idea of the supposed meanings II and III.[5] At least one of these meanings is based, partly at least, on cognate evidence—which Clines himself discussed ably in 1992.

A change of policy appears in volume II. This and future volumes will "include also the 'new' words that have been recognized or proposed (rightly or wrongly) in the scholarly literature, especially of the last fifty years" (p. 9). Clines notes that "many of the proposals depend on the existence of a cognate word", and that "Cognate languages are . . . often our source for the meanings of the words that are already in the lexicographical tradition" (p. 9). The so-called "new" words in the *Dictionary* are marked with an asterisk, and bibliographical references are given at the end of the volume. But no cognates are recorded, and "No judgments have been offered . . . about the probability of the proposals that have been made. Rather, we have thought it valuable in itself to bring (or, keep) the range of proposals before the scholarly public, leaving it in each case to them to make their own decisions in the light of the evidence" (p. 10).

The introduction of bibliographical references concerning "new" words is welcome—especially since it is often difficult to find the relevant information without help. The failure to record the philological evidence for such theories is in accord with the principles of the *Dictionary*. It would, however, surely have been more helpful to readers to give them the relevant philological information, since they are "to make their own decisions in the light of the evidence". They therefore need the evidence. Cognate languages are not the only evidence, but, in these cases at least, they are a highly important part of it. Further, while one can understand the reluctance to offer judgements, and the conviction that some issues are "ultimately irresolvable" (p. 10), one may question whether this is the most appropriate policy for a dictionary. Many readers will want and expect to learn the judgement of the author of a dictionary, even though not all readers will agree with every judgement. In fact, judgements about the meanings of words are made in the *Dictionary* when the meanings are "old" ones, and it is difficult to see why some judgements should not be offered about at least some "new" words.

III

Earlier in this article, I made a distinction between the use of cognate languages to shed light on the meanings of Hebrew words and their

[5] I am grateful to Professor H.G.M. Williamson for this point.

use in the study of etymology. While not all dictionaries give etymological information, it is surely appropriate for some to do so. Moreover, in the case of Hebrew the two purposes sometimes overlap; and to say that does not necessarily involve the equation of meaning with etymology, which Elwolde rightly rejects.

Sometimes comparison with other languages may lead to the revision of etymological theories. Elsewhere, I have discussed the fact that the discovery of the Ugaritic cognate of Hebrew *šulḥān*, "table", has shown the etymology of the Hebrew word in BDB to be mistaken (Emerton 1994, pp. 54–5). In the same article (pp. 65–6) I commented on *w^ešinnantām* in Deut. vi 7, the second-person masculine singular *piʿel* perfect with *waw* consecutive of *šānan* with the third-person masculine plural pronominal suffix, which refers back to "these words" in verse 6. The context shows that the meaning is something like "to teach" or "to tell". BDB regards this verb as a form of the verb *šānan*, "to sharpen", whose Arabic cognate iş *sanna*. The connexion with the meaning "to sharpen" is explained as follows: it means "teach the words *incisively*: Germ. 'einschärfen'". In Ugaritic, however, there is a verb *ṯnn*, beginning with *ṯ*, not a sibilant, and it denotes doing something a second time, repeating. It is probably a by-form of Ugaritic *ṯny*, related to Arabic *ṯana*(*y*) and Aramaic, *t^enāʾ*, and also Hebrew *šānâ*; cp. also *tnh*, which is used in the *piʿel* in Judg. v 11, xi 40; and *t^enâ* in Ps. viii 2 is probably to be repointed as a form of the same verb (cp. Driver 1950, p. 48).

Comparative study can sometimes help to distinguish between two homonymous roots. There is a noun *ʿebrâ* in Hebrew that appears to mean "anger" or the like. BDB also gives to the related verb in the *hithpaʿel* the meaning "be arrogant, infuriate oneself". BDB relates these words to the verb *ʿābar* "to pass through or over"; *ʿebrâ* is thus explained as "overflowing rage, fury". Yet as far back as the 18th century J.D. Michaelis drew attention to the existence of two different roots in Arabic distinguished by the fact that each begins with a different cognate of the Hebrew consonant *ʿayin*. One of them, *ʿabara* with the Arabic laryngeal *ʿain*, is cognate with the Hebrew verb *ʿābar*. The other root begins with the velar consonant *ghain*. Lane renders *ġabira*, "*He bore rancour, malevolence, malice*, or *spite*; or *had enmity*, or *violent hatred, in his heart*", and the noun *ġibrun* "*Rancour, malevolence*, or *spite*, or *concealed enmity and violent hatred*". So it was that Michaelis (*Supplementa* p. 1824) compared Hebrew *ʿebrâ* with Arabic *ġabrun*, "residuum inimicitiae". Buhl, who does not mention

Michaelis, compares the same Arabic root with Hebrew *ʿebrâ*, and also compares Aramaic *taʿăbûrāʾ* (or *taʿăbōrāʾ*), "anger". Further, he notes that the transliteration of *b^eʿabrôt* in Ps. vii 7 as βεγαβρωθ in the Hexapla represents the Hebrew letter *ʿayin* by the Greek letter *gamma*, and argues that this points to Arabic *ghain* rather than *ʿain*. A similar view was presented by G.R. Driver in 1922 (p. 69; cp. 1951, pp. 185–6). Further, in 1963 (p. 381) I pointed to evidence that may imply that *ʿbr* in Syriac means "to be angry" in one place. In Ps. lxxix 41 the Hebrew text has *hitwâ*, which is translated παρώξυναν in the LXX, *grgw* in the Peshiṭta, and "concitaverunt" by Jerome. The Syro-Hexaplar records Aquila's rendering as *ʿbrw*, which makes no sense in its usual meaning, but does make sense and agrees with the other versions noted, if it means "to cause to be angry".

It must be granted that malevolence is not the same as anger, and some may hesitate to offer a translation of *ʿebrâ* that attributes malevolence to God. Yet, when the contexts in which *ʿebrâ* occurs are examined, it appears that, to say the least, God has ill will towards evildoers, and the meaning may not be far from anger. It seems likely that the distinction between the two roots *ʿbr* in Hebrew is sound, and that they correspond to the two roots in Arabic.

IV

Any attempt to justify the use of cognate languages to determine the meaning of Hebrew words must acknowledge that the method has often been misused, and that appropriate caution has not always been exercised. If a case is to be presented for the use of the method, it must defend only a sober, careful and disciplined application.

The case for the method is simple: it is that it has produced a sufficient number of convincing results to justify its continued use. The results are apparent, not only in the use of cognate languages to shed light on Hebrew meanings, but also in the interpretation of another North-West Semitic language, namely, Ugaritic. The hypothesis that the alphabet of the Ras Shamra tablets was used to write a Semitic language was part of the process of deciphering the script, and the translation depended on identifying Semitic cognates. While many obscurities remain in the Ugaritic texts, the fact that we can read and understand a large part of them depends on the use of the comparative method. If the method produced satisfactory results in the study of Ugaritic, why should it not help in the understanding of Hebrew?

There is room in this article to give only a small number of examples of ways in which it may be claimed that the use of other Semitic languages has helped us to understand the meanings of Hebrew words. There is no need to repeat here what I have already said about the verb *šānan* in Deut. vi 7, and I shall comment on a few different examples.

First, it was suggested by Dhorme three quarters of a century ago that the Hebrew noun *nepeš* sometimes denotes, not the soul or self, but the throat or neck (cp. Dürr). The suggestion was based on a comparison with Accadian *napištu* as well as consideration of the contexts in which the Hebrew noun appears. It is now also possible to compare the Ugaritic noun *npš*, where the context sometimes favours the meaning "throat". It would, I think, be generally accepted that this explanation of Hebrew *nepeš* is justified in some verses (e.g. Isa. v 14; Hab. ii 5; Ps. cv 18). The source of the discovery of the meaning "throat" or "neck" was a cognate language, and it was confirmed by another Semitic language (Ugaritic) as well as by study of some contexts in which the Hebrew noun appears.

Second, there is a Ugaritic verb *ṯtʿ*, which is shown by the context, where it is parallel to *yrʾ*, "to fear", to mean "to be afraid" (*CTA* 5 [*KTU* 1.5] II 7; 6 [*KTU* 1.16] VI 30). This meaning was recognized by Ginsberg (pp. 46, 67). Similarly in Phoenician, the Karatepe inscription (*KAI* 26 A ii 4) has a word *štʿ*, which appears to be a verb with a similar meaning. As Ginsberg pointed out in 1936, and others recognized when the Karatepe inscription was published, *tištāʿ* (parallel to *tîrāʾ*) and *wᵉništāʿâ* in Isa. xli 10 and 23, respectively, should be understood as forms of a verb *šātaʿ*, rather than derived—less plausibly—from *šāʿâ*, "to gaze", and so to gaze about in anxiety or at each other in rivalry, as was formerly believed (so, for example, BDB). Although "to be afraid" is not so very different from what was previously thought to be the meaning (apart from the idea of rivalry), the precise root and meaning were learned solely from the Ugaritic and Phoenician texts. According to N.H. Tur-Sinai (in his discussion of *štʿ* in the continuation of Ben Yehuda's *Dictionary*, p. 7593), Jewish exegetes of the past were uncertain whether to derive the verb in Isa. xli from *šʿh* or *štʿ*. It does not appear, however, that they knew of any examples of *štʿ* apart from these two verses.

Eitan noted in 1924 (p. 8) that *tištāʿ* in verse 10 is parallel to *tîrāʾ*,

but his other reasons for arguing that the verbs in verses 10 and 23 are forms of *štʿ*, "to be afraid", are inconclusive or inadequate or unconvincing. Thus, although *wᵉništāʿeh* might have been expected from a root *šʿh* in verse 23, there are analogies for *wᵉništāʿâ* in the MT (cp. GK § 75 *l*). Similarly, the fact that the Peshiṭta has *ttrhb* in verse 10 may be an attempt to explain the verb as a form of *šāʿâ*, and Eitan fails to observe that the same version has *wnštʿʾ*, from the Syriac root *šʿʾ*, in verse 23. Further, Eitan compares the Arabic verb *šatiʿa*, "to be sad and agitated", for which he cites Kazimirski (whose name he spells "Kasimirski"), p. 1190 ("Ȇtre triste *ou* agité, troublé par la faim *ou* quelque maladie"), and Wahrmund (p. 969: "niederschlagen, ungeduldig sein [in Hunger, Krankheit]"). He fails to comment on the fact that the normal Arabic cognate of the Hebrew consonant *shin* is *sin*, not *shin*; and one might have expected him to hold that the Tiberian pointing is wrong and that the Hebrew verb was *śātaʿ*. Without mentioning that problem, he notes that there is also an Arabic root *stʿ*. He does not give the meaning, but refers to Kazimirski, p. 1150 (a mistake for 1050). Kazimirski records under this root only *mistaʿun*, "1. Toujours agile et infatigable. 2. Contracté, ramassé et replié sur soi-même"; Eitan presumably had in mind the second meaning. The meanings of neither Arabic root seem sufficiently close to, let alone identical with, "to be afraid". In any case, Ugaritic bears witness that the first radical of the Hebrew verb was not originally a sibilant, but an interdental (to which, of course, Hebrew *shin* regularly corresponds).

Third, the verb *rḥp* is used (in the *piʿel*) twice in the Old Testament: *wᵉrûaḥ ʾĕlōhîm mᵉraḥepet ʿal-pᵉnê hammāyim* in Gen. i 2, and *ʿal-gôzālāyw yᵉraḥēp* in Deut. xxxii 11. The subject of the verb in the latter verse is a *nešer*, an eagle or vulture, and so the verb denotes something that a bird does above its young. It is unnecessary here to describe in detail all the suggestions that have been made about these verses. It will suffice to note what Skinner says about Gen. i 2 after recording some of the varied renderings in the ancient versions: "It is impossible to say whether 'brood' or 'hover' is the exact image here, or in" Deut. xxxii 11 (p. 18). One cognate was known at the time when he wrote, namely, Syriac *rḥp*, which is used in the *paʿel*. But, as Skinner says, "The Syriac vb. has great latitude of meaning", which offers the Hebraist less help than could be wished. Another cognate is now, however, provided by the Ugaritic verb *rḫp*. It is found in contexts that make it plain that it denotes a bird's movements in the air, i.e., some kind of flight: *CTA* 18 (*KTU* 1.18) IV 20, 31; 19 (*KTU* 1.19) I 32 (where the reading is not clear). The same meaning is probably also found in *KTU* 1.108 8. Whether the kind of flying is hovering is uncertain, but possible. The subject of the verb is *nšrm*, the plural of the cognate of Hebrew *nešer*. While the Ugaritic evidence does not constitute absolute proof that the verb in Deut. xxxii denotes some kind of flight, rather than brooding, it offers strong support for that view. An assessment of its meaning in Gen. i 2 is related to the problem of the significance of *rûaḥ* in this verse.

Fourth, although D. Winton Thomas's theory about a second root *ydʿ* should be rejected, there is a much stronger case for his belief that the Hebrew verb *šānâ* sometimes means "to be, or to become, high, or exalted in rank". He based his theory on a comparison with the Arabic verb *saniya* with such a meaning, the Syriac noun *šanāʾ*, "sublimitas, maiestas, honor magnus", and the contexts of several verses. I have discussed this theory elsewhere (1974) and compared it with the same or similar suggestions by other scholars. Although not all Thomas's suggestions about particular verses are convincing, others seem probable. In 1974 and 1978 I suggested that a similar explanation would solve the problems of two other verses.

Fifth, Exod. xxxii 4 tells how Aaron took the gold rings given by the Israelites and says *wayyāṣar ʾōtô baḥereṭ wayyaʿăśēhû ʿēgel massēkâ*. The *Revised Standard Version* translates these words as follows: "and fashioned it with a graving tool, and made a molten calf". The difficulty that a graving tool seems inappropriate to make an image that was cast has long been recognized.

Some have sought to explain the noun *ḥereṭ* from, or as a wrong vocalization of, *ḥārîṭ*, which is used of an article of women's dress in Isa. iii 22, and of a purse in which silver was wrapped in 2 Kings v 23—or perhaps a cloak, as Loewenstamm maintains (1975, pp. 336–7; contrast 1967, p. 487; cp. Gevirtz). The verb *wayyāṣar* is then derived from *ṣûr* or *ṣārar*, "to bind". So Noth translates the relevant clause: "und er (Aaron) schnürrte es (das Geld) in einem Beutel zusammen" (p. 422). According to this solution of the problem, the words *wayyāṣar ʾōtô baḥereṭ* give incidental information about the way in which Aaron handled the gold, and the statement plays no organic role in the story. That is possible, though it would be an advantage to the theory if it involved such a role.

There is an ancient tradition that understands Aaron's action to be part of the making of the calf and thus gives *ḥereṭ* a more important place in the story (cp. Driver 1946, p. 210, and 1969, pp. 465–6). Targum Pseudo-Jonathan contains a double translation, of which the second is *ûr^e^mā' yātêh b^e^ṭupsā'*, "and he threw it [the gold] into a mould". The Neofiti targum contains only this rendering. Similarly, the Peshiṭta renders *ḥereṭ* by *ṭupsā'*. The Targum of Onkelos translates *ḥereṭ* by *zēpā'*, and Loewenstamm takes the word to be related to Accadian *zipu*, which he renders "a casting mold for copper vessels" (1967, p. 485). The *CAD* Z, p. 86, notes *ze'pu* (*zīpu*), whose meanings include "mold for casting metal objects"; von Soden: "*zi'pu, zīpu* III . . . 'Gussform'". The Vulgate has *opere fusorio*, "by casting", This interpretation of *ḥereṭ* is also found in the midrash *leqaḥ ṭôb* (Buber, p. 202). Saadia (Derenbourg, p. 128), Al-Fasi (Skoss I, p. 582; cp. p. xlvi, n. 52), Ibn Janaḥ (Neubauer, p. 247) and Abu Sa'id (Kuenen, p. 246) have *qālabun*, which means "a mould into which metal is poured" (Lane). (Cp. Torrey, pp. 259–60; and Driver 1946, p. 210, and 1969, pp. 465–6.) Qimḥi notes that some understand *ḥereṭ* here to mean *dāpûs*, "mould" (Biesenthal and Leberecht, p. 118).

Attempts have been made to justify the rendering "mould" in Exodus. Holzinger (p. 150) notes the theory of B. Stade that *ḥereṭ* should be emended to *ḥārîṭ*, "Tasche; hier vielleicht Gußform", and *wayyāṣar* to *wayyiṣṣōq*: "und er goß es in eine Form". Similarly, Ehrlich emends the verb to *wayyiṣṣōq* and supposes that *ḥereṭ* means "Gussform": "was die Etymologie dieses *ḥrṭ* betrifft, so heisst das Verbum kratzen, auskratzen, und daraus ergibt sich leicht der Begriff 'Höhlung', 'Receptakel'; vgl. *ḥryṭ* Tasche, Säckel" (p. 390). Noth, however, comments on Stade's theory that "es ist reine Willkür, aus der Bedeutung Beutel/Tasche auf eine allgemeine Grundbedeutung 'Behälter' zurückzuschliessen und wiederum aus dieser hypothetischen Grundbedeutung eigens für Ex. xxxii 4 eine spezielle Bedeutung Schmelztiegel/Gussform abzuleiten" (p. 420). Similarly, Loewenstamm comments "there are no linguistic grounds to sustain this interpretation for the word *ḥrṭ*" (1967, p. 487).

Driver, however, has found a cognate. In 1919, when he was in Damascus, he visited a jeweller's workshop and enquired about the names of the objects that he saw there. Among them was "a crucible or mould full of molten gold and [he] called it a *ḫarīṭah*, which at once reminded me of the *ḥereṭ* used by Aaron in making the golden calf" (1969, p. 465; cp. 1946, p. 210). Given the well-attested tradition that *ḥereṭ* in Exod. xxxii 5 means "mould", that there is an Arabic noun meaning "mould" to whose consonants those of *ḥereṭ* correspond, and that the meaning fits the context whereas "graving tool" does not, there is a strong case for translating the Hebrew word "mould" in this verse.

If Driver's explanation of *ḥereṭ* is accepted, it is unnecessary to emend the verb *wayyāṣar*, for *ṣûr* may mean "to fashion" as well as "to delineate", It may be a by-form of *yāṣar*, "to form, fashion". Alternatively, the consonants may be vocalized *wayyēṣar*, from *yāṣar*, and there is no need to follow Noth (p. 421) in thinking that *yāṣar* is so closely associated with the work of a potter that it cannot be used of what a metal-worker does.

Of the countless suggestions that have been made I have considered above only a few. Many theories that have been advanced are weak and should be rejected. But others are strong, and I believe that all those considered above deserve to be taken seriously. For example, the theory that *nepeš* sometimes means "throat" or "neck" seems to be as near certain as is possible in this kind of study. I noted above Clines's statement that it "is incorrect" to say that "the function of noting the cognates is to indicate how it is that we know the meaning of the Hebrew word to be such and such". He rightly says that "there is usually a quite complex set of evidences for such matters". Indeed, though the evidence for understanding *nepeš* in this way may not be complex, it involves, not only comparison with a cognate, but also its clear suitability to the context of several verses. Nevertheless, it was comparison with Accadian *napištu* that led Dhorme to make the suggestion: that is how scholars came to know that *nepeš* might have the relevant meaning. It is also interesting that the same combination of cognate and context led scholars to see that, in Ugaritic too, *npš* sometimes means "throat". *nepeš* is a particularly good example, but there are other good ones too. Comparison with cognates has shed light on the meaning of Hebrew words and has a part to play in Hebrew lexicography.

V

There is thus a scale of probability for theories ranging between virtual certainty to improbability. There are some for which a reasonable case can be made, but for which a very high degree of probability cannot be claimed. We shall consider just one example.

Num. xvi 1, which introduces the story of the rebellion of Korah, and also of Dathan and Abiram, begins with the verb *wayyiqqaḥ*: "And Korah . . . and Dathan and Abiram took . . ." But the verb has no object.[6]

It has been argued that the story in this chapter is a combination of two originally independent stories. The absence of an object for the verb has been explained as the result of clumsy work by the redactor who combined the stories. Barr notes this solution to the problem and favours it ("Philology and Exegesis", p. 59; *Tradition and Interpretation*, pp. 49–50; *Heythrop Journal*, pp. 389, 398). It is, indeed, likely that two stories have been combined, Nevertheless, this explanation involves postulating editorial incompetence in producing an ungrammatical sentence. Although that is possible, it is reasonable to enquire whether sense can be made of the passage without ascribing such a mistake to the redactor.

Other scholars have sought to make sense of the text by conjectural emendation. That too is possible; but, once again, before resorting to such a solution, one needs to ask whether any other answer can be found.

It is possible that there is ellipsis of the object, although we do not know of an exact parallel with the verb *lāqaḥ* that fits the context. Or perhaps *lāqaḥ* had some special connotation that is unattested elsewhere in Hebrew. B.A. Levine (p. 405) suggests that the verb may here have had "an extended meaning". He compares Accadian *leqû*, "to take", in the sense of "'grasping' facts or knowledge". Similarly, Accadian *aḫāzu* can be used of "grasping" facts. (He could also have compared the Hebrew noun *leqaḥ*, which can denote "teaching", "understanding" or the like.) Levine suggests that the sense of the verse "may be that the persons named 'grasped' what was happening and consequently confronted Moses with their grievances". He does not, however, explain what he thinks "was happening" or how it relates to the rest of the Hebrew text. In any case, having made the suggestion, Levine explains the text differently and translates it: "Korah . . . took counsel". For this interpretation of the text he appeals to the Jewish tradition that the verse means that "he drew the leaders of the courts among them with words". He compares *qᵉḥû ʿimmākem dᵉbārîm* in Hos. xiv 3, which he translates "take counsel among yourselves

[6] Milgrom, pp. 130, 312–13, surveys ways in which the verse was understood in the versions and by medieval Jewish scholars, and attempts by modern scholars to deal with the problem.

with words"—though it may be questioned whether the idea of taking counsel is present there. Levine, however, is aware of the difficulty of Num. xvi 1, and he comments "When all is said, the opening verse of Numbers 16 defies certain interpretation" (p. 401).

Among the various renderings in the ancient versions is the one ascribed to "the Hebrew" in the Hexapla, namely, ὑπερηφανεύθη, "behaved arrogantly". Meek suggested (pp. 167–8) that the Hebrew text used by the translator read *wayyāzed* instead of *wayyiqqaḥ*, but the difference from the consonants of the MT is so great that the suggestion is unconvincing. A more plausible suggestion was made by G.R. Driver in 1948 (p. 238). He compared the Arabic verb *waqiḥa*, "was bold, impudent". He suggested that *wayyiqqaḥ* should be pointed *wayyāqaḥ*, the *hiphʿil* of a verb **yqḥ*, and translated "and . . . acted shamelessly", which fits the context well. Driver does not mention Eitan who in 1924 (p. 20) had also explained Num. xvi 1 with the help of the Arabic verb, though without mentioning the reading in the Hexapla. Eitan did, however, mention (p. 21) the LXX's rendering of *yiqqāḥăkā* in Job xv 12 as καὶ ἐτόλμησεν (cp. the Peshiṭta's *ʾttrym*). Driver also mentions this verse (p. 235) and suggests that the verb should be vocalized *yōqīḥăkā* (*yôqîḥăkā*), "wherein has thy heart emboldened thee?" This is one of the places where Driver believes that the Greek bears witness to a meaning of a Hebrew verb that was known to the translator. Driver also suggests that the same verb is to be found in Prov. vi 25 (1948, pp. 235–6) and Hos. iv 11 (1950, p. 215).

Neither Eitan nor Driver seems to have known that this suggestion for Num. xvi 1 had been anticipated in 1796 by J.F. Gaab, who compared with the Hebrew the Arabic verb "*wqḥ* perfrictae frontis, pauci pudoris fuit" (pp. 113–14; on pp. 21–2 he found the same verb in Gen. xxx 15). He pointed the Hebrew *wayyēqaḥ* or *wayyīqaḥ*: "Einmahl bezeugten sich Korach—nebst Datan—unverschämt".[7]

It cannot be claimed for the theory that there was a Hebrew verb *yāqaḥ* that it has the same degree of probability as, for example, the view that *nepeš* sometimes means "throat" or "neck". It is possible that the problem of Num. xvi 1 should be explained in some other

[7] I am grateful to Professor Rudolf Smend for sending me photocopies of the relevant pages of this book and for biographical information about Gaab. I first learned of Gaab's work on this verse from E.F.C. Rosenmüller, *Scholia in Vetus Testamentum* 3 (3rd edn, Leipzig, 1824), ad loc.

way—though it is not clear that any other theory has an advantage over it. It is plausible and deserves to be recorded as a possibility. There are many theories in this category.

VI

It would be possible to multiply examples of the use of cognate languages in Hebrew lexicography, some poor, some plausible, and some that should be accepted without hesitation. It seems justified to claim that the method has proved itself, whatever doubts may remain in some cases. It must be used with caution; but when so used it can produce satisfactory results, and its evidence deserves to be recorded—together with other evidence—in any substantial scholarly lexicon, in the interests of etymology and of justification for the meanings recorded. I believe that we need to combine the approaches of Driver and Danby—and also any more recent approaches that have proved their value. In a sense, both Driver and Danby were right.

LIST OF WORKS CITED

L. Alonso Schökel, *Diccionario bíblico hebreo-español* 1 (Valencia, 1990).

J. Barr, *Comparative Philology and the Text of the Old Testament* (Oxford, 1968), 2nd edn, with reprints of "Philology and Exegesis" (see below) on pp. 362–87, and "Ugaritic and Hebrew 'ŠBM'?" (see below) on pp. 388–411, and also "Limitations of etymology as a lexicographical instrument in Biblical Hebrew" on pp. 412–36 (Winona Lake, 1987).

———, "Ugaritic and Hebrew 'ŠBM'?", *JSS* 18 (1973), pp. 17–39.

———, "Hebrew Lexicography", in P. Fronzaroli (ed.), *Studies on Semitic Lexicography* (Florence, 1973), pp. 103–26.

———, "Philology and Exegesis", in C. Brekelmans (ed.), *Questions disputées de l'Ancien Testament* (Gembloux and Leuven, 1974), pp. 39–61; 2nd edn, ed. by M. Vervenne under the title, *Continuing Questions in Old Testament Method and Theology* (Leuven, 1989).

———, "Semitic Philology and the Interpretation of the Old Testament", in G.W. Anderson (ed.), *Tradition and Interpretation* (Oxford, 1974), pp. 31–64.

———, "After Five Years: a Retrospect on Two Major Translations of the Bible", *Heythrop Journal* (1978), pp. 381–405.

W. Baumgartner—see L. Koehler.

BDB = F. Brown, S.R. Driver and C.A. Briggs, *A Hebrew and English Lexicon of the Old Testament* (Oxford, 1907).

J.H.R. Biesenthal and F. Leberecht, *Rabbi Davidi Kimchi Radicum liber* (Berlin, 1847).

S. Buber, *mdrš lqḥ ṭwb hmkwnh psyqtʾ zwṭrtʾ* 2 (Wilna, 1880).

F. Buhl—see W. Gesenius.

CAD—The Assyrian Dictionary (Chicago 1956–).

D.J.A. Clines, "Was there an *ʾbl* II in Classical Hebrew?", *VT* 42 (1992), pp. 1–10.
———, (ed.), *The Dictionary of Classical Hebrew* I (Sheffield, 1993), and II (1995).
CTA = A. Herdner, *Corpus des textes en cunéiformes alphabétiques découvertes à Ras Shamra-Ugarit de 1929 à 1939* (Paris, 1963).
M.J. Dahood, "Mišmar 'Muzzle' in Job 7_{12}", *JBL* 80 (1961), pp, 270–1.
———, review of H.-J. Kraus, *Psalmen* (Neukirchen Kreis Moers, 1960), *Biblica* 42 (1961), pp. 383–5.
———, review of *Semitica* 12, *Biblica* 45 (1964), pp. 129–30.
———, review of *The Torah* (Philadelphia, 1962), *Biblica* 45 (1964), pp. 281–3.
———, "Ugaritic lexicography", in *Mélanges Eugène Tisserant* (Rome, 1964), pp. 81–104.
———, *Psalms I* (Garden City, 1965); *II* (1968); *III* (1970).
J. Derenbourg, *Œuvres complètes de R. Saadia ben Iosef al-Fayyoûmî* 1: *Version arabe du Pentateuque* (Paris, 1893).
E.P. Dhorme, "L'emploi métaphorique des noms de parties du corps en hébreu et en akkadien", *RB* 29 (1920), pp. 465–506, especially pp. 482–3; reprinted as a book under the same title (Paris, 1923); see especially pp. 18–19.
G.R. Driver, "Some Hebrew Roots and their Meanings", *JTS* 23 (1922), pp. 69–73.
———, review of Skoss (see below), *JTS* 47 (1946), pp. 209–11.
———, "Misunderstandings in the Old Testament", *WO* 1/3 (August 1948), pp. 234–8.
———, "Problems of the Hebrew Text and Language", in *Alttestamentliche Studien Friedrich Nötscher zum 60. Geburtstag gewidmet* (Bonn 1950), pp. 46–61.
———, "Hebrew Roots and Words", *WO* 1/5 (August 1950), pp. 406–15.
———, "Problems in the Hebrew Text of Proverbs", *Biblica* 32 (1951), pp. 173–97.
———, "Things Old and New in the Old Testament", in *Mélanges de l'Université Saint-Joseph* 45/38 (Beirut, 1969), pp. 463–78.
L. Dürr, "Hebr. *nepeš* = akk. *napištu* = Gurgel, Kehle", *ZAW* 43 (1925), pp. 262–9.
A.B. Ehrlich, *Randglossen zur hebräischen Bibel* 1 (Leipzig, 1908).
I. Eitan, *A Contribution to Biblical Lexicography* (New York, 1924).
J.F. Elwolde, "The Use of Arabic in Hebrew Lexicography: Whence?, Whither?, and Why?", in W. Johnstone (ed.), *William Robertson Smith: Essays in Reassessment* (Sheffield, 1995), pp. 368–75.
J.A. Emerton, "Notes on Three Passages in Psalms Book III", *JTS* NS 14 (1963), pp. 374–81. This article is wrongly attributed to A. Guillaume in the list of contents on p. iii.
———, "Notes on Jeremiah 12_9 and on some suggestions of J.D. Michaelis about the Hebrew words *naḥā, ʿæbrā* and *jadăʿ*", *ZAW* 81 (1969), pp. 182–91.
———, "A Consideration of Some Alleged Meanings of *ydʿ* in Hebrew", *JSS* 15 (1970), pp. 145–80.
———, "The meaning of *šēnāʾ* in Psalm cxxvii 2", *VT* 24 (1974), pp. 15–31.
———, "The 'Second Bull' in Judges 6:25–28", *Eretz-Israel* 14 (1976), pp. 52*–55*.
———, "A further consideration of D.W. Thomas's theories about *yādāʿ*", *VT* 41 (1991), pp. 145–63.
———, "The work of David Winton Thomas as a Hebrew scholar", *VT* 41 (1991), pp. 287–303.
———, "What Light has Ugaritic Shed on Hebrew?", in G.J. Brooke, A.H.W. Curtis and J.F. Healey (ed.), *Ugarit and the Bible* (Münster, 1994), pp. 53–69.
J.F. Gaab, *Beiträge zur Erklärung des ersten, zweiten und vierten Buchs Moses* (Tübingen, 1796).
W. Gesenius and F. Buhl, *Hebräisches und aramäisches Handwörterbuch über das Alte Testament* (17th edn, Berlin, 1915).
W. Gesenius, R. Meyer, H. Donner and U. Rüterswörden, *Hebräisches und Aramäisches Handwörterbuch über das Alte Testament* 1 (18th edn, Berlin, etc., 1987).
S. Gevirtz, "*ḥereṭ* in the Manufacture of the Golden Calf", *Biblica* 65 (1984), pp. 377–81.

H.L. Ginsberg, *The Ugarit Texts* (Hebrew) (Jerusalem, 1936).
GK = A.E. Cowley (ed.), *Gesenius' Hebrew Grammar as edited and enlarged by the late E. Kautzsch* (2nd edn, Oxford, 1910 = the 28th German edn).
A. Guillaume, "A Contribution to Hebrew Lexicography", *BSOAS* 16 (1954), pp. 1–11.
———, "Hebrew and Arabic Lexicography. A Comparative Study", *Abr-Nahrain* 1 1959–60 (1961), pp. 3–35; "... II", 2 1960–61 (1962), pp. 5–35; "... III", 3 1961–2 (1963), pp. 1–10; "... IV", 4 1963–4 (1965), pp. 1–18. The volumes are cited above according to the actual year of publication.
H. Holzinger, "Das zweite Buch Mose oder Exodus", in E. Kautzsch and A. Bertholet (ed.), *Die Heilige Schriften des Alten Testaments* 1 (4th edn, Tübingen, 1922), pp. 97–161.
W. Johnstone, "*yd*ʿ II, 'be humbled, humiliated'?", *VT* 41 (1991), pp. 49–62.
KAI = H. Donner and W. Röllig, *Kanaanäische und aramäische Inschriften* Wiesbaden, 1962–4).
A. de B. Kazimirski, *Dictionnaire arabe française* (Paris, 1860).
KBL = L. Koehler and W. Baumgartner, *Lexicon in Veteris Testamenti Libros* (Leiden, 1953).
L. Koehler, W. Baumgartner and J.J. Stamm, *Hebräisches und Aramäisches Lexikon zum Alten Testament* (Leiden, 1967–95).
L. Kopf, "Das arabische Wörterbuch als Hilfsmittel für die hebräische Lexikographie", *VT* 6 (1956), pp. 286–302.
KTU = M. Dietrich, O. Loretz and J. Sanmartín, *Die keilalphabetischen Texte aus Ugarit* 1 (Kevelaer and Neukirchen-Vluyn, 1976).
A. Kuenen, *Libri Exodi et Levitici secundum arabicam pentateuchi Samaritani versionem ab Abū-Saʿīdo conscriptam* (Leiden, 1854).
E.W. Lane. *An Arabic-English Lexicon* (London, 1863–93).
B.A. Levine, *Numbers 1–20* (New York, etc., 1993).
S.E. Loewenstamm, "The Making and Destruction of the Golden Calf", *Biblica* 48 (1967), pp. 481–90.
———, "The Making and Destruction of the Golden Calf—a Rejoinder", *Biblica* 56 (1975), pp. 330–43.
L. Maurin, "Himilcon le Magonide. Crises et mutations à Carthage au début du ive siècle avant J.-C.", *Semitica* 12 (1962), pp. 5–43.
T.J. Meek, "Some Emendations in the Old Testament", *JBL* 48 (1929), pp. 162–8.
J.D. Michaelis, *Supplementa ad lexica hebraica* (Göttingen, 1792).
J. Milgrom, *Numbers* (Philadelphia and New York, 1990).
A. Neubauer, *The Book of Hebrew Roots by Abu 'l-Walîd Marwân ibn Janâḥ otherwise called Rabbî Yônâh* (Oxford, 1873–5).
M. Noth, "Zur Anfertigung des 'Goldenen Kalbes'", *VT* 9 (1959), pp. 419–22.
J. Skinner, *A Critical and Exegetical Commentary on Genesis* (2nd edn, Edinburgh, 1930).
S.L. Skoss, *The Hebrew-Arabic Dictionary of the Bible ... of David Ibn Abraham Al-Fasi* 1 (New Haven, Conn., 1936); 2 (1945).
W. von Soden, *Akkadisches Handwörterbuch* (Wiesbaden, 1965–81).
D.W. Thomas, "A Note on *wenôdaʿ lākem* in I Samuel vi. 3", *JTS* NS 11 (1960), p. 52.
C.C. Torrey, "The Foundry of the Second Temple at Jerusalem", *JBL* 55 (1936), pp. 247–60.
N.H. Tur-Sinai, continuation of E. Ben Yehuda, *A Complete Dictionary of Ancient and Modern Hebrew* 16 (Jerusalem, 1959).
C. Virolleaud, *La déesse Anat* (Paris, 1938).
A. Wahrmund, *Handwörterbuch der arabischen und deutschen Sprachen* 1 (Giessen, 1877).

ON READING BIBLICAL POETRY: THE ROLE OF METAPHOR

by

ADELE BERLIN
College Park, Maryland

I am concerned in this essay with biblical Hebrew poetry[1] and with the study of biblical Hebrew poetry. My concerns can be organized around three questions: (1) How may we approach the reading of a biblical poem? (2) What makes the poem poetic? (3) What is the place of the study of biblical poetry within the larger field of biblical studies? In chiastic order, I begin with the last question, which will lead to the second and then to the first.

There has been no period during the last few centuries when literary approaches to the Bible have enjoyed more popularity and success than in the last two or three decades. One might expect that these literary approaches would have concentrated on the study of poetry, for what genre could be more literary? But a survey of published works, such as that done by Mark Allan Powell in *The Bible and Modern Literary Criticism*, suggests that this has not occurred. Powell lists 1749 entries, divided into six parts, including theory, methodology, evaluation, and criticism of individual books of the Bible. When we look at the listings under individual books, we find confirmed what most of us already knew: that the main focus of the literary study of the Bible has been narrative, and, more specifically, four narrative works: Genesis (54 entries), Samuel–Kings (58 entries), Ruth (14 entries), and Jonah (15 entries). Now it is not hard to explain this disproportionate attention. Narratology has received more critical study among literary scholars than other areas of literature, and bold new theories and methods were brought to bear on it. So it is only natural that narratological knowledge was applied to the Bible; and the parts

[1] In using this term, or the shorter term "biblical poetry", I am waging a quiet battle against the use of the term "Hebrew poetry" to refer to poetry in the Hebrew Bible. "Hebrew poetry" is a much broader term, encompassing all poetry written in Hebrew from biblical to modern times.

of the Bible most obviously amenable to narratology are precisely those just listed.

While there is still more work to be done on narrative, the most blatant absences are in the area of poetry, the very area that would seem to have the loudest claim to literary analysis. The book of Lamentations, roughly the size of Ruth and Jonah, has three entries; and Psalms, comparable in size to Genesis, has only twenty. My rough estimate is that there are three studies of narrative to every one study of poetry. Again, the reasons derive from the interests and focus of secular literary criticism, where the majority of the texts are not poetic and where the innovative theories grew out of non-poetic genres (if they grew out of texts at all). While it is good, and in fact inevitable, that we will apply to the Bible the focus and methods that others are applying to their literatures, there is a danger here. To ignore poetry in the Bible is to produce a much larger lacuna than to ignore poetry in, say, 20th century English literature—simply because poetry forms a much larger part of the literary corpus in pre-modern times than it does in modern times.

Now biblicists have not really been ignoring poetry. They have been studying it from non-literary perspectives—in recent years mostly from linguistic perspectives with emphasis on the formal aspects of meter, parallelism, and structural devices like repetition and word patterning. In addition, commentaries on poetic books and chapters have been interpreting biblical poetry, although often this has been done more philologically than poetically. I would argue that we need to attend more to biblical poetry *qua* poetry—to give more attention to the *meaning* of a poem and to how a poem achieves its meaning. That is, to develop ways of reading poetry. We have some fine models in the work of Luis Alonso Schökel, Robert Alter, Harold Fisch, Francis Landy (especially in *Paradoxes of Paradise*), and Meir Weiss.

A good starting-point in the quest for reading strategies is the study of metaphor. In some theories of poetry, beginning with Aristotle, metaphor is the defining characteristic of poetry. While it is generally not taken as such by most modern biblicists, and scant attention has been paid to it in a systematic way,[2] most descriptions of biblical

[2] That is, relative to the attention that has been heaped upon other aspects of poetry. There are some systematic studies of metaphor, going back as far as Robert Lowth. See Alonso Schökel, pp. 95–141; Brensinger; Caird; Watson, pp. 251–72. An example of the treatment of a specific metaphor is Nielsen. There are many fine studies of metaphors in specific passages.

poetry include metaphor, or the broader term "figurative language", along with or as secondary to the formal features of parallelism and meter. A few scholars have come close to privileging metaphor above parallelism.[3] Luis Alonso Schökel (p. 95) says that "Images are the glory, perhaps the essence of poetry." Northrop Frye (p. 54) stated that "we have to consider the possibility that metaphor is not an incidental ornament of biblical language, but one of its controlling modes of thought".

Francis Landy has remarked, in a particularly instructive statement, on the centrality of metaphor in distinguishing poetry from prose.

> Prose perceives the world through relations of contiguity, temporal and spatial, i.e. metonymy; poetry expresses it metaphorically, through relations of likeness and difference. ("Poetics and Parallelism", p. 72)

Landy's description of (poetic) metaphor is very close to that of John Briggs and Richard Monaco, who distinguish between the poetic and non-poetic uses of metaphor.

> In the everyday use of metaphors for clarification or persuasion, the emphasis is nearly always on the similarity between terms; in poetic metaphor *it is on the tension of both the similarities and dissimilarities between them* (Briggs and Monaco, p. 6; italics in the original).

Landy's use of the terms "likeness and difference" and Briggs' and Monaco's "similarities and dissimilarities" call to mind my own use of "equivalence and contrast" in connection with parallelism. Parallelism juxtaposes lines that are, from a linguistic perspective, equivalent on one level while being different on another. Parallel lines contain grammatical and semantic equivalents but are rarely identical. They are the same and yet different; and it is the productive tension between the sameness and the difference that makes parallelism so effective. Robert Alter and James Kugel have advocated a similar view of parallelism although they framed it in a non-linguistic description: parallel lines reframe a thought and develop it further. However one describes it, the combination of likeness and difference is the essence of the relationship between parallel lines.

I will take the next step here, perhaps a leap, and suggest that metaphor and parallelism are two sides of the same coin—counterparts

[3] These scholars espouse different theories of metaphor. I cite them here merely as illustrations of the centrality of metaphor in some literary discussions of the Bible.

of the same phenomenon in a different dimension. They share a functional similarity in structuring the type of perception of the world that poetry engenders. We could say that parallelism operates in the linguistic dimension the way metaphor operates in the conceptual dimension.[4] Parallelism juxtaposes verbal similarities and differences while metaphor juxtaposes non-verbal similarities and differences. It is through the coherent interpretation of both of these types of juxtapositions that meaning is achieved.

Once again I call upon the words of Francis Landy, whose statement I am about to reinterpret. He said of parallelism: "Two halves of the clause are juxtaposed and held to be alike; the basic form of parallelism is metaphor" ("Poetics and Parallelism" p. 81). Landy was using the term "metaphor" in the Jakobsonian sense of the principle of equivalence. He did not, I assume, intend us to understand "metaphor" as "figurative language". He did not mean "metaphor" in its literal sense, but used it figuratively to explain parallelism. I would use the term "parallelism" to explain metaphor; and I mean it quite literally. The basic form of metaphor is parallelism, in the sense of the contiguous or syntagmatic arrangement of paradigmatic elements such that unlikes become alike. The inevitable conclusion is that both parallelism and metaphor are the defining characteristics of biblical poetry.

It follows, then, that, as Patrick Miller suggested more than a decade ago, our next step should be to explore poetic metaphors in the Bible. There are many competing theories of metaphor—linguistic, cognitive, pragmatic, philosophic. To understand them all and apply them to an analysis of biblical metaphor is a worthy task that I would encourage biblical scholars to undertake. But I do not have the fortitude to do so now, so I will simply point to a number of paths that one might take. I will aim for a balance between identifying principles or wide-spread phenomena and interpreting their particular force in specific passages.

Every society has its common, or stock, metaphors, and they are a window onto that society's world-view. Take, for example, the sky, *šāmayim*. In addition to an image of height and the locus of God's presence, how is the sky pictured in biblical poetry? There are four

---

[4] This is close to, but not identical with, the classical formulation of figures of speech and figures of thought.

categories into which most of the images involving the sky may be placed.

1. The sky is personified with verbal and auditory abilities; the sky praises, tells, rejoices, listens.

y^ehall^elûhû šāmayim wā'āreṣ	(Ps. lxix 35);
w^eyôdû šāmayim pil'ăkā	(Ps. lxxxix 6);
haššāmayim m^esapp^erîm k^ebôd-'ēl	(Ps. xix 2);
wayyaggîdû šāmayim ṣidqô	(Ps. l 6 = xcvii 6);
ronnû sāmayim	(Isa. xliv 23);
yiśm^eḥû haššāmayim	(Ps. xcvi 11);
šim'û šāmayim	(Isa. i 2);
ha'ăzînû haššāmayim	(Deut. xxxii 1).

In these verses the sky is a metonymy for the world, a world that bears witness to God's greatness.

2. The sky is a thin material, easily shaped.

hannôṭeh kaddōq šāmayim	(Isa. xl 22);
nôṭeh šāmayim kay^erî'â	(Ps. civ 2);
w^enāgōllû kassēper haššāmāyim	(Isa. xxxiv 4);
lû'-qāra'tā šāmayim	(Isa. lxiii 19).

The sky, again a metonymy for the world, is malleable in God's hands.

3. The sky is pictured as having parts of a building—doors, columns, and windows.

dal^etê šāmayim	(Ps. lxxxviii 23);
'ammûdê šāmayim	(Job xxvi 11);
'ărubbōt haššāmayim	(Gen. vii 11; 2 Kgs vii 2, 19).

This image contrasts with the malleability of the sky in the previous set of verses. Here the sky is a strong and solid structure.

4. The sky is a source of provisions: grain, food, water. This is a more circumscribed category and does not refer to ordinary provisions. In Ps. lxxviii 24 manna is "grain of (or from) the sky", and in Ps. cv 40 the quail is "the food/meat of (or from) the sky", Job xxxviii 37 speaks of "bottles of the sky" in the sense of the source of precipitation.

The examples in categories 3 and 4 are expressed in grammatical constructions employing the status constructus. This suggests another way of pursuing the study of metaphors: through a linguistic analysis of their structures. This approach was used by Lida Knorina in an unpublished paper entitled "The Range of Biblical Metaphors in *smikhut*".[5] Knorina attempted to ascertain the rules governing the interpretation of metaphors that occur in *smikhut* constructions. She noted that in one model the image in the MODIFIER is transferred as a metaphorizing property to the HEAD, as in *lēb hāʾeben* "heart of stone" (Ezek. xi 19); *qešet rᵉmiyyâ* "a bow of deceit" (Hos. vii 16). In a second model, the image in the HEAD is transferred through a metaphorizing predicate to the object of the metaphor. An example is *zalʿăpôt rāʿāb* "storms of famine" (Lam. v 10). Knorina further differentiates types according to the specific relationship that pertains between the two terms in the construction. In the course of defining these relationships she notes that "collections or containers", often used in non-metaphorical *smikhut* constructions, seem to lend themselves to metaphorical use: *ṣᵉrôr haḥayyîm* (1 Sam. xxv 29); *kôs ḥămātô* (Isa. li 17); *kap naḥat* (Eccl. iv 6). Knorina's work, which is too technical to present here in detail, is a contribution towards a linguistic explanation of the process whereby these types of metaphors may be interpreted.

Exploring categories of images and analysing the linguistic construction of metaphors are just two of many approaches to the study of metaphor. In the remainder of this paper I will present interpretations of selected metaphors in specific contexts. I have limited my analysis to short passages, and therefore have not addressed the equally important issue of metaphors that structure entire poems.

Metaphor involves more than a simple comparison or equation of one object with another. By placing the two objects in juxtaposition, a relationship between them is established such that their qualities may become interchanged. This can be seen in Ps. xlii 2–3:

kᵉʾayyāl taʿărōg ʿal-ʾăpîqê māyim
kēn napšî taʿărōg ʾēlekā ʾĕlōhîm
ṣāmᵉʾâ napšî lēʾlōhîm

As a deer longs for streams [ʾ*pyqy*] of water,
So my soul longs for you, O God.
My soul thirsts for God. . . .

[5] Lida Knorina was a Russian linguist who died on 4 June 1994. Her husband, Vladimir Borshchev, sent me her paper after her death.

Water, the life-sustaining element, is equated with God; and the psalmist's thirst for God is like the deer's thirst for water. It is a natural, intuitive thirst for a basic substance. Thus the qualities of the deer-image are transposed to the psalmist. But "longing" is not an emotion usually associated with a deer. It is a human emotion, transposed from the psalmist's longing for God on to the deer. The verb that one would expect in *v.* 1 in connection with the deer, "to thirst", is used for the psalmist in *v.* 2. There is a cross-over effect: the deer longs (like a human) for water, and the human being thirsts (like a deer) for God.

This passage exemplifies the interplay between metaphor and parallelism. By using "to long" in the first two lines and "to thirst" in the third, a sense of incrementation is created, of the type we have come to expect in parallelism. Is "thirsting" stronger than "longing"? If so, the psalmist's need for God is even greater than the deer's need for water. The psalmist's need is first equated with the deer's and then it surpasses it.

The psalm continues the image of sustaining water in *v.* 4 with "my tears have become daily and nightly food". This is no doubt invoking the common association between water and food (*leḥem*) but again it is unexpected. Tears should be equated with water, not with food. Another increment is occurring. Food is more nourishing than water, and taken together, food and water constitute total sustenance. Earlier we deduced that the psalmist needs God more than the deer needs water. Now we may deduce that God is not only water, he is food, too. He is the psalmist's complete diet, his only sustenance. And instead of the life-sustaining protection of God, the psalmist has only a symbol of despair, tears.

Even stock images like water can be used creatively. Let us see how the same term found in Ps. xlii 2, *ʾāpîq*, "stream", is used in two other passages.

Job vi 15:

ʾaḥay bāgᵉdû kᵉmô-nāḥal
kaʾăpîq nᵉḥālîm yaʿăbōrû

My companions are as treacherous as a wadi,
Like a wadi-stream [*ʾpyq*] they vanish [or: that vanishes].

The image is taken from nature: the wadis that flow with water in the winter and are dried up in the summer. The primary transfer of qualities in Job vi 15 is from the water to the companions. They are treacherously inconsistent like the wadis; they are unreliable, changing with the seasons. The choice of water imagery may also suggest that, like water, the companions should be life-giving, and therefore their betrayal is all the more disappointing. But there is also a transfer in the other direction. One does not normally think of wadis as traitors, yet that is what is suggested here in a hint of personification of the wadis.[6] Interpreters usually feel compelled to decide whether the verb *yaʿăbōrû* refers to the companions or to the wadi-stream. The first is grammatically easier to justify (a plural verb and a plural subject); however, the second is not impossible. (The plural verb may be influenced by the plural *nᵉḥālîm*; cf. the following verse.) But to choose one to the exclusion of the other is to lose the poetic ambiguity, for the verb may refer to both antecedents. (Compare the verb *yaṣlîaḥ* in Ps. i 3.) In fact, through the use of this verb, and also *bāgᵉdû* and through the effect of the parallelism, there is an exchange of qualities between the companions and the wadi-stream so that the image is doubly fused. The companions act like a wadi-stream in that they vanish; and the wadis become, by implication, like the companions in that they are treacherous.

The same natural image is used for the opposite effect in Ps. cxxvi 4.

> *šûbâ yhwh ʾet-šᵉbîtēnû [ketib: šbwtnw] kaʾăpîqîm bannegeb*
>
> Restore our fortunes, O Lord, like streams [*ʾpyqym*] in the Negev.

Here the stream is not an image of treachery but an image of hope: the return of the streams in the rainy season. The restoration of fortunes will be like the streams in their cyclical return, and therefore inevitable. The notion of the yearly cycle continues in the Psalm's next two verses with the image of sowing and reaping, correlating with a transition from sorrow to joy.

Sometimes there are multiple metaphors linked to one subject. One intriguing example is Ps. xix 5b–6:

[6] Although the verb *bāgad* does not occur elsewhere with water, Raymond de Hoop pointed out to me the use of *paḥaz* "unstable as water" in Gen. xlix 4. The link between *pḥz* and *bgd* is forged in Zeph. iii 4: *nᵉbîʾehā pōḥăzîm ʾanšê bōgᵉdôt*. Water is unstable in that, not being a solid, it does not retain its shape and is difficult to contain—it may ooze away. The wadis are "traitors" in that they lack consistency; they are sometimes present and sometimes gone.

lassĕmes śām ʾōhel bāhem
w^e hûʾ k^e ḥātān yōṣēʾ mēḥuppātô
yāśîś kegibbôr lārûṣ ʾōraḥ

For the sun he set a tent therein [in the sky],
Which is like a bridegroom coming out from his wedding chamber.
It strains eagerly like a powerful man about to run a course.

There is a flood of intertwined imagery here that recalls images elsewhere in the Bible and yet employs them in different ways. The sky as a tent is found in Isa. xl 22, but there the tent is a thin, flimsy thing, to show how easily God can arrange the sky. The idea of a tent in the sky for the sun is unusual, and the image it conveys is not readily apparent.[7] The sun emerging from this tent, itself a metaphor, is compared in a simile to a bridegroom emerging from his wedding chamber. This image is usually interpreted to mean that just as the bridegroom emerges joyful and bright, so does the sun rise in brilliant joy.[8] One might add the notion of the crown or headdress traditionally worn by the groom (see Isa. lxi 10 and Song iii 11); the rising sun is crowned with radiant splendor, like a groom. But, although commonly accepted, this interpretation may not draw out the full potential of the image. We will look more deeply into it.

The image of the bridegroom is followed by an equally masculine one of a powerful runner. What makes the connection stronger is the use, at the beginning of 6b, of the verb *yāśîś*, a verb usually translated "rejoice" and often found in association with "bride and groom" (Isa. lxii 5; Jer. vii 34, xvi 9, xxv 10, xxxiii 11). It may seem at first that we have another case of crossover—the use of a verb in the second line referring to the *gibbôr* that is more appropriate to the *ḥātān* in the previous line. But I do not think that *yāśîś* means "rejoice" here. And, I would add, the interpretation of *yāśîś* as "rejoice" has tended to obfuscate the bridegroom image in the preceding line. The more appropriate interpretation of *yāśîś* is in connection with strength. Support for this is found in Job xxxix 21, in the description of the horse.

yaḥp^e rû bāʿēmeq w^e yāśîś b^e kōaḥ

He paws with force, he *yāśîś* with strength.

---

[7] Perhaps an abode for the sun below the horizon.

[8] Or, as Ibn Ezra says, people greet the rising sun with joy.

The verb *yāśîś* would seem to mean "be eager, ardent, strain with excitement". Its use with the horse and with the sun imagined as a runner poised at the starting-gate betokens a swift and powerful force. The sun as a powerful force, an anticipation, as it were, of thermodynamics, becomes itself a metaphor in Judg. v 31: "So may all your enemies perish, O Lord, but may his loyal ones be like the sun rising in its power." In Ps. xix, as in Judg. v, the sun is linked with *gibbôr* or *g^{e}bûrâ*. The sun is an emblem of masculine power. Returning to the bridegroom coming out from his wedding chamber, one may see this as an image of virility as much as an image of radiance.[9]

On occasion, the same image may recur in close proximity with a new twist that gives a jarring effect, reinforcing the power of the image, as in the following two examples from Isaiah. The first is "Sodom and Gomorrah".

Isa. i 9–10:

> Had not the Lord of Hosts left us some survivors,
> We would have been *like Sodom*,
> Looked *like Gomorrah*.
> Hear the word of the Lord,
> You chieftains of *Sodom*;
> Give ear to our God's instruction,
> You folk of *Gomorrah*.

Because the Sodom-and-Gomorrah image has two different connotations, Isaiah is able to use it for two different effects. He first invokes the association of Sodom and Gomorrah with total destruction, suggesting that the destruction that he describes might have been, but for the grace of God, as catastrophic. But then, in an arresting reversal, he calls upon the association of Sodom and Gomorrah with total corruption, equating his present audience with the wickedness of Sodom and Gomorrah, which must inevitably lead them to a similarly catastrophic end.

The second image is "like a garment" in Isa. li 6–8:

> Raise your eyes to the heavens,
> And look upon the earth beneath.
> Though the heavens should evaporate like smoke,

[9] For an enlightening reading of the entire psalm see Fisch, *Poetry with a Purpose*, pp. 120–6.

And the earth wear out *like a garment*,
And its inhabitants in like manner die out,
My salvation shall stand for ever.
My deliverance shall not cease.
Listen to me, you who know the right,
You people with my teaching in its heart.
Fear not human insults,
And be not dismayed at their jeers.
For the moth shall eat them up *like a garment*,
The caterpillar shall eat them like wool.
But my deliverance shall endure for ever,
My salvation through the ages.

The image of the earth wearing out like a garment makes the earth, which does not wear out nearly so quickly, seem ephemeral compared to the permanence of God's victory. Then, in verse 8, the jeering enemy will be eaten as a moth eats a garment, making the enemy not only ephemeral but powerless before the attack of a small insect which will come to punish it.

While the single use of "Sodom and Gomorrah" and "being eaten like a garment" would be effective, the reuse of these images strengthens the rhetorical effect by forcing the audience to revisualize the image in a different context, with a different range of associations.

To sum up, I have suggested that metaphor is as important a constituent of poetry as parallelism, and that they both achieve their effects through the juxtaposition of things that are alike and yet different. I have suggested some directions that a study of metaphor might take, and have offered interpretations of specific passages. I have not addressed the interesting question how we recognize metaphors; nor have I discussed over-arching metaphors drawn from the biblical narrative itself—like the creation and the exodus. I would again stress the importance of the study of biblical metaphor, for to understand the Bible's use of imagery is to perceive the network of relationships in the biblical text and in the view of the world that it represents. Therein lies the meaning of the biblical message.

BIBLIOGRAPHY

Alonso Schökel, Luis, *A Manual of Hebrew Poetics* (Rome, 1988).

Alter, Robert, *The Art of Biblical Poetry* (New York, 1985).

Berlin, Adele, *The Dynamics of Biblical Parallelism* (Bloomington, Indiana, 1985).

Brensinger, Terry Lee, *Lions, Wind and Fire. A Study of Prophetic Similes* (unpublished Dissertation, Drew University, 1985).

Briggs, John, and Monaco, Richard, *Metaphor: The Logic of Poetry* (New York, 1990).

Caird, G.B., *The Language and Imagery of the Bible* (London and Philadelphia, 1980).

Fisch, Harold, "The Analogy of Nature, a Note on the Structure of Old Testament Imagery", *Journal of Theological Studies*, NS 6 (1955), pp. 161–73.

———, *Poetry with a Purpose* (Bloomington, Indiana, 1988).

Follis, Elaine R. (ed.), *Directions in Biblical Hebrew Poetry* (Sheffield, 1987).

Frye, Northrop, *The Great Code* (London, 1982).

Knorina, Lida, "The Range of Biblical Metaphors in *smikhut*" (unpublished paper, 1994).

Kugel, James, *The Idea of Biblical Poetry. Parallelism and Its History* (New Haven, Conn., 1981).

Kuntz, J. Kenneth, "Recent Perspectives on Biblical Poetry", *Religious Studies Review* 19/4 (1993), pp. 321–7.

Landy, Francis, *Paradoxes of Paradise. Identity and Difference in the Song of Songs* (Sheffield, 1983).

———, "Poetics and Parallelism: Some Comments on James Kugel's *The Idea of Biblical Poetry*", *JSOT* 28 (1984), pp. 61–87.

Miller, Patrick D., "Meter, Parallelism, and Tropes: The Search for Poetic Style", *JSOT* 28 (1984), pp. 99–106.

Nielsen, Kirsten, *There is Hope for a Tree. The Tree as Metaphor in Isaiah* (Sheffield, 1985).

Noppen, J.-P. van, *Metaphor. A Bibliography of Post-1970 Publications* (Amsterdam and Philadelphia, 1985).

———, *Metaphor II. A Classified Bibliography of Publications 1985 to 1990* (Amsterdam and Philadelphia, 1990).

Powell, Mark Allan, *The Bible and Modern Literary Criticism* (New York, 1992).

Preminger, A., and Brogan, T.V.F., *The New Princeton Encyclopedia of Poetry and Poetics* (Princeton, 1993).

Watson, Wilfred G.E., *Classical Hebrew Poetry. A Guide to its Techniques* (Sheffield, 1984).

Weiss, Meir, *The Bible from Within* (Jerusalem, 1984).

THE END OF THE MALE CULT PROSTITUTE: A LITERARY-HISTORICAL AND SOCIOLOGICAL ANALYSIS OF HEBREW *QĀDĒŠ-QĔDĒŠÎM*

by

PHYLLIS A. BIRD
Evanston, Illinois

In this article I shall argue that the predication of a class of "male cult prostitutes" in ancient Israel on the basis of occurrences in the MT of the terms *qādēš* and *qĕdēšîm* is questionable on literary, linguistic, and sociological grounds. Briefly summarized, the arguments are as follows: (1) the expression "male cult prostitute" does not correspond to any ancient locution; (2) the institution as reconstructed in the secondary literature does not make sense in terms of current understandings of the social and religious organization of ancient Israel and the ancient Near East; (3) the textual evidence exhibits no first-hand knowledge of the institution. The discussion focuses on the textual evidence, interpreted in the light of literary-historical and sociological considerations.[1]

Linguistic considerations

The linguistic argument concerns the terminology commonly used to translate the Hebrew terms, and applies equally to the masculine and feminine forms of the noun. It is independent of questions of historicity or assumed function(s). Nevertheless, because the nomenclature has had a determining effect on the way the phenomenon has been conceived, and hence on the way the textual evidence has been interpreted, the issue of terminology becomes a substantive consideration.

[1] This article is drawn from a larger study of *qĕdēšâ/qĕdēšîm* and assumes an understanding of the feminine term that cannot be fully explicated here. The treatment of the masculine forms is also necessarily abbreviated.

The expression "cultic (or 'sacred') prostitute", as a combination of terms referring on the one hand to the sacred sphere and on the other to profane sexual commerce,[2] does not correspond to the Hebrew lexeme, which points only to a sacred or cultic identification;[3] nor does it have a counterpart in any ancient Semitic usage.[4] No compound term linking the ideas of cultic service and prostitution is found in any of the cultures for which the institution of "sacred prostitution" has been posited. The Akkadian evidence is particularly clear in showing that the prostitute (*ḫarimtu*) and the several classes of cult-related women, including the *qadištu*, belong to quite distinct social and literary contexts.[5] Thus the concept of "sacred prostitution" rep-

[2] Prostitution is the granting of sexual access for payment (Gagnon, p. 592). Because terms for prostitutes and prostitution are used at times more broadly to describe promiscuous sexual relations or lewd behavior, usually by a woman (see the *Oxford English Dictionary*, s.v. "prostitute" for English usage), it is often difficult to determine the exact nature of practices characterized as "prostitution", especially in polemical accounts. In Hebrew, the female prostitute is designated by a participle (*zônâ*) from a root used to describe indiscriminate and/or illicit sexual activity, especially on the part of an unmarried woman. A secondary, metaphorical use of the root to describe Israel's illicit "affairs" with foreign gods has resulted in confusion and conflation of meanings in the secondary literature, which cannot be analysed here. There is no masculine professional noun from this root corresponding to *zônâ*. Male (homosexual) prostitution is poorly attested in the Hebrew Bible, the single occurrence of an apparent reference to a male prostitute (described as a "dog" [*keleb*]) is treated below. See Bird (1989a), pp. 120–1; Bird (1993); cf. Goodfriend.

[3] *qādēš* (m.)/*qĕdēšâ* (f.) is a *qaṭil*-type noun from the common Semitic root *QDŠ* meaning "holy" or "sacred". A literal rendering would be "Geweihter", "consecrated person". All other Hebrew formations from this root exhibit a sense of holiness or relationship to a deity or a sanctuary (BDB, pp. 871–4; *HALAT*, pp. 1003–8). The cognate languages demonstrate the same range of meanings and usage (Costecalde; Müller; Xella).

[4] Wacker (pp. 51–2) credits the expression, as well as the conception, to British anthropologists of the Victorian era. See esp. Frazer (1914), pp. 41, 51, 70, 71; and William Robertson Smith, whose 1889 *Lectures on the Religion of the Semites* referred to "temples of Semitic deities thronged with sacred prostitutes" (p. 436). Wilhelm (p. 511) argues that A.H. Sayce (1883) was the first to connect Herodotus' remarks in Klio 199 (= 1.199) with temple prostitutes, identifying them with the *qadištu*s of Assyrian texts. A basis for the modern expression may be found in the usage of Classical and Patristic authors, who describe the activities of women at various sanctuaries as prostitution—but this language is always used of someone else's practice (either ancient or foreign).

[5] Based on my analysis of *qadištu* and *ḫarimtu* texts. See Westenholz, pp. 250–5, 262; Gruber (1986), pp. 139-46. While van der Toorn (1992) argues against "narrowing down" the activities of the *qadištu* to those of a prostitute, he asserts that "the term does at times refer to a prostitute" (p. 512). Since no texts are cited, it is impossible to determine what evidence he has in mind. His argument that the *qadištu* operated together with the *ḫarimtu* and the *ištarītu* under the patronage of Ishtar, the goddess of love (p. 512) falsely infers common activity from common identification with a goddess of many roles. Moreover, the identification is problematic. Westenholz (p. 251) argues that the *qadištu* had a special

resents an outsiders' interpretation of an institution or activities regarded as strange and generally abhorrent.

The interpretation that has dominated modern discussion of the subject is that of Sir James Frazer, who assembled a collection of texts from western Asia reporting a variety of practices described as "sacred prostitution" and provided an interpretative construct of a common underlying myth-and-ritual pattern.[6] It is this construct, centered in the notion of copulating deities and their human representatives as the essential feature of "fertility cult religion", that continues to play a determining role in discussions of ancient Near Eastern religion.[7] Only in recent years have dissenting voices begun to sound—from a number of different directions.[8]

Frazer's main contribution to the ideas current in his time was his insistence that the sexual activity of women with strangers reported in antiquity for various temples of western Asia, and characterized as "prostitution", was to be understood as fundamentally religious, hence as "*sacred* prostitution".[9] What requires note is the fact that

---

relationship to a male deity (Adad is named in a number of texts), in contrast to the *ḫarimtu*, who is associated with a female deity. None of Wilhelm's examples of temple prostitutes includes *qadištu*s.

[6] The theory is articulated in Frazer's study of the cult of Adonis, first appearing in the two-volume work, *Adonis, Attis, Osiris: Studies in the History of Oriental Religion* (London, 1906; expanded 1907), which was incorporated into the third edition of *The Golden Bough* (1914). See Oden, pp. 137–8; Wacker, pp. 52–3. For a critique of the classical sources to which Frazer and others appealed, see Oden, pp. 138–52; and n. 8 below.

[7] Oden, pp. 138–40. Cf. Pope; Fauth. A concept of "sacred marriage" undergirds most constructions of "sacred prostitution" (e.g., Fauth, p. 24). See Renger (1975) for a history and critique of the idea. Cf. Wacker, p. 53, n. 8.

[8] E.g., Oden, pp. 140–7; van der Toorn (1992), p. 510; Westenholz, p. 263; Frymer-Kensky, pp. 199–202. While van der Toorn rejects the notion of ritual sex, he continues to use the term "cultic prostitution" in the limited sense of "prostitution that was profitable to, and at times organized by, the temple and its administration" (p. 510). Under this designation he includes "occasional prostitution" engaged in by women without other means to pay vows (pp. 511–12), prostitutes organized or engaged by temples as a source of temple income, and cultic personnel (such as the "consecrated persons") who might also be employed by the temple in prostitution as a source of revenue (p. 512). I find this combination of practices under a cover term that lacks ancient attestation problematic. Wilhelm finds evidence of prostitutes among the classes of temple personnel at some temples (pp. 514–24), but no evidence of ritual/cultic prostitution, nor of *qadištu*s as prostitutes.

[9] Frazer (pp. 57–61) rejected the theory that derived this "religious prostitution" from a "purely secular and precautionary practice of destroying a bride's virginity before handing her over to her husband" (p. 57). As proponents of this theory he cites L.R. Farnell, "Sociological hypotheses concerning the position of women in ancient religion", *ARW* 7

the primary data on which the theory is built are descriptions of *female* activity—of the most varied sorts.[10] Little attention has been given to the men whose role in the sacred drama is equally essential and who are identified variously as male worshippers, priests, the king, and "sacred men".[11] It is this orientation to the female role, inherent in the notion of prostitution,[12] and exhibited in the textual evidence, that presents one of the most serious problems for interpreting the biblical *qdšym*.

I have argued that the English expression, "sacred prostitution" (and its modern language equivalents), has no counterpart in ancient Semitic texts, although it may have a root in classical usage. A biblical basis for this association of ideas is clearly laid, however, in the juxtaposition (but not union) of *zwnh* "prostitute/harlot" and *qdšh* in the Hebrew Bible. It is this association, in a manner that makes the former term define the latter,[13] that has been decisive for the history of interpretation and translation of Hebrew *qdšh*/*qdš*.[14] And it is an association focused on the feminine form of the term. Thus in the Bible as well as the texts from classical antiquity, the institution interpreted as "sacred/cultic prostitution" is conceived on a female model.

(1904), p. 88; M.P. Nilsson, *Griechische Feste* (Leipzig, 1906), pp. 366–7; and Fr. Cumont, *Les religions orientales dans le paganisme Romain* (2nd edn, Paris, 1909), pp. 361–2 (Frazer, p. 57, n. 1).

[10] A primary objection to standard descriptions of "sacred prostitution" must be their indiscriminate use of evidence of the most disparate sorts in terms of personnel, time, place, and frequency of occurrence. See Westenholz, p. 261.

[11] Frazer is an exception to this rule, since his interest in priest-kings and the Adonis myth led him to focus on the male role. But he recognizes a wide range of players, including the Hebrew *qdšym*, whom he describes as "strange clergy" (p. 18), avoiding the term "prostitute", which he reserves for their female counterparts (not partners), the "sacred women" (*qdšwt*). See below.

[12] Prostitution is an overwhelmingly female institution, designed to serve male interests. The rare incidence of male (homosexual) prostitution in the ancient Near East likewise serves male interests. See Bird (1993).

[13] Each occurrence of *qdšh*/*qdšwt* in the Hebrew Bible involves a polemical identification with *zwnh* by means of parallelism or interchange. The identification assumes a distinction, but also a judgement; the reader is meant to understand that the "consecrated woman" is "simply" a kind of prostitute. It is possible that *qdšh* came to function in some Hebrew uses as a "euphemism" for *zwnh*, much as "courtesan" in English. See Bird (1989a), pp. 125–6.

[14] All the major modern English versions employ the term "prostitute" (or an equivalent), either in combination with "cult"/"temple"/"sacred" or alone, in translating all occurrences of the feminine noun. See Henshaw (p. 219) for other modern and ancient versions. Cf. BDB: "temple-prostitute" ("= harlot", Gen. xxxviii 21–2); *HALAT*: "Geweihte, Kult-prostituierte". For translation of the masculine forms, see below.

Sociocultural considerations

The notion of male cult prostitution is derived from the conception of the female form on the basis of the common terminology—attested only in Biblical Hebrew.[15] Attempts to understand the *qdš* as the male counterpart of a "female cult prostitute" fall into two distinct categories. Where the model of prostitution dominates, the *qdš* is understood as a homosexual prostitute, in keeping with the form of the "secular" institution (hence *KJV* "sodomite"). The alternative interpretation is guided by the "sacred marriage" model with its view of the female role as representing the goddess in the ritual union of the sexes. The male role is then conceived as analogous. Both construals are deeply problematic, however, even under the (now questionable) assumption that sexual activity had an essential place in the Canaanite cult.[16]

First, homosexual intercourse has no place in a fertility cult. It fails to support, and in fact threatens, the primary symbolism of the cult (as commonly reconstructed), which centers in the union of male and female.[17] As cultic activity, it produces neither symbol nor effect appropriate to its assumed functions. A variant of the homosexual model points to classes such as the Akkadian *assinnu* or male devotees of a goddess who castrated themselves in her honor.[18] Such interpretations rest in part on questionable understandings of the assumed models and lose connection with the female institution they are thought to imitate or complement—or involve contorted identifications of disparate symbol systems.[19] The notion of homosexual

[15] Cognate terms are confined to a single gender in each cultural/linguistic area (see below). The Hebrew Bible is the only corpus containing both masculine and feminine forms, and Deut. xxiii 18 is the only text in which they appear together.

[16] An identification of the *qdšwt/qdšym* with Canaanite practice is typically assumed by commentators, often improperly described as "syncretism". That, I believe, is how the biblical writers intend them to be understood, although they are never explicitly identified as "Canaanite" or pagan. But such theopolitical constructions can not be taken as historical data; moreover, references to *qdšwt/qdšym* appear only in sources far removed from any time in which "Canaanites" might have formed a recognizably distinct presence in the land.

[17] Consequently, Frazer (p. 73) objected to the rendering of *qdšym* as "sodomites" in the English Bible of his day (*KJV*).

[18] See Marglin, p. 311; and Albright (pp. 153–4), who equates the "male prostitutes (*qĕdēshîm*)" with the *cinaedi* or *galli* known to classical writers and the *kulu'u, asinnu*, and *kurgarrû* of cuneiform sources. He further identifies them with the *kĕmārîm*, whom he characterizes as "eunuch priests"—an identification, and characterization, that appears to be pure speculation.

[19] Exhibited, e.g., by Marglin, who interprets various examples of male transvestitism and self-castration as means of identification with the goddess, but also describes the

prostitution makes sense only if the *qdšym* are understood simply as male prostitutes who operate at sanctuaries alongside their female counterparts, offering a choice of sexual partners to male worshippers.[20]

The alternative interpretation is equally problematic in its notion of analogous function and assumed complementarity of roles. In the case of the *qdšh*, the priest(s) or male worshippers are the assumed partners, with the *qdšh* representing the goddess. But who are the partners of the *qdšym*, and what deity do they represent? The idea of providing sexual service to female worshippers analogous to that provided by female "cult prostitutes" assumes a view of women's roles that runs counter to what we know both of the cultus, as organized essentially with males in mind, and of socially sanctioned sexual relations, which are designed primarily to serve male needs and desires.[21] It seems unlikely that any Israelite man would allow his wife or daughter to have intercourse with a stranger, even a "sacred man", at a sanctuary. The notion of analogous function fails to recognize the characteristic asymmetry of sexual roles, rights, and expectations that is the mark of patriarchal societies.[22]

I have argued that both the nomenclature used to describe *qdšym* in modern interpretation and the general conceptions of the class or institution are inappropriate to the term's ancient Near Eastern social

---

practitioners as representing a dying and rising god—the husband or son of the goddess, who symbolizes the death and rebirth of nature (pp. 311–12).

[20] This would appear to be the view of van der Toorn (1992), since he denies a ritual interpretation and argues that "the parallelism between *qĕdēšâ* and *zônâ* . . . favors the idea that the *qĕdēšîm* engaged primarily in sexual activities" (p. 512). In arguing for prostitution "as a source of profits for the temple", he cites 2 Kgs. xxiii 7 as evidence (p. 511) (—understanding the m.pl. as a gender-inclusive term?). His discussion of prostitution for payment of vows is entirely oriented to women's lack of independent sources of income (pp. 511–12; cf. idem 1989). Thus his conclusion surprises by including men in this category: "the phenomenon of women—*and, occasionally, men*—prostituting themselves in order to obtain money to pay vows was known and to some extent accepted" (p. 512; emphasis added). He offers no evidence or argument for this extension, and by explaining the practice in terms of the peculiar socioeconomic circumstances of women, he renders the male "counterpart" even more enigmatic.

[21] See Bird (1987), esp. pp. 401–3; Bird (1992), pp. 952–3. Frazer's speculation that the *qdšym* in the Jerusalem temple (2 Kgs xxiii 7) played the role of Tammuz/Adonis to the women weeping for Tammuz (Ezek. viii 14) (p. 17) combines mourning rituals with "sacred marriage" rites and is not supported by either text. Elsewhere, Frazer suggests that barren women might resort to intercourse with the "holy men" in the hope of obtaining offspring from them (p. 78)—an example of secondary function at best, which transforms symbolic action into literal. The notion also rests on a misinterpretation of theophoric names as designating divine offspring.

[22] Bird (1992), p. 953. See Rosaldo.

and religious context. The implications of my critique may be summarized as follows:

(1) The term "sacred prostitute" should be rejected *as a translation* of *qdš(h)*, because it incorporates into the name of the class an identification with prostitution that is lacking in the Hebrew term. The biblical writer may believe that the *qdš(h)* is "simply" a prostitute, but that message is conveyed in the MT through the literary environment in which the consecrated (wo)man is placed. In the case of *qdšh*, the Hebrew reader is led to draw this conclusion by the juxtaposition of the term with *zwnh*. The reader of a modern translation should be allowed to do likewise.

(2) The argument concerning nomenclature entails no judgement about the actual role and/or activity of the *qdš(h)*, including the question whether (s)he engaged in any form of sexual activity and under what conditions.[23] It does point to cognate usage as an essential source for interpreting the Hebrew terms, in combination with literary analysis that attends to the distinctive contexts of MT/Israelite usage.

(3) Any attempt to reconstruct a male class on the basis of evidence for a female class is problematic because of the prevailing pattern of asymmetry of sexual roles and the absence of ancient Near Eastern parallels.

(4) The models of prostitution and/or "sacred marriage" to explain the role of the *qdšh* are questionable in the light of recent scholarship and especially problematic when extended to a male class.

Cognate evidence[24]

Akkadian and Ugaritic texts contain references to classes of persons bearing the title "consecrated person" (Akk. *qadištu*, Ug. *qdš*) associated

[23] While it has become increasingly doubtful that sexual intercourse involving cultic personnel ever played a role in the *ritual* performed in ancient Near Eastern sanctuaries, it would appear to be as difficult to deny sexual activity on the part of ancient religious professionals as for their modern counterparts. Whether the biblical texts present us with a debased form of an institution or simply a polemical portrait is difficult to determine without extra-biblical evidence for the same period and milieu. Cognate evidence from Mesopotamia and Ugarit contains no sign of the sexual associations exhibited in the MT's use of the Hebrew terms. The evidence cited by Wilhelm for prostitutes under temple administration involves the ordinary terms for prostitutes and prostitution, *ḫarim/ntu* and *ḫarim(t)ūtu* (pp. 12–16).

[24] It is impossible here to review, or even summarize, this important evidence. Gruber

with priests and temples in liturgical roles, but also (in Mesopotamia) involved in a variety of activities whose relationship to the cult is not apparent from the preserved records. Akkadian texts know only a female class, attested in more than 70 citations in the *CAD*.[25] Ugaritic evidence is thus far confined to male references, most in lists of professions, where *qdšm* follows *khnm* ("priests"), suggesting a class of "lay" temple servants.[26]

On the basis of the cognate evidence, and other Hebrew uses of the root *QDŠ*, we should expect Hebrew *qdš(h)* to describe a comparable class of persons set apart for cult-related service. The form of the service and the deity for whom it is performed are not determined by the title and may be expected to vary from place to place. The fact that classes identified by the term "consecrated" appear to be confined to a single sex at any given place is instructive, however,

(1986) and Westenholz give the fullest treatments available to date. See also Costecalde, cols 1377–9, 1368–72; Renger (1967), pp. 179-84.

[25] Most of the texts do not permit precise determination of the *qadištu*'s functions and duties or of the deity to whom she was dedicated. The Code of Hammurapi (CH § 181) names the *qadištu* alongside two other classes of cult-related women, the *nadītu* and *kulmašītu*, in an inheritance law treating the case of a daughter "given to a god" by her father. In other texts *qadištu*s are associated with birthing (a special "house" where the midwife helps the woman in labor is called *bīt qadišti* "house of the *qadištu*" in the Old Babylonian version of Atra-hasis (Lambert and Millard, pp. 62–3, line 290), translated "house of the prostitute"[!]) and wet-nursing (VAS 7 10 1–3; VAS 37 13–17; Ana ittišu VII iii 11–14). The clearest example of ritual activity is found in a Middle Assyrian text (*KAR* 154) describing a procession from the temple of Adad in Assur. A group of *qadištu*s accompany the priest (*šangû*), "intoning" and "prolonging" the *inḫu*-chant at each stop on the route, and in conclusion consume the remains of the sacrificial offerings together with the priest, *qadištu*s are also associated with purification rituals involving the sprinkling of water: (Lambert, *BWL*, p. 160, lines 5–9; *KAR* 321–7). In first millennium Babylonian texts (*Maqlû* III 40–55, V 51–60, VI 26–31; *Šurpu* III 116–17, VIII 69) *qadištu*s are identified with sorceresses and witches, suggesting a development in which their powers associated with exorcism and/or their independence of family/male control led to a demonizing of the class (Westenholz, p. 253). See Gruber (1986), pp. 139–46; Westenholz, pp. 250–5.

[26] Von Soden, pp. 329–30. The texts are *KTU* 4.29:3; 4.36:2; 4.38:2; 4.68:73; 4.126:7. A ritual text (*KTU* 1.112:21) specifies that a *qdš* is to sing (*w qdš yšr*). An Akkadian text from Ugarit records the king's elevation of a man from the class/status of **qadšu* (*ina qadšutti iššīma*) to that of *maryannu*, including a tax exemption to him and his sons—evidence, as von Soden (p. 330) observed, that the *qdš* at Ugarit could marry and have children. Two occurrences of the f. noun *qdšt* are attested in what appear to be names or components of names (*KTU* 4.69 V 11; RS 17.36:14). The interpretation of both is disputed. Cf. Westenholz, pp. 249–50; Gruber (1986), p. 147. I am inclined to see it as deriving from the epithet of a deity, "the Holy one" (cf. the goddess Qudshu), rather than the professional noun "consecrated person". I do not think one can posit a class of female hierodules on the basis of this evidence.

for evaluating the biblical evidence. This represents a general pattern of ancient Near Eastern cultic organization, illustrated by J. Renger's study of the "priesthood" in the Old Babylonian period. Among the many classes of religious specialists treated in this study, none but the EN and the various classes of "prophets" include male and female specialists under a common designation.[27] It appears to be a general rule that cultic personnel of the type described as "priests" or "priestesses" were distinguished by gender-specific titles and functions,[28] while "charismatic" or "oracular" specialists might include both men and women under a single title (as in Israel), with identical, or comparable, functions.[29]

Literary-historical considerations

Key factors in my analysis are the distribution of the terms in the canonical text and the contexts of use. The feminine noun *qĕdēšâ* (pl. *qĕdēšôt*) occurs five times in the Hebrew Bible—and nowhere else in the extant corpus of West Semitic texts. The Hebrew usage is confined to three passages: Gen. xxxviii 21–2 (sg., 3 times); Hos. iv 14 (pl.); Deut. xxiii 18 ([EVV. 17] sg.). In the Deuteronomy text, which is also the latest of the three,[30] *qdšh* is complemented by the masculine

---

[27] Renger (1967), p. 113.

[28] This is the class described by Renger (1967, p. 112) as "Kultpriester (einschließlich der 'Priesterinnen')"—in contrast to "Wahrsager und Wahrsagerinnen" and "Beschwörungspriester" (all male). The term "priestess" as a designation of various classes of cult-related women is misleading in suggesting status and function analogous to priests. Akkadian lacks a comprehensive term for the various classes of cult-related personnel, as does Hebrew. I have adopted the Greek term "hierodule", in its primary etymological meaning of "sacred servant/slave", as a cover term for all classes of persons attached to sanctuaries other than male priests. Cf. English "religious" in its use as a substantive to designate members of religious communities. Gender-specific titles in the West Semitic realm include *khn* and Hebrew *lwy*. *khnt* in the Eshmunazar sarcophagus inscription (*KAI* 14.15) does not represent a class of priestesses, but is the title of a royal widow who has assumed the headship of the national cult as well as the state (see Bird 1987, pp. 416–17, n. 35).

[29] Cf. Westenholz (p. 254), who contrasts a Mesopotamian system of "gender-differentiated ecclesiastical role specialization" to the North Syrian system. In suggesting a contrast, she is misled, I believe, by the two occurrences of *qdšt* at Ugarit, which she interprets as evidence for a class of female cult personnel (pp. 249–50). She does not observe the divergent pattern for prophetic/oracular specialists, common to both regions, perhaps because of their looser relationship to the cult.

[30] The tendency in recent pentateuchal and prophetic studies to situate most, if not all, of the composition in the post-exilic period makes it difficult to compare dates or establish sequences for individual texts. I am nevertheless persuaded that the language and tone

term *qādēš*—in the highly unusual order of feminine-masculine.[31] The four remaining occurrences of the masculine noun, excluding the questionable reading in Job xxxvi 14,[32] are all found in the Deuteronomistic History (DH): 1 Kgs. xiv 24, xv 12, xxii 47 (EVV. 46), and 2 Kgs xxiii 7. Thus, apart from the Job reference, the masculine noun is confined to Deuteronom(ist)ic literature. All the masculine forms postdate the independently occurring feminine forms, while the only passage that combines both presents them in the same order of appearance, viz. female first, then male.

My assessment of the Genesis and Hosea texts leads me to conclude that the term *qdšh*/*qdšwt* in these passages describes a class of cult-related women[33] associated with outlying sanctuaries in pre-Josianic times, at least through the mid-8th century BCE in the northern kingdom. Contextual evidence associates them with surviving "Canaanite" practices (Adullamite location in Gen. xxxviii 21–2; "Baal" worship, "fertility cult", and idolatry in Hosea).[34] Despite these associations, however, the Hosea text clearly places the *qdšwt* in a milieu of Israelite worship, addressing Israelite priests and (male) worshippers with charges of unfaithfulness. Canaanites have long vanished, and foreigners play no role. Instead, practices of earlier days, reinforced by a royally sponsored Baal cult, have led to the "Canaanization" of the YHWH cult. The *qdšwt* belong, I suggest, to the persisting forms of Israelite cultic life that were rooted in indigenous tradition, but came to be viewed as incompatible with Yahwistic practice (as the *bmwt* and *mṣbwt*). I believe we must reconstruct a class of female attendants at the rural shrines representing a form of cultic service on the part of women that may once have had a recognized place in Israelite worship, but was ultimately rejected.[35] One might see an earlier

of the prohibition in Deut. xxiii 18 make it extremely difficult to view the Hosea and Genesis texts as later compositions.

[31] This reversal of the normative sequence in gender-differentiated pairs is so unusual that commentators frequently "restore" the expected order when discussing the passage.

[32] This reference is excluded from analysis here because the reading/interpretation of *qdšym* is problematic, its occurrence in the Elihu speeches places it in the latest stratum of the book and considerably later than all other references, and interpreters invariably appeal to the usage of Deuteronomy and the DH in attempting to explain it. Thus the weight of the evidence is in the Deuteronom(ist)ic uses. See Appendix.

[33] The cultic context is explicit in Hos. iv 14. Cf. Wacker, pp. 58–9.

[34] See Bird (1989a), pp. 122–6; (1989b), pp. 83–9.

[35] The reasons are no longer accessible to us, but they may have included the difficulty of controlling the behavior of the women attached to the sanctuary (thus their reputation as "prostitutes")—or of controlling the priests and male worshippers (see following note).

attestation of the class in the references to women serving at the entrance to the tent of meeting[36] or in the role of Miriam leading the praise of YHWH at the sea.[37] The sexual inuendo of the biblical texts represents an evaluative judgement and cannot be taken as role definition.

Deut. xxiii 18 (EVV. 17)

Although the verse is complete in itself, it is linked editorially with the following verse, creating a complex that appears as an isolated unit within the series of laws in this chapter.

> (18 [EVV. 7]) *lʾ-thyh qdšh mbnwt yśrʾl wlʾ-yhyh qdš mbny yśrʾl*
> (19 [EVV. 18]) *lʾ-tbyʾ ʾtnn zwnh wmḥyr klb byt yhwh ʾlhyk lkl-ndr ky twʿbt yhwh ʾlhyk gm-šnyhm* (xxiii 18–19 [EVV. 17–18])

> (18 [EVV. 17]) There shall be no *qdšh* from the daughters of Israel, and there shall be no *qdš* from the sons of Israel.
> (19 [EVV. 18]) You shall not bring the fee of a harlot or the hire of a "dog" into the house of YHWH your God for [payment of] any vow, for both of them are an abomination to YHWH your God.

The coupling of *vv.* 18 and 19 brings *qdšh* into parallelism with *zwnh*, as in each of the other occurrences of *qdšh*/*qdšwt*. But here *zwnh* is paired with a masculine term, *klb* "dog", which has commonly been understood to designate a male prostitute.[38] In this context, the previously unattested *qdš* appears to represent a class corresponding to *klb*, and the two verses are typically read as parallel prohibitions treating two types of "prostitutes", "cultic" and "secular".

The verses are not parallel in structure,[39] however, or in content. The first proscribes the existence of a "professional" class (female and male) within the Israelite population; the second prohibits an action: dedication of income from sexual commerce (female and male). The

---

[36] Exod. xxxviii 8; 1 Sam. ii 22. Note that the accusation in 1 Sam. ii 22 is against the sons of Eli (legitimate priests) for lying with the women, not against the women.

[37] Burns (pp. 39–40, 47–8, 121–3) argues that the evidence of the oldest traditions points to a cultic or liturgical role for Miriam and that the designation "prophet" stems from a later period when this was the only legitimate religious office recognized for women.

[38] This usage is not attested elsewhere in the MT, and the interpretation is disputed. Cf. Goodfriend, pp. 507–9; Gruber (1983), pp. 167–76; (1986), p. 133, n. 1; Stager, p. 36. Whatever the original meaning, the Deuteronomic author of *v.* 18 seems to have understood the paired terms of the older prohibition (*v.* 19) as references to gender-differentiated forms of a common institution, or at least comparable practices. However *klb* is interpreted, it is secondary to *zwnh*.

[39] *Pace* Seitz, p. 252; cf. L'Hour, pp. 475–97.

first is formulated in impersonal third-person style and consists of duplicate sentences, each with its own verb; the second is formulated in second-person (m.sg.) apodictic style and employs a single verb with a double object. The impression of parallelism is created by the occurrence in successive verses of the noun pairs *qdšh-qdš* and *zwnh-klb*, each in the highly unusual female-male word order. It is a parallelism created by editorial activity, based on an identification of *qdšh* and *zwnh*.

Separate origins for the two prohibitions have been widely acknowledged, but the meaning and manner of their union, as well as the age and intention of the component parts, are subject to widely differing interpretations.[40] Most commentators find a common subject matter in the two verses, which they characterize as "religious/cultic prostitution".[41] In fact, the argument for independent origins has been based, in part, on the assumption that both laws treat the same institution.[42] A common cultic orientation does appear to unite the verses and set them off from the surrounding ethical prohibitions.

The present form of the unit, as well as its location within the chapter, is best explained by viewing *vv.* 18 and 19b as interpretative additions to an older apodictic law, whose primary concern, like that of the two following laws, was, broadly speaking, "money matters" (prohibited forms of payment of vows and prohibited forms of income). In contrast, *v.* 18 stands close in its thought and formulation to the prohibitions that open the chapter, which address the question: who may belong to Israel? Thus it orients the paired verses to what precedes, while *v.* 19 is tied to what follows.[43]

---

[40] See Merendino, p. 316; Seitz, pp. 303–11, 184–6.

[41] Driver, p. 264; von Rad, p. 147 (German, p. 106); Mayes, p. 319; Phillips, pp. 156–7. Cf. Hooks, pp. 170–1; L'Hour, pp. 495–6. The tradition of equating the activity represented by the two verses is ancient, exhibited already in the LXX and Targums Pseudo-Jonathan and Neofiti; but that common activity was seen as simple prostitution. It appears that, as in Gen. xxxviii, where the LXX translates both *zwnh* and *qdšh* by πόρνη, the more common term has provided the clues for understanding the rarer term. For that reason, the unusual double translation of *v.* 18 in the LXX bears special note. Following an initial translation with terms for prostitutes (πόρνη/πορνεύων; cf. πόρνη for *zwnh*, *v.* 19), a second rendering is given using terms for initiates into mystery cults (τελεσφόρος/τελισκόμενος). On the LXX rendering elsewhere, see below.

[42] Cf. Seitz: "Nach *v.* 18, dem Verbot weiblicher und männlicher Qedeschen in Israel, ist das Verbot, den Ertrag aus der kultischen Prostitution zur Erlösung von Gelübden zu verwenden, überflüssig" (p. 252).

[43] Although the chapter appears to be a miscellany of originally independent laws or complexes expanded by later additions, those relating to cultic matters (membership in

The secondary nature of *v.* 18 is suggested by considerations of form as well as content. The impersonal third-person formulation contrasts with the second-person apodictic form of the series into which it has been inserted (*vv.* 16–17, 19, 20–1, 22–4, 25–6). Similar impersonal formulations occur in this section of Deuteronomy only in xxii 5 and xxv 13–15. Both stand out from the surrounding material in subject matter and form, and both conclude with the identical declaration, *ky tʿbt yhwh ʾlhyk kl ʿśh ʾlh* "for everyone who does these things is an abomination to YHWH your God" (xxii 5, xxv 16).[44]

The *tʿbt yhwh* formula also follows xxiii 18, but not directly. It is attached instead to the old apodictic clause in *v.* 19a, which it reinterprets in the light of *v.* 18, directing attention to the practitioners rather than the payment and strengthening the parallel between the two classes mentioned in *vv.* 18–19 through the pointed addition of *gm šnyhm* "both of them".[45]

Vv. 18 and 19b represent the work of the author who combined and framed older laws to create the interpreted collection that formed the core of Deuteronomy. They exhibit the characteristic Deuteronomic concern to define and preserve the distinctness of Israel over against "the nations". The nature of the language employed in *v.* 18, with its blanket prohibition and lack of any contextual clues, makes it impossible to determine what first-hand knowledge, if any, the author had of *qdšh* or *qdš*. In relation to Hos. iv 14, whose indirect reference to *qdšwt* in a richly detailed account of activities at the rural sanctuaries

---

the assembly and the purity of the camp) are otherwise confined to *vv.* 2–15, with *vv.* 16–17 (treatment of an escaped slave) introducing an ethical interest that continues in *vv.* 20–1 (lending on interest) and following.

44 The *tʿbt yhwh* formula appears in most cases to represent the work of a Deuteronomic editor, introduced into older collections of laws as commentary identifying the practices with Canaanite practice (Mayes, p. 189). See also L'Hour, p. 503; Seitz, p. 186; Weinfeld, pp. 268–9, 323.

45 Others have argued for an original connection to *v.* 19a (Driver, p. 265; L'Hour, p. 497—with "hire" and "price" as the antecedents) or *v.* 18 (Merendino, pp. 284–7; Mayes, p. 320—with *qdšh* and *qdš* as antecedents). The unusual use of the emphatic *gm šnyhm* as a pointedly inclusive expression suggests, however, that it was not an original part of either prohibition but was introduced at the time that *v.* 18 was added to 19a in order to encompass both sets of practices/practitioners. Merendino (p. 284) rightly notes its uneasy fit with 19a, which really describes a single action with two objects (as in xvii 1, which uses the singular pronoun *hwʾ*), but I do not think it formed an original unity with *v.* 18. It belongs rather to the expansion and reinterpretation of the older sentence in 19a. It is not male and female practitioners that are linked by the *gm šnyhm* of 19b, but the two classes of activity described in *vv.* 18 and 19a. Both types are declared *tʿbt yhwh*. Cf. Merendino, p. 287; Frevel, pp. 644–5.

attests a currently flourishing institution, this latest reference to *qdšh*, and first reference to a previously unknown *qdš*, appears decidely non-specific, and, one might argue, intentionally vague.[46] No hint of an institutional locus is provided for the proscribed classes, and the general language, gender-inclusive formulation, and mimicking construction of the two-fold prohibition suggest secondary, rather than first-hand knowledge.

V. 18 is a Deuteronomic creation, expanding the theme of cult and sex introduced by the old prohibition in *v*. 19a, and drawing on a "popular" association of *zwnh* and *qdšh* attested in Hosea and earlier traditions from Judah. In order to make the proscription "complete", like the parallel clause relating to prostitution, the author extended it to include male as well as female practitioners. This earliest Hebrew attestation of the masculine noun *qdš* is, in my view, a literary creation, introduced for comprehensiveness and balance.[47] It is derived from the feminine form, by which it must be interpreted.[48] The resulting word pair, found only here, contrasts with the *zwnh-klb* pair, whose unmatched terms reflect the characteristic asymmetry of sexual roles, and terminology, in patriarchal societies.[49]

---

[46] Note that Hosea's critique does not target the *qdšwt* (or *zwnwt*) directly, but rather the entire cultic practice and more particularly its male (priestly) overseers and adherents.

[47] In arguing for the artificial construction of *this reference* I do not rule out the possibility of the existence of a class of male cult personnel in some way analogous to the *qdšh* attested in Hos. iv and Gen. xxxviii and/or corresponding to the male class by the same name attested in the Ugaritic texts—although I believe the lack of evidence for gender-inclusive classes of hierodules makes this extremely unlikely. I also do not rule out *a priori* the possibility that other Hebrew texts, presently known or yet to be discovered, may provide evidence for the existence of such a class in Israel. I do insist that it is methodologically unsound to equate the Hebrew and Ugaritic terms (as it is equally unsound to equate Akkadian *qadištu* and the Hebrew cognate *qdšh* in a manner that assumes a common institution) without attention to the literary and social contexts in which both are found. In particular, literary constructions may not be converted into sociological or historical data without consideration of their historical setting and rhetorical aims.

[48] Interpretative dependence on the feminine term is indicated—by word order and the weight of the better-known term—even if the independent existence of the masculine form is affirmed. The parallel masculine term *klb* also provides interpretative clues.

[49] Gruber's proposal of distinct meanings for *qdšh* and *qdš* may appear to support this argument, but it is based on faulty analysis. Although Gruber insists that both masculine (Ugaritic) and feminine (Akkadian) cognates refer exclusively to cultic functionaries, with no associations of prostitution (1986, pp. 138–48; 1983, pp. 169–71), he appeals to cognate usage only in interpreting the Heb. masculine nouns. For the feminine terms he looks to Hos. iv 14 and Gen. xxxviii, arguing that Heb. *qdšh* is a synonym of *zwnh*, with no cultic association. Thus he interprets the second terms in Deut. xxiii 18, 19 as referring to cultic functionaries (1986, pp. 133–4), but the first as referring to prostitutes, juxtaposing moral and cultic prohibitions in gender-specific alternation within each verse. This analysis

However one assesses the construction of this text, the appearance of *qdš* in Deut. xxiii 18 is *by itself* insufficient to establish either the existence of a class of male hierodules or the nature of their activity. It is evidence only for the author's view that an institution defined by its female form (*qdšh*), and in some way analogous to prostitution, was not to be tolerated in Israel in any form, female or male.

qdš/qdšym *in the Deuteronomistic history*

The remaining biblical evidence is confined to the books of Kings.[50] Four occurrences of the masculine noun are attested in the DH, none of them paralleled by feminine forms, which are totally lacking in this corpus, or by references to prostitutes of either sex.[51] All appear in the regnal summaries of Judean kings, in the evaluations of the king's actions in relation to the cult. None can be dated earlier than the 7th century.[52]

The first three texts are clearly interrelated and form a series. Arranged in the order of their appearance and isolated from their contexts, the essential statements are as follows:

---

violates the strong internal parallelism of both verses, expressed in *v*. 18 by gender variants of a common term; and it ignores the socio-religious context of the prohibitions. Gruber's argument for a special development of Heb. *qdšh* from a basic root meaning of "set apart" must also be rejected, both for its faulty analogy to the root ḤRM and for the putative etymology, which Costecalde (cols 1356–61 and 1392–3) has shown to be totally lacking in support.

[50] On Job xxxvi 14, see n. 32 above and Appendix.

[51] The literary environment of the masculine terms is entirely different from that of the independently occurring feminine terms. One consequence of this differentiation may be seen in the LXX translation, which never uses the term πόρνη or its cognates to translate *qdš(h)* where an association with *zwnh* is lacking—or when a cultic context is evident, as in Hos. iv 14. In the LXX of Kings uncertainty and confusion about the meaning of the term is evidenced in different translations for each occurrence of *qdš* or *qdšym*, including transliteration in 2 Kgs xxiii 7. See Dion, pp. 44–6; Wacker, p. 61.

[52] A key question for the interpretation of these references is whether any of them represents pre-Dtr usage or derives from pre-Dtr sources. Despite differing views of the redaction history of Kings, none of the various reconstructions places any of the *qdš/qdšym* texts earlier than the 7th century. See Lowery, pp. 12–32. I agree with Hoffmann that the regnal summaries of the DH, as a whole, contain little archival material and none that has not been selected and shaped to serve the author's own purposes, but I do not share his view of a single exilic, or post-exilic, author nor his extreme scepticism about the nature of the sources. I would place the primary author closer to Josiah's time, give greater weight to unique formulations within the composition, and recognize more extensive work by secondary hands.

wgm-qdš hyh b'rṣ
Also (the) *qdš* was in the land.
(1 Kgs xiv 24: Rehoboam)

wyʿbr hqdšym mn-h'rṣ
He expelled the *qdšym* from the land.
(1 Kgs xv 12: Asa)

wytr hqdš ʾšr nšʾr bymy ʾsʾ ʾbyw bʿr mn-h'rṣ
Now the remnant of the *qdš*, that was left in the days of his father Asa, he exterminated from the land.
(1 Kgs xxii 47: Jehoshaphat)

The series presents the history of an institution attested only for the southern kingdom and existing "in the land" at the time of the division of the monarchy.[53] Its representatives are removed as the first action of Judah's first reforming king (Asa), and the remaining traces are exterminated by his son Jehoshaphat (*ca.* 873–49 BCE). Thus according to the view represented in these texts, the institution was eradicated from the southern kingdom by the mid-9th century BCE.

The final reference (2 Kgs xxiii 7) is curiously indirect, describing "houses" (*bty hqdšym*) within the temple where women were engaged in weaving for (the) Asherah.[54] The text records the destruction of these structures as a part of Josiah's reforms:

wytṣ ʾt-bty hqdšym ʾšr bbyt yhwh ʾšr hnšym ʾrgwt šm btym lʾšrh

And he broke down the houses of the *qdšym*, where the women were weaving "houses" for the Asherah.

The text presents numerous problems and exhibits a number of distinctive features, which set it apart from those in 1 Kings. First, it

---

[53] No account is given of its introduction. It is therefore presumably to be understood as a "holdover" from earlier practices, associated with the aboriginal inhabitants of the land.

[54] It is not always possible to determine whether a particular occurrence of *ʾšrh* represents the goddess herself or a cult object, especially when prefaced by the preposition *l* (Frevel, pp. 535–6, 546–7). I have capitalized all references to the f.sg. noun, even where it clearly represents an object. In my view, a connection with the goddess of the same name is maintained (and exploited) in these references. The use of the article (whether by the author or editor or the Masoretic vocalizers) may be a way of "belittling" the goddess by objectifying her (cf. *htmwz*, Ezek. viii 14). See Olyan, p. 2, n. 7; and Frevel (p. 924), who maintains the polysemous character of the term. Frevel's massive study of Asherah in Israelite religion and literature became available to me only after I had completed this article. Earlier studies of significance for this question include Olyan; Day; and Smith, pp. 110–44, 270–94. J.M. Hadley's Ph.D. dissertation *Yahweh's Asherah in the Light of Recent Discovery* (Cambridge University, 1989) was not yet published at the time of this writing.

contains a degree of specificity lacking in all other references and is commonly held to represent a first-hand report from archival records. Second, it is the only passage that locates the *qdšym* in the temple, and the only one suggesting an association with the cult of Asherah. All other references in the DH locate the *qdš/qdšym* vaguely "in the land", and 1 Kgs xv separates the notice of their expulsion from its account of the removal of the Asherah image. Finally, it describes no action against the *qdšym* themselves, but only against their "houses"—which are further defined by reference to the activity of women engaged in weaving for the Asherah.

Thus the one passage that appears to contain first-hand knowledge of the installations and activities it describes seems to know nothing of *qdšym*, or at least is unable to report any action against them—an astonishing fact given the proscription of Deut. xxiii 18 and the Deuteronomists' interest in ascribing every possible reform to Josiah and, more especially, conformity to the Deuteronomic law.

1 Kgs xiv 24

In the Deuteronomist's introduction to the reign of Rehoboam, the typical evaluation formula is expanded to present a comprehensive portrait of the cultic sins of the state.

> (22) *wyʿś yhwdh*[55] *hrʿ bʿyny yhwh wyqnʾw ʾtw mkl ʾšr ʿśw ʾbtm bḥṭwʾtm ʾšr ḥṭʾw.* (23) *wybnw gm-hmh lhm bmwt wmṣbwt wʾšrym ʿl kl-gbʿh gbhh wtḥt kl-ʿṣ rʿnn.* (24) *wgm-qdš*[56] *hyh bʾrṣ ʿśw kkl htwʿbt hgwym ʾšr hwryš yhwh mpny bny yśrʾl.* (xiv 22–4)

> (22) Judah did what was evil in the eyes of YHWH, and (they) provoked him to jealousy with their sins which they committed, more than all their fathers had done. (23) They too built for themselves high places, and pillars, and asherim on every high hill and under every green tree. (24) Also *qdš* was in the land. They did according to all the abominations of the nations which YHWH drove out before the people of Israel. (xiv 22–4)

[55] MT; LXX Ροβοαμ; cf. 2 Chr. xii 14. The standard opening formula is modified here in the MT so that the judgement that is normally focused on the king is directed against the people. See Montgomery, pp. 268, 272–3; Gray, pp. 341–2; Jones, pp. 276–7; cf. Noth, p. 323.

[56] Gk σύνδεσμος. The *BHS* apparatus assumes *qešer* "conspiracy" (as in 2 Kgs xi 14) in the Hebrew *Vorlage*. See Montgomery, p. 273; Dion, p. 45.

Two features of the account bear note: the general and formulaic nature of the statements, in contrast to the following description of Shishak's campaign (*vv.* 25–8),[57] and the disjunctive and restricted nature of the statement concerning *qdš*.

The language of *vv.* 22, 23, and 24b is wholly and characteristically Deuteronomistic and aims to describe the apostasy of the southern kingdom at the beginning of the divided monarchy.[58] This apostasy is summarized in *v.* 23 by the threefold enumeration of *bmwt, mṣbwt* and *ʾšrym*, which serves throughout the DH to identify the basic forms of cultic perversion and the targets of cultic reform.[59] But *qdš* has no place in this catalog, and the singular form stands out alongside the series of plural cult objects or installations. The awkward syntax of the clause, which interrupts a sequence of active m.pl. verbs describing actions of the people, also marks it as a later addition to the original Dtr summary.[60] The standard Dtr list targets the continuing worship at the *bmwt*, with their attendant cultic symbols that have come to represent pagan worship. No personnel other than (legitimate) priests are associated with these sanctuaries in the earliest edition of the DH (2 Kgs xxiii 9), and it is only a later hand that has distinguished the priests of the *bmwt* as *kmrym* ("idolatrous priests") (see below). Thus it appears that Dtr did not know of any illegitimate cult personnel operating at the *bmwt* and did not connect the *qdš(ym)* with these installations.[61]

The notice concerning the presence of *qdš* "in the land" is not an original part of the Dtr summary, nor can it be regarded as resting on a pre-Dtr source. Like the Dtr catalog which it supplements, it serves to account for an abuse targeted in later reforms by locating it in the earliest period of the southern monarchy. But unlike the *bmwt*, which represent an ongoing abuse terminated only in Josiah's reforms, the *qdš(ym)* are effectively removed in the first reported reform and play no further role in Dtr's account of cult and kingship, apart from the "clean-up" credited to Jehoshaphat (1 Kgs xxii 47) and the indirect

---

[57] See Hoffmann (pp. 36–7) on the style of the cultic notices.

[58] This summary is generally reckoned to the primary stratum of Deuteronomistic redaction (Jones, p. 543).

[59] Hoffmann, p. 76; cf. pp. 336, 350, 354, 355–6; Noth, p. 329.

[60] Noth, p. 330; Jones, pp. 277–8. Cf. Hoffmann, p. 76, who regards it as an "inhaltlich abgesagte Nachtrag", but not a literary addendum. See also Lowery, pp. 68, 72.

[61] Deuteronomy, which does not use the term *bmwt* in this sense, also treats *qdš* and *qdšh* apart from the *mṣbwt* and *ʾšrym*.

mention in relation to Josiah's reforms. The notice in 1 Kgs xiv 24 is an attempt by a later hand to correct an "omission" in the record by recording the presence of a class whose removal heads the list of Asa's reforms in xv 12. Its secondary character is supported by the only other occurrence of the m.sg.coll. (1 Kgs xii 47), which is even more clearly an addendum.[62]

The meaning and function of these two notices, including their common use of the singular form, can be understood only in relation to 1 Kgs xv 12, on which they both depend. Since scholarly discussion has focused on xiv 24, however, as the first appearance of the term in the DH, a brief account of prevailing views at this point will serve to identify the major interpretative issues.

Hoffmann's understanding may be taken as representative, at least with respect to the form of the noun and its referents. He understands the term as belonging to Dtr's attempt to describe the pagan practices of Rehoboam's reign in the light of Dtn cult prescriptions and with an eye to later reforms. Here *qdš* is singled out, he argues, as a particularly offensive feature of the Canaanite cult, standing, *pars pro toto*, as "typical". As Hoffmann (pp. 76–7) understands it, "das Stichwort *qdš* steht hier kollektiv für *qdšym* und *qdšwt*, was genau dem zugrundeliegenden dtn Verbot (Dtn. 23, 18f.) entspricht". Hoffmann's view of the term as collective and inclusive of both sexes is shared by most commentators,[63] who also point to Deut. xxiii 18 by way of interpretation. But his assertion of "exact" correspondence is hardly accurate and exposes the problem of attempting to derive this usage directly from the Deuteronomic prohibition. Any attempt to represent the gender-inclusive formulation of Deut. xxiii 18 would surely use the plural, rather than selecting one of the paired terms. We should rather

---

[62] The two notices need not stem from the same hand, but they are both late and appear to share a common understanding of the term. See below.

[63] A collective interpretation is required in 1 Kgs xxii 47 (*ytr hqdš*) and is recognized for both texts by BDB and *HALAT*. It does not, however, require that the collectivity be understood as comprising both males and females, though that has been the view of most modern scholars. Proponents of a gender-inclusive interpretation include Burney (p. 193); Noth (p. 330); Gray (p. 343); and Jones (p. 227). Montgomery (p. 268) is one of the few who treats the reference as exclusively male. His interpretation collapses the references of Deut. xxiii 18 and 19: "they [the 'Sodomites' of the *AV* translation of 1 Kgs xiv 24] are the 'dogs' whose hire may not be brought into YHWH's house (Dt. 23. 18f.), which caste of 'dogs' appears among the Phoenician hierodules". The LXX translates with a singular noun (σύνδεσμος) in xiv 24, but a plural (τῶν σύμπλοκῶν) in xxii 47 (= 3 Kgdms xvi 28)—both referring, however, to action/ritual rather than officiants (Dion, pp. 44–5; see below).

expect on the basis of Deut. xxiii 18 that the m.sg. would represent a deliberate emphasis on the male form of the institution, either to the exclusion of the female class, or as the dominant form. That exclusive masculine interpretation is in fact the understanding that has dominated English translations.[64]

1 Kgs xv 12

The summary of Asa's reign begins with the standard introductory formula (*vv.* 9–10) followed by the judgement that "Asa did what was right in the eyes of YHWH, like David his father" (*v.* 11). This judgement, shared only by Hezekiah and Josiah, is supported in *vv.* 12–15 by evidence that presents Asa as the first cult reformer in the southern kingdom. The catalog of reform actions is headed by a reference to *qdšym*.

> (12) *wyʿbr haqqĕdēšîm mn-hʾrṣ wysr ʾt-kl-hgllym ʾšr ʿśw ʾbtyw* (13) *wgm ʾt-mʿkh ʾmw wysrh mgbyrh ʾšr ʿśth mplṣt lʾšrh wykrt ʾsʾ ʾt-mplṣth wyśrp bnḥl qdrwn* (14) *whbmwt lʾ-srw rq lbb-ʾsʾ hyh šlm ʿm-yhwh kl-ymyw* (15) *wybʾ ʾt-qodšê ʾbyw wĕqodšo*[65] *byt yhwh ksp wzhb wklym*
>
> (12) He expelled the *qdšym* from the land and removed all the idols which his ancestors had made. (13) Also Maacah, his mother: he removed her from being queen mother, because she had made an "abominable image" for (the) Asherah;[66] and Asa cut down her "abominable image" and burned it in the Kidron valley. (14) But the *bmwt* did not depart. Nevertheless Asa's heart was wholly true to YHWH all his days. (15) And he brought the "holy things" of his father and his own "holy things(s)" into the house of YHWH: silver and gold and vessels. (1 Kgs xv 12–15).

---

[64] KJV, JPS 1917: "sodomites"; JPS: "male prostitutes" (cf. Luther: "Hurer"); *NEB, REB*: "male prostitutes attached to the shrines/house of the LORD"; *RSV, NRSV, JB*: "male cult/temple/sacred prostitutes"; Chicago: "male devotees of the fertility cult" (omitting "male" in 2 Kgs xxiii 7). Only the *NAB* ("cult/temple prostitutes") and Chicago in 2 Kgs xxiii 7 ("devotees of the fertility cult") translate in gender-neutral terms (though not explicitly inclusive), while the *TEV* renders with explanatory paraphrases specifying male and female (e.g., 1 Kgs xv 12: "male and female prostitutes serving at the pagan places of worship"). The four occurrences of the masculine nouns are translated in identical fashion in each version (with only minor stylistic variations in the *JB* and *TEV*), except for Chicago, whose gender-neutral rendering in 2 Kgs xxiii 7 appears to reflect the reference to women in the verse. No distinction is made between the singular and plural forms in any of these versions, with all using plurals throughout.

[65] Kt; Qr *qodšê*.

[66] On the problems of translating *mplṣt lʾšrh* see commentaries and Frevel, pp. 535–7.

What is immediately striking in comparing this catalog of actions with the summary characterizing Rehoboam's reign is the concreteness and particularity of description; here we encounter specific actions and unique terms, which have long suggested that the account must rest on an archival source.[67] The otherwise unattested *mplṣt* of *v.* 13 and the associated action of deposing the queen mother from her rank or office stand at the center of the notice and point to an historical source. Similar evidence for a special source is commonly seen in the notice concerning the *qĕdēšîm*, which opens the account, and the note on the *qodāšîm* that closes it.[68] But the presence of clearly Deuteronomistic language in *vv.* 12b and 14 has led Hoffmann to reopen the question concerning the extent of the Deuteronomist's hand in the passage, as well as the nature and extent of his source.[69]

In my view, the picture of reform has been built upon a kernel of tradition concerning the removal of the queen mother and her image of/for Asherah, although even this historical notice appears to have been shaped in its present form by the reference to the Asherah in 2 Kgs xxiii 6, especially its burning in the Kidron Valley.[70] Around this central account of palace cleansing[71] a larger picture of reforms has been constructed in broad generalizing terms. It begins with Asa's expulsion (*ʿBR* Hiphil) of the *qdšym* from the land, coupled with the removal (*SWR* Hiphil) of "all the idols (*gllym*) which his fathers had made" (*v.* 12).

V. 12b appears to be wholly Deuteronomistic in its formulation,[72] but what of 12a with which it is paired? The verb is unique in this context and the expression *hʿbyr mn-hʾrṣ* is found only in the parallel

[67] Noth, p. 336; Gray, p. 347; cf. Jones, pp. 282–3.

[68] Those who see *v.* 15 as based on archival sources include Noth (p. 337); and Montgomery (p. 275). Cf. Jones (p. 284), who views the verse as Deuteronomistic, along with Würthwein (1977, p. 188) and Hoffmann (pp. 90–1).

[69] Hoffmann, pp. 87–93. Cf. Spieckermann (pp. 184–5), who questions the literary integrity of *vv.* 12–13. Noth (pp. 336–7) also recognized Deuteronomistic elements in the cultic summary, esp. in *v.* 14b (a Dtr addition) and *v.* 12b (a Dtr summary of individual items mentioned in his source).

[70] See Hoffmann, pp. 88, 221–2; Spieckermann, p. 186; Lowery, p. 94; Frevel, p. 538.

[71] The temple is not mentioned at this point and appears only in the concluding reference to the dedicated objects (*v.* 15). Only Hezekiah and Josiah are explicitly identified with the cleansing of the Jerusalem temple. I believe Lowery (p. 94) is right in seeing a court power struggle as the essential historical datum in the account of Asa's reform, in which, however, her cult object, interpreted as a sign of devotion to Asherah, is exploited by the Deuteronomistic author to link Asa with Josiah. Cf. Hoffmann, p. 91; Frevel, p. 538.

[72] Hoffmann, pp. 347–8, 359–60, 364–5.

2 Chr. xv 8 and in the later passage Zech. xii 2. But recognition of the unique language of 12a, and the absence of *qdšym* from the standard Dtr cultic inventory, does not immediately confer the status of a first-hand historical report on this notice. The vagueness of the language, both with respect to the action (*ʿBR* Hiphil) and the location (*mn-hʾrṣ*), suggests some distance from the event and/or uncertainty about its exact nature. If an historical source lay behind the notice, it apparently included no reference to specific actions. It seems more likely that the composition and placement of this report are determined solely by the author's view of the history of cultic reform in the southern kingdom.

What then does the Deuteronomist understand by this notice, and why is it placed at the head of the reform account? In contrast to the actions reported in *vv*. 13 and 15, which center on Jerusalem and the royal cult, the action of *v*. 12 refers broadly to "the land", suggesting a dispersed phenomenon, or simply vagueness about the location of the *qdšym*. It also suggests an effort to extend the reform action beyond the capital to include the (whole) land controlled by the Judean king.[73] Whatever the intention, the statement lacks operational specificity, while conveying a sense of total removal.[74] In both respects it corresponds to the prohibition of Deut. xxiii 18, which simply declares that there shall be no *qdšh* or *qdš* among the Israelite population. This class of persons has no place in Israel.[75]

Asa is presented then as acting in accordance with the Deuteronomic command. The implication is that from Asa's time onward the *qdšym* were no longer an issue in the continuing cultic abuses of the southern kingdom. And in fact they play no role in Dtr's account of recurrent apostasy until the reforms of Josiah. Asa, as the first southern monarch to take action against abuses of the cult, moved first, according to the Deuteronomist, to rid the land of persisting "Canaanite" cult functionaries, whose practices were viewed, in accordance with Deut. xxiii 18, as particularly abhorrent and incompatible with Yahwistic practice. *Vv*. 12b–14 target alien, or syncretistic, cult objects and installations.

---

[73] Cf. 2 Chr. xv 8 (*mkl-ʾrṣ yhwdh wbnymyn*), which spells out the territorial claim, adding Benjamin (and cities taken in Mt. Ephraim).

[74] Cf. Spieckermann, pp. 188–9, n. 73; Noth, p. 336; Hoffmann, p. 88, n. 48.

[75] Here, as with the two other references in 1 Kings, the LXX has a term for activities rather than actors, τὰς τελετὰς "initiation ceremonies", suggesting that the Greek translator read the consonants as *qiddūšîm* (Dion, pp. 44–5, n. 11).

Whatever the sources available to the author for Asa's reign, the formulation of this notice, as it now appears, is dependent, I believe, on Deut. xxiii 18—and 2 Kgs xxiii 7, the only other occurrence of the m.pl. *qdšym*. While the latter text supplies no further information concerning the nature or activities of the *qdšym*, the reference to women in the same verse may serve to reinforce the gender-inclusive interpretation suggested by Deut. xxiii 18. On the basis of these two sources, I believe that *qdšym* in 1 Kgs xv 12 must be understood inclusively. The reference here does not describe a class of male cult functionaries, or any class composed exclusively of males; nor does it constitute historical evidence for a class of male practitioners alongside the *qdšwt* known from Hosea and Gen. xxxviii. It testifies only to the author's belief, based on Deut. xxiii 18, that there must have been male as well as female practitioners—or to his uncertainty about the exact nature of the class, which he covers with a "generic" plural, using the expression found in his Josianic source.

I find no evidence of a pre-Dtr source in *v.* 12a, despite the otherwise unattested **hʿbyr*. My interpretation reckons *v.* 12a to the primary Deuteronomistic author. *V.* 12b is also Deuteronomistic, but the language, especially *gllym*, is late Dtr, and *qdšym* and *gllym* do not occur elsewhere together.[76] The original Dtr composition, without *v.* 12b, stands much closer to 2 Kgs xxiii 6–7, having only two items, *qdšym* and Asherah—but here without any apparent relationship to one another.[77]

1 Kgs xiv 24a is one step further removed from historical knowledge of the institution. A later hand has supplied the needed "historical" notice concerning the *qdšym* removed in Asa's reforms, matching the language of his source by locating them "in the land". But why

---

[76] *gllym* has an entirely different distribution from *qdšym*, or the cultic catalog associated with the *bmwt*. In Deuteronomy it occurs only in the late passage, Deut. xxix 16, while all its other occurrences in Kings (1 Kgs xxi 26; 2 Kgs xvii 12, xxi 11, 21, xxiii 24) are found in passages commonly assigned to a second level of Deuteronomistic redaction. In the account of Josiah's reforms the reference to *qdšym* belongs to the annalistic source (*v.* 7), while *gllym* appears in a late Dtr expansion (*v.* 24).

[77] In striking contrast to 2 Kgs xxiii 7, where the *qdšym* are located in the temple and appear to be intimately related to the Asherah cult, they are not connected here with either the Asherah or the temple. The author's failure to make the connection, and thus exploit more narrowly the parallels between the two reforms, suggests that he was uncertain about the relationship of the *qdšym* to the Asherah, or knew of no association of the two. Consequently, he uses the term in his Josianic source to create a broad statement about alien cult personnel reflecting the prohibition of Deut. xxiii 18.

did he opt for the singular *qdš* if he was dependent on xv 12, and how did he understand the term? Despite current scholarly opinion that understands the singular collectives as sharing the gender-inclusive meaning imputed to the plurals, I suggest that the redactor responsible for this addendum understood the m.pl. of xv 12 as a reference to a male class. Even if the term is meant to designate a "species" of activity (Montgomery, pp. 268, 273), it defines it by association with the male role. But why this focus on the male? Is it perhaps a way of stressing the revulsive character of this alien phenomenon? Assuming the interpretative tradition of Deut. xxiii 18, which suggests an analogy to prostitution, one may expect that the imputed practice would have been understood as "natural", though disapproved, for women (as in Hos. iv 14). For men, however, it would be viewed as "unnatural" and therefore deeply repugnant, illustrative of the perversions of Canaanite religion.[78]

However one understands the author's intentions in this usage, I believe one must conclude that he had no historically reliable knowledge of the class or institution he describes. This reference can tell us nothing about its nature, function, or distribution, except that the author understood it to belong to the earliest period of Judah's existence as a state—and even that need be no more than an inference from xv 12.

1 Kgs xxii 47 (EVV. 46)

The notice in 1 Kgs xxii 47 (E 46) attributing an action against the *qdš* to Asa's successor Jehoshaphat is clearly an addendum, since it follows the reference to sources, which normally forms part of the concluding formula, and is separated from the evaluation formula with its notice concerning the persistence of the *bmwt* (*vv.* 43–4 [EVV. 42–3]).[79] It is also lacking in the Old Greek (together with *vv.* 48–50), which might suggest an even later hand than that exhibited in xiv 24. The standard concluding formula begins in *v.* 46 [EVV. 45], but is interrupted in the MT by the following notice:

---

[78] Cf. the consistent *KJV* rendering of the masculine forms with "sodomite". Another reason for singling out the masculine term might be a recognition that the female institution continued to exist, at least into the later monarchy, while a corresponding male form was unknown, and therefore assumed to have been eradicated.

[79] On the order of *vv.* 41–51 in the MT and versions and various suggestions for improving the text, see Hoffmann, pp. 93–5, esp. n. 74.

wytr hqdš ʾšr nšʾr bymy ʾsʾ ʾbyw bʿr mn-hʾrṣ

Now the remnant of the *qdš*, that was left in the days of his father Asa, he exterminated from the land. (1 Kgs xxii 47 [EVV. 46])

The notice is a harmonizing one so far as it attempts to relate Jehoshaphat's action to that of his father, but also distinguish it by use of a different verb, emphasizing complete eradication.[80] What has occasioned this qualification of Asa's reforms, and on what authority does it rest? It appears that the author wants to qualify the notion that Asa completed the removal of the *qdšym* and to credit Jehoshaphat with some of the action. It is hardly the work of the same hand that composed the summary of Asa's reforms, since it take pains to acknowledge both the earlier action and its incompleteness. The use of the collective singular form links it to the notice in xiv 24, a notice, judged to reflect concern for systematic presentation rather than historical memory. Does this same author, or a later editor, know or believe that the institution persisted after the time of Asa's reforms, or does he, in the absence of specific historical data, simply want to depict Jehoshaphat as "carrying through" the action begun by his father? (See Hoffmann, pp. 93, 95–6.)

Hoffmann is right, I believe, in connecting this notice to the developing tradition magnifying Jehoshaphat as a reformer that is reflected in the greatly expanded account of 2 Chr. xvii–xx (there restricted to the political and judicial spheres). The glossator responsible for this notice apparently wanted to claim some type of cultic reform for Jehoshaphat. Since the *bmwt* remained and Asa is credited with removing *all* the idols, only one item of the previously listed cultic perversions offered a possibility of further action, viz. the *qdšym*. Their removal was formulated in sufficiently vague language to invite, or permit, qualification, and thus allowed Jehoshaphat a place among the cult reformers.

Parallel texts in Chronicles

While the Chronicler draws on sources for his political history of Jehoshaphat's reign that are not reflected in the Deuteronomistic

[80] *Pace* Spieckermann (pp. 188–9, n. 73), who speculates that *wyʿbr* in xv 12 represents an accidental transposition from an original *wybʿr*. Cf. Noth, p. 336; Hoffmann, p. 88, n. 48.

summary, his account of the king's cultic actions reveals no source beyond the DH, recast or replaced by his own appraisal. The same appears true of the parallel accounts relating to Rehoboam and Asa's reigns. But if Chronicles offers no independent information about cultic practice and reforms during the reigns of Judah's first kings, it does provide an evaluation of those recorded by the Deuteronomists. Most striking is the Chronicler's elimination of all references to *qdšym*/*qdš* (see Japhet, p. 706; Dion).

In the Chronicler's summary of Rehoboam's reign (2 Chr. xii 13–14), which follows closely the parallel in 1 Kgs xiv 21–22a, the whole account of Judah's cultic abuses in *vv*. 23–4 has been eliminated and replaced by the summary statement that "he (Rehoboam here, instead of Judah in Kings) did evil, for he did not set his heart to seek the LORD".[81] In contrast, the account of Asa's reforms contains a long expansion (2 Chr. xv 9–15),[82] but opens with a recasting of 1 Kgs xv 12 that combines the two parallel statements into one, eliminating the reference to the *qdšym*: "Asa . . . took courage and removed the abominations (*wyʿbr hšqwṣym*) from the whole land of Judah and Benjamin" (*v*. 8).[83] In the four chapters devoted to Jehoshaphat's reign (2 Chr. xvii–xx), the only cultic action ascribed to him is a report of his removal of the *bmwt* and *ʿšrym* from Judah, and a qualifying clause in the condemnation announced by the seer Jehu: "Nevertheless, some good is found in you, for you destroyed the asherahs out of the land (*ky bʿrt hʾšrwt mn-hʾrṣ*)" (2 Chr. xix 3). The language appears to be derived from the notice in 1 Kgs xxii 47, with *ʾšrwt* substituted for *qdš*.[84]

---

[81] See Japhet, p. 682. Cf. Auld (pp. 107, 111), whose posited common source behind the DH and Chronicles lacked any reference to *qdš(ym)* in the case of Rehoboam. The source for Asa's reign, according to Auld, contained a notice of their removal, which the Chronicler altered slightly (p. 108).

[82] The Chronicler has also prefaced his own introductory summary of the reform actions in 2 Chr. xiv 3–5 [EVV. 2–4]. See Japhet, pp. 702–3, 705; cf. Williamson, pp. 255–9.

[83] Although *šqwṣym* is most commonly used to represent objects, I am inclined to see its use here as an attempt to represent both of the terms in the DH source (*qdšym* and *gllym*) in a way that obscures the exact nature of the original referents. The use of *hʿbyr* and the expanded reference to territory appears to reflect 1 Kgs xv 12a. Cf. Japhet, pp. 702, 716; Myers, p. 88; Williamson, pp. 259, 269.

[84] Although neither Japhet nor Williamson sees dependence on Kings in this notice, the isolation of the *ʾšrwt* (not associated here with *bmwt*, *mṣbwt*, or *bʿlym*) and the description of their extermination (*BʿR Piel*) "from the land" closely reflects the language of 1 Kgs xxii 47 (EVV. 46). Cf. Dion (pp. 42–3), who also finds dependence on the Kings passage.

The reason for the Chronicler's elimination of the *qdš(ym)* from his account lies, I believe, in his theology, not in his (mis)understanding of his sources. Chr's view of Judah's religious practice, even its perverted forms, permitted no recognition of the existence of *qdšym*. In this he represents the Deuteronomic prohibition as realized: the asherahs, altars, and pillars are destroyed as commanded, and the *qdšym* do not exist.[85]

Summary of references in 1 Kings

The three references to *qdšym*/*qdš* in 1 Kings are interdependent and may not be counted as separate historical attestations. The two latest notices, xiv 24 and xxii 47, explicate the presuppositions and extend the credit for the action reported in xv 12. Neither brings new historical information about the institution. They do, however, appear to reconceive it—as an exclusively male, or male-defined, phenomenon. Thus the ambiguous m.pl. of xv 12, formulated and interpreted in relation to Deut. xxiii 18 and 2 Kgs xxiii 7 as a gender-inclusive category, is (re)interpreted by a later hand as designating a class of male hierodules. This move represents a sharpening of the polemic against the abominable practices of the "nations", but it is a purely literary move, describing a remote past, not a reflection of changed practice or new historical evidence. The "male cult prostitute" is a literary creation of a later age, beginning with the shadowy complement of the *qdšh* in Deut. xxiii 18 and culminating in the collective representation of male hierodules by a late Deuteronomistic editor.

1 Kgs xv 12 is the only independent witness of the three, but is of questionable value as historical evidence. The language and location of the notice suggest a controlling theological interest and

[85] The substitutions in the notices taken from DH and shaped to suit the Chronicler's interests cannot therefore be used as evidence for the Chronicler's understanding of the *qdšym* (e.g., as images or asherahs), since he appears to have substituted objects of one order (cult objects, which can be removed or destroyed) for those of another (cult personnel, whose existence is denied). Cf. Dion (pp. 47–8), who argues from the confused renderings of the LXX that the authors had no knowledge of the institution represented by *qdš(ym)* in their Hebrew *Vorlagen* (pp. 44–7), but finds it "hard to believe that [the Chronicler] did not understand the meaning of *qādēš*" in his sources (p. 47). The Chronicler stands closer to his source and its cultural world than the LXX translators, but his "knowledge" of *qdš(ym)* is entirely dependent on Deuteronomy and Dtr. Their literary constructions have resulted in Chr's literary suppression of the institution they created.

dependence on Deut. xxiii 18, and 2 Kgs xxiii 7. Here Asa is presented as the first great reformer, carrying out the Deuteronomic prohibition against pagan cult functionaries, of both sexes. It is possible, and I believe likely, that the notice concerning the purge of the *qdšym* represents nothing more than the Deuteronomist's schematic view of the stages of reform and apostasy that culminated in Josiah's reforms. The scheme that eliminates the *qdšym* in the first reform is clearly an artificial one, just as the restriction of the references to the southern kingdom. It suggests nevertheless that, unlike the *bmwt* and their attendant cult objects, hierodules, of either sex, played a minor role, if any, in the cult toward which Josiah's reforms were directed.[86]

2 Kgs xxiii 7

The final occurrence of *qdšym* differs from all other attestations of the masculine noun in the concreteness, specificity and complexity of the report in which it is found; in its association with the temple, Asherah cult, and women weavers; and in the indirect nature of the reference. It stands at the center of a detailed account of Josiah's cultic reforms. While assessments differ markedly concerning the nature and extent of original material in this account, most scholars reckon

[86] The fact that Hosea does not directly attack the *qdšwt*, suggests that the absence of any clear reference to this class of female hierodules in the DH is insufficient evidence for concluding that they did not exist in the southern kingdom. The case of an assumed male counterpart cannot be assessed in the same way, however, because a class of male hierodules would present a challenge of quite a different order to the recognized, and contending, priestly classes and/or other (male) religious specialists.

I cannot agree with Lowery's conclusion that "cult prostitution was a normal part of First Temple Yahwism throughout the period of the monarchy" (p. 93; cf. p. 70), but he is one of the few who recognize the problem of the absence of any reference to *qdšym* between the time of Jehoshaphat and Josiah (pp. 89–93). He is right, I believe, in connecting attention to the *qdšym* with Deuteronomic interests (p. 93), although his arguments are weakened by failure to distinguish between the masculine and feminine forms of the noun and lack of clarity concerning the redactional history of Kings. Noting the absence of any attention to "cult prostitution" prior to the mid-8th century [Hosea], he concludes that "it apparently was not a part of the reform consciousness which motivated Hezekiah's reform" (p. 93; cf. pp. 89–91). "By the time of Josiah's reform", however, "abolition of cult prostitution was an established tenet of the deuteronomic program", he argues, with consequences for the Dtr presentation of Judah's cultic history (p. 93). His own proposal assumes Josiah's abolition of the practice: "the Asa-Jehoshaphat cult prostitute reforms most likely are a fictional device to explain why Hezekiah did not abolish cult prostitution in Judah. If, on the other hand . . . [they] are historical, they had very little success, as the Josiah reform shows" (p. 93; cf. p. 72).

v. 7 to the earliest stratum or source material.[87] As the report now reads, actions directed toward the temple appear at several points (*vv.* 4, 6–7, 11, 12b), but only *vv.* 6–7 refer to cultic installations within the temple itself. These two verses, with their common interest in (the) Asherah, appear to describe the core action of the reform—at least as it relates to Jerusalem and the national/central shrine.[88]

The basic account appears to have detailed actions directed toward cult objects and installations identified with the worship of other deities.[89] Attention to personnel appears in the earliest form of the account only in relation to the *bmwt*, where it is directed to the rights and duties of the (legitimate Yahweh) priests who had served at the outlying, and now defunct, sanctuaries.[90] Only at a later stage are the Judahite priests of the *bmwt* recast as alien or idolatrous, distinguished by the designation *kmrym*, and subjected to extermination (*v.* 5).[91] The only other personnel named as objects of the reform appear in a late appendix (*v.* 24), reporting the eradication of a miscellany of proscribed practices/practitioners (*ʾbwt* "mediums" and *ydʿnym* "wizards") and objects (*trpym, gllym*, and *šqṣym*). In the chapter as a whole the reference to *qdšym* is anomalous; it does not fit the pattern of accommodating legitimate, though tainted, cult personnel or extirpating illegitimate religious specialists.

---

[87] Among those who view *v.* 7 as stemming from archival, or pre-Dtr, records are Noth (p. 80), Nelson (p. 81), and Spieckermann (pp. 425–7). Jones (pp. 616–17) and Würthwein (1984, pp. 414–18) see Dtr expansion of an historical report in this verse, while Hoffmann (p. 217) rejects any attempt to identify a pre-Dtr *Vorlage* by literary-critical means. He nevertheless assumes an historical report or tradition concerning the destruction of the *qdšym*-houses, and historical memory behind the description of their function, although the present text witnesses only to Dtr's systematic reflection (p. 231).

[88] Lohfink (pp. 38–9) argues that the center of the account in *vv.* 4–14 is the centralization of the YHWH cult in Jerusalem by the action against the cult of the *bmwt*, reported in *vv.* 8–9. His analysis of the logic in Dtr's construction of this account is convincing. But temple cleansing and centralization are closely related, and the actions reported in *vv.* 6–7 direct attention forcefully to the temple itself, which must be purged before the outlying cult centers are desecrated. For Lohfink's literary analysis of *vv.* 1–24 as a Dtr composition, see pp. 38–47.

[89] Although the *bmwt* clearly belonged to the history of YHWH worship, by the time of this account they are associated with alien cults and must therefore be "defiled" (*v.* 8a).

[90] The northern *bmwt* are treated separately (*vv.* 15, 19), and their priests (viewed as illegitimate) are slaughtered (*v.* 20).

[91] Whatever the history of Heb. *kmrym*, its three uses in the MT (2 Kgs xxiii 5; Hos. x 5; Zeph. i 4) all designate priests of foreign gods, introducing a distinction in nomenclature unattested in pre-exilic texts. Here the use with the copulative perfect (*whšbyt*) marks it as belonging to the later redaction of the account. See Jones, p. 618; Spieckermann, pp. 84–6; Würthwein (1976), p. 415; McKay, pp. 36–7. The LXX transliterates (χωμαρειμ), as it does *qdšym* (see below).

Although the text has usually been understood as recording the removal of the *qdšym*,[92] a careful reading shows that is not the case. Moreover, the notice in which *qdšym* appears is set in the context of action against the Asherah cult, which must be considered in assessing the reference.

(6) *wyṣʾ ʾt-hʾšrh mbyt yhwh mḥwṣ lyrwšlm ʾl nḥl qdrwn wyśrp ʾth bnḥl qdrwn wydq lʿpr wyšlk ʾt-ʿprh ʿl-qbr bny hʿm* (7) *wytṣ ʾt-bty hqdšym ʾšr bbyt yhwh ʾšr hnšym ʾrgwt šm btym lʾšrh*

(6) He brought out the Asherah from the house of YHWH, outside Jerusalem, to the brook Kidron, and burned it at the brook Kidron, and beat it to dust and cast its dust on the grave(s) of the common people. (7) And he broke down the house(s) of the *qdšym*, which were in the house of YHWH[93] where the women wove "houses"[94] for (the) Asherah (2 Kgs xxiii 6–7).

---

[92] So, e.g., Lowery, p. 70; cf. p. 72. Cf. Würthwein (1984), p. 457.

[93] There are two interrelated problems relating to the object of *wytṣ*: the nature of the structure(s) and its/their location. *btym* appears strange as a term to describe structures within the temple building, and thus most commentators interpret *byt yhwh* as referring to the larger temple complex, with its courts, storehouses, work rooms, etc. Interpreting the first relative clause as modifying *hqdšym*, rather than *bty* (*NEB*/*REB*), is a problematic solution, in my view, and is not followed by most translators, although it is attested in the LXX (Lucianic readings, however, place the "house" [οἶκον] in the "house of the Lord"). Identifying the *qdšym* directly with the temple makes the absence of any reported action against them even more striking.

The LXX and Targum read *byt* (sg.) instead of MT *bty*. Other uses of *byt*/*btym* that may serve as analogies are *byt nkth* "(his) treasure house" and *byt klyw* "(his) armory (house of weapons)", both in 2 Kgs xx 13 (= Isa. xxxix 2) in a series of terms describing what Hezekiah showed the envoys of Merodach-baladan, concluding with the summary term *ʾwṣrtyw*. Cf. *byt hʾwṣr* (Mal. iii 10), designating the temple storehouse for tithes, whose location in relation to the temple or other structures is unspecified, and *byt ʾwṣr ʾlhyw* "the treasure house of his God" (Dan. i 2), as the place where Nebuchadnezzar brought the vessels from the temple in Jerusalem. Other structures called *byt* which might have been incorporated into larger building complexes are the *byt hnšym* "harem/women's house" (Est. ii 9, 11), and various terms for prisons or guard houses, such as *byt hklʾ* (1 Kgs xxii 27 [= 2 Chr. xviii 26]; 2 Kgs xvii 4; Jer. xxxvii 15, 18; Isa. xlii 1; cf. *bty klʾym* Isa. xlii 22) and *byt mšmrt* (2 Sam. xx 3). In Ezek. xlvi 24 *byt* [for *bty*? see the *BHS* note] *hmbšlym* describes "kitchens" in the outer courtyard (*hḥṣr hḥyṣnh*) of the temple. All but Isa. xlii 22 employ the sg. *byt*, which may favor the notion of an original singular in 2 Kgs xxiii 7. The plural may be explained by metathesis and/or inadvertant assimilation to *btym* in the second half of the verse. Only *byt nšym* defines *byt* by reference to a class of persons. See Stinespring, pp. 534–47; Meyers, pp. 1021–7.

[94] MT *bāttîm* ("houses") is inappropriate as an object of *ʾrqwt* and is generally emended, either to read *kuttōnîm* (unattested m.pl. of *kĕtōnet* "tunic") on the basis of the LXX transliteration Χεττιειν and Luc. στολάς (Burney, p. 359; Gray, p. 730)—hence "vestments"—or interpreted in the light of Arab. *batt* "woven garment", represented elsewhere in Biblical Hebrew in the spelling *bad, baddîm* (as material of priestly garments)—hence "linens"

The essential content of *v.* 7 is the destruction of some type of structures[95] associated with the temple, whose significance for the reform program is spelled out by reference to their use in the Asherah cult. The defining qualifier is the final *ʾšr* clause, not *hqdšym.*[96] In most interpretations, however, attention has focused on the *qdšym* as the target of the action, with the reference to weaving operations treated as little more than an antiquarian notice authenticating the account as a first-hand report. Little consideration has been given to the question of how the women and their activity might be related to the *qdšym*, and all attempts to specify the relationship involve serious problems. The following is a synopsis of major arguments relating to the two primary options: (1) viewing the weavers as a sub-class of the *qdšym*, or (2) viewing them as a distinct group. Each is open to multiple constructions, of which only a few can be considered here.

The nšym *as a category of the* qdšym

The use of the article with *nšym*, indicating a definite group or collectivity, suggests—but does not require—an understanding of the women as a component of a previously named or understood class,[97]

or "vestments" (*HALAT; BHS*; Montgomery, p. 539; Driver, p. 107; Jones, p. 619). All the proposals are problematic, and I am inclined to view the text as corrupt, especially in view of the two occurrences of *bty(m)* in the verse. See Frevel, pp. 686–8, for an exhaustive survey of proposals.

[95] I adopt the MT's plural for ease of reference, although I am inclined to see the sg. *byt* as most likely original.

[96] This interpretation seems to be required by the common theme of eradication of the Asherah cult that unites *vv.* 6–7. Yet the initial identification of the structures is provided by *hqdšym*, and the awkwardness of introducing a second descriptive qualifier requires note—especially when *qdšym* appears to be the "better known" term and represent the more offensive activity. That the two have never elsewhere been associated also requires explanation. Some view the second *ʾšr* clause as an addition by a later editor who no longer knew the meaning of *qdšym* (Benzinger, p. 192, who equates the "Weberinnen" with the "Kedeschen"). Others see it as heightening the charge by adding service of a foreign deity (idolatry) to a prohibited cult practice (Hoffmann, p. 231, who describes the women's activity as "'nebenamtliche' Beschäftigung der Bewohner dieses Hauses"). All attempts to explain the double definition of the houses involve interrelated judgements about the meaning of *qdšym* and the women's activity, as well as the literary history of the verse. I am not persuaded by Wacker's attempt to relate the second *ʾšr* clause to *byt yhwh*, rather than *bty hqdšym* (p. 59, n. 25).

[97] Joüon § 137. See, e.g., Jer. vii 17–18. A closer parallel to the usage here, however, and one favoring the second option, is found in Ezek. viii 14, where women alone are specified, as a particular group that is further defined by the following participles: *whnh-šm hnšym yšbwt mbkwt ʾt-htmwz* "there sat (the) women weeping for Tammuz".

for which *qdšym* appears as the logical, and only, antecedent. One might then view the activity of the women as evidence for an Israelite class of hierodules comparable to those identified by the terms *qadištu* and *qdš(m)* in Akkadian and Ugaritic texts. While such persons appear to have exercised some types of liturgical functions, they may also have performed other types of cult maintenance service, appropriate to their sex, such as the weaving recorded here.[98]

There are several problems with this interpretation, however. First, the women are not called *qdšwt*. Thus it is difficult to see them as representative of the class identified as *qdšym*. One explanation might be that they do not represent the female counterparts of the male hierodules, but rather their female dependents—like the women of priestly families or prophetic guilds. In that case, however, their activity does not define or exemplify the class, which is determined by the male role.

An alternative interpretation might lie in positing a separate development of the masculine and feminine forms of the noun, in which the feminine form acquired sexual connotations lacking in the masculine. The feminine term *qdšh* might consequently be reserved for a special class of women operating at the rural shrines (and identified with prostitutes), while women performing the normal cultic roles might simply be known as women of the *qdšym* (class). But this explanation also fails to illumine the male role, or assumes a generic meaning for *qdšym* in which the sole representatives are female, an unlikely development.

The most serious obstacle to any attempt to reconstruct a class of cultic personnel comprising both males and females under a common title is the absence of ancient models (noted above). The pattern of gender-differentiated cultic as well as professional service attested throughout the ancient Near East, including Israel, leaves little place for common or shared professional activity[99]—and none for shared

[98] Cf. the description of two women in Old Babylonian Ur as "weaver-women of the god El of the Amorites" (*UET* V 393, cited by Diakonoff, p. 228). On the problems of interpreting this weaving as a form of cultic service, see Frevel, pp. 692-8. Attempts to see this expression as a euphemism for sexual intercourse (Murmelstein, pp. 223–5; de Moor, cols 476–7; cf. Würthwein 1984, p. 457) are unconvincing and have found little following. Such concealment of the "true" activity of the women is at cross purposes with the intention of condemnation in the verse.

[99] Some activities, such as weaving or baking, that were originally women's activities performed in the home, were engaged in by men outside the home (commercial production or in palace or temple industry). Models and reliefs from Egypt show men and women

quarters. Guild organization based on family units is the general rule for male professions (e.g., priests, diviners, scribes, merchants).[100] Even prophets, the major exception to the rule of gender-differentiated nomenclature and activity in both Israel and Mesopotamia, appear to have been organized according to the male guild principle when they are found in groups. Female prophets are never identified with these groups—and women of the prophetic bands are never called prophets.

We must consequently reject the common interpretation of the structures of 2 Kgs xxiii 7 as residential quarters.[101] The pattern of residence for women associated with the cult is cloistered (spatially separated and restricted) residence for single women within the temple complex, or a marriage relationship with residence outside the cult precinct.[102] Male cult personnel appear to have lived in families in or near the sanctuary precinct, with all the male members employed in cultic service. Apart from palace eunuchs or slaves there appear to have been no classes of single males residing together.[103] Consequently, the term *byt/bty hqdšym* cannot designate a residence, leaving only the option of a work area associated with this class. But here too a gender-inclusive interpretation must be rejected. The notion that the *byt/bty hqdšym* designated a common work area for the activities of male and female votaries, a kind of "house of the 'religious', or temple auxiliary" draws on western models and assumes a generic use of the term *qdšym* that is not otherwise attested. It also makes the term *qdšym* virtually contentless in this verse, since only the women's work is specified. In the final analysis I do not believe we can include the women in the category identified here by the term *qdšym*.

---

in the same scene or structure engaged in common work (beer making [*ANEP*, pp. 153, 154]; baking [p. 154]; and harvesting [p. 91])—but in different tasks. Two weaving scenes (p. 42, nos 142, 143) contain only female figures.

[100] Cf. the all-male Ugaritic lists of professional groups, including *khnm* and *qdšm*.

[101] It is widely assumed that the *bty hqdšym* are residences (e.g., Hoffmann, p. 230: "Wohnungen der Kultprostituierten")—without any attempt to envision the living arrangements of a non-familial group comprising both sexes. See Bird (1987), pp. 406–7.

[102] Cf. Harris (1964); (1976), p. 962. We learn of female prostitutes living together (1 Kgs iii 16–17), but have no evidence for male prostitutes.

[103] The status and marital options of the three Jewish youths in Dan. i 3–7 are not clear from the narrative. The identity and functions of the *ntynym* are disputed. Cody (pp. 116–69, 186) understands them as temple servants. Weinberg (pp. 368–70), believes they were originally artisans in the royal administration, who belonged to the lowest social class of the post-exilic community and were organized by families. A "house of the Nethinim" (*byt hntynym*) is mentioned in Neh. iii 31, suggesting that they lived together; *v*. 26 locates them on the Ophel. Ugaritic evidence points to married *qdšm*, with families.

The nšym *as a group distinct from the* qdšym

The association of two groups with the same structures has suggested that they were somehow related, if not in common activity, at least in common identification with the Asherah cult. In the usual interpretation of *qdšym* as "male cult prostitutes", this text appears to provide the critical link with the fertility cult represented by the goddess. The fact that such an identification with Asherah is made nowhere else, however, is a strong argument from silence. Moreover, the conceptual link is problematic, as noted above. And the reconstruction of a sexual role for the male hierodules leaves the reference to the associated women's activity even more striking in its total lack of sexual innuendo.

An identification of the *qdšym* with the cult of Asherah is easier to imagine if the class is reconstructed along the lines suggested by the Ugaritic evidence, with the *qdšym* functioning perhaps as liturgical leaders in rituals related to (the) Asherah, alongside the priests who presided over the YHWH cult.[104] The women then are simply devotees, engaged in the kind of cultic service women typically perform, and do not constitute a professional class. The argument from silence challenges this reconstruction as well, but it has less force in the case of a (once) legitimate, or at least widely tolerated, institution than in the case of an abhorrent and clearly illegitimate one. Is it possible that a class of "consecrated men" functioned within the YHWH cult in pre-Josianic times, with special duties relating to the Asherah (which seems to have been a fairly constant feature of the pre-Deuteronomic cult)?[105] As minor cultic officials, or simply assistants, of non-priestly status, there would be no reason to single them out in the recurring critique of the Asherah, since it is the cult symbol, and the deity it represents, that is the main focus of interest.

Or should we view the *qdšym* as a more general class of cultic functionaries within the YHWH cult, without a particular association

---

[104] In my view, the Asherah cult in Israel must be understood within the YHWH cult. Whatever form it took, it appears not to have involved sacrifices or a separate priesthood. Contrast the cult of Baal, who has his own "house" (1 Kgs xvi 52), altar (Judg. vi 25–6; 1 Kgs xvi 32), priests (2 Kgs x 19), and prophets (1 Kgs xviii 19; 2 Kgs x 19—I regard the reference to prophets of Asherah in 1 Kgs xviii 19 as a late, literary creation; note the Hexaplaric asterisk; see commentaries and Smith, pp. 271–2, n. 4). Cf. Smith, pp. 80–97; Frevel, p. 916.

[105] Olyan; cf. Frevel, pp. 927–9.

with Asherah, a class that may have fallen out of favor with the Deuteronomists or simply lost its position to reorganization of the cult or rivalry with other classes of cult personnel? Has the Deuteronomist perhaps reinterpreted an old term, drawing on the well-established negative associations of the feminine term, and connecting the class to the deposed Asherah? I believe we must entertain the possibility that the reference to *qdšm* in this text stems from historical memory of a class of male cult personnel functioning within the Jerusalem temple in the pre-Josianic cult.[106] They may be hidden in several ways in our far from adequate sources.

It may be possible to conceive of such a class within the Israelite cult at some point in its early history—but they are no longer present in Josiah's time. In the final analysis, the text rules out any interpretation that would place *qdšym*, however conceived, in the temple as a functioning institution at the time of Josiah's reforms. The action reported in the verse is directed against the structures, not the *qdšym*—and the link with the Asherah is made only through the activity of the women. A Deuteronomistic author, familiar with the prohibition of Deut. xxiii 18, would surely not have failed to report any action against *qdšym* or any word of their fate if he had a source indicating their presence in the temple. And he would hardly have needed to add a reference to women's weaving operations to explain the destruction of their houses, which seems only to diffuse the critique by pointing to a different kind of offense. The clear impression conveyed by this text is that the *qdšym* by which the houses are identified are no longer there.

A satisfactory interpretation of this text must understand it both as a Dtr composition and as an account based on historical memory—and that necessitates a double reading. The Deuteronomist is bound here to his source, and is thus unable to provide any of the information about the detestable class of *qdšym* that Deuteronomy leads us to expect. His hand is still evident in this text, however, as Hoffmann has rightly seen.[107] The Deuteronomist has reinterpreted his source by

---

[106] My reasoning is quite different from that of Lowery, who interprets the silence concerning the *qdšym* between the reigns of Jehoshaphat and Josiah as a sign of acceptance of an institution of cultic prostitution (p. 91). His view of this "flourishing" institution is based entirely on female examples, as treated by Lang and Wolff (p. 92). Reconstructing a male institution requires a distinct set of considerations.

[107] Hoffmann identifies *ntṣ* as a characteristic term of Dtr's reform vocabulary (pp. 255, 342–3; cf. Spieckermann, p. 92) and notes Dtr's use of *ʾšr* clauses (pp. 240, 265, 364).

emphasizing the destruction of structures identified by the term *qdšym* and underlining their location in the temple. Whatever *qdšym* may have meant in a pre-Dtr source, the term cannot be read in a Dtr text apart from the associations of Deut. xxiii 18. The traditional interpretation that has understood this reference in the light of the Deuteronomic prohibition, with its intimations of cult-related sex exemplified by both male and female practitioners, has understood it as the Dtr author intended.

The Deuteronomist has exploited the shock value of *qdšym* in his source to suggest abhorrent practices going on in the temple. His source, however, exhibits a quite different interest. The primary target of Josiah's action is the Asherah cult (cult symbol and support complex), which had established itself within the temple. The issue here is idolatry (in Deuteronomic terms), or religious "syncretism", related to an Israelite popular cult; the issue with the *qdšym* is sexual immorality involving "foreign" cult personnel—and these are not related. The two qualifiers of the "house" point in different directions, a case of Dtr using his source to compound accusations. But Dtr's use does not explain the original meaning of *qdšym*, which remains an enigma.[108]

The Deuteronomist is consistent in his presentation of the *qdšym*. He has allowed the term in his source to carry the full weight of Deuteronomic censure, but he knows that the *qdšym* are no longer on the scene. He accounts for their absence by attributing their removal to Asa, not simply from the temple, however, but from the land. I take this as an indication of his uncertainty about the exact nature and location of the class that has left its name on a temple structure, but is otherwise unattested in any historical source—unlike the Asherah.

An alternative reading

Thus far I have interpreted the term in 2 Kgs xxiii 7 as the Deuteronomistic author intended it to be understood, but have been unable to locate or explain the historical presence behind the term. But perhaps

The latter criterion is less compelling here, since the final *ʾšr* clause does not fit Hoffmann's categories of Dtr usage.

[108] It is significant that here alone, of all occurrences of *qdšh/qdš(ym)*, the LXX transliterates (καδησειμ, Luc. καδησιν), rather than translates, indicating uncertainty about the meaning of the term.

Dtr's interpretation involves a more radical reinterpretation of the key term in his source. Perhaps the *qdšym*-house(s) did not refer to *qĕdēšîm* at all. I suggest an alternative reading of the original source, prompted by a clue contained in the account of Asa's reforms (1 Kgs xv 12–15). There the Deuteronomistic author has framed his summary of the cultic reforms with opening and closing statements that employ as their key terms m.pl. nouns from the same root: *qĕdēšîm* (*v*. 12) and **qodāšîm* (*qdšy ʾbyw wqdšw, v*. 15)—terms that are identical in their consonantal spelling. Asa's first act is to remove *qĕdēšîm* from the land; his final act is to bring *qodāšîm* into the temple. His purge of alien votaries is paralleled by his deposit of votive offerings. *V*. 15 echoes the notice in 1 Kgs vii 51, which concludes the account of the building and furnishing of the temple with the notice that "Solomon brought in the votive gifts of his father David (*wybʾ šlmh ʾt-qdšy dwd ʾbyw*) . . . and put [them] in the treasuries of the temple (*ntn bʾṣrwt byt yhwh*)." It is these storehouses for the dedicated gifts (*ʾṣrwt hqdšym*, 1 Chr. xxviii 12; cf. *byt hʾwṣr*, Mal. iii 10), I suggest, that were intended by the original reference in, or behind, 2 Kgs xxiii 7—storehouses appropriated for the service of the Asherah cult.

In this reading the structure(s) where the women performed their weaving was/were originally designated *byt/bty haqqodāšîm*, storehouse(s) for the votive objects, emptied by Hezekiah in payment of tribute to Sennacherib (2 Kgs xviii 15–16) and converted into workshops for the Asherah introduced by Manasseh (2 Kgs xxi 3, 7). Josiah's destruction of these desecrated structures along with his burning of the Asherah removed all vestiges of this cult and destroyed its base of operation. But of *qĕdēšîm* the text provides no evidence, either as a class of male hierodules or as a gender-inclusive category of temple servants. According to the original text or source, there never were any *qĕdēšîm* in the temple.[109]

If this interpretation of *qdšym* in 2 Kgs xxiii 7 is rejected, we are left with a term that must still be recognized as our sole historical

[109] It is difficult to determine at what stage in the transmission of the text/tradition this reinterpretation took place, but if the author who juxtaposed *qĕdēšîm* and *qodāšîm* in 1 Kgs xv 12, 15 was also responsible for the present form of this text, it is difficult to attribute the move to misunderstanding. It is, however, a move that makes sense as a heightening of offense by allusion to the abominations of Deut. xxiii 18. But the author could do no more than cast aspersions, because his source reported no action against any *qdšym*. The present vocalization could represent a later interpretation, but it clearly antedates the LXX, whose transliteration reflects the MT vocalization.

evidence for a class of male hierodules who are no longer present in Josiah's time and unattested in any earlier source. The author of our earliest witness to the masculine term, Deut. xxiii 18—which may be roughly contemporary with the Josianic source—is so uncertain about the nature of the class that he can only present it as analogous to the *qdšh*.[110] The problem remains that the Deuteronomists, through whom alone we encounter the *qdš(ym)*, permit us no reliable access to any institutionally meaningful phenomenon behind the term.

Conclusions

The consequences of this investigation of *qdš/qdšym* in the HB may be summarized as follows:

1. The m.sg. noun in its earliest attestation (Deut. xxiii 18) is a literary creation derived from the feminine noun *qdšh*, to which it is appended as a complement. It is introduced to give comprehensiveness and balance to a Deuteronomic prohibition of cult-related sex, in a new law directed against alien cult personnel paralleling an older law banning temple income from prostitutes of both sexes.

2. The m.pl. noun (1 Kgs xv 12; 2 Kgs xxiii 7) is confined to Deuteronomistic usage and is dependent for its interpretation on Deut. xxiii 18. It is thus to be understood as a generic term, intended as a comprehensive reference to male as well as female practitioners—a term to cover all possibilities—but precisely in this intention, implausible as historical description.

3. The m.sg.coll. usage (1 Kgs xiv 24, xxii 47) is dependent on the m.pl. usage and has no independent base. It appears to represent an interpretation of the m.pl. form as referring primarily or exclu-

---

[110] We cannot point to the other occurrences of the noun in 1 Kings as corroborating evidence, since they are later and show literary dependence on the earlier sources. They do, however, serve to underscore the absence of the phenomenon in their own day by their unanimous testimony that the class had long vanished. Their view of the institution as belonging to the earliest period of the southern monarchy reinforces the notion that the authors lacked historically reliable knowledge—and exacerbates the problem of explaining a persisting "memory" of this class in a 7th-century document. One might suggest that the *qdšym* ceased to exist, or function, under Hezekiah, or at least at some point close enough to Josiah's time to leave their name, since the Dtr notices are clearly schematic. Although I am open to such a possibility, it does not answer any of the questions raised above about the place and function of the class, and the silence of the sources outside the highly restricted and artificial Deuteronom(ist)ic references.

sively to males, emphasizing the repugnant associations with male homosexual activity suggested by the parallelism with *klb* in Deut. xxiii 18–19.

4. The m.pl./coll. usage has no historical grounding accessible through the biblical references. There is no historical evidence for the existence in Israel/Judah of male hierodules, or cult prostitutes, known as *qdš(ym)*, either as a legitimate class of cultic servants or as devotees of a Canaanite cult. The content and connotations of the term appear to have been derived from the independently attested feminine forms of the noun and the latter's association with illicit sexual activity.

5. There is no historical evidence for identification of *qdšym* (or *qdšwt*) with the cult of Asherah.

Appendix: Job xxxvi 14

The reference occurs in the fourth Elihu speech, in a segment dealing with the discipline of suffering. *V.* 14 continues a discourse on the fate of those who fail to respond appropriately to divine chastisement (*v.* 12). *V.* 13 characterizes the subjects, while *v.* 14 describes their fate:

(13) *wḥnpy-lb yśymw ʾp*
lʾ yšwʿw ky ʾsrm
(14) *tmt*[111] *bnʿr npšm*
wḥytm bqdšym

(13) The impious in heart cherish anger;
they do not cry for help when he binds them.[112]
(14) Their self/existence shall die in youth,
their life in *qdšym*.

I have translated *v.* 14 literally in order to show what I think is the major problem in the usual translation of *bqdšym* as "among the *qdšym*" or "as the *qdšym*". The parallelism in the verse is similar to that in *v.* 11 ("They will complete their days in prosperity [*baṭṭôb*] and their years in pleasantness [*bannĕʿîmîm*]", ABC:BC), but with a chiastic reversal in the final colon (ABC:CB).

[111] Reading impf. (*tāmūt*) for MT jussive (*tāmōt*).

[112] The meaning of several of the terms and constructions in this verse is disputed, but the sense of failing to cry out in response to trials is clear. See commentaries.

The consonantal text appears to be firmly attested, and understood by the Vulgate (*inter effeminatos*) and Targum (*hyk mry znw* "like male prostitutes") as the same term found in Deut. xxiii 18, interpreted in the traditional manner. The LXX, however, has read the consonants differently, rendering ὑπὸ ἀγγέλων (= *baqqĕdōšîm*; cf. xv 15). This rendering differs from all other treatments of *qdšh*/*qdš* in the LXX. Elsewhere, the Greek translators have either used terms related to cultic practices, or to prostitution where the context provided this clue; or they have simply transliterated (as in 2 Kgs xxiii 7). Because of differing translation practices within the LXX, I do not think that much weight can be placed on this comparison, but it does serve to show ancient recognition of a problem in the interpretation of this text.[113] In my view, neither LXX nor MT yields a satisfying sense, because they require different interpretations of the same preposition in the parallel cola.

Modern attempts to interpret *qdšym* in this text typically appeal to Deut. xxiii 18, understood as a reference to a homosexual prostitute, and draw conclusions about the dissolute lifestyle and early death of such persons. The following English translations are illustrative: *NRSV* "They die in their youth, and their life ends in shame (note: Heb *ends among the temple prostitutes*)"; *REB* "so they die in their prime, short-lived as male prostitutes";[114] they "die in the bloom of their youth or live among the male prostitutes of the temple"; JPS: "They die in their youth; [Expire] among the depraved".

Commentators are somewhat freer to consider alternatives, but wherever they connect their reading with *qĕdēšîm*, they are bound by traditional views of "male (cult) prostitutes". Thus Rowley (p. 229) specifies "male prostitutes" for the "cult prostitutes" of the *RSV* note and cites Duhm's view that "these persons, attached to the shrines for infamous purposes, commonly died early". Pope (p. 233) elaborates: "the orgiastic excesses imposed on the hierodules so debilitated them that their predisposition to precocious mortality became proverbial".[115]

Dhorme observes that the parallelism of *ḥyh* and *npš* is typical of the style of Elihu (p. 543), and notes that the parallelism of *bqdšym* with *bnʿr* invites interpretation of the plural as an abstract term similar

---

[113] See Dion (p. 46) for an interpretation of the "holy ones" as destroying angels.

[114] Cf. *NEB*: "like male prostitutes (note: Cp. Deut. 23. 17) worn out (note: prob. rdg; Heb. unintelligible)".

[115] Cf. Habel, p. 192; Driver and Gray, p. 276.

to *nĕʿûrîm* "youth", *bĕḥûrîm* "adolescence", etc. Arguing that "the infamous part incumbent on [the male sacred prostitute] presupposes quite a youthful age", he infers that "the abstract *qĕdēšîm* connotes this age which borders on adolescence" (p. 544), and translates "their life ends in adolescence!" (p. 543). Gordis (p. 415) suggests a double connotation of "shameful youth".[116] Van Selms also insists that the preposition *b* must have the same meaning in both parts of the verse, proposing a reading of *baqqodāšîm*, understood in the sense of "voortijdig", as the fruit of a tree in its fourth year after planting, which is *qōdeš* to YHWH (Lev. xix 23). Thus he translates: "hun bestaan voortijdig" (pp. 146–7).

I do not think that any of the proposed meanings of *qĕdēšîm* make sense here, though a parallel to *nōʿar* seems to be required. I am inclined to view the text as corrupt or concealing some other term or meaning of the root. In any case, this reference clearly postdates the references in DH and, when read as *qĕdēšîm*, is understood by all interpreters in terms of the Deuteronom(ist)ic usage. Consequently, it cannot be treated as supplying independent content to the term. The most one can argue for this attestation, assuming the term is correctly transmitted, is that the *term* was still known in the post-exilic period—perhaps in the sense that it had come to have in the latest Dtr uses, as a class of male prostitutes associated with the Canaanite cult, and thus as an institution known only by tradition from remote times. This is at best testimony to a "proverbial meaning", not an historical institution.

ABBREVIATIONS OF TRANSLATIONS OF THE BIBLE

AV	*Authorized Version* of 1611 (= *KJV*)
Chicago	*The Complete Bible: An American Translation* (Chicago, 1939)
JB	*Jerusalem Bible*
JPS 1917	Jewish Publication Society version of 1917
KJV	*King James Version* of 1611 (= *AV*)
Luther	German translation of Martin Luther (edn of *ca.* 1950)
NAB	*New American Bible*
NEB	*New English Bible*

[116] Cf. Alonso Schökel and Sicre Diaz (p. 520), who support the translation of the *Nueva Biblia Española* ("mueren a la edad de los efebos"). They note, however, that the comparison set up by the parallelism within the verse is "inesperada sorprendente".

NJB *New Jerusalem Bible*
NRSV *New Revised Standard Version*
REB *Revised English Bible*
RSV *Revised Standard Version*
TEV *Today's English Version*

Works Cited by Author's Last Name Only

W.F. Albright, *Archaeology and the Religion of Israel* (5th edn, Garden City, New York, 1969; 1st edn, Baltimore, 1942).

A.G. Auld, *Kings Without Privilege: David and Moses in the Story of the Bible's Kings* (Edinburgh, 1994).

I. Benzinger, *Die Bücher der Könige* (Freiburg i. B., 1899).

P.A. Bird, "The Place of Women in the Israelite Cultus", in P.D. Miller, P.D. Hanson, and S.D. McBride (ed.), *Ancient Israelite Religion: Essays in Honor of Frank Moore Cross* (Philadelphia, 1987), pp. 397–419.

——— 1989a, "The Harlot as Heroine in Biblical Texts: Narrative Art and Social Presupposition", *Semeia* 46 (1989), pp. 119–39.

——— 1989b, "'To Play the Harlot': An Inquiry into an Old Testament Metaphor", in P.L. Day (ed.), *Gender and Difference* (Minneapolis, 1989), pp. 75–94.

———, "Women (OT)", *ABD* VI (1992), pp. 951–7.

———, "Prostitution", in B.M. Metzger and M.D. Coogan (ed.), *The Oxford Companion to the Bible* (Oxford, 1993), pp. 623–4.

C.F. Burney, *Notes on the Hebrew Text of the Books of Kings* (Oxford, 1903).

R.J. Burns, *Has the Lord Indeed Spoken Only Through Moses? A Study of the Biblical Portrait of Miriam* (Atlanta, 1987).

A. Cody, *A History of Old Testament Priesthood* (Rome, 1969).

C.B. Costecalde, "Sacré (et sainteté), I. La racine 'qdš' et ses dérivés en milieu ouest-sémitique et dans les cunéiformes; II Sacré et sainteté dans l'Ancien Testament, A. and B.", *DBSup* X (1985), cols 1346–414.

J. Day, "Asherah in the Hebrew Bible and Northwest Semitic Literature", *JBL* 105 (1986), pp. 385–408.

P.E. Dion, "Did Cultic Prostitution Fall into Oblivion during the Postexilic Era? Some Evidence from Chronicles and the Septuagint", *CBQ* 43 (1981), pp. 41–8.

S.R. Driver, *A Critical and Exegetical Commentary on Deuteronomy* (Edinburgh, 1895).

W. Fauth, "Sakrale Prostitution im Vorderen Orient und im Mittelmeerraum", *JAC* 31 (1988), pp. 24–39.

J. Frazer, *The Golden Bough: A Study in Magic and Religion*, 3rd edn, Part IV *Adonis, Attis, Osiris* 1 (London, 1914).

C. Frevel, *Aschera und der Ausschliesslichkeitsanspruch YHWHs: Beiträge zu literarischen, religionsgeschichtlichen und ikonographischen Aspekten der Ascheradiskussion* (2 vols) (Weinheim, 1995).

T. Frymer-Kensky, *In the Wake of the Goddesses: Women. Culture, and the Biblical Transformation of Pagan Myth* (New York, 1992).

J.H. Gagnon, "Prostitution", in D.L. Silk (ed.), *The International Encyclopedia of the Social Sciences* (New York, 1969), XII, pp. 592–8.

E.A. Goodfriend, "Prostitution (Old Testament)", *ABD* V (1992), pp. 505–10.

J. Gray, *I & II Kings. A Commentary* (2nd rev. edn, London and Philadelphia, 1970).

M.I. Gruber, "The *qādēš* in the Book of Kings and in Other Sources" (Heb.), *Tarbiz* 52 (1983), pp. 167–76.

———, "Hebrew *qedēšāh* and her Canaanite and Akkadian Cognates", *UF* 18 (1986), pp. 133–48.

R. Harris, "The *nadītu* Woman", in *Studies Presented to A. Leo Oppenheim* (Chicago, 1964), pp. 106–35.
———, "Woman in the Ancient Near East", *IDBSup* (1976), pp. 960–3.
R.A. Henshaw, *Female and Male: The Cultic Personnel: The Bible and the Rest of the Ancient Near East* (Allison Park, Pennsylvania, 1994).
H.-D. Hoffmann, *Reform und Reformen. Untersuchungen zu einem Grundthema der deuteronomistischen Geschichtesschreibung* (Zurich, 1980).
S.M. Hooks, *Sacred Prostitution in Israel and the Ancient Near East* (unpublished Ph.D. diss., Hebrew Union College, Cincinnati, 1985).
J. L'Hour, "Les interdits *tô'ēbā* dans le Déuteronome", *RB* 71 (1964), pp. 481–503.
S. Japhet, *I & II Chronicles: A Commentary* (London and Louisville, 1993).
G.H. Jones, *1 and 2 Kings* (2 vols) (London and Grand Rapids, 1984).
P. Joüon, *Grammaire de l'Hébreu Biblique* (Rome, 1923).
W.G. Lambert, *Babylonian Wisdom Literature* (Oxford, 1960).
W.G. Lambert and A.R. Millard, *Atra-hasīs, the Babylonian Story of the Flood* (Oxford, 1969).
N. Lohfink, "Zur neueren Diskusssion über 2 Kön 22–23", in N. Lohfink (ed.), *Das Deuteronomium: Entstehung, Gestalt und Botschaft* (Leuven, 1985).
R.H. Lowery, *The Reforming Kings: Cults and Society in First Temple Judah* (Sheffield, 1991).
F.A. Marglin, "Hieroduleia", in M. Eliade (ed.), *The Encyclopedia of Religion* VI (New York, 1987), pp. 309–13.
A.D.H. Mayes, *Deuteronomy* (London and Grand Rapids, 1979).
J. McKay, *Religion in Judah under the Assyrians 732–609 BC* (Naperville and London, 1973).
R.P. Merendino, *Das deuteronomische Gesetz: ein literarkritische, gattungs- und überlieferungsgeschichtliche Untersuchung zu Dt. 12–26* (Bonn, 1968).
C. Meyers, "The Temple", *Harper's Bible Dictionary* (San Francisco, etc., 1985), pp. 1021–9.
J.A. Montgomery and H.S. Gehman, *A Critical and Exegetical Commentary on the Books of Kings* (Edinburgh, 1951).
J.C. de Moor, "*'ăšērâ*", *TWAT* I (1972), cols 473–9.
H.-P. Müller, "*qdš* heilig", *THAT* II (1979), cols 589–609.
B. Murmelstein, "Spuren altorientalischer Einflüsse im rabbinischen Schrifttum. Die Spinnerinnen des Schicksals", *ZAW* 81 (1969), pp. 215–32.
J.M. Myers, *2 Chronicles* (Garden City, New York, 1965).
R.D. Nelson, *The Double Redaction of the Deuteronomistic History* (Sheffield, 1981).
M. Noth, *Könige* 1 (Neukirchen-Vluyn, 1968).
R.A. Oden, *The Bible Without Theology: The Theological Tradition and Alternatives to It* (San Francisco, 1987).
S.M. Olyan, *Asherah and the Cult of Yahweh in Israel* (Atlanta, 1988).
A. Phillips, *Deuteronomy* (Cambridge, 1973).
M.H. Pope, "Fertility Cult", *IDB* 2 (1962), p. 265.
G. von Rad, *Deuteronomy, A Commentary* (Philadelphia and London, 1961); E. tr. of *Das fünfte Buch Mose: Deuteronomium* (Göttingen, 1956).
J. Renger, "Untersuchungen zum Priestertum in der altbabylonischen Zeit", *ZA* N.F. 24 (1967), pp. 110–88.
———, "Heilige Hochzeit. A. Philologisch", *RLA* IV, fasc. 4–5 (1975), pp. 251–9.
M.Z. Rosaldo, "Women, Culture, and Society: A Theoretical Overview", in M.Z. Rosaldo and L. Lamphere (ed.), *Women, Culture, and Society* (Stanford, 1974), pp. 17–42.
G. Seitz, *Redaktionsgeschichtliche Studien zum Deuteronomium* (Stuttgart, 1971).
M.S. Smith, *The Early History of God: Yahweh and the Other Deities in Ancient Israel* (San Francisco, 1990).
W.R. Smith, *Lectures on the Religion of the Semites* (Edinburgh, 1889).
W. von Soden, "Zur Stellung des 'Geweihten' (*qdš*) in Ugarit", *UF* 2 (1970), pp. 329–30.

H. Spieckermann, *Juda und Assur in der Sargonidenzeit* (Göttingen, 1982).
W.F. Stinespring, "Temple, Jerusalem", *IDB* IV (1962), pp. 534–60.
K. van der Toorn, "Female Prostitution in Payment of Vows in Ancient Israel", *JBL* 108 (1989), pp. 193–205.
———, "Cultic Prostitution", *ABD* V (1992), pp. 510–13.
M.-T. Wacker, "Kosmisches Sakrament oder Verpfändung des Körpers? 'Kult Prostitution' im biblischen Israel und in hinduistischen Indien: Religionsgeschichtliche Überlegungen im Interesse feministischer Theologie", *BN* 61 (1992), pp. 51–75.
J.P. Weinberg, "*Nethînîm* und 'Söhne der Sklaven Solomos' im 6.–4. Jh. v. u. Z.", *ZAW* 87 (1975), pp. 355–71.
M. Weinfield, *Deuteronomy and the Deuteronomic School* (Oxford, 1972).
J.G. Westenholz, "Tamar, *Qedēšā, Qadištu,* and Sacred Prostitution in Mesopotamia", *HTR* 82 (1989), pp. 245–65.
G. Wilhelm, "Marginalien zu Herodot Klio 199", in I.T. Abusch, J. Huehnergard, and P. Steinkeller (ed.), *Lingering Over Words: Studies in Ancient Near Eastern Literature in Honor of William L. Moran* (Atlanta, 1990), pp. 505–24.
H.G.M. Williamson, *1 and 2 Chronicles* (London and Grand Rapids, 1982).
E. Würthwein, *Die Bücher der Könige. Das erste Buch der Könige, Kap. 1–16* (Göttingen, 1977); *1. Kön. 17–2. Kön. 25* (1984).
——— "Die josianische Reform und das Deuteronomium", *ZTK* 73 (1976), pp. 395–423.
P. Xella, QDŠ. "Semantica del 'sacro' ad Ugarit", in *Materiali Lessicali ed Epigrafici* I (Rome, 1982), pp. 9–17.

WORKS CITED (APPENDIX)

J. Alonso Schökel and J.L. Sicre Diaz, *Job: Commentario teológico y literario* (Madrid, 1983).
E. Dhorme, *A Commentary on the Book of Job* (London, 1967), E. tr. of *Le livre de Job* (Paris, 1926).
S.R. Driver and G.B. Gray, *A Critical and Exegetical Commentary on the Book of Job* (Edinburgh, 1921).
R. Gordis, *The Book of Job: Commentary. New Translation, and Special Studies* (New York, 1978).
N.C. Habel, *The Book of Job* (Cambridge, 1975).
M. Pope, *Job* (Garden City, New York, 1965).
H.H. Rowley, *Job* (London, 1976).
A. van Selms, *Job II* (Nijkerk, 1983).

THE AGE OF DECIPHERMENT: THE OLD TESTAMENT AND THE ANCIENT NEAR EAST IN THE NINETEENTH CENTURY

by

KEVIN J. CATHCART
Dublin

According to the Introduction in J.B. Pritchard's *Ancient Near Eastern Texts*, "the importance of Assyriology for Biblical studies was widely heralded through the spectacular announcements of George Smith".[1] This is a reference to Smith's translations of a cuneiform account of the flood, which he gave in a paper read to the Society of Biblical Archaeology in December 1872, and to his identification of fragments of an account of creation, which he communicated in a letter to the London *Daily Telegraph* in March 1875. Cuneiform materials which were considered relevant for the study of the Old Testament were published in E. Schrader's *Die Keilinschriften und das alte Testament*, a work which appeared first in 1872 and was translated into English in later years.[2] A wider range of ancient Near Eastern texts was used in the Danish work of V. Schmidt, *Syriens Oldtid belyst ved Ikke Bibelske Kilder*.[3]

Yet how many biblical scholars are familiar with the significant, if less spectacular, discoveries which were made during the thirty years or more previous to Smith's announcements? The present writer, for one, would have only a limited appreciation of the nature and scope of the unflagging efforts made by the pioneers of decipherment and their immediate followers, if he had not systematically read several thousand pages of largely unpublished correspondence and papers of

---

[1] (Princeton, 1950) p. xiii; (3rd edn, 1969), p. xix.

[2] (Giessen, 1872) The rapid progress of cuneiform studies and Old Testament studies is reflected by the appearance of a second edition (Giessen, 1883), and a third edition by H. Zimmern and H. Winckler (Berlin, 1903). An English translation of the second edition was published by O.C. Whitehouse, *The Cuneiform Inscriptions and the Old Testament*, 2 vols (London, 1885–8).

[3] 2 vols (Copenhagen, 1872).

some of the early pioneers. Two scholars in particular, Edward Hincks (1792–1866) and Peter le Page Renouf (1822–97), corresponded with many of the Egyptologists and Assyriologists of the time.[4]

It should be remembered, however, that the decipherments of ancient Egyptian and Mesopotamian cuneiform were not accepted by everybody. Charles Wall, the Professor of Hebrew at Trinity College, Dublin, wrote to Hincks in March 1842: "I thank you for your paper which I got last night and have read over today—I can only say that I regret to see so much ingenuity and talent thrown away in the effort to support an erroneous theory. For my part, I have long since dismissed from my mind the subject of Egyptian hieroglyphics, together with Champollion's merits or demerits, and am at present engaged in preparing for the press proof of the spurious nature of the vowel letters in the text of the Hebrew Bible."[5] In later years the same academic heaped scorn on Hincks's work in Mesopotamian cuneiform, saying: "It appears to me no better than mere moonshine and I have very little doubt that if as much Chinese were laid before you as you have samples of Assyrian cuneiform writing, and if you applied the same industry and ingenuity to the investigation, you could coin as plausible fragments of a language from one set of materials as from the other."[6] In 1863, Renouf felt it necessary to publish a refutation of G.C. Lewis's claim that the decipherment of Egyptian was bogus.[7]

In this paper, the principal concern is with some aspects of Egyp-

[4] A fair portion of Hincks's correspondence was published by his grandson, E.F. Davidson, *Edward Hincks. A Selection from his Correspondence with a Memoir* (Oxford, 1933). See also K.J. Cathcart, "Edward Hincks (1792–1866): a biographical essay", in K.J. Cathcart (ed.), *The Edward Hincks Bicentenary Lectures* (Dublin, 1994), pp. 1–29. This writer is preparing an edition of Hincks's extensive correspondence and unpublished papers. Renouf's correspondence is equally voluminous, but little of it has been published. Some of Renouf's letters to Hincks are in Davidson, pp. 110–11, 115–16, 126–7, 223–4, 243. See also W.H. Rylands, G. Maspero and E. Naville (ed.), *The Life-Work of Sir Peter le Page Renouf*, 4 vols (Paris, 1902–7), esp. vol 4, pp. v–cxxxiii (a biography of Renouf, probably written by his daughter Edith). Permission to cite or refer to correspondence of Edward Hincks and Peter le Page Renouf was kindly given by Cambridge University Library, the Department of Western Antiquities at the British Museum, and the Griffith Institute, Ashmolean Museum, Oxford.

[5] GIO/H 539. (GIO/H = Griffith Institute, Ashmolean Museum, Oxford: Hincks correspondence.)

[6] GIO/H 542 (letter dated 29 August 1850).

[7] "Sir G.C. Lewis on the Decipherment and Interpretation of Dead Languages", *Atlantis* 4 (1863), pp. 23–57. In this article Renouf refers to Lewis's *An Historical Survey of the Astronomy of the Ancients* (London, 1862). Note, however, that in the same year, Lewis also published *Suggestions for the Application of the Egyptological Method to Modern History* (London, 1862).

tian and Mesopotamian discoveries in the 19th century and how they were related to the study of the Bible.

When Hincks wrote to Sir Robert Peel in 1842 to ask for an increase in his income so that he might continue his Egyptological studies, he informed him that he gave much of his spare time to the study of Egyptian because he felt it "might be of the greatest service to the cause of Christianity, as illustration of Biblical history and of Biblical language".[8] It must be said, however, that in Hincks's Egyptological publications and correspondence, the Old Testament is not so frequently mentioned. This is true also, as far as it can be judged, for the writings and letters of many of the other Egyptologists with whom Hincks and Renouf corresponded. The date of the Exodus was discussed from time to time. For example, Hincks told Samuel Birch that he was "quite satisfied that the Exodus was in the time of the Hyksos",[9] and Renouf wrote to Hincks: "As to the time of the Exodus I confess that the reasons for placing it at a late date seem to me very cogent, in spite of the fatal difficulty of 1 Kings VI.1 which I freely acknowledge myself unable to get over."[10]

There was great preoccupation with the chronology of ancient Egypt, and the publication of new chronological schemes naturally unsettled those who held the biblical chronology to be correct. In 1848 Hincks reviewed three books on ancient Egypt including the first volume of the English translation of a major work by C.C.J. Bunsen.[11] In this review he says: "We by no means accept this low view of the historical element in the Bible; but we are not prepared to denounce the man who does so as an infidel."[12] Just over ten years later he reviewed a further volume of Bunsen's work.[13] At the end of his long, rather tedious and highly critical review, which is largely concerned with Egyptian chronology, Hincks concludes by saying about Bunsen: "sceptical as regards the Bible, he is credulous to an extreme as to

[8] BL Add. Ms. 40517 f. 293r.

[9] BM/WAA, letter 2915 (dated 17 October 1865).

[10] GIO/H 479 (letter dated 30 January 1863).

[11] "Egypt and the Bible", *The Dublin University Magazine* 32 (1848), pp. 371–88, esp. 386–8. The work by Bunsen appeared in German as *Aegyptens Stelle in der Weltgeschichte. Geschichtliche Untersuchung in Fünf Büchern* (Hamburg, 1845–57) and in English under the title *Egypt's Place in Universal History; an Historical Investigation in Five Books* (London, 1848–67).

[12] Hincks (n. 11), p. 387.

[13] "Bunsen's Egypt", *The Dublin University Mazagine* 54 (1859), pp. 20–32. This was a review of vol. 3 of *Egypt's Place in Universal History* (London, 1859).

everything that he reads elsewhere".[14] John Rogerson has dealt at some length with Bunsen's place in 19th-century English Old Testament scholarship, pointing out H. Ewald's high regard for Bunsen and Bunsen's friendship with the Egyptologist, C.R. Lepsius.[15] Hincks's disagreement with Bunsen and Lepsius on chronological matters was seized upon by one correspondent as support for his own stand against what he called "the anti-Mosaic scheme of Bunsen and Lepsius".[16] It is fair to say that early Egyptologists, who had anything to say about the Bible, usually made moderate, though not necessarily correct statements. For example, the French scholar F.J. Chabas wrote in a letter to Hincks: "my studies lead me to believe firmly that the chronological tables derived from scripture are not long enough; that of course large allowances should be made, though it is not impossible that the numbers of the Septuagint could suffice".[17] Sometimes Egyptologists would write on biblical subjects quite separately from their special field. Here mention can be made of C.W. Goodwin's interesting essay "On the Mosaic Cosmogony" in the well-known volume *Essays and Reviews*,[18] or even Renouf's long review of W. Smith's *A Dictionary of the Bible*.[19]

Every Old Testament Scholar who has studied the development of monotheism in Israelite religion is acquainted with Pharaoh Amenhotep IV's break with the established religion of Egypt and his changing his name to Akhenaten. We are not concerned here with the unconvincing view that this pharaoh's exclusive worship of the god Aten was linked to the founding of the first monotheistic faith. Suffice it to say that it is probable that the cult of Aten had developed before Amen-hotep IV had come to the throne. As early as 1842, Samuel Sharpe and Edward Hincks were exchanging letters about the erasure of names in ancient Egypt,[20] and in February 1844 a remarkable paper

[14] Hincks (n. 13), p. 32.

[15] *Old Testament Criticism in the Nineteenth Century: England and Germany* (London, 1984), pp. 121–9.

[16] GIO/H 93 (letter from H. Browne, dated 11 April 1844).

[17] GIO/H 102 (letter dated 28 December 1863).

[18] London, 1860, pp. 207–53. For a biography of Goodwin, cf. W.R. Dawson, *Charles Wycliffe Goodwin 1817–1878: A Pioneer in Egyptology* (Oxford, 1934). Goodwin and Renouf were good friends.

[19] 3 vols (London, 1863). Renouf's review appeared in *The Home and Foreign Review* 4 (1864), pp. 623–66.

[20] There is a letter (GIO/H 492) dated 10 February 1842 from Sharpe to Hincks, on the subject of the erasure of names and the political motivation behind it.

by Hincks was read to the Royal Irish Academy "On the Defacement of Divine and Royal Names on Egyptian Monuments".[21] He had observed that at the temple of Karnak the name of Amen-hotep III, Akhenaten's father and one of the great kings of ancient Egypt, had been deliberately defaced, but in such a way that it was the name Amun in the cartouche that had been damaged. Hincks was not slow to see the significance of his observation. The "Sun-worshippers" had launched attacks against the temples and priesthood of Amon-Re in Thebes, and had pursued their religio-political cause even to the extent of erasing the name of the god Amun wherever it was found. The full extent of what happened in the reign of Akhenaten was of course not known in Hincks's lifetime, but his observations on the defacement of the names were shrewd.

For Old Testament scholars, the most significant development in ancient Near Eastern studies during the 19th century was, without doubt, the decipherment of Mesopotamian cuneiform.[22] Towards the end of the 18th century, the Danish explorer Carsten Niebuhr visited Persepolis and made the first accurate copies of the inscriptions there. It was observed that there were three different kinds of inscriptions, written with three different sets of characters. The first set contained simple signs, about forty in number; the second set contained more complicated ones, about one hundred; finally the third set had several hundred complex signs. Because of its prominence, the first kind of writing was taken to represent Persian. G.F. Grotefend, a Göttingen school-teacher, applied the names of kings of the Achaemenid dynasty to the groups of signs and discovered that Hystaspes, Darius and Xerxes fitted. Though this was a remarkable achievement by Grotefend, he did not fully decipher the Persian cuneiform script. The values of most of the letters were established by E. Burnouf and C. Lassen, and in 1846 Hincks added the finishing touches to the understanding of Old Persian cuneiform.[23] It so happened that H.C. Rawlinson, a

---

[21] *Transactions of the Royal Irish Academy* 21 (1846), Polite Literature, pp. 105–13. The contributions of Hincks and Sharpe on this subject are discussed by J.D. Ray, "Edward Hincks and the Progress of Egyptology", in Cathcart (n. 4), pp. 67–9.

[22] The only satisfactory account of the decipherment is by P.T. Daniels, "Edward Hincks's Decipherment of Mesopotamian Cuneiform", in Cathcart (n. 4), pp. 30–57.

[23] For discussion of the decipherment of Old Persian and bibliographical references, see M. Pope, *The Story of Decipherment: From Egyptian Hieroglyphic to Linear B* (London and New York, 1975), pp. 85–110. Note also Hincks, "On the first and second Kinds of Persepolitan Writing", *Transactions of the Royal Irish Academy* 21 (1846), Polite Literature, pp. 114–31.

British soldier and diplomat in India and Persia, had also taken an interest in cuneiform inscriptions and he became famous for his daring labours in making accurate copies of the inscriptions inscribed on the rock face of the side of a mountain at Behistun in Iran. It is generally accepted that Rawlinson independently deciphered the Persian inscriptions though he knew the work of Burnouf, Grotefend and Lassen. His accurate rendering of the Old Persian text from Behistun was published in London in 1846.[24] Hincks, who already had a masterly control of Old Persian, wrote a glowing thirteen page review-article of Rawlinson's work.[25]

Accounts of decipherment generally give much attention to Rawlinson's work in Old Persian. This is unsatisfactory on two accounts. First, as was mentioned above, Old Persian had already been deciphered when Rawlinson published his Behistun texts. Secondly, the Old Persian texts were not as extensive or important as those in Akkadian. It is the decipherment of Mesopotamian cuneiform that is more important and interesting for Old Testament scholars. The term "Mesopotamian cuneiform" refers to the writing system used for Akkadian, Elamite and Urartian as distinct from the unrelated Persian one. With regard to the language of the second kind of writing at Persepolis, the language which we now call Elamite, the Danish scholar Niels Westergaard published important results in 1845.[26] The paper by Hincks, which was read to the Royal Irish Academy on 9 June 1846 (cf. n. 23), dealt with the Old Persian and Elamite parts of the Persepolitan inscriptions. However, there is a postscript to this article in which he announces that he has made some progress in reading the inscriptions in the third Persepolitan or Babylonian writing.[27] He is able to state that both the Assyrian and Babylonian languages appear to have much in common with the Semitic Languages. During the next five years, in a series of brilliant papers between 1846 and 1852, Hincks accomplished the basic decipherment of Akkadian.

At a meeting of the British Association for the Advancement of

---

[24] *The Persian Cuneiform Inscription at Behistun, decyphered and translated, with a Memoir* (London, 1846) = *JRAS* 10 (1846–7) [entire volume].

[25] "Some Passages of the Life of King Darius, the Son of Hystaspes, by Himself", *The Dublin University Magazine* 29 (1847), pp. 14–27.

[26] "On the Deciphering of the Second Achaemenian or Median Species of Arrowhead Writing", *Mémoires de la Société Royale des Antiquaires du Nord* (1844), pp. 271–439 + 14 plates; "Zur Entzifferung der Achämenidschen Keilschrift zweiter Gattung", *Zeitschrift für die Kunde des Morgenlandes* 6 (1844), pp. 337–466 + 2 plates.

[27] Hincks (n. 23), p. 131.

Science at Edinburgh in July 1850, Hincks distributed a lithograph which illustrated how he had successfully applied his knowledge of the Semitic languages to elucidate the writing system and he announced "in opposition to all other writers, that the characters had all definite values; . . . though the language of the Assyrians was Semitic, their mode of writing was not".[28] This is further elucidated in a paper published in 1852.[29] Hincks's statement is so important that an extract is given here:

> It has been assumed by all other investigators, that the mode of writing used in the Assyrio-Babylonian inscriptions was contrived with a view to represent the words of the language of those inscriptions. This language is unquestionably of the family commonly called the Semitic; and it is therefore taken for granted, that the characters used in the inscriptions represent Semitic letters. I can have no doubt whatever that this is a mistake; and moreover, that it is one of so serious a nature as to render it impossible for those who labour under it to attain any accurate knowledge of the grammar of the language. I am myself fully satisfied, and I hope in the present paper to satisfy all who will take the trouble to follow my arguments, that the characters *all* represent syllables, and that they were originally intended to represent a non-Semitic language. Instead of the vowels being unrepresented, or only represented by points, as in all Semitic writing that was first applied to a Semitic language, we have in the cuneatic inscriptions every vowel definitely expressed. The Semitic language appears in a disguise similar to what the Maltese does in Roman letters, or the Punic in the well-known passage of Plautus.
>
> Again, it has been taken for granted, that the only method of ascertaining the value of the characters is the analysis of known proper names. It appears to me, however, that, the characters representing what I have just stated that they do, this method can only lead to approximate, as distinguished from accurate, knowledge. The way by which I have sought to obtain accurate knowledge is by analyzing verbs and nouns, especially such as have three radicals, of which none is liable to be omitted or altered. I assume two principles: first, that the characters which occur in different inflexions of the same root, if they be not the same, must contain the same consonant differently combined with a vowel; secondly, that characters which occur in like forms of different roots, contain

[28] "On the Language and Mode of Writing of the ancient Assyrians", *Report of the Twentieth Meeting of the British Association for the Advancement of Science; held at Edinburgh in July and August 1850* (1851), p. 140 + 1 plate.

[29] "On the Assyrio-Babylonian Phonetic Characters", *Transactions of the Royal Irish Academy* 22 (1852), Polite Literature, pp. 293–370.

> the same vowel in the same position, differing only in the consonant. The former principle shows which characters express different functions of the same consonant; the latter shows which are like functions of different consonants.[30]

This is not the place to present the details of Hincks's progress in the decipherment of cuneiform. It has been done recently, in a most effective way, by P.T. Daniels.[31] He has made the point that "the great inscription at Bisitun—so often hailed as the key to decipherment—in fact played no role whatsoever in the interpretation of cuneiform writing. It provided valuable confirmation of earlier results, of course."[32] Furthermore, Daniels is the first scholar to recognize the crucial role of Hincks's work on the Van inscriptions. In December 1847, Hincks presented a paper on these inscriptions to the Royal Asiatic Society, which was published together with a supplement in 1848.[33] The Van inscriptions are in the Urartian language, but Hincks's discussion of them is of far-reaching importance for the understanding of the process of decipherment. As Daniels says: "it most clearly lays out the reasoning behind the assignment of values to cuneiform signs, and it shows great astuteness in working out the grammar of the unknown language we call Urartian . . . in the reading of cuneiform, this article, 'On the Inscriptions at Van,' is the keystone".[34]

One of the most celebrated archaeological discoveries of the 19th century is the four-sided stone obelisk, known as the Black Obelisk of Shalmaneser III, which was discovered by A.H. Layard in 1846.[35] Ever since its discovery, Old Testament scholars have been interested in it because of the mention of Jehu son of Omri, Hadad-ezer (Adad-idri) of Damascus and Hazael of Damascus. Hincks published a translation of the Black Obelisk in 1853.[36] He wrote the name Adad-idri as *Ban*-idri but added the following footnote: "Ban-idri is evidently

[30] Hincks (n. 29), p. 295.
[31] Daniels (n. 22), pp. 30–57.
[32] Daniels (n. 22), p. 50.
[33] "On the Inscriptions at Van", *JRAS* 9 (1848), pp. 387–449.
[34] Daniels (n. 22), pp. 38, 42.
[35] For the text and translation of the inscriptions on the Black Obelisk see E. Michel, "Die Assur-Texte Salmanassars III (858–824) (7. Fortsetzung)", *Die Welt des Orients* 2/2 (1955), pp. 137–57; "Die Assur-Texte Salmanassars III (858–824) (8. Fortsetzung)", *WO* 2/3 (1956), pp. 221–33. A recent study of the interpretation of this monument is O. Keel and C. Uehlinger, "Der Salmanassar III und Jehu von Israel auf dem Schwarzen Obelisken aus Nimrud", *Zeitschrift für Katholische Theologie* 116 (1994), pp. 391–420.
[36] "The Nimrûd Obelisk", *The Dublin University Magazine* 42 (1853), pp. 420–26.

the Benhadad of Scripture; the Septuagint read the name with a final *r* instead of *d*. This seems to determine the value of the divine name, which is the first element in that of the king; and yet other considerations lead me to suspend my opinion on that question."[37] This illustrates the combination of acute observation and sensible caution which characterize Hincks's work generally. Overall, Hincks's translation of the Black Obelisk text is remarkably good. Rawlinson had already published a translation in 1850,[38] but he missed the most interesting aspect of the monument for Old Testament studies, namely the meaning and significance of the caption above the second sculptured relief on side one of the obelisk. The scene in the relief shows an Israelite king, bringing tribute to Shalmaneser. Rawlinson says: "The second line of offerings are said to have been sent by 'Yahua, son of Hubiri', a prince of whom there was no mention in the annals, and of whose native country therefore I am ignorant."[39] But in 1851 Hincks identified *IA-ú-a mar Hu-um-ri-i* as "Jehù son of Omri". A diary entry of 21 December 1851 says: "Thought of an identification of one of the obelisk captives—with Jehu, king of Israel, and satisfying myself on the point wrote a letter to the *Athenaeum* announcing it."[40] In the unpublished translation prepared for the Trustees of the British Museum in 1853, he renders this part of the inscription as follows: "The tribute of Yahu (Yahua) dhur Humri, silver, gold, bowls of gold, *chains* of gold, goblets of gold, *jars* of gold, tin, khu*tar*ut, royal *linen*, and *staves with sharpened ends*; I received it."[41] It compares favourably with a modern translation—for example, that by T.C. Mitchell: "Tribute of Jehu son of Omri, silver, gold, a golden bowl, a golden vase, golden tumblers, golden buckets, tin, a staff for the king, [and] hunting spears, I received."[42] Hincks's writing of the name Yahua is noteworthy in the light of recent discussions of the Assyrian form. J. Hughes tentatively suggests that [I]*IA-ú-a* = **Yehu'a*.[43]

---

37 Hincks (n. 36), p. 422.

38 "On the Inscriptions of Assyria and Babylonia", *JRAS* 12 (1850), pp. 401–83.

39 Rawlinson (n. 38), p. 447.

40 The diary entry is cited in Davidson, (n. 4), p. 167. (Read "captives" for Davidson's meaningless "Cophetus"!) The letter, dated 22 December 1851, appeared in "Nimrud Obelisk", *The Athenaeum*, No. 1251 (1851), pp. 1384–5.

41 BL Add Ms 22097 f. 17r. Hincks explains "dhur Humri" as "child of Omri" in his notes to the translation.

42 *The Bible in the British Museum* (London, 1988), p. 47.

43 *Secrets of the Times. Myth and History in Biblical Chronology* (Sheffield, 1990), pp. 183–4, n. 55.

Before leaving this discussion of the Black Obelisk, it should be observed that Hincks sometimes replaces the accounts given on the obelisk by those from the longer annals in other inscriptions. In this he anticipates the procedure followed by modern scholars. This can be illustrated by giving Hincks's version of the eighteenth year together with A.L. Oppenheim's version for comparison. The comparison also shows how generally accurate was Hincks's translation made 145 years ago.

Hincks:

> In my eighteenth year, I crossed the Euphrates for the sixteenth time. Khazail (i.e., Hazael) of Damascus, relying on the multitude of his soldiers, collected his soldiers in great numbers. He took up a strong position upon Saniru, a mountain range opposite to Libnana (i.e., Lebanon). I fought with him, and defeated him. I slew in battle 16,000 of his warriors, and deprived him of 1121 of his chariots, 460 of his *moving towers*, and his camp.[44]

Oppenheim:

> In the eighteenth year of my rule I crossed the Euphrates for the sixteenth time. Hazael of Damascus . . . put his trust upon his numerous army and called up his troops in great number, making the mountain Senir . . ., a mountain facing the Lebanon, to his fortress. I fought with him and inflicted a defeat upon him, killing with the sword 16,000 of his experienced soldiers. I took away from him 1,121 chariots, 470 riding horses as well as his camp.[45]

On 13 April 1853 a paper by Hincks "On Certain Ancient Arab Queens" was read to the Royal Society of Literature.[46] It challenged Rawlinson's contention that the Sheba of the Old Testament, whose queen visited Solomon, was in the northern part of Arabia, and, therefore, not far from the land of Israel.[47] There was no doubt in

---

[44] Hincks (n. 36), pp. 423–4.

[45] *ANET*, p. 280. The same passage is given by D.J. Wiseman in D. Winton Thomas (ed.), *Documents from Old Testament Times* (London, 1958), p. 48, though with an incorrect caption (*Black Obelisk*). Wiseman's notes on the passage show that the error is probably due to an oversight. Rawlinson's translation (n. 38, p. 441), made some years earlier, is wide of the mark, and Hincks's version shows how much progress had been made.

[46] *Transactions of the Royal Society of Literature*, Second Series 5 (1856), pp. 162–4.

[47] As there are no references in Hincks's paper, it is not possible to say where he found Rawlinson's view expressed.

Hincks's mind that the queen of Sheba was "the Queen of the South" and "her kingdom in 'the uttermost parts of the earth', that is, evidently, on the shores of the Indian Ocean".[48] Rawlinson had observed that in the annals of Tiglath-pileser III, a queen of the Arabs was named among sovereigns paying tribute. In his opinion there could only have ever been one single Arab tribe governed by a queen; and therefore the country of this queen must be the Sheba of the Old Testament. Since this country, tribe and its queen were certainly in the north, then it followed, Rawlinson argued, that Sheba was too. It was this argumentation with which Hincks took issue. Before proceeding with Hincks's refutation, it should be mentioned that the annals of Tiglath-pileser III list Zabibe, queen of the Arabs, as one of several leaders who paid tribute to the Assyrian king in 738 B.C.[49] Hincks read these annals with relative ease, though he read the queen's name as *ḫābiba*, "the affectionate". Her true name, Zabibe, probably derives from Arabic *zabīb*, "raisin".[50] Now Hincks readily agreed with Rawlinson that the country over which Zabibe was queen lay in the north of Arabia. But he differed completely from him on the rarity of queens among the Arabs. Because he was so familiar with the cuneiform texts which he had studied in the British Museum, he was able to point out that according to a historical inscription of Esarhaddon, the latter Assyrian king made a certain Tabûa queen in Adumatu, biblical Dumah, and imposed a tribute of 65 camels.[51] Sennacherib had formerly captured Adumatu and deported Tabûa as a young girl to Nineveh where she grew up. Here, then, Hincks was able to point out a second Arab tribe governed by a queen. Clearly the queen of Sheba's rulership was not unique.[52]

On 25 June 1855 a paper by Hincks "On certain animals mentioned in the Assyrian inscriptions" was read before a meeting of the Royal

---

[48] Hincks (n. 46), p. 162.

[49] Among the leaders mentioned are Rezin of Damascus, Menahem of Samaria and Hiram of Tyre. See I. Eph'al, *The Ancient Arabs* (Jerusalem and Leiden, 1982), pp. 82–3; H. Tadmor, *The Inscriptions of Tiglath-Pileser III, King of Assyria* (Jerusalem, 1994), pp. 68–9.

[50] Eph'al, p. 82, n. 247.

[51] Eph'al, pp. 43–4, 122–8, where details of the Neo-Assyrian records are given.

[52] For other Arab queens, see the index in Eph'al, p. 249 (sub Arab). Eph'al's work supersedes N. Abbott, "Pre-Islamic Arab Queens", *AJSL* 58 (1941), pp. 1–22. Eph'al (p. 88) also discusses the nomadic (= North Arabian) Sabaeans, who are mentioned in the inscriptions of Tiglath-pileser III, but were distinct from the sedentary Sabaean population in South Arabia.

Irish Academy.[53] In this paper Hincks expressed the hope that "the knowledge of zoology possessed by some of those who may hear it read will enable them to throw light on points which mere philological research has left in obscurity".[54] Anyone who has been involved in making a translation of the Bible will know of the difficulties in identifying the precise meaning of certain Hebrew words which seem to refer to various species of animals and birds. Hincks bewailed the fact that Assyrian sculptures contained fewer representations of animals accompanied by names, compared with Egyptian sculpture, painting and texts. A more serious problem for Hincks and his contemporaries was the correct interpretation of the cuneiform signs—Sumerian logograms were often taken to be Akkadian words. For example the Sumerian logographic signs for "horse", KUR.RA (= Akk. *sīsu*) were read as if they were the writing for an Akkadian word *kurra*. Hincks has mixed success with words for camels and elephants. He notes that in the Black Obelisk camels with two humps are sculptured in two places and comments that in both instances they are called "*habba* whose humps are double".[55] Then he goes hopelessly astray by suggesting that *habba* stands for *halba*. He believes that Hebrew *habbîm*, in *šenhabbîm*, stands for *halbîm*, of which *halab* would be the singular. In his opinion, *halab* on its own signifies an elephant, but with the determinative of beasts of burden prefixed to it gives the sense "camel".[56] It is clear that Hincks did not grasp the logographic status of the signs A.AB.BA in ANŠE.A.AB.BA.MEŠ. (= Akk. *gammalē*, "camels"). Of course, he was not helped by the fact that Akk. *gammalu* is sometimes represented by the logographic signs GAM.MAL.

Hincks also discusses at length the animals which he refers to as *amsi*.[57] He notes that they are repeatedly mentioned in the inscriptions, and that there is frequent reference to their teeth or tusks. It is quite extraordinary that Hincks did not immediately identify these animals as "elephants", though, as seen above, he had already erroneously identified a word *halab*, as the word for "elephant". AM.SI, a reading which he distrusted, was in fact a correct one, but was the Sumerian for "elephant", to be read *pīru* in Akkadian (cf. Hebrew *pîl*.). By 1857,

[53] *Proceedings of the Royal Irish Academy* 6 (1855), pp. 251–60.
[54] Hincks (n. 53), p. 252.
[55] Hincks (n. 53), p. 253.
[56] Hincks (n. 53), p. 253.
[57] Hincks (n. 53), pp. 259–60.

however, Hincks had worked out the correct meaning of AM.SI and he renders it by "elephants" in his translation of those parts of the inscription of Tiglath-pileser I used for the famous "test case" to prove that Babylonian and Assyrian cuneiform had been deciphered.[58] Hincks translated vi 70–5 of the inscription as follows:

> I killed four (sic) great male elephants in the land of Rasan and on the banks of the Khabur. I took captives four elephants that survived. I brought their skins and their tusks, along with the elephants that survived, to my city Assur.[59]

Apart from the mistake in the numeral at the beginning of the passage (and it may be nothing more than a *lapsus calami*), Hincks's version is quite good. A. Kirk Grayson's modern translation reads:

> I killed ten strong bull elephants in the land Harran and the region of the River Habur (and) four live elephants I captured. I brought the hides and tusks (of the dead elephants) with the live elephants to my city Assur.[60]

In the same 1857 "test case", Rawlinson rendered AM.SI by "buffaloes" and Fox Talbot simply wrote *amsi* in despair.

What is remarkable in the discussion of these animal names so far is that by and large he read the signs correctly, but did not recognize their logographic values. Hincks was rather more successful with other words for animals. In the inscriptions of Tiglath-pileser III, the word *anaqātē* occurs several times.[61] It is not a common word, but Hincks worked out its correct meaning "she-camels", citing Aramaic *ʾᵃnāqâ*, which has a cognate in Arabic *nāqa*.[62] It is interesting to note that he refers to the second Targum of Esth. i 2 for an example of *ʾᵃnāqâ*. An examination of the Targum, however, reveals that this

---

58 The results of the "test case" were published in *Inscription of Tiglath Pileser I, King of Assyria, BC 1150 as translated by Sir Henry Rawlinson, Fox Talbot, Esq., Dr Hincks, and Dr Oppert* (London, 1857). The publication also appeared as "Comparative Translations of the Inscription of Tiglath Pileser I", *JRAS* 18 (1861), pp. 150–219.

59 *JRAS* 18 (1861), pp. 202–3.

60 *Assyrian Rulers of the Early First Millennium BC: I (1114–859 BC)* (RIM/AP 2; Toronto, 1991), p. 26.

61 *CAD*, A/II, p. 112. It occurs only in the plural.

62 See M. Sokoloff, A *Dictionary of Jewish Palestinian Aramaic of the Byzantine Period* (Ramat-Gan, 1990), p. 166. Cf. D. Talshir, "ʾnqh šhyʾgmlh" (Heb.), in M. Bar-Asher et al. (ed.), *Hebrew Language Studies presented to Professor Zeev Ben-Ḥayyim* (Jerusalem, 1983), pp. 219–36.

word does not occur there. Hincks gives no reference to the source of his information, but he may have used J. Buxtorf's *Lexicon Chaldaicum, Talmudicum et Rabbinicum*, which cites a view that *ʾnqʾ* "camelus foemina" should be read for *ʾynqʾ* "avis nomen" in Targum Esth. i 2.[63] Actually, *ʾynqʾ* means "suckling".[64] Hincks would have been on secure ground, if he had mentioned the other reference for *ʾᵃnāqâ* given by Buxtorf, that is, Lamentations Rabba 49.27.

Some of Hincks's more interesting comments perhaps, are on the Akkadian word *nāḫiru*. He has read in the inscriptions how the Assyrian king Tiglath-pileser I boasts that he has killed the *nāḫiru* in the sea. He has noted that there is mention of the teeth and tusks of the *nāḫiru* and has discovered also that representations of the *nāḫiru* were set up at the palace gates. He thinks that the *nāḫiru* is some rare sea monster and asks: "what cetaceous animal, or fish, could be found in the Levant, which would satisfy these statements?"[65] He seems not to have thought of the whale. Indeed, it is interesting to compare a remark by Hincks with a note in the entry for *nāḫiru* in the Chicago *Assyrian Dictionary*. Hincks writes: "*nahir* . . . according to the Hebrew value of the root, would signify the 'snorter'".[66] The note in the *Assyrian Dictionary* reads: "the word means 'spouter', describing the blowing of a whale".[67]

On 3 June 1896, T.K. Cheyne wrote to Renouf for advice about several alleged Egyptian etymologies for Biblical Hebrew words, including *bᵉhēmôt* (Job xl 15) and *timśōk* (Job xl 25).[68] Renouf replied that the scholars who had made the proposals did not have "anything more than a smattering of Coptic" and did not know "anything of the prior stages of the language".[69] This somewhat curt and dismissive reply was written the year before he died. Renouf recalls, however, that more than thirty years earlier, J.B. Morris, once E.B. Pusey's assistant, had written to him with questions about the possible Coptic

[63] J. Buxtorf, *Lexicon Chaldaicum, Talmudicum et Rabbinicum* (Basel, 1639), p. 147.
[64] M. Jastrow, *A Dictionary of the Targumim, the Talmud Babli and Yerushalmi, and the Midrashic Literature* (New York, 1903), p. 53. In the 19th-century J. Levy also gives *ʾynqʾ*, "*N.pr.* eines grossen Vogels". Cf. *Chaldäisches Wörterbuch über die Targumim* (Leipzig, 1867), p. 43.
[65] Hincks (n. 53), p. 259.
[66] Hincks (n. 53), p. 258.
[67] *CAD*, N/I, p. 137.
[68] GIO/R 30.
[69] GIO/R 31.

etymology of *b^{e}hēmôt*.[70] This illustrates well how some philological problems have exercised scholars' minds decade after decade.

In this paper, an attempt has been made to show the extent and quality of the research carried out by some 19th-century scholars. It is clear that much can be learned from the history of scholarship in the fields of Old Testament and ancient Near Eastern Studies.

---

[70] Cambridge University Library/Acton Papers: Ad Ms 8119/I/R 85. The letter is dated September 1859.

DES OUTILS POUR LE DÉVELOPPEMENT DE L'HERMÉNEUMATIQUE SÉMITIQUE NORD-OCCIDENTALE[1]

par

JESÚS-LUIS CUNCHILLOS
Madrid

Introduction ou avant-propos

En 1980, lors du Xème Congrès de l'I.O.S.O.T à Vienne, l'auteur du présent exposé vous entretenait du *mal'āk*, le chargé d'affaires, le messager; en somme sur les communications au IIIème et IIème millénaire av. J.C. Le même intervenant vous parlera aujourd'hui de communications qui concernent la fin du IIème et le début du IIIème millénaire après J.C. Les choses ont tellement changé en si peu de temps!

Pour faciliter la compréhension de mon discours permettez-moi de vous en indiquer les trois parties qui sont comme les trois moments, passé, présent et futur d'un projet:

I° La Banque de Données Philologiques Sémitiques Nord-occidentales (BDFSN).

II° Le système de gestion de la Banque de Données: Siamtu II (Système intégré d'analyse morphologique des textes ougaritiques).

III° L'herméneumatique.

I° La BDFSN (Banque de données philologiques sémitiques nord-occidentales)[2]

I *Définition*

Nous appelons banque de données l'accumulation organisée sur un support informatique des données qu'utilise une science. Elle est

[1] Je tiens à remercier tous le membres de l'équipe et d'autres qui sont redévables à tant des titres. En particulier MM et Mmes. J. Cuena, A. García-Serrano, J.-P. Vita, R. Cervigón, J.-M. Galán, J.-A. Zamora, G. Bourgeat et M. Molina.

[2] Une première approche en a été faite dans "Realizaciones informáticas del Sistema

comparable à un magasin doté d'un service de gestion informatique des produits. S'agissant de données philologiques, la gestion informatique inclut toutes les applications susceptibles d'analyser et de comprendre les données philologiques dans leurs développements, dans leurs contextes, et dans les textes. "Une banque de données peut et doit être le point de départ d'une spécialité scientifique."[3]

II *Le projet*

1. Le plan complet de l'œuvre a été publié à la p. IV de la *Concordancia de Palabras Ugariticas (CPU)*.[4] Nous y renvoyons pour le détail. Dans une premiere phase, la banque de données se limite à l'ugaritique. Ultérieurement, s'intègreront les données des autres langues sémitiques nord-occidentales: phénicien, hébreu, araméen, amorite, moabite, amonite, edomite, ainsi que le matériel linguistique nord-occidental d'El Amarna.

2. L'équipe. L'Equipe d'Étude du Sémitique Nord-occidental (ESN) de l'Institut de Philologie du CSIC a élaboré le projet de recherche *Création d'une Banque de données Philologiques du Sémitique nord-occidental.*[5] Jusqu'à ce jour, il n'existait pas de projet de création d'une telle Banque de Données.[6] L'ESN est devenu Laboratoire d'Hermé-

---

integrado de análisis morfológico de textos ugariticos (SIAMTU)", *Biblica* 73 (1992), pp. 547–9. Nous y renvoyons le lecteur.

[3] J.-L. Cunchillos, J.-P. Vita, *Banco de Datos Filologícos Semiticos Noroccidentales (BDFSN). Primera parte. Datos ugariticos, I: Textos ugariticos* (Madrid, 1993), p. XVIII. Cité *TU*. L'affirmation permettrait une discusion que nous n'allons pas établir ici. Sur les problèmes de la science et la philosophie de la science voir entre autres M. Bunge, *La ciencia. Su método y su filosofía*. (Buenos Aires [Argentina], 1981); J. Lohse, *A Historical Introduction to the Philosophy of Science* (Oxford, 1980); R.K. Merton, *The Sociology of Science. Theoretical and Empirical Investigations* (Chicago, 1973).

[4] J.-L. Cunchillos, J.-P. Vita, *Concordancia de Palabras Ugariticas en morfologia desplegada (CPU)*, 3 vols (Madrid et Zaragoza, 1995).

[5] Creación de un Banco de Datos Filológicos Semíticos Noroccidentales (PB 89/0040). Le projet a été approuvé puis financé par le Ministère de l'Education et de la Science espagnol, MEC (Direction générale de la Recherche scientifique et technique). La suite en est le projet PB 93/0107. Le 22 juillet 1994 la même Direction a approuvé et financé un deuxième projet de 5 ans.

[6] Le projet le plus proche est le CATS (Computer Assisted Tools for Septuagint Studies) de R.A. Kraft et E. Tov commencé à la fin des années soixante dans le but de produire un dictionnaire de la traduction grecque de la Bible connue comme la LXX. (Voir R.A. Kraft et E. Tov, "Computer assisted Tools for Septuagint Studies", *Bulletin of the International Organisation for Septuagint and Cognate Studies* 14 [1981], pp. 22–40). En 1993, l'objectif n'avait pas encore été atteint. Ce couteux projet ne manque pas d'interêt en dépit de défauts de conception, comme le reconnaissent les auteurs. (Voir par exemple leurs

neumatique car son champ de recherche exigeait cette évolution. Il déborde en effet le champ du seul sémitique nord-occidental et permet l'intégration de spécialistes de l'informatique et d'autres champs de recherches linguistiques.

III *Les problèmes à résoudre et les critères adoptés*[7]

1. Ecriture ou langue? Comme critère de sélection nous avons choisi la langue et non l'écriture, simplement parce que notre objet d'étude est la langue. On pourrait créer une autre application complémentaire pour travailler sur l'écriture. Dans la BDFSN sont donc exclus les textes écrits en cunéiformes alphabétiques mais en langue hittite, hourrite ou akkadienne; sont inclus, par contre, les textes écrits en cunéiformes syllabiques mais en langue ugaritique.[8] Ainsi on a intégré la colonne ugaritique des vocabulaires polyglotes.[9]

2. L'unité reconnaissable et classifiable. Introduire un matériel philologique dans une base de données implique de nombreux choix.

> il convient de décider l'unité minimale à traiter et les sous-unités suceptibles d'être traitées et utilisées. Toutes doivent être identifiées et identifiables à tout moment. L'individualité de chaque unité ou sous-unité doit être susceptible de généralisation à certains moments pour pouvoir constituer une science, en même temps qu'est respectée sa singularité (*TU*, p. XIII).
>
> L'unité reconnaissable et classifiable d'une tablette est la ligne. De là que chaque ligne de la tablette devient une fiche différente. Chaque fiche contient les champs suivants: sigle, ligne de texte avec tous les accidents épigraphiques, texte nettoyé des accidents épigraphiques, analyse (racines et lexèmes), contexte matériel, contexte significatif et notes (*Biblica* 73 [1992], p. 551).

---

commentaire dans E. Tov et B.G. Wright, "Computer-assisted Study of the criteria for assessing the Literalness or Translation Units in the LXX", *Textus* 12 [1985], pp. 149–87.) Nous voyons d'autres défauts de conception. Les travaux publiés ne sont pas toujours convaincants pour le spécialiste, d'abord parce que n'a pas été soigné suffisamment le passage du support informatique au support papier qui a ses exigences propres, ensuite parce que l'état des travaux publiés ne dépasse par le niveau statistique. (Voir par ex. A. Kraft et E. Tov, *LXX, Computer Assisted Tools for Septuagint Studies (CATSS)* 1 *Ruth* [Atlanta, 1986].)

[7] Sur ce thème voir nos observations déjà publiées dans *Biblica* 73 (1992), p. 551.

[8] Ce qui nous a conduit à faire entrer cinq textes déjà publiés mais absents de *KTU*: ce sont 00–5.24; 00–5.26; 00–5.27; 00–7.222.

[9] Voir *TU*, Vocabulaires, pp. 757–65.

C'est ce que nous écrivions en 92. Depuis ont été ajoutées de nouvelles rubriques,[10] mais elles sont plus opératives pour l'ordinateur que pour le chercheur.

3. Le Texte de base, point de départ d'une édition critique. Le texte de base et la banque de données, sont et restent toujours ouverts.[11]

Le point de départ a été le texte de la collation la plus récente et complète des textes ugaritiques[12] au moment de la mise en œuvre de la Banque de donées. Nous avons apporté à ce texte une série de modifications déjà explicitées ailleurs (*Biblica* 73 [1992], pp. 549–50). On y a joint les textes publiés depuis 1976 (pp. 550, et 555). Les nouveaux textes sont intégrés au fur et à mesure de leur publication.[13] L'ensemble se distingue par le préfixe 00- et constitue le texte de base. Ce texte sert de point de départ au chercheur et c'est pourquoi sont ajoutées les collations comme on le verra plus loin. D'autre part, dans les cas controversés, la décision ne peut être prise qu'au moment du commentaire de texte quand la critique interne impose une lecture ou une autre. Nous n'avons pas prétendu faire une nouvelle collation des tablettes. Certains collègues ne l'ont pas compris. Ils n'ont pas perçu le concept de banque de données et ses répercussions dans le travail critique. C'est ainsi que nous comprenons un paragraphe de O. Loretz:

> In *TU* dürfe ausserdem zu wenig in Betracht gezogen worden sein, dass auch bei einer *Textbank* das Problem des Bekenntnisses zur eigenen Lesung nicht zu umgehen ist. *Dieser wesentliche Teil einer Textaussgabe lässt sich vorläufig noch nicht an die Maschine delegieren.* Wenn sich die Autoren ängtslich einer eigenen Meinung und Entscheidung enthalten und diese von den Benützern ihres Buches verlangen, so werden diese sehr oft aus vielfältingen Gründen nich in der Lage sein, dieses Versäumnis der Herausgeber selbst nachzuholen.[14]

---

[10] Les nouvelles rubriques sont les suivantes: nº de tablette, nº de base qui indique la correspondance entre la numération de chaque ligne de collation et le nº de ligne dans le Texte Complexe.

[11] C'était déjà notre conclusion dans *Biblica* 73, (1992), p. 555.

[12] M. Dietrich, O. Loretz, J. Sanmartín, *Die keilalphabetische Texte aus Ugarit Einschliesslich der keilalphabetischen Texte ausserhalb Ugarits* 1 (Kevelaer et Neukirchen-Vluyn, 1976). Citée *KTU*. La deuxième étion élargie vient de paraître, *The Cuneiform Alphabetic Texts from Ugarit, Ras Ibn Hani and Other Places (KTU: second, enlarged edition)* (Münster, 1995).

[13] Voir J.-L. Cunchillos, J.-P. Vita, "Banco de Datos Filologicos Semiticos Noroccidentales (BDFSN). Primera parte: Datos ugariticos. Suplemento 1993", *Sefarad* 54 (1994).

[14] O. Loretz, *UF* 25 (1993), p. 498. Il s'agit du compte-rendu de *TU*. Au contraire P. Merlo dans son compte-rendu du même livre dans *SEL* 11 (1994), pp. 135–6, a compris parfaitement l'intention des auteurs de *TU*. Souligné de l'auteur de cette conférence.

Loretz confond un texte imprimé avec une banque de données qu'il appelle "banque de texte", il prète aux auteurs de *TU* l'intention de laisser à la machine la décision de choisir la lecture, interprète comme "peur des auteurs" l'effort de rationalisation qui consiste à prendre les décisions au moment où la connaissance du texte l'exige sans céder à des critères d'autorité, d'amitié ou de nationalité.

Le texte de base n'est qu'un point de départ. Les collations postérieures, les possibilites qu'offre l'application "texte complexe" (voir plus loin) et l'intervention des spécialistes à chaque phase du commentaire des textes font que l'on s'achemine vers un nouveau texte de base;[15] par ailleurs les erreurs constatées obligent à des corrections du texte de base tout au long de la constitution de la BDFSN.[16] Dans tous les cas la BDFSN prend acte du changement du texte 00- dans une note individualisée en indiquant les motifs. Bref, le texte de base est remis en question tout au long du chemin qui conduit au commentaire de texte.

Saisir les textes en homogénéisant les signes épigraphiques a été notre première tache scientifique. Elle comprend la création de types aproprlés (typographie informatique) et des signes diacritiques épigraphiques, ainsi que d'un système de référence des textes. Mais il faut prendre en compte la rationalité de l'informatique et l'inutilité d'utiliser deux numeros ASCII quand un seul suffit. Il est urgent de se mettre d'accord sur a) les phénomènes ou accidents épigraphiques qu'il est nécessaire de connoter; b) les signes conventionnels qu'il convient d'utiliser.[17]

Cette fois encore, l'informatique peut être l'occasion idéale d'appliquer une rigueur accrue. Le laboratoire d'Herméneumatique de Madrid ouvre ses portes à tous ceux qui souhaitent contribuer à la normalisation des connotations épigraphiques ou de tout autre phénomène qui pourrait

---

[15] Voir la liste dans *Biblica* 73 (1992), pp. 555–7, complétée par *Sefarad* 54 (1994), pp. 145–7. Il faut y ajouter de petits fragments antérieurs à 1976 et non inclus jusqu'à maintenent dans les collections de textes en langue ugaritique. Ce sont les suivants: Ritual RS 24.285, *Ugaritica V* (Paris, 1968), p. 511: *tk*. A reçu dans la BDFSN le sigle 00–1.177:16; Jurisprudencia: RS 16.180, *PRU* 3 (1955), p. 41 (pl. LX): [. . .]*š*[. . .]. A reçu dans BDFSN le sigle 00–3.10:17; Administracion. Ce chapitre s'enrichit de RS 16.291, *PRU* 3 (1955), p. 198 (pl. XCIV): *-l-ni///-dni*. A reçu dans la BDFSN le sigle 00–4.786:8; RS 19.64, *PRU* 6 (1970), nº 163; *ak* . . ., selon J. Nougayrol, ibid., p. 121, il n'existe pas de copie cuneiforme. A reçu dans la BDFSN le sigle 00–4.787.

[16] Voir la première liste dans *Sefarad* 54 (1994), pp. 147–9.

[17] Voir J.-L. Cunchillos, José Manuel Galán, "Filología e informática. Epigrafía ugarítica", *Sefarad* 56 (1996), pp. 161–70.

se présenter. Nous envisageons la création d'une page dans World Wide Web d'Internet sur l'Herméneumatique et ses problèmes dans laquelle apparaitraient les opinions et solutions de chacun.

4. *Les collations*. Personne ne doute de l'importance de disposer dans la BDFSN ou dans *TU* de toute l'information transmise par les différentes lectures et de leurs confrontation aux collations antérieures ou postérieures.

a. Critères de sélection. Premièrement nous avons retenu comme collation tout travail présenté comme tel par son auteur. Un lecteur attentif pourra vérifier les résultats de chacune des collations.[18] Deuxièmement nous aurions pu saisir tout le texte de la collation dans l'ordinateur, le reproduire dans *TU* et ensuite dans les Concordances. Cela eût signifié la répétition inutile de passages lus de la même manière dans les différentes collations, et par voie de conséquence la falsification des statistiques de fréquence de mots, etc. Nous avons donc choisi de faire une sélection rigoureuse et d'introduire uniquement les informations philologiques nouvelles ou différentes.

b. L'usage: le texte complexe. Ici l'ordinateur reproduit la démarche du chercheur qui travaille sur une collation, consulte les autres et remplace dans le texte qu'il commente les lectures de la collation de base par les lectures postérieures. Ici se posent deux problèmes:

1º Un problème de contenus. Dans l'automatisation complète, le critère adopté est le suivant: toute collation postérieure substitue la précédente mais seulement dans les lignes sélectionnées. Certains penseront qu'eût été préférable une radicalisation du type: toute collation postérieure remplace la précédente et à toutes les lignes du texte. C'eût été plus facile pour l'ESN mais injuste pour ceux qui firent les premières collations et lirent correctement la plus grande partie de la tablette, souvent près de 100%. Le critère suivant est également discutable: "toute nouvelle collation substitue la collation antérieure mais seulement dans les lignes selectionnées". La dernière collation n'est pas toujours la meilleure, en effet.

Solution. Le chercheur qui disposera de SIAMTU II sur Internet pourra appeler les lignes des collations antérieures qu'il désire et s'il possède SIAMTU II sur CD-ROM il pourra même introduire dans son exemplaire de la BDFSN toutes les lignes de texte qu'il souhaite.

[18] Pour plus de détails sur les collations voir *TU*, pp. XIX–XX.

2° Un problème de numérotation

Les changements de numérotation des lignes. Non seulement les auteurs des collations donnent des lectures différentes. Assez souvent ils lisent une ou plusieurs lignes de plus que leurs prédecesseurs ou bien considèrent comme recto ce que les autres considèrent comme verso, etc. Imagine-t-on la complexité que ces changements de numérotation signifient pour l'automatisation? Sans doute, il eût été plus facile pour l'ESN de changer la numérotation des lignes données par le dernier épigraphiste et de l'adapter à la numérotation du premier, indiquant en note le changement. Une fois encore, nous avons respecté au maximum le travail des spécialistes. Les lignes apparaissent toujours avec le numéro qui leur est affecté par chaque épigraphiste.

Solution adoptée. L'ordinateur dispose d'une liste de référence indiquant les correspondances de lignes des différentes collations. Ceci allège le travail du chercheur qui peut s'épárgner l'effort de repérage de la ligne 00–1.103:12 comme identique à la 10–1.103:46 et à la 11–1.103:12. etc.... La complexité est telle que nous sommes sûrs de faire l'économie de quelques crises de nerfs!

5. Séparer des chaînes graphématiques (substantif ou verbe précédé d'une particule *w, b, l, k*). Certaines collations maintiennent unies *w*, mais aussi *b*, *l* ou *k* avec les mots suivants, car ces graphèmes se trouvent ainsi unis sur la tablette. Il n'est pas facile de savoir dans tous les cas si *k* ou *l* appartiennent ou non au radical suivant. Une autre application fournit à l'usager la liste de mots qui commencent par *w, l, b*, ou *k*, susceptibles d'être séparés en deux, avec leurs références. L'ordinateur procède en comparant, par exemple, la chaîne *w*xxx, de laquelle il coupe le *w*, et en confrontant le résultat avec la liste des mots qu'il a tirés auparavant du texte propre. Si le mot xxx existe dans la liste, l'ordinateur propose à l'usager de séparer définitivement le *w* du mot suivant. L'utilisateur peut à ce moment valider la séparation, la repousser ou douter. Dans le premier cas, l'ordinateur écrira *w*.xxx dans le texte propre. Dans le second, il laissera les chaînes ensemble et dans le troisième il écrira les deux solutions dans le texte propre. Ceci permet de prendre la décision exacte au moment scientifiquement le plus opportun. Les choix faits dans chaque cas seront reflétés dans les Concordances et autres travaux ultérieurs.

Naturellement ce que nous venons d'expliquer pour le *w*- sert également pour le *b*, le *l* ou le *k*, ou n'importe quelle autre chaîne graphématique divisible, en suivant la même démarche.

6. Unir les chaînes graphématiques: le cas des mots coupés sur deux lignes. Parfois les scribes ugaritains écrivaient le commencement d'un mot à la fin d'une ligne et sans indication supplémentaire continuaient à la ligne suivante. Pour pouvoir donner un traitement informatique à ces mots, il est nécessaire d'identifier les deux fragments et de traiter les deux parties comme un seul mot.

L'application recherche dans chaque ligne la dernière chaîne graphématique et la première de la ligne suivante et vérifie automatiquement si les deux chaînes réunies forment un mot existant dans la liste que l'ordinateur tire du texte propre. S'il le trouve, il le propose au chercheur, comme dans le cas antérieur, pour validation, rejet ou doute. Dans le premier cas, l'ordinateur écrit le mot complet sur la première ligne du texte propre. Dans le second, il laisse le texte en l'état, dans le troisième, il inscrit les deux options dans le texte propre, mais en écrivant le mot complet sur la première ligne pour que la référence soit celle de la première ligne. N.B. le texte propre d'accidents épigraphiques devient un fichier dans lequel apparaissent les mots avec leurs références.

7. Contenu de la BDFSN. "La BDFSN, dans son état actuel, réunit les textes trouvés à Ras Shamra, Ras Ibn Hani ou ailleurs, publiés et originellement rédigés en langue ugaritique" (*TU*, p. XIV). L'option philologique qui suppose donner priorité à la langue sur l'écriture, entraine d'autres options. La BDFSN ne prend pas en compte les documents écrits en cunéforme alphabétique mais en langue hourrite ou akkadienne. Par contre elle intègre la colonne ugaritique des vocabulaires polyglottes ou, bien que ce soit moins important, n'importe quel mot ugaritique apparu dans un texte akkadien.[19]

Des textes originaux continuent à apparaître, qui enrichissent la Banque de données. En 1992 nous écrivions: "Tout est prêt pour que chaque nouvelle collation ou nouveau texte qui sera publié à l'avenir soit introduit immédiatement dans la Banque de Données. L'actualisation de la banque de données philologiques doit être permanente" (*Biblica* 73 [1992], p. 550). Il en est ainsi désormais.

L'ouvrage *Banco de datos filológicos semíticos noroccidentales*

[19] Ainsi par exemple, Ritual: RS 24.285, *Ug*. V (1968), p. 511: *tk*. Reçoit dans BDFSN le sigle 00–1.177:16; Jurisprudencia: RS 16.180, *PRU* 3 (1955), p. 41 (lám. LX): [. . .]*s̀*[. . .]. Reçoit dans BDFSN le sigle 00–3.10:17; Administración: Ce chapitre s'enrichit de: RS 16.291, *PRU* 3 (1955), p. 198 (lám. XCIV): *-l-ni///-dni*. Reçoit dans BDFSN le sigle 00–4.785:10; RS 18.116, *PRU* 6 (1970), nº 118 (lám. XLI): [. . .].*rʿym*. Reçoit dans BDFSN le sigle 00–4.786:8.

(BDFSN). Primera parte: Datos ugaríticos, I Textos ugaríticos[20] est disponible sur le marché. On y trouve les données à partir desquelles sont élaborés tous les travaux ultérieurs. *TU* contient aussi 62 nouveaux textes qui reçoivent les numeros corrélatifs dans le genre auquel ils appartiennent et 136 nouvelles collations[21] publiés depuis 1976.

Le livre est organisé en chapitres qui correspondent aux genres littéraires connus à Ugarit à ce jour.[22] Mais un *Suplemento* (*Sefarad* 54 [1994], pp. 143–50), déjà publié, contient les nouveaux textes et collations déjà parus et arrivés à la direction avant le 31 décembre 1993. De même a été publié la première édition électronique qui inclut dans la série pertinente les textes et collations du *Suplemento* 1993.[23] Dans l'édition électronique de *TU* sont corrigés les erreurs qui ont été détectés. L'édition électronique est le fidèle reflet du contenu de la BDFSN au moment de sa publication.

La *Concordancia de Palabras Ugaríticas (CPU)*[24] vient de sortir. On y trouve tous les mots tels qu'ils se présentent dans les textes, puis les chaînes graphématiques restituables, suivies des chaînes graphématiques restituables unilitères, des chaînes graphématiques sans restitutions et des index.

Les livres sont des reflets en support papier de la Banque de données informatique. Mais plus importante que les livres est l'existence de la Banque de données en base de données relationnelle des documents ugaritiques et collations publiées jusqu'en décembre 1994.

"La BDFSN inclut les données philologiques indispensables pour un traitement informatique ultérieur en concordances et autres usages scientifiques assistés par ordinateur. Elle prétend être un point de départ et non un aboutissement. C'est là que réside son interêt" (*TU*, p. XVI).

La BDFSN va être complétée par un fichier de bibliographie. Quand

---

[20] Edité par J.-L. Cunchillos, et J.-P. Vita avec la collaboración de toute l'équipe (Madrid, 1993), 906 + XXI pages.

[21] Voir la liste complète dans *CPU*, pp. 2781–6.

[22] 1-Mítica, 2-Epica, 3-Ritual, 4-Hipiatría, 5-Correspondencia, 6-Jurisprudencia, 7-Administración, 8-Ejercicios escolares, 9-Vocabularios, 10-Inscripciones, 11-Fragmentos varios.

[23] J.-L. Cunchillos, J.-P. Vita, *Edición electrónica de Textos ugaríticos* (incluidos los *Addenda et Corrigenda* del Suplemento '93) Banco de datos filológicos semíticos noroccidentales (BDFSN). Primera parte: Datos ugaríticos, I: Textos ugaríticos (Madrid, CSIC, 1994), 3 disquettes de 1,4 Mbs.

[24] J.-L. Cunchillos, J.-P. Vita, "Banco de Datos Filológicos Semíticos Noroccidentales (BDFSN), Primera parte: Datos ugaríticos", *II: Concordancia de Palabras Ugaríticas en morfología desplegada*. 3 volúmenes. (Madrid-Zaragoza, 1995), 2876 páginas.

l'utilisateur appelera un texte, il pourra obtenir aussi, s'il le souhaite la bibliographie spécifique à cette tablette.[25]

La banque de données s'enrichira d'un fichier d'images comprenant les photos des tablettes et des inscriptions. Les deux fichiers, texte et image seront connectés pour que le chercheur puisse en disposer sur l'écran.

Une Banque de données a besoin d'un système de gestion des données. Si par ailleurs elle s'enrichie d'un ensemble d'outils informatiques qui permettent de parcourir le chemin de la reconnaissance du texte dans son aspect morphologique, la Banque de données a besoin d'un système de gestion des données et des outils. Cet ensemble reçoit le nom de SIAMTU II (Système intégré d'analyse morphologique des textes ugaritiques).

II° Le gestionnaire de la BDFSN: SIAMTU II

> La banque de données ne serait qu'une accumulation de données si ces dernières ne pouvaient être mises en relation entre elles. D'où, la nécessité d'une base relationnelle".[26] "Le spécialiste a des exigences de mise en relation qu'il faut analyser, rationaliser et programmer dans la base de données. Ainsi surgissent les applications informatiques (*TU*, p. XVI).

La création d'une base de données relationnelle dotée de ses propres applications n'est possible qu'avec l'intervention constante d'un spécialiste, dans ce cas, sémitiste. Il faut en effet synthétiser et réduire à la plus simple expression des connaissances grammaticales de base. Cette fois ce n'est plus le chercheur qui tire profit de la machine mais la machine qui met à profit les connaissances du chercheur. Ainsi commence l'interaction sémitiste-machine.

---

[25] Le contenu de l'information est celui publié par l'auteur, *La Trouvaille Epigraphique de l'Ougarit, (Ras Shamra—Ougarit V, 2) Bibliographie* (Paris, 1991), et constamment mis à jour.

[26] Les projets situés dans le même champ que le nôtre ne dépasent pas le stade du traitement de texte, c'est le cas de Dietrich, Loretz et Sanmartín, (n. 11), ce qui rend impossible tout travail ultérieur sur les textes. R.E. Whittaker publia une concordance, *A Concordance of the Ugaritic Literature* (Cambridge, Mass., 1972), mais soit il ne créa pas soit il ne conserva pas de banque de donnée.

I *Définition*

SIAMTU II est un développement du logiciel de gestion de base de données *4ème dimension* sur Macintosh, système 7, pourvu des caractères *Ilu* et *Mutu* de création propre. Cet ensemble d'outils informatiques est destiné à aider le chercheur dans la reconnaissance morphologique du texte. Bientôt SIAMTU II sera disponible aussi pour PC et Unix.

II *Fonctions*

Les fonctions principales de SIAMTU II sont au nombre de huit:

1. *Fonction de consistance.* C'est la fonction qui mantient à tout moment les relations établies entre les données. La saisie d'une nouvelle donnée dans la BDFSN entraîne une série de procédures ayant comme but de maintenir les rapports entre données établis auparavant. Ainsi

(a) dans les Concordances chaque mot est accompagné de son contexte matériel, c'est à dire non seulement de la ligne à laquelle il appartient, mais aussi de la précédente et de la suivante. Le contexte matériel est établi automatiquement par SIAMTU. Si l'on corrige une ligne de texte, on corrige automatiquement le contexte matériel des lignes affectées par les modifications introduites.

L'objectif est de maintenir actualisées les concordances de mots: *Concordancias de palabras ugariticas (CPU)*, et de racines: *Concordancia de Raices Ugaríticas (CRU).*

(b) Le texte propre ou nettoyé des accidents épigraphiques est établi automatiquement par l'application (*Biblica* 73 [1992], p. 552). Il existe dans la rubrique *texte* de nombreux signes épigraphiques qui ne sont pas des mots: parenthèses, crochets, marques de rayures, *circelli*, etc. SIAMTU sans toucher au texte, le nettoie des accidents épigraphiques et l'enregistre.

Par ailleurs, il arrive qu'une collation propose différentes lectures d'un graphème séparant les différents lectures d'une ou de plusieurs lettres au moyen du signe "/". L'ordinateur développe automatiquement les divers mots signalés par la barre oblique. Quand les propositions sont établies entre deux mots le signe utilisé est ///. L'ordinateur interprète automatiquement les différentes lectures.

Le tiret est aussi le signe adopté par SIAMTU pour accompagner des mots incomplets précédés ou suivis de crochets dans le *texte* quand la tablette est en mauvais état. Par exemple, si dans le texte apparait *š*[, dans le texte propre aparaitra .*š*-.; si dans le texte apparait]*š*, dans le texte propre aparaitra .-*š*.; si le texte transcrit]*š*[, l'ordinateur sortira .-*š*-. L'application extrait les chaînes graphématiques en éliminant les accidents épigraphiques. Le texte propre est la base de la liste de mots existants dans leur réalisation morphologique. Cette liste est le point de départ de la Concordance de mots ugaritiques (*CPU*).

(c) Au moyen de la fonction—*effacer une ligne de texte, une ligne de collation, une fiche du lexique*, on peut éliminer ou défaire automatiquement toutes les connexions, et elles sont multiples, liées au sigle.

2. *Fonction de tri ou mise en ordre*. Toutes les selections demandées sont ordonnées alphabétiquement selon la séquence hébraïque imposée par C.H. Gordon.[27] Pour cela ont été crées les caractères *Mutu* sur les-quels travaille le système de façon invisible pour l'usager.

3. *Fonctions d'analyse morphologique* des mots. L'analyseur morphologique montre toutes les possibilités morphologiques de chaque forme verbale avec des indications précises de personne, aspect, conjugaison, etc. Pour les formes verbales on obtient la racine, les préfixes, les infixes, les affixes et la conjugaison selon la morphologie et les ressources existantes dans le lexique. Pour les substantifs on obtient le genre, le nombre. Par ailleurs sont signalés les anthroponymes, toponymes, théonymes, gentilices, etc. s'ils ont été répertoriés auparavant dans le lexique. L'analyseur distingue également les adverbes, les prépositions et les conjonctions.

Chaque texte ou mot nouveau intégré à la banque de données, donnera naissance à la concordance correspondante. L'application permet son usage et son impression.

L'ordinateur établit une liste avec les références des localisations où apparait la racine. Il organise alphabétiquement les racines et génère la Concordance par racines dans le contexte matériel. Les Concordances pourront être consultées directement à l'écran ou imprimées. Elles pourront être totales ou partielles.

L'analyseur morphologique devient un banc d'essai pour les théories morpholinguistiques que l'on veut tester.

L'analyseur morphologique est prévu pour l'ougaritique mais il est facilement adaptable à n'importe quelle langue sémitique. Cet outil est également un nouveau produit.[28]

---

[27] *Ugaritic Grammar* (Roma, 1940); *Ugaritic Handbook* (Roma, 1947); *Ugaritic Manual* (Roma, 1955); *Ugaritic Textbook* (Roma, 1965).

[28] Complètement nouveau par rapport à celui décrit dans *Biblica* 73 (1992), pp. 553–4.

4. *Fonction de restitution de chaînes graphématiques incomplètes*, fragments de mot. Cette fonction permet de recupérer 1/6 du vocabulaire autrement perdu. La grande majorité des *chaînes graphématiques incomplètes* est susceptible d'une ou plusieurs restitutions. Les propositions de restitution sont fondées sur le vocabulaire existant dans la banque de données au moment de la demande. Cela signifie que l'introduction d'un mot nouveau peut affecter une ou plusieurs chaînes graphématiques.

Le croisement des résultats de cette fonction avec les résultats des fonctions statistiques et d'analyse littéraire permet des résultats encore plus satisfaisants. Ces résultats pourront encore être améliorés le jour où l'on disposera des photos des tablettes en mettant à profit une technique qui permettra de développer ce que nous appelons déjà l'épigraphie informatique.

5. *Fonction statistique*. (a) Nombre d'occurences d'un mot ou d'une racine dans une ligne, dans un texte, dans un genre littéraire; (b) pourcentage de l'usage d'un mot ou d'une racine dans un genre littéraire.

6. *Fonction d'analyse littéraire*. Pour le moment, cette fonction se limite au vocabulaire. Elle permet d'obtenir le vocabulaire propre à un, deux ou plusieurs genres littéraires, le vocabulaire commun à tous les genres littéraires. Cette fonction sera développée à l'avenir.

7. *Fonction de recherche et d'affichage*. Chercher et afficher les lignes d'un document (une ligne, un ensemble des lignes ou les lignes d'une unité littéraire avec ou sans les collations); les mots qui apparaissent dans un document (tablette ou ligne de texte); les racines qui apparaissent dans un document (tablette ou ligne de texte); les chaînes graphématiques d'un document (tablette ou ligne de texte).

N.B. 1ª Les recherches peuvent être simples ou combinées selon des critères divers.

2ª Toutes les sélections antérieures peuvent servir de point de départ pour de nouvelles sélections ou pour naviguer à l'intérieur de la Banque de Données.

8. *Modification de la Banque de Données*:

a. Ajouter une ligne de texte, une ligne de collation, une fiche du lexique.

b. Corriger une ligne de texte, une ligne de collation, une fiche du lexique.

Les possibilités d'intervention grâce à la fonction de modification sont multiples:

1° on peut vérifier si le sigle existe.

2° que le genre littéraire correspond à celui repéré pour d'autres lignes du même document.

3° Etroitement liées aux procédures antérieures, les références de chaque mot ou chaîne graphématique s'obtiennent automatiquement.

4° Veut-on vérifier si une chaîne graphématique du texte a été coupé? Si la réponse est positive, l'ordinateur propose de la diviser.

5° Il arrive parfois que sur la tablette les mots soient coupés sur deux lignes. Si la dernière chaîne graphématique de la ligne antérieure jointe à la première chaîne de la ligne que l'on vient d'introduire, forment un mot déjà identifié, l'ordinateur avertit l'usager de la présence d'un mot coupé sur deux lignes.

6° Les chaînes graphématiques, des mots ou des chaînes graphématiques incomplètes, sont enregistrées avec leurs références.

7° L'ordinateur avertit de la présence de nouveaux mots et donne la possibilité de les analyser morphologiquement.

8° Le système repère de nouvelles chaînes graphématiques incomplètes et propose de restituer les tirets pour compléter un mot.

9° *Effacer une ligne de texte, une ligne de collation, une fiche du lexique.*

III *Possibilités d'utilisation*

SIAMTU II permet à l'usager:

1° d'intégrer dans la BDFSN tout nouveau texte et toute nouvelle collation publiés et de leur faire parcourir le chemin informatique tracé par les textes précédents.

2° d'introduire de nouvelles fiches du lexique.

3° de corriger une ligne du texte de base ou d'une collation ainsi que les fiches du lexique.

4° d'effacer ou de supprimer des lignes du texte, des collations ou des fiches du lexique.

5° de chercher un document entier ou une partie avec ou sans collation.

6° Constituer un texte composé avec le texte de base et les collations souhaitées par l'usager.

7° L'usager dispose de la possibilité de chercher de mots et des racines, ainsi que de consulter ou de construire lui-même à son usage des Concordances totales ou partielles de mots en morphologie déployée ou des concordances totales ou partielles de racines.

8° d'analyser morphologiquement tous les mots.

> Dans l'analyse des mots apparaissent plusieurs solutions possibles. Une d'entre elles doit être correcte pour le cas analysé. C'est du ressort du chercheur-utilisateur de décider celle qu'il considère comme la bonne dans tous les cas ou celle qu'il considère possible pour une forme déterminée, ou correcte dans un cas précis. Si aucune n'était bonne, l'usager peut faire une proposition et l'ordinateur l'enregistre (*Biblica* 73 [1992], p. 553).

Dans ce dernier cas, lorsque l'usager écrit la racine, l'ordinateur vérifie si elle existe déjà dans le lexique. Si elle n'est pas présente, il ouvre une fiche vierge pour que l'utilisateur saisisse la nouvelle racine et complète la fiche. L'application vérifie également si le préfixe et le suffixe supposés par le spécialiste sont présents dans la liste des préfixes et suffixes.

L'usager a la possibilité d'inclure, parmi les analyses morphologiques, différentes racines qu'il considère probables ou possibles. Ses décisions se reflèteront dans les Concordances. Dans le cas où l'on choisirait plusieurs solutions, la racine (et le contexte qui l'accompagne) apparaitront dans les Concordances sous chacun des radicaux sélectionnés.

Les études ugaritiques ne sont pas suffisamment avancées pour que nous puissions assurer dans tous les cas que la racine indiquée est correcte. Nous donnons donc diverses possibilités: certaines analyses seront confirmées à l'avenir, d'autres non. Mais la confirmation ou le rejet s'établiront à un niveau ultérieur et il est bon que le spécialiste en soit conscient.

L'analyseur morphologique a été conçu comme un outil qui facilite la création de concordances de racines. Mais c'est aussi un outil magnifique pour le chercheur. En traitant toutes les possibilités d'analyse morphologique il le prévient de ne pas écarter une possibilité peu fréquente.

> La plus grande partie des erreurs de grands spécialistes dans l'interprétation d'un texte tient au fait qu'ils ont analysé un mot en le rattachant à un radical bien connu et à la sémantique correspondante; en réalité il s'agissait d'un autre radical et le mot se décomposait autrement (*Biblica* 73 [1992], p. 554).

9° SIAMTU II permet à l'usager d'obtenir des propositions de restitution pour toute chaîne graphématique incomplète. La décision finale du choix de la restitution parmi les possibilités offertes par l'ordinateur est de la compétence du chercheur.

10° SIAMTU II permet à l'usager de chercher des sélections selon des critères divers et croisés.

11° de naviguer à l'intérieur de la banque de donnée en prenant comme point de départ n'importe quelle sélection.

12° SIAMTU II permet aussi à l'usager d'obtenir le nombre d'occurences d'un mot ou d'une racine dans une ligne, dans un texte, dans un genre littéraire.

13° Obtenir le pourcentage d'un mot ou d'une racine à l'intérieur d'un genre littéraire, de plusieurs genres littéraires ou de toute la littérature ougaritique.

14° Obtenir le vocabulaire complet d'un genre littéraire, ou bien le vocabulaire propre et exclusif à un, deux ou plusieurs genres littéraires.

15° "L'application permet . . . d'afficher et d'imprimer les textes" (*Biblica* 73 [1992], p. 553), ou n'importe quelle selection effectuée par l'usager.

Au fur et à mesure que nous progressions dans la création de SIAMTU, nous prenions conscience des avantages du support informatique sur le support papier. C'est l'expression d'un phénomène culturel qui affecte autant les sciences humaines que le reste de la société. Il convient donc d'intégrer les nouvelles technologies à notre culture de recherche.

Quand il dessine un ouvrage, une concordance, l'auteur doit prendre des décisions qui reflètent sa manière de le concevoir. Certains concepts sont clairs et tous les spécialistes les acceptent. Souvent, il faut prendre des décisions qui pourraient être aussi valables et acceptables à l'opposé. Quand on utilise le support papier, les décisions prises sont irréversibles une fois réalisée l'impression. Le moindre changement suppose de refaire l'ouvrage. Dans la pratique, une vingtaine d'années. Quand on travaille sur support informatique, les décisions peuvent rester ouvertes dans de nombreux cas, et permettre à l'usager de prendre parti pour l'une ou l'autre. Changer d'avis, refaire le produit ou le mettre à jour est une affaire de quelques jours. L'usager peut disposer d'une version informatique actualisée, corrigée et augmentée chaque année ou même chaque jour si le produit SIAMTU II est disponible sur Internet.

Pour le moment, trois livres sont le fruit du système informatique SIAMTU. Vous aurez remarqué que nous avons fréquemment fait allusion aux options prises. Depuis le début, nous avons pensé à l'usager. En effet, comme éditeurs de la concordance imprimée, nous avons été contraints de délimiter, choisir telle ou telle solution. Nos décisions ne peuvent être appréciées par tous. Quand vous serez en possession de SIAMTU, vous pourrez faire ce que bon vous semble et modifier le contenu à votre guise, selon vos critères, tout cela avec un effort minimum et sans avoir à réécrire les textes et aucune des applications que compte SIAMTU.

Si nous décidons de changer les sigles, la concordance sera générée sans obligation de changer le reste.

Si nous décidons de connoter un nouveau phénomène épigraphique ou de changer tel ou tel signe épigraphique, la concordance sera générée sans obligation de changer le reste.

Si nous décidons un changement dans la coupure des mots, nous pouvons générer la concordance sans changer le reste.

Si nous décidons d'introduire de nouvelles lignes de collations non existantes dans BDFSN ou des collations qui viennent de paraître, nous pouvons générer la concordance sans changer le reste.

De même si nous introduisons de nouveaux textes, ce qui ne saurait tarder, nous pouvons générer la concordance sans changer le reste.

Si nous décidons de faire une nouvelle analyse morphologique de tel ou tel morphème et le cas peut être assez fréquent, nous pouvons générer la concordance sans changer le reste.

Si nous décidons de mettre à disposition un contexte matériel plus large, il suffirait d'une indication au programmeur.

Si en outre, nous disposons de la bibliographie et des images sur le support informatique, quand apparaissent un nouvel article ou de nouvelles photographies d'une tablette, nous pourrons générer la concordance sans avoir à changer ou à réécrire le reste.

Nous n'aurons pas davantage de problèmes pour choisir le papier, le format du livre, la taille et le type de lettre, la couleur de la couverture. Sur le support informatique, vous pouvez changer le format des lettres, chercher les pages, les textes, les mots, etc.

Vous pourrez introduire de nouvelles fiches de votre collation favorite, y compris celles que nous avons jugées négligeables. Vous pourrez construire avec elles votre *TU* ou faire la Concordance totale ou partielle que vous souhaitez. Et si vous n'osez pas, le laboratoire d'herméneumatique peut le faire pour vous.

Avec SIAMTU, vous pourrez modifier ce que vous désirez ou proposer vos idées et les discuter avec les membres du laboratoire d'herméneumatique.

En fait le but de la BDFSN c'est l'herméneumatique.

III° L'herméneumatique

I *Définition*. L'herméneumatique est un néologisme formé par acronymie et composé de herméneu (de herméneu[tique] du grec ἑρμηνεύω, "interprét/er") et -matique de [infor]matique.[29] La signification de herméneumatique est donc "interprétation automatique". Par ce terme on veut indiquer tout le processus d'automatisation informatique dans l'interprétation des textes.

Les principes herméneumatiques concernent le contexte archéologique, la phonétique, la morphologie, la syntaxe, la critique interne littéraire (structure du texte, stylistique), la critique historique et la critique externe littéraire et historique. Mais l'application de ces principes dépend beaucoup de la maîtrise de l'herméneute, de son expérience et de son art. L'art de l'herméneute dépend de sa sensibilité à la littérature, au texte, à un genre et à une culture déterminés. L'expérience d'un chercheur n'est autre que le fruit de la création dans son cerveau, à force de pratiquer cet exercice, de systèmes experts qu'il exerce, une fois crées, de manière inconsciente.

II *L'objet de l'herméneumatique*
est la formalisation de règles herméneutiques destinées à obtenir le plus grand degré possible d'automatisation dans l'interprétation de textes. L'herméneumatique prétend réaliser l'automatisation de tout le processus d'interprétation critique des textes.

Ceci dit, réussir l'interprétation automatique d'un texte peut paraître, en l'état actuel des choses, une utopie. Personne ne peut prétendre actuellement réaliser l'interprétation automatique, complète et parfaite du texte. Mais on peut prétendre autre chose: ouvrir le chemin en marchant. Et encore, créer les outils informatiques d'aide au chercheur pour chaque étape à parcourir dans l'interprétation du texte.

La première tâche à réaliser est peut-être celle de faire comprendre aux philologues à quel point l'ordinateur optimise la méthode de travail. L'ordinateur introduit des concepts différents de ceux avec lesquels le chercheur travaille. Le philologue devra connaître peu à peu ces concepts s'il veut tirer profit des possibilités que lui offre l'informatique.

---

[29] Je remercie mon collègue le Dr Leonardo Gómez Torrego, del Instituto de Filología del CSIC, spécialiste de grammaire de la langue espagnole pour l'aide apportée dans la définition scientifique du terme inventé par l'auteur de cette conférence.

Du point de vue du philologue, l'objectif est de détecter d'abord et de formaliser ensuite chacune des étapes qui constituent le circuit herméneutique ou phase de reconnaissance du texte. Nous appelons reconnaissance du texte tous les progrès critiques que doit réaliser le chercheur pour atteindre la compréhension critique du texte. L'idée de base est de connaître le chemin de reconnaissance critique d'un texte et de le décrire dans ses moindres détails.

L'écrivain parcourt un chemin depuis la première idée créative du texte jusqu'au produit externe à lui-même qu'est le texte. Le lecteur part du texte, objet qui s'offre à sa compréhension et doit reconnaître tous les codes que consciemment ou inconsciemment l'auteur a utilisés, depuis la langue, l'époque à laquelle il écrit, la culture à laquelle il appartient, etc. Le lecteur dont nous parlons est un lecteur critique, capable de reconnaître les codes utilisés par l'auteur et de vérifier qu'ils sont corrects. Le chemin critique de reconnaissance du texte est bien connu de certains spécialistes en particulier de ceux qui se consacrent à l'étude des documents anciens.

La possibilité de formaliser ces méthodes d'interprétation des textes, bien connues des biblistes et autres herméneutes, il faut se la représenter comme une interaction (*TU*, p. XIII) entre informatique et sciences humaines mais également en sens inverse entre sciences humaines et informatique.

Nous entrons dans une étape interdisciplinaire (philologue et informaticien). Un dialogue interdisciplinaire large est nécessaire. Le spécialiste doit décrire de la manière la plus claire possible quels sont ses besoins et ses objectifs. Il doit en outre, écouter l'informaticien qui lui précisera les possibilités de la machine et de ses langages de programmation. Le spécialiste doit résumer et concrétiser au maximum les étapes et les critères qu'il utilise dans la pratique de sa discipline. Il exerce ainsi de façon explicite un effort de rationalisation de son savoir qui le surprendra lui-même. Cette étape l'aide à développer ses propres connaissances et favorise le progrès de la science en général et de sa spécialité en particulier. La construction d'une base relationnelle avec applications propres à une discipline a l'avantage d'obliger le spécialiste qui la constitue à faire participer de la rationalisation informatique toutes les techniques et ressources qu'il utilise dans sa spécialité. Chemin faisant, il récupère la confiance dans sa propre discipline et découvre à quel point son savoir est science.

En général, le philologue a tendance à décrire comme une tache ce qui en réalité en constitue plusieurs. Il n'est pas habitué à disséquer ses démarches. Il travaille en réalité avec des *systèmes experts* qu'il s'est crée à son insu et qui fonctionnent dans l'ordinateur de son cerveau.

Un système expert est un système informatique fondé sur les connaissances d'un groupe d'experts, et destiné à résoudre un problème donné. Il est composé de *bases de connaissances* et d'un *moteur d'inférence*. Dans les bases de connaissance on tésorise dans la représentation adéquate, l'expérience professionnelle des spécialistes. Le moteur d'inférence est un programme qui utilise ces connaissances et les combine pour résoudre le problème.

Dans ce travail interdisciplinaire, philologie et informatique, l'objectif premier est de connaître les étapes des systèmes experts utilisés par le spécialiste philologue. L'informaticien joue le rôle de miroir qui renvoie au philologue son message traduit aux possibilités de la machine. Sous l'impulsion ou la pression de l'informaticien, le philologue prend conscience du fait que sa démarche se décompose en réalité en actes multiples, reliés entre eux selon la logique de la machine qui réduit tout à des zéros ou des uns (le courant électrique ne passe pas; le courant électrique passe). Une fois localisé l'acte, le passage, l'informaticien doit le formaliser.

Notre effort actuel de recherche scientifique se centre sur la mise à jour de ces circuits inconscients qu'utilise l'herméneute. Pour y parvenir, nous utilisons l'ordinateur à qui il faut indiquer les moindres étapes formalisées en langage informatique. Si les étapes qui conduisent à la compréhension d'un texte sont bien décrites et bien formalisées, l'ordinateur doit être capable de les reproduire. S'il n'y parvient pas, c'est que le facteur humain qui a analysé le circuit de la connaissance ou reconnaissance d'un texte a échoué. Alors on recherche l'erreur, on la corrige et l'on continue dans la recherche du circuit de reconnaissance du texte, jusqu'à ce que l'ordinateur soit capable de le reconnaître intégralement.

L'ingénierie. Une fois connu le chemin de la reconnaissance d'un texte et décrit dans ses différentes étapes, on peut passer à la phase de l'ingénierie linguistique. C'est un travail similaire à celui d'un ingénieur chargé de la fabrication. Il faut décomposer la reconnaissance du texte en phases de travail avec des objectifs précis à atteindre pour chaque phase. Il s'agit donc de créer les outils informatiques adéquats à chaque phase.

Il s'agit de construire des outils qui remplacent une partie du travail effectué par le chercheur de façon répétitive, des outils ouverts qui puissent être améliorés. Ainsi on ne peut comparer une concordance imprimée qu'on ne peut plus modifier avec une concordance en support informatique, ouverte, où le lecteur-chercheur peut disposer de ce que d'autres ont déjà élaboré et en même temps modifier ce qu'il souhaite.

En outre, chaque étape que nous parcourons, chaque outil informatique, qu'il s'agisse de systèmes experts ou d'environement, pourront être améliorés avec l'intervention d'autres spécialistes plus savants dans l'un ou l'autre aspect de l'étape parcourue. Pour ajouter ces connaissances ultérieures, il ne sera plus nécessaire de reécrire tout le livre mais simplement de donner des instructions précises que l'on pourra incorporer à l'outil.

III *Les ideés sousjacentes*

1. Une matière objet d'étude, banc d'essai pour déceler et formaliser le trajet herméneutique: l'ugaritique.

Les philologues, biblistes, classiques ou modernes ont pu élaborer une méthode complète d'interprétation d'un texte, mais l'étude du Proche Orient Ancien présente un intérêt spécial. Le bibliste, l'helléniste ou le philologue latiniste ou germaniste, etc. ont toujours compté avec une tradition sur laquelle ils ont pu s'appuyer si nécessaire. Le spécialiste en cultures du Proche-Orient Ancien, excepté le bibliste, se trouve dans une situation particulière. Chaque tablette est un original qu'il faut déchiffrer et comprendre dans son texte et son contexte. Chaque unité minimale, comme le mot, peut le conduire à chercher son origine inconnue, sa signification de base et naturellement, à refaire partiellement la grammaire, surtout la syntaxe. Une tablette est fréquemment une énigme avec plusieurs inconnues. En outre, le sens le plus évident n'est pas toujours pertinent. Tout ceci exige de disposer d'instruments de travail comme dictionnaires et grammaires de toutes les langues du même groupe et des groupes proches.

Le processus cognitif-interprétatif que parcours le chercheur devant une tablette du IIème millénaire av. J.C. est très complet par l'exigence même de la matière. Il nous parait donc qu'il s'agit d'un terrain nouveau où l'on peut tenter de comprendre la ligne du processus cognitif-interprétatif dans chacune de ses phases et étapes.

Si en parcourant ce chemin, nous découvrions un des maillons de la chaîne de reconnaissance d'un texte, ce serait une grande satisfaction pour tout philologue commentateur de textes. Peut-être, nous qui nous consacrons aux textes anciens, avons-nous dans les mains, sans le savoir, un de ces chaînons. Il s'agirait d'une grande contribution des études de l'antiquité à la plus stricte modernité et actualite!

Le linguiste moderne est par l'objet de son étude très éloigné de l'ordinateur ignorant à qui il faut tout apprendre. Dans la reproduction artificielle de l'intelligence humaine, dans la branche du langage, on a toujours travaillé en partant des langues contemporaines, par exemple, anglais-russe, dont on connait le dictionnaire et la grammaire. Dans ce cas, il s'agit d'enseigner à l'ordinateur une langue dans un état déjà très avancé.

L'interprète des tablettes du IIème millénaire av. J.C. au contraire est plus proche de l'ignorance de l'ordinateur car il ne connait pas d'avance les structures syntaxiques de la langue qu'il interprète et ne peut compter que sur un nombre réduit de personnes capables de l'aider. A ces handicaps correspondent cependant quelques avantages. L'interprète des tablettes doit parcourir de manière complète la ligne de l'interprétation. S'il escamote la moindre étape, l'interprétation correcte n'a pas lieu. Cette situation l'a conduit à se fabriquer mentalement des systèmes experts, systèmes peut-être plus simples mais en définitive aussi plus complets que ceux que reproduit le linguiste moderne et donc plus proches de la machine à laquelle il faut tout apprendre depuis le début. En effet, au début, il ne dispose pas de dictionnaire, ni de grammaire, et quand il commence à en disposer, l'apparition d'un nouveau texte peut l'obliger, et fréquemment c'est le cas, à revoir aussi bien le lexique disponible que la grammaire la plus élaborée à ce jour. En outre, il est bien connu que la compréhension du texte ne s'achève pas à la connaissance de la sémantique des lexèmes ni à la connaissance de la syntaxe grammaticale. Il y a dans chaque texte des éléments structuraux, pas toujours grammaticaux, qu'il faut trouver et comprendre. L'interprète du texte doit trouver la structure sous-jacente, parfois inconsciente à son propre auteur, dont les éléments et l'assemblage sont fondamentaux pour la compréhension du texte. Ces éléments structuraux ne sont pas tous les mêmes dans chaque culture ou langue, ni dans chaque genre littéraire. Les genres littéraires ont aussi leurs marqueurs propres qui servent à les distinguer entre eux. Il convient de les découvrir et ensuite de les cataloguer laissant ouvert le fichier pour son enrichissement ultérieur grace à d'autres découvertes.

Partir d'une langue morte, inconnue jusqu'à 1929 et qu'il a fallu déchiffrer est un avantage. La langue est inconnue aujourd'hui encore en grande partie, ce qui oblige les spécialistes à utiliser des techniques éprouvées pendant plus de cent ans mais qui n'ont jamais été formalisées.

Par contre, tout ne se réduit pas à des facilités!

2. L'existence de méthodes d'interprétation des textes qui ont fait leurs preuves. Nous en parlons au pluriel. L'herméneumatique doit s'étendre à toutes les méthodes utilisées par les exégètes et autres herméneutes des textes. En fait nous utiliserons seulement la méthode historico-critique, mais nous estimons que d'autres méthodes sont posssibles et doivent également être formalisées et traitées. La banque de données peut aussi être un banc d'essai pour les méthodes.

Dans l'application de la méthode historico-critique, les étapes peuvent se résumer ainsi: (1) critique interne: analyse philologique (étymologie, évolution phonémique, morphologique et sémantique), analyse littéraire (genre littéraire, structure, syntaxe), analyse historique, synthèse; (2) critique externe: philologique, littéraire et historique.

L'unité minimale du texte, le mot, est soumis à l'étude philologique de son origine et de son évolution phonétique, morphologique et sémantique. Le mot est étudié aussi comme partie d'un ensemble qui est l'unité littéraire de manière à ce qu'une fois établis les éléments structurels, les autres données cadrent parfaitement avec chacun des éléments qui composent cette unité. Tout ceci constitue la critique interne.

Vient ensuite la critique externe: le document doit être compris dans le contexte littéraire (sans négliger le genre littéraire) et historique, non seulement de la culture à laquelle il appartient, mais aussi en relation avec les cultures qui l'entourent.

Seulement quand le circuit complet a été parcouru, on peut affirmer que l'on a compris le texte et procéder à son commentaire.

3. Le développement de l'herméneumatique exige enfin une autre condition: l'existence de spécialistes capables d'utiliser les méthodes mises à l'essai. La méthode historico-critique développée par les biblistes doit être étendue aux textes des cultures du Proche-Orient. Celles-ci ont déjà pris leurs distances vis-à-vis de la Bible. Elles y ont gagné d'éliminer les arguments d'autorité religieuse, mais pas nécessairement ceux d'autorité "académique" ou de "prestige" qui s'immiscent parfois dans une argumentation scientifique.

Nous sommes fortement redevables aux méthodes herméneutiques utilisées par les biblistes. C'est pour cela que nous tenions à exposer les prémices de notre recherche devant une assemblée de biblistes. Nous savions aussi que vous seriez à même de comprendre notre recherche et en même temps nous voulions ainsi rendre hommage à tous ceux et celles dont nous avons tant appris.

Les études bibliques ont affronté dans les deux siècles écoulés les défis de la critique littéraire[30] d'abord, puis de la critique archéologique et historique.[31] Cela a permis aux biblistes d'élaborer des méthodes d'analyse des textes qui ont fait leurs preuves. Il s'agit maintenant d'accepter le défi informatique c'est à dire le dialogue interdisciplinaire avec l'informatique en tenant compte de toutes ses possibilités. Il s'agit donc d'une participation active des exégètes au développement des nouvelles technologies.

Voilà ce que nous avons commencé à réaliser en partie, seulement en partie, mais suffisemment pour être optimistes.

Le chemin qui nous reste à parcourir peut être résumé ainsi:

– *Du mot à la phrase, de l'analyse morphologique à l'analyse syntaxique*. L'analyseur syntaxique est dans la phase de création, outil d'aide à la recherche de la syntaxe de la phrase. L'analyseur syntaxique des textes donnera naissance aux concordances syntaxiques en support informatique, indispensables pour le traitement scientifique des textes.

– *De la syntaxe à la sémantique*. Au moyen d'un environnement informatique construit par l'équipe dont font partie les Professeurs José Cuena et Ana Garcia-Serrano du Département d'Intelligence Artificielle de l'Université Polytechnique de Madrid, on essaiera la réalisation d'un prototype de Système expert d'aide à l'interprétation des textes du sémitique nord-occidental.

L'analyse syntaxique permettra la génération de *Concordances dans le contexte significatif*. Réalisées de même que les précédentes à partir des racines de mots, le contexte sera dans ce cas la phrase sémantique complète dont fait partie le mot étudié. Cette concordance ne pourra être réalisée qu'à partir de textes parfaitement connus, analysés et étudiés.

– *De l'analyse sémantique au commentaire de textes*. Recherche et localisation des structures qui composent l'armature d'un texte. Ici on arrive définitivement à la connaissance du document ancien, source de l'histoire.

C'est à ce moment que le philologue abandonne le texte qui doit

---

[30] Voir par ex. H. Cazelles, *Introduction critique à l'Ancien Testament. Introduction à la Bible II* (nouvelle édition, Paris, 1973), pp. 107–39, 151–9.

[31] Voir par ex. Cazelles, pp. 140ss., 250ss.

être repris par l'historien. C'est à ce moment que l'historien doit commencer à penser et à construire sa Banque de données historiques.

SIAMTU II n'est qu'une étape. Les possibilités que l'intelligence Artificielle offre à la recherche dans le domaine de l'herméneumatique sont encore à découvrir. Il est trop tôt pour parler de résultats. Il est prévu de le faire, dans un autre cadre sans doute, d'ici à trois ans.

Pour les trois années à venir, notre but est l'étude de la syntaxe et un essai d'automatisation.[32] L'équipe interdisciplinaire travaille au dessin et à la réalisation des modèles. Nous avons commencé par identifier les bases de connaissances qu'utilisent les ugaritologues (et sans doute d'autres spécialistes) et nous arrivons au résultat suivant: (1) une base archéologique; (2) une base épigraphique; (3) une base phonétique et phonologique; (4) une base morphologique; (5) une base syntaxique; (6) une base littéraire; (7) une base historique. Il s'agit maintenant d'établir les règles qui régissent chacune de ces bases de connaissance. Nous avons établi les règles épigraphiques,[33] phonétiques et morphologiques et nous commençons à établir les règles syntaxiques.

L'équipe informatique[34] réalise actuellement les taches de dessin du

---

[32] Voici une brève bibliographie sur le traitement informatique du langage naturel: J. Allen, *Natural Language Understanding* (Menlo Park, California, 1987); J.R. Carbonell, "Politics, automated ideological reasoning", *Cognitive Reasoning* 2 (1978), pp. 27–51; K.M. Colby, R.C. Parkison, W.S. Faught, "Conversational language comprehension using integrated Pattern-Matching and Parsing", *Artificial Intelligence* 9 (1977), pp. 111–34; R. Duda, J. Gaschnig, P. Harb, "Model Design in the Prospector Consultant System for Mineral Exploration", dans D. Michie (ed.), *Expert Systems in the Microelectronic Age* (Édimbourg, 1979), pp. 153–67; E.J. Fillmore, "The case for case", dans E. Bach, R.T. Harms (ed.), *Universals in Linguistic Theory* (New York, 1968), pp. 1–88; P.S. Jacobs, L.F. Rau, "Innovations in text interpretation", *AI* 63 (1993), pp. 143–91; F.C.N. Pereira, D.H.D. Warren, "Definite clause grammars for language analysis—a survey of the formalism and a comparison with augmented transition networks", *AI* 13 (1980), pp. 231–78; F.C.N. Pereira, *SRI Technical Note 275* (Menlo Park, California, 1983); G. Sabah, "Knowledge representation and Natural language Understanding", *AICOM* V-6, N:3/4, (December 1993); E.D. Sacerdoti, "Language access to distributed data with error recovery", *Fifth International Joint Conference on Artificial Intelligence* 1 (Cambridge, Mass., 1977), pp. 196–202; R.C. Schank, R.P. Abelson, *Scripts, Plans, Goals and Understanding: an Inquiry into Human Knowledge Structure* (Hillsdale, New Jersey, 1977); S.M. Shieber, "An Introduction to Unification-based approaches to grammars", *CSLI Lecture Notes* 41 (Stanford University, 1986); J. Weizenbaum, "ELIZA, a computer program for the study of natural language communication between man and machine". *Comm. ACM* (Association for Computing Machinery) 9,1 (New York, January 1966), pp. 36–45; Y. Wilks, "An intelligent analyzer and understander of english", *CACM* 18 (1975), pp. 264–74; T. Winograd, *Understanding Natural Language* (Édimbourg, 1972); W. Woods, "Transition network grammars for natural language analysis", *CACM* 13, 10 (October 1970), pp. 591–606.

[33] Voir J.-L. Cunchillos, J.-M. Galán (n. 17).

[34] Je remercie le professeur Anna García-Serrano, membre de l'équipe de recherche, l'aide apportée dans la rédaction de ce passage.

support logiciel à développer. Cette équipe participe depuis plusieurs années à des projets de développement de systèmes fondés sur des connaissances de deuxième génération. Ces travaux ont donné lieu à la première version d'un environement du logiciel général KSM (Knowledge Structure Manager)[35] qui actuellement s'utilise dans d'autres domaines avec des financements européen et espagnol.

La configuration à développer, dont l'architecture est fondée sur la connaissance, doit être modulaire, susceptible de croissance, explicatif et redéfinissable, caractéristiques propres à un travail de recherche tel que la connaissance des langues ugaritique et phénicienne. De même seront importants les aspects d'interface pour les usagers.

L'objectif immédiat du projet est de réaliser l'analyse de la Correspondance ugaritique en vue d'obtenir une réponse du système parmi ces possibilités:

(a) Acceptation du texte avec diverses formes de traduction.

(b) Rejet du texte avec justifications à l'appui.

(c) Proposition de formes à intégrer qui, soit permettent de repousser des alternatives du texte acceptées; ou bien permettent de valider certaines parties du texte, repoussées auparavant.

(d) Assimilation des nouvelles formes acceptées par les experts.

La méthodologie de dessin est fondée sur la proposition de structuration des connaissances des Unités Cognitives du Professeur Cuena. Elle permet le dessin du système en vue de l'identification de la connaissance disponible, et son usage en vue des tâches à réaliser. Le dessin se réalise à trois niveaux de description: niveau de connaissance, niveau symbolique et niveau d'implementation (réalisation).

Conclusions

L'apparition de l'informatique a signifié un progrès formidable pour tous les chercheurs obligés à écrire. Désormais, la pensée ne devient plus un texte au moyen du stylet, du calame, du crayon, de la plume ou du stylo, causes instrumentales dans la plus pure tradition scolastique. Ces outils ont été supplantés par la machine qui ne peut plus être

[35] J. Cuena Véase, M. Molina, "KSM: An environment for knowledge oriented design of applications using structured knowledge architectures", dans K. Brunnstein, E. Raubold (ed.), *Information Processing '94: Proceedings of the IFIP 13th World Computer Congress Hamburg, Aug–Sept 1994* II: *Applications and Impacts* (Amsterdam, London et North-Holland, 1994).

> considérée comme simple cause instrumentale. Son action quadruple l'efficacité de l'écrivain en augmentant la rapidité de transmission de la pensée à l'écrit. La même efficacité se prolonge dans l'édition, l'impression et la publication du texte (*Biblica* 73 [1992], p. 547).

L'informatisation ne se réduit pas au traitement de texte. Les bases de données relationnelles offrent de nombreux avantages pour notre travail. Mais il est indispensable de créer des applications adaptées à la spécialité pour lesquelles la contribution du spécialiste, qu'il soit philologue ou historien, est indispensable.

Même les plus exigents en matière de rigueur trouvent dans la machine le professeur le plus exigent qu'ils aient jamais eu. Le chercheur découvre que ses collègues sont moins rigoureux qu'il ne le croyait et plus tard vérifie aussi que lui-même est inégal dans l'usage de cette rigueur dont il se targue. Dans ce domaine influent en effet aussi bien les velléités d'école que les vélléités personnelles. Fréquemment surviennent des changements d'opinion qui ne sont pas explicités car ils sont généralement inconscients. Le niveau de conscience se situe à un niveau de compréhension plus élevé pour le chercheur qui attribue une moindre importance aux débuts considérés à la portée de n'importe qui. C'est ainsi qu'il se trompe fréquemment dans son appréciation.

Nous ne sommes pas très loin du jour où nous pourrons vous proposer un livre électronique interactif. Vous pourrez alors disposer sur l'écran non seulement des textes, des concordances, de la bibliographie et des photos du texte sur lequel vous désirez travailler. Vous disposerez également d'un glossaire, au début simple, mais que vous pourrez enrichir des connaissances existantes. Le support informatique se convertit ainsi en un instrument complet de travail. Avec l'application informatique, vous disposerez des livres de référence que vous utilisiez auparavant assidument. Vous pourrez travailler commodément, éviter la tâche fastidieuse de devoir réécrire un texte pour la centième fois, vous pourrez faire des recherches rapides sans avoir à feuilleter les pages d'un livre, des recherches au rythme de l'électronique.

Ceci est le futur immédiat, mais futur. Nous savons que nous avons besoin encore du livre en support papier. Pour cela nous l'avons édité. Mais en même temps nous avons fabriqué l'application informatique pour que le support papier vieillisse avec plus de dignité sachant que les recherches, les compléments, les mises à jour, les changements se trouveront sur le support informatique. Dès que possible, nous fabriquerons le livre électronique avec tous les avantages du support informatique, outre ceux qui lui sont propres et nous le mettrons à la disposition des chercheurs pour qu'ils puissent s'habituer à passer du livre imprimé au livre électronique.

Il ne s'agit pas de promouvoir que tous les spécialistes se consacrent directement à construire des outils ou applications informatiques, des systèmes experts ou des environements. Du moins pouvons-nous réserver aux herméneumaticiens le même respect que nous avons toujours professé aux lexicographes par exemple.

Je souhaiterais signaler aussi que l'informatique nous offre le support ideal pour que nous travaillons en équipe chacun apportant depuis son lieu de travail les améliorations qui lui paraissent convenables. Le Laboratoire d'herméneumatique ouvre ses portes aux collegues qui souhaiteraient participer à l'amélioration des applications existantes.

La BDFSN peut être mise immédiatement à disposition des spécialistes soit au moyen d'actualisations périodiques soit plus rapidement encore par connexion sur Internet. Cette dernière solution permettra à n'importe quel collègue du monde entier de consulter la BDFSN actualisée de jour en jour, de minute en minute.

Ainsi se justifie la création d'un réseau international de *Correspondants* de la BDFSN.

Leurs noms en toutes lettresfigureront à la suite des noms de l'équipe, dans l'écran d'affichage WWW que le laboratoire d'herméneumatique ouvrira sur le réseau Internet.

Toutes les améliorations ou progrès communiqués, aprouvés par la direction et incorporés à la BDFSN, seront identifiés en note par le sigle du correspondant. Un correspondant particulièrement actif pourra faire partie de l'équipe de la BDFSN, s'il le souhaite.

RESURRECTION IMAGERY FROM BAAL TO THE BOOK OF DANIEL

by

JOHN DAY
Oxford

A more precise and fuller title for this essay would be "Death and Resurrection Imagery from Baal to the book of Daniel *via* Hosea and the so-called 'Isaiah Apocalypse'". I hope to demonstrate that the first clear reference to the literal resurrection of the dead in the Old Testament in Dan. xii 2 is a reinterpretation of the verse in Isa. xxvi 19 about resurrection, which I shall argue refers to restoration after exile, rather than literal life after death. Isa. xxvi 19 in turn, I shall argue, is dependent on the death and resurrection imagery in the book of Hosea, especially on a reinterpretation of Hos. xiii 14. Finally, the imagery of death and resurrection in Hosea (both in chapters v–vi and in xiii–xiv), which likewise refers to Israel's exile and restoration, is directly taken over by the prophet from the imagery of the dying and rising fertility god, Baal.

That Baal was regarded as a dying and rising god cannot seriously be disputed.[1] In the Ugaritic Baal myth we read of his being swallowed by Mot, the god of death, and it is declared several times that "Mightiest Baal is dead, the prince, Lord of the earth has perished". He is buried by Anat and lamented in the customary way by her and El. The land becomes hot, dry and parched, for Baal has taken the rain, wind and most of the dew with him into the underworld. Then El has a vision in which the heavens rain oil and the ravines run with honey. El rejoices and declares, "mightiest Baal is alive, for the prince, Lord of the earth exists". Baal then resumes his throne. (See *KTU* 1.4.VIII–1.6.VI.)

Hosea, of course, was highly polemical against the cult of Baal. But polemic can sometimes involve taking up one's enemies' imagery and reusing it for one's own purposes. It was W.W. Graf Baudissin

[1] *Contra* H.M. Barstad, *The Religious Polemics of Amos, SVT* 34 (1984), pp. 150–1, who fails to note all the evidence which I cite here.

in his book *Adonis and Esmun*[2] who first argued that Hosea took up the imagery of death and resurrection from a fertility deity. But strange to say, he does not mention Baal in this connection, but rather speaks of Adonis and Eshmun, since, prior to the discovery of the Ugaritic texts, he had to depend on late classical sources, which curiously do not mention the death and resurrection of Baal. Subsequently, a number of scholars[3] have argued that it was from Baal that Hosea drew his imagery. But some other scholars[4] have questioned this.

One point that has frequently been claimed is that Hosea is referring not to death and resurrection but rather to illness and healing.[5] The following points, however, may be made in favour of seeing death and resurrection imagery in Hos. v–vi.[6] First, in support of the resurrection understanding of Hos. vi 2 it may be noted that the verbs employed are the hiphil of *qûm* "raise up" and the piel of *ḥāyâ* "revive": "After two days he will revive us (*yeḥayyēnû*); on the third day he will raise us up (*yeqîmēnû*), that we may live before him." In all the other places in the Old Testament where these two verbs (*ḥyh, qwm*) appear as word pairs the meaning clearly relates to resurrection from death, not simply healing. This is the case in Isa. xxvi 14, 19 and Job xiv 12, 14. Secondly, three verses later, in Hos. vi 5, the prophet implies that the people are dead: "Therefore I have hewn them by the prophets; I have slain them by the words of my mouth . . ." Thirdly, in Hos. v 14 Hosea uses the image of a lion carrying off its prey and says "and none shall rescue". Elsewhere in the Old Testament the image of the lion carrying off its prey implies certain death (cf. Amos iii 12; Jer. ii 30; Mic. v 7, E. tr., 8). This is clear elsewhere in the book of Hosea itself, as we see from Hos. xiii 7, 9, where Yahweh's

---

[2] (Leipzig, 1911), pp. 404–16. Cf. H.G. May, "The fertility cult in Hosea", *AJSL* 48 (1932), pp. 74–8.

[3] E.g. R. Martin-Achard, *From Death to Life* (Edinburgh and London, 1960), pp. 81–6 (E. tr. of *De la mort à la résurrection, d'après l'Ancien Testament* [Neuchâtel and Paris, 1956]). F.F. Hvidberg, *Weeping and Laughter in the Old Testament* (E. tr., Leiden and Copenhagen, 1962), pp. 126–31.

[4] Cf. W. Rudolph, *Hosea* (Gütersloh, 1966), pp. 136–7; D.N. Freedman and F.I. Andersen, *Hosea* (Garden City, 1980), p. 420. See below n. 9 for the more nuanced position of G.I. Davies.

[5] E.g., J.L. Mays, *Hosea* (London, 1969), p. 95; H.W. Wolff, *Dodekapropheton I. Hosea* (Neukirchen, 1961), p. 149 (E. tr., *Hosea* [Philadelphia, 1974], p. 117); Rudolph (n. 4), p. 135; G.I. Davies, *Hosea* (London and Grand Rapids, 1992), p. 161.

[6] Those supporting the view that death and resurrection are envisaged here include Baudissin (n. 2), pp. 404–7; Martin-Achard (n. 3), pp. 80–6; Freedman and Andersen (n. 4), pp. 418–20; B.C. Pryce, *The Resurrection Motif in Hosea 5:8–6:6: an exegetical Study*. (Ph.D. dissertation, Andrews University, Ann Arbor, 1989), *passim*.

devouring Israel like a lion is explicitly said to be equivalent to destruction.

The last observation brings me to my fourth and most decisive argument, which has been strangely neglected by scholars writing on this subject. This is the fact that there are a whole series of parallel images between Hos. v–vi and xiii–xiv, and in the latter it is made abundantly clear that the image is that of death and resurrection, not merely illness and healing. That death is envisaged in Hos. xiii is shown by *v*. 1, "he [i.e. Ephraim] incurred guilt through Baal and died", *v*. 9, where Yahweh states, "I will destroy you, O Israel", and *v*. 14, which speaks of Israel as being in the grip of Death and Sheol. Now the parallels between Hos. v–vi and xiii–xiv are as follows. Hos. v 14 says, "For I will be like a lion to Ephraim, and like a young lion to the house of Judah. I, even I, will rend and go away, I will carry off, and none shall rescue"; we may compare Hos. xiii 7–8, "So I will be to them like a lion, like a leopard I will lurk beside the way. I will fall upon them like a bear robbed of her cubs, and I will tear open their breast, and there I will devour them like a lion, as a wild beast would rend them." Hos. vi 1 states, "Come let us return to the Lord; for he has torn, that he may heal us; he has stricken, and he will bind us up"; compare Hos. xiv 2 (E. tr. 1), "Return, O Israel to the Lord your God . . ." and xiv 5 (E. tr. 4), "I will heal their faithlessness . . ." Hos. vi 3 reads, "he will come to us as the showers, as the spring rains that water the earth", which may be compared with Hos. xiv 5 (E. tr. 4), "I will be as the dew to Israel". Since, as we have seen, Hos. xiii–xiv clearly imply death and resurrection, this must likewise be the case in Hos. v–vi, where the identical imagery is used. Interestingly, Hos. xiv 5 (E. tr. 4) speaks of Yahweh's healing Israel's faithlessness: the use of the verb "heal" in Hos. vi 1 therefore does not require something less than death in Hos. v–vi, as has sometimes been claimed.[7]

Granted that Hos. v–vi and xiii–xiv allude to Israel's death and resurrection, are we to suppose that this imagery derives from Baal? One strong argument in favour of this that has not previously been noted by other scholars[8] is to be found in Hos. xiii 1, where we read

---

[7] Cf. scholars cited above in n. 5.

[8] I have myself noted this earlier in passing in "Baal", *Anchor Bible Dictionary* 1 (New York, 1992), p. 549, and in "Ugarit and the Bible: do they presuppose the same Canaanite Mythology and Religion?", in G.J. Brooke, A.H.W. Curtis and J.F. Healey (ed.), *Ugarit and the Bible* (Münster, 1994), p. 42.

that "Ephraim . . . incurred guilt through Baal and died". This must surely be deliberately ironical. For Hosea it is not Baal who dies and rises but Israel who dies through worshipping Baal, followed, if repentant, by resurrection. In keeping with this Hos. vi 3 associates Israel's resurrection with the rain ("he will come to us as the showers, as the spring rains that water the earth"), and Hos. xiv 6 (E. tr. 5) likewise mentions the dew as bringing about renewed fertility in Israel ("I will be as the dew to Israel . . ."). This is striking, since in the Ugaritic Baal myth we read that Baal took the rain and two of the dew goddesses with him when he went into the underworld, and it is implied that they reappeared when he rose again.

A further striking parallel with Baal mythology occurs in Hos. xiii 14–15. In *v.* 14 Israel is said to be in the grip of Death (*māwet*) and Sheol, and in the following verse we read that Israel's "fountain will dry up, his spring will be parched". Similarly, in the Ugaritic Baal myth, when Baal goes down into the realm of Mot (Death) we read that the land becomes dry and parched.[9] Again, the resurrection of Israel in Hos. xiv is symbolized by fertility in nature, just as Baal's resurrection ensured the fertility of the land in Canaanite mythology.

One final possible parallel occurs in both Hos. v 14 and xiii 7–8. Yahweh is depicted as destroying Israel like a ravenous beast. Similarly, in the so-called Hadad text (*KTU* 1.12), which provides a variant on the main Baal myth, Baal appears to owe his death to ravenous beasts, which is followed by dryness, though the text is not wholly clear. It is perhaps also relevant to note that Mot's appetite is compared to that of a lion in *KTU* 1.5.I.14.

However, in arguing that Hosea takes over the image of Baal's death and resurrection and applies it to Israel, I would not appeal, as some have done, to the reference in Hos. vi 2 to Israel's resurrection on the third day. Some scholars have claimed that this was derived from a fertility god.[10] Thus, we have evidence of the celebration of the resurrection of the Egyptian god Osiris on the 19th Athyr, two days after his death on 17th Athyr (cf. Plutarch, *De Iside et Osiride*, 13, 356 C; 19, 366 F), and the resurrection of the Phrygian god Attis took place on 25th March, three days after his death (22nd March), according to Firmicus Maternus, writing of 4th century Rome.

---

[9] Davies, (n. 5), p. 297, finds it attractive to see influence from the myth of Baal's swallowing by Mot here, even though he rejects this in the case of Hos. v–vi (p. 61).

[10] E.g., Baudissin (n. 2), pp. 408–10; Martin-Achard (n. 3), pp. 83–3.

But these are both very late, and influence from Osiris or Attis on Hosea is most unlikely. Also very late, but nearer geographically and culturally, is Lucian, *De Syria Dea* 6, who states that at Byblos the faithful expected the resurrection of Adonis "on another day", though this is very vague. However, nowhere do we hear of a third-day resurrection of Baal—the god whose imagery influenced Hosea—and it is far more likely that "on the third day" is a poetic way of saying "after a short while". We may recall that Hebrew *ʾetmôl* or *tᵉmûl šilšōm*, literally "yesterday, the third day", means "formerly", and in Luke xiii 32 Jesus says, "Behold I cast out demons and perform cures today and tomorrow and the third day I finish my course" (cf. *v*. 33).

Just as imagery from Baal's death and resurrection has influenced the book of Hosea, so the next stage of my argument is that the book of Hosea has influenced the reference to resurrection in Isa. xxvi 19: "Your dead shall live, their bodies[11] shall rise, the dwellers in the dust shall awake and sing for joy,[12] for your dew is a dew of light, and the earth shall give birth to the shades."

In support of this claim I would first point out that there is a whole series of parallels between Hos. xiii–xiv and Isa. xxvi–xxvii—eight in number—all occurring in the same order, with one minor exception. As I have already pointed out in an earlier article,[13] these parallels are as follows:

(i) Israel knows no lords/gods but Yahweh. Hos. xii 4. Cf. Isa. xxvi 13 (LXX).
(ii) Imagery of birthpangs but child refuses to be born. Hos. xiii 13. Cf. Isa. xxvi 17–18.
(iii) Deliverance from Sheol. Hos. xiii 14 (LXX, etc.). Cf. Isa. xxvi 19.
(iv) Imagery of destructive east wind symbolic of exile. Hos. xiii 15. Cf. Isa. xxvii 8.
(v) Imagery of life-giving dew. Hos. xiv 6–8 (E. tr. 5–7). Cf. Isa. xxvi 19.

---

[11] Following the Targum and Peshiṭta I read "their bodies" (*niblōtām*) for the M.T.'s "my body" (*nᵉbēlātî*), which does not seem appropriate here.

[12] Instead of the M.T.'s imperatives *hāqîṣû* and *wᵉrannᵉnû* I read the imperfects *yāqîṣû* and *wîrannᵉnû* with the support of 1QIsa[a], LXX, Aquila, Symmachus and Theodotion.

[13] "A case of inner Scriptural interpretation: the dependence of Isaiah xxvi.13–xxvii.11 on Hosea xiii.4–xiv.10 (Eng. 9) and its relevance to some theories of the redaction of the 'Isaiah Apocalypse'", *JTS*, NS 31 (1980), pp. 309–19.

(vi) Israel blossoming and like a vineyard. Hos. xiv 6–8 (E. tr. 5–7). Cf. Isa. xxvii 2–6.

(vii) Condemnation of idolatry, including the Asherim. Hos. xiv 9 (E. tr. 8). Cf. Isa. xxvii 11.

(viii) The importance of discernment; judgement for the wicked. Hos. xiv 10 (E. tr. 9). Cf. Isa. xxvii 11.

One of the verses in Hosea that corresponds to the resurrection verse, Isa. xxvi 19, it will be noted, is Hos. xiii 14, "Shall I ransom them from the power of Sheol? Shall I redeem them from Death? O Death, where are your plagues? O Sheol, where is your destruction? Compassion is hid from my eyes." This, of course, is saying the opposite of Isa. xxvi 19. However, we know from the LXX and the other ancient versions (similarly, 1 Cor. xv 55) that Hos. xiii 14 was widely interpreted in a positive sense in the ancient world, "I *shall* ransom them from the power of Sheol, I *shall* redeem them from Death . . .", and this was clearly how the author of Isa. xxvi 19 interpreted it. What is most striking, and adds considerably to the evidence for the dependence of Isa. xxvi 19 on Hos. xiii 14 at this point, is the fact that the immediately preceding verses in both Hosea and Isaiah have the imagery of a woman in labour pains but the child not presenting itself (Hos. xiii 13; cf. Isa. xxvi 17–18), something too remarkable to be ascribed to mere coincidence. It is further possible that Isa. xxvi 19 shows dependence on the other resurrection passage, Hos. vi 2–3, since both passages employ the verbs *ḥyh* and *qwm* to describe the resurrection, as well as the imagery of light: compare "his going forth is sure as the *dawn*" in Hos. vi 3 with "your dew is a dew of *light*" in Isa. xxvi 19.

Granted that we have found the sources of the imagery in Isa. xxvi 19, the further question arises as to its meaning. Is there here a literal belief in life after death (as in the book of Daniel) or is the resurrection symbolism simply an image for national restoration (as in Hos. vi 1–3 and Ezek. xxxvii)? Scholarly opinion is quite divided on this question.[14] In favour of the literal life after death view it is sometimes

[14] For example, literal resurrection here is supported by G.F. Hasel, "Resurrection in the theology of Old Testament Apocalyptic", *ZAW* 92 (1980), pp. 272–5, and É. Puech, *La Croyance des Esséniens en la Vie Future: Immortalité, Résurrection, Vie Éternelle?* 1 (Paris, 1993), p. 71, whereas communal restoration is maintained by H. Wildberger, *Jesaja* 2 (Neukirchen, 1978), p. 995, and R.E. Clements, *Isaiah 1–39* (Grand Rapids and London, 1980), p. 16.

argued that the contrast with the wicked rulers in Isa. xxvi 14 is with those who are literally dead, "They are dead, they shall not live; they are shades, they will not arise; to that end you have visited them with destruction and wiped out all remembrance of them." However, since the imagery of Isa. xxvi 14 could similarly be taken either metaphorically or literally, this verse does not provide a decisive argument. What does provide a strong, if not decisive, argument in favour of the metaphorical interpretation of the resurrection as national restoration, comparable to Ezek. xxxvii, is the fact that the very next chapter, in Isa. xxvii 8, actually speaks of the exile: "By expelling her,[15] by exiling her, you did contend with her; he removed them with his fierce blast in the day of the east wind." Isa. xxvii 8 most naturally refers back to the distress referred to in Isa. xxvi, including xxvi 19. Moreover, as we have noted above, Isa. xxvi 19 and xxvii 8 have their sources in two adjacent verses in Hos. xiii, namely *vv.* 14 and 15, which further supports our reading Isa. xxvi 19 in the light of xxvii 8.

Now we come to the final stage of literary dependence in my argument, namely the claim that Isa. xxvi 19 has in turn influenced Dan. xii 2. This seems in every way likely. The language of the two verses is very similar, both of them referring to awaking (hiphil of *qîṣ*) from the dust (*ʿāpār*) in connection with resurrection. As we have already noted, Isa. xxvi 19 declares, "Your dead shall live, their bodies shall rise, the dwellers in the *dust shall awake* and sing for joy"; with this we may compare Dan. xii 2, which predicts, "And many of those who sleep in the *dust* of the earth *shall awake*". Now at last the language of resurrection has been "remythologized", speaking as it does of a literal renewal of life in an afterlife, and no longer simply of national restoration.

The view that Dan. xii 2 was dependent on Isa. xxvi 19 at this point is made all the more credible by the fact that Dan. xii shows other evidence of dependence on the book of Isaiah. The last but one word of Dan. xii 2, *dērāʾôn* "abhorrence", used of the destiny of the wicked in the phrase "everlasting abhorrence" (*l*^{e}*dir*^{e}*ʾôn ʿôlām*) occurs only once elsewhere in the Old Testament, namely in Isa. lxvi 24, where it is likewise used of the eschatological judgement of the wicked:

[15] Reading *b*^{e}*saʾs*^{e}*āh* for *b*^{e}*saʾss*^{e}*â*, as the following word *b*^{e}*šal*^{e}*ḥāh*, which is probably an explanatory gloss, suggests that we have here *b*^{e} + inf. constr. + 3rd p.s. fem. suffix. The verb is a *hapax legomenon* and is probably a pilpel form, and likely to be cognate with Arabic *saʾsaʾa* "to shoo away". Cf. G.R. Driver, "Some Hebrew verbs, nouns and pronouns", *JTS* 30 (1929), pp. 371–2.

"And they shall go forth and look on the dead bodies of the men that have rebelled against me, for their worm shall not die, their fire shall not be quenched, and they shall be an *abhorrence* (*dērā'ôn*) to all flesh."

Interestingly, there is clear evidence that Dan. xii was also dependent on another passage containing death and resurrection imagery,[16] namely, the fourth Servant song in Isa. lii 13–liii 12.[17] The very next verse, Dan. xii 3, speaks of the resurrected righteous as "those who turn many to righteousness (*maṣdîqê hārabbîm*)", language which clearly echoes Isa. liii 11, where the suffering and resurrected Servant is described as one "who makes many to be accounted righteous (*yaṣdîq . . . lārabbîm*)". The next verse (Dan. xii 4) then speaks of these martyrs as "the wise" (*hammaśkîlîm*), which seems to take up the verb *yaśkîl* used of the suffering Servant in Isa. lii 13, where the original meaning was probably "[he] will prosper", rather than "[he] will be wise". However, since a modern scholar of the stature of C.C. Torrey[18] was of the opinion that it was the root *śkl*, "to be wise" in Isa. lii 13, there is no reason why an ancient writer like the author of Dan. xii should not have thought the same. Isa. liii's idea of the vicarious death of the Servant[19] has also probably influenced the imagery in Dan. xi 35, "and some of those who are wise shall fall, to refine and to cleanse among them and to make them white. . . ." This interpretation of Isa. liii is clearly the source of the idea that the Maccabean martyrs' deaths were atoning in their effect, which we find in 2 Macc. vii 37–8; 4 Macc. vi 27–9, xvii 22 and xviii 4.

If the thesis I have put forward is correct, we must assume that the resurrection imagery had its ultimate origin in Canaanite Baal mythology, that it was "demythologized" in prophets such as Hosea and in the "Isaiah apocalypse" as a way of referring to Israel's

---

[16] R.N. Whybray, *Thanksgiving for a Liberated Prophet* (Sheffield, 1978), pp. 79–106, has argued that Isa. liii does not allude to death and resurrection but rather to imprisonment and release, but the piling up of so much language to do with death cannot be so easily explained away. In any case, the writer of Dan. xii clearly interpreted Isa. liii in this way.

[17] Cf. H.L. Ginsberg, "The oldest interpretation of the Suffering Servant", *VT* 3 (1953), pp. 400–4.

[18] *The Second Isaiah* (Edinburgh, 1928), pp. 252, 415.

[19] Whybray (n. 16), pp. 29–76, has attempted to deny that there is vicarious suffering in Isa. liii, but this seems a *tour de force*. He has no explanation of the use of the word *'āšām*, "guilt offering", used of the Servant in Isa. liii 11, other than to suggest that the text is corrupt (pp. 63–6).

restoration after exile, and then "remythologized" in the book of Daniel, where it again refers to literal life after death.

Assuming this thesis to be correct, we cannot claim that the Jewish belief in resurrection was derived from the Zoroastrians, as has sometimes been supposed.[20] One can, of course, see the attractions of such a standpoint: the belief in individual resurrection emerged in Israel only after the period when the Jews had been subject to the rule of the Persians, contacts with whom were friendlier than with the previous harsher Assyrian and Babylonian imperial powers. Moreover, although the problem of dating Zoroastrian sources is notoriously difficult, we do have indisputable evidence that the Zoroastrians already believed in resurrection by *ca.* 350 B.C. from the writer Theopompus,[21] who lived about that time. However, when we come to examine the Zoroastrian belief carefully, we find that it differs considerably from the Jewish notion. As has been pointed out by others, the Jewish sources repeatedly speak of death as a sleep, and resurrection as an awakening from it (e.g. Isa. xxvi 19; Dan. xii 2; 2 Esdras vii 32), whereas such a concept is completely alien to the Zoroastrians. However, in keeping with the ultimately Canaanite origin which I have postulated, it is interesting to note that we have some evidence that the Canaanites conceived resurrection as an awakening from sleep. Thus, Menander, as reported by Josephus (*Antiquities*, 8.5.3, § 146), refers to the festival of the resurrection of the Tyrian god Herakles (i.e. Melqart) as his ἔγερσις—an awakening from a condition similar to sleep. Also, we may note, much earlier, in the Ugaritic texts (*KTU* 1.19.III.45), Aqhat's death is referred to as "sleep" (*šnt*; cf. *qbr*, "grave", in the previous line).

The re-emergence of resurrection imagery in a literal sense in the book of Daniel and later Jewish apocalyptic may therefore be seen as yet a further example of the recrudescence of myth that has been detected in other aspects of apocalyptic symbolism.

---

[20] Cf. W. Bousset, *Die Religion des Judentums im späthellenistischen Zeitalter* (2nd edn, Berlin, 1906), pp. 577–94; M. Boyce, *A History of Zoroastrianism* 2 (Leiden, 1982), p. 193, and 3 (Leiden, 1991), p. 404; B. Lang, "Street theater, raising the dead, and the Zoroastrian connection in Ezekiel's preaching", in J. Lust (ed.), *Ezekiel and his Book* (Leuven, 1986), pp. 297–316.

[21] As reported by Plutarch, *De Iside et Osiride*, 46, Diogenes Laertius, *Proemium*, 9; and Aeneas of Gaza, *De Animali Immortalitate* 77.

ON THE DEVELOPMENT OF WISDOM IN ISRAEL

by

KATHARINE J. DELL
Cambridge

Those who work on wisdom are used to giving their papers at the end of the week.[1] Although there is no doubt that the study of wisdom is now firmly on the scholarly agenda, there is still the feeling that it can be dealt with separately, marginalized a little from the main business of the Old Testament.[2] It is not hard to see where this picture of wisdom as rather a separate, self-contained entity has sprung from. The main aspect of the literature cited in this regard is that it does not contain reference to Yahweh's self-revelation in the Exodus, in the promise to David or in the election of Israel as the covenant people. Rather, its theology is that of creation,[3] a doctrine not combined with the election traditions of Israel until a relatively late stage in its development.[4] Furthermore, its subject matter is very different from other Old Testament material: pithy, proverbial sayings, reflection on the meaning of life and on the relationship of the creator God to human beings in the context of retributive justice. The arguments are well-rehearsed, and yet I suggest that there has been in recent years a growing feeling of unease with this attempt to separate wisdom from the rest of the Old Testament. It has been noted that wisdom influence is to be found in a number of books, particularly in the

---

[1] Having said this, I am assured by the Secretary of the Congress, Dr G.I. Davies, that this was unintentional programming and I would like to thank him for his helpful comments on earlier drafts of this article. I would also like to thank Professor R.N. Whybray for his remarks and Professor J.A. Emerton for his kind invitation to read a paper at this Congress.

[2] R.E. Clements, *Wisdom in Theology* (Carlisle, 1992), discusses this in the opening chapter of his book.

[3] W. Zimmerli, "The Place and Limit of Wisdom in the Framework of Old Testament Theology", *SJT* 17 (1964), pp. 146–58, made the oft-quoted remark that "Wisdom thinks resolutely within the framework of a theology of creation" (p. 148).

[4] G. von Rad, *Old Testament Theology* 1 (Edinburgh and London, 1962), E. tr. of *Theologie des Alten Testaments* 1 (Munich, 1957).

prophets,[5] in some psalms,[6] and in parts of the Pentateuch (especially in Gen. i–xi). A natural-law type ethic has also been found in the prophets,[7] and wisdom seen as a biblical precedent for natural theology.[8] In this article I shall suggest that the reason wisdom has been marginalized is that a now-dated view of its development has been too dogmatically maintained, one which has made it sit uneasily alongside the main development of the religion of Israel as posited by scholars.

While most scholars work with the presupposition that religion develops over time, there is often little agreement about the exact nature of the development, its precise boundaries, direction and social context. When J. Wellhausen[9] posited his theory of the development of the religion of Israel there was a great deal of optimism concerning the possibility of being able to trace a development through the relative dating of the sources of the Pentateuch. However, since then, there has been increasing uncertainty about the developments for which he argued. As R.N. Whybray writes in his book *The Making of the Pentateuch: a Methodological Study*:[10]

> The truth is that despite the immense labour of recent generations in the fields of ancient Israelite religion and theology, it is still as difficult as it was in the time of Wellhausen to plot the course of the history of religious ideas in Israel with sufficient precision to pinpoint the moment at which this or that theological notion arose. Indeed, the Wellhausenian confidence with regard to this matter has given way to a state of great uncertainty.

Until recently, studies in wisdom seemed to be an exception to this statement as there appeared to be a remarkable consensus on the

[5] Notably on Amos, see S. Terrien, "Amos and Wisdom", in B.W. Anderson and W. Harrelson (ed.), *Israel's Prophetic Heritage* (London, 1962), pp. 108–15; and on Isaiah, see J.W. Whedbee, *Isaiah and Wisdom* (Nashville and New York, 1971).

[6] Notably the wisdom psalms whose identification is not always easy to decide; see R.E. Murphy, "A consideration of the classification 'Wisdom Psalms'", *SVT* 9 (1962), pp. 160–1, and J.K. Kuntz, "The canonical wisdom psalms of ancient Israel—their rhetorical, thematic and formal dimensions," in J.J. Jackson and M. Kessier (ed.), *Rhetorical Criticism*, (Pittsburgh, 1974), pp. 186–222.

[7] J. Barton, "Natural Law and Poetic Justice in the Old Testament", *JTS* NS 39 (1979), pp. 1–14.

[8] J.J. Collins, "The Biblical Precedent for Natural Theology", *JAAR* 45 (1977), pp. 35–62.

[9] *Prolegomena to the History of Israel* (Edinburgh, 1885), E. tr. of *Prolegomena zur Geschichte Israels* (2nd edn, Berlin, 1883).

[10] (Sheffield, 1987), p. 108.

question of how wisdom developed in ancient Israel. This is illustrated by a survey of any standard introduction to the wisdom literature from around a decade ago, such as J.L. Crenshaw's *Old Testament Wisdom: an Introduction*,[11] in which you will find the following widely accepted picture. On the level of social context, a threefold structure is advanced: wisdom is found at its simplest in the form of maxims and observations which originated in the family or clan, it became a literary and educational endeavour in the court and school, and then developed into more theological concerns in a wider cultural and intellectual setting.[12] On a literary level, there was seen by some earlier scholars[13] to be a development from simple to more complicated: from one-limbed sayings to multi-limbed ones, from maxims to instructions, although Crenshaw himself saw diversity in genre as the key-note of wisdom and did not raise the question of the development of literary forms in relation to each other.[14] On the theological level it went from being largely secular in its concerns[15]—finding patterns in life, drawing together unlike phenomena, to a gradually more Yahweh-oriented theology which saw God as moving from the limits to the centre of the quest to understand life, a pattern very much established by G. von Rad's work, *Wisdom in Israel*.[16] Another issue aired in Crenshaw's book is the relationship of Israelite wisdom to that of the ancient Near East, a relationship which is felt to be very close: Crenshaw assumes the literary dependence of Prov. xxii 17–xxiv 22 on the Egyptian Instruction of Amenemope,[17] he argues for

[11] (Atlanta 1981; London, 1982). These arguments were formulated in response to contemporary discussion amongst scholars, and Crenshaw's views have not remained static. In fact, in 1981 Crenshaw played down the role of schools in contrast to H.J. Hermisson and B. Lang and put more emphasis on the role of family and clan in the formulation of wisdom sayings, a stress he would now want to place more firmly.

[12] Crenshaw (n. 11), pp. 94–6. Wisdom's later development in wider intellectual circles was argued by R.N. Whybray in *The Intellectual Tradition in the Old Testament, BZAW* 135 (Berlin, 1974), in which he argued that the distinctions between groups of sages, prophets and priests began to break down, so that, for example, Jesus, son of Sira, could take on the role not just of teacher but of lawyer too, and the author of the Wisdom of Solomon could act in a more spiritual and priestly role alongside that of the wise man.

[13] E.g. W. Baumgartner, *Israelitische und altorientalische Weisheit* (Tübingen, 1933); J. Schmidt, *Studien zur Stilistik der alttestamentlichen Spruchliteratur* (Münster, 1936).

[14] This idea was rejected by some scholars, e.g. W. McKane, *Proverbs* (London and Philadelphia, 1970). For Crenshaw's discussion see (n. 11) pp. 219–22.

[15] Crenshaw qualifies use of the word 'secular' stating that "wisdom contained a religious element from the beginning" (p. 92), but then later when speaking of "court wisdom" he writes "the adjective 'secular' characterizes this kind of wisdom" (p. 94).

[16] (London, 1972), E. tr. of *Weisheit in Israel* (Neukirchen-Vluyn, 1970).

[17] (n. 11) pp. 98–9. This view was first set forth by A. Erman, "Eine ägyptische Quelle

a close relationship of theological ideas such as that between the feminine personification of wisdom and Maʿat,[18] and he supports the positing of schools in Israel based on the Egyptian model[19] and hence the picture of wisdom as the medium of education for all men of prominence.[20]

It would be widely accepted today that this picture is open to serious challenge. In the last ten years or so a different model has been emerging, which has led not only to the break-up of this picture but also to increasing uncertainty whether one can chart a development at all. In this article I wish to show the areas in which this standard picture has been challenged and to point the way towards a fresh approach to the development of wisdom in Israel, one which leaves open the possibility of a less linear conception of its development.

Three main changes in scholarly approach have occasioned the emergence of the different model for understanding wisdom which I shall attempt to outline here. The first has to do with social context. It is still held that wisdom may well have originated in the family—in fact, such a setting is now thought to be more appropriate for many proverbs than the court or school.[21] For example, it is argued that the references to father/mother and son in the proverbs should be taken at face value rather than being thought to represent teacher and pupil in the context of a school education. The family is now seen to have a very significant educative role, not just in the earliest period of Israelite wisdom before the time of the monarchy, but during the whole of Israel's history, with a particular emphasis developing during and after the Exile with the break-up of old patterns of national life.[22] Thus the linear development of proverbs from an oral context to a

---

der Sprüche Salomos", *Sitzungsberichte der preussischen Akademie der Wissenschaften*, Phil.-hist. Kl. 15 (Berlin, 1924), pp. 86–93.

[18] See B.L. Mack, *Frau Weisheit* (Düsseldorf, 1975).

[19] This was propounded most fully by E.W. Heaton in *Solomon's New Men* (London and New York, 1974). He argued for the growth of an administrative class in Israel to administer Solomon's new state. This group were seen to be largely separate from the rest of society, which accounted for the lack of interest in covenant and law in the wisdom literature. The interest of the sage was in practical, administrative, secular matters.

[20] This led to the quest for wisdom forms in other literature, in prophets such as Amos and Jeremiah and in the narratives of the Pentateuch. See D.F. Morgan, *Wisdom in The Old Testament Traditions* (Oxford, 1981).

[21] This has also been argued in reference to Egyptian parallels, see H. Brunner, *Altägyptische Weisheit. Lehren für das Leben* (Zürich and Munich, 1988).

[22] This idea is put forward by Claudia V. Camp in *Wisdom and the Feminine in the Book of Proverbs* (Sheffield, 1985), which I shall discuss later.

literary one has also been challenged—maxims would have gone on being used in an oral context through the centuries. The precise social context of such sayings is impossible to chart, and the quest for such a context becomes less significant, these sayings almost taking on an ahistorical nature, in that they are timeless and universal.

So what has led to this shift in opinion? A main area of new research has been into the proverbial traditions of other primitive cultures. The work of F. Golka[23] on African parallels has been influential in suggesting a return to older views that regarded wisdom as an oral folk tradition rather than as a literary product of educational schools.[24] There has been a corresponding move away from a strong emphasis on Egyptian parallels. It is now argued that the positing of schools of wisdom in Israel at the time of the monarchy is by no means verifiable.[25] This thesis was largely built on the seemingly remarkable parallels between Prov. xxii 17–xxiv 22 and the Instruction of Amenemope. Literary dependence was thought to be likely and along with this a correspondence in the educational, school context known to have existed for the Egyptian work. Against such views, first the point is made that, whilst there may be a more literary context for Prov. xxii 17–xxiv 22, this should not dominate our entire picture of the context of the book of Proverbs.[26] In any case, positing a literary context for parts of wisdom should not lead to the assumption that "literary" means "educational" or that "educational" presupposes an administrative class or court setting. There no doubt were educated people in Israel but precisely when and where to locate them in a historical setting is highly uncertain. We do not know the extent of written education, nor can we assume that it was the sole preserve of one particular group or class.[27] Second, the links with Amenemope

---

[23] *The Leopard's Spots* (Edinburgh, 1992). Studies of the oral patterns of non-literate peoples in general suggest that the origins of proverbs do not have to be literary.

[24] C. Westermann, *Roots of Wisdom* (Edinburgh, 1995), E. tr. of *Wurzeln der Weisheit* (Göttingen, 1990). R.N. Whybray writes of the proverbs on wealth and poverty "There is nothing in them to suggest that they were composed as tribal law or to form part of a system of education": *Wealth and Poverty in the Book of Proverbs* (Sheffield, 1990), p. 74.

[25] S. Weeks, *Early Israelite Wisdom* (Oxford, 1994). Weeks writes, "The biblical and epigraphic evidence adduced for schools seems very weak indeed and can certainly not support any hypothesis of an integrated school system. If the existence of schools cannot be proved, though, it cannot be disproved either: all we can say for certain is that it should not be presumed" (p. 153).

[26] R.N. Whybray, *The Composition of the Book of Proverbs* (Sheffield, 1994).

[27] One of the arguments used to support this claim was that a number of proverbs

are now considered to have been overstated, in terms of both content and context.[28] The assimilation of the Israelite social context to an Egyptian one is now thought to be an uncertain presupposition to make (see Weeks [n. 25]). Egypt was a far greater international power than Israel and the administrative and educational system was developed many centuries before Israel even came into being as an independent monarchic state. Whilst interaction of ideas between Egyptian and Israelite cultures is probably undeniable, this can be assumed without also holding that the institutions were the same. Furthermore, whilst E.W. Heaton's thesis of a Solomonic enlightenment in the 10th century B.C.[29] with an opening up of the administrative state serviced by a class of educated courtiers is an attractive one, it remains a thesis for which concrete evidence is non-existent. There is also some doubt whether a group of "the wise" ever existed.[30] In addition, the attribution of all the wisdom books except Job to Solomon could well be nothing more than a post-exilic literary device at a time when pseudonymity was becoming more important. Moreover, the reference in

---

concern the king, and it was argued that only courtiers would be in a position to speculate on the king and his position. However, Golka's work has challenged this by demonstrating in reference to African parallels that it is the commoner rather than the courtier who is generally interested in the king and his relationship to them. Golka establishes by reference to African parallels that this is the case in early oral cultures. As regards post-exilic interest in the king, we may recall an older view that placed Proverbs in the post-exilic period, one of the grounds being that after the Exile kings would have been the kind of people one might have met socially. Some proverbs are highly critical of the king and would not be obvious candidates for a close court setting, others moderate and play down royal power and glorification (e.g. compare the royal sayings in Proverbs to Ps. xlv which is highly likely to have a court setting). There is a tendency here towards generalization, for whole sections of proverbs do not mention the king at all—Prov. i–ix, for example, one of the more literary sections that might have been a more obvious section with possible court connections. See my forthcoming article in *King and Messiah*.

[28] R.N. Whybray, "The Structure and Composition of Proverbs 22:17–24:22", in S.E. Porter, P. Joyce and D.E. Orton (ed.), *Crossing the Boundaries: Essays in Biblical Interpretation in Honour of Michael D. Goulder* (Leiden, New York and Köln, 1994).

[29] (n. 19) building on von Rad (n. 4).

[30] Although Ben Sira refers to such a group of "the wise", we do not know how technical a term that was and at what date such a formal group might have come into being—it may have been a generic term to refer to people of skill and education rather than a particular group of people (see R.N. Whybray, *The Intellectual Tradition in the Old Testament, BZAW* 135 [Berlin, 1974]). The reference in Jer. xviii 18 does not afford conclusive evidence but, if adopted, would place such a group at a time just before the Exile at the earliest. Weeks (n. 25) argues that the thrust of this passage is to stress "counsel" as a source of divine guidance for the nation. This does not rule out its focus on a particular group however; cf. Ezek. vii 26 which has "elders" in place of "wise".

I Kings iv 23–4 to the wisdom activity of Solomon bears little resemblance to what is actually found in the main bulk of the wisdom literature.

This leads us on to the second area of change which concerns literary history. There seem to be emerging two bodies of opinion: those who believe, as I have just discussed, that the oldest proverbial tradition was predominantly oral, and those who see it as a literary tradition. E.W. Heaton in his last book,[31] where he is less dogmatic about the precise social context of what he terms the "school tradition", speaks of an ongoing literary tradition with its roots in preexilic Israel, basing his arguments largely on ancient Near Eastern parallels, but one dislodged from precise historical moorings. This area of discussion too is taking on a more ahistorical nature. Two issues emerge from this. First, we face the problem that we do not know when the transition from oral transmission to literary activity took place,[32] but what we do know is that there was significant literary activity from the time of the Exile, possibly from before it at the time of Josiah or even Hezekiah.[33] There was in the work of W. McKane (n. 14) and others a high confidence in tracing literary developments in the monarchy period in order to perceive development, but the recent work of Whybray (see n. 26) has shown this to be a highly uncertain exercise. Whilst we also have evidence elsewhere in the Old Testament of the literary influence of wisdom—in the prophets for example—we have equally good evidence that oral sayings found their way into what is now written material[34] and we would be hard pushed to divide oral sayings from literary formulations and to know which material was primary and which secondary redaction. We should not therefore rule out the possibility of a more literary setting for wisdom, but this may belong more naturally to a period later than the so-called Solomonic era. Second, we must beware of falling into

[31] *The School Tradition in the Old Testament* (Oxford, 1994).

[32] See R.N. Whybray, *Proverbs* (London and Grand Rapids, 1994), pp. 14–15.

[33] The reference to the "men of Hezekiah" in Proverbs leads R.B.Y. Scott, "Solomon and the Beginnings of Wisdom in Israel", *SVT* 3 (1955), pp. 262–79, to argue that his reign was a time of significant literary activity. Recently, however, M. Carasik, "The men of Hezekiah", *VT* 44 (1994), pp. 289–300, has argued that this cannot be maintained with any certainty. He concludes, "The citation of the 'men of Hezekiah' in Prov. xxv 1 could just as well be exegetical as it could historical . . . the court of Hezekiah can no longer be considered the first, fixed point in the transmission of wisdom literature" (p. 300).

[34] C. Fontaine, *Traditional Sayings in the Old Testament* (Sheffield, 1982).

the trap of generalizing about wisdom. Recent work by Whybray (see n. 26) has stressed the need to treat the different parts of the book of Proverbs separately. He argues that Prov. x 1–xxii 17 form the section most likely to have existed in an oral form probably from early times, but Prov. i–ix, xxii 17–xxiv 22 and xxiv 23–4 have a decidedly more developed literary cast and so are likely to belong to a more literary tradition. He posits that an affluent, urban, educated context can be found for these sections, whilst Prov. x 1–xxii 17 belong to a relatively prosperous middle class.[35] He sees the former as a development from the latter in linear historical terms.

The third area of changing thought is in the theological realm. For some time the word "secular" has been felt to be inappropriate as a description of the proverbs in the light of the basic religious presupposition of all the material.[36] It was largely the positing of an educational context for proverbs, in common with Egypt, that led to an emphasis on the material that is not specifically Yahwistic.[37] When this presupposition is removed, the possibility of a more distinctively Israelite content and context comes into play. Wisdom was defined by G. von Rad as "a practical knowledge of the laws of life and of the world, based upon experience" ([n. 4] p. 418 = German, p. 415). The basic form of the proverb enabled the wise man to observe an order in seemingly paradoxical phenomena. The keynote of early wisdom was thought by von Rad to be a determinism based on the idea of order—again in common with Egyptian wisdom—in which God took a minor role. He wrote, "For wisdom, questions of faith entered in only on the periphery of its field . . . it is reason, and not faith, that must verify and admit that pride goes before a fall, that a dish of herbs where there is love is better than an ox where there is hatred" and so on (p. 435 = p. 433). He did however stress, against McKane, the theological aspect of such wisdom. He continues, "What this wisdom teaching has to say only passes over into theology where

[35] Whybray writes "The tenor of these proverbs suggests that those who speak in them are themselves neither rich nor poor in the sense in which they use these terms, but are people of moderate means who consider that increased prosperity may well be within their means, yet are equally aware of the possibility of falling into destitution" ([n. 24] pp. 60–1).

[36] This has also been seen to be an inappropriate description of the Egyptian Instructions: Brunner (n. 21).

[37] McKane (n. 14) argued for example that the proverbs were largely secular in their concern and only later subjected to a thorough "Yahwehization".

the subject-matter contains some kind of pointer or reference to Yahweh, his activity, or what pleases or displeases him" (p. 437 = p. 435). So God gives a kind of divine verdict on human actions so that the avoidance of evil, for example, instead of just setting the wise man on the right path is accompanied by the idea that "by the fear of Yahweh a man avoids evil" (Prov. xvi 6). This assessment was not confined to the book of Proverbs. Narratives such as the Joseph and Succession narratives were seen by von Rad as literary gems from the Solomonic enlightenment in which human activity was at the centre of concern, with God directing the action at certain points.[38] The explicit development of a theology of wisdom was thought to have grown out of these early roots. So von Rad saw a transition from God on the periphery of wisdom to a gradual perception of God at the centre of it as wisdom itself became a means of revelation. He wrote,

> At a later date, not precisely ascertainable, there was a decided movement into the realm of theology. Wisdom teaching became the custodian of centralities of the faith and approached man's environment with the whole import of the quest for salvation—it asked about the meaning of Creation. . . . Indeed, in odd inversion of its origin, it increasingly became the form *par excellence* in which all Israel's later theological thought moved (pp. 449–1 = pp. 438–9).

Confidence in human ability was the starting point of wisdom, only later did the anthropocentric give way to the more theocentric as confidence in the wisdom quest started to diminish. This view of the theological development that took place in wisdom led to the late dating of Prov. i–ix on the grounds that these chapters contained the most references to God. However, even within this section there was found evidence of development: many instructions were seen as primarily secular, with first a religious element and second an explicitly Yahwistic element, notably the phrase "the fear of the Lord", being added.[39]

---

[38] The appropriateness of aligning these narratives alongside the experiential wisdom that has God at its limits has recently been questioned by Weeks (see n. 25), who sees the Joseph narrative in particular as maintaining the centrality of God's actions rather than human ones.

[39] R.N. Whybray, *Wisdom in Proverbs* (London, 1965). However, Whybray has recently modified his opinion that there is a systematic "Yahwehizing" redaction in Prov. i–ix, holding merely that there are some later additions to the material to make the religious connection explicit (see [n. 32], p. 25).

This picture of the development of wisdom was challenged in some quarters, notably by H.H. Schmid[40] who argued for wisdom being imbued, even in its earliest stages, by religious ideas. Schmid writes, arguing from parallel developments in Egyptian and Mesopotamian wisdom,

> Like that of other nations, in its earlier stages it [Israelite wisdom] presupposes a relationship between God and the world which later becomes an explicit theology of wisdom and incorporates more and more of the "official" religion. This development can be seen in Proverbs 1–9, post-canonical wisdom literature, and the LXX of Proverbs, but also within "old wisdom" itself (p. 145).

He argues that Israel never perceived the world apart from God, and finds that even in the most worldly parts of Israelite wisdom literature, where explicit references to Yahweh are few, there are many verses with a religious character. Furthermore, the phrase "the fear of the Lord" is not only found in Prov. i–ix; it also appears in Prov. xiv 26–7. In the earliest sections of Proverbs Yahweh does not simply maintain an existing order, rather he plans what happens in life: every event comes from him and what seems good to human beings may not seem so to God, hence accounting for the seeming incomprehensibility of his actions from the human angle. Schmid suggests that instead of moving from early maxims about life as represented by the proverbs to a more Yahweh-centred, cosmological wisdom, the development in wisdom went the other way, from being more cosmological to less so. He argues this in part in relation to parallel developments in Egypt and Mesopotamia, but then sees as distinctively Israelite a development into a greater anthropocentrism and a link with morality. He postulates a shift from the act-consequence relationship which has Yahweh in control to a behaviour-consequence relationship which involves personalization of the cosmological into "what will happen to me if I do not" (Prov. ix–xi; Sir. xxi; Wisd. iii–v). This anthropologizing of wisdom in itself leads to a hardening of ideas about right and wrong actions and paves the way for the later identification of wisdom with the law. He writes,

> Like the law in post-exilic Judaism wisdom ceases to be a way of relating to reality and becomes a reality of its own, fixed, eternal, static

[40] *Wesen und Geschichte des Weisheit: Eine Untersuchung zur altorientalischen und israelitischen Weisheitsliteratur, BZAW* 101 (Berlin, 1966).

> and absolute. The unity of the cosmos is no longer a perceived unity, but a theoretical, dogmatically defined unity, a matter of speculative theology, rather than of practical living in tune with the orders of the world (p. 151).

So von Rad saw a more maxim-based wisdom as leading to a more theological wisdom,[41] Schmid saw it the other way round. Is there any way of deciding between these different views? One aspect of von Rad's work that I have always found puzzling is that, when characterizing early wisdom as less theological than later wisdom, he still sees God as directing the act-consequence relationship which has an order of its own, as in the Joseph and Succession narratives. He also acknowledges that God is at the limits of a human quest which at times perceives its own limitations. He cites in this connection maxims which speak of the limiting of human possibilities by God: a human being may deliberate a great deal, but the right answer comes from Yahweh, as in Prov. xix 21, "Many are the plans in the heart of a man, but it is the purpose of Yahweh that is established." He argues that recognition of the limits to mastering life then led those who practised it into a more theological construction of reality—it was borne out of the failure of the human quest to discern everything, a tendency made explicit in Job and Ecclesiastes. But this quest was never perceived as being without God, as evidenced in von Rad's analysis of the Joseph and Succession narratives and according to the maxims which see God at the limits. I suggest that it is, once again, the presupposition that one set of perceptions has to develop from the other that leads to this confusion, and that a view that holds these two—the human quest and the God-given dimension—in tension may be more satisfactory. Schmid is also too tied in to ideas about linear development. Once one acknowledges that the experiential side of wisdom is not divorced from divine revelation, nor is the divine revelation outside a grounding in human experience, one can see the tension. However, this recognition of a tension does not nullify the attempt to make the distinction.

So where does all this leave us as we try to characterize the development of wisdom in Israel? One factor that has been stressed

[41] Interestingly, von Rad modified his sharply evolutionary view of wisdom's development in his later work *Wisdom in Israel* and saw the rational and the religious as less differentiated stages in Israelite thought (p. 61 = German, p. 86).

in recent scholarship is the importance of recontextualization. Material that may well have had a fixed character from early times finds a new relevance in a later period and is recontextualized in that context.[42] This can involve a shift from oral to written, or can reflect stages of written composition. In the area of social context R.E. Clements has recently suggested in *Wisdom in Theology* (Cumbria, Michigan, 1992) that the proverbs may well have found an important context at the Exile amongst those dispersed outside Israel and that wisdom received its decisive development at this time. He argues that old structures of cult, court and temple had broken down, thus creating a theological vacuum which was filled by the wisdom literature. He sees the Exile as a major point of development of the sayings in the light of a new universal relevance and a new practical and theological role. He writes,

> For a time wisdom held a unique key to understanding the new world in which the Jews found themselves among the nations (pp. 25–6).

He continues,

> Once prophecy had provided the *raison d'être* for the coming into being of the state of dispersion and the physical distancing of a majority of Jews from the formal temple cultus, wisdom laid out the basis for a more far-reaching rewriting of the Israelite world view. No longer was this to be drawn from the mythological traditions associated with the Jerusalem temple worship, but from the concept of a world order established at creation by God through the exercise of wisdom (p. 32).

Interestingly, Heaton makes this distinction too between a moral and intellectual school tradition and what he calls a religious and institutional "seminary" tradition attended by priests and teachers of the Law. He sees each institution having a different concept of authority. He writes, "The school tradition embraced the world including the whole creation, whereas the instruction of the seminary was rooted in the nation's past" ([n. 19] p. 186). These views have much in common with those of older scholars such as C.H. Toy who placed Proverbs in the post-exilic period on the grounds that a non-nationalistic culture did not exist among the Jews until they were scattered throughout the world.[43] We may note in connection with this Westermann's view on

---

[42] E.g. on Ecclesiastes, G.T. Sheppard, "The Epilogue to Qoheleth as Theological Commentary", *CBQ* 39 (1977), pp. 182–9.

[43] *The Book of Proverbs* (Edinburgh, 1899).

the increasingly universal context of Proverbs as it becomes a literary artifact. We may also take account of Claudia Camp's views on the possibility of a new post-exilic contextualization of Proverbs. She argues that rather than a hardening of ideas in the post-exilic period there was a reorientation of old perspectives in a new context which has the family at the centre of concern in contrast to a preoccupation with the cult. She writes,

> The themes and organization of the book of Proverbs thus reflect and support the renewed recognition accorded to the importance of the family in the kingless sociological configuration of the exilic and post-exilic period. Predictably, given wisdom's traditional emphases the orientation was toward the family rather than the cult as the critical source of social organization and the arena of God's blessing ([n. 22] p. 253).

There is little agreement as to precisely which concerns shaped the material in its literary form. However, that recontextualization gave to the material a fresh literary form seems likely.[44] If we are to speak in terms of a school tradition, as Heaton still does, it could well be a mainly post-exilic phenomenon, formulating in literary terms earlier oral material as well as generating its own literary masterpieces. It would be closely tied in to family education rather than a product of a Solomonic court, although one might want to look again at older views which found schools of wisdom in the Persian period for the youth of the Jewish bourgeoisie. However, evidence to decide this issue is sparse. For the earliest social context of wisdom we may have to take a lesson from modern sociological study that society is never represented by one view alone, and we need to be open to the possibility of parallel and sometimes contradictory developments, the precise boundaries of which are impossible to chart and date.

On a literary level, the work of Whybray (n. 26) on the difficulty of dating earlier and later material supports the possibility that the book of Proverbs may well have been essentially shaped during the exilic or early post-exilic period with regard to its written form. Although oral and literary material probably existed already in some form, it was at this time that there was the kind of context in which the book of Proverbs would have begun to take on its main literary character at a time of recontextualization. In terms of the development

[44] See G.T. Sheppard's views on canon-consciousness in *Wisdom as a Hermeneutical Construct, BZAW* 151, Berlin, 1980, cited by Camp (pp. 185–6).

of wisdom chronologically this would put Proverbs into closer literary, historical and theological relationship with Job and Ecclesiastes, books which attack the easy optimism of the just rewards theory upheld in Proverbs. However, it has to be said that scholars seem to have reached a certain impasse on the issue of the development of forms—recent work has demonstrated the precariousness of the enterprise and the uncertainty of its conclusions. We are perhaps better off looking at the final form of a work rather than trying to see it in terms of literary development. Prov. i–ix, for example, cannot be conclusively shown to be later than the rest of the book on purely literary grounds;[45] the evidence is more weighted towards the theological, but even then there is uncertainty over which parts of the material are redactional additions designed to recontextualize the work.[46]

We should now turn to address theological concerns. It is possible in my view to see wisdom in its earliest form as consisting of two elements, the humanistic, aphoristic wisdom which involved the quest for knowledge from the human side with God at the limits, and a more cosmological wisdom concerned with the affirmation of the creator God with links with much other Old Testament material. These elements are both likely to have had early origins and I see the two aspects as held in tension in the wisdom literature. I might mention here the views of L.G. Perdue[47] who sees cosmological and anthropological as held together in dialectic rather than the one having developed out of the other, a tension he finds particularly in the book of Job. It may be that we have been trying to force into a historical development theological presuppositions that are not of that nature and are essentially ahistorical. We should perhaps open up the possibility of a world view having existed that was not historically bound in the same way that the main salvation history was. When discussing creation, Westermann makes a division between the saving acts of God as time-bound within the acts of history, and blessing from God as a constant action and thus beyond the temporal sequence of history, describing it as "the power that furthers life, growth and increase, and

[45] Whybray no longer sees the possibility of dating instruction and maxim forms in terms of one developing out of another, or of one being later than another. He sees them as coming from different strands of the tradition.

[46] Camp sees the redactional elements as those creating a new context using the figure of woman wisdom, whilst Whybray argues that the redactional shaping is of a more explicitly Yahwistic nature.

[47] *Wisdom in Revolt* (Sheffied, 1991).

preserves creation from danger and damage".[48] B. Gemser[49] spoke of a picture of a horizontal and a vertical revelation, the two existing alongside and in tension and J. Léveque[50] of a contrapuntal relationship between the two main themes of wisdom (these being concern for a structuring of the created, and the existence of humanity) and the rest of the Old Testament. There is a strong likelihood in my view of a cosmology from wisdom which saw God in all things as creator, that existed alongside and in tension with a more maxim-based wisdom, which nevertheless uses images from the created world to illuminate human behaviour, that started from human experience and saw God at its limits. However, neither is ever conceived of apart from God.

I suggest that before the Exile the material can be more profitably looked at in this more ahistorical way than in terms of linear development, this being more feasible as an approach only as social context and recontextualization in literary terms become more clearly defined. I would argue that a two-pronged tradition of cosmology and anthropology clearly comes together in Proverbs with a weighting towards the human quest for wisdom. The Exile could have provided a context for the fixing of the material in a more developed literary formulation. This was followed in the early post-exilic period by the production of Job and Ecclesiastes, in part as a critique of the picture found in Proverbs. Job can be seen as representing the tension between the two prongs of the tradition, the dialogue between Job and the friends representing the limits of the more humanistic debate, and the relationship between Job and God representing the clash of the anthropocentric with the cosmological.[51] Ecclesiastes too illustrates both sides of the tradition: a use of proverbial wisdom, be it often to contradict, and yet an appeal to the cosmological God and his unpredictability in poems such as iii 1–11.[52] This tension can also be evidenced in

---

[48] *Der Segen in der Bibel und im Handeln der Kirche* (Munich, 1968), E. tr., *Blessing in the Bible and the Life of the Church* (Philadelphia, 1978). Westermann pursued these ideas mainly in speaking of the J narrative in the Pentateuch and of the way the J writer had incorporated primal elements with the revelatory acts of God in history.

[49] "The spiritual structure of Biblical Aphoristic Wisdom", in J.L. Crenshaw (ed.), *Studies in Ancient Israelite Wisdom* (New York, 1975), pp. 208–19.

[50] "Le contrepoint théologique apporté par la réflexion sapientelle", in C. Brekelmans (ed.), *Questions disputées de l'Ancien Testament* (Louvain, 1974), pp. 183–202.

[51] As argued by Perdue (n. 47).

[52] In my view the epilogue of Ecclesiastes illustrates the move of the wisdom tradition in a more anthropological direction with the first establishing of the connection with law. See K.J. Dell, "Ecclesiastes as wisdom: consulting early interpreters", *VT* 44 (1994), pp. 301–29.

the hymns to wisdom in Prov. viii 22–3; Job xxviii; Sir. xxiv and Wisd. vii 22–viii 2 in their movement between God's creative activity and human perception. The pattern of these poems shows a move from God to man and back again to man's need to respond to God for the acquisition of life (but often his folly in not doing so). The purpose of God is to reveal himself to human beings and the aim of humanity is to find life—this is mediated by the figure of Wisdom in these poems. They also show the complete dependence of humanity upon the cosmological God and support the idea that there was never a wisdom perceived without God.

This discussion leads us back to the two broader issues of scholarly interest with which I began this article. The first is the possibility that we should be questioning the whole attempt to find linear development in early Israelite religion and to relate that development to specific contexts. This is a preoccupation that we can trace back to Wellhausen (see n. 10 above), and maybe we have been too committed to it. On the level of forms, content and context, whilst there is certainly change in the course of time, pinning that down precisely is a vexed task, hampered chiefly by lack of evidence. The second area is to link up this debate regarding wisdom with the question how one can characterize the theology of the Old Testament in general. The question how creation thought fits into the overall theology of the Old Testament has gradually become for scholars a more central concern. Whereas von Rad (n. 4) saw creation as a late and subordinate part of Old Testament theology, explicitly linked with the redemptive acts of God in history only in exilic literature notably in Deutero-Isaiah, Schmid[53] saw it as a central concept inseparable from the concept of order from early times. Schmid writes, "the controlling background of OT thought and faith is the view of a comprehensive world order and, hence, a creation faith in the broad sense of the word—a creation faith that Israel in many respects shared with her environment".[54] One

---

[53] Schmid expresses this in developmental terms seeking to ground creation in the development of Israel's history, depicting the historical development of the conception of order in Yahwistic belief from the nomadic stage through the adaptation of Canaanite conceptions down to the development of Israel's own specific conceptions of order. He thought that there was a decline of the old political order at the time of exile and a crisis of the conception of order associated with it, conceptions going back to the promises to the patriarchs and the covenant.

[54] H.H. Schmid, "Creation, Righteousness, and Salvation: 'Creation Theology' as the Broad Horizon of Biblical Theology", in B.W. Anderson (ed.), *Creation in the Old Testament* (London and Philadelphia, 1984), pp. 110–11.

weakness in von Rad's assertion of the exilic development of a doctrine of creation was that it sat uneasily beside obviously pre-exilic creation passages, most notably Gen. ii–iii which can be shown to have close links with Prov. x 1–xxii 17 in its interest in human beings and their limitations. There is also evidence of psalms containing largely mythological references to creation, such as Ps. viii, xix, xciii and civ[55] (as opposed to exilic works such as P in Gen. i which demythologize the creative acts),[56] and there is the work of scholars such as S. Mowinckel[57] on the nature of the early Israelite cultus as an Autumn New Year Festival, a large element of which would be creation-based. In common with all primitive cultures, part of the faith of early Israel would surely have been one featuring creation ideas. It is the view of G. Lindeskog[58] that the exodus theme and the creation theme were two elements of equal standing in early Israel, the creation theme having largely derived from Canaanite origins.[59] Through this kind of work therefore profound links are being forged between the thought-world of wisdom and the theology of the Old Testament as a whole. It may be then that the time is ripe for us to reconsider other aspects of the theology of the Old Testament that have tended to be assumed to be late, such as the rise of individualism and universalism, both key characteristics of wisdom, in the light of the place we should give to wisdom thought in the overall progression of religious ideas and in a spirit of reviewing the linear developments to which we may have become overcommitted.

---

[55] G. von Rad in "The Theological Problem of the Old Testament Doctrine of Creation", *The Problem of the Hexateuch and Other Essays* (Edinburgh and London, 1965), pp. 131–43 = *Gesammelte Studien zum Alten Testament* (Munich, 1958), pp. 136–47, sees Ps. viii, ix and civ as "real evidence for an unadulterated doctrine of creation which stands on its own ground" (p. 144), although he does not consider them at length because they are perceived as on the periphery of Old Testament theology and possibly of alien origin.

[56] This text too can be seen as "wisdom" or as "wisdom literature", depending on one's definition of the terms.

[57] *The Psalms in Israel's Worship* (Oxford, 1962).

[58] "The Theology of Creation in the Old and New Testaments", *The Root of the Vine: Essays in Biblical Theology: Festschrift for A. Fridrichsen* (London, 1953), pp. 1–22.

[59] This has been supported since Lindeskog by evidence from Ugarit. Canaanite parallels include the idea of the kingdom of God, the theme of the struggle with chaos, and that of the mountain of God which in Jerusalem is identified with Zion.

WHAT THE BOOK OF PROVERBS IS ABOUT

by

MICHAEL V. FOX
Madison, Wisconsin

I. *At the heart of Proverbs*[*]

What is the book of Proverbs about?

First of all, is this a reasonable question to ask of a collection of collections of mostly independent sayings and poems? I believe it is, because, in brief, despite its unquestionable diversity and lack of overall structure, the book constitutes a meaningful textual unit, one shaped by a series of intentional acts. Selection is a powerful form of creativity, and the redactors who chose to preserve some proverbs but not others, as well as the scribes who added sayings of their own, all impressed their intentions on the material as it grew into a book.[1] But it was above all the author of chs i–ix who imbued the anthology with a certain conceptual unity by giving the older collections a hermeneutical setting, explaining what proverbs are and what claims they make upon us. This author is the one primarily responsible for the distinctive themes I will discuss, but (as indicated by the references below to the other collections) he was building on ideas well represented in the older material.[2]

---

[1] I do, however, leave aside Agur's words from my overview. The passage is an addition whose purpose, as I read it, is to repudiate the core idea of Proverbs, an idea that Agur defines by opposition. Agur asserts that while he does not have even human (let alone angelic) *bînâ*, and that he has not learnt *ḥokmâ*, he does have the more important "knowledge of holiness", which comes from God's word (vs. 5). According to Prov. ix 10, wisdom *is daʿat qᵉdōšîm* (cf. ii 5).

[2] Walther Zimmerli draws a suggestive distinction between the older wisdom of Prov. x–xxxi, which is supposedly unreflective and undogmatic, and the later, reflective or theological wisdom of i–ix: "In Prov. 1–9 ändert sich das äussere Bild, indem nun die zusammenfassende Reflexion über die Weisheit einsetzt, man ihre Bedeutung ganz grundsätzlich zu erkennen und zu rühmen beginnt" ("Ort und Grenze der Weisheit im Rahmen der alttestamentlichen Theologie", in *Les Sagesses du Proche-orient ancien* [Paris, 1963], pp. 121–38; at 131). The treatment of this theme in Prov. i–ix is well described as a "zusammenfassende Reflexion über die Weisheit", but it is found in the earlier collections and it is not reducible to the concept of wisdom as a personal being.

I will approach the question of Proverbs' central message by means of literary comparison, to determine the ideas in Proverbs that stand out against its background. Background is not the thing itself; it is the foil against which individuality is defined. Comparison shows us what *not* to take for granted, what *not* to expect.

For this task we require two axes of comparison. One is native, the collectivity of works of all types which were accessible, directly or indirectly, to the authors of Proverbs; this is *partly* preserved in the Bible. Works later than Proverbs, including Qohelet and (in my view) the wisdom psalms,[3] having been shaped under Proverbs' influence, do not in principle affect my thesis, but, as it happens, they rarely violate it. The other axis is international, the long-lived genre of Wisdom Literature, in which Proverbs is unmistakably rooted. I refer to the well-defined genre of instructions; I do not include the amorphous set of works commonly designated speculative wisdom.[4]

II. *Wisdom in Proverbs*

Unique to Proverbs is the concern for wisdom in and of itself, not only as the specific teachings of the sages but as a faculty and type of knowledge that transcends them.[5]

[3] The perimeters of the wisdom psalm genre have been demarcated with some precision by means of linguistic criteria by Avi Hurvitz, *Wisdom Language in Biblical Prosody* (Hebrew) (Jerusalem, 1991). Hurvitz identifies Pss xix 8–15, xxxiv, xxxvii, cxi–cxii, and cxix as sapiential. (Ps. cxi he considers sapiential on condition that it is paired with cxii.) I would include Ps. i because of its schematic wicked-righteous contrast, its praise of study, and its proverbial ending contrasting the two "ways", which is a basic topos in Proverbs. Other psalms exhibit isolated Wisdom usages or show affiliations with speculative wisdom (esp. Pss xlix, lxxiii, and lxxxviii), which is a separate genre.

Wisdom psalms draw on Wisdom phraseology, motifs, ideas, and sayings, probably using Proverbs itself as their source. One reason for this assumption is that sapiential features that are scattered in Psalms are concentrated in certain passages in Proverbs and often embedded in well-organized literary structures. Moreover, the linguistic features that mark the Wisdom psalms are common in Proverbs but unusual in Psalms. In a few verses it is possible to see how the Psalm is reusing a particular line in Proverbs. For example, the use of derivatives of *šʿšʿ* "play" (noun and verb) in Ps. cxix 16, 24, 47, etc. is a (somewhat artificial) combination of the unique and contextually natural reuse of *šʿšʿ* and *ḥokmâ* in Prov. viii 30–1; see ibid., pp. 100–2. The hypothesis of a common source, which Hurvitz allows as a possibility, is superfluous and unlikely, since the association of *šʿšʿ* and *ḥokmâ* is an integral part of the extended figure in Prov. viii 30–1, whereas it is by no means a commonplace in Wisdom Literature.

[4] For foreign Wisdom books mentioned and editions used, see the list at the end of the present article.

[5] The specific words of instruction are also called *ḥokmâ* (ii 2, v 1). There is a wisdom

Proverbs uses a number of near-synonyms to refer to wisdom—notably *ḥokmâ, bînâ, tᵉbûnâ, daᶜat, śēkel* and *lēb*. These all signify types of cognitive powers which may be put to any use the possessor wishes and comprise the faculty and the associated knowledge in one, with no necessary implication of ethical application.[6] Though Proverbs assigns ethical connotations to the wisdom words, this is not a lexical shift. Proverbs does not suddenly give the wisdom words an idiosyncratic or technical meaning; they mean what they always meant. What has changed is what Proverbs says *about* the concept they represent.

None of the wisdom words, not even *ḥokmâ*, is exactly synonymous with the word "wisdom" as now commonly used in English, for "wisdom" denotes the judicious use of intellectual powers in pursuit of moral goals and long-term goods.

I will survey five themes peculiar to Proverbs. The absence of these themes from other biblical literature makes it improbable that they were distributed throughout Israelite proverbial tradition and came into the collections of Proverbs by random gathering. Moreover, the virtual absence of these proverbs from foreign Wisdom excludes the possibility that they were unthinkingly drawn into Proverbs as components of traditional wisdom. They are the deliberate differentia of the book of Proverbs and signal its unique message.

These themes (together with other, less novel statements about wisdom and the wise) combine to convey a powerful and unparalleled principle: wisdom, meaning the entire range of intellect and knowledge, is the necessary and sufficient condition of ethical-religious behavior.

---

beyond the latter that the pupil is required to aim at: wisdom itself, *haḥokmâ*—an entity comprehending but transcending the particular teachings. This distinction is clear in Prov. ii, in which the father tells his son to begin his education by absorbing and storing up his words (vs. 2), but also to call to wisdom and seek it (vs. 3). The instructions the son is to imbibe are not yet wisdom in the greater sense, for ultimately it is God who "grants wisdom" (vs. 6). The apparent tautology in iv 7a, *rēʾšît ḥokmâ qᵉnēh ḥokmâ* "The first step to wisdom is: Get wisdom!", is resolved by applying the two usages of the word: in order to attain the faculty of wisdom one must first take in the particular wisdom teachings.

[6] Bernhard Lang says that "The Israelite . . . makes no distinction between smart and wise. *Ḥokmah* denotes both wisdom proper and smartness; both concepts have equal value" (*Wisdom and the Book of Proverbs* [New York, 1986], p. 14). The first sentence is a Whorfian confusion of semantic fields with national mentalities. The second sentence, however, is a valuable insight, *ḥākām* is often best translated "smart".

III. *Where Proverbs differed*

1. *Praise of wisdom*

It hardly requires demonstration that many proverbs extol wisdom and its benefits.[7] Praise of wisdom may be identified as the main theme of Prov. i–ix in its present form. One poem (iii 13–20) eulogizes wisdom at length, as does Lady Wisdom's self-praise in ch. viii.

This theme is to be distinguished from the praise of something else by calling it or its doer wise. For example, the sentence "with the modest is wisdom" (Prov. xi 2b) commends modesty rather than wisdom. This sort of statement *is* paralleled in other literature. In contrast, the saying, "the wisdom of the clever man guides his way" (xiv 8a), points to a benefit of wisdom.[8]

(1) In the Bible
Wisdom is never praised elsewhere in the Bible prior to Proverbs. Of questionable dating is Job xxviii 15–19, which calls wisdom incomparably precious but insists that it is accessible only if reduced to ethical behavior and piety (vs. 28). Qohelet occasionally endorses wisdom, meaning practical good sense, which he regards as helpful though fragile. Elsewhere various things are commended as wise, for it is assumed that wisdom, like wealth, is desirable, but no one isolates wisdom as an object of praise.

(2) In foreign wisdom
The Egyptian sages undoubtedly had an appreciation for knowledge. Their task was to impart a knowledge of *maʿat*, rectitude in speech and behavior.[9] The goal of the teachings, in Amenemope's words, is to "make the ignorant wise (*rḫ*)" (§ 30). Such statements, however, do not praise knowledge; they take its benefits for granted.

When the Egyptian sages do laud knowledge, it is almost always

[7] These benefits include prosperity (xxiv 3–4), pleasing one's parents (xxix 3a), honor (iii 35a, iv 8–9), power (xxiv 5), safety (iii 23–4, iv 6, xxviii 26) and life (iii 22a, xvi 22a). In sum, wisdom is more precious than any jewels (viii 11).

[8] This verse, we may note, ascribes *ḥokmâ* to the *ʿārûm* "clever man", a word that is ethically neutral and often refers to unscrupulous cunning.

[9] Cf. "I have caused you to know righteousness" [*bw mʿ3t*] in your heart, that you may do that which is honest [*ʿq3*] before you" (Pap. Beatty IV, vso 6, 8–9). S. Morenz, *Egyptian Religion* (Ithaca, New York, 1973), pp. 120–5, discusses cognizance of *maʿat* as a pillar of Egyptian religion.

with reference to the father's own teachings or to education with specific content, most often verbal and scribal skills.[10] The Egyptian prologues, when they are at all expansive (as in Amenemope), promise to inculcate particular virtues and skills (mainly effective speech) not to teach wisdom as such. Ptahhotep concludes with a lengthy encomium on the virtue of hearing, by which he means attention to the father's instructions (§ 39; lines 534–63). This is not exactly wisdom but rather a prerequisite to it.

Praise of wisdom is paralleled in Egyptian Wisdom Literature, but only skimpily, even when a variety of terms for wisdom and knowledge are allowed.[11] Ptahhotep says, "A wise man [*rḫ*] is recognized by his wisdom [*rḫt.f*], the nobleman [*sr*] by his good actions".[12] Merikare commends knowledge for the power it bestows: "The understanding man [*sꜣꜣ*] is a [wall? school?] for the nobles. Those who know his knowledge [*rḫ*] will not attack him".[13] This sentence may, however, be read narrowly, with reference to knowledge of verbal rhetoric, for speech is "stronger than all fighting".[14] There are a few arguable cases elsewhere,[15] but they do not add up to a prominent theme.

There is even less of this theme within the Mesopotamian Wisdom Instructions.[16] A true parallel is presented by Aḥiqar (lines 94a–95), who says that wisdom is precious to the gods. I will treat this passage below in conjunction with personification.

---

[10] For example, "The educated man lives off the house of the fool" (Anii, 5, 9–10); and "All you say will be done, if you are skilled [read *sšꜣ*] in the writings" (Anii, 7, 4). The teacher of Merikare urges: to "Open (the books) and read, that you may be come surpassing in knowledge [*rḫ*]. Thus a talented man [*ḥmww*] becomes educated [*sbꜣyw*]" (Helck X3–4 = P 3, 11–4, 1).

[11] The main Egyptian wisdom-words are *rḫ*(*t*) ("knowledge", "wisdom"); *ʿrq* ("skill", "perceptiveness"); *sšsꜣ*/*šsꜣ* ("skill", "erudition"); *sꜣr* ("learned wisdom"); *ḥmw* ("craft", "expertise"); *siꜣ* ("insight", "perception", "understanding"), with its variants *sꜣꜣ* and *sꜣt, sꜣrt*. There are also cognate verbal and adjectival forms. The distinctions among these terms are not entirely clear, and all can be translated "wisdom" or "wise" in certain contexts. The best discussion of this terminology is Nili Shupak, *Where Can Wisdom Be Found?* (Göttingen, 1992), pp. 217–29.

[12] This is preceded by "The wise nourishes his soul with what endures, so that it goes well with him on earth" (lines 524–5). This seems to mean that the astute man studies the example of his predecessors.

[13] Helck IX5–6 = P 9–10.

[14] IX2 = P 8.

[15] For example, "Sluggishness does not befall a man of understanding [*sꜣꜣ*]" ("A Man for His Son" I4). As I see it, this does not describe a benefit (non-sluggishness) of being an insightful man, but rather says that it is dull-minded to be sluggish. But even if we accept such debatable cases as praise of wisdom, they do not change the picture much.

[16] The instruction of Shuruppak concludes: "The gift of wisdom [is like] the stars (of

2. *Wisdom as righteousness*

Proverbs, of course, proclaims the virtues and rewards of righteousness at length, as do all Wisdom books. What is different in Proverbs is the mutual implication of righteousness and wisdom. No one would deny that the righteous are wise and that it is wise to be righteous. More problematic is whether a *ḥākām*—which, again, means smart and knowledgeable but not necessarily virtuous—is ipso facto righteous. The book of Proverbs affirms this equation and speaks of the righteous man's wisdom.

Most prominently, the Prologue binds wisdom and righteousness by presenting as the book's goal the teaching of "righteousness, justice, and rectitude" along with wisdom of various sorts (i 3). Indeed, "righteousness, justice, and rectitude" are identified appositionally with "the teaching of perspicacity (*mûsar haśkēl*)".

According to another programmatic discourse, Prov. ii, wisdom is tantamount to righteousness. When God gives you wisdom (ii 6), *then* you will understand "righteousness and justice—every good course" (ii 9), because "wisdom will have entered your heart, and knowledge will be pleasant to your soul" (ii 10).

The intrinsic ethical virtue of wisdom receives figurative expression in viii 6–9, in which Lady Wisdom declares that all her words are honest and just.

Proverbs places wisdom-words in synonymous parallelism with terms for righteousness. The "paths of wisdom" *are* the "routes of rectitude" (iv 11). Wisdom and righteousness entail each other in various ways. The righteous man speaks wisdom (x 31) and possesses knowledge (xi 9). The man of good sense walks straight (xv 21).

Proverbs is teaching that *ḥokmâ*, the same smartness and savvy that makes for success in practical matters, the same wisdom that is nigh to cunning and shrewdness (viii 12), is also a force making for virtue. Conversely, moral wisdom—which is the sages' real concern—yields practical benefits. This bold and, indeed, disputable assertion would be a banality if the words for wisdom had a built-in ethical valence.

heaven)" (line 278; Alster, p. 51). This probably refers not to wisdom generally but to Shuruppak's abundant teachings, for which the goddess Nisaba is praised in the following lines (279–82).

(1) In the Bible

Deut. xvi 19b sets *ṣaddîqîm* parallel to *ḥăkāmîm*. Ps. xxxvii 30, a reformulation of Prov. x 31a, declares that the righteous man speaks wisdom and justice. Isaiah, whose connections with wisdom have been long recognized,[17] comes the closest to identifying wisdom as a component in ethics.[18] Still, what Isaiah demands is not wisdom generally but rather a particular form of knowledge, namely cognizance of God's ways and will. Isaiah does not suppose that *ḥokmâ* or *daʿat* in itself guarantees rectitude (see xxix 14, xlvii 10). Qohelet pairs the wise with the righteousness in vii 16–17 and ix 1aα.

(2) In foreign wisdom

The Egyptian sages' intention is to inculcate knowledge of *maʿat*. But knowledge in and of itself is not a precondition or guarantor of this prime virtue.

3. *Wisdom as piety*

Proverbs regards wisdom as a personal relationship with God that is both emotional and cognitive. Wisdom starts from and leads to fear of Yahweh and knowledge of God, expressed in the thematic declaration, "The fear of the Lord is the beginning of knowledge" (i 7a; cf. viii 13a, ix 10, xv 33a, xxxi 30b).[19] Learning and intellectual growth lead also to knowledge of God (ii 5), meaning awareness of God's will (see, e.g., Hos. iv 1, vi 6) and the way he acts in history.

---

[17] On Isaiah's connection to wisdom see Johannes Fichtner, "Jesaja unter den Weisen", *ThZ* 74 (1949), pp. 75–80. While it is unnecessary to locate Isaiah in a class of "wise men", he has undoubtedly picked up a number of locutions and concepts characteristic of Wisdom Literature.

[18] See Isa. xxix 24 and xi 2. In the latter, the phrase *rûaḥ daʿat wᵉyirʾat yhwh* "the spirit of knowledge and the fear of Yahweh", does not exactly equate wisdom with fear of the Lord, but it does combine them in describing the righteous ruler. When Isaiah says that Judah is not an *ʿam bînôt* "a people of understanding" (xxvii 11), he is assuming that this intellectual failing is manifest in their moral one. The difficult xxxvi 6 promises wisdom, knowledge, and fear of Yahweh.

[19] Prov. viii 13a and ix 10 are probably later insertions, and the words *yirʾat yhwh* in xxxi 30b may be a replacement for *nᵉbônâ*, represented by the LXX's συνετή. Furthermore, given the suspension of i 7 between the Prologue and the first discourse, the possibility must be granted that it too is a later insertion, though it works well as an introductory motto. Thus the evidence for the theme of wisdom as piety may belong in part to a stage later the authorship of the poems in which it is imbedded. But these later scribes did not invent the theme and, in any case, they too shared in the composition of the book. A pietistic tendency is in evidence in the wisdom psalms and Ben Sira as well.

Since knowledge is piety, hating knowledge is equivalent to rejecting fear of Yahweh: "fools despise wisdom and discipline" (i 7b; and see the antithesis in i 29). The possibility of a holy fool, or even of a godly simpleton, does not come into Proverbs' purview.[20] The *petî*, "simpleton" or "callow youth", is not pious. To be sure, he *can* learn, but until he does, he is lumped together with fools and sinners (i 22, 32).

This theme belongs to a complex of ideas that McKane assigns to a later, "Yahwistic", revision of wisdom. I cannot on this occasion situate myself in relation to William McKane's historical schema,[21] except to observe that some of the key characteristics of the revision he postulates are to be found among the peculiar themes that my approach identifies and probably do belong to a later stage than the bulk of the proverbial material.[22]

(1) In the Bible
Ps. cxi 10a identifies piety with wisdom, using the maxim found in Prov. i 7a. Isaiah (xi 2), probably under Wisdom influence, joins wisdom and religious conscience, "the fear of Yahweh", in listing the endowments of the ideal ruler: *rûaḥ daʿat wᵉyirʾat yhwh* (but see n. 18). Job xxviii 28a defines human wisdom as piety. The polemical tone of the chapter shows it is not just confirming a self-evident axiom.

(2) In foreign wisdom
Some Egyptian instructions, particularly Anii and Amenemope, promote the virtue of personal piety, but they do not link this virtue to wisdom.

The belief that piety leads to wisdom and wisdom to piety belongs almost exclusively to Proverbs.

4. *Wisdom as obligation*

Given the ethical-religious virtues of wisdom, it is no surprise that Proverbs requires man to seek and acquire wisdom. In short, "Get

---

[20] Ben Sira mentions this possibility in xix 24.
[21] *Proverbs* (London, 1970), pp. 10–22 and *passim*, developing the arguments of his *Prophets and Wise Men* (London and Naperville, Ill., 1965).
[22] In brief, I believe that the turning point in the history of Israelite Wisdom is the introduction of the wisdom theme rather than with an infusion of religious concerns, which were important in Wisdom Literature from the start.

(*qᵉnēh*) wisdom, get understanding" (iv 5a). Note the global formulation—learn wisdom—with no further definition of the type of knowledge to be acquired.

Various proverbs exhort the reader to "get" or "take" wisdom (iv 7, viii 10, 33, xviii 15a, xxiii 23), to "understand" or "know" it (viii 5, xxiv 14), to "call" to it (ii 3), to "seek" it (ii 4, xviii 15b). Other passages proclaim the value of "finding" it (iii 13–20, viii 35). Put figuratively, people are obliged to answer the summons of Lady Wisdom (i 20–3, ix 4–5; cf. vii 4). Such demands may seem self-evident, but consider that there is a reasonable alternative: to require simply the doing of the right thing.

The obligation to get wisdom is also a bond of love. Wisdom and mankind are drawn together by a sort of eros.[23] Wisdom delights in man and seeks him, almost seems to need him. Man, in turn, must love wisdom (iv 6, viii 17a; cf. 21). God set the example by taking delight in wisdom as she played before him during creation (viii 30aβ).[24]

(1) In the Bible

While wisdom is universally (and almost by definition) esteemed as useful and valuable, nowhere else in the Bible or in foreign Wisdom is the acquisition or love of wisdom demanded or even advised, except so far as this is identified with the study of Torah in Deut. iv 6 and some wisdom psalms.

(2) In foreign wisdom

The Egyptian instructions include many exhortations to learn and obey the author's teachings and to study the ancient writings, but they never demand the pursuit or love of wisdom apart from specific teachings or types of knowledge.[25] Wisdom's value is regarded as instrumental

---

[23] On the role of eros in Prov. i–ix see, *inter alia*, R.E. Murphy, "Wisdom and Eros in Proverbs 1–9", CBQ 50 (1988), pp. 600–3. Claudia V. Camp, *Wisdom and the Feminine in the Book of Proverbs* (Sheffield, 1985), pp. 97–103, 275–8. Gerhard von Rad (*Weisheit in Israel* [Neukirchen-Vluyn, 1970], p. 217) aptly calls this a "geistige Eros".

[24] The MT's *wāʾehyeh šaʿăšūʿîm*, lit. "I was delights" (plural of abstraction), implies this. To be *šaʿăšūʿîm* is to be a source of delight to someone else (see, e.g., Isa. v 7; Jer. xxxi 20; Ps. cxix 24). This is brought out in the LXX's probably exegetical rendering of Prov. viii 30aβ, ἐγὼ ἤμην ᾗ προσέχαιρεν "I was that in which he took delight".

[25] A possible exception is Ptahhotep, whose prologue advertises the book as "instructing the ignorant in knowledge (*rḫ*), in the norms of fine speech" (lines 47–8). "Knowledge" and "norms of fine speech" might be appositional or additive (Egyptian generally uses

rather than intrinsic. Supporting this distinction is the fact that learning in Proverbs (and, subsequently, Qohelet and Ben Sira) is described as seeking wisdom. In Egyptian Wisdom Literature, the pupil need not seek, but only "hear" the teachings and "receive" them.

5. *Wisdom as a person*

In three passages (i 20–33, viii 1–36, ix 1–6+11–12), wisdom is personified as a superhuman female, intermediate between the divine and the human. In some other passages we see a partial or inchoate personification, in which wisdom is spoken of in terms appropriate to a human without being consistently depicted as such; for example, "Say to wisdom, you are my sister, and call understanding (your) acquaintance" (vii 4; cf. ii 3, iii 16–18, and iv 8–9). Since full personification is latent in the inchoate form, the figure of Lady Wisdom is best regarded as a natural literary development, an expansion of a one trope of several used to describe wisdom. But the development arrives at something qualitatively different from a trope. Wisdom's personification, especially in ch. viii, becomes a *mythos*. We may use the Greek term to recall Plato's use of the word: an extended narrative metaphor that serves as an explanatory model in areas where understanding requires the poetic imagination.[26]

The unforgettable mythos of wisdom, especially as it appears in ch. viii, casts its light throughout the book and almost imposes on the reader a certain concept of wisdom. The reader is taught to think of wisdom as an entity that, once created, is autonomous, atemporal, and unitary, separate from individual actions, thoughts, and minds, including God's. This entity manifests itself in the specific teachings of the wise and in the sage's knowledge and is the prerequisite of their being. Unbounded by space and time, it permeates space and time like a form of energy.

Much has been written about what Lady Wisdom represents, but on one level this is quite clear. She is identified explicitly as wisdom. If *ḥokmâ* meant something entirely different from what it means

---

no word for "and"). In the former case, the line is not promising knowledge generally but skill in rhetoric.

[26] "These myths are not allegories; they are not symbolic paraphrases of demonstration. They are poetic creations which give in the immediacy of an imaginative picture a sense of the atmosphere, the beauty, the validity of some human aspiration, some human faith, some human vision which the senses cannot touch nor the methods of dialectic prove" (Irwin Edman, *The Works of Plato* [New York, 1928], p. xxxii).

elsewhere, if it meant, for example, "Weltordnung" or "Ordnungsgeheimnis" (thus von Rad [n. 23], p. 204), the personification passages would be only deceptively connected to their context. Instead, Lady Wisdom is the wisdom that resides in people's hearts and in wise teachings.

Less has been said about *how* she exists, her ontological status. In my view, the wisdom that the figure represents is an archetype. It is the perfect and transcendent archetype of which all human wisdom is an imperfect reflection or realization. This archetype exists objectively, and not only as an abstraction or as a intellectual construct. This description may sound abstruse but, I think, it is actually close to the surface: transcendent wisdom has the same name as the human wisdom that is described at length in Prov. i–ix, but unlike the latter it existed prior to creation and thus outside time. It dwells in special proximity to God. It is not exactly a divine faculty, for it is something God "acquired" (viii 21), which he must have done by creating it.[27] It is somehow external to him, existing as the object of his thought, "before him". This archetypal wisdom now presents itself to man. The wise things human beings can learn, such as the teachings of Proverbs, are thus instances of a universal, atemporal wisdom and are a means to reaching or "finding" the latter.

(1) In the Bible

The Bible knows personification, such as of cities and peoples, or, occasionally, of abstractions such as of justice and truth (Isa. lix 14; cf. Ps. lxxxv 11) Wisdom, however, is never personified elsewhere.

(2) In foreign wisdom

In spite of the freedom with which Egyptians created both divine hypostases and literary personifications,[28] they never did this in

[27] The ancient debate whether *qānānî* in Prov. viii 22 means "acquired" or "created" seems to me moot. The verb *qānâ* unquestionably means "acquire" in the great majority of occurrences, and this is the only *lexical* meaning the word can carry into context. But there are various ways of acquiring something, and one of them is creation. This must be the *contextual* meaning of the verb here, as is confirmed by the parallel verbs in vss 24–5, which refer to the production of something new. One difficulty in dealing with this question is that English "acquire" connotes that the object was already in existence, but this is not the case with *qānâ*.

[28] This happens in the New Kingdom tale "Truth and Falsehood" (transl. Lichtheim, II, pp. 211–13). The brothers in the tale personify abstractions but are not gods. Their names are not written with the divinity determinative, and truth (*maʿat*) is represented as a male, whereas the divine hypostasis of *maʿat* is female. Falsehood (*grg*) is never a divinity.

Wisdom literature. The God Sia, "Perception", important in creation, does not appear in Wisdom Literature. *Rḫt* "knowledge" etc., the concept closest to *ḥokmâ*, is never hypostasized. *Maʿat*, contrary to Christa Kayatz's influential theory, is not the model for Wisdom in Prov. viii, and in any case the *goddess* Maʿat has no role in Egyptian Wisdom Literature.

A significant parallel to the personification of wisdom is to be found in the Aramaic Aḥiqar, lines 94a–95. This famous passage, if the usual reconstruction is correct, treats wisdom as a person: she is given rulership for ever. But this is just a passing metaphor, for wisdom is immediately spoken of as a treasure, precious to the gods and "laid away" (*šymh*) in heaven. It does seem that conceptually, and perhaps historically, this is a step on the way to Proverbs' treatment of wisdom. But full and consistent personification of wisdom remains one of the differentia of the book of Proverbs and its successors.

IV. *Proverbs' claims for wisdom*

Proverbs was the first to assert the intellectual foundations and prerequisites of piety and righteousness and to insist on the obligation to seek wisdom apart from any specific virtue. Putting it another way, one who wants to be smart or learned, a *ḥākām*, must embrace the ethical-religious wisdom taught by the sages. Any thinking that runs counter to these teachings is not so much a misuse of *ḥokmâ* as its absence.

Proverbs insists that human intelligence and knowledge is indispensable for individual and social well-being. The book shows no awareness of other sources of ethics, such as revelation or national tradition. It does not deny them or try to replace them, but it never looks in their direction. The divine and universal status of the wisdom teachings comes from their participation in the transcendent wisdom-archetype, which is ever in immediate association with God.

This idea of knowledge as the foundation of ethics is the core of Proverbs. It is *raison d'être* of Proverbs as a book, as a literary unit meant to be read as a whole as well as being dipped into for good advice. This ethics provides an intellectual framework for the miscellaneous pragmatic counsels and observations, such as "Wealth adds many friends, but a poor man is alienated from his friend" (xix 4) or "A gift in secret assuages anger . . ." (xxi 14a). Whatever the reason such sayings were originally collected, they now have a role in wisdom as a system. Their importance is not, as sometimes thought, that they provide empirical data contributing to the description of the world order (which is a doubtful scholarly construct),[29] nor even that they are conducive to social harmony[30] (some are not). The importance of these pragmatic maxims is that, being identified as wisdom, they manifest the transcendental power that produces piety and righteousness as well as practical benefits.

V. *Virtue and knowledge*

Why does Proverbs subsume all virtues in wisdom? Precedent shows that the sages could have told us wise, pious, and virtuous things to do and left it at that. Other moralists, such as the prophets, value wisdom only so far as it promotes righteous behavior and recognition of God's will. Since the prophets never demand wisdom as a virtue in its own right, we may conclude that they would have been satisfied with simple obedience to God's commands alongside faith in his governance of history. The foreign sages too sought to shape a moral, prudent, and tranquil character while placing little importance on knowledge and intellectual faculties in themselves, independent of their objects.

The idea underlying Proverbs' new focus is that morality is founded on knowledge. I would epitomize Proverbs' core claim by the Socratic principle that "virtue is knowledge" or "virtue is wisdom, either in whole or in part".[31] In other words, the possession of moral knowledge is a necessary and sufficient condition of being good, and hence of doing the good. This is not formulated theoretically; it is an attitude, a basic premise that comes to expression through a constellation of themes.

[29] See my essay, "World Order and Ma'at: A Crooked Parallel", *JANES* 23 (1995), pp. 37–48.

[30] Carole R. Fontaine, *Traditional Sayings in the OT* (Sheffield, 1982), p. 170 and *passim*, maintains that the promotion of *šālôm* in daily life was the purpose of traditional wisdom, to which many of the observations and sayings in Proverbs probably belong.

[31] Plato develops the idea mainly in the *Protagorus*; see esp. 352a ff. In Aristotle's formulation of Platonic ethics: "All virtues are forms of knowledge" (ἐπιστήμας γὰρ ᾠετ᾽ ἐῖναι πάσας τὰς ἀρετάς), so that knowing justice and being just must go together" (*Eth. Eud.* 1216b, cf. *Eth. Nic.* 1144b). In the *Meno* Socrates calls virtue both ἐπιστήμη "knowledge"

Ruled by this principle, Proverbs leaves no room for a knowledgeable man acting foolishly or wickedly. Again we can apply Socrates' words: "knowledge is a noble and commanding thing, which cannot be overcome, and will not allow a man, if he only knows the difference of good and evil, to do anything which is contrary to knowledge, but that wisdom will have strength to help him?[32] If someone does evil or folly, he must be on some level ignorant. He may be a moral pervert, an *ʾěwîl*, who confounds good and evil; or a dullard, a *k*ᵉ*sîl*, who is too lax and smug to learn what is right and wrong; or at best a naif, a *petî*, who lacks the moral discipline to discern and resist misdirection. Conscience (a word that etymologically and originally meant consciousness, awareness) demands the application of thought and presupposes moral knowledge. Hence intellect, when it follows its course honestly to the end, is a moral virtue—wisdom, in the valenced sense of the English word.

VI. *Proverbs' new path*

Through the development of the wisdom theme, the author-redactors of Proverbs introduced two profound innovations.

First, by exalting wisdom as the precondition and guarantor of all virtues, the sages recast the ancient Hebrew tradition of ethical and practical maxims to supply a Jewish equivalent of Greek philosophy, which is the employment of unaided human reason in the search for truth and the principles of effective and ethical behavior. I would not assume direct influence or suppose that the sages had read Greek philosophy, but, at most, postulate stimulus diffusion: a response to a vague awareness of the existence of Greek philosophical thinking, which would have been possible fairly early in the Hellenistic period. Here we recall an unparalleled aspect of the "obligation" theme: the love of wisdom, in other words, φιλοσοφία. We may note also that

---

(87d) and σοφία "wisdom" (88d). In the *Meno*, however, his own position on the issue is elusive.

The thesis that virtue is knowledge assumes that one does what he truly believes is good (Aristotle disputes this). Thus one does the truly good so far as he knows what this is. Knowledge of this sort must be of a deep sort, in other words, a conviction.

[32] *Prot.* 352c. Translation from Norman Gulley, *The Collected Philosophy of Socrates* (New York, 1968), p. 95. The quoted sentence is phrased as a rhetorical question calling for affirmation. Gulley provides a lucid discussion of Socratic ethics, including the "moral paradoxes" that "virtue is knowledge" and "no one does wrong willingly" (ch. 2).

early Greek philosophy was commonly gnomic and epigrammatic in form, and thus could seen comparable to traditional proverbial forms.

Second, the redactor-sages laid the foundation for a new religious attitude, one which makes learning—also called *ḥokmâ*—an intrinsically religious and ethical duty, whose fulfillment is a realization of a transcendent potential, in the sense that it exists on a plane beyond the individual and is superior even to humanity as a whole. This attitude is brought to fuller expression in Ben Sira's identification of Torah and wisdom (xxiv, esp. vs. 23) and is, in fact, already implicit in the wisdom psalms with their praise of learning God's law. This principle is further refined in the rabbinic tenet of *tôrâ lišmāh*, study for its own sake, according to which study of God's word, and not only its fulfillment, is an act and obligation of piety. In their search for knowledge of Torah, the *ḥăkāmîm*, which for the rabbis meant scholars of Torah, were embarked on a sacred task. But that was true of the *ḥăkāmîm* of Proverbs as well.

FOREIGN WISDOM BOOKS MENTIONED AND EDITIONS USED

Egyptian:

Amenemope: H.O. Lange, *Das Weisheitsbuch des Amenemope* (Copenhagen, 1925);
Anii (Pap. Boulaq IV): E. Suys, *La Sagesse d'Ani* (Rome, 1935);
Instruction of a Man to His Son: W. Helck, *Die Lehre des Djedefhor und Die Lehre eines Vaters an Seinen Sohn* (Wiesbaden, 1984);
Merikare: W. Helck, *Die Lehre für König Merikaṛe* (Wiesbaden, 1977);
Pap. Beatty IV: A.H. Gardiner, *Hieratic Papyri in the British Museum*, 3rd Series (London, 1935), pls 37–44;
Ptahhotep: Z. Žába, *Les Maximes de Ptahhotep* (Prague, 1956).
For translations see Helmut Brunner, *Altägyptische Weisheit* (Zürich, 1988), and (in part) Miriam Lichtheim, *Ancient Egyptian Literature* I–III (Berkeley, Cal., 1973–80).

Mesopotamian:

Shuruppak (Sumerian): B. Alster, *The Instructions of Suruppak* (Copenhagen, 1974);
Counsels of Wisdom (Akkadian): W.G. Lambert, *Babylonian Wisdom Literature* (Oxford, 1960), pp. 95–107;
Shube'awilum (R.S. 22.439): Jean Nougayrol et al., *Ugaritica* 5 (Paris, 1968), pp. 273–97;
Aḥiqar (Aramaic): J.M. Lindenberger, *The Aramaic Proverbs of Ahiqar* (Baltimore, 1983).
Statements about Sumero-Akkadian Wisdom texts are based on the translations of Alster and Lambert.

CHASING SHADOWS? THE QUEST FOR THE HISTORICAL GODDESS[1]

by

JUDITH M. HADLEY
Villanova, Pennsylvania

The worship of deities other than Yahweh in Israel and Judah has long been a matter of interest. Recent archaeological discoveries have reopened the debate on the worship of various goddesses in ancient Israel and Judah. Ever since the discovery of the Kuntillet ʿAjrud and Khirbet el-Qom material, interest in the worship of Asherah in particular has been building. On the basis of these finds, together with other supporting evidence such as the Taanach cultic stands and the numerous female pillar figurines from 8th century Judah, and especially the discovery of the Ugaritic material, many scholars now agree that the goddess Asherah was worshipped as the consort of Yahweh in both Israel and Judah during the period of the Israelite monarchy (for a full discussion of this material see Hadley 1994 and Hadley forthcoming, and the references there).

Taking this archaeological evidence as background material, the present study will briefly consider those biblical passages in which the "evolution" of the meaning of asherah can be seen from that denoting a goddess in her own right during the Monarchy period to referring to solely an object by the time of the exile. Then we will turn to a similar process that is occurring with the goddess Astarte, paying particular attention to the mention of Astarte in the book of Deuteronomy as a part of a common idiom referring to the fertility of the flock. Anat will not be considered, as she appears in the Hebrew Bible only in the context of personal or place names. Finally, the personification of Wisdom as a woman in the book of Proverbs and several deuterocanonical books will be briefly considered, in the light

[1] Parts of this article are taken as summary excerpts from longer, fuller treatments to be found in Hadley 1994, Hadley 1995, and Hadley in the press. I wish to express my thanks to E.J. Brill; Othmar Keel, editor of *Orbis Biblicus et Orientalis*; and Chris Scarles of Cambridge University Press for permission to reproduce those paragraphs here.

of the apparent attempt to eradicate the worship of goddesses such as Asherah and Astarte in Israel and Judah.

The biblical passages that best illustrate the "demotion" of the goddess Asherah to solely an object can be seen in those passages in the books of Kings in which Asherah is referred to in the singular, together with the parallel accounts in Chronicles where the term appears in the plural. For example, in 1 Kings xv 13 and its parallel account in 2 Chr. xv 16, Asa removes Maacah his (grand?)mother from the position of Queen Mother because she made a *mipleṣet*, "horrid thing" (BDB, p. 814a), for the asherah. It is then this *mipleṣet* which Asa cuts down (*krt*), beats into dust (*dqq*, Chronicles only), and burns (*śrp*) in the Kidron. As there is no mention of the removal of the asherah, scholars have interpreted asherah here to refer to the goddess.

The word *mipleṣet* occurs in the Hebrew Bible only in these two verses. What exactly it is remains open to speculation, especially since the word denotes a feeling of abhorrence to an unspecified object, and not necessarily the object itself. But since the object here is cut down and burned, which is the same treatment often afforded to the wooden cultic object of the goddess, it is reasonable to assume that *mipleṣet* in this instance referred to something similar to an asherah, and may in fact have been an (explicit?) image of the goddess.

The parallel account in 2 Chr. xv 16 mentions asherah in the singular, against all other places where the Chronicler uses the plural. The Chronicler has also changed the word order here, from *mipleṣet lāʾăšērâ* to *laʾăšērâ miplāṣet* (in pause). Perhaps we are intended to read "because she made a *mipleṣet* in the function of an asherah". To add to the confusion, the LXX has a variant reading here, which mentions Astarte instead of Asherah. This may indicate that by the time of the Chronicler (*ca.* mid 4th century BCE; cf. Williamson 1982, p. 16), the term "asherah" had ceased to mean either the goddess or the cult symbol associated with the goddess, and the distinction between the two ideas had become obscured. Therefore, when the Chronicler envisioned an asherah, the image brought to mind was only a wooden object. This may be the reason the Chronicler had a tendency to speak of the asherah in the plural. In the Kings passage, however, the combination of asherah and *mipleṣet* was baffling, especially if the Chronicler was not acquainted with the goddess Asherah in whose image the original *mipleṣet* was made. The LXX writer, as well, evidently did not immediately recognize the term asherah as referring to a deity, since the variant reading in the LXX refers to Astarte (for more on these and the following passages see Hadley forthcoming).

Perhaps a clearer example is to be found in 2 Kings xxi 7, and its parallel account in 2 Chr. xxxiii 7. Here, Manasseh places an image (*pesel*) of the Asherah in the temple. The first part of v. 7 reads *wayyāśem ʾet-pesel hāʾăšērâ ʿăšer ʿāśâ babbayit*. The parallel account in 2 Chr. xxxiii 7 states that Manasseh set up *ʾet-pesel hassemel*, replacing *hassemel* for *hāʾăšērâ*. The etymology of *semel* is uncertain, but as the only places outside the Hebrew Bible in which it occurs are several Phoenician and Punic inscriptions (*KAI* 26, 41, and 33 which has *smlt*), many recent scholars believe that it came into Hebrew from the Phoenician (cf. McKay 1973, pp. 22–3, and Schroer 1987, pp. 25–7, both of whom include discussions on the various interpretations of *semel*, and cf. also Dohmen 1984, pp. 263–6). It is evidently some type of image, perhaps anthropomorphic, and may be related to the *sēmel haqqinʾâ* in Ezek. viii 3, 5.[2] If so, it is interesting that the term asherah is no longer used, almost as if the goddess (or at least her connection with the statue) had been forgotten.[3] Thus it is not proven that the Chronicler knew that *semel* stood for a representation of an actual deity; it may have been considered as simply another "idol". Furthermore, in the summary of Manasseh's rule in 2 Chr. xxxiii 19, the Chronicler relates that Manasseh set up *ʾăšērîm* as well as *pᵉsīlîm*. It may be that the writer understood the asherah to be an "idolatrous" object like the *pesel*, and not a goddess. Therefore, when considering the comment in 2 Kings xxi 7 that Manasseh made a *pesel* for the Asherah, the Chronicler could not understand how an idol could be made for another type of idol, and so changed the text to read that Manasseh made both *ʾăšērîm* and *pᵉsīlîm*.

Therefore, it is possible to trace a process by which the term asherah in the Hebrew Bible changed from denoting a goddess and her image to merely an object.[4] The passages in the Hebrew Bible which mention

---

[2] Cf. McKay 1973, p. 22 and Ackerman 1992, pp. 60–1. Schroer believes that the *semel* mentioned both here in 2 Chr. xxxiii 7 and in Ezek. viii 3, 5 may be a statue of Asherah in the form of a suckling cow (1987, p. 41).

[3] McKay believes that the Chronicler may have referred to Manasseh's idol in this verse as a *semel* precisely because it represented some Phoenician goddess, probably Asherah, especially in the light of Dtr.'s reference to the asherah which Ahab set up (1973, p. 23). Williamson is of the opinion that if this is correct, then "the change probably already stood in the text of Kings that the Chronicler was following, since it is unlikely that he himself would have still known the precise significance of the word" (1982, p. 391).

[4] For the exact opposite view, see Miller 1986, who states "Either the feminine deity was implicitly absorbed in Yahweh from the beginning along with all other divine powers

asherah are largely condemnatory, and can be attributed to Dtr. or later (Hadley 1994, pp. 237–8). It may be, then, that for whatever reason, religious reformers in the time of Josiah and later wanted to eradicate the worship of Asherah, whether it was the wooden cultic symbol or the goddess herself. But during the centuries before this, as shown by the finds from Taanach, Kuntillet ʿAjrud, and Khirbet el-Qom, Asherah has appeared paired with Yahweh in most positive ways. But since the biblical text was significantly composed or edited by the Deuteronomistic school or even later, this positive attitude toward either Asherah the deity or asherah the cultic symbol is not immediately apparent. In fact, the author of Deuteronomy goes to great pains to point out in xvi 21 that the asherah standing next to the altar of Yahweh is an object, and nothing more. The use of *nṭʿ*, "plant" (used with asherah only in this verse) and of *kol-ʿēṣ*, "any kind of tree", help to underscore the physical nature of the object (and see below for a similar de-deification of Astarte in Deuteronomy). Evidently, this attempt to de-personalize the term worked, for a gradual shift in the understanding of asherah can be traced, right through to the time of the Chronicler, when it appears that the distinction between Asherah the goddess and asherah the cultic pole has become totally obscured, with the term asherah denoting merely some type of object, as the goddess Asherah and her worship was gradually eradicated.

A similar shift can be seen in the treatment of Astarte in the biblical text. Astarte is a well-known North-West Semitic goddess, known from Ugarit (cf. *ʿṯtrt* in *KTU; CTA; UT; TWAT*; Perlman 1978; Day 1992, among others) and elsewhere throughout the Levant, Egypt and Cyprus (*CAD; TWAT; KAI*; Driver 1913, pp. 62–3; Burney 1920, n. on pp. 58–9; Stadelmann 1967, pp. 96–110; Giveon 1967; Gray 1970, pp. 275–6; Delcor 1974; 1979; Helck 1983). Scholars are agreed that the goddess is mentioned in the Hebrew Bible, but in the altered form of Ashtoreth (plural Ashtaroth). Many of these scholars believe that this vocalization of *ʿaštōret* is a deliberate scribal distortion of *ʿaštart*. These scholars believe that this distorted vocalization reflects the vowels of the Hebrew word *bōšet* "shame" (Moore 1898, n. on p. 70;

and so had no independent existence or character, or the radical integration of divine powers in the male deity Yahweh effectively excluded the goddess(es). . . . In Israelite religion, of course, this was not a slow process that can be traced. The feminine dimension of deity is absorbed or absent from the beginning" (p. 245).

Driver 1913, p. 62; Burney 1920, p. 58; Robinson 1972, p. 139; McCarter 1980, p. 143; Soggin 1981, p. 39; Day 1992, p. 492). This term (bosheth) is further used in place of the divine name Baal in some personal names such as Ishbaal/Ishbosheth or Merib-baal/Mephibosheth, and may have been used in the divine name Molech (Burney 1920, p. 58; Robinson 1972, p. 139; Day 1992, p. 492). If this were the case, then it would seem that the scribes of the Hebrew text did not view Astarte (or her Hebrew Bible equivalent Ashtoreth) in a positive light (but see also Cooper 1990, who argues that ashtoreth is a natural Hebrew transcription of the Phoenician form of Astarte, and it [as well as molech] has nothing to do with bosheth).

The term Ashtoreth appears nine times in the Hebrew Bible as a goddess, three times in the singular *ʿaštōret* (1 Kings xi 5, 33; 2 Kings xxiii 13), the other six times in the plural *ʿaštārōt* (Judg. ii 13, x 6; 1 Sam. vii 3, 4, xii 10, xxxi 10). A further four times, the term appears in Deuteronomy in the context of an idiom (Deut. vii 13, xxviii 4, 18, 51).

In all three passages where Ashtoreth is mentioned in the singular, she is called the god of the Sidonians (1 Kings xi 5, 33), or, in the case of 2 Kings xxiii 13, the abomination of the Sidonians. The term *šiqqūṣ*, generally translated here as "abomination", basically denotes an "idol". This may be a further example of the idea of a deity being replaced by an object (see below).

The plural form Ashtaroth appears in the books of Judges and 1 Samuel, often paired with Baal, and usually in a negative, polemical sense. The two passages in Judges, ii 13 and x 6, appear in the Dtr. summary accusation against the apostasy of the people by forsaking Yahweh and serving other deities. Most earlier commentators take the plural form of Astarte here as referring to various local manifestations of the deity (Driver 1913, p. 63; Burney 1920, p. 58; Martin 1975, p. 35; Gray 1986, p. 245), although Soggin believes that in the language of Deuteronomy and the Deuteronomistic History, the terms "Baal and Astarte" are used as the embodiment of the "idolatrous" Canaanite cult, and are therefore more symbolic of polytheism in general, rather than referring to any specific deities (Soggin 1981, p. 39). Moore notes that in Akkadian *ilāni u-ištārati* is used to denote "gods and goddesses" (Moore 1898, n. on p. 70). The *CAD* also takes *ištaru* as a common noun, similar to the use of Hebrew *ʾēl* (see also Burney 1920, n. on p. 59, who notes that even Ishtar in the singular is used for "goddess", alongside *ilu* for "god").

As in the book of Judges, the plural forms of the name in 1 Samuel are seen as references to the local manifestations of the deity, or, together with baalim, as typical terms for male and female deities in general (McCarter 1980, pp. 143, 215). Of the four times Astarte is mentioned in 1 Samuel (vii 3, 4, xii 10, xxxi 10), twice she is again paired with Baal in a polemical fashion (1 Sam. vii 4 and xii 10), and is used in a general sense as a "foreign" deity in 1 Sam. vii 3. This attitude conforms well to the theme of Deuteronomy and the position of Dtr.

The last passage mentioning Astarte in 1 Samuel (xxxi 10) is in a very much different context from the others. Here, the Philistines, at the defeat of Saul, placed his armour in the temple of Astarte (Ashtaroth) and fastened his body to the wall at Beth-shan (1 Sam. xxxi 10). Many scholars wish to emend the pointing of Ashtaroth in the plural here, to the singular Ashtoreth, to reflect more accurately the goddess Astarte, and perhaps in the light of the LXX reading τὸ Ἀσταρτεῖον, "the Astarteion" (cf. Ackroyd 1971, p. 228; McCarter 1980, p. 441). A full examination of this passage is beyond the scope of this article (but see Hadley in the press); however, from this brief survey it is to be noted that all the references to the goddess Astarte in the Hebrew Bible are to be found in the books of the Deuteronomistic History, and all of them identify her as a "foreign" deity, and are polemical in nature. It may furthermore be instructive that the parallel passage in Chronicles to 1 Sam. xxxi 10, in 1 Chr. x 10, omits any reference to Astarte, and instead reads "the temple of their gods". Chronicles does, however, refer to a temple of Dagon, which is lacking in the 1 Samuel account. There are also other differences between the two accounts, such as the hanging up of Saul's body on the walls of Beth-shan in 1 Samuel, but the fastening of Saul's head in the temple of Dagon in 1 Chronicles. This leads some scholars to believe that there is more than one account of the death of Saul (cf. Ackroyd 1977, p. 5; Williamson 1982, pp. 93–4; Japhet 1993, pp. 226–8). Japhet believes the Chronicler omitted any reference to Beth-shan because to the Chronicler, Beth-shan had always been Israelite (instead of the D view that it was Canaanite until David took it; cf. Josh. xvii 11–12; Judg. i 27; 1 Kings iv 12), and so a "Philistine" temple in Beth-shan would have been an anomaly for the Chronicler, who therefore recorded an unspecified "temple of Dagon", somewhere in Philistine territory (Japhet 1993, p. 228; see also Ackroyd 1977, p. 5).

On the other hand, the Chronicler may not know of the existence of a goddess Astarte, at least in Israel. That the cult of Astarte continued into Greco-Roman times in the ancient Near East is not in question; but the Chronicler may not have felt that the goddess was relevant to any account of the history of Israel and Judah. Nowhere in the books of Chronicles is the goddess mentioned. Admittedly, this is an argument from silence, but even in two accounts where the goddess is mentioned in what may be a parallel account in Dtr. (the first in the Solomon narratives, the second in 1 Sam. xxxi 10/1 Chr. x 10 noted above), the goddess is notably absent from the Chronicler's account. Of course, this may in part depend on the Chronicler's use of Dtr. as a source, which is not proved for either passage, especially the Solomon narratives. Even so, if any reference to Astarte were lacking in the narrative material that the Chronicler was using for the account, then that might further indicate the polemical nature of Dtr.'s views. The question thus remains: did the Chronicler omit reference to Astarte, or did Dtr. add it?

So again we appear to have a case where a goddess is treated polemically and in a negative fashion in Dtr., but it is nevertheless still possible to identify a deity behind the references. And yet by the time of the Chronicler, all reference to that deity appears to be lost, or deliberately omitted. And, as in the case of Asherah, but even more clearly, in between these two positions lies the treatment of the term in the book of Deuteronomy. We will now turn to the idiom found in the book of Deuteronomy.

Astarte is mentioned only four times in the book of Deuteronomy (apart from a fifth time where it denotes a place name), where the word appears in the idiom *ʿštrwt ṣʾnk* in Deut. xxviii 4 and 18, and spelled defectively in Deut. vii 13 and xxviii 51. All four instances are in the context of blessings (vii 13 and xxviii 4) or parallel curses (xxviii 18, 51). (For a full discussion of these verses see Hadley in the press.) The blessing extends to all aspects of Israelite life, including a pledge that God will love, bless, and multiply the Israelites. The fruitfulness extends not only to the Israelite community, but also to their flocks and herds, and their grain, wine, and oil. Not only will the Israelites be fruitful, but Yahweh will also keep disease and barrenness from both people and animals (Deut. vii 13–15; and cf. Driver 1895, p. 103; Mayes 1979, p. 187).

Perhaps the most well-known discussion about Astarte and the fertility of the flocks in Deuteronomy is that by Delcor. Delcor mentions the previous interpretation that the idiom in Deuteronomy indicates that Astarte had an ancient representation in the form of a sheep. He mentions, however, that to date, nowhere in Palestine have any figurines been found of Astarte in the form of an ewe (Delcor 1974, p. 8). The whole question of the iconography of Astarte needs to be re-evaluated, however, especially in the light of more recent studies of the so-called "Astarte figurines". Many scholars now identify the deity represented by some of the types of female figurines as Asherah, and not Astarte. A full examination of the female figurines is beyond the scope of this study (see Hadley forthcoming, and Pritchard 1943; Holland 1975; Tadmor 1982; Keel and Uehlinger 1992). Rather, there are far more images of deities represented with caprids than with sheep (cf. Keel and Uehlinger 1992; Delcor 1974, Table 1 also notes a Greek bronze that shows Aphrodite [= West Semitic Astarte] sitting on a goat). Some scholars believe that the deity represented with two goats on a 13th century BCE ivory from Minet el-Beida is Astarte (cf. Pope 1965a, p. 251; *TWAT*, pp. 461–2; and for a depiction of the relief see *ANEP*, p. 464). This has led Taylor to surmise that Athtart at Ugarit (= Astarte) was particularly associated with the "wild goat" (1982, p. 103). However, as mentioned, the deity represented by many of these depictions is now open to question, or else they may just represent fertility aspects of the goddesses in general.

Nevertheless, this fertility motif goes well with the translation of "Ashtaroth of the flock" as the "flocks of your sheep" or "increase of your flocks". This translation as "flocks of your sheep" is the understanding of the LXX, the Peshiṭta and the Vulgate (cf. Delcor 1974, p. 8).

It may be that Astarte's connection with fertility of the land and animals, and her connection with sheep (although not necessarily in response to an ancient "representation" as a sheep), has led to the development of the idiom in Deuteronomy "the Astartes of the flock". Any association she had with goats would fit in well with this designation, since *ṣ'n* includes both sheep and goats. We may get further insight into this idiom by a brief examination of its "companion" idiom, "the Sheger of the herd", or the "increase of cattle".

The phrase *'štrwt ṣ'nk*, "issue of your flock", seems to be a "fixed idiom", which appears together with the idiom *šgr 'lpyk* (*šᵉgar 'ălāpekā*), "the increase of your cattle". The two terms are in parallel in all four passages in Deuteronomy and do not occur elsewhere in the Hebrew Bible (although *šgr* as "firstborn of your flock" appears in Exod. xiii 12; although this interpretation is slightly more nuanced, the basic interpretation remains that of fertility and increase of herds). *šgr* is known from the Ugaritic texts, also as a fertility deity (*KTU* 1.5.3.16, 17 = *UT* 67:111:16, 17; *KTU* 1.148.31; some scholars, however, contest Sheger as a deity, especially at Deir ʿAlla; see Frevel 1995, p. 459, n. 1557, for some of these). Astarte and Sheger are listed together in *KTU* 1.148.31, where they both are allocated a sheep as an offering (and cf. Nougayrol et al. 1968, p. 584; Fisher 1975, p. 305; Gibson 1978, p. 70). The use of *šeger* and *ʿaštārôt* here as common nouns is parallel to the use of *dāgān* in these verses as "grain". Dagon is a Canaanite deity, mentioned in the Hebrew Bible in 1 Chr. x 10 noted above, as well as elsewhere and at Ugarit (indeed, Dagon also appears in *KTU* 1.148, in line 26).

In this way, both deities, Astarte and Sheger, are reduced to merely their functions, and are distanced from any divine identification (and for both sides of the issue, see *TWAT*, cols 461–2; Loretz 1990, p. 87; Keel and Uehlinger 1992, pp. 166–8; Frevel 1995, pp. 457–8). Delcor asks the question whether perhaps the idiom started first, and then the deity grew out of that, in a manner similar to that of a hypostasis. He agrees, however, that the chronology of the attestations of deity and idiom necessitate that the deity came first, before the idiom (Delcor 1974, p. 14). This still leaves us with the de-personalized use of these names in Deuteronomy then, despite the presumption that the deities are known within the larger Palestinian area.

This apparent "de-personalization" or "de-deification" of deities is evidently common to Deuteronomy, which does not (as far as I know) list a single "foreign" deity by name in the whole book (with the possible exception of "Baal of Peor" in iv 3, although even in that context Baal probably refers to "foreign deity" in general). "Foreign" deities are instead called "other gods", or some similar general notation is used. On the other hand, deities such as Shegar, Astarte, Dagon and Asherah noted above are treated as common nouns. This may be an attempt by the author(s) of Deuteronomy to eradicate the worship of other deities by "reducing" them to merely their roles, and to then grant the control of these roles to Yahweh. In this way the power of the other deities is severely curtailed, and Yahweh is given dominion over them, and ultimate control over their previous jobs as well.

Evidently, this attempt worked, for by the late exilic period and later our Hebrew sources seem to ignore or be unaware of even the names of some of these deities. Thus we read in Jeremiah that the

Israelites made cakes for and worshipped the "Queen of Heaven" (Jer. vii 16–20, xliv 15–19, 25). Much has been written on this deity in recent years, and a full analysis is beyond the scope of this study (cf. Ackerman 1989; Koch 1988; Olyan 1987; Delcor 1982; Rast 1977; Culican 1976; Patai 1976). Many scholars identify the "Queen of Heaven" with West Semitic Astarte, although others have made their case for other deities such as Babylonian Ishtar, Asherah, and Anat, among others (see the sources above and the references there). However, it may be that the author or editor of Jeremiah knew of worship of some "foreign" goddess in Israel, but had no idea of her name, apart from a more general designation "Queen of Heaven". Furthermore, since the "head" goddess at a particular place was often called "Queen of Heaven" (cf. the designation on the stele dedicated to Antit [= Anat?] at Beth-shan in Rowe 1930, pp. 32–3 and Pl. 50.2; Rowe 1940, pp. 33–4 and Pl. LXVI.1; Kempinski 1975, p. 215; Mazar 1993, pp. 218, 220; and also Asherah as "Mistress of the Gods" at Ugarit, etc.), then it may be that the term "Queen of Heaven" refers more to a general role than to any specific goddess.

By the time of the Chronicler, this distancing of the deity and the job description has evidently worked well enough that, although the Chronicler knows that the Philistines worship a god called Dagon, perhaps the Chronicler is unaware that the deity Astarte was ever worshipped in Israel or Judah, and so in 1 Chr. x 10 we read that Saul's armour was placed in the temple to "their gods", no longer associated with Astarte. Thus the de-personalization of Astarte is complete, as she has moved from being a well-known and presumably widely worshipped deity in Palestine to becoming an abstraction of fertility in a Hebrew idiom, to total silence on the part of the latest biblical writers.

So where have all the goddesses gone? If Asherah and Astarte are no longer known as deities, and even the worship of the "Queen of Heaven" appears to be little understood, what has happened to the goddess in ancient Israel and Judah?

I believe that the answer may lie in some curious way with the figure of Lady Wisdom in the book of Proverbs as well as in the deuterocanonical books of Ben Sira, Baruch, and the Wisdom of Solomon. The personification of Wisdom as a woman is a much-discussed topic, and cannot be covered fully here, but a few comments are in order (for a discussion of possible divine connections to wisdom see Hadley 1995 and the references there, and also Lang 1986, who perhaps amongst modern scholars advocates most strongly the divinity of *ḥokmâ* in the Hebrew Bible).

The main texts which appear to give divine status to Lady Wisdom are Prov. i, viii and ix; Job xxviii (although Wisdom is not explicitly personified here); Ben Sira i 1–10 and xxiv 1–22; Baruch iii 9–iv 4; and Wisdom of Solomon vii–ix, although other more isolated passages in Prov. i–ix, Ben Sira and Wisdom also appear to give Lady Wisdom divine status. The consensus is that these texts in their present form are all relatively late (cf. Emerton 1979, p. 229), although the dating of Prov. i–ix and Job xxviii are disputed (see below).

Many suggestions have been made for the origin of the portrait of Lady Wisdom. Some look to goddesses, e.g., Egyptian Maʿat or Isis, Canaanite Astarte, Mesopotamian Inanna, or even to a Persian provenance (cf. Conzelmann 1971, pp. 230–1, and the references listed there, including Ringgren 1947; cf. also Lang 1986; Hölscher 1937; Rankin 1936; Boström 1935). Others see her as a hypostasis of God's Wisdom.[5] Conzelmann sees her not only as a hypostasis, but also as a Person (1971, p. 232). Still others prefer to explain the apparent divine imagery as a literary device.[6] In a very different vein, C.V. Camp, while admitting some echoes of goddesses, sees the image as an abstraction from women sages and counsellors (and biblical stories about them; cf. Camp 1985; 1987, pp. 45–76; 1990, pp. 185–203; and Schroer 1990, p. 45). Another recent suggestion has been advanced by M.D. Coogan, that the divine attributes given to Lady Wisdom in Prov. i–ix and especially Job xxviii (as elsewhere in the deuterocanonical books) is a legitimization of the worship of more "established" goddesses in Israel and Judah, such as Asherah (Coogan 1993; I wish to thank Professor Coogan for furnishing me with a rough draft of this communication). It is my opinion that the apparent apotheosis of Lady Wisdom in the biblical literature is not a legitimization of the worship of "established" goddesses, but rather is a literary

---

[5] Cf. e.g., Marcus 1950–1, pp. 57–171, who follows the definition of hypostasis as given by Ringgren 1947; and Whybray 1972, p. 50. It should be noted, however, that the term "hypostasis" has no agreed definition; cf. Cazelles 1984, p. 53. It apparently comes from Christology, in an attempt to provide some degree of individuality while still maintaining a monotheistic theology.

[6] Murphy, who believes that wisdom cannot be a hypostasis or distinct person because of the strict monotheism of the post-exilic period, may be the most vocal advocate of this view; see e.g., Murphy 1978, pp. 35–42; 1981, pp. 21–34; 1986, pp. 87–95; 1990, pp. 133–49; etc.

compensation for the eradication of the worship of these goddesses.

The passage in Proverbs which may give the best support to viewing *ḥokmâ* as a deity is Prov. viii 22–31, where Wisdom declares herself to be the first of all of Yahweh's creations/acquisitions/children, and to have been present when Yahweh established the heavens and set the boundaries of the sea. (For a full analysis of this passage see Hadley 1995 and the references there.)

Additionally, Prov. iii 19 indicates that Yahweh "by wisdom founded the earth; by understanding he established the heavens". Since Yahweh obviously needs Wisdom in order to create the heavens and the earth, then Yahweh must have been acquainted with Wisdom before the acts of creation could be performed. Although some scholars see this passage as poetic imagery (cf. e.g., Whybray 1972, p. 51, among others), others believe the passage identifies Wisdom as a divine or at least personified figure (see above, and Ben Sira i 1–9).

However, the question still remains; is this apparent apotheosis of Lady Wisdom a result of her actually being (or having been) a deity as such, or is it a literary device of some sort? To try to answer this question, we will now briefly turn to Job xxviii.

The uniqueness of the book of Job and its lack of historical allusions have created difficulties for scholars in determining a date for the book. Nevertheless, most scholars date it to somewhere between 700 and 200 BCE, with perhaps the majority of scholars placing it in the early post-exilic period.[7] As far as ch. xxviii is concerned, some scholars believe that it is an independent poem, or "Hymn to Wisdom", whereas others believe that the poem was still written by the author of Job.[8]

---

[7] For example, Pope 1965b, after an extended discussion of the previous suggestions for the date of the book of Job (pp. xxx–xxxvii), declines to give it a more precise dating apart from the 7th century BCE for the dialogue. Gordis 1965, pp. 216–18, places it between 500 and 300 BCE, with probabilities favouring the 5th rather than the 4th century (and see also the relevant notes on p. 361). Gibson 1985, p. 3, dates the book to around 600 BCE, but he "would not object if it were dated a little later". Janzen 1985, p. 5 believes that it was "written in the exile", and Habel 1985, p. 42, tentatively suggests a date somewhere in the post-exilic era. See the commentaries and the discussions there for more opinions.

[8] So Gibson 1985, pp. 188–9, who also notes that Andersen 1976 and Westermann 1981 hold similar positions; Gordis 1965, p. 278, and repeated in 1978, p. 298; Janzen 1985, p. 187, etc.; one notable exception being Pope 1965b, p. xviii. For a good survey of the various positions see Habel 1985, pp. 391–2, who himself believes that this chapter is the poet's "personal reflection on the debate thus far".

Vv. 1–11 describe the activities of humanity in the search for precious metals and stones, but the question "But where shall wisdom be found?" in *v*. 12 and the answer in *vv*. 13–19 lead one to realize that the most precious acquisition of all is inaccessible to human beings, and cannot be bought for any price. Even Abaddon (Sheol) and Death (who are personified here) have only heard rumours of it (*vv*. 20–2). Only God knows the way to Wisdom, and noted Wisdom's presence in creation (*vv*. 23–7).

Vv. 23–7 are perhaps the most instructive. Especially, the verbs *yabbîṭ*, "looks to", and *yir'eh*, "sees", in *v*. 24 may indicate that God is seeking for Wisdom, which has her own independent existence and origin. *V*. 23 may also suggest that Wisdom lies elsewhere, and that even God must "find" Wisdom by following a path that leads to her own special abode. Nevertheless, most commentators are reluctant to attribute divine status to Lady Wisdom.

So how, then, are we to view this personified figure, with seemingly divine attributes, re-emerging in the late exilic period? Perhaps the best interpretation of the apparent apotheosis of *ḥokmâ* in Israelite wisdom literature is that the gradual eradication (or assimilation into Yahweh) of legitimate goddesses such as Asherah and Astarte has prompted a counter reaction (perhaps even subconsciously) where the feminine needs to be expressed. Georgi follows a similar view, seeing a shift in Wisdom from an abstraction to a person to a heavenly character, taking her place at the side of Yahweh, which in pre-exilic times was filled by other female figures such as Asherah (at Kuntillet ʿAjrud) and Anat (at Elephantine). He further notes, however, that now Wisdom is not the wife of Yahweh, but rather the daughter (Georgi 1988, p. 246). Similar situations to this may be seen in the Hosea's imagery of Israel as the bride of Yahweh, and the "demotion" of Asherah into a hypostasis of Yahweh and the "reduction" of Astarte into a common idiom meaning fertility discussed above. Now, here in the wisdom literature, can be seen a female figure of Lady Wisdom with seemingly divine attributes, but still very much "under the thumb" of Yahweh, which may be an attempt at satisfying this apparent need for the feminine to be represented in the deity.

Where have all the goddesses gone? The shadow of the goddess looms large over the biblical text, but further light to be shed on the topic will only bring the shadows into greater relief, rather than dispel them altogether as the biblical editors may have intended.

WORKS CITED

Ackerman, S., "'And the Women Knead Dough': the Worship of the Queen of Heaven in Sixth-century Judah", in P.L. Day (ed.), *Gender and Difference in Ancient Israel* (Minneapolis, 1989), pp. 109–24.

———, *Under Every Green Tree: Popular Religion in Sixth-Century Judah* (Atlanta, 1992).

Ackroyd, P.R., "The Chronicler as Exegete", *JSOT* 2 (1977), pp. 2–32.

———, *The First Book of Samuel* (Cambridge, 1971).

Andersen, F.I., *Job* (London, 1976).

Boström, G., *Proverbia Studien: die Weisheit und das fremde Weib in Spr. 1–9* (Lund, 1935).

Brown, F., Driver, S.R., and Briggs, C.A., *A Hebrew and English Lexicon of the Old Testament* (BDB) (Oxford, 1907).

Burney, C.F., *The Book of Judges* (London, 1920).

Camp, C.V., "The Female Sage in Ancient Israel and in the Biblical Wisdom Literature", in J.G. Gammie and L.G. Perdue (ed.), *The Sage in Israel and the Ancient Near East* (Winona Lake, 1990), pp. 185–203.

———, *Wisdom and the Feminine in the Book of Proverbs* (Sheffield, 1985).

———, "Woman Wisdom as Root Metaphor: A Theological Consideration", in K.G. Hoglund et al. (ed.), *The Listening Heart: Essays in Wisdom and the Psalms in Honor of Roland E. Murphy* (Sheffield, 1987), pp. 45–76.

Cazelles, H., "La Sagesse de Proverbes 8, 22: Peut-elle être considérée comme une hypostase?", in A.M. Triacca and A. Pistoia (ed.), *Trinité et Liturgie* (Rome, 1984), pp. 51–7.

Conzelmann, H., "The Mother of Wisdom", in J.M. Robinson (ed.), *The Future of Our Religious Past: Essays in Honor of Rudolf Bultmann* (New York, 1971), pp. 230–43.

Coogan, M.D., "The Goddess Wisdom—'Where can she be found?': Literary Reflexes of Popular Religion", communication given at the Society of Biblical Literature Meetings in Washington D.C., November 1993.

Cooper, A., "A Note on the Vocalization of *ʿaštōret*", *ZAW* 102 (1990), pp. 98–100.

Culican, W., "A Votive Model from the Sea", *PEQ* 108 (1976), pp. 119–23.

Day, J., "Ashtoreth", in D.N. Freedman (ed.), *The Anchor Bible Dictionary* 1 (New York, 1992), pp. 491–4.

Delcor, M., "Astarté et la fécondité des troupeaux en Deut. 7,13 et parallèles", *UF* 6 (1974), pp. 7–14.

———, "Le culte de la 'Reine du Ciel' selon Jer. 7,18; 44,17–19,25 et ses survivances", in W.C. Delsman et al. (ed.), *Von Kanaan bis Kerala* (Kevelaer and Neukirchen-Vluyn, 1982), pp. 101–22.

———, "Le personnel du temple d'Astarté à Kition d'après une tablette phénicienne (cis 86 A et B)", *UF* 11 (1979), pp. 147–64.

Dietrich, M., Loretz, O., and Sanmartín, J., *Die keilalphabetischen Texte aus Ugarit* 1 (*KTU*) (Kevelaer and Neukirchen-Vluyn, 1976).

Dohmen, C., "Heisst Semel 'Bild, Statue'?", *ZAW* 96 (1984), pp. 263–6.

Donner, H., and Röllig, W., *Kanaanäische und Aramäische Inschriften* (*KAI*), (Wiesbaden, 1962–4, 2nd edn, 1966–9).

Driver, S.R., *A Critical and Exegetical Commentary on Deuteronomy* (Edinburgh and New York, 1895).

———, *Notes on the Hebrew Text and the Topography of the Books of Samuel* (2nd edn, Oxford, 1913).

Emerton, J.A., "Wisdom", in G.W. Anderson (ed.), *Tradition and Interpretation: Essays by Members of the Society for Old Testament Study* (Oxford, 1979), pp. 214–37.

Fisher, L.R. (ed.), *Ras Shamra Parallels*, 3 vols (Rome, 1972, 1975, 1981).

Frevel, C., *Aschera und der Ausschließlichkeitsanspruch YHWHs* (Weinheim, 1995).

Gelb, I.J., Landsberger, B., and Oppenheim, A.L. (ed.), *The Assyrian Dictionary (CAD)* (Chicago, 1956–).
Georgi, D., "Frau Weisheit oder das Recht auf Freiheit als schöpferische Kraft", in L. Siegele-Wenschkewitz (ed.), *Verdrängte Vergangenheit, die uns bedrängt: Feministische Theologie in der Verantwortung für die Geschichte* (München, 1988), pp. 243–76.
Gibson, J.C.L., *Canaanite Myths and Legends* (2nd edn, Edinburgh, 1978).
———, *Job* (Edinburgh and Philadelphia, 1985).
Giveon, R., "Ptah and Astarte on a Seal from Accho", in G. Rinaldi and G. Buccellati (ed.), *Studi sull'oriente e la Bibbia* (Genova, 1967), pp. 147–53.
Gordis, R., *The Book of God and Man: A Study of Job* (Chicago and London, 1965).
———, *The Book of Job: Commentary, New Translation and Special Studies* (New York, 1978).
Gordon, C.H., *Ugaritic Textbook* (*UT*), (Rome, 1965).
Gray, J., *Joshua, Judges, Ruth* (Grand Rapids and Basingstoke, 1986).
———, *I & II Kings: A Commentary* (2nd edn, London, 1970).
Habel, N.C., *The Book of Job* (London and Philadelphia, 1985).
Hadley, J.M., *Evidence for a Hebrew Goddess: The Cult of Asherah in Ancient Israel and Judah* (Cambridge, forthcoming).
———, "The Fertility of the Flock?: The De-personalization of Astarte in the Old Testament", in B. Becking and M. Dijkstra (ed.), *On Reading Prophetic Texts: Exegetical Essays in Memory of Fokkelien van Dijk-Hemmes* (Leiden, 1996), pp. 115–33.
———, "Wisdom and the goddess", in J. Day, R.P. Gordon and H.G.M. Williamson (ed.), *Wisdom in Ancient Israel: Essays in Honour of J.A. Emerton* (Cambridge, 1995), pp. 234–43.
———, "Yahweh and 'his Asherah': Archaeological and Textual Evidence for the Cult of the Goddess", in W. Dietrich and M.A. Klopfenstein (ed.), *Ein Gott allein?: JHWH—Verehrung und biblischer Monotheismus im Kontext der israelitischen und altorientalischen Religionsgeschichte*, OBO 139 (Freiburg, Schweiz; and Göttingen, 1994), pp. 235–68.
Helck, W., "Zur Herkunft der Erzählung des sog. 'Astartepapyrus'", in M. Görg (ed.), *Fontes atque pontes* (Wiesbaden, 1983), pp. 215–23.
Herdner, A., *Corpus des tablettes en cunéiformes alphabétiques* (*CTA*), 2 vols, Mission de Ras Shamra 10 (Paris, 1963).
Holland, T.A., *A Typological and Archaeological Study of Human and Animal Representations in the Plastic Art of Palestine During the Iron Age* (D.Phil. dissertation, Oxford, 1975).
Hölscher, G., *Das Buch Hiob* (Tübingen, 1937).
Janzen, J.G., *Job* (Atlanta, 1985).
Japhet, S., *I & II Chronicles* (London and Louisville, 1993).
Keel, O., and Uehlinger, C., *Göttinnen, Götter und Gottessymbole* (Freiburg, 1992).
Kempinski, A., "Beth-Shean: Late Bronze and Iron Age Temples", in M. Avi-Yonah (ed.), *Encyclopedia of Archaeological Excavations in the Holy Land* 1 (London and Jerusalem, 1975), pp. 213–15.
Koch, K., "Aschera als Himmelskönigin in Jerusalem", *UF* 20 (1988), pp. 97–120.
Lang, B., *Wisdom and the Book of Proverbs: An Israelite Goddess Redefined* (New York, 1986).
Loretz, O., *Ugarit und die Bibel: Kanaanäische Götter und Religionen im Alten Testament* (Darmstadt, 1990).
Marcus, R., "On Biblical Hypostases of Wisdom", *HUCA* 23 (1950–1), pp. 157–71.
Martin, J.D., *The Book of Judges* (Cambridge, 1975).
Mayes, A.D.H., *Deuteronomy*, (London and Grand Rapids, 1979).
Mazar, A., "Beth-Shean", in E. Stern (ed.), *The New Encyclopedia of Archaeological Excavations in the Holy Land* 1 (Jerusalem, 1993), pp. 214–23.

McCarter, P.K., *1 Samuel: A New Translation with Introduction, Notes & Commentary*, (Garden City, 1980).
McKay, J.W., *Religion in Judah Under the Assyrians: 732–609 BC* (London, 1973).
Miller, P.D., "The Absence of the Goddess in Israelite Religion", *Hebrew Annual Review* 10 (1986), pp. 239–48.
Moore, G.F., *A Critical and Exegetical Commentary on Judges* (Edinburgh, 1895).
Müller, H.P., "'štrt", *Theologisches Wörterbuch zum Alten Testament* (*TWAT*) 6 (Stuttgart, 1989), cols 453–63.
Murphy, R.E., "Hebrew Wisdom", *JAOS* 101 (1981), pp. 21–34.
———, "Proverbs and Theological Exegesis", in D.G. Miller (ed.), *The Hermeneutical Quest* (Allison Park, Pennsylvania, 1986), pp. 87–95.
———, *The Tree of Life: An Exploration of Biblical Wisdom Literature* (New York, 1990).
———, "Wisdom—Theses and Hypotheses", in J.G. Gammie et al. (ed.), *Israelite Wisdom: Theological and Literary Essays in Honor of Samuel Terrien* (Missoula, 1978), pp. 35–42.
Nougayrol, T., Laroche, E., Virolleaud, C., and Schaeffer, C.F.A., *Ugaritica V*, Mission de Ras Shamra 16 (Paris, 1968).
Olyan, S.M., "Some Observations Concerning the Identity of the Queen of Heaven", *UF* 19 (1987), pp. 161–74.
Patai, R., "The Goddess Cult in the Hebrew-Jewish Religion", in A. Bharati (ed.), *The Realm of the Extra-Human* (The Hague, 1976), pp. 197–210.
Perlman, A.L., *Asherah and Astarte in the Old Testament and Ugaritic Literatures* (Ph.D. dissertation, Berkeley, 1978).
Pope, M.H., "'Aṯtart, ʿAštart, Astarte", in H.W. Haussig (ed.), *Wörterbuch der Mythologie* (Stuttgart, 1965a), pp. 250–2.
———, *Job* (Garden City, 1965b).
Pritchard, J.B. (ed.), *The Ancient Near East in Pictures* (*ANEP*) (2nd edn with Supplement) (Princeton, 1969).
———, *Palestinian Figurines in Relation to Certain Goddesses Known Through Literature*, (New Haven, Conn., 1943).
Rankin, O.S., *Israel's Wisdom Literature* (Edinburgh, 1936).
Rast, W.E., "Cakes for the Queen of Heaven", in A.L. Merrill and T.W. Overholt (ed.), *Scripture in History & Theology: Essays in Honor of J. Coert Rylaarsdam* (Pittsburgh, 1977), pp. 167–80.
Ringgren, H., *Word and Wisdom: Studies in the Hypostatization of Divine Qualities and Functions in the Ancient Near East* (Lund, 1947).
Robinson, J., *The First Book of Kings* (Cambridge, 1972).
Rowe, A., *The Four Canaanite Temples of Beth-Shan: Part 1 The Temples and Cult Objects*, Publications of the Palestine Section of the University Museum, University of Pennsylvania 2 (Philadelphia, 1940).
———, *The Topography and History of Beth-Shan* (Philadelphia, 1930).
Schroer, S., *In Israel gab es Bilder: Nachrichten von darstellender Kunst im Alten Testament* (Fribourg and Göttingen, 1987).
———, "Weise Frauen und Ratgeberinnen in Israel", *BN* 51 (1990), pp. 41–60.
Soggin, J.A., *Judges: A Commentary* (London and Philadelphia, 1981).
Stadelmann, R., *Syrisch-Palästinensische Gottheiten in Ägypten* (Leiden, 1967).
Tadmor, M., "Female Cult Figurines in Late Canaan and Early Israel: Archaeological Evidence", in T. Ishida (ed.), *Studies in the Period of David and Solomon and Other Essays* (Winona Lake and Tokyo, 1982), pp. 139–73.
Taylor, J.G., "The Song of Deborah and Two Canaanite Goddesses", *JSOT* 23 (1982), pp. 99–108.
Westermann, C., *The Structure of the Book of Job* (Philadelphia, 1981). E. tr. of *Der Aufbau des Buches Hiob* (2nd edn, Stuttgart, 1977).
Whybray, R.N., *The Book of Proverbs* (Cambridge, 1972).
Williamson, H.G.M., *1 and 2 Chronicles* (Grand Rapids and London, 1982).

ZUM VERHÄLTNIS VON TEXTKRITIK UND LITERARKRITIK: ÜBERLEGUNGEN ANHAND EINIGER BEISPIELE[1]

von

ARIE VAN DER KOOIJ
Leiden

I. *Einleitung*

Wie bekannt haben die Funde von Bibeltexten in Qumran zu einem erneuerten wissenschaftlichen Interesse an der Textüberlieferung der alttestamentichen Bücher in der Zeit vom 3. Jh. v. Chr. bis zum 2. Jh. n.Chr. geführt. Ein grosser Teil dieser Texte macht klar, dass der massoretische Text (MT) auf eine altehrwürdige Tradition zurückgeht; daneben sind aber Texte gefunden worden, freilich meistens in fragmentarischer Form, die eine andere Textform gewisser Bibelbücher bezeugen, und die auf Grund von bedeutsamen Unterschieden zum MT als alternative Editionen bezeichnet werden können. Da in bestimmten Fällen diese Qumrantexte mit LXX übereinstimmen, haben diese Funde auch die Untersuchungen zur LXX in starkem Masse gefördert.

Vor allem seit den achtziger Jahren wird in mehreren Publikationen die These vorgelegt, dass es sich bei alternativen Editionen manchmal um Textformen handelt, die älter sind als MT bzw. Proto-MT. Es wird betont, man soll in solchen Fällen damit rechnen, dass die bezeugte Textform, die ganz markante Unterschiede zu MT aufweist, eine Phase der Entstehungsgeschichte eines Buches darstellt. Texthistorische Untersuchungen betreten also das Gebiet der literarkritischen bzw. redaktionskritischen Arbeit. In den einschlägigen Arbeiten handelt es sich vor allem um die folgenden Bibelbücher: Josua, Samuel, Könige, Jeremia, Ezechiel und Psalmen.[2]

---

[1] Ich danke Prof. Adrian Schenker ganz herzlich für die Korrekturlesung des Deutschen.

[2] Die Titel der Veröffentlichungen sind meistens vielsagend: z.B. E. Tov, "L'incidence de la critique textuelle sur la critique littéraire dans le livre de Jérémie", *RB* 79 (1972), S. 189–99; "La Septante de Jérémie au service de la critique littéraire" (Titel einer Abteilung

Die Verknüpfung zwischen Textkritik und Literarkritik ist nicht neu. Vgl. schon im 19. Jahrhundert A. Kuenen zum Text des Exodus und J. Wellhausen zum Text der Samuelbücher. Und weiter ist auf *BHK*3 und *BHS* zu verweisen, die in ihrem kritischen Apparat auch literarkritische Notizen (z.B. Glossen) enthalten.[3]

In seiner anregenden Arbeit *Textual Criticism of the Hebrew Bible*[4] widmet E. Tov ein ganzes Kapitel dem Verhältnis zwischen Textkritik und Literarkritik (Kap. 7). Er betont, dass es in Fällen von anderen Editionen, die auch als ältere Editionen zu betrachten sind, um grosse Unterschiede ("sizable differences") zwischen MT und LXX/Qumran handelt, d.h. Unterschiede nicht im Sinne von Buchstaben oder einzelnen Wörtern, sondern von Sätzen, Versen und Perikopen und manchmal auch im Sinne von einer anderen Reihenfolge von Kapiteln. Er weist darauf hin, dass diese Editionsarbeit nicht von Kopisten, sondern von Autoren ("authors-scribes") gemacht worden ist (S. 314). Die früheren Editionen, so führt er weiter aus, seien einmal als endgültige Texte gemeint gewesen und als solche publiziert, wurden aber in einer späteren Zeit revidiert und bearbeitet mit der Absicht, eine ältere Textform zu ersetzen. Dabei geht Tov vom Modell des literarischen Wachstums aus: der kürzere Text eines Buches gehe dem längeren voran.

Zum Verhältnis der textkritischen und literarkritischen Methoden ist er der Meinung, dass die letztere sich mit der Entstehungsphase eines Buches, die erstere aber mit der Transmissionsphase beschäftigen soll. Es erhebt sich natürlich die Frage, wo die Entstehungsphase endet und die Transmissionsphase anfängt. Hier wird folgende Position eingenommen: die Entstehungsgeschichte eines Buches endet, sobald der Proto-MT auf der Bühne erscheint. Die Textkritik soll nämlich versuchen denjenigen Text oder diejenige Edition eines Buches festzustellen, "which has been accepted as binding (authoritative) by Jewish tradition" (S. 317).

---

in P.M. Bogaert [Hrsg.], *Le Livre de Jérémie* (Leuven, 1981); D. Barthélemy, D.W. Gooding und J. Lust, E. Tov, *The Story of David and Goliath. Textual and Literary Criticism* (Fribourg, Göttingen, 1986); J. Lust (Hrsg.), *Ezekiel and His Book. Textual and Literary Criticism and their Interrelation* (Leuven, 1986).

[3] Siehe A. Kuenen, *Historisch-critisch onderzoek*, tweede, geheel omgewerkte uitgave I,1 (Haarlem, 1885), S. 73–81; J. Wellhausen, *Der Text der Bücher Samuelis* (Göttingen, 1871), S. ix–xiii. Vgl. auch D. Barthélemy, "L'enchevêtrement de l'histoire textuelle et de l'histoire littéraire dans les relations entre la Septante et le texte Massorétique", in A. Pietersma und C. Cox (Hrsg.), *Be Setuaginta* (Mississauga, 1984), S. 21–40.

[4] (Minneapolis, Assen/Maastricht, 1992), S. 313–49.

Tov bemerkt schliesslich, dass dies alles nicht gilt für Editionen, die eine spätere Phase attestieren, und nicht zur Entstehungsgeschichte des Proto-MT gehören. Es gehe dabei um "literary developments subsequent to the edition of M" (S. 316), und er verweist auf "midrashic developments" in den Büchern LXX Könige, LXX Esther, und LXX Daniel.

Zum Verhältnis zwischen Textkritik und Literarkritik haben sich auch andere Gelehrte geäussert.[5] H.J. Stipp ist der Meinung, die Textkritik und Literarkritik sollen zusammengehen, da die Textüberlieferung in eine Periode zurückreicht, in der Texte noch bearbeitet wurden. Der Proto-MT sei deshalb nicht das Ziel der Textkritik: "Textkritik fällt diachrone Urteile [. . .] und betreibt Vorstufenrekonstruktion, wenn und solange die Erklärungs-bedürftigkeit der Daten dies erfordert".[6] Es ist weiter noch darauf hinzuweisen dass er wie auch E. Ulrich[7] den Proto-MT nicht wie Tov und andere[8] in die Periode seit dem 3. Jh. v.Chr. *neben* anderen Textformen, sondern als Endergebnis eines Prozesses textlicher Bearbeitungen bis ins 1. Jh. n.Chr. ansetzt.

Es dürfte klar sein, dass diese neue Entwicklung in der texthistorischen Arbeit von grosser Bedeutung für die alttestamentliche Wissenschaft ist. Doch erheben sich auch Fragen. Die folgenden seien hier genannt:

– Wie verhalten sich die Textkritik und die Literarkritik bzw. die Redaktionskritik? Ist die Literarkritik von der Textkritik abhängig, oder hat sie ja auch einen eigenen Platz neben der Textkritik inne?

– Wie weiss man, ob eine Edition älter als Proto-MT sei oder eine nachherige Ausgabe darstelle?

– Warum soll man eine frühere, vormassoretische Edition eines Buches redaktionsgeschichtlich, d.h. als Phase in der Entstehungschichte eines Buches betrachten? Dies ist keinesfalls zwingend;

---

5 Vgl. u.a. J.H. Tigay (Hrsg.), *Empirical Models for Biblical Criticism* (Philadelphia, 1985).

6 "Das Verhältnis von Textkritik und Literarkritik in neueren alttestamentlichen Veröffentlichungen", *BZ*, NF 34 (1990), S. 33.

7 "The Canonical Process, Textual Criticism, and Later Stages in the Composition of the Bible", in M. Fishbane und E. Tov (Hrsg.), "*Sha'arei Talmon*". *Studies in the Bible, Qumran, and the Ancient Near East Presented to Shemaryahu Talmon* (Winona Lake, 1992), S. 267–91.

8 Siehe A.S. van der Woude, "Pluriformity and Uniformity. Reflections on the Transmission of the Old Testament", in J.N. Bremmer and F. García Martínez (Hrsg.), *Sacred History and Sacred Text in Early Judaism* (Kampen, 1992), S. 151–69.

– Ist der Proto-MT Ziel der textkritischen Arbeit oder die vormassoretische Edition, der Prae-MT?

Es ist unmöglich, in diesem Referat diese und andere Fragen ausführlich zu besprechen. Anhand einiger Beispiele von grossen textlichen Unterschieden, die als Zeugen einer früheren Edition betrachtet werden, nämlich Jos. xx; 1 Sam. xvii, und Jer. xxxiii, möchte ich einige Überlegungen vorlegen.

II. *Einige Beispiele*

Josua xx

Während MT von Targum, Peschiṭta und Vulgata bezeugt ist, stellt LXX Jos. einen Text dar, den man als eine andere Edition bezeichnen darf: an einigen Stellen enthält sie einen kürzeren Text, bietet dagegen an anderen Stellen bedeutende Ergänzungen, und dazu findet man auch Fälle einer anderen Reihenfolge von Versen. Tov spricht von zwei "literary strata", wobei LXX die ältere Textphase repräsentiere.[9] Auf Grund der Annahme, dass die griechische Übersetzung als ziemlich wörtlich anzusehen sei, liege es nicht nahe, die Unterschiede dem Übersetzer zuzuschreiben; sie seien vielmehr Zeugnis für eine andere hebräische Vorlage.[10]

Ein Vergleich zwischen MT und LXX Jos. ergibt, dass die meisten Unterschiede von geringem Umfang sind. Es liegt nur ein Fall eines längeren Textes in MT vor, der zur Kategorie der "sizable differences" gehört: Jos. xx. MT und LXX Jos. xx 1–6 weisen auffallende Differenzen auf: die Verse 4, 5, 6aα und 6b sind nicht von LXX bezeugt.

(1) Und der Herr redete zu Josua und sprach:
(2) Rede zu den Söhnen Israels und sprich: Bestimmt euch die Zufluchsstädte, von denen ich durch Mose zu euch geredet habe,

---

[9] (Anm. 4), S. 327: "Two Literary Strata of Joshua". Dort weitere Literatur zum Verhältnis zwischen MT und LXX Jos. Siehe jetzt auch L. Mazor, *The Septuagint Translation of the Book of Joshua. Its Contribution to the Understanding of the Textual Transmission of the Book and its Literary and Ideological Development* (Ph.D. Dissertation, Hebrew University of Jerusalem, 1994).

[10] Zur Bedeutung von 4QJosua[a] siehe die Reiträge von A. Rofé und E. Ulrich in G.J. Brooke und F. García Martínez (Hrsg.), *New Qumran Texts and Studies* (Leiden, 1994), S. 73ff. und S. 89ff.

(3) damit dorthin ein Totschläger fliehen kann, wenn er jemanden aus Versehen, *ohne Vorsatz*, erschlagen hat; und sie sollen euch zur Zuflucht dienen vor dem Bluträcher.
(4) *Und er soll zu einer von diesen Stadten fliehen und sich an den Toreingang der Stadt stellen und vor den Ohren der Altesten jener Stadt seine Sache vortragen. Sie aber sollen ihn zu sich in die Stadt aufnehmen und ihm einen Ort anweisen, damit er bei ihnen wohnen kann.*
(5) *Wenn dann der Bluträcher ihn verfolgt, so dürfen sie ihm den Totschläger nicht ausliefern, denn er hat seinen Nächsten ohne Vorsatz erschlagen, und ohne dass er von gestern und ehegestern her einen Hass gegen ihn gehabt hat.*
(6) *Und er soll in jener Stadt wohnen bleiben,* bis er vor der Gemeindeversammlung vor Gericht gestanden hat, *(bzw.) bis zum Tode des Hohenpriesters, der in jenen Tagen vorhanden sein wird. Dann darf der Totschläger wieder in seine Stadt und in sein Haus zurückgehen, in die Stadt, aus der er geflohen war.*
(Die kursivierten Teile sind nicht von LXX bezeugt)

A. Rofé und andere haben mit guten Gründen argumentiert, dass die Plusse in MT literarkritisch gesehen sekundär sind.[11] LXX stimmt also mit einem Text überein, der literarkritisch rekonstruiert werden kann.

Zunächst ist aber zu fragen: geht LXX auf eine Vorlage ohne diese Zusätze zurück oder hat der Übersetzer seine (längere) Vorlage gekürzt, um damit Kap. xx eindeutiger mit dem parallelen Passus in Num. xxxv zu harmonisieren? Beides ist ja denkbar. Hinsichtlich der zweiten Möglichkeit könnte man einwenden, dass es im Lichte des ziemlich wörtlichen Übersetzungsstils nicht nahe liege, der Autor von LXX Jos. habe seine Vorlage gekürzt wiedergegeben. Doch bin ich dessen nicht sicher, dass sich eine ziemlich wörtliche Übersetzungstechnik einerseits und literarische Initiativen wie Kürzungen andererseits sich gegenseitig ausschliessen, zumal da LXX Jos. Spuren von literarischen Initiativen im Sinne von hinzugefügten Versen aufweist (siehe weiter unten). Es gibt jedoch andersartige Hinweise dafür, dass nicht der längere, sondern der kürzere Text dem Autor von LXX Jos. vorlag.

Jos. xx gehört m.E. zur priesterschriftlichen Redaktion des Josuabuches, einer Redaktion, die in den Kap. xx–xxi auf die parallelen Passagen im Buche Numeri zurückgeht. Der kurze Text von Jos. xx

[11] A. Rofé, "Joshua 20: Historico-Literary Criticism Illustrated", in Tigay (Anm. 5), S. 131–47; M. Fishbane, "Biblical Colophons, Textual Criticism and Legal Analogies", *CBQ* 42 (1980), S. 443–6; E. Cortese, *Josua 13–21. Ein priesterschriftlicher Abschnitt im Deuteronomistischen Geschichtswerk* (Freiburg [Schweiz], Göttingen, 1990), S. 79–80.

stimmt mit Num. xxxv 11–12[12] überein, und das bedeutet wohl, dass dieser kürzere Text die ältere Version darstellt.

Das ruft die Frage hervor, woher dann die Zusätze in MT Jos. xx stammen. Cortese redet von "einem nachpriesterlichen Redaktor" (S. 80), während Tov und Rofé die Bearbeitung einer deuteronomistischen Hand zuschreiben.[13] Rofé bemerkt dazu, dass es sich bei diesem "deuteronomistic stratum" (S. 145) um eine Bearbeitung handle, "composed too late to be introduced into all manuscripts, and therefore happened not to appear in the Vorlage of the Septuagint" (ibid.). Es ist jedoch die Frage, ob die Zusätze in Jos. xx einer deuteronomistischen Hand entstammen. Die Textteile enthalten nämlich Elemente sowohl aus D als aus P.

D-Elemente: vor allem V. 4–5 (vgl. Deut. xix 4–6,11–12),
P-Elemente: V. 6 (vgl. Num. xxxv 25,28).

Es handelt sich offenbar um einen Autor, der sowohl P als D kannte, sodass man die Zusätze als nachpriesterlich und/oder als nachdeuteronomistisch bezeichnen kann. Wir haben es hier also mit einer Bearbeitung zu tun, ausgeführt von einem schriftgelehrten Autor, für den es kein "P" und "D" mehr gab. Das führt zu einer relativ späten Periode. Man vergleiche zum Beispiel die Tempelrolle, in der Texte des Pentateuch, die einmal verschiedenen Kreisen (P und D) entstammten, ohne Unterschied im Rahmen einer Neukomposition verwendet werden. MT Jos. xx stellt deshalb wohl das Ergebnis einer späten Bearbeitung dar, was auch immer ihr Grund gewesen sein mag. Es ist von daher wahrscheinlich, dass der Autor von LXX Jos. die bearbeitete Version von Jos. xx noch nicht kannte.

Literarkritik und Textgeschichte gehen in diesem Fall also deutlich zusammen. Es ist zu betonen, dass die Literarkritik ihren eigenen Platz inne hat; denn beim literarkritischen Verfahren von MT Jos. xx kommt man ohne LXX aus. Auf die Frage, ob die Bearbeitung von Kap. xx Teil einer umfassenden Redaktion des Josuabuches gewesen ist, kann hier nicht eingegangen werden. Es sei jedoch darauf hingewiesen, dass die Bearbeitung von Kap. xx ein von priesterschriftlichen und deuteronomistischen[14] Händen abgefasstes Josuabuch voraussetzt.

---

[12] Siehe Cortese (Anm. 11), S. 80.

[13] Tov (Anm. 4), S. 330: "The layer of additions [. . .] contains words and sections from Deuteronomy 19 which are meant to adapt the earlier layer to Deuteronomy". Rofé (Anm. 11), S. 145.

[14] Einschliesslich des späten, "nomistischen" Dtr (z.B. Kap. xxiii: MT und LXX). Siehe

1 Samuel xvii

Wie bekannt, zählt MT 1 Sam. xvii 58 Verse und LXX nicht mehr als 32. Wir haben es mit einem langen und einem kurzen Text derselben Geschichte zu tun. (Es ist interessant zu sehen, dass der philistäische Held, Goliat, in der langen Version lang [6 Ellen und eine Spanne]!, aber in der kurzen Version etwas kürzer ist [4 Ellen und eine Spanne]!)

Zur texthistorischen Frage der relativen Chronologie gehen die Meinungen auseinander. Das gilt u.a. für die interessante Arbeit von D. Barthélemy, D.W. Gooding, J. Lust und Tov, die im Rahmen einer Joint Research Venture (eine nachfolgenswerte Initiative!) 1 Sam. xvii–xviii von verschiedenen Seiten her ausführlich diskutiert haben (siehe Anm. 2). Lust und Tov sind der Meinung, dass die LXX eine kürzere Version der David-Goliat Geschichte bezeuge, die eine Phase der Redaktionsgeschichte dieses Textes widerspiegele; demgegenüber repräsentiere MT eine sekundäre Kombination der Kurzfassung und einer zweiten Parallelfassung derselben Geschichte. Barthélemy und Gooding dagegen vertreten die Auffassung, dass die MT Fassung die primäre sei. Es könnte ja sein, dass die Kurzfassung der LXX eine ältere Textphase widerspiegelt. Aber methodisch gesehen vermisst man in der Argumentation eine eigenständige literarkritische Analyse von Proto-MT 1 Sam. xvii. Eine solche Analyse ist wichtig, um der Frage nachzugehen, ob sie zu demselben Schluss führen wurde, d.h. ob auch auf Grund von einer von LXX unabhängigen literarkritischen Analyse des Proto-MT argumentiert werden kann, dass die LXX Form eine ältere Phase des Textes biete, wie das in Jos. xx der Fall ist. Wie ich an anderer Stelle diskutiert habe, führt sie nicht zu demselben Schluss.[15] Das bedeutet m.E., dass LXX eine sekundäre Textfassung bezeugt, sei es auf der Ebene der Vorlage, sei auf der Ebene der Übersetzung. Es wäre an sich schon seltsam, wenn die LXX der Bücher Samuelis redaktionsgeschichtlich gesehen eine ältere Stufe repräsentiere; man würde dann nicht nur in 1 Sam. xvii–xviii, sondern auch anderswo einen kürzeren Text erwarten (vgl. schon Wellhausen [Anm. 3], S. ix).

---

dazu R. Smend, *Die Entstehung des Alten Testaments*, (Stuttgart, ^{2}1981), S. 115.

[15] A. van der Kooij, "The Story of David and Goliath: The Early History of Its Text", *ETL* 68 (1992), S. 118–31 (dort weitere Literatur).

Jeremia xxxiii

Ein faszinierender Fall stellt das Jeremiabuch dar: der hebräische MT ist weit umfangreicher als die Septuaginta-Übersetzung dieses Buches; dazu liegt auch ein Unterschied in der Reihenfolge der Kapitel vor: die Völkerorakel stehen nicht nur an anderer Stelle, sondern diese Kapitel weisen ausserdem eine andere Reihenfolge auf. Wie allgemein angenommen wird, stellen beide Texte zwei verschiedene Editionen des Jeremiabuches dar. Interessanterweise haben die Textfunde aus Qumran diese Sachlage bestätigt: einige Fragmente gehen mit MT zusammen, zwei andere (4QJer^{b} und 4QJer^{d}) machen klar, dass es eine hebräische Fassung gegeben hat, die der LXX nahe stand. Offenbar liefen im hellenistischen Zeitalter zwei Textversionen des Jeremiabuches um, eine längere und eine kürzere.[16]

Mancher Gelehrte ist der Meinung, dass die Langfassung des MT eine spätere Phase der Entstehungsgeschichte des Buches widerspiegelt als die Kurzfassung der LXX.[17] Die Alternative, LXX als Zeuge einer sekundären Bearbeitung anzusehen, sei deshalb nicht plausibel, weil LXX Jer. eine wörtliche Übersetzung darstellt und es von daher nicht naheliegt, die Unterschiede zwischen MT und LXX dem Übersetzer zuzuschreiben. Das heisst: LXX Jer. bezeuge eine kürzere Vorlage als MT, und diese Kurzfassung gehe gemäss dem Modell des literarischen Wachstums eines Buches der Langfassung des (Proto-)MT voraus.

Es ist unmöglich hier auf die vielen Detailfragen und Detaildiskussionen einzugehen. Sehen wir uns als Beispiel einer grossen Differenz zwischen MT und LXX die Sachlage von Kap. xxxiii näher an.

Jer. xxxiii 14–26 ist der langste Passus, der in LXX Jer. nicht belegt ist. Diese Passage enthält eine Prophezeiung von Heil für Israel und Juda. Sie werden als Volk in Gerechtigkeit und Frieden leben, weil, wie V. 17–18 sagt, der Herr versprochen hat, es werde David nie an einem Nachfolger fehlen, der auf dem Thron von Israel sitzt, und den

---

[16] Man darf nicht ausschliessen, dass es drei Versionen gegeben hat: die beiden von Qumran bezeugten Textforme und die LXX als dritte, denn man kann nicht einfach annehmen, dass eine Handschrift wie 4QJer^{b} stets mit LXX übereingestimmt hat; vgl. die Unterschiede zwischen 4QJer^{d} und LXX, und im Falle der Samuelbücher diejenige zwischen 4QSam^{a} und LXX Sam.

[17] Für Literaturangaben sei verwiesen auf P.M. Bogaert, "Le Livre de Jérémie en perspective. Les deux rédactions antiques selon les travaux en cours", *RB* 101 (1994), S. 363–406, und H.J. Stipp, *Das masoretische and alexandrinische Sondergut des Jeremiabuches* (Freiburg [Schweiz], Göttingen, 1994).

levitischen Priestern werde es nie an einem fehlen, der Brandopfer und Speisopfer in Rauch aufgehen lässt und Schlachtopfer zurichtet allezeit. In V. 19–22 ist von zwei Bünden die Rede, einem mit David, und einem anderen mit Levi; sie werden nachdrücklich als ganz feste Ordnungen proklamiert: sie sind unverbrüchlich wie die Schöpfungsordnung der regelmässigen Wechsel von Tag und Nacht. Das bedeutet also, dass die nationale Existenz Israels gesichert sein wird, denn auf den beiden Institutionen, dem Königtum und dem Priestertum, beruht der Bestand von Israel als Staat (*gwy*). Wie aus V. 23 hervorgeht, gab es Leute, die diese Erwählung der "beiden Geschlechter", und damit sind ja wohl die Geschlechter von David und Levi gemeint,[18] anzweifelten und damit die Existenz von Israel als Nation für unsicher hielten (V. 23–4). In den letzten Versen, 25–6, wird in Anknupfung an V. 24b betont, dass die Zukunft des Volkes ("der Nachkommen Jakobs") sichergestellt sei, wobei wie in V. 15–16 das Motiv der Leitung dieses Volkes auf das Königtum zugespitzt wird: es werde aus Davids Nachkommen Herrscher (Plural) über die Nachkommen Abrahams, Isaaks und Jakobs geben. Im Zentrum von Jer. xxxiii 14–26 stehen also zwei Bünde, der Bund mit David und der Bund mit Levi. Die beiden Institutionen, das Königtum und das Priestertum, werden als die Grundpfeiler der nationalen Existenz Israels gesehen.[19]

Es sind in den letzten Jahren mehrere Arbeiten erschienen, in denen die Frage des umfangreichen Minus von Jer. xxxiii 14–26 in LXX behandelt worden ist.[20] Mit guten Gründen wird argumentiert, dass diese Passage redaktionskritisch gesehen innerhalb MT Jer. einen relativ späten Text darstellt. Obwohl die Abwesenheit dieses Passus in LXX nicht bedeuten muss, dieser Passus habe es in der Vorlage noch nicht

---

[18] Siehe dazu A. Schenker, "La rédaction longue du livre de Jérémie doit-elle être datée au temps des premiers Hasmonéens?", *ETL* 70 (1994), S. 286.

[19] Nach P.M. Bogaert ("Les mécanismes rédactionnels en Jér. 10,1–16 (LXX et MT) et la signification des suppléments", in Bogaert [Anm. 2], S. 236) wäre der Grund des ganzen Passus, die Rolle der Priester hervorzuheben, während Y. Goldman (*Prophétie et royauté au retour de l'exil* [Freiburg (Schweiz), Göttingen, 1992], S. 27–8) gerade die Versteile über die Priester (in V. 21–2) als sekundär ansieht; s.E. liege der Nachdruck auf dem Königtum (in Zusammenhang mit der Nation).

[20] Bogaert (Anm. 19) und ders., "*Urtext*, texte court et relecture: Jérémie xxxiii 14–26 TM et ses préparations", in *Congress Volume: Leuven 1989, SVT* 43 (Leiden, 1991), S. 236–47; J. Lust, "Messianism and the Greek Version of Jeremiah", in C.E. Cox (Hrsg.), *VII Congress of the International Organization for Septuagint and Cognate Studies, Leuven 1989* (Atlanta, 1991), S. 87–122; ders., "The Diverse Text Forms of Jeremiah and History Writing with Jer. 33 as a Test Case", *JNSL* 20 (1994), S. 31–48; Goldman (Anm. 19),

gegeben, nimmt man meistens an, dass dies der Fall gewesen ist, weil, wie z.B. Rudolph sagt: "ein Grund für G, es wegzulassen, ist nicht zu erkennen" ([Anm. 20] S. 217). Man hat darauf hingewiesen, dass der Text von Jer. xxxiii 14ff. mit Hilfe von anderen Passagen in Jer. wie xxiii 5–6, xxix 11, und xxxi 35–7 verfasst sei. Am wichtigsten ist wohl die Beziehung zwischen xxxiii 15–16 und xxiii 5–6, denn es ist klar, dass der Autor von xxxiii 15–16 den Text von xxiii 5–6 als Quelle benutzt hat.

Synopse: MT xxxiii 15–16 und xxiii 5–6

בימים ההם ובעת ההיא	הנה ימים באים נאם יהוה
אצמיח לדוד צמח צדקה	והקמתי לדוד צמח צדיק
	ומלך מלך והשכיל
ועשה משפט וצדקה בארץ	ועשה משפט וצדקה בארץ
בימים ההם תושע יהודה	בימיו תושע יהודה
וירושלם תשכן לבטח	וישראל ישכן לבטח
זה אשר יקרא לה יהוה צדקנו	זה שמו אשר יקראו יהוה צדקנו

Neben weitgehenden Übereinstimmungen gibt es auch Unterschiede; die wichtigsten sind folgende: das Minus von *wmlk mlk whśkyl*, die Änderung von Israel zu Jerusalem und damit zusammenhängend die Übertragung des Ehrennamen, *yhwh ṣdqnw*, vom Davidspross auf Jerusalem. Der Autor von xxxiii 15–16 hat seine Quelle auf kreative Weise benutzt. Es handelt sich um ein schönes Beispiel einer Transformation, wie M. Fishbane nachgewiesen hat.[21] Goldman und Lust sind jedoch der Meinung, die Sachlage sei verwickelter, da LXX Jer. xxiii 5–6 eine andere und ältere Vorlage als MT voraussetze. Dagegen stelle MT xxiii 5–6 das Ergebnis einer Bearbeitung dar, die eine nähere Übereinstimmung mit xxxiii 15–16 beabsichtigte.[22]

Der LXX Text von Jer. xxiii 5–6 lautet wie folgt:

> 5) Ἰδοὺ ἡμέραι ἔρχονται, λέγει κύριος, καὶ ἀναστήσω τῷ Δαυιδ ἀνατολὴν δικαίαν καὶ βασιλεύσει βασιλεὺς καὶ συνήσει καὶ ποιήσει κρίμα καὶ δικαιοσύνην ἐπὶ τῆς γῆς.
>
> 6) Ἐν ταῖς ἡμέραις αὐτοῦ σωθήσεται Ιουδας, καὶ Ισραηλ κατασκηνώσει πεποιθὼς καὶ τοῦτο τὸ ὄνομα, ὃ καλέσει αὐτὸν κύριος[23] Ιωσεδεκ ἐν τοῖς προφήταις.

S. 9–64; Schenker (Anm. 18), S. 286–9. Siehe auch Stipp (Anm. 17), S. 133–6; W. Rudolph, *Jeremia* (Tübingen, ³1968), S. 217–19.

[21] *Biblical Interpretation in Ancient Israel* (Oxford, 1985), S. 471–3.

[22] Goldman (Anm. 19), S. 45–7, und Lust, "Messianism" (Anm. 20), S. 89–93.

[23] J. Ziegler hält κύριος für sekundär, aber siehe dazu Goldman (Anm. 19), S. 46.

Wichtiger Punkt ist der Name des neuen Herrschers: MT *yhwh ṣdqnw*, LXX Ιωσεδεκ. Lust und andere argumentieren, der Name der LXX (hebräisch *yhwṣdq*) sei als die ältere Lesart zu betrachten, weil mit diesem Namen König Zedekia gemeint sei.[24] Das würde bedeuten, dass das Orakel von xxiii 5–6 in Originalfassung vorexilisch datiert werden kann. Der Name *yhwṣdq* sei späterhin in Bezug auf xxxiii 15–16 in *yhwh ṣdqnw* geändert worden.[25]

Es erhebt sich die Frage, ob damit nicht eine zu verwickelte Erklärung geboten wird: einerseits stelle xxxiii 15–16 eine Transformation von xxiii 5–6 dar, aber andererseits habe der Autor von xxxiii 15–16 seine Quelle xxiii 5–6 mit dem neuen Text harmonisiert. Das leuchtet nicht ein, denn erstens fragt man sich warum die Harmonisierung nicht besser durchgeführt worden ist, und zweitens setzt eine Transformation voraus, dass der Autor von xxxiii 15–16 einen hebräischen Text von xxiii 5–6 mit dem Namen *yhwh ṣdqnw* benutzt hat. Wenn es eine Namensänderung von *Iosedek* zu *yhwh ṣdqnw* gegeben hat, ist es wahrscheinlicher dass sie stattgefunden hat, bevor Jer. xxxiii 15–16 abgefasst wurde (cf. Stipp [Anm. 17], S. 136).

Aber es muss gefragt werden, ob der Name Iosedek älter ist als der Name in MT. Zur These, dass Iosedek als ursprünglicher Name auf Zedekia anspielt, erheben sich folgende Bedenken:

– eine solche positive Heilserwartung hinsichtlich König Zedekia ist im Lichte von Passagen wie Jer. xxi 7 und xxiv 8ff. nicht wahrscheinlich;

– das Orakel xxiii 5–6 steht in einem Kontext (V. 1–4: MT cf LXX), der eine nachexilische Situation vermuten lässt;[26]

– der Name Iosedek als alternative Name für Zedekia ist theoretisch nicht unmöglich, liegt aber nicht auf der Hand, denn er ist als Name für Zedekia nicht belegt.

Auch wenn man davon ausgeht, *Io-sedek* sei nicht als Variante zu *Zedek-ia* aufzufassen, sei jedoch für älter als der MT Name zu halten, ist es aus anderen Gründen fraglich, ob dieser Name zum ursprünglichen Wortlaut des Heilsorakels gehörte. Es wäre ja sehr ungewöhnlich,

---

[24] Lust, "Messianism" (Anm. 20), S. 89–93 (dort weitere Literatur).

[25] Goldman (Anm. 19), S. 46–7, und Lust, "Diverse Text Forms" (Anm. 20), S. 40. Lust nimmt auch an, dass diese Änderung des Namens in xxiii 5–6 ebenfalls zur Folge hatte, dass der neue Name wie in xxxiii 16 auf Jerusalem Bezug nimmt. Das ist im Lichte der Suffixe in xxiii 6 nicht wahrscheinlich.

[26] Cf. R.P. Carroll, *Jeremiah; a Commentary* (London, 1986), S. 639. Vgl. auch Stipp (Anm. 17), S. 110.

dass ein Heilsorakel, in dem ein zukünftiger neuer König angekündigt wird, den konkreten Namen dieses Herrschers bieten würde. Dagegen gibt der MT Name, der als Symbolname zu verstehen ist (wie Immanuel in Jes. vii), einen guten Sinn ab.

Es empfiehlt sich also, LXX Jer. xxiii 5–6 anders zu deuten. Den Namen, den der griechische Text enthält, findet man auch in anderen Teilen der LXX: es handelt sich dabei stets um ein Mitglied des hohenpriesterlichen Geschlechts, den Vater von Josua (Hag. i 1,14; Sach. vi 11; 1 Esdras v 5,47,54; Sir. xlix 12, u.a.). Es liegt von daher nahe, Iosedek in LXX Jer. xxiii 6 mit diesem bekannten Namen zu verbinden.[27] Das bedeutet, dass dieser Text einen Herrscher im Sinne von einem Hohenpriester-Fürsten im Auge hat.

Dagegen könnte man einwenden, dass der Passus von Jer. xxiii vom davidischen Königtum redet, und dass diese Stelle kontextuell gesehen als Fortsetzung von Kap. xxii fungiert, wo es sich ebenfalls um davidische Könige handelt. Aber die Idee, dass die Linie der vorexilischen Könige von nach-exilischen Hohenpriestern fortgesetzt wurde, war damals nicht unbekannt. Man findet sie zum Beispiel in 1 Esdras, einem Buch, das ebenfalls dem 2. Jh. v.Chr. entstammt. In dieser Schrift, die als eine Neukomposition zu bezeichnen ist, fängt es mit dem König Josia an und endet ganz nachdrücklich mit dem Hohenpriester Esra. Dieses Legitimationsinteresse der damaligen Zeit spiegelt sich auch im (hebräischen) Sirachbuch wider: in dem *Laus Patrum*, Kap. xxxxiv–l, wird ja der Hohepriester Johanan (Onias) als der legitime Nachfolger von Aaron/Pinchas *und* von den davidischen Königen präsentiert.[28] Ein ganz wichtiger Passus ist in diesem Zusammenhang Sir. xlv 24–5:

> Darum richtete er (Gott) auch ihm (Pinchas) eine Ordnung auf, einen Bund des Heils, um das Heiligtum zu versorgen, sodass ihm und seinen Nachkommen gehören solle das Hohepriesteramt in Ewigkeit, und auch (richtete er ihm auf) seinen Bund mit David, dem Sohn des Isai aus dem Stamme Juda: das Erbe des Feuers vor seiner Herrlichkeit, das Erbe Aarons für all seine Nachkommen.[29]

[27] Vgl. auch W. McKane, *Jeremiah* I (Edinburgh, 1986), p. xxv.

[28] Siehe dazu E. Janssen, *Das Gottesvolk und seine Geschichte* (Neukirchen-Vluyn, 1971), S. 28 (S. 22: der Hohepriester [hat] auch die königlichen Funktionen übernommen); T.R. Lee, *Studies in the Form of Sirach 44–50* (Atlanta, 1986).

[29] Zu dieser Übersetzung siehe vor allem P.C. Beentjes, *Jesus Sirach en Tenach* (Nieuwegein, 1981), S. 186–92.

Der Bund mit David wurde offenbar als Teil des Bundes mit Pinchas betrachtet. Auf diese Weise war es ideologisch gesehen möglich, die hohepriesterliche Leitung des Volkes als legitime Fortsetzung der vorexilischen Könige zu präsentieren. Das wirft auch Licht auf unsere Stelle in LXX Jer. xxiii: es war für einen damaligen Schriftgelehrten kein Problem, einen Text über David mit dem Hohenpriesteramt in Verbindung zu bringen.[30]

Der Name Iosedek in LXX Jer. xxiii 6 lässt sich also als eine Deutung verstehen, die die Absicht hatte, eine hohepriesterliche Leitung als Garantie einer heilvollen Zukunft für Juda und Jerusalem zu proklamieren. Das heisst, dass der Name Iosedek, sei er vom Übersetzer eingetragen oder von ihm bereits in seiner Vorlage vorgefunden, sekundär im Vergleich mit dem Namen in MT zu betrachten ist.

Es ist nun auf die Frage einzugehen, was diese Sicht der Dinge für Jer. xxxiii 14–26 bedeutet. Wie wir gesehen haben, besagt diese Passage, dass zwei Bünde, der Bund mit David und der Bund mit Levi, für die nationale Existenz Israels konstitutiv sind. Demgegenüber hat unsere Analyse von LXX Jer. xxiii 5–6 ergeben, dass dieser griechische Text die Ideologie eines Priester-Fürsten in Übereinstimmung mit Texten wie Sir. xlv 24–5 widerspiegelt. Mir scheint, man hat Jer. xxxiii 14–26 ausgelassen, weil diese Stelle eher das "dyarchische" Prinzip bezeugt und nicht das "monarchische" wie in Sir. xlv 24–5.[31] Kompositionstechnisch gesehen handelt es sich dann um eine Auslassung aus ideologischen Gründen, die vermutlich im 2. Jh. v.Chr. anzusetzen ist. Jer. xxxiii 14–26 ist als Teil des langen Jeremiatexts wohl älter, weil 4QJer[a], ein wichtiger Qumranzeuge dieser Textform, um 200 v.Chr. datiert wird, und weil man mit W. Rudolph und Carroll annehmen darf, dass dieser Passus in der persischen Zeit abgefasst worden ist.[32]

---

[30] Es erhebt sich die Frage, welches Parteiinteresse hinter dieser Deutung steht (zu dieser Fragestellung im allgemeinen siehe unten).

[31] Zu diesen beiden Prinzipien siehe jetzt D. Goodblatt, *The Monarchic Principle. Studies in Jewish Self-Government in Antiquity* (Tübingen, 1994), S. 6–76. Wegen der ideologischen Unterschiede zwischen Sir. xlv und Jer. xxxiii liegt es nicht nahe, beide Stellen mit einander zu verbinden, wie Lust, "Diverse Text Forms" (Anm. 20), S. 41–2, und Schenker (Anm. 18), S. 287, vorschlagen.

[32] Siehe Rudolph (Anm. 20), S. 219, und Carroll (Anm. 26), S. 639. Dazu auch A. Laato, *Josiah und David Redivivus* (Stockholm, 1992), S. 117. Eine Datierung im 2. Jh. v.Chr. (B. Duhm [siehe Goldman (Anm. 19), S. 23–4] und Schenker [Anm. 18], S. 283–4) ist im Lichte von 4QJer[a] unwahrscheinlich.

III. *Überlegungen*

Zum Schluss möchte ich einige Überlegungen vorführen, die bei der Diskussion der obengenannten Beispiele als Voraussetzungen eine Rolle spielten oder als Bemerkungen zu bestimmten Fragen zu betrachten sind.

(1) Autoren der schriftlichen Übersetzungen der biblischen Bücher im frühen Judentum waren Leute, die zum Kreis der Schriftgelehrten gehörten. Das geht aus dem Aristeasbrief hervor; ferner weist die Arbeit von Jesus Sirach in diese Richtung, und man denke auch an die Übersetzungen wie jene von Aquila, Symmachus, und die Targumim. Es war keine Kleinigkeit, die literarischen Texte der Tradition der Vorväter[33] übersetzen zu können. Man musste dafür wie jeder Schriftgelehrte im (lauten) Lesen (ἀνάγνωσις) der biblischen Bücher geübt sein und in ihnen eine hinreichende Kenntnis erworben haben (vgl. Sirach, Prolog, 7–11). Weiter war eine gute Kenntnis des Hebräischen und des Griechischen erforderlich, wie im Aristeasbrief gesagt wird (par. 121). Dass diese Kenntnisse nicht immer so gross waren, wie man wunschen würde, ist eine andere Sache.

(2) Ein Text wie LXX Jer. ist in einer Periode der frühjüdischen Religionsgeschichte entstanden, die von einer intensiven Schriftgelehrsamkeit geprägt war. Das Interesse galt nicht nur dem Gesetz, sondern auch den Prophezeiungen. Es ist zu beachten, dass man davon überzeugt war, dass die Prophezeiungen auf die damalige Zeit, bzw. auf die nahe Zukunft bezogen wurden. Diese Sicht spricht nicht nur aus den Pescharim von Qumran (die zugleich deutlich machen, dass eine solche aktualisierende Interpretation Sache von gelehrten und führenden Priestern war), sie ist auch klar erkennbar aus einem Text wie Sir. xxxvi 14:

> und richte auf die Prophezeiungen, die in deinem Namen ergingen.[34]

Bezüglich des Jeremiabuches stellt Dan. ix ein bekanntes Beispiel dar; dort bemüht man sich, die 70 Jahre aus Jer. xxv und xxix mit dem 2. Jh. v.Chr. zu verknüpfen.[35] Man darf wohl sagen, dass die nationale

---

[33] Aus Sirach, Prolog 10, geht hervor, dass die biblischen Bücher damals als πάτρια βιβλία bezeichnet wurden.

[34] Vgl. auch Tob. xiv 2–11.

[35] Zum damaligen Interesse an Jeremia vgl. auch 2 Makk. ii 1ff.

Krise, die Identitätskrise, um es modern zu sagen, in der ersten Hälfte des 2. Jh. v.Chr. das Interesse an den Prophezeiungen gefördert hat.

(3) Das damalige Judentum kannte viele Parteien und Strömungen. Es ist also damit zu rechnen, dass Schriftgelehrte(-Übersetzer) in ihren Arbeiten bestimmte Ideen zur Geltung gebracht haben, die gewisse Interessen einer Partei widerspiegeln. A. Geiger hatte diesen Gesichtspunkt seinerzeit nachdrücklich hervorgehoben in seiner Arbeit *Urschrift und Uebersetzungen der Bibel in ihrer Abhängigkeit von der innern Entwicklung des Judenthums* (Breslau, 1857).[36] Ein sehr bekanntes Beispiel stellt der Samaritanische Pentateuch dar mit seiner Propaganda für Garizim/Sichem als der von Gott gewählte Stätte für den samaritanischen Tempel. Anderswo habe ich ausgeführt,[37] dass 1QJes[a] einige Lesarten bietet, die im Lichte von anderen Qumrantexten als Legitimation der Qumranbewegung gemeint sind; diesen Text könnte man somit als den "Essenischen Jesaja" bezeichnen. Auch LXX Jes. stellt ein interessantes Beispiel dar: sie enthält eine Deutung, die den Bau eines jüdischen Tempels in Ägypten, in Leontopolis, zu legitimieren versucht.[38]

(4) Zur Frage, ob eine Auslassung wie die von Jer. xxxiii 14–26 (vgl. auch 1 Sam. xvii) einem Übersetzer zuzuschreiben wäre, möchte ich folgende Überlegungen vorführen. Es wird oft gesagt, es sei unwahrscheinlich, dass ein Autor einer wörtlichen Übersetzung auch editionsmässig gearbeitet habe. Diese Argumentation scheint mir nicht zwingend zu sein. Es ist fraglich, ob man Bücher wie LXX Jer. als eine wörtliche Übersetzung einstufen soll. Zwar gibt es auf Wortebene Fälle von wörtlichen und hebraisierenden Wiedergaben, aber auf lexikalischer Ebene und auf der Ebene des Satzes und der Perikope liegen auch freie Wiedergaben vor.[39] Aber wie man den Übersetzungsstil

---

[36] Vgl. zu dieser Fragestellung auch F.E. Deist, *Witnesses to the Old Testament* (Pretoria, 1988), S. 198–201; E. Ulrich, "The Bible in the Making: The Scriptures at Qumran", in E. Ulrich and J. VanderKam (Hrsg.), *The Community of the Renewed Covenant* (Notre Dame, 1994), S. 84.

[37] *Die alten Textzeugen des Jesajabuches* (Freiburg [Schweiz], Göttingen, 1981), S. 87–92.

[38] Ibid., S. 50–5.

[39] Neuere Arbeiten wie die von Stipp (Anm. 17), S. 17–58, und G. Fischer, *Das Trostbüchlein. Text, Komposition und Theologie von Jer. 30–31* (Stuttgart, 1993), S. 33–78, bieten wichtige Observationen. Das Verhältnis zwischen MT und LXX wird jedoch meistens auf Wortebene analysiert, während dem Satz und dem breiteren Kontext nur wenig Beachtung findet. Was Übereinstimmungen zwischen 4QJes[b] und LXX Jer. betrifft, ist zu bedenken, dass sie auch einem gemeinsamen exegetischen Verfahren oder eben einem gemeinsamen schriftgelehrten Kreis entstammen können.

eines Werkes auch beurteilen mag, die grosse Frage ist, wie sich dieser Stil einerseits und eventuelle literarische oder editorische Initiativen andererseits zueinander verhalten. Diese Frage trifft auch für das Verhältnis zwischen dem Stil des Kopierens und demjenigen der eventuellen literarischen Initiativen im Sinne von umfangreichen Hinzufügungen oder Auslassungen.[40] Es gibt Hinweise dafür, dass nicht nur eine freie, sondern auch eine wörtliche Stil von Übersetzen bzw. Kopieren mit literarischen Initiativen zusammengehen kann (man vergleiche z.B. 4QpaleoExod^{m}, Sam. Pent., LXX Jos., LXX Job). Es liegt nicht nahe, diese Initiative einem Kopisten oder einem Übersetzter im Sinne eines Dolmetschers zuzuschreiben, sondern vielmehr einem schriftgelehrten Autor: er konnte beides machen, übersetzen bzw. kopieren und edieren. Kurz gesagt, man soll m.E. klar zwischen Übersetzungstechnik bwz. Stil des Kopierens einerseits und Kompositionstechnik bzw. Editionstechnik andererseits unterscheiden.

Es ist in diesem Zusammenhang zu beachten, dass die Periode der letzten zwei Jahrhunderte v. Chr. nicht nur eine Zeit intensiver Schriftgelehrsamkeit war, sondern auch von grosser literarischer Kreativität. Viele neue Schriften wurden abgefasst (Tobit, Judith, nichtbiblische Qumranschriften). Für unsere Fragestellung ist vor allem wichtig, dass literarische Werke entstanden, die auf biblischen Texten basieren: Neukompositionen wie 1 Esdras, die Tempelrolle, Texte die man zur Kategorie der "rewritten Bible" rechnet, ebenso Texte, die man als "parabiblical compositions" bezeichnet. In einer solchen Situation überrascht es nicht, wenn dann auch Neueditionen von biblischen Büchern (im Sinne von Bearbeitungen von überlieferten Bibeltexten) auf der Bühne erschienen (vgl. 4QpaleoExod^{m}, LXX Könige, LXX Job, LXX Daniel). Das Phänomen der verschiedenen Editionen wäre deshalb zuerst im Rahmen der damaligen grossen literarischen Kreativität zu untersuchen, bevor man auf ältere Texte und Traditionen aus vorhellenistischer Zeit schliesst. Was Bearbeitungen des biblischen Textes betrifft, sei hervorgehoben, dass auch der Proto-MT eine bestimmte Edition darstellt, d.h. Spuren von literarischer Aktivität aufweist (siehe auch unten).

(5) Kehren wir schliesslich zur Frage zurück, die im Anfang dieses Beitrages genannt wurde, nämlich der nach dem Ziel der Textkritik. Man kann mit Tov einverstanden sein, dass die Textkritik Sache der

---

[40] Es handelt sich hier nicht um kleinen Hinzufügungen oder Auslassungen als Teil eines Übersetzungsstils.

Transmissionsphase ist und Literarkritik Sache der Entstehungsgeschichte eines Buches. Aber wie wir gesehen haben fängt die Transmissionsphase s.E. erst mit dem Proto-MT eines Buches an. Es ist jedoch die Frage, ob man den proto-massoretischen Text als das Ziel der textkritischen Arbeit betrachten soll, und nicht eine ältere Form des Textes, den Prae-MT eines Buches. Mit Prae-MT meine ich eine ältere Textform, die sich einerseits orthographisch vom Proto-MT unterscheidet, andererseits auch in gewissen Fällen einen älteren, von Qumran und LXX bezeugten Text darstellt, der nachher bearbeitet worden ist.[41] Interessante Beispiele sind: Dtn. xxxii 43[42] und Jos. xx 4–6 (siehe oben).

Es empfiehlt sich, beim textkritischen Verfahren die Textüberlieferung der MT Tradition so weit wie möglich zu rekonstruieren zu versuchen (cf. Stipp). Das ist ja auch das Ziel, das wir im Rahmen des Projektes einer Neuedition der *Biblica Hebraica, Editio Quinta* genannt, vor Augen haben. In den *Guidelines for Contributors*[43] heisst es: "The aim of this edition in rendering judgments in its apparatus is to indicate the earliest attainable form(s) of the text based on the available evidence." Dabei sind Konjekturen miteingeschlossen, "as a means of explaining the evidence of textual transmission" (ibid.).

In Fällen von (grossen) Unterschieden, die mit anderen Editionen zu tun haben, ist im Rahmen dieses Projektes festgelegt, diese Lesarten im Apparat als literarisch ("literary") zu bezeichnen. Es bleibt natürlich zu untersuchen, ob es sich dabei im Vergleich zum Proto-MT um ältere, prae-massoretische oder um alternative bzw. sekundäre Differenzen geht. Wie es in der gängigen textkritischen Arbeitsweise

[41] Zum Unterschied zwischen Proto-MT und Prae-MT siehe vor allem D. Barthélemy, *Critique textuelle de l'Ancient Testament* 3: *Ézéchiel, Daniel et les 12 Prophètes* (Fribourg, Göttingen, 1992), S. cii–cxiv. Ob man den Prae-MT als eine Phase der Entstehungsgeschichte eines Buches ansieht, hängt davon ab, wie man "Buch" definiert (im Sinne von Proto-MT oder nicht). Es steht m.E. noch dahin, ob LXX oder Qumran wirklich Textformen bieten, die redaktionskritisch gesehen eine Vorstufe eines Buches darstellen. Die Differenzen sind meistens von geringem Umfang. Es wäre eine andere Sache, wenn z.B. eine Textform von Josua bezeugt wurde, die noch nicht von P oder von DtrN bearbeitet worden war.

[42] Siehe A. van der Kooij, "The Ending of the Song of Moses: On the Pre-Masoretic Version of Deut. 32:43", in F. García Martínez u.a. (Hrsg.), *Studies in Deuteronomy in Honour of C.J. Labuschagne on the Occasion of his 65th Birthday*, *SVT* 53 (Leiden, 1994), S. 93–100.

[43] Version Effective August 14, 1994 (Distributed January, 1995). Formulated by R.D. Weis and G.J. Norton, O.P., on the basis of decisions of the General Editorial Committee (Deutsche Bibelgesellschaft), S. 4.

eine bekannte Praxis ist, bei der Entscheidung von kleinen Differenzen philologische, stilistische oder exegetische Argumente miteinzubeziehen, so liegt es in Fällen von grossen Differenzen nahe, literarkritische bzw. redaktionskritische Argumente miteinzubeziehen. Vor allem in solchen Fällen brauchen Textkritik und Literarkritik einander. Wie es anhand von Jos. xx und 1 Sam. xvii dargelegt wurde, sei es nochmals betont, dass die literarkritische Analyse des Proto-MT dabei ihren eigenen Platz inne hat.

LA PLACE DU SACRIFICE DANS L'ANCIEN ISRAËL

par

ALFRED MARX
Strasbourg

En qualifiant le sacrifice d'"élément païen de la religion d'Israël" et en considérant le système sacrificiel de P comme un système artificiel et sans âme,[1] J. Wellhausen a fortement influé sur l'attitude des exégètes. Car, par ce jugement dépréciatif, il a contribué dans une large mesure à les détourner de cette forme du culte dont de toute manière ils ne savaient trop que faire. Et le peu d'intérêt qu'ils ont manifesté pour le sacrifice a conduit, par ricochet, à ancrer dans les esprits l'idée que le culte sacrificiel n'était somme toute qu'un élément marginal de la religion de l'ancien Israël.

Or, il suffit d'une simple revue des multiples mentions du sacrifice pour constater que tel est loin d'être le cas.

Du seul point de vue quantitatif, il apparaît que le sacrifice occupe une place non négligeable dans la Bible hébraïque.[2] La première partie du Lévitique lui est presqu'entièrement consacrée. Le dernier tiers du livre de l'Exode, les Nombres, les visions d'Ez. xl–xlviii, le Chroniste lui réservent une part substantielle. En fait, la plupart des livres bibliques y font référence,[3] que ce soit dans le cadre de lois cultuelles ou dans des psaumes, dans des oracles de jugement comme dans des oracles de salut, dans des sentences, des réflexions sapientiales, ou encore dans des narrations: pas moins d'une soixantaine de narrations, dans

[1] Voir *Geschichte Israels* 1 (Berlin, 1878), respectivement pp. 439 et 84. Voir aussi p. 80: "Die Seele . . . war entwichen, die Schale geblieben, und auf deren Ausbildung ward nun alle Kraft verwandt." Cf., près d'un siècle plus tard, ce jugement de C. Lévi-Strauss qui, opposant le sacrifice au système classificatoire, écrit "le système du sacrifice représente un discours particulier, et dénué de bon sens quoiqu'il soit fréquemment proféré", *La pensée sauvage* (Paris, 1962) p. 302.

[2] Pour une revue des différents textes, voir R. Rendtorff, *Studien zur Geschichte des Opfers im alten Israel* (Neukirchen-Vluyn, 1967), pp. 6–73, et, sauf pour les données de P, R.J. Thompson, *Penitence and Sacrifice in Early Israel outside the Levitical Law* (Leiden, 1963).

[3] Les seuls livres à ne jamais y faire expressément référence sont Abdias, Nahum, Aggée (mais voir ii 11–13), Ruth, Cantique des cantiques, Lamentations et Esther.

la Genèse, l'Exode, les Nombres, les prophètes antérieurs, chez le Chroniste, mais aussi dans les livres de Jérémie, Jonas, Job, mettent en scène l'offrande de sacrifices. D'une certaine manière, le culte sacrificiel apparaît ainsi comme le trait d'union entre les différents milieux et entre les différentes époques. Et ne serait-ce que pour cette raison, il mérite l'attention des exégètes.

Ce que l'on pressent, au vu de ces données, de l'importance du sacrifice, est corroboré par la place que lui confèrent les mythes et autres textes fondateurs. Le premier geste de piété attribué aux descendants du couple primordial est une offrande de produits de la terre et de premiers-nés (Gen. iv 3–4). Et le premier réflexe que l'on prête à Noé, au sortir de l'arche, après le déluge, est de construire un autel en vue d'y offrir un gigantesque holocauste, dont on rapporte qu'il a eu pour conséquence d'amener Yhwh à lever la malédiction qu'il avait prononcée sur la terre et à prendre l'engagement de garantir l'alternance régulière des temps et des saisons (Gen. viii 20–2).[4] Bien plus, le sacrifice est intrinsèquement ancré dans les institutions d'Israël: l'offrande de sacrifices fait partie des obligations que Yhwh impose à Israël au Sinaï au moment où il le constitue comme son peuple, et ce aussi bien en Ex. xxxiv 10–26 que dans le Code de l'alliance, dans le Code deutéronomique tout comme dans le Code sacerdotal. Et c'est par des sacrifices qu'est scellée l'alliance avec Yhwh, au pied du Sinaï (Ex. xxiv 3–8)[5] et à l'arrivée en Terre promise (Jos. viii 30–5; cf. Deut. xxvii 1–8).

La place du sacrifice dans l'existence d'Israël est particulièrement mise en évidence par les multiples circonstances où il est offert. En faisant abstraction des données de P et d'Ez. xl–xlviii, qui exigeraient un traitement spécifique, on constate qu'une offrande sacrificielle intervient dans les cas suivants:

Offrir des sacrifices est d'abord une obligation à laquelle doit se soumettre tout Israélite. Dans le cadre de l'alliance du Sinaï, il doit apporter à Yhwh, en tant que propriétaire du pays, les premiers-nés (Ex. xxii 28, xxxiv 19–20; Deut. xv 19; voir aussi Ex. xiii 2, 12–15) et les prémices (Ex. xxiii 19, xxxiv 26; Deut. xviii 4; xxvi 1–11), à quoi s'ajoutera la dîme (Deut. xiv 22–9, xxvi 12–15). Et il doit se

[4] Pour cette interprétation de Gen. viii 21–2, voir R. Rendtorff, "Genesis 8, 21 und die Urgeschichte des Jahwisten", *KeDo* 7 (1961), pp. 69–78.

[5] Sur ce rituel, voir E.W. Nicholson, "The covenant ritual in Exodus xxiv 3–8", *VT* 32 (1982), pp. 74–86.

présenter devant lui au sanctuaire trois fois par an et y offrir des sacrifices (Ex. xxiii 14, 17, xxxiv 23, 24; Deut. xvi 16; pour une description très vivante d'une telle fête voir 1 Sam. i 1–20), ce que fera Salomon, selon l'auteur de 1 Rois ix 25.

Mais ce sont surtout les autres circonstances, celles où l'initiative de l'offrande vient du sacrifiant, qui permettent de se rendre compte de l'importance du sacrifice dans la vie d'Israël. Les narrations constituent sur ce point une source particulièrement précieuse.[6] Car non seulement elles nous donnent un certain nombre d'indications rituelles très concrètes en précisant, dans la plupart des cas, qui est le sacrifiant, quel type de sacrifice est offert, quelle en est la matière et quel est le lieu où il est offert, et en permettant de mettre en corrélation ces différents éléments. Mais elles nous renseignent aussi sur les différents types de situations dans lesquelles intervient l'offrande d'un sacrifice et sur les effets qu'on lui prête. Sans doute, ces sources n'ont aucun caractère systématique et exhaustif, et l'inventaire des circonstances, largement tributaire du hasard, ne saurait être complet. De plus, les textes en question proviennent d'époques et de milieux différents et reflètent ainsi des systèmes sacrificiels différents, de sorte qu'il n'est guère possible, sur la seule base de ces narrations, de retracer l'évolution des formes et des conceptions du sacrifice. Mais les multiples situations qui apparaissent au fil des narrations nous montrent quelles sont les principales fonctions que l'on attribuait au sacrifice, et permettent de dégager des constantes qui constituent une sorte de commun dénominateur par delà les milieux et les époques.

Plus de la moitié de ces narrations, dont la plupart se trouvent dans les livres des Juges et de Samuel, portent sur des sacrifice censés avoir été offerts antérieurement à la construction du Temple.

Nombre de narrations ont pour objet l'exercice du culte. Les récits concernés s'intéressent tout particulièrement aux situations inaugurales, en soulignant généralement le rôle du roi, qui a le privilège d'offrir les premiers sacrifices: inauguration du Temple (1 Rois viii 62–4// 2 Chr. vii 4–6), consécration du Temple (2 Chr. vii 7),[7] du Temple

[6] Sur ces textes cf., classés par ordre chronologique, W. Zwickel, *Der Tempelkult in Kanaan und Israel. Studien zur Kultgeschichte Palästinas von der Mittelbronzezeit bis zum Untergang Judas* (Tübingen, 1994), pp. 285–339, et, classés par types de sacrifices, I. Willi-Plein, *Opfer und Kult im alttestamentlichen Israel. Textbefragungen und Zwischenergebnisse* (Stuttgart, 1993), pp. 71–90. Cf. aussi L. Rost, *Studien zum Opfer im Alten Israel* (Stuttgart, 1981).

[7] Pour cette interprétation, voir A. Marx, *L'offrande végétale dans l'Ancien Testament* (Leiden, 1994), pp. 125–6.

purifié (2 Chr. xxix 20–36,[8] xxxiii 16) ou reconstruit (Esd. vi 16–17), inauguration d'un autel (1 Rois xii 33) ou d'un nouvel autel destiné à remplacer l'ancien (2 Rois xvi 10–13). Certains de ces récits mettent le sacrifice en relation avec la mise en place d'un nouveau culte: le culte consécutif à la fabrication d'une représentation divine sous la forme d'un taurillon (Ex. xxxii 1–6), celui qui résulte de la substitution de Yhwh à Baal (Jug. vi 25–32), la première fête d'automne célébrée par Jéroboam à Béthel (1 Rois xii 33). Quelques récits révèlent le lien étroit du sacrifice avec l'arche: après avoir procédé au rite qui permet la levée des sanctions contre les Philistins,[9] *v*. 14, les habitants de Beth-Shèmesh saluent le retour de l'arche par des sacrifices (1 Sam. vi 15); l'offrande par David de sacrifices permet de transporter l'arche sans encombre et de la conduire jusqu'à la Cité de David (2 Sam. vi 13//1 Chr. xv 26), où elle est saluée par de nouveaux sacrifices royaux (2 Sam. vi 17–18//1 Chr. xvi 1–2); et le transfert de l'arche au Temple nouvellement construit s'accompagne de sacrifices offerts par Salomon et par toute l'assemblée d'Israël (1 Rois viii 1–6//2 Chr. v 2–7). Enfin, le livre d'Esdras fait état d'une utilisation de sacrifices en vue de la purification. Il rapporte, en effet, qu'à leur arrivée à Jérusalem, au retour d'Exil, les compagnons d'Esdras offrirent des holocaustes et des sacrifices "pour les péchés" (Esd. viii 31–6).

La diversité des situations dans lesquelles intervient une offrande sacrificielle est surtout révélée par ceux des récits qui rapportent l'offrande d'un sacrifice dans un contexte non cultuel. Lorsque l'on fait l'inventaire de ces situations, on constate qu'un sacrifice est souvent offert en cas de crise, et tout particulièrement en cas d'agression. Des sacrifices sont ainsi offerts, sur le champ de bataille, avant l'engagement et alors que l'ennemi s'apprête à passer à l'attaque (1 Sam. xiii 5–12), ou à l'instant même où il monte à l'assaut (1 Sam. vii 7–10), ou lorsque la situation de l'assiégé est désespérée et que la défaite semble inéluctable (2 Rois iii 26–7). Des sacrifices sont aussi offerts, au sanctuaire, dans le cadre d'un rituel pénitentiel, en relation avec une consultation oraculaire, après la perte d'une bataille et avant le prochain engagement (Jug. xx 24–8), mais également à l'issue d'une

---

[8] Sur ce rituel, voir J. Milgrom, "Hezekiah's Sacrifices at the Dedication Services of the Purified Temple (2 Chr. 29:21–24)", in A. Kort et S. Morschauser (éd.), *Biblical and Related Studies Presented to Samuel Iwry* (Winona Lake, 1985), pp. 159–61.

[9] Pour cette interprétation du *v*. 14 (voir aussi 2 Sam. xxi 1–14; Job xlii 7–10), voir A. Marx, "Sacrifice de réparation et rites de levée de sanction", *ZAW* 100 (1988), pp. 189–94.

guerre intestine qui s'est révélée fatale pour l'une des composantes du peuple (Jug. xxi 1–4). C'est aussi par un sacrifice que le peuple réagit au réquisitoire de l'ange de Bokim et à sa condamnation d'Israël (Jug. ii 1–5). Pareillement, c'est dans ce cadre pénitentiel, après la dévastation du pays par les armées babyloniennes, que la délégation venue de Sichem, Silo et Samarie se propose d'offrir des sacrifices dans les ruines du Temple (Jer. xli 4–8). On peut encore citer ici le sacrifice offert par David, à l'instigation du prophète Gad, au lieu même où se trouve l'ange destructeur, quand sévit la peste qui décime son peuple (2 Sam. xxiv 18–25//1 Chr. xxi 18–27). Mais il n'y a pas que les situations de crise. On offre aussi des sacrifices pour sceller une alliance (Gen. xxxi 54)—du moins là où il s'agit de groupes apparentés (cf. Ex. xxiii 32, xxxiv 12!)—, pour célébrer une victoire (Jug. xvi 23–4; 1 Sam. xv 14–15, 21; cf. 1 Sam. xiv 32–5), la levée d'un siège (2 Chr. xxxii 21–3), l'intronisation d'un roi (1 Sam. xi 14–15; 1 Chr. xxix 20–2), la venue d'un hôte de marque (Ex. xviii 1–12;[10] Nb. xxii 39–40), l'heureux achèvement d'une entreprise: c'est ainsi qu'à son retour de Gabaon, où il avait reçu de Yhwh les gages d'un règne prospère, Salomon offre des holocaustes et des *šᵉlāmîm* (1 Rois iii 15) et qu'à l'issue de la reconstruction des murailles de Jérusalem le peuple exprime sa joie par des sacrifices (Neh. xii 27–43). Des sacrifices sont également effectués, parfois par de simples individus, comme geste spontané de piété (Jug. xiii 16–23), en action de grâce (Jon. i 16) ou encore pour accomplir un voeu prononcé dans une situation de détresse (Jug. xi 29–40; 2 Sam. xv 7–12; cf. 1 Sam. i 21; Jon. i 16; cf. aussi ii 10). Et c'est ce type de situation qui a dû être le plus habituel. D'autres récits encore font état de sacrifices offerts lors d'une séparation et d'un changement de statut (1 Sam. i 24–5; 1 Rois xix 19–21). Mais les sacrifices peuvent aussi servir à la divinitation: Balaam fait offrir des sacrifices en vue de recevoir une parole de Yhwh (Nb. xxiii 1–6, 13–17, 27–30); et les sacrifices offerts par le patriarche Israël, sur le chemin de l'Egypte (Gen. xlvi 1–4), et par Salomon, au début de son règne (1 Rois iii 4–14//2 Chr. i 3–13)[11] débouchent sur un songe au cours duquel Dieu s'adresse

[10] Mais cf. A. Cody, "Exodus 18,12: Jethro Accepts a Covenant with the Israelites", *Bib.* 49 (1968), pp. 153–66, selon qui il s'agit ici d'un repas d'alliance (voir aussi Thompson, pp. 70–1).

[11] Tandis que le livre des Rois tend à séparer le sacrifice du songe par la précision "à Gabaon", au début du *v.* 5, le livre des Chroniques, tout au contraire, met les deux événements en rapport en soulignant que ce songe a lieu au cours de la nuit qui suit l'offrande de l'holocauste.

au sacrifiant. Ils permettent même à Yhwh de se manifester en tant que tel: c'est grâce à un sacrifice que Gédéon reconnaît un ange de Yhwh dans son interlocuteur anonyme (Jug. vi 17–24); et c'est à travers un holocauste que Yhwh démontre, à la face de tout Israël, qu'il est seul Dieu (1 Rois xviii 20–40).

Cet inventaire montre que des sacrifices sont apportés à Yhwh tant par une collectivité, ou par son représentant que par des individus ordinaires, et ce dans des situations très diverses, comme sacrifices réguliers et obligatoires ou comme sacrifices spontanés et occasionnels. Dans tous les cas, ces sacrifices marquent des temps forts. Ils expriment l'hommage de ses sujets au divin suzerain, et leur soumission. Ils constituent des redevances à celui à qui appartient le pays et tout ce qui y vit et, par là même, font participer Yhwh à la prospérité de son peuple. Ils l'associent à la joie de ses fidèles. Et, surtout, ils permettent à Israël de faire appel à Yhwh, pour le consulter ou, comme ultime recours, lorsque l'intégrité d'Israël est en jeu, afin de l'amener à intervenir en vue de modifier le cours normal des choses: Les narrateurs raconteront comment, à la suite de ces sacrifices, la situation s'est débloquée et s'est retournée en faveur d'Israël.

L'offrande de sacrifices rythme ainsi la vie des Israélites et imprègne leur existence. Le rituel sacrificiel est suffisamment familier pour que, incité par l'inconnu venu lui annoncer la naissance d'un fils, Manoah sache comment offrir un sacrifice (Jug. xiii 16–23), pour que le jeune Isaac sache quelle est la victime habituelle d'un holocauste (Gen. xxii 7) et pour que les prophètes puissent utiliser la métaphore sacrificielle pour décrire l'intervention de Yhwh contre Israël (Soph. i 7–8) ou contre ses ennemis (Es. xxxiv 5–7; Jer. xlvi 10; Ez. xxxix 17–20)[12] mais aussi pour annoncer le retour des exilés (Es. lxvi 20). Les occasions d'offrir des sacrifices sont suffisamment nombreuses pour que le prétexte d'un sacrifice—sacrifice spontané réunissant les anciens d'un village (1 Sam. xvi 1–5; cf. aussi 1 Sam. ix 12–13), sacrifice régulier du clan (1 Sam. xx 6, 29),[13] accomplissement d'un voeu (2 Sam. xv 7–12) ou sacrifice inaugural d'un règne (2 Rois x 18–25)—apparaisse comme une excuse parfaitement valable et suffise à déjouer toute suspicion ou inquiétude (mais cf. 1 Rois i 9–10, 18–19, 25–6!). L'attachement au sacrifice est suffisamment grand pour que

[12] Sur cette métaphore, voir S. Grill, "Der Schlachttag Jahwes", *BZ*, NF 2 (1958), pp. 278–83.

[13] Sur le *zèbaḥ hayyāmîm*, voir M. Haran, "*zebaḥ hayyamîm*", *VT* 19 (1969), pp. 11–22.

Jérémie puisse évoquer le bonheur futur par l'image de pélerins affluant à Jérusalem pour y apporter leurs offrandes à Yhwh (Jer. xvii 26; cf. xxxiii 11, 18).

La question qui, dès lors, se pose est la suivante: d'où vient cette importance attribuée au sacrifice? On sait que pour R. Girard[14]—dont le diagnostic sur la nature de la société rejoint celui fait par Yhwh en Gen. vi 13!—le sacrifice a pour fonction de canaliser la violence en la déchargeant sur une victime.[15] Mais, indépendamment même d'autres considérations, cette explication ne s'accorde guère avec le type de situation où le sacrifice est offert.

La solution pourrait bien être apportée par la loi sur l'autel d'Ex. xx 23(sic!)–26, texte qui a généralement été étudié du point littéraire, historique ou archéologique, mais dont on n'a pas véritablement mesuré l'importance pour l'interprétation du sacrifice.[16]

Le texte se présente sous la forme d'un discours de Yhwh, comme une instruction destinée à Israël. Son auteur l'a clairement conçu comme une unité:[17] les *v.* 23, 24a et 25 sont reliés entre eux par la construction *ʿāśâ* inacc.—2° masc.—*l*ᵉ,[18] les *v.* 24a, 25 et 26, par le mot *mizbéaḥ*

---

[14] *La violence et le sacré* (Paris, 1972).

[15] Pour une critique de la thèse de Girard, du point de vue de la Bible hébraïque, voir A. Marx, "Familiarité et transcendance. La fonction du sacrifice d'après l'Ancien Testament", in A. Schenker (éd.), *Studien zu Opfer und Kult im Alten Testament* (Tübingen, 1992), pp. 1–14 (voir pp. 1–5).

[16] Cf. cependant M. Görg, "Der Altar—Theologische Dimensionen im Alten Testament", in J. Schreiner (éd.), *Freude am Gottesdienst: Aspekte ursprünglicher Liturgie* (= Fest. J.G. Plöger) (Stuttgart, 1983), pp. 291–306. Sur cette loi voir notamment E. Robertson, "The Altar of Earth (Exodus xx. 24–26)", *JSS* 1 (1948), pp. 12–21; D. Conrad, *Studien zum Altargesetz: Ex 20, 24–26* (Marburg, 1968); J. Halbe, *Das Privilegrecht Jahwes Ex 34, 10–26* (Göttingen, 1975), notamment pp. 369–76, 441–4; A. Phillips, "A fresh look at the Sinai pericope", *VT* 34 (1984), pp. 39–52, 282–94; L. Schwienhorst-Schönberger, *Das Bundesbuch (Ex 20,22–23,33). Studien zu seiner Entstehung und Theologie* (Berlin et New York, 1990), pp. 287–99 (histoire de la recherche et place dans le Code de l'Alliance); Y. Osumi, *Die Kompositionsgeschichte des Bundesbuches Exodus 20,22b–23,33* (Freiburg, Suisse, et Göttingen, 1991), pp. 80–5, 156–62, 185–95; B. Renaud, *La théophanie du Sinaï Ex 19–24. Exégèse et théologie* (Paris, 1991), pp. 61–4, 164–6; Fr. Crüsemann, *Die Tora. Theologie und Sozialgeschichte des alttestamentlichen Gesetzes* (München, 1992), pp. 201–5; J.M. Sprinkle, *"The Book of the Covenant". A Literary Approach* (Sheffield, 1994), pp. 35–49. Sur les *v.* 22–3, voir D. Patrick, "The Covenant Code source", *VT* 27 (1977), pp. 145–57; J.P. Oberholzer, "The Text of Ex. 20, 22.23", *JNSL* 12 (1984), pp. 101–5.

[17] Cf. aussi Sprinkle (n. 16), pp. 37–9, ainsi que, mais uniquement pour les *v.* 24–6, Osumi (n. 16), pp. 80–3. En règle générale, on estime que le texte est constitué de plusieurs couches rédactionnelles.

[18] Le passage du pluriel, *v.* 23, au singulier, *v.* 24–6—ou, inversement, du singulier au pluriel—est, comme l'a souligné R. Albertz, une construction rhétorique intentionnelle (*Religionsgeschichte Israels in alttestamentlicher Zeit* 1 [Göttingen, 1992], p. 284). Cf. aussi Sprinkle (n. 16), pp. 39–40.

et par la préposition *ʿal*, avec *mizbéaḥ* comme complément. L'unité du texte se trouve d'ailleurs curieusement corroborée par le décompte du nombre de mots, lequel fait apparaître qu'il comporte cinquante-sept mots, ce qui correspond à la valeur numérique de *mizbéaḥ*!

L'auteur de cette péricope l'a composée avec grand soin et, ainsi que le note Sprinkle ([n. 16] pp. 36, 39), l'a rédigée de manière à lui donner une structure concentrique.

Les *v*. 23 et 26 en forment le cadre extérieur. Construits de la même manière, ils sont constitués chacun de deux hémistiches de cinq mots, chacun de ces versets étant, par ailleurs, introduit par la négation *lōʾ*, laquelle est reprise, associée au même verbe, au *v*. 23, à un verbe différent, au *v*. 26, dans le second hémistiche. Ces deux versets énoncent un certain nombre d'interdits en relation avec l'autel: l'interdiction d'une représentation divine, devant laquelle on offrirait des sacrifices, *v*. 23,[19] et l'interdiction de faire des marches sur l'autel, afin que la nudité du sacrificateur ne soit pas vue sur l'autel, *v*. 26.

Les *v*. 24a et 25, pour leur part, en forment le cadre intérieur. Également de longueur identique, ils sont, quant à eux, introduits chacun par une proposition affirmative, respectivement *mizbéaḥ . . . taʿăśèh lî, ʾim mizbéaḥ . . . taʿăśèh lî*. Ils portent principalement sur la fabrication de l'autel, plus précisément, sur la nature des matériaux qui doivent être utilisés. Les deux versets envisagent deux types d'autel. Le premier de ces deux versets, *v*. 24a, énonce ce qui est la norme, à savoir un autel de terre, et indique quels sont les types de sacrifices et la matière sacrificielle utilisée. La désignation de ces sacrifices comme *ʿōlōt* et *šᵉlāmîm*—et non *zᵉbāḥîm*—, montre clairement que l'auteur a en vue, non le culte privé, mais les sacrifices d'intérêt national.[20] L'autre verset, *v*. 25, envisage le cas d'un autel en pierre brute et motive l'interdiction d'utiliser des pierres taillées pour la construction de l'autel.

Le lien entre les versets 24a et 25 est interrompu par le *v*. 24b. Placé très exactement au centre de ce dispositif et mis en valeur par ce double cadre, le *v*. 24b se détache, en outre, de par son vocabulaire et son contenu spécifiques. En effet, tandis que le reste de la péricope prend la forme d'une loi, énoncée à la deuxième personne, et porte

---

[19] On notera une corrélation entre le *v*. 23bβ et Ex. xxxii 31bβ—ici en séquence inverse—ainsi qu'avec le récit du culte célébré devant le "veau d'or", Ex. xxxii 1–6. Voir aussi Oberholzer (n. 16), p. 103; Albertz (n. 18), p. 284 n. 162.

[20] Sur les *šᵉlāmîm* voir R. Schmid, *Das Bundesopfer in Israel. Wesen, Ursprung und Bedeutung der alttestamentlichen Schelamim* (München, 1964).

sur les conditions extérieures du sacrifice, le texte est ici rédigé à la première personne et se présente comme une promesse: "en tout lieu où je ferai souvenir mon nom, je viendrai vers toi et je te bénirai". Une promesse dont on notera qu'elle est rédigée crescendo, de manière à culminer dans l'annonce de la bénédiction: *ʾazkîr ʾèt-šᵉmî*—trois mots—, *ʾābôʾ ʾélèkā*—deux mots—*ûbéraktîkā*—un seul mot. Cette promesse, insérée au coeur de la loi sur l'autel comme dans un écrin, nous révèle deux choses: premièrement que l'autel, qui est le lieu du sacrifice, est par excellence le lieu où Yhwh vient à la rencontre de son peuple; deuxièmement, que cette rencontre débouche sur une bénédiction pour Israël. Par cette promesse, Yhwh valide l'aspiration d'Israël à établir une communication avec lui. Mais cette communication ne peut aller que dans le sens ciel-terre—Yhwh descendant auprès des hommes—, toute tentative humaine d'atteindre le ciel étant placée sous le sceau de la condamnation divine (Gen. xi 1–9). Et, par ailleurs, en revendiquant l'initiative—"en tout lieu où *je* ferai souvenir mon nom"—Yhwh prévient toute interprétation magique du sacrifice, qui mettrait Yhwh à la disposition de l'homme.[21]

Mais il y a plus. Toute la portée de ce texte a, en effet, été masquée par ce dogme selon lequel la loi sur l'autel formerait le début du Code de l'alliance, de sorte que l'on n'a pas assez remarqué les liens qui unissaient ce discours divin au premier discours de Yhwh, au début d'Ex. xix. Car, à y regarder de plus près, on constate que ces deux textes sont tous deux introduits de la même manière,[22] par une formule en trois temps qui, telle quelle, n'apparaît nulle part ailleurs dans la Bible hébraïque: introduction du locuteur, à savoir Yhwh, et du destinataire du discours, Moïse (Ex. xx 22aα//xix 3bα), puis instruction de s'adresser aux enfants d'Israël, en utilisant la formule *kōh tōʾmar ʾèl/lᵉ* (Ex. xx 22aβ//xix 3bβ)—un type de formule utilisé ailleurs, en relation avec Israël, uniquement en Ex. iii 14 et 15[23]—, enfin interpellation d'Israël sous la forme d'une référence à une intervention passée de Yhwh qu'Israël a vue, *ʾattèm rᵉʾîtèm kî/ʾăšèr* suivie d'un verbe à la 1ère personne référant à cette action passée (Ex. xx 22b//

[21] En faveur de la lecture *ʾazkîr*, voir aussi J.J. Stamm, "Zum Altargesetz im Bundesbuch", *ThZ* 1 (1945), pp. 304–6.

[22] Voir aussi Patrick (n. 16), pp. 145–7, qui, toutefois, isole les *v.* 22–3 de la suite et estime qu'avec xix 3b–8 et xxiv 3–8 ils forment le cadre narratif du Code de l'Alliance.

[23] Cf. aussi Ez. xxxiii 27. Les seuls autres emplois de la formule *kōh tōʾmar ʾèl/lᵉ*, avec Yhwh pour sujet mais avec un autre objet, se trouvent en 2 Sam. vii 8//1 Chr. xvii 7; Jer. xxiii 37, xlv 4, avec un autre sujet, en 2 Sam. xi 25; 1 Rois xii 10//2 Chr. x 10.

xix 4a), formule dont les seules autres attestations se trouvent en Jer. xliv 2 et, avec un sujet différent (respectivement Moïse et Josué) et un verbe à la 3° personne, en Deut. xxix 1 et Jos. xxiii 3.

Une correspondance à ce point étroite entre les deux introductions ne peut qu'attirer l'attention du lecteur et laisse présager une correspondance entre les deux discours divins qui suivent, au début d'Ex. xix et à la fin d'Ex. xx. Et de fait, lorsque l'on examine le contenu de ces deux discours, on s'aperçoit qu'ils portent sur les mêmes thèmes. Tous deux, en effet, contiennent une promesse (Ex. xix 5b6a, xx 24bβ) et culminent dans l'annonce de la venue de Yhwh, *ʾānōkî bāʾ ʾélèkā*, respectivement *ʾābôʾ ʾélèkā* (Ex. xix 9aα//xx 24bα),[24] celle-ci étant accompagnée d'instructions relatives à cette venue, instructions concernant les fidèles, en Ex. xix 10–13, instructions relatives à la construction et à l'aménagement du lieu où Yhwh vient, en Ex. xx 23–24a, 25–6. Toutefois, nos deux textes diffèrent par la forme que prend cette venue et par la perspective dans laquelle celle-ci s'effectue. Le premier discours débouche sur une théophanie spectaculaire (Ex. xix 16a, 18–19; cf. xx 18a) et terrifiante (Ex. xix 16b; cf. xx 18b–19), où la voix de Yhwh tonne du haut des cieux (Ex. xx 19, 22b), cette théophanie étant destinée à affermir l'autorité de Moïse (Ex. xix 9aβ).[25] Le second discours, au contraire, annonce une venue de Yhwh ayant pour unique objet la bénédiction d'Israël (Ex. xx 24b).

Cette correspondance entre les deux discours ne saurait, de toute évidence, être fortuite. En les rapprochant comme il l'a fait, leur auteur aura incontestablement voulu rapprocher aussi les deux types de théophanies qu'ils décrivent, celle du Sinaï et celle de l'autel, la première, qui constitue un événement unique du passé, dont Yhwh a l'entière initiative et qui est liée à un lieu géographique bien précis, extérieur au pays de Canaan et inaccessible à Israël, la seconde, reproductible en tout temps et en tout lieu, *b^{e}kol-hammāqôm*, à l'intérieur des frontières de la Terre promise. Dans cette perspective, tout autel devient Sinaï—comme Moïse était monté, *ʿālâ*, au Sinaï, Ex. xix 3 (cf. aussi xix 12, 13, 20, 23, 24) le sacrificateur monte sur l'autel, Ex. xx 26. Et telle est probablement la raison pour laquelle l'autel doit être fait de matériaux à l'état brut, terre ou pierre. Et tout

[24] Sur l'emploi du verbe *bôʾ* en relation avec la venue de Yhwh, voir H.D. Preuss, *bôʾ*, *TWAT* I (Stuttgart, 1973), col. 562–8.

[25] Sur la théophanie du Sinaï, voir J. Jeremias, *Theophanie. Die Geschichte einer alttestamentlichen Gattung* (Neukirchen-Vluyn, 1965), pp. 100–11.

sacrifice devient la reproduction, sous une forme atténuée, de la théophanie du Sinaï, que se concentre toute entière dans le feu de l'autel, signe visible de la venue de Yhwh (Jug. vi 21, xiii 20; 1 Rois xviii 38; 1 Chr. xxi 26) et qui, selon P et le Chroniste, est d'origine divine (Lev. ix 24; 2 Chr. vii 1). De là l'importance du feu dans la procédure sacrificielle, de préférence, par exemple, à la libation ou au simple dépôt. Car le feu qui brûle sur l'autel n'est pas seulement le moyen de transmettre la matière sacrificielle à Yhwh, il est aussi, d'une certaine manière, la face visible de Yhwh.[26] De là aussi, parce que Yhwh est présent sur l'autel,[27] l'interdiction de toute image de Yhwh—qui, de toute manière; serait superflue du fait de la présence de Yhwh lui-même—et de marches sur l'autel pour que Yhwh ne voie pas la nudité du sacrificateur (cf. Deut. xxiii 15?). Le sacrifice apparaît ainsi, à la lumière de cette correspondance, comme la reproduction cultuelle de la théophanie du Sinaï. Il peut être défini comme un rite mimétique donné par Yhwh à Israël pour lui permettre, chaque fois que nécessaire, chaque fois qu'il le souhaite, de reproduire, en tout temps et en tout lieu, la théophanie du Sinaï, en la domestiquant et en la canalisant de manière à faire venir Yhwh en vue d'obtenir sa bénédiction.

Cette interprétation est expressément corroborée par plusieurs des narrations sacrificielles.

Parmi celles des narrations qui font état de sacrifices liés à l'exercice du culte, cette fonction théophanique est clairement mise en évidence en 2 Chr. vii 1—le feu qui descend du ciel et enflamme le sacrifice manifeste la gloire de Yhwh—mais aussi en 2 Chr. xxix 20–30 et en Gen. xxii 1–19. En 2 Chr. xxix, le rituel de consécration du Temple, consécutif à sa purification, culmine dans l'offrande d'un holocauste, laquelle est accompagnée de chants et de sonneries de trompettes, *v.* 27–30. Et, ainsi que l'indique l'attitude des assistants, cet holocauste débouche sur la venue de Yhwh: à la fin de l'holocauste, tous les présents s'inclinent et se prosternent, tandis que les lévites louent Yhwh, *v.* 29–30. En Gen. xxii, de même, l'holocauste a en vue l'adoration, *hištaḥăwâ*, de Yhwh (*v.* 5), ce qui suppose, concrètement, que Yhwh vient auprès du fidèle à la suite de son holocauste.

---

[26] Pour ce lien de Yhwh avec le feu voir V. Hamp, "*ʾēš*", *TWAT* I (Stuttgart, 1973), col. 457–63.

[27] Voir aussi Am. ix 1; Ps. xliii 4.

Un certain nombre de récits de sacrifices indiquent expressément que cette venue de Yhwh a pour objet une intervention en faveur d'Israël. Les sept holocaustes offerts par Balaq à l'instigation de Balaam sont destinés à faire venir Yhwh auprès de Balaam, *qārâ* ni . . . *liqra*ʾ*t* (Nb. xxiii 3; cf. aussi *v.* 4, 15, 16) afin qu'il lui communique ses instructions, *śîm dābār b*ᵉ*pèh* (Nb. xxiii 5, 16; cf. aussi *v.* 3), et ont pour résultat de déjouer les plans de Balaq et de changer la malédiction en bénédiction (Nb. xxiii 11, 27). Les sacrifices offerts par le patriarche Israël à Béer-Shéva, au moment où il quitte le pays de Canaan pour aller en Egypte, débouchent, la nuit suivante, sur des visions, *mar*ʾ*ōt*, au cours desquelles Dieu le rassure et lui promet sa présence à ses côtés (Gen. xlvi 1–4). De même, c'est dans la nuit qui suit l'offrande par Salomon de mille holocaustes à Gabaon, que Dieu lui apparaît, *rā*ʾ*â* ni., pour l'inviter à formuler un voeu, et lui accorde sagesse, fortune, victoire sur ses ennemis et gloire (1 Rois iii 4–14 et surtout// 2 Chr. i 3–13). L'offrande par Samuel d'un *ʿôlâ kālîl*, à l'instant même où les Philistins attaquent Israël, entraîne l'intervention immédiate, *ʿānâ*, de Yhwh, qui frappe les Philistins de panique, *hāmam* pi., et leur inflige une défaite (1 Sam. vii 7–10). Et l'holocauste du roi de Moab, assiégé par Israël et ses coalisés, déclenche une grande fureur, *qèṣèp gādôl*, contre Israël, fureur qui ne peut être que celle du dieu de Moab (2 Rois iii 26–7).[28] Selon le Chroniste, les holocaustes et *š*ᵉ*lāmîm* offerts par David pendant la peste débouchent sur la venue de Yhwh dans le feu, *ʿānâ*, pour s'adresser aussitôt à l'ange destructeur afin de lui demander de rengainer son épée (1 Chr. xxi 26–7). Toutes ces narrations démontrent la formidable efficacité des sacrifices, en particulier de l'holocauste, et confirment le rôle qui leur est attribué par Ex. xx 24, à savoir faire venir Yhwh pour qu'il bénisse Israël, cette bénédiction pouvant prendre de multiples formes.

La théophanie peut même constituer un objectif en soi. Tel est le cas de l'holocauste d'Elie, au sommet du Carmel, destiné à manifester, par le feu divin qui tombe sur l'holocauste, que c'est Yhwh qui est Dieu (1 Rois xviii 30–9). Et l'holocauste que Yhwh demande à Gédéon d'offrir a pour but d'installer Yhwh à la place de Baal (Jug. vi 25–7). Cette fonction théophanique du sacrifice permet aussi de rendre compte de l'offrande d'un sacrifice lors de la seconde tentative de transférer l'arche de la maison de Oved-Edom à la Cité de David (2 Sam. vi 13//

---

[28] Il est à noter que, de tous les sacrifices offerts à d'autres dieux (Nb. xxv 2; Jug. xvi 23–24; 2 Rois x 18–25), c'est ici le seul à se voir attribuer un effet positif.

1 Chr. xv 26): en offrant à Yhwh un sacrifice de communion[29]—Yhwh étant déjà présent dans l'arche (2 Sam. vi 6–7!), il n'est pas nécessaire de le faire venir par l'offrande d'un holocauste—David détourne Yhwh de l'arche et concentre sa présence sur le sacrifice, de sorte que l'arche est en quelque sorte rendue "profane" et peut donc être manipulée désormais sans danger.

Si donc le sacrifice, et plus précisément l'holocauste, a pour fonction de faire venir Yhwh—et Levine a très bien analysé cette fonction de l'holocauste, qu'il définit comme un rite d'attraction[30]—, l'objectif visé est, on l'a vu, multiple. Cet objectif est précisé par le sacrifiant, et ce, de différentes manières. Il peut être spécifié par les rites qui accompagnent le sacrifice: prière (1 Sam. vii 9; 1 Rois xviii 36–7; 1 Chr. xxi 26; 2 Chr. vi 12–42; cf. aussi Jug. vi 17–18), rites de pénitence (Jug. ii 4–5, xx 26, xxi 2–4; Jer. xli 5–6), séjour du fidèle au sanctuaire en vue d'une incubation (Gen. xlvi 2; 1 Rois iii 5// 2 Chr. i 7), lecture de la loi (Ex. xxiv 3, 7; Jos. viii 34–5), etc.... Mais il peut aussi être indiqué par la nature même du rituel sacrificiel (Nb. xxiii 4), la place du sacrifice dans la séquence rituelle (2 Sam. vi 13),[31] la forme des rites (Ex. xxiv 6, 8, pour le rite du sang), ou encore par la nature des sacrifices associés à l'holocauste: *minḥâ*, pour signifier l'hommage, *šᵉlāmîm*, dans le cas d'un sacrifice d'intérêt national, sacrifice de communion ordinaire, que l'on peut aussi offrir indépendamment de tout autre sacrifice, là où l'on veut inviter Yhwh à prendre part à un repas.

En parcourant ainsi ces différentes narrations il est frappant de constater que dans aucune d'entre elles le sacrifice n'est offert en vue

---

[29] Les victimes utilisées, *šôr* et *mᵉrî'*, sont les victimes habituelles du sacrifice de communion. Cf. 1 Rois i 9, 19, 25. Pour *mᵉrî'*, cf. Ez. xxxix 18; Am. v 22. En remplacant ces victimes par des taurillons et des béliers, le texte parallèle de 1 Chr. xv 26 a considéré ce sacrifice comme étant un holocauste. La fonction de ce sacrifice a été diversement comprise. Pour Thompson, par ex., il s'agit d'un sacrifice d'action de grâce offert à la suite d'un départ sans incident ([n. 2] p. 113). Pour De Robert, au contraire, ce sacrifice est destiné à se rendre Yhwh propice (A. Caquot et Ph. De Robert, *Les livres de Samuel* [Genève, 1994], p. 417).

[30] B.A. Levine, *In the Presence of the Lord. A Study of Cult and Some Cultic Terms in Ancient Israel* (Leiden, 1974), pp. 22–7. Mais Levine a surtout insisté sur la fonction de l'holocauste comme un moyen de s'assurer de l'état d'esprit de Yhwh (voir p. 25).

[31] Le sacrifice est ici offert après six pas et est ainsi associé au nombre sept. Dans le parallèle des Chroniques, ce sont d'ailleurs sept taurillons et sept béliers qui constituent la matière du sacrifice (1 Chr. xv 26). Cf. Jos. vi 3–4 où, après une sextuple circumambulation de la ville, Yhwh se manifeste le septième jour lors de la septième circumambulation (*v.* 12–21). Pour le lien du nombre sept avec la théophanie cf. aussi Nb. xxiii 1, 14, 29.

d'inciter Yhwh à modifier son attitude envers son fidèle. Les quelques récits que, de prime abord, on penserait pouvoir alléguer, ne permettent pas, en réalité, de justifier une telle interprétation. L'holocauste apporté à Yhwh par Noé à l'issue du déluge—dont le caractère unique est souligné par le fait qu'il est constitué d'un exemplaire de chacune des espèces animales pures (Gen. viii 20), et non des seules espèces domestiques, comme il est de règle—est destiné à rétablir la communication avec Yhwh, et non à le faire changer d'avis. Il est d'ailleurs significatif que Noé n'ait pas effectué ce sacrifice au moment de l'annonce du déluge. Même s'il a pour résultat d'amener Yhwh à prendre un certain nombre d'engagements, tel n'est pas l'objectif recherché. Le sacrifice, que Moïse et Aaron prétextent devant Pharaon devoir offrir, n'est pas destiné à écarter la peste ou l'épée, mais celles-ci sanctionneraient l'absence de ce sacrifice (Ex. v 3). Les sacrifices qu'offre David pendant la peste (2 Sam. xxiv 18–25//1 Chr. xxi 18–27) le sont à l'instigation de Gad (2 Sam. xxiv 18)/de l'ange (1 Chr. xxi 18)—autrement dit, par un messager divin—, alors même que Yhwh a déjà pris la décision de la faire cesser (2 Sam. xxiv 16// 1 Chr. xxi 15).[32] Des textes tels que 1 Sam. xxvi 19, où David propose de disposer favorablement Yhwh à son égard en lui faisant sentir une *minḥâ*, sont tout à fait isolés. Sans doute, il est toujours hasardeux de solliciter les silences des textes. Il n'en est pas moins significatif qu'aucune narration n'attribue au sacrifice la fonction de mettre fin à un châtiment envoyé par Yhwh, tel que maladie, famine, sécheresse ou guerre: telle est la fonction de la prière, du jeûne ou encore de la repentance. Et jamais il n'y sert à procurer au sacrifiant descendance, richesse ou protection. Le sacrifice n'est pas destiné à rendre Yhwh propice, ni à apaiser son courroux: sa fonction s'inscrit entièrement dans le cadre fixé par Ex. xx 24, à savoir faire venir Yhwh—et cette venue est à comprendre dans un sens très concret, Yhwh étant présent dans le feu de l'autel—, et ce afin qu'il bénisse son peuple, mais aussi pour l'associer à sa joie, consécutive à la bénédiction reçue.

---

[32] Ce sacrifice est généralement interprété comme un sacrifice d'action de grâce. Ainsi, par ex., Thompson (n. 2), p. 116, ou encore A.A. Anderson, *2 Samuel* (Dallas, 1989), p. 287. Même à supposer que dans une forme ancienne du texte le sacrifice devait servir à inciter Yhwh à mettre fin à la peste (voir, par exemple, Thompson [n. 2], pp. 116–17; Fr. Stolz, *Das erste und zweite Buch Samuel* [Zürich, 1981], p. 303. Cf. aussi A. Caquot, [n. 30], p. 642), dans la forme actuelle du texte, il intervient après que Yhwh a déjà pris cette décision, et ce aussi bien en Samuel que dans le texte parallèle des Chroniques.

Le sacrifice, en tant qu'il permet d'établir et de maintenir la communication avec Dieu, vitale pour l'existence d'Israël, occupe ainsi une place essentielle dans l'ancien Israël. Ainsi que l'a établi Girard, il constitue, pour Israël comme pour toute société primitive, le fondement même de la société. En faire un rite marginal serait parfaitement contraire à la réalité historique.

THE ROOTS OF ANICONISM: AN ISRAELITE PHENOMENON IN COMPARATIVE PERSPECTIVE

by

TRYGGVE N.D. METTINGER
Lund

1. *The problem*

The Decalogue commandment in Exod. xx 4, "thou shalt not make unto thyself any graven image," seeks to enshrine a cult without images, worship that is exclusively aniconic. The problem I am going to discuss is this: where are we to look for the roots, the ultimate origin of Israelite aniconism?[1]

There is now an emerging consensus that the express ban on images is fairly late and to be found only in literature from the period after 722 BCE. Studies by Zimmerli, Dohmen and myself point in this direction.[2] This consensus gives rise to the question: what practices were followed prior to the express prohibition of images? Was the earlier Israelite cult a cult of images and therefore "iconic"? Or are we to reckon with a long-standing tradition of aniconism with truly ancient origins? Did Israelite aniconism emanate from theological reflection, perhaps on the nature of the deity and divine transcendence or on man as the image of God? Or is aniconism the cultic corollary of Israel's bias against kingship? Or, again, is aniconism an inheritance from the putative nomadic past of ancient Israel?

There have been attempts to answer such questions and a great amount of serious research has been devoted to the prohibition on images by Bernhardt, Keel, Dohmen, Hendel, Uehlinger, Loretz and

---

[1] This problem is discussed in detail in my recent monograph (Mettinger 1995a), where the reader will find extensive documentation.

[2] See Zimmerli 1969 and 1974, Mettinger 1979, Dohmen and also Uehlinger 1989 and 1993, pp. 281–2. On 1 Sam. v 1–5 (the statue of Dagon) as a possible indication of an early date for the programmatic aniconic stance, see Mettinger 1995a, p. 196, and contrast Zwickel 1994b. On 2 Kgs xvi 17, see Zwickel 1993.

others.[3] In one respect, however, one notes an alarming lack of scholarly attention: Israelite aniconism has never been properly studied in the light of the comparative material from the surrounding cultures. One simple observation demonstrates that comparative data do merit attention: in addition to the religion of Israel another major Semitic religion has developed a prohibition on images. I refer, of course, to Islam, where a prohibition on images was clearly promulgated in the edict of the Caliph Yazid II in 721 CE. The Hadith and numismatic evidence take us back in time to the 690s CE (see Mettinger 1995a, p. 77). Though this is admittedly rather late, we must ask: is it mere coincidence that two major Semitic religions attest the same attitude toward images? What, then, do the comparative data indicate concerning the roots of aniconism?

The difficulty of the problem is clearly pronounced by two distinguished biblical scholars. One of them, Gerhard von Rad, states it in the following way:

> Here becomes manifest something of the mystery of Israel, something of her nature as a stranger and a sojourner among the religions. Anyone who seriously devotes himself to a study of religions as they appear and their worship of images can find absolutely no way of transition from them to Israel's prohibition of images . . . (1962, pp. 214–15 = German, pp. 227–8).

The other, Werner H. Schmidt, writes that,

> Since once again any real analogy is lacking, the prohibition of idols cannot be derived from the surrounding world. Religio-historical inquiry keeps on running up against the first and second commandments in the Old Testament, but the two also form the boundary beyond which historical research has not hitherto been able to pass (p. 77 = German, p. 83).

What I shall make here is, indeed, nothing less than an attempt to reconstruct the situation prevailing in periods prior to the express formulation found in the Decalogue. The tool that I shall use to penetrate this barrier is the material from the surrounding cultures.

Before we proceed any further, I must define the term "aniconism".[4] I shall use it to refer to cults where there is no iconic representation

[3] See Bernhardt, Keel, pp. 37–45, Mettinger 1979, Dohmen, Hendel, Uehlinger 1989 and 1993, pp. 278–88, and Loretz in Dietrich and Loretz, 1992, pp. 77–182.

[4] For definitions and terminology, see Mettinger 1995a, pp. 18–27.

of the deity (anthropomorphic or theriomorphic) serving as the dominant or central cultic symbol.[5] It goes without saying that this definition includes sacred emptiness or "empty-space aniconism"—attested in the case of the empty cherubim throne in the Solomonic temple. But we are not concerned only with sacred emptiness: cults using aniconic symbols may also be considered to be instances of aniconism, that is, "material aniconism".

At this juncture I should like to call attention to the striking parallelism between the cultic paraphernalia in Jerusalem and at Arad: in Jerusalem we find the empty cherubim throne in the holy of holies.[6] At Arad we find one or maybe several *maṣṣēbôt* in the holy of holies.[7] In my opinion, the findings at Arad signal the importance of stelae for a proper understanding of the issue before us. There are thus two basic sub-types of aniconism: "empty-space aniconism" and "material aniconism".

There is, however, still another distinction that is highly important to us. We must maintain a distinction between the mere absence of images, on the one hand, and the programmatic demand for a cult without images, the repudiation of iconic objects, on the other. I shall call the first type *de facto* aniconism, the other programmatic aniconism. *De facto* aniconism probably tended to be tolerant, while programmatic aniconism, having been subjected to the rigours of theological reflection, was likely characterized by a conscious and programmatic attitude which may have lead to outright iconoclasm.

From an epistemological point of view it is clear that the actual, physical absence of images is hard or even impossible to prove since evidence for such absence can always be classified as an argument from silence. On the other hand, the category of "material aniconism" provides some much-needed corroborative evidence. Material objects classified as aniconic, objects that functionally take the place of the image in the cult, may have survived and may be recovered in archaeological excavations. Thus, cult archaeology becomes an important aspect of our efforts.[8]

---

[5] Note that the overwhelming majority of votive figures (offerings) representing deities do not seem to have served as the central cultic image in the context in which they were found; see Mettinger 1995a, p. 27.

[6] See Mettinger 1982, pp. 19–37, with literature, and my article "Cherubim" in Mettinger 1995b.

[7] On Arad, see Mettinger 1995a, pp. 143–9.

[8] For criteria for defining a cultic context for archaeological finds, see Mettinger 1995a, pp. 141–3.

2. *The evidence*

1. *Gades, Tyre, Phoenicia*

In order to solve our problem and answer our question we must take an excursion far afield from Palestine, to Spain, or, to be more exact, to Gades[9] on the island Santipetri, 18 km SE of present-day Cádiz. Here we encounter the unusual circumstance that there is written evidence to the effect that the cult was aniconic. This is found in Silius Italicus (1st century CE) and Philostratus (3rd century CE). The latter says that "In the shrine they say there is maintained a cult both of one and the other Hercules [i.e., the Greek and Tyrian Hercules], though there are no images of them; altars however there are . . ." (*Vita Apollon. Thyan.* V, 5). And the former says: "But the fact that there were no statues or familiar images of the gods filled the place with solemnity and sacred awe" (*Punica* III, 30–1).[10]

To bring evidence from a cult place in Spain to bear on a problem related to the ancient Near East is by no means far-fetched. Gades was an early Phoenician settlement, founded by the Tyrians. Even the name is Phoenician, attesting the root *gdr*, as is obvious from the forms Gadeira and Gadir. The cult is a cult for the Tyrian Hercules or Melqart.

The references to aniconism at Gades have been judged quite differently by various scholars. Corinne Bonnet in her monograph on Melqart pointed out that imperial coins depict Hercules Gaditanus as a statue in his temple and was not inclined to view the cult as a parallel of Israelite aniconism (p. 213, and on the coins also p. 230). García y Bellido, on the other hand, assumes that there were two distinct cults at Gades and holds that, even if the Greek Heracles required an anthropomorphic representation, the Tyrian, Phoenician Heracles-Melqart did not (pp. 110–114). D. van Berchem writes in the same vein and makes an explicit reference to "la vieille interdiction sémitique, si abondamment illustrée par l'Ancien Testament" (p. 84). Pierre Rouillard assumes two subsequent phases with a transition from aniconic to iconic cult at Gades (Lipiński and Rouillard, p. 183).

---

[9] On Gades, see Mettinger 1995a, pp. 86–90.

[10] Instead of Duff's translation "but no statues . . . filled . . .", I adopt the interpretation of "nullus" suggested by Spaltenstein, 1986, p. 180.

The cult at Gades may represent Phoenician practice. That this is a real possibility is made clear by Ernest Will's study (especially pp. 8–9). Will compiles and compares information on the cults at Gades and Tyre, found in various writers. At both sites he finds (a) a sacred olive tree, (b) a sacred fire and (c) stelae. The stelae serve as aniconic symbols of the divine. Will's results are confirmed by the observation that blood is important as sacrificial matter at both Gades and Tyre (see Mettinger 1995a, p. 192 n. 223 with references).

In the case of Tyre,[11] it is true that there is an anthropomorphic iconography for Tyrian Melqart, either the late, Hellenized one (Heracles) or an earlier one, known from Bar Hadad's Melqart stele found in the vicinity of Aleppo. However, neither of these can be regarded as the canonical iconography of Melqart. In contrast to this, one may adduce an aniconic iconography, attested on Tyrian coins from the 3rd and 4th centuries CE (fig. 1, p. 233). The mintage on these coins clearly portrays two stelae or betyls, an olive tree and a flaming incense altar standing together. The stelae are also mentioned by various ancient authors; the earliest allusions to them seem to appear in Ezek. xxvi 11, xxviii 14, 16.

It may be added parenthetically that my conclusion as to the importance of stelae as aniconic symbols in certain Semitic contexts is confirmed by Herodian of Syria. In his history of the Roman Empire, Herodian describes the temple at Emesa (Homs) in Syria, which was erected at the beginning of the 3rd century CE for the Semitic god Elagabalus and states that the cultic object of this sanctuary was,

> no actual man-made statue of the god, the sort Greeks and Romans put up; but . . . an enormous stone, rounded at the base and coming to a point on the top, conical in shape and black, . . . sent from heaven [διοπετής, lit. "fallen from Zeus"]. (V, 3, 4–5).

This object is also known from a coin from Emesa.[12] It was obviously what is sometimes referred to as a betyl (βαίτυλος) by both ancient sources and modern scholars. For this Semitic cult we thus note, just as at Gades, the absence of images *and* the presence of an aniconic object, "an enormous stone".

Turning from Tyre to Sidon,[13] we find a different form of aniconic

[11] On Tyre, see Mettinger 1995a, pp. 90–100.
[12] See Mettinger 1995a, p. 85, fig. 5.3.
[13] On Sidon, see Mettinger 1995a, pp. 100–6.

iconography. In the first place, some sixteen votive sphinx thrones, most of them of less than natural size, have been found in the vicinity of Sidon. These thrones are mostly empty, but a hole in the seat or an anathyrose seems to imply that the throne was occupied by some object. Of course, this could have been a seated deity, but some indications point in a different direction. One item, a throne from Khirbat et-Tayyiba, displays two stelae sculptured in low relief on the interior side of the back (fig. 2). Soyez mentions a throne bearing a parallelepipedal betyl. Another remarkable item is the so called "trône Seyrig" (fig. 3), the seat of which is occupied by a spherical object. Still another of this series is a throne from Sidon with the seat at such a steep incline that it is incapable of receiving any object (fig. 4). This was obviously a case of an empty throne.

The coins from Sidon (see for instance fig. 5) should be added to the evidence mentioned thus far. The impression on these is a composition depicting a globular object, housed within in a four-columned shrine on a two-wheeled vehicle, the "car of Astarte". The spherical object either rests on a podium or else is supported by two figures which are probably stylized sphinxes. If the latter is true, the composition depicts a spherical object on a sphinx throne, just as in the case of the "trône Seyrig".

What we find at Sidon is thus a *configuration* consisting of a sphinx throne plus either an aniconic object (stele or globe) or just the empty space. One is tempted, indeed, to draw the daring conclusion that "stelae equal empty space". If correct, this sheds light on the iconography of two Israelite Iron Age sanctuaries: one at Arad, where we find stelae, and the other in Solomonic Jerusalem, where we find an empty cherubim throne.

We have seen that the Phoenician world provides evidence for what I have chosen to call material aniconism, mostly in the form of cults focussed on stelae or betyls. The question that now presents itself is this: is this type of aniconism limited to the Phoenicians or do we also find it in other realms of the ancient Semitic world? The answer to this question is clearly that it is so found. I must here limit myself to a brief review of the evidence. A detailed account is provided in my recent monograph *No Graven Image? Israelite Aniconism in its Ancient Near Eastern Context* (1995).

2. *The Nabateans*[14]

The major representation at Petra of the Nabatean national god Dusares is described in some detail in Suidas' *Lexicon*, compiled in the 10th century CE, but certainly based on earlier sources. We read in Suidas that Dusares' symbol was a black stone:

> The image [ἄγαλμα] is a black stone, square and unshapen, four feet high by two feet broad. It is set on a base of wrought gold. To this they offer sacrifice and for it they pour forth the victim's blood, that being their form of libation (*Lexicon* 2, p. 173; translation from Patrich, p. 51).

The stone obviously represents the deity and appears as the recipient of libations of blood. Nabatean aniconism has been thoroughly treated in a groundbreaking monograph by Joseph Patrich (1990). The evidence comprises among other things a number of coins with aniconic representations of the deities (see for instance fig. 6).

3. *Pre-Islamic Arabia*

Whether the Nabateans were Arabs—as their proper names seem to indicate—or of some other origin, it is worthy of note that the same type of cult is found in pre-Islamic Arabia.[15] The open-air sanctuaries consisted of a *temenos*, properly marked off by stones. The central cult stone (*nuṣuḇ*) was the recipient of sacrificial libations of blood which were shed into the pit (*ġabġab*) in front of it. The circumambulation (*ṭawāf*) of the holy stone was an important part of the ritual. Already Wellhausen pointed out that the rare cases of anthropomorphic images should probably be attributed to foreign imports and are hardly characteristic of original Arabic religion (p. 102).

4. *Bronze Age Syria*

When we turn to Bronze Age Syria[16] we notice that there is now growing documentary evidence for the prominence of stelae in cults which I regard as West Semitic. This evidence includes texts from Mari and Emar which attest a term for stele, *sikkānu*, a derivative

---

[14] On the Nabateans, see Mettinger 1995a, pp. 57–68.
[15] On Arabia, see Mettinger 1995a, pp. 69–79.
[16] On Bronze Age Syria, see Mettinger 1995a, pp. 115–34.

of the root *skn*, "to dwell", and related to Hebrew *škn*. It also comprises archaeological finds of stelae, such as the one in Ninni-Zaza's temple in Mari (date: pre-Sargonic), or the two slabs in Temple N in Ebla or the two stelae in Temple D at the same site (date: Middle Bronze Age), or the cultic paraphernalia of the open cult place at Qatna (date: probably Middle Bronze Age).

5. *Iron Age Palestine*

What, then are we to say about Israel, about Iron Age Palestine?[17] I suspect that the reader may be tempted at this point to remind me of the passages where *maṣṣēbôt* are prohibited, just as images (Deut. xvi 22; 2 Kgs xviii 4, etc.). Such texts, however, are hardly representative of the situation prior to the reign of Hezekiah. There are solid indications to the effect that, during Iron Age I and the major part of Iron Age II, Israel regarded the *maṣṣēbôt* cult as a legitimate expression of religious worship. Both textual evidence (Gen. xxviii; Hos. iii 4) and archaeological finds point in this direction. I shall here just briefly enumerate the most important archaeological evidence without indulging in any detailed comments.

– Arad. There were one or several *maṣṣēbôt* in the holy of holies. Date: Iron Age II (either Solomonic, the Y. Aharoni-Z. Herzog chronology, or 7th century, D. Ussishkin's revision).

– Lachish. Cult room 49 in Stratum V (Iron Age IIA) and the open high place excavated under the *adyton* of the Hellenistic temple, as well as a pit in a nearby street, provide good examples of *maṣṣēbôt*.

– Beth-shemesh. A stratum that probably met its end in 701 BCE. contained an open-air high place with *maṣṣēbôt* in use during Iron Age II.

– Tirzah. According to the reconstruction by R. de Vaux and Chambon a basin and a *maṣṣēbâ* stood at the centre of the open place just inside the city gate. Date: Iron Age II. The installation was in use from the 10th century onwards (probably even after 722 BCE).

– Taanach. A basin and an arched slab seem to represent a similar arrangement to the one at Tirzah. Date: Iron Age IIA. Admittedly, Taanach and Tirzah are controversial cases.

---

[17] On Palestine, see Mettinger 1995a, pp. 153–97; on the Iron Age finds, see pp. 143–68. For a general presentation of Palestinian cult places from the Iron Age, note Zwickel 1994a, pp. 201–84.

– Megiddo. The "Schumacher-Ussishkin sanctuary", Locus 340 within building 338 in Area BB, seems to have been a cultic installation with *maṣṣēbôt* forming the focal point of the cultic paraphernalia. Date: Iron Age IIA (Stratum VA–IVB). In Area AA, Locus 2081 contained a number of cultic items among which were a *maṣṣēbâ*. Date: Iron Age IIA.

– Tel Dan. Quite recently, four different *maṣṣēbôt* shrines have been found in the gate square. Date: Iron Age II. Three of these shrines belong to the 9th–8th centuries, while the other may be from the time around the Assyrian conquest.

Let me summarize what I have said so far. Among the Phoenicians, Nabateans, pre-Islamic Arabs and Israelites, and also in Bronze Age Syria, we have found what I should like to term a "material aniconism" in the form of cults focussed on standing stones. In my opinion, this evidence indicates the existence of a shared West Semitic cult type and an aniconism common to the West Semites.

If we focus on the Israelite Iron Age phenomenon, the *maṣṣēbôt* cults just referred to, one can of course raise the question about its immediate origin. Could it be that this type of cult was a Yahwistic import, carried into Palestine by an immigrating YHWH-group, coming from the south? The finds of numerous cult places with stelae in the Negeb, notably in the Uvda Valley and at Timna,[18] might support such a conclusion. I personally believe that the cult of the earliest YHWH-worshippers was aniconic and was a type of *maṣṣēbôt* cult. However, I must also emphasize that this type of "material aniconism" seems to have been an established practice in Palestine and Syria long before the emergence of ancient Israel, and long before the immigration of groups worshipping YHWH. That this is so is supported by a number of Bronze Age finds, made in Palestine. Let me briefly mention the following sites:[19]

– Hartuv. This site near Beth-shemesh in the Shephelah revealed a hall which housed nine standing stones lining the inner face of the southern long wall. Date: Early Bronze Age I.

– Tel Kitan. A cult place with a temple featured a row of 8 stelae standing in front of the temple, parallel to its façade. Date: Middle Bronze Age IIB.

---

[18] See U. Avner and Mettinger 1995a, pp. 168–74.

[19] For details, see Mettinger 1995a, pp. 175–91. See also Zwickel 1994a, pp. 17–203, who gives a general presentation of Bronze Age cult places in Palestine.

– Tell el-Hayyat. The new temple of phase 3, Middle Bronze Age IIB, had a similar installation of stelae in the court.

– Megiddo. The holy precinct in Area BB, a place that holds cultic associations for centuries. The south-west corner of square N13, above altar 4017, was spotted with stelae. Date: Middle Bronze Age IIB (Stratum XII, 1750–1700 BCE or somewhat earlier).

– Gezer. A row of large monoliths. Date: Middle Bronze Age IIC (or perhaps Late Bronze Age).

– Shechem. A striking find of a huge stele is connected with temple 2. It stood in the forecourt, to the east of the entrance, and close to the altar. Date: Late Bronze Age.

– Hazor. Stelae have been found at various loci at Bronze Age Hazor. The stelae sanctuary (Shrine 6136) in Area C in the lower city is the most renowned of these finds. Date: Late Bronze Age (Stratum 1b and 1a, 14th–13th centuries BCE). One could also mention an open-air cult place in Area A on the mound, with a stele and a bowl. Date: Late Bronze Age (Stratum XIV and XIII, 14th–13th centuries BCE).[20]

It thus seems clear that the cult of stelae was widespread in Palestine long before the Iron Age.

3. *Conclusions and final remarks*

The problem I have discussed in this article is that of the origin of Israelite aniconism. My objective has been, not to demonstrate that all cult in ancient Israel was aniconic—it certainly was not—but to bring to light a tradition of aniconic worship of YHWH with deep roots in earlier West Semitic cults.[21] The evidence discussed here sheds new light on the phenomenon of Israelite aniconism and seems to justify the following conclusions:

1. There are compelling reasons to make two important distinctions: first, a distinction must be observed between *de facto* aniconism

[20] On a find at Beth-shan which I took to be a stele, Mettinger 1995a, pp. 189–90, see now Zwickel 1994a, p. 174.

[21] I am well aware of cases like the bull figurine from the Bull Site (Mettinger 1995a, pp. 153–5) or of textual evidence such as 1 Kgs xv 13; 2 Kgs xxi 7 or again of the Assyrian texts about the spoliation of images (on which see Mettinger 1995a, pp. 69, 84, 136 and 194–5). However, I do not find this material alters the essential fact established by my investigation, viz., that there was a long-standing tradition of aniconic cult among the West Semites, including the Israelites.

and the programmatic repudiation of images, the iconoclastic attitude. As soon as our quest for origins is redirected, from a search for ancient parallels to the Israelite ban on images, to a search for cases of *de facto* aniconism, our eyes are opened to the neglected ancestry of the Israelite phenomenon. Second, we must make a distinction between "empty-space aniconism" and "material aniconism". As soon as we recognize the last-mentioned type as a form of aniconism,[22] our quest for the genesis of aniconism is transformed from a quixotic search for the empty space (which hardly leaves archaeological traces) to a search for tangible material objects such as aniconic stones like stelae/*maṣṣēbôt*.

2. The range of discovery of aniconic stelae indicates that aniconism was a shared feature of West Semitic cults. Israelite aniconism originally belonged to this wider frame of reference.[23] Moreover, aniconism in Islam is probably not a direct descendant but rather a late cousin of the Israelite phenomenon. Both originally go back to West Semitic "standing stones aniconism".

3. Israelite aniconism as such (*de facto* aniconism) is no late innovation. It is as old as Israel itself. The express prohibition of images is just the conclusion of centuries of development, and this continuum of development spans the distance between early West Semitic *de facto* aniconism and late Israelite iconoclasm.

4. Israelite aniconism as such, her *de facto* aniconism, is not the result of theological reflection. Instead, it must be seen as an inherited convention of religious expression on the level of cult and ritual. Various attempts to explain this *de facto* aniconism as deriving from specific Israelite beliefs are to be considered disproven. Israelite aniconism does not derive from any specific notions of God, such as divine transcendence.

As for the development that led from *de facto* aniconism to the programmatic stance and the express prohibition of images, we shall, however, have to reckon with specific theological and religio-political ideas as important factors in the process. Besides, we should be wise to see the concept of the empty throne as an important intermediary between standing stones aniconism and the prohibition of images.

---

[22] The fact that a number of stelae from Ugarit had reliefs with iconic representations of deities does not basically affect the fact that West Semitc stelae were generally aniconic; see Mettinger 1995a, pp. 122–7, 128–9, 134.

[23] On aniconism and aniconic tendencies in Egypt and Mesopotamia, see Mettinger 1995a, pp. 39–56.

I must here finally call attention to a typological contrast between West Semitic cults on the one hand and Mesopotamian (and Egyptian) on the other. West Semitic cult in its genuine form has three characteristics:

(a) The cult place is an open-air *temenos* with stelae as symbols of the divine.

(b) The sacrificial procedure is ritual slaughter and a communal meal.

(c) The sacrificial offering by preference is blood.

In addition, there is a taboo on the use of pork for cultic purposes. The West Semitic cults offer an unmistakable contrast when compared with the temples, divine images and the idea of the care and feeding of the gods of the Mesopotamian cults.[24]

5. My discussion of Israelite aniconism also alerts us to a characteristic feature of Israel's cultural relationship with its *Umwelt*. This relationship has important elements of both continuity and contrast: continuity so far as Israelite aniconism has a West Semitic pedigree, contrast so far as the express veto on images represents a specific Israelite development, seemingly unparalleled for centuries in the ancient world. Later on, the Nabateans and early Islam take a similar step. I have traced a development that runs from West Semitic aniconism to Israelite iconoclasm. The roots of Israelite aniconism are found in the West Semitic world. The express ban on images, however, belongs to Israel's *differentia specifica*.[25]

Addition to the proofs: For a discussion of the Israelite developments, see now T. Mettinger, "Israelite Aniconism: Developments and Origins", forthcoming in K. van der Toorn (ed.), *The Image and the Book: Iconic Cults, Aniconism, and the Veneration of the Holy Book in Israel and the Ancient Near East*, Leuven (Peeters).

---

[24] On this contrast, see Mettinger 1995a, pp. 191–3, and cf. pp. 29–32. Note the convergence of my results and those of Houston (especially pp. 124–81) in his study of the taboo on pork as sacrificial matter. That there were a number of temples in the West Semitic area (see most recently Zwickel 1994a) does not alter the fact that the most typical and genuine West Semitic cult place was the open-air cultic site, while the most typical Mesopotamian locus for cultic activities was the temple.

[25] I wish to thank Dr Michael S. Cheney, of Edmonton, who scrutinized my English.

REFERENCES

Herodian—*Herodian* I and II (*Loeb Classical Library*), with an English translation by C.R. Whittaker (London and Cambridge, Mass., 1969 and 1970.

Philostratus—*Philostratus. The Life of Apollonius of Tyana* . . . I (*LCL*), with an English translation by F.C. Conybeare (Cambridge, Mass., and London, 1912).

Silius Italicus—*Silius Italicus Punica* I and II (*Loeb Classical Library*), with an English translation by J.D. Duff (Cambridge, Mass., and London, 1927 and 1934).

Suidas—*Suidae Lexicon*. 1–5 ed., A. Adler (Teubner) (Leipzig, 1928–38).

Avner, U. 1993. "*Maẓẓebot* sites in the Negev and Sinai and their significance", in A. Biran and J. Aviram (ed.), *Biblical Archaeology Today 1990* (Jerusalem), pp. 166–81.

Bernhardt, K.-H. 1956. *Gott und Bild. Ein Beitrag zur Begründung und Deutung des Bilderverbotes im Alten Testament* (Berlin).

Bonnet, C. 1988. *Melqart. Cultes et mythes de l'Héraclès tyrien en Méditerranée* (Leuven and Namur).

Cook, A.B. 1940. *Zeus. A Study in Ancient Religion*, 3:2 (Cambridge).

Dietrich, M. and O. Loretz, 1992. *"Jahwe und seine Aschera": Anthropomorphes Kultbild in Mesopotamien, Ugarit und Israel. Das biblische Bilderverbot* (Münster).

Dohmen, C. 1985 *Das biblische Bilderverbot. Seine Entstehung und seine Entwicklung im alten Testament* (Bonn).

García y Bellido, A. 1963. "Hercules Gaditanus", *Archivo Español de Arqueologia* 36, pp. 70–153.

Hendel, R.S. 1988. "The social origins of the aniconic tradition in ancient Israel", *CBQ* 50, pp. 365–82.

Hill, G.F. 1910. *BMC Phoenicia = Catalogue of the Greek Coins of Phoenicia* (London).

——— 1922. *BMC Arabia = Catalogue of the Greek Coins of Arabia, Mesopotamia and Persia* (London).

Houston, W. 1993. *Purity and Monotheism. Clean and Unclean Animals in Biblical Law* (Sheffield).

Keel, O. 1977. *Jahwe-Visionen und Siegelkunst. Eine neue Deutung der Majestätsschilderungen in Jes 6, Ez 1 und 10 und Sach 4* (Stuttgart).

Lipiński, É. and P. Rouillard. 1992. "Gadès." *Dictionnaire de la civilisation phénicienne et punique* (Turnhout), pp. 181–3.

Mettinger, T.N.D. 1979. "The veto on images and the aniconic God in ancient Israel", in H. Biezais (ed.), *Religious symbols and their functions* (Stockholm), pp. 15–29.

——— 1982. *The Dethronement of Sabaoth. Studies in the Shem and Kabod Theologies* (Lund).

——— 1994. "Aniconism—a West Semitic context for the Israelite phenomenon?", in W. Dietrich and M.A. Klopfenstein (ed.), *Ein Gott allein? Jhwh-Verehrung und biblischer Monotheismus im Kontext der israelitischen und altorientalischen Religionsgeschichte* (Fribourg and Göttingen), pp. 151–78.

——— 1995a. *No Graven Image? Israelite Aniconism in its Ancient Near Eastern Context* (Stockholm).

——— 1995b. "Cherubim", in K. van der Toorn, B. Becking and P.W. van der Horst (ed.), *Dictionary of Deities and Demons in the Bible* (Leiden, New York and Köln), cols 362–67.

Metzger, M. 1985. *Köningsthron und Gottesthron. Thronformen und Throndarstellungen in Ägypten und im Vorderen Orient* . . . (Kevelaer and Neukirchen-Vluyn).

Patrich, J. 1990. *The formation of Nabatean art. Prohibition of a graven image among the Nabateans* (Jerusalem).

Rad, G. von. 1962. *Old Testament Theology* I (Edinburgh and London), = *Theologie des Alten Testaments* I (4th edn, Munich, 1962).

Schmidt, W.H. 1983. *The Faith of the Old Testament. A History* (Oxford), = *Alttestamentlicher Glaube in seiner Geschichte* (Neukirchen-Vluyn, 1983).
Spaltenstein, F. 1986. *Commentaire des Punica de Silius Italicus (livres 1 à 8)* (Geneva).
Uehlinger, C. 1989. Review of C. Dohmen 1985, *BO* 46, cols 410–19.
——— 1993. "Northwest Semitic inscribed seals, iconography and Syropalestinian religions of Iron Age II", in B. Sass and C. Uehlinger (ed.), *Studies in the iconography of Northwest Semitic Inscribed Seals* (Fribourg and Göttingen), pp. 257–88.
Van Berchem, D. 1967. "Sanctuaires d'Hercule-Melqart", *Syria* 44, pp. 73–109 and 307–38.
Wellhausen, J. 1897. *Reste arabischen Heidentums* (2nd edn, Berlin).
Will, E. 1950–1. "Au sanctuaire d'Héraclès à Tyr. L'olivier enflammé, les stèles et les roches ambrosiennes", *Berytus* 10, pp. 1–12.
Zimmerli, W. 1969. "Das zweite Gebot" (orig. publ. in 1950), in W. Zimmerli, *Gottes Offenbarung* (2nd edn, Munich), pp. 234–48.
——— 1974. "Das Bilderverbot in der Geschichte des alten Israel", in W. Zimmerli, *Studien zur alttestamentlichen Theologie und Prophetie* 2 (Munich), pp. 247–60.
Zwickel, W. 1993. "Die Kultreform des Ahas (2 Kön xvi 10–18)", *SJOT* 7, pp. 250–62.
——— 1994a. *Der Tempelkult in Kanaan und Israel* (Tübingen).
——— 1994b. "Dagons abgeschlagener Kopf (1 Samuel v 3–4)", *VT* 44, pp. 239–49.

Illustrations

Fig. 1. Tyrian coin with steale. Copper, 31 mm. Hill, *BMC Phoenicia*, pl. 33, no. 14. From Cook 1940, p. 980, fig. 785.
Fig. 2. Throne from Khirbat et-Tayyiba. Limestone. Height: 0.47m. Date: 2nd century BCE. Drawing by Per Helin after Metzger 1985, no. 1200.
Fig. 3. Phoenician throne with a spherical object on the seat. Exact provenance unknown. Bronze. Height: 7 cm. Roman period. Drawing by Per Helin after Metzger 1985, no. 1202.
Fig. 4. Throne from Sidon with seat so steeply inclined that it must have been empty. Height: 0.45 m. Date: 59–60 CE. Drawing by Per Helin after Metzger 1985, no. 1201.
Fig. 5. Coin from Sidon, depicting the "car of Astarte". Ae, 25 mm. Drawing by Per Helin after Hill, *BMC Phoenicia*, pl. 24, no. 8.
Fig. 6. Coin of Nabatean Adraa with dome-shaped betyl. Ae, 27 mm. Drawing by Per Helin after Hill, *BMC Arabia*, pl. 3, no. 5.

1. Coin of Type

2. Phoenician votive throne

3. Phoenician votive throne

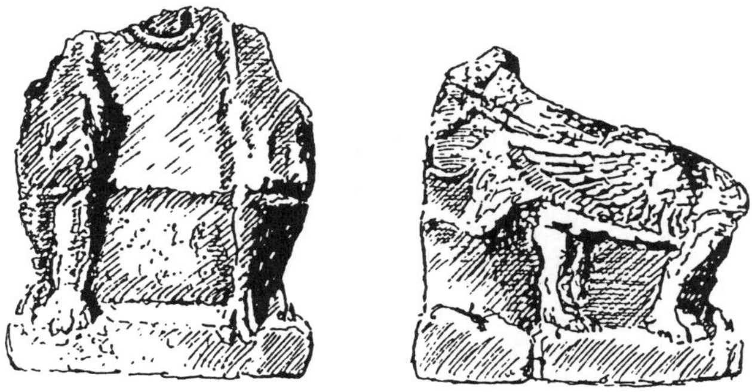

4. Phoenician votive throne

5. Coin of Sidon

6. Nabatean coin

FROM TRADITION TO CRITICISM: JEWISH SOURCES AS AN AID TO THE CRITICAL STUDY OF THE HEBREW BIBLE

by

ALEXANDER ROFÉ
Jerusalem

The book of Psalms in the Hebrew Bible opens with a poem which extols the virtue of the man who "delights in the Torah of the Lord and recites his Torah day and night": *bĕtôrat yhwh ḥepṣô ûbĕtôratô yehgeh yômām wālāylâ* (Ps. i 2). The same practice is enjoined to Joshua in an interpolation extant in the first chapter of the canonical collection of Prophets (Josh. i 8): "Let not this book of the Torah cease from your lips, but recite it day and night": *lōʾ-yāmûš sēper hattôrâ hazzeh mippîkā wĕhāgîtā bô yômām wālāylâ*. It appears yet again as a promise interpolated in Isa. lix 21. Here, those in Jacob who turned back from sin have a covenant bestowed on them, the contents of which is that the Lord's words—here meaning his commandments—will never cease from their lips, etc.: *ûdĕbāray ʾăšer-śamtî bĕpîkā lōʾ-yāmûšû mippîkā*. The presence of this ideal of assiduous study of the Torah—an ideal phrased in similar expressions—at three crucial points of the biblical canon, indicates that the last phases of the formation of the Hebrew Bible must be considered as Proto-Pharisaic.[1] Or, in other words, the emerging Judaism of late Persian and early Hellenistic times is responsible for the authorship of the most recent layers in the creation of the Hebrew Bible.

This perception can be put to use in biblical criticism. When our textual witnesses are at variance, sometimes the fact should not be explained as due to mechanical mistakes made by the copyists, but rather to the intrusion of midrashic elements into biblical manuscripts. The same criterion is applicable in the field of higher criticism. In those passages where the critic suspects the interference of a late hand,

[1] Cf. my remarks in "The Piety of the Torah-Disciples at the Winding-up of the Hebrew Bible: Josh. 1:8; Ps. 1:2; Isa. 59:21", in H. Merklein et al. (ed.), *Bibel in juedischer und christlicher Tradition—Fs. Johann Maier* (Frankfurt a.M., 1993), pp. 78–85.

he is advised to check whether the suggested interpolation shows marks of the lore and law that developed in Second Commonwealth Judaism. And in case of a positive answer, his historico-literary arguments will find a reliable confirmation. All in all, the task of discerning primary and secondary elements in the Biblical books, ancient and late components therein, can be assisted by the recognition of the specific character of Jewish creativity in late-biblical and early post-biblical times.

At least four types of Jewish elaborations can be detected in the Hebrew Bible: literary, theological, legal and legalistic.[2] They are present in many of the books, but especially obtain in the Torah and in the Former Prophets. The task of gathering and studying them all is certainly a rewarding one. In the frame of the present paper, however, I shall limit myself to one segment only: literary elaborations of aggadic nature which were introduced into the Hebrew Bible by Jewish scribes.[3]

One of the trends that have been pointed out in Jewish Aggadah is the spurious identification of two biblical heroes who share the same name or the same patronym.[4] A well-known instance of this course is the identification of Obadiah the steward of the palace of King Ahab (mid-4th century BCE), mentioned in 1 Kings xviii, with the prophet Obadiah who prophesied against Edom after the fall of Jerusalem (1st half of the 6th century BCE), nearly three hundred years later.

The identification is made in the Babylonian Talmud, Tractate Sanhedrin 39b as follows:

> "The vision of Obadiah. Thus says the Lord God concerning Edom" (the book of Obadiah, vs. 1). Why particularly Obadiah against Edom? R. Isaac said: The Holy One blessed be He, said: Let Obadiah, who has lived with two wicked persons [i.e., Ahab and Jezebel] and yet has not taken example from their deeds, come and prophesy against wicked Esau [i.e. Edom] who lived with two righteous persons [i.e., Isaac and Rebekah] and yet did not learn from their deeds.

---

[2] Otherwise called "nomistic". I have offered a sample of them in my essay: "The Nomistic Correction in Biblical Manuscripts and its Occurrence in *4QSam*[a]", *RdQ* 14 (1989), pp. 247–54.

[3] With the term *ʾaggādâ*, from which the adjective "aggadic" is derived, I designate the Jewish literary, mostly legendary, material embedded in the Talmudim and Midrashim.

[4] I. Heinemann, *The Methods of Aggadah*[2] (Hebrew; Jerusalem and Tel Aviv, 1954), pp. 29–30.

The same aggadic feature appears to have affected the transmission of biblical manuscripts. There are two prophets with similar names: Micaiah, a prophet to king Ahab, about 850 BCE, and Micah, the titular of a book of prophecies, who flourished in Judah some 120 years later. Now, concerning the former, at the end of the story about him, in 1 Kgs xxii 28a, one reads that he told the king:

If you safely return home, the Lord has not spoken through me! Then we read:

> And he said: "Listen you peoples, all of you" (1 Kgs xxii 28b).

What is the meaning of this last sentence? Who are the peoples referred to? Could he refer in this way to Israel and Judah? And what is the need for this last call for attention right here? But if we take into account that these very same words open the prophecy of Micah (Micah i 2), then we are led to conjecture that it was some late scribe who tried to identify this Micaiah of 1 Kgs xxii with Micah the Morashtite, whose book is part of the prophetical canon.[5]

What favours this conclusion is the fact that the sentence mentioned—"And he said: Listen you peoples, all of you"—is not represented by the LXX^{B} and the Lucianic manuscripts. Apparently, it did not appear in the Hebrew *Vorlage* of the Old Greek.

Thus we reach a two-fold conclusion: (1) aggadic elements sometimes penetrated biblical manuscripts; (2) it is difficult to assume that the conservative archetype of the MT accepted such additions in late periods; most probably they belong to pre-Hasmonean times, i.e. before 167 BCE; hence a relatively early date for the origin of Jewish Aggadah is suggested.

An additional characteristic of Jewish Aggadah, in a sense opposite to the one just mentioned, is its tendency to reshape a biblical narrative by casting new roles in it. In this way the narrative's plot is either vivified, as more action obtains, or sometimes rationalized, as heroes are made to act in a more consistent way. The means for this remodelling of narratives are both the addition of new characters and the differentiation of actions by attributing distinct roles to the heroes of the biblical story.

The former type, the addition of new characters, appears, for instance, in the Genesis Apocryphon, a Jewish legendary reworking of Genesis,

---

[5] This late scribe should not be identified with a Dtr author or redactor; *pace* E. Ball, "A Note on 1 Kings XXII. 28", *JTS*, n.s. 28 (1977), pp. 90–4.

dated by scholars to the 1st century BCE. In the biblical story of Abram and Sarai in Egypt, two *personae* only take an active part: Abram and Pharaoh; the third one, Sarai, is passive (Gen. xii 10–20). The Genesis Apocryphon, unsatisfied with this sobriety, adds two more *personae*: Hyrqanos, a minister of Pharaoh, and Lot, Abram's nephew. Their exchange brings home to Pharaoh the reason for his predicament:

> Then Hyrqanos came to me and begged me to come and pray over the king and lay my hands upon him that he might be cured, for [he had seen me] in a dream. But Lot said to him. "Abram, my uncle, cannot pray for the king, while his wife Sarai is with him. Now go, tell the king", etc.[6]

This feature obtains in the LXX, in 1 Sam. i 14. The MT reads here:

> And Eli said to her: how long will you be drunk, etc.

But the LXX:

> The servant of Eli said to her, etc.

It seems to me that a late scribe considered it improper for Eli to misjudge the personality of Hannah in such a way. Therefore, the mistake was attributed to his servant—a suitable subject invented for this purpose.[7]

An additional character is also inserted into the story relating how the wife of Jeroboam comes to enquire of the prophet Ahijah concerning her sick child. In the MT the prophet directly addresses her (1 Kgs xiv 6):

> As Ahijah heard the sound of her feet while she was coming through the door, he said: Come in, wife of Jeroboam! Why are you disguised? I have a harsh message for you.

In the LXX, however, the story is related in the large plus which appears there after 1 Kgs xii 24. There, in the verse conventionally designated as 24k, we read as follows:

---

[6] I have followed the translation of J.A. Fitzmyer, *The Genesis Apocryphon of Qumran Cave I*[2] (Rome, 1971), p. 65.

[7] Another possibility to be taken into account is the presence of secondary assimilation to an analogous biblical story. In this case, the servant of Eli would assume the role first attributed to Gehazi in the Shunammite story, 2 Kgs iv 27; cf. Y. Zakovitch, "Assimilation in Biblical Narratives", in J.H. Tigay (ed.), *Empirical Models for Biblical Criticism* (Philadelphia, 1985), pp. 175–96.

> When she came into the town to Ahijah the Shilonite, Ahijah said to his servant: Go out towards Ano the wife of Jeroboam and say to her: Come in, do not tarry, for thus says the Lord: A harsh message I am sending to you.[8]

It appears that the presence of a servant is designed to lend respectability to the old blind prophet: he is not dwelling alone, since a young man assists him.

This midrashic phenomenon, now, explains a variant reading in the recently published manuscript 4QExod[b].[9] Exod. ii 3 MT, and so all ancient versions read:

> When she (scil. Moses' mother) could hide him no longer, she got a wicker basket for him and caulked it with bitumen and pitch. She put the child into it and placed it among the reeds by the bank of the Nile.

4QExod[b] goes hand in hand with MT, but for a slight variation: Moses' mother instructs her slave-girl, who places the basket among the reeds by the bank of the Nile: *wtʾmr lšpḥth lky [wt]śym ʾwtw bswp*, etc.

How should we construe this peculiar reading? Did the midrashic interpreter introduce a slave-girl in order to spare the mother the cruel act of exposing her baby? This is a possible explanation, although for that purpose the interpolator could have availed himself of another figure present on the scene—Moses' sister who was standing by. More plausibly, a different tendency was here at work. Josephus describes Moses' father, Amram, as one of the noblest Hebrews (Ant. Jud. II 9,3[210]). The Babylonian Talmud too assures us that Amram was most prominent in his generation, and therefore he was imitated by everybody when he first divorced Jochebed and later remarried her (Sotah 12a). If so, one cannot depict the leader's wife as one who did everything by herself; certainly, she had a slave-girl who took the basket to the Nile. Thus the midrash interpreter added: "And she said to her slave-girl: 'go'!"

The slave girl of Moses' mother in 4QExod[b] joins former witnesses to demonstrate how elements of Second Commonwealth midrashic lore penetrated biblical manuscripts, appearing nowadays in our textual witnesses: the MT, the LXX, the Samaritan Pentateuch and the Qumran Scrolls.

---

[8] Cf. Z. Talshir, *The Alternative Story of the Division of the Kingdom: 3 Kingdoms 12:24a–z* (Jerusalem, 1993), pp. 85–8, 90–2, 172–94, 219 and n. 116.

[9] E. Ulrich, F.M. Cross et al., *Qumran Cave 4. VII, DJD* XII (Oxford, 1994), p. 87 (pl. XIV, 31).

Besides, there is a methodical lesson to be learnt here. 4QExod[b] presents a nice symmetry between both "mothers" of Moses, Jochebed and Pharaoh's daughter. The one sent her slave girl to place the basket in the reeds; the other sent her maid to take the basket out of the reeds. A nice symmetry, indeed, yet a secondary one. Which proves once again the irrelevance of such structures which some present-day scholars adduce in order to establish the unity and originality of the Scriptures. To be sure, the midrashic interpolator inadvertently created the symmetry. And if one wonders at the logic of the Midrash, how does it happen that the wife of Amram, the Hebrew leader, goes on hire as a wet-nurse? There is no need to worry: the God of Midrash will solve that puzzle too![10]

More widespread appears to be the second type, i.e. the attribution of distinct roles to heroes already on the stage. A few instances only can be offered here for this category.

In the story of Gen. xiv, one reads about the kings of Sodom and Gomorrah who, being defeated in battle, fled and fell into bitumen-pits (Gen. xiv 10). The Genesis Apocryphon (xxi 32–3) endeavours to improve the tale: the king of Sodom was routed and fled while the king of Gomorrah fell into the bitumen-pits.[11] Plausibly, this differentiation of the lot of the two kings was brought about by the fact that the king of Sodom later re-emerges in the story at the celebration of the victory of Abram by Melchizedek (Gen. xiv 17, 21, 22).

The Bible tells that when Pharaoh caught up with the Israelites at the Reed Sea they reacted with fear and complaint:

> Greatly frightened, the Israelites cried out to the Lord. And they said to Moses: "Was it for want of graves in Egypt that you brought us to die in the wilderness? What have you done to us, taking us out of Egypt? Is this not the very thing we told you in Egypt, saying: 'Let us be, and we will serve the Egyptians, for it is better for us to serve the Egyptians than to die in the wilderness'" (Exod. xiv 10–12).

---

[10] Cf. A. Rofé, "Moses' Mother and her Maid according to 4QExod[b]" (Hebrew), *Beit Miqra* 40 (1994/5), pp. 197–202.

[11] Cf. Fitzmyer (n. 6), p. 71. A similar diversification in contradiction to Scripture was done in the Babylonian Talmud concerning the sons of Eli: Hophni sinned, Phinehas did not sin (B. Shabbat 55b). This aggadah was probably imported from the land of Israel; cf. J. Heinemann, *Aggadah and its Development* (Hebrew; Jerusalem, 1974), pp. 166–7.

Later Jewish legend assigned here three or even four roles.[12] The Tannaitic Midrash Mekhilta deRabbi Ishmael commented:

> The Israelites at the Reed Sea were divided into four groups. One group said: "Let us throw ourselves into the sea". One said: "Let us return to Egypt". One said: "Let us fight them". And one said: "Let us cry out against them" (Bešallaḥ: Wayehi, par. II, end).

Pseudo Philo's Liber Antiquitatum Biblicarum reads:[13]

> Tunc, considerantes metum temporis, Israel filii in tres divisiones consiliorum diviserunt sententias suas. Nam tribus Ruben et tribus Ysachar, et tribus Zabulon, et tribus Symeon dixerunt: Venite mittamus nos in mare. Melius est enim nos in aqua mori, quam ab inimicis concidi. Tribus autem Gad, et tribus Aser, et tribus Dan et tribus Neptalim dixerunt: Non, sed revertamur cum eis, et si voluerint donare nobis vitam, serviamus eis. Nam tribus Levi et tribus Iuda, et Ioseph et Beniamin dixerunt: Non sic, sed accipientes arma nostra, pugnemus cum eis, et erit Deus nobiscum (x 3).

The Samaritan Memar Merqa has a similar homily:

> They were divided at the sea into three divisions. Each division made a statement and the great prophet made a reply corresponding to each statement. The first division said: "Let us . . . go back to Egypt and let us serve the Egyptians . . . for it would have been better for us . . . than to die in the wilderness". The great prophet Moses said: "You shall never see them again". The second division said: "Let us flee from the Egyptians into the desert". The great prophet Moses said to them: "Stand firm, and see the salvation of the Lord, which He will work for you today". The third division said: "Let us arise and fight against the Egyptians". The great prophet Moses said to them: "The Lord will fight for you, and you have only to be still".[14]

It is impressive that the basically same aggadah appears in three utterly distinct sources. This wide distribution indicates, in my opinion, that the core of the legend must have been relatively old, perhaps

---

[12] Cf. the discussion by Joseph Heinemann (preceding note), pp. 92–3. He convincingly argues that there were originally three roles only; the fourth being just a duplication of the third.

[13] G. Kisch, *Pseudo-Philo's Liber Antiquitatum Biblicarum* (Notre Dame, Ind., 1949), p. 141. E. tr. in M.R. James, *The Biblical Antiquities of Philo* (London, 1917), p. 104.

[14] J. MacDonald, *Memar Marqah* II: The Translation, *BZAW* 84 (Berlin, 1963), p. 167; cf. Z. Ben-Hayyim, *Tibat Marqe* (Jerusalem, 1988), pp. 274–5.

going back to Hasmonean times, when the question how to behave when overtaken by the Seleucid army was a crucial one. In any case, there is no doubt that this diversification of roles, perpetrated by the Jewish aggadah, animated the biblical story ever more.[15]

With this phenomenon in mind we come to discuss the scene at the gate in Ruth iv. In vss 9–10, Boaz addresses the elders and all the people: "You are witnesses today", etc. In vs. 11 "all the people at the gate and the elders answered: We are witnesses. May the Lord make the woman who is coming into your house like Rachel and Leah", etc.

The LXX reads vs. 11 differently:

> All the people at the gate answered: "We are witnesses". And the elders said: "May the Lord make the woman, etc."

There has been dissent among commentators whether the MT or the LXX should be preferred.[16] In favour of the former, one can summon as a witness the chiasmus of vs. 11 *vis-à-vis* vs. 9: "Boaz said to the elders and all the people" (vs. 9) . . . "All the people and the elders said to Boaz" (vs. 11). Chiasmus is indeed a beloved figure of speech in ancient Hebrew diction. On the other hand, how appropriate is this diversification of roles?: the people function as witnesses, the elders follow suit and attach their blessing.

However, now that we have identified the phenomenon of diversification of roles in biblical stories as characteristic of Jewish aggadah, there can be little doubt that the MT represents the primary text and the LXX is secondary.

Was there a Hebrew *Vorlage* before the reading of the LXX in Ruth iv 11? Two facts militate in favour of this hypothesis: (1) the diversification of roles in biblical stories characterizes Jewish Palestinian aggadah, as pointed out above. (2) We have already noted how aggadic elements crept into the MT in 1 Kgs xxii 28 and into 4QExod^b in ii 3.

The Greek translation of Ruth has been recognized as a late version originating in Palestine.[17] Indeed, it has points of contact with Aquila,

[15] Further instances of this characteristic of Jewish Midrash are quoted and discussed in my essay: "Ruth 4:11 LXX: A Midrāshic Dramatization" (Hebrew), in M.V. Fox et al. (ed.), *Texts, Temples, and Traditions: A Tribute to Menahem Haran* (Winona Lake, Indiana, 1996), pp. 119*–124*.

[16] Bibliographical references have been given in my article, mentioned in the preceding note.

[17] Cf. M. Harl, G. Dorival and O. Munnich, *La Bible grecque des Septante* (Paris,

such as the translation of *šadday*—ἱκανός, and with proto-Theodotion, when rendering *gam* by καί γε. Nevertheless, it seems possible, and even probable, that the deviation from the MT in Ruth iv 11 is not the work of the late translator, otherwise known as faithfully adhering to a proto-MT text; Ruth iv 11 reflects, in my view, a Hebrew variant that originated in Jewish lore in Hellenistic and Roman times.

Let us move to consider an additional trait of Jewish aggadah as reflected by a biblical manuscript, this time by 4QSam[a].

A few years ago, F.M. Cross published a fragment from this Qumran scroll which contains a plus over against the MT. This plus, placed between 1 Sam. x 27[a] and 27[b], runs, in English translation as follows:

> [Na]hash, king of the Ammonites, sorely oppressed the Gadites and the Reubenites and gouged out a[ll] their right eyes and struck ter[ror and dread] in Israel. There was not left one among the Israelites bey[ond the Jordan who]se right eye was no[t go]uged out by Naha[sh king] of the [A]mmonites; except that seven thousand men [fled from] the Ammonites and entered [J]abesh-gilead. [About a month later etc.][18]

In Cross's opinion, this passage, also attested by Josephus, is original.[19] In my view, the passage is secondary.[20] It reflects an established feature of Jewish legend as elaborating the biblical characters, namely, the transformation of a one-time trait into a constant one. This is achieved by the duplication or even the multiplication of one deed of the biblical hero in question. For instance, according to Genesis, Abraham was tested once (ch. xxii); the book of Jubilees counts seven tests (xvii 17) or even ten (xix 18), the latter number repeatedly appears in the rabbinic sources (Abot v 3 et *passim*). Thus Abraham becomes the symbol of a righteous man who stands the test. An opposite case: Doeg the Edomite slandered the priest Ahimelech in the presence of Saul (1 Sam. xxii 9), but, according to the Talmud, Doeg had already incited Saul against David even before the latter was brought to court

1988), pp. 83–111. I have benefited from the advice of Dr P.G. Borbone (Turin) on this point.

[18] F.M. Cross, "The Ammonite Oppression of the Tribes of Gad and Reuben: Missing Verses from 1 Samuel 11 found in 4QSamuel[a]", in E. Tov (ed.), *The Hebrew and Greek Texts of Samuel* (Jerusalem, 1980), pp. 105–19; reprinted in H. Tadmor and M. Weinfeld (ed.), *History, Historiography and Interpretation* (Jerusalem, 1983), pp. 148–58.

[19] Cf. the preceding note. The same opinion is held by Cross's disciples: E.C. Ulrich, *The Qumran Text of Samuel and Josephus* (Missoula, Montana, 1978), pp. 166–9; P.K. McCarter, *I Samuel* (Garden City, New York, 1980), pp. 198–200.

[20] Cf. A. Rofé, "The Acts of Nahash according to 4QSam[a]", *IEJ* 32 (1982), pp. 129–33. An expanded Hebrew version has been published in *Beit Miqra* 30 (1985), pp. 456–62.

(B. Sanh. 93b), and once again after the battle with Goliath (B. Yeb. 76b). Thus Doeg is implicitly defined as the defamer *par-excellence* (cf. Ps. lii) and is deprived in the Mishna of any share in "the world to come" (San. x 2).

If, now, the acts of Nahash in 4QSam[a] are examined in the light of this pattern, one may conclude that the same aggadic trait is present here. The single proposition of Nahash who wanted to shame Israel has been turned into a means of constant subjection. Nahash is now depicted as an inveterate "eye gouger", a fact that stresses both Israel's distress and Saul's subsequent victory.

Therefore, this extra passage of 4QSam[a] is an aggadic interpolation. It has no consequence whatsoever for the history of Israel in the 11th century BCE. At the same time, it submits some extremely important evidence for the intrusion of late legend into biblical manuscripts. Further instances of such intrusions can be found in the LXX account of Jeroboam's rebellion and 1 Esdras's narratives concerning the restoration of Judah in the time of Darius I.

Keeping this aggadic feature in mind, we are now able to transcend the realm of textual evidence into the perilous territory of historico-literary criticism. Namely, assisted by the criterion of aggadic qualities, we shall attempt to discern secondary layers in the biblical literature.[21]

In the story of Elisha at Dothan, the prophet is surrounded by a strong Aramean army. His servant is dismayed; Elisha reassures him: "Have no fear; there are more on our side than on theirs" (2 Kgs vi 16). Then we read (vss 17–18): "Elisha prayed saying: 'Lord, please, open his eyes and let him see.'" And the Lord opened the servant's eyes and he saw, lo, the hill was covered with horses and chariots of fire, all about Elisha. And they came down to him. Elisha prayed to the Lord, saying: "Strike, please, this people with a blinding light." And he struck them, etc.

We note in the first place that the fiery horses and chariots all about Elisha do not have any function in the dénouement. Everything is done by the Lord who intervenes directly to rescue his prophet. Besides, vss 17–18a are circumscribed by a *Wiederaufnahme: wayyitpallēl ʾĕlišāʿ wayyōʾmar yhwh*, and again *wayyitpallēl ʾĕlišāʿ ʾel-yhwh wayyōʾmar*; this stylistic feature often indicates the presence of an

[21] A fuller treatment of the following topic has been offered in my essay: "Eliseo a Dotan (2 Re 6, 8–23): Saggio di critica storico-letteraria coll'ausilio della tradizione giudaica", *RivBiblt* 43/1–2 (1995) (= *Fs. E Galbiati*), pp. 45–54.

interpolation.[22] Finally, what concerns us here, the verse in question presents the aggadic feature we have just discussed: duplicating a deed or an event associated with a biblical hero, thus making it his constant characteristic. In the story of Elijah's ascension to heaven (2 Kgs ii 1–18)—a narrative that belongs to the cycle of Elisha—fiery horses and chariots came down from heaven one single time in order to separate the master, Elijah, from his disciple Elisha. In the present story, in vss 17–18a, it is presumed that the fiery cavalry was always at the disposal of the prophet, always there, invisible, but ready to intervene. A single and singular trait has become a constant one.

This does not exhaust the aggadic quality of the verse in question. A salient characteristic of Jewish midrash is the literal and concrete interpretation of expressions that originally were figurative or abstract.[23] In this way the midrash often furbishes Scripture with dramatic or hyperbolic episodes that gratify listeners and readers. Some instances are adduced here to illustrate this point.

"Do I lack madmen?", asks Achish, king of Gath, disgusted at the sight of David's exhibitions (1 Sam. xxi 16). The midrash, however, takes the "madmen" literally, and supplies the information that Achish already had two madwomen at home: his wife and daughter.[24]

"The God of my father . . . delivered me from the sword of Pharaoh", says Moses (Exod. xviii 4). When was this?, inquires the midrash, and tells that, before his flight to Midian, Moses had been arrested and condemned to death; a sword was already at his throat, an actual sword, when an angel coming down from heaven confused the executioner; thus the Egyptians "seized the angel and let Moses go".[25]

More instances can be adduced, but I will limit myself to one from the books of Chronicles, because it proves that this midrashic feature is not a late Jewish creation, but rather an early one, already present in the mid-4th century BCE. Concerning Obed-edom it is said in the books of Samuel that "the Lord blessed him and his house" (2 Sam.

---

[22] Cf. M. Anbar, "La 'reprise'", *VT* 38 (1988), pp. 385–98, with reference to preceding contributions.

[23] Heinemann (above, n. 4), pp. 118–19; J. Fraenkel, *The Methods of Aggadah and Midrash* (Hebrew; Givataim, 1991), 1:96–7.

[24] *Midrasch Tehillim* (Shoher Tov), ed. by S. Buber (Vilna, 1891; repr. Jerusalem, 1976/7), p. 246.

[25] *Mechilta d'Rabbi Ismael*, ed. by H.S. Horovitz and J. Rabin (Frankfurt, 1931; repr. Jerusalem 1959/60), p. 192.

vi 11). Chronicles repeats this (1 Chr. xii 14), but then comments on it with a midrashic concretization, asserting that Obed-edom had eight sons and sixty-two descendants,—seventy in all?—because the Lord had "blessed him" (1 Chr. xxvi 4–8, esp. 5b).[26]

To come back now to the episode of Elisha at Dothan, it is this midrashic quality that we find in the relation of vs. 17 *vis-à-vis* vs. 16. Elisha had said: "There are more on our side than on theirs"—vaguely meaning that divine assistance is stronger than the Aramean force. The midrashic exposition, however, takes him literally; who are these "more", these *rabbîm*? It is the divine cavalry that had come to rescue the prophet (vs. 17). Consequently, the qualification of 2 Kgs vi 17–18a as being interpolated is confirmed: they attribute a literal, concrete sense to the preceding verse. Vs. 16 is Scripture, while vs. 17 and the beginning of vs. 18 are its midrash.

If this method is correct, I would like to point out some consequences. On the one hand, we have possibly gained an additional tool furthering our research. The critical argumentation will be strengthened and enriched. On the other hand, we all know that power impels moderation. Once we have at our disposal a wider knowledge concerning the authors active at the winding up of biblical literature, we must restrain our conjectures concerning alleged contributions of redactors, interpolators, glossators. A legitimate hypothesis in historico-literary criticism is one that can sufficiently account for the conceptions of the diverse authors of a literary work.

BIBLIOGRAPHICAL NOTE

In addition to the literature quoted in the footnotes, I record here a few items relevant to our subject. Some of these works were brought to my attention by Professor I.L. Seeligmann and Dr A. Toeg of blessed memory, and by Dr H. Eshel at Bar-Ilan University.

E.J. Bickerman, "The Historical Foundations of Post-Biblical Judaism", in L. Finkelstein (ed.), *The Jews: Their History, Culture and Religion* (New York, 1949), p. 80.

J. Boksenboim, "Shear-Jashuv—Concerning Chapters 7–8 in Isaiah" (Hebrew), *Beit Miqra* 22 (1987/8), pp. 35–50.

[26] Cf. I.L. Seeligmann, "The Beginnings of *Midrash* in the Books of Chronicles" (Hebrew), *Tarbiz* 49 (1979/80), pp. 14–32, ad p. 15; idem, *Studies in Biblical Literature* (Hebrew; Jerusalem, 1992), pp. 454–74, ad p. 455.

U. Cassuto, "The Israelite Epic" [1944], in his: *Biblical and Oriental Studies*, II, E. tr. by I. Abrahams (Jerusalem, 1975), pp. 69–109.
D. Daube, "Zur fruehtalmudischen Rechtspraxis", *ZAW* 50 (1932), pp. 148–59.
M. Fishbane, *Biblical Interpretation in Ancient Israel* (Oxford, 1985).
M. Goshen-Gottstein, "Hebrew Syntax and the History of the Bible Text", *Textus* 8 (1973), pp. 100–6.
S. Japhet, *The Ideology of the Book of Chronicles and its Place in Biblical Thought*, E. tr. by A. Barber (Frankfurt a.M., 1989), pp. 176–91.
Y. Kaufmann, *History of the Religion of Israel* IV [1956], E. tr. by C.W. Efroymson (New York, 1977), pp. 380–430.
M. Lerner, *Torat Hammišna* (Hebrew; Berlin, 1914/15).
A. Rofé, *Introduction to Deuteronomy*—Part I and Further Chapters (Hebrew; Jerusalem, 1988).
———, "The Editing of the Book of Joshua in the Light of 4QJosh[a]", in G.J. Brooke (ed.), *New Qumran Texts and Studies* (Leiden, 1994), pp. 73–80.
A. Roifer [Rofé], "The Breaking of the Heifer's Neck" (Hebrew), *Tarbiz* 31 (1961/2), pp. 119–43.
I.L. Seeligmann, "Voraussetzungen der Midrashexegese", *SVT* 1 (1953), pp. 150–81.
A. Toeg, "Exodus XXII, 4: The Text and the Law in the Light of the Ancient Sources" (Hebrew), *Tarbiz* 39 (1969/70), pp. 223–31, 419.
———, "Does Deuteronomy XXIV, 1–4 Incorporate a General Law on Divorce?", *Dine Israel* 2 (1970), English Section, pp. v–xxiv.
J. Weingreen, "Exposition in the Old Testament and in Rabbinic Literature", in F.F. Bruce (ed.), *Promise and Fulfilment: Essays Presented to . . . S.H. Hooke* (Edinburgh, 1963), pp. 187–201 (with references to his preceding contributions).
Th. Willi, *Die Chronik als Auslegung* (Göttingen, 1972).
I. Willi-Plein, *Vorformen der Schriftexegese innerhalb des Alten Testament, BZAW* 123 (Berlin and New York, 1971).
Y. Zakovitch, *An Introduction to Inner-Biblical Interpretation* (Hebrew; Even-Yehuda, 1992).

CENT ANS DE BOTANIQUE AU PROCHE-ORIENT ANCIEN

par

HEDWIGE ROUILLARD-BONRAISIN
Paris

"Botanique!"[1] Avec ce mot en viennent immédiatement à la pensée les noms prestigieux des botanistes du temps passé, les taxinomistes des dix-huitième et dix-neuvième siècles, d'abord limités à l'étude de la flore d'Europe, ensuite étendant leurs recherches et leurs études à celle du Proche-Orient ancien. Et l'on risque de se dire qu'il s'agit là d'une science poussiéreuse, voire obsolète, dont vaut tout juste une rapide consultation s'agissant d'essayer d'identifiér telle plante, pour tenter, autant que possible, de faire correspondre une classe ou une essence précise à un nom, bref de mettre une réalité sous un mot.

Je voudrais montrer, d'une part, que ce terme recouvre un champ beaucoup plus vaste, d'autre part que cette discipline a encore devant elle de beaux jours, car elle a su se diversifier, s'adapter aux ramifications et évolutions de la recherche et offrir cent ans plus tard un bel éventail de réussites et de possibilités encore ouvertes. C'est le contraire d'une science fossile, simplement parce qu'un travail d'observation, de description, d'enregistrement et de classification a de longue date été entrepris et qu'il est désormais achevé. Fait, et bien fait, il n'est donc plus à faire. Toutefois la flore, si elle reste globalement constante, n'en a pas moins évolué avec les conditions historiques et climatiques. Il faut donc prendre en compte cette évolution, la décrire l'expliquer.

[1] En choisissant ce sujet je n'avais pas conscience, mais peut-être le choix était-il cependant inconsciemment déterminé, que l'Université de Cambridge possède de prestigieux jardins botaniques couvrant une vingtaine d'hectares: trésor de plantes avec sa rocaille unique, plantée selon un système géographique, son jardin parfumé, ses plates-bandes retraçant, par massifs chronologiques, les plantes introduites dans le pays, son jardin d'hiver et sa serre d'espèces rares. Fondé en 1760 pour découvrir les vertus des plantes "for the benefit of mankind" le jardin fut déplacé à son actuel emplacement en 1847. Son rôle primitif perdure. Ce chef-d'œuvre attire toujours botanistes professionnels et amateurs éclairés pour ses parterres systématiques contenant chacun un seul ordre naturel. Jardins d'hiver et jardins d'été y brillent également, les serres abritent les plantes les plus exotiques.

Jusqu'au premier tiers du xxème siècle on procédait par classification descriptive, comme fait encore F.-M. Abel en 1933 dans sa *Géographie de la Palestine* I: *Géographie physique et historique* (Paris). Puis les méthodes ont changé en accord avec les préoccupations. Ce sont d'abord les études de terrain, au premier chef l'archéologie, qui, en fonction d'intérêt nouveaux, usent de nouvelles techniques susceptibles d'analyser et de reconstituer le milieu végétal des sites fouillés. D'autre part, on s'est mis à étudier les pratiques hydro-agricoles traditionnelles en elles-mêmes. Les modes de culture au Proche-Orient ont fait l'objet d'approches pluridisciplinaires éclairant des aspects aussi variés que l'étude de l'habitat, des systèmes agricoles, des structures socio-économiques. Enfin, last but not least on ne saurait oublier l'explication des mythes, ni le vaste champ de l'iconographie, qui articule le symbolique sur le botanique, par le canal de l'art.

La botanique traditionnelle reposait sur deux activités complémentaires: d'une part identifier les plantes évoquées dans les textes ou représentées (problèmes ponctuels de sémantique, d'herméneutique, analyse), de l'autre recueillir la plus grande quantité possible (extension, somme, collection, synthèse) d'individus répertoriés, classés. Ce sont pour ainsi dire ses deux jambes.

D'emblée elles ont avancé de conserve, les voyageurs érudits ont collecté et classé leurs observations, qui ont alimenté les identifications et traductions des historiens et exégètes. Souvent, d'ailleurs, c'étaient les mêmes qui circulaient, observaient, consignaient, puis, retournant à leurs textes, y appliquaient leurs trouvailles (voir les notations de Flavius Josèphe dans les *Antiquités judaïques*).

Pèlerins et néanmoins savants, les voyageurs d'Europe septentrionale ont visité les pays bibliques pour en étudier la flore et la faune. Ainsi Leonhardt Rauwolf de Hollande dont les collections de plantes (1583–6) seront publiées par J.V. Grenovius en 1775. Evoquons les fructueux voyages de J.P. Tournefort (*Relations d'un voyage au Levant* [Lyon, 1717–18]), de Pier Forsskal de Danemark (1761–2) et de F. Haselquist (1777–8), ces deux derniers élèves du grand botaniste suédois Carolus Linnaeus.

Vint l'époque romantique, où s'unissent l'esprit des Lumières et le goût des voyages en Orient. Le Suisse Edmond Boissier a laissé, en sa monumentale *Flora orientalis* (Genève et Bâle, 1867–88), l'une des sources encore de nos jours les plus fiables sur la flore proche-orientale. L'idéal demeure encyclopédique. Cédons au plaisir de citer quelques phrases de sa préface: écrites dans le beau style personnel de l'époque, elles illustrent merveilleusement l'attitude de ces érudits du xixème siècle, tour à tour voyageurs enthousiastes, infatigables arpenteurs et vérificateurs intransigeants:

"Au printemps de 1846, venant de l'Arabie Pétrée, je me rendais de Gaza à Jérusalem, j'herborisais dans les environs de la ville, au mont des Oliviers, sur les pentes par lesquelles on descend de Béthanie à Jéricho, sur les rivages de la mer Morte et à St-Saba. Je traversais toute la Palestine jusqu'à Naplouse, le mont Carmel, Nazareth, le Thabor jusqu'à Tibériade et à Banias vers les sources du Jourdain, parcourant ces collines et ces vallées où le Sauveur des hommes admirait la beauté du Lys des champs et tirait de la nature tant de comparaisons pour ses enseignements divins. Je visitai ensuite Damas . . . j'allai camper quelques jours dans les belles forêts qui s'étendent au pied du mont Cassius . . . Je passai encore quelques jours dans la partie supérieure du Liban, à Eden et aux Cèdres, je descendis dans la Coelésyrie . . .

"Noë, pharmacien de Trieste, attaché à la Commission qui devait fixer les frontières de la Turquie et de la Perse, a fait, en 1851, un assez long séjour à Bagdad et à Mohammera en Babylonie, et m'a envoyé une collection intéressante de cette contrée peu connue.

"La Flore du littoral de la Phénicie et des pentes occidentales du Liban est mieux connue que celle des autres parties de la Syrie, grâce aux investigations persévérantes de deux botanistes, M. Blanche et Gaillarot, auxquels je suis heureux de témoigner ici toute ma reconnaissance pour le zèle avec lequel ils ont exploré ces contrées et les nombreux et préciaux matériaux qu'ils n'ont cessé e m'envoyer. M. Blanche, vice-consul de France à Tripoli, herborise, depuis 1847, sur le littoral, principalement autour de Beyrouth et de Tripoli, sur les pentes et les sommités du Liban; il a, en outre, fait le voyage de Palmyre, à travers le désert Syrien, et a rapporté un précieux herbier de cette contrée inexplorée."

On le voit, le maître d'œuvre collabore avec de nombreux résidents européens au Proche-Orient, reçoit d'eux de précieuses informations sur des flores extrêmement locales qu'eux seuls peuvent explorer systématiquement, voire exhaustivement. Mais il a à cœur de contrôler pour vérifier:

"Le Dr Lorent a voyagé, en 1842 et 1843, en Syrie et s'est rendu d'Alep à Erzerum. Il a recueilli quelques plantes qui ont été décrites par le prof. Hochstetter, à la suite des *Wanderungen im Morganlande* de Lorent et font maintenant partie de l'herbier de l'Université à

Tübingen; mes démarches répétées pour en obtenir communication sont demeurées inutiles et c'est à regretter, car les espèces nouvelles, proposées par Hochstetter, sont généralement des doubles emplois et il eût été utile d'en débrouiller la synonymie par la comparaison des échantillons."[2]

Boissier semble paradigmatique non seulement d'une méthode à une époque donnée, donc forcément bornée par les limites techniques de cette époque, mais encore d'une science à partir de laquelle s'est développée la botanique proche-orientale depuis 130 ans. C'est elle qui en a défini les contours, les traits généraux et particuliers.

Sa flore orientale couvre six régions:

1° Grèce et Turquie d'Europe.

2° Crimée, provinces transcaucasiennes avec le Caucase.

3° Egypte jusqu'à la 1ère cataracte; Arabie septentrionale jusqu'au Tropique.

4° Asie mineure, Arménie, Syrie, Mésopotamie.

5° Perse, Afghanistan, Beloutch.

6° Turkménistan oriental jusqu'au 45ème degré de latitude qui coupe le lac Aral en sa moitié.

Il divise l'Orient en quatre régions botaniques:

1° Europe moyenne: côtes du Pont et de la Perse septentrionale.

2° Région méditerranéenne littoral et zone inférieure de Grèce et de Turquie d'Europe, îles de Méditerranée, côte méridionale de Crimée, côtes occidentale et méridionale d'Anatolie, de Syrie et de Palestine.

3° Région orientale proprement dite: climats extrêmes: plateaux d'Anatolie, Arménie, Syrie, Perse, Afghanistan, Belutchistan, plaines de Mésopotamie et Turkménistan.

4° Régions du dattier: déserts. Egypte, Arabie septentrionale ont Oman; versants méridionaux et littoraux brûlants de Perse et du Belutchistan.

Boissier expose[3] les difficultés, fort instructives, rencontrées à son époque. Il a pu voir et décrire la quasi totalité des espèces énumérées. Il regarde cette flore d'Orient comme le point de départ, la base d'additions, rectifications, corrections de toutes sortes. Cela à Genève, en janvier 1867. Il prévoit donc, sans pouvoir l'imaginer totalement, ce que sera l'avenir.

---

[2] Boissier, préface, pp. xxiv–xxv.

[3] Pp. xxix–xxxiv de sa préface.

Le nombre d'ouvrages de recherche en botanique proche-orientale est trop vaste pour que nous en dressions la liste. Ce serait d'ailleurs fastidieux, et ne servirait pas notre dessein, qui est d'éclairer des lignes essentielles.[4] Ils sont parus en maintes langues, dans des périodiques, des encyclopédies, des dictionnaires. Le noyau en est constitué d'ouvrages de théologiens et de savants du Proche-Orient soucieux d'identifier les noms bibliques pour les traduire et les étudier. Les publications de cette sorte apparurent peu après les traductions classiques de la Bible. La plupart figurent dans la somme d'I. Löw[5] et chez A.L. Moldenke.[6] On est frappé par de fortes divergences voire des contradictions, des erreurs d'identification, une certaine confusion.

Die Flora der Juden (Vienne et Leipzig) est remarquable par son étendue et l'étude philologique des plantes attestées dans les écrits talmudiques et autres littératures juives. Quatre volumes, rédigés entre 1924 et 1938, constituent une somme analytique abondant en listes de noms hébraïques munis de leur traduction, et émanant de toutes sources connues. Toutefois, malgré une ample bibliographie et une information exhautive sur la botanique biblique, l'ensemble laisse sans identification de nombreux noms, d'autres restant difficilement acceptables compte tenu du contexte. Chef d'œuvre nécessairement imparfait.

Il me paraît important de s'attarder sur quelques figures majeures, car elles ont fait la botanique proche-orientale, spécialement biblique. Ces auteurs de sommes, aux xixème et xxème siècles, étaient conjointements des hommes de terrain, des savants classificateurs, et des esprits soucieux de religion. Nous retrouverons les hommes de terrain avec les archéologues contemporains.

L'exposé, par I. Löw, de sa démarche, illustre une méthode différente de celle de Boissier, mais non opposée. Elle est délibérément phénoménologique, au sens où elle prend en compte, et les phénomènes, et le regard, l'attitude interrogatrice de celui qui les examine. Ce n'est sans doute pas un hasard s'il élabore sa *Flora der Juden* sensiblement dans les décennies (trois premiers tomes 1923–28, tome iv 1934, début de la recherche 1874) au cours desquelles Hüsserl produit ses recherches.

---

[4] M. Zohary le fait parfaitement, dans sa préface à *Plants of the Bible. A Complete Handbook to all the Plants* (Cambridge, 1982).

[5] *Die Flora der Juden*, 1938, volume iv.

[6] *Plants of the Bible* (Waltham, Mass., 1952).

"Die Beziehungen der Juden zur Pflanzenwelt sind, wie das ganze jüdische Leben, durchweg mit religiösen Anschauungen und Bräuchen verwoben. Gesetzliche Bestimmungen führten die Rabbinen zu eingehender Beschäftigung mit der Flora ihrer Umgebung, wie sie gesetzliche Bestimmungen zur Kenntnis der Flora zwangen. Homiletische Vorträge, moralische Erörterungen führten zu sinniger Auslegung pflanzlicher Erscheinungen. Halacha und Aggada bewahren einen Schatz volkstümlicher Naturkenntnis . . . Meine Flora ist der erste Versuch, ein annähernd volständiges Bild der Beziehungen der Juden zum Pflanzenreich zu zeichnen."[7]

La tâche que se fixe Löw est, certes, de déterminer quelles sont les plantes des sources juives, d'identifier les noms de plantes hébraïques et araméennes, cherchant solution dans la série des familles de plantes naturelles, mais tout autant, et cela nous intéresse plus, d'établir quelles étaient les plantes connues des Juifs, ainsi que leur émergence historique. Définir les relations du monde des plantes à la loi, aux récits et au folklore.

Ses sources sont fabuleusement riches. Il n'apparaît pas comme un homme de terrain, mais de textes: Mishna, Nouveau Testament, Apocryphes, Pseudépigraphes, Josèphe, Coran, Targumim, Talmud, Midrashim, Geonim, écrits médicaux, Qaraïtes, jargon, jardins et parcs, Halaka, rites, plantes de la cuisine juive, mesures, commerce et agriculture, folklore, superstitution, Aggada et poésie, symbolique, art, étoiles, kabbale et alchimie. L'étude de la flore se déploie sur fond d'un vaste éventail, encyclopédique encore, totalité des savoirs sur totalité des activités humaines.

Après lui place ne peut plus exister que pour l'ethnographie systématique. Celle-ci trouvera son maître en G. Dalman,[8] dont le grand œuvre, *Arbeit und Sitte in Palästina: Sammlung wissenschaftlicher Monographien*,[9] paru peu avant l'achèvement de la *Flora* de Löw, témoigne d'une autre approche. Il a conscience de représenter la fin d'une époque et d'en ouvrir une autre, dont nul ne sait au juste quelle elle sera. Au début de son tome premier, *Jahreslauf und Tageslauf*, il expose, en une vivante et touchante préface, humaine, évocatrice de personnages concrets et amis, les circonstances dans

[7] *Die Flora der Juden* IV (1934), p. 2.
[8] Dalman a d'abord lui-même publié *Die Pflanzen Palästinas*, s'inscrivant dans la tradition taxinomique classique.
[9] 14 volumes (Gütersloh, 1928–37).

lesquelles il a rédigé son grand œuvre. Ce texte constitue une profession de foi et un discours de la méthode indépassables: rien qu'à le lire et à consulter cette somme, mine de renseignements, on comprend qu'après lui la botanique proche-orientale devait changer, à la fois parce qu'il a si bien défriché le sujet qu'il n'y a plus guère à faire, et parce que, comme lui-même le pressent dès 1927, la modernisation (il n'envisage que celle menée par les Anglais!) va à ce point modifier l'aspect du pays, qu'il ne sera plus possible de pratiquer l'ethnologie et la phytogéographie comme il le fit. Il a conscience d'être l'un des derniers témoins de la vie en Palestine ancienne. Du point de vue ultérieur qui est le nôtre, tout finit bien, dans la mesure où il a achevé la tâche nécessaire que lui seul, héritier d'une lignée de voyageurs en Orient, pouvait mener à bien et que d'ailleurs il n'est plus possible de remplir comme lui: il faut donc se tourner vers d'autres centres d'intérêt, adopter d'autres méthodes sans pour autant mépriser l'acquis de siècles d'observations, de collections et de classifications. La mutation radicale s'est produite après lui, accélérée ces dernières décennies, mais jusqu'alors le temps spatial était resté étale, jusqu'à la fin de l'empire ottoman.

Sa préface explique comment son œuvre est autant une somme de vie et d'expérience que d'érudition. Ce fait s'accorde avec son attitude face à l'élucidation des textes bibliques: selon lui, c'est d'un certain type de comparatisme consistant en la confrontation entre les données antiques, notamment vétérotestamentaires, et la réalité palestinienne contemporaine, que jaillira la lumière sur l'antiquité.

Il conte avec verve comment, dès 1899, lors d'un long séjour à Alep, il prit contact avec Bédouins et paysans, revint en 1900 entre Sud-Liban et Hermon, apprit à connaître l'économie paysanne, descendit ensuite vers le Sud pour traverser toute la Palestine jusqu'à Hébron et Ein Geddi, puis passa en Transjordanie et remonta à Damas, où il arriva en mai. "Auf dieser Weise legete ich einen Grund zy einer durchaus nicht vollständigen, aber doch vielseitigen Kenntnis des palästinischen Volkslebens, zumal ich auch in Aleppo Gelegenheit hatte . . . zu erfahren, worin die Palästinischen Sitte sich von der nordsyrischen unterscheidet." Après un séjour en Egypte, Dalman arriva à Jaffa en 1902, mandaté pour la création du Deutsche Evangelische Institut Jerusalem. Jusqu'en juin 1914 il poursuit un travail fondamentalement ethnographique. Il y retournera après la guerre, en 1921 et 1925. Il séjourne, en particulier, à l'asile des lépreux, qui lui apportent de riches témoignages personnels. Il définit sa méthode comme une nécessaire immersion pour cueillir, collecter, comprendre et faire comprendre. Il a conscience d'œuvrer à la constitution d'un témoignage authentique, celui d'une vie et d'une culture en voie de disparition. La modernisation induite par les Anglais et l'immigration juive demeurent inachevées, les transformations décisives dues à la guerre (machinisme et électricité) n'ont pas encore atteint ce coin d'Orient: il invite à le suivre, en premier lieu les habitants arabes de Palestine, avant qu'ils ne subissent l'influence occidentale et d'abord européenne, avertissement qui, à y réfléchir, est un paradoxe, un comble!

Dalman se voit comme un théologien, mais refuse l'éclairage ponctuel et superficiel de passages bibliques, il en réclame l'inscription dans un contexte global. Il veut comparer le domaine judéo-chrétien avec les formes encore vivantes de travail, les us et coutumes, notamment arabes en Palestine. Il cherche à combler un fossé.

Son matériau est multiple: textes bibliques et judéo-palestiniens, littérature grecque, fouilles archéologiques, histoire des religions au Proche-Orient. Quelque 70 ans plus tard, il reste le type du savant européen théologien protestant, à une époque relativement exempte des conflits, encore larvés, qui devaient éclater à partir de 1947. Loin de la pure classification, son souci d'un savoir global se coule dans une démarche ethnologique intégrant l'ensemble des activités humaines. Il ouvre ainsi la voie aux études ultérieures qui, renonçant à l'idéal encyclopédique, se spécialiseront dans l'une ou l'autre des multiples directions où il fit œuvre de pionnier.

A l'autre extrémité de notre siècle un savant comme Michaël Zohary[10] nous mène aux cent ans annoncés: centenaire du début de recherches systématiques comme celles de Löw et fin du vingtième siècle, qui vit l'achèvement de recherches taxinomiques entamées dès les premiers siècles de l'ère chrétienne, et systématisées à compter du xviiième siècle.

Chaque entreprise a su compléter les précédentes, et non les répéter. Mais désormais la forêt des travaux s'est à ce point épaissie et diversifiée que s'y impose une orientation.

Il y aura l'étude de données historico-économiques fournies par les

[10] Expert dans la botanique et l'écologie du Proche-Orient, il a occupé la chaire de Botanique à l'Université Hébraïque de Jérusalem. Il est l'auteur, entre autres, de *Geobotanical Foundations of the Middle East* (Stuttgart et Amsterdam, 1973); *A New Analytical Flora of Israel* (Tel-Aviv, 1976); *The Plant World* (1978); *Vegetable Landscapes of Israel* (1980); *Plants of the Bible. A Complete Handbook to all the Plants* (Cambridge, 1982).

textes et la numismatique. Les sujets sont si nombreux que l'on ne saurait tous les évoquer, mais seulement repérer les grandes lignes, les allées principales. Et celles-ci ont d'abord été dessinées par les chercheurs qui ont retenu les sujets les plus pertinents à cause, et de la richesse de la documentation, et de leur antique portée. Ainsi les fameux cèdres du Liban, élément symbolique s'il en est dans la Bible hébraïque, mais parce qu'il repose sur une réalité géographique et économique essentielle, à savoir des forêts florissantes relevant d'un monopole d'Etat, et fournissant en bois toutes les flottes du Proche-Orient. Il est mille façons de les aborder, dont une particulièrement féconde, consistant à analyser "L'exploitation des cèdres du Mont Liban par les rois assyriens et néo-babyloniens."[11] Celle-ci est, de l'avis des spécialistes, la plus étudiée, mais aussi la plus mal connue. Les questions posées à ce sujet illustrent parfaitement l'ampleur d'un problème qui pouvait a priori paraître ponctuel. S'y trouve toute la gamme des sujets "écologiques".

D'abord s'impose une discussion de terminologie: "le terme akkadien *erēnu* (*erinnu*, ^{giš} ERIN) désigne-t-il bien 'le cèdre' et quelle espèce de 'cèdre'? Les botanistes en distinguent généralement aujourd'hui quatre espèces différentes: le *cedrus atlantica*, le *cedrus deodara*, le *cedrus brevifolia* et le *cedrus Libani*. dont on trouve encore des peuplements dans les montagnes du Liban, les Monts Alaouites, l'Amanus et le Taurus."[12] Il faut jongler entre les appellations akkadiennes, hébraïques, araméennes, grecques, égyptiennes.

Ignorant l'étendue des forêts antiques, on a du mal à estimer la déforestation des cèdres du Mont Liban. Botanique se conjugue d'autant plus avec histoire et géographie: les forêts de cèdres étaient sans doute à l'époque historique moins abondantes qu'on ne le croit. Considérations économiques: comment l'acquisition de bois de cèdre s'insère-telle dans le système tributaire assyrien? Valeur hautement symbolique de l'opération même d'abattage du bois de cèdre. Prise en compte des *realia*: difficultés du transport des grumes de cèdre. Les botanistes d'aujourd'hui sont convoqués pour évaluer la taille des antiques cèdres. Epigraphistes et historiens s'accordent à penser que les rois assyriens préférèrent exploiter les cèdres de l'Amanus.

---

[11] J. Elayi, *Journal of the Economic and Social History of the Orient* 31 (1988), pp. 14–41. Pour les problèmes d'identification, voir, entre autres: A. Nibbi, "Some remarks on the cedar of Lebanon", in *Discussions in Egyptology* 28, (1994), pp. 36–53.

[12] J. Elayi, ibid., p. 15.

L'intérêt de telles études est de confronter les textes anciens à l'épreuve des faits diversement attestés, pour corriger les impressions fausses données par les premiers: ainsi semble-t-il que la réputation mythique des cèdres du mont Liban ait largement outrepassé leur exploitation réelle par les rois assyriens et néo-babyloniens, exploitation en réalité "limitée à la valeur symbolique de leur abattage et prestigieuse de leur usage". Autrement dit, le serpent se mord la queue: valeur symbolique → prestige → abus → valeur mythique.

La conclusion, à savoir que "l'exploitation des cèdres du Mont Liban a joué un rôle très limité dans le déboisement de cette montagne. L'importance de ce rôle a été exagérée parce que les *Annales* assyriennes l'ont amplifié pour servir la propagane royale, et parce que l'image du roi abatteur de cèdres a été utilisée dans l'*Ancien Testament* comme symbole détestable de l'oppression assyro-babylonienne",[13] éclaire la réalité historico-botanique à de multiples niveaux, les uns permettant d'élucider les autres: comment un phénomène limité (l'exploitation des cèdres du Mont Liban par les rois assyro-babyloniens) fut amplifié par une propagande hostile, cette propagande n'étant, comme il est courant, pas née de rien, mais résultant de la propagande assyrienne inverse.

Dans un autre ordre d'idées, les techniques les plus fines et sophistiquées se mettent au service de la botanique. C'est le cas de la dendrochronologie, qui s'attache à dater les arbres d'après le diamètre de leurs anneaux. Elles sont, en particulier, la tâche de "The Malcolm and Carolyn Wiener Labotary for Aegean and Near Eastern Denrochronology", qui à Porsuk/Ulukišta, en Turquie, traitent en tout 64 arbres, dont le genévrier (314 ans), le cèdre (288), le pin (200).[14] Le "cross-dating" ou datation croisée interne permet les plus féconds résultats. Les poutres trouvées à Porsuk n'ayant pas été équarries, l'écorce existante fournit des informations sur l'année, parfois sur la saison même à laquelle fut coupé le bois.

Par ailleurs, Porsuk recèle des trésors de charbon de bois fort ancien et bien préservé, dont l'exploitation ne fait que commencer. Les anneaux d'arbres peuvent être datés relativement à d'autres sites anatoliens du Bronze. La plupart du bois étudié à Porsuk fut coupé dans les années 1431/1432, soit 200/201 ans après le bois de Acemhüyük et 258/259

---

[13] Ibid., p. 41. Voir aussi, entre autres, H. Cazelles, "Qui aurait visé, à l'origine, Isaïe ii 2–5?", *VT* 30 (1980), pp. 409–20.

[14] Voir, par exemple, "Dendrochronological investigation at Porsuk/Ulukišta, Turkey. Preliminary report 1987–1989", *Syria* 69 (1992), pp. 379–87.

ans après le bois de Kültepe. On obtient ainsi une chronologie du Moyen Bronze II, dont la fin se relie au Bronze récent et au Fer.

Alors que ce matériau était jusque récemment, rejeté avec indifférence, que seules comptaient les traces des activités artistiques, culturelles et domestiques de l'activité humaine, désormais la reconstitution du paléoenvironnement à l'aie des bois restés sur le sol livre des informations sur la température de l'époque, le niveau des nappes aquifères et même sur l'emplacement de leurs berges, tous paramètres qui ont varié au cours des siècles, et influé sur les sites habités et les modes de vie. La carbonisation du bois n'est pas moins féconde en renseignements. Il est également surprenant de constater combien l'homme a anciennement connu et apprécié les qualités des différentes essences de bois et su les utiliser. Les tombes, avec leur matériel funéraire, fournissent des restes ligneux sous la forme de traces de rouilles visibles, les fragments de bois ayant été transformés en oxyde de fer. Les procédés radiographiques et radiotomographiques médicaux s'appliquent au bois.

La dendrochronologie est une vaste science dont la première étape est une datation, relative ou absolue, d'une pièce de bois. On arrive à connaître la façon méthodique dont la forêt était exploitée, puis régénérée dès l'âge du Bronze. Bois et, d'une manière générale, végétaux, sont d'humbles témoins parfois plus crédibles qu'archives et chroniques toujours tendancieuses, ou que des critères stylistiques imprécis, fluctuants et subjectifs.

Au total, s'il est toujours justifié de se poser la question "Was war ein elon?",[15] on peut désormais, de manière plus globale, faire jouer à diverses fins l'étude des techniques et pratiques hydro-agricoles traditionnelles: les modes de culture au Proche-Orient ancien sont susceptibles d'approches pluridisciplinaires éclairant des aspects aussi variés que l'étude de l'habitat, des systèmes agricoles, des structures socio-économiques, sans oublier l'explication des mythes comme c'est le cas pour Ugarit le pays de Baʿal, de la culture à la pluie.[16] Haddu est le "contrôleur des eaux du ciel et de la terre" selon l'inscription assyro-araméenne de Tell Fekherye. ʿAnat sa consœur et parèdre est sans doute à la fois la personnification et la maîtresse des sources. Le constat de l'existence de cultures intensives et de cultures d'été trahit la nécessité de l'irrigation, pour atténuer les irrégularités

[15] G. Greiff, in *ZDPV* 76 (1960), pp. 162–70.
[16] P. Bordreuil, 1989.

pluviométriques. Le cycle de Baʿal serait dû au besoin ressenti par les Ugaritains d'expliquer et de conjurer le risque de sécheresse saisonnière en donnant de la réalité météorologique une version mythologique mettant en scène des combats de dieux.

La pluie, substance de Baʿal, reste prisonnière de la terre durant l'été. La déesse ʿAnat, sœur de Baʿal et personnification des sources, recueille cette pluie dans ces réservoirs d'où jaillit l'eau de la terre, même l'été. La déesse solaire Shapshu ramène ensuite Baʿal au ciel par l'évaporation, visible sous la forme de nuages. Or une région boisée se trouvait à l'est du Ṣapon et Ṣalḫu, dont le nom évoque l'arrosage, convient à un sanctuaire de source, peut-être à la naissance du Nahr el Kebir. ʿAnat est aussi "ʿAnat des labours et des champs", qu'un fragment lacunaire présente comme une génisse. Une tablette de Ras Ibn Ḥani nous apprend la présence de bovins dans deux villages de la région frontalière septentrionale de l'Ugarit. L'on aboutit à une représentation du taureau Baʿal et de la génisse ʿAnat dans la région du mont Ṣapon couverte alors de forêts et de prairies, où paissent les troupeaux de bovins.

Envisageons des perspectives nouvelles s'inspirant de l'état actuel de la recherche. Grâce aux plus fines approches de l'archéologie, à l'étude des systèmes socio-économiques, des techniques hydro-agricoles, à la philologie (entre autres, toponymie), à l'histoire des rites, des textes administratifs, religieux, mythiques, on peut arriver:

– à de ponctuelles et précises mises au point, circonscrites à la culture en telle région du Proche-Orient à telle époque;
– à des études comparatives de proche en proche;
– à de vivants tableaux de la culture au Proche-Orient à telle époque, comparant les régions, les mœurs, les rites;
– à de plus vastes histoires des cultures, des échanges, des importations, des disparitions et apparitions d'espèces.

Des cercles tangents, puis sécants.

Rêver d'une histoire sociale des légumes, des fleurs, des arbres, des plantes ornementales et comestibles en lien avec les fêtes et les saisons, histoire qui, un peu à la manière de J.-M. Pelt,[17] comme le tentaient déjà Dalman et Löw en leur temps, intégrerait tous les savoirs antérieurs, anciens et modernes et les nouerait en un splendide bouquet, sans que cependant les fleurs que sont les modestes études ponctuelles ne perdent leur utilité, leur nécessité.

[17] Voir, entre autres, *Fleurs, fêtes et saisons* (Paris, 1994).

DAS SPÄTDEUTERONOMISTISCHE GESCHICHTSWERK GENESIS I–2 REGUM XXV UND SEINE THEOLOGISCHE INTENTION

von

HANS-CHRISTOPH SCHMITT
Erlangen

I

Es ist eine ständige Gefahr der exegetischen Forschung, sich stärker an herrschenden bibelwissenschaftlichen Theorien zu orientieren als an Textbefunden. So wird in der neueren Pentateuchexegese im Schatten der Arbeiten von Martin Noth[1] fast nur noch nach Zusammenhängen im Rahmen der ersten vier Mosebücher, des sogenannten Tetrateuch, gefragt. Dagegen wird der Beobachtung, daß der Pentateuch keine in sich geschlossene Größe darstellt, sondern zumindest auf eine Fortsetzung im Josua- und im Richterbuch angelegt ist, die im 19. und am Beginn des 20. Jh.s einen der Eckpfeiler der Pentateuchforschung darstellte,[2] viel zu wenig Beachtung geschenkt.

Problematisch ist dabei zum andern, daß durch die Tetrateuchhypothese[3] das Deuteronomium als Teil des Pentateuch an den Rand

[1] *Überlieferungsgeschichtliche Studien* (Halle, 1943); *Überlieferungsgeschichte des Pentateuch* (Stuttgart, 1948).

[2] Daß der Pentateuch auf eine Fortsetzung im Josuabuch hin angelegt ist, hat bereits Alexander Geddes (*The Holy Bible* I [London, 1792], S. XXI) festgestellt: "To the Pentateuch I have joined the Book of Joshua both because I conceive it to have been written by the same author and because it is a necessary appendix to the history contained in the former books." Vgl. im übrigen J. Wellhausen, *Die Composition des Hexateuchs* (3. Aufl., Berlin, 1899); H. Holzinger, *Einleitung in den Hexateuch* (Freiburg, 1893); O. Eißfeldt, *Hexateuch-Synopse* (Leipzig, 1922).

[3] Vgl. schon M. Noth, *Überlieferungsgeschichte* (Anm. 1), S. 247–71. Voraussetzung für die Vorstellung von einem Tetrateuch ist die Annahme, daß die vorpriesterlichen und priesterlichen Pentateuchschichten im wesentlichen nur in den Büchern Genesis bis Numeri erhalten sind, "da die Landnahmeerzählung von JE schon bei der Einbettung in P verloren ging und P eine solche nicht kannte" (O. Kaiser, Art. "Tetrateuch", *BHH* III [Göttingen, 1966], Sp.1957). Bemerkenswert ist, daß sich selbst noch in der von E. Blum vertretenen Theorie der Pentateuchentstehung diese Engführung auf den Tetrateuch als herrschend erweist: So setzt er für seine "D-Komposition das sog. 'deuteronomistische Geschichts-

gerückt ist. Die Bedeutung, die das Deuteronomium und die deuteronomistischen Schichten für die Theologie des Pentateuch besitzen, wird so nicht mehr genügend berücksichtigt.

Nun ist es zu Recht Konsens der neueren Forschung, daß die Schichten des Deuteronomiums nur im Zusammenhang des sog. Deuteronomistischen Geschichtswerkes sachgemäß verstanden werden können. Wer das Deuteronomium und seine deuteronomistischen Bearbeitungsschichten als Bestandteil des Pentateuch ernst nehmen will, muß daher zunächst einmal den Zusammenhang zwischen Deuteronomium und dem sog. Deuteronomistischen Geschichtswerk in seine Überlegungen einbeziehen. Als Größe, die vom alttestamentlichen Textbefund her als Interpretationsbasis der Pentateuchforschung zugrunde gelegt werden muß, ist daher der Textzusammenhang von Genesis–2 Könige anzusehen.

II

Wie der Zusammenhang von Pentateuch und den Büchern des sog. Deuteronomistischen Geschichtswerks zustande gekommen ist, ist somit nicht eine Randfrage der Pentateuchkritik, die man—wie dies in vielen neueren Arbeiten zum Pentateuch geschieht—anhangsweise behandeln kann. Vielmehr fallen in der Bestimmung des Verhältnisses von Deuteronomistischem Geschichtswerk und Tetrateuch zentrale Vorentscheidungen für die Frage nach der Entstehung des Pentateuch.

Es ist das Verdienst von John Van Seters,[4] diese Frage wieder in den Mittelpunkt der Pentateuchforschung gerückt zu haben, wobei er sich vor allem auf die Arbeiten von Hans-Heinrich Schmid[5] und Martin Rose[6] stützen kann. In seinem Werk *In Search of History*, S. 323, 355–61, geht er davon aus, daß das von Dtn. i–2 Reg. xxv reichende und aus der Exilszeit stammende Deuteronomistische Geschichtswerk das grundlegende Dokument für Israels Historiographie darstellt. Erst nach dem Deuteronomistischen Geschichtswerk ist die weitere israelitische Geschichtsschreibung in mehr oder weniger direktem Bezug auf dieses Werk entstanden. Eines dieser Geschichtswerke ist nach

---

werk' voraus" (*Studien zur Komposition des Pentateuch* [Berlin und New York, 1990], S. 164) und beschränkt sie deshalb auf die Bücher Genesis bis Numeri.

[4] *In Search of History* (New Haven, Conn., und London, 1983), S. 248.

[5] *Der sogenannte Jahwist* (Zürich, 1976).

[6] *Deuteronomist und Jahwist* (Zürich, 1981).

Van Seters (S. 361) der Jahwist, der in spätexilischer Zeit etwa gleichzeitig mit Deuterojesaja[7] als Ergänzung zum Deuteronomistischen Geschichtswerk abgefaßt worden sei. Der Jahwist verstehe sich somit als Prolog zu diesem Geschichtswerk und sei auch bewußt als ein solcher abgefaßt worden. Die die neuere Pentateuchforschung bestimmende Frage, weshalb keine vom Jahwisten stammende Landnahme überliefert ist, findet daher bei Van Seters eine Antwort, die dem Zusammenhang von Pentateuch und Deuteronomistischem Geschichtswerk besser gerecht wird als die Nothsche Tetrateuchhypothese.

Van Seters lehnt es in diesem Zusammenhang allerdings ab, den Jahwisten als einen deuteronomistischen Redaktor zu verstehen, der ihm vorliegende Quellen im Sinne des Deuteronomistischen Geschichtswerks bearbeitet hat. Vielmehr hebe sich der Jahwist durch seinen Universalismus und sein Verheißungsverständnis deutlich von der deuteronomistischen Theologie ab.[8] Die theologischen Strukturen, die auf einen von Gen. i bis 2 Reg. xxv reichenden Zusammenhang weisen, kommen daher bei Van Seters nicht hinreichend in den Blick.

Als problematisch erweist sich außerdem die von Van Seters vorgenommene Abgrenzung der priesterlichen Schicht. Van Seters versteht sie als eine zusätzliche, jetzt nachexilische Erweiterung, die von Gen. i bis ins Richterbuch ([Anm. 4] S. 343) reicht, dort aber von ihm nur noch sehr unscharf bestimmt werden kann (vgl. S. 345, Anm. 79). Es ist einer der wenigen noch bestehenden Konsense der Pentateuchforschung, daß sich die priesterliche Schicht durch einen spezifischen Stil von den übrigen Schichten des Pentateuch bzw. des Hexateuch abhebt. Wenn nun Van Seters große Teile des Josuabuches und im Richterbuch den einleitenden Passus Jdc. i 1–ii 5 und ii 22–iii 4 auf die priesterliche Schicht zurückführt,[9] dann muß er diesen Konsens durchbrechen. Es kommt somit zu dem nicht überzeugenden Ergebnis, daß sich die von ihm angenommene priesterliche Schicht aus heterogenen Bestandteilen zusammensetzt und teils aus Stücken mit priesterlichem Stil und teils aus solchen mit deuteronomistischem Stil besteht.

---

[7] Vgl. J. Van Seters, *Prologue to History* (Zürich, 1992), S. 330.

[8] Vgl. hierzu vor allem "The so-called Deuteronomistic Redaction of the Pentateuch", in J.A. Emerton (ed.), *Congress Volume: Leuven 1989, SVT* 43 (Leiden u.a., 1991), S. 58–77, und (Anm. 7), S. 227–45.

[9] (Anm. 4) S. 337–43. Vgl. dagegen R. Smend, *Die Entstehung des Alten Testaments* (4. Aufl., Stuttgart u.a., 1989), S. 115–16.

Es fragt sich, ob die richtige Beobachtung von Van Seters, daß im Deuteronomistischen Geschichtswerk mit nachexilischen Bearbeitungen zu rechnen ist, so interpretiert werden muß, daß man sie auf die priesterliche Schicht des Pentateuch zurückführt. Schon R.N. Whybray hat in seiner Arbeit über *The Making of the Pentateuch*,[10] in der er ansonsten die These von Van Seters weitgehend übernommen hat, auf diese Schwachstelle der Van Seterschen Argumentation hingewiesen. Whybray hat dabei vor allem darauf aufmerksam gemacht, daß die weitverbreitete Auffassung, P sei nachexilisch zu datieren, durch beachtenswerte neuere Arbeiten zum Stil und zur Theologie von P in Frage gestellt ist ([Anm. 10] S. 231). Die alte Auffassung von Julius Wellhausen,[11] daß die Redaktion des Hexateuch im Geist der Priesterschrift durchgeführt wurde, die in modifizierter Form auch noch der Auffassung von P als abschließender Redaktions- bzw. Kompositionsschicht zugrundeliegt,[12] kann nicht mehr ohne weiteres vorausgesetzt werden. Vielmehr wird eine der Hauptaufgaben der folgenden Ausführungen darin bestehen, zu überprüfen, ob die Endgestalt des Pentateuch nicht stärker "deuteronomistisch" als "priesterlich" bestimmt ist.

Es stellt sich daher die Frage, ob die Erklärung, die Rudolf Smend[13] für eine späte Bearbeitung des Deuteronomistischen Geschichtswerks gegeben hat, dem Textbefund nicht gerechter wird. Smend hat anhand der teilweise gleichen Befunde im Josua- und im Richterbuch, die Van Seters für seine priesterliche Bearbeitung in Anspruch nimmt, die These von einer spätdeuteronomistischen Redaktion des Deuteronomistischen Geschichtswerks vertreten. In seiner Arbeit "Das Gesetz und die Völker" hat er gezeigt, daß die Vorstellungen von Jos. xiii 2–6 und Jdc. i 1–ii 5, die Van Seters seiner priesterlichen Schicht zuweist und denen es um "die Unvollständigkeit des Landbesitzes und die Forteexistenz fremder Völker im Land"[14] geht, mit der eindeutig "deuteronomistischen" Abschiedsrede Josuas in Jos. xxiii in Zusammenhang

[10] (Sheffield, 1987), S. 232.

[11] Vgl. u.a. *Prolegomena zur Geschichte Israels* (6. Aufl., Berlin, 1905), S. 383–4, wo Wellhausen von "der priesterlichen Schlußbearbeitung des Hexateuchs" spricht.

[12] Vgl. hierzu nur F.M. Cross, "The Priestly Work", in *Canaanite Myth and Hebrew Epic* (Cambridge, Mass., 1973), S. 293–325; R. Rendtorff, *Das Alte Testament* (Neukirchen-Vluyn, 1983), S. 166–74; aber auch Smend (Anm. 9), S. 46 (endredaktionelle Zusätze gehören "in Geist und Sprache zur Tradition von P").

[13] "Das Gesetz und die Völker" (1971), in *Die Mitte des Alten Testaments* (München, 1986), S. 124–37; vgl. auch (Anm. 9), S. 114–25.

[14] Smend, *Mitte* (Anm. 13), S. 129.

zu sehen sind, die auch Van Seters der deuteronomistischen Schicht des Josuabuches zuweist. Auch hier geht es um die "übriggebliebenen Völker" (xxiii 4, 7, 12), die Jahwe nur dann gemäß seiner Zusage vertreiben wird (xxiii 5, 13; vgl. dazu besonders Jdc. ii 3), wenn sich die Israeliten nicht mit ihnen einlassen und nicht ihre Götter verehren (xxiii 7). Die von Van Seters beobachteten Erweiterungen des Deuteronomistischen Geschichtswerks sind also nicht auf eine priesterliche Schicht zurückzuführen, sondern auf eine späte deuteronomistische Schicht, für die man allerdings auf das von Smend gebrauchte Siglum DtrN (nomistischer Deuteronomist) verzichten und stattdessen, einem Vorschlag Otto Kaisers folgend,[15] das Siglum DtrS (spätdeuteronomistisch) benutzen sollte. Wie bereits Smend[16] gezeigt hat, ist diese späte Redaktionsschicht nämlich auf mehrere Hände einer spätdeuteronomistischen schriftgelehrten Schule zurückzuführen, deren Tendenz nur zum Teil als nomistisch bezeichnet werden kann.

Hinter den Zuweisungen von Jos. xiii 1ff.* und Jdc. i 1–ii 5 an P durch Van Seters steht jedoch eine Beobachtung, die für die Pentateuchforschung von entscheidender Bedeutung ist. Zu Recht weist Van Seters ([Anm. 4] S. 331–42) darauf hin, daß die in Jdc. i 1–ii 5 vorliegenden Vorstellungen nicht auf das Deuteronomistische Geschichtswerk beschränkt sind, sondern daß es sich hier um eine auch im Tetrateuch vorhandene Schicht handelt. Van Seters (S. 341) findet entsprechende Auffassungen über die Distanz Israels zu den Völkern vor allem in den auf das Westjordanland bezogenen Landverteilungsanweisungen von Num. xxxiii 50–6, die er zur priesterlichen Pentateuchschicht rechnet, die aber—wie vor allem Norbert Lohfink[17] herausgearbeitet hat—durch einen "Priesterschriftliches und Deuteronomistisches mischenden Charakter" auffallen. Bemerkenswert ist, daß auch Smend ([Anm. 9] S. 115) den Abschnitt Num. xxxiii 50–5 als eine Stelle ansieht, die in Beziehung zu seiner spätdeuteronomistischen Schicht des Deuteronomistischen Geschichtswerks steht. Aufgrund dieses Befundes spricht daher einiges dafür, daß die spätdeuteronomistische Bearbeitung des Deuteronomistischen Geschichtswerks nicht auf dieses Werk beschränkt ist, sondern eine Schicht darstellt, die

---

[15] *Grundriß der Einleitung* 1 (Gütersloh, 1992), S. 129.

[16] *Mitte* (Anm. 13), S. 125–6. Zu nichtnomistischen Tendenzen innerhalb der spätdeuteronomistischen Schicht vgl. nur Dtn. xxx 6 und dazu Kaiser (Anm. 15), S. 130.

[17] Die "Schichten des Pentateuch und der Krieg", in *Studien zum Pentateuch* (Stuttgart, 1988), S. 255–315, S. 307.

Tetrateuch und Deuteronomistisches Geschichtswerk miteinander verbinden will.

Im folgenden wird zu fragen sein, ob sich diese These einer gleichzeitigen Redaktion von Tetrateuch und Deuteronomistischem Geschichtswerk an weiteren Befunden bewährt. Vor allem muß geklärt werden, inwieweit anhand dieser Befunde eine gemeinsame—Tetrateuch und Deuteronomistisches Geschichtswerk übergreifende—theologische Intention erkennbar ist.

Angesichts der Kürze der zur Verfügung stehenden Zeit muß ich mich dabei auf wenige Beobachtungen beschränken. Zunächst soll gezeigt werden, daß das Motiv der Distanz Israels zu den Völkern und ihren Kulten eine den Gesamtkomplex Gen. i–2 Reg. xxv strukturierende Funktion besitzt. Dabei ist auch zu fragen, inwieweit die Motive des "Glaubens" an Jahwe (*hæʾæmîn*) und der "Reue Gottes", die beide im Kontext der genannten Theologie der Distanz zu den Völkern belegt sind, mit dieser Struktur von Gen. i–2 Reg. xxv in Zusammenhang stehen, was nicht bedeuten muß, daß diese Vorstellungen erst auf die spätdeuteronomistische Schicht zurückgehen: Die hier zu untersuchenden Texte können durchaus eine längere Vorgeschichte durchlaufen haben, bevor sie in der spätdeuteronomistischen Schicht ihre Funktion erhielten.

Als nächstes muß die Frage nach einem gemeinsamen Verheißungsverständnis von Deuteronomistischem Geschichtswerk und Tetrateuch gestellt werden. Gerade wegen des von ihm angenommenen unterschiedlichen Verhältnisses von Verheißung und Gehorsam gegenüber dem Gesetz hat Van Seters ja Bedenken gegenüber einer durchgängigen deuteronomistischen Theologie im Tetrateuch und Deuteronomistischen Geschichtswerk erhoben.

Schließlich ist auch kurz nach der religionsgeschichtlichen Situation zu fragen, die zur Entstehung dieses umfassenden spätdeuteronomistischen Geschichtswerks Anlaß gegeben hat.

III

Wir beginnen mit der Frage, ob sich für Tetrateuch und Deuteronomistisches Geschichtswerk eine gemeinsame Struktur erkennen läßt. Bemerkenswert ist, daß Rudolf Smend (*Mitte* [Anm. 13], S. 124–37) für die Frage nach einer beide Geschichtswerke übergreifenden spätdeuteronomistischen Redaktion zunächst einmal nur auf Texte des

Josua- und des Richterbuches und dann auf wenige Stellen in Deuteronomium, Numeri und Exodus verweisen konnte. In der neueren Forschung ist aber nur die These von einer spätdeuteronomistischen Schicht des Deuteronomistischen Geschichtswerks breit rezipiert worden. Dabei wurden vor allem durch die Arbeiten von Walter Dietrich, Timo Veijola, Ernst Würthwein, Gwilym H. Jones und Mark A. O'Brien, auf die ich mich im folgenden stütze, große Teile des Richterbuches und der Samuel- und Königsbücher auf diesen spätdeuteronomistischen Redaktor zurückgeführt.[18] Die Smendsche Frage nach den Beziehungen dieser Schicht zum Pentateuch ist demgegenüber—soweit ich sehe—kaum weiterverfolgt worden. Im folgenden wird daher nach Themen Ausschau gehalten werden müssen, die sowohl für das Deuteronomistische Geschichtswerk als auch für den Pentateuch von Wichtigkeit sind und die daher für eine beide Komplexe übergreifende Redaktion sprechen.

Die neuere Diskussion über das Deuteronomistische Geschichtswerk hat vor allem gezeigt, daß die von Smend für die spätdeuteronomistische Schicht des Josua- und des Richterbuches herausgearbeitete Thematik des Gesetzesgehorsams Israels angesichts des Götzendienstes der mit Israel zusammenlebenden Heiden auch in den Samuel- und Königsbüchern zentrale Bedeutung besitzt. So wird in dem letzten großen Deuteabschnitt des Deuteronomistischen Geschichtswerks (2 Reg. xvii 7–20), der über den Untergang Israels (und auch Judas) reflektiert, nicht mehr wie im ursprünglichen Deuteronomistischen Geschichtswerk (vgl. xvii 21–3) die Sünde Jerobeams als die entscheidende Verfehlung Israels herausgestellt, sondern vielmehr der Umstand, daß die Israeliten den Völkern gefolgt sind und die vom Deuteronomium (vgl. u.a. xviii 10–11) verbotenen Bräuche der Vorbewohner des Gelobten Landes geübt haben. Dabei herrscht in der neueren Forschung[19] weitgehend Übereinstimmung darüber, daß diese Reflexion über die

---

[18] Vgl. dazu u.a. W. Dietrich, *Prophetie und Geschichte* (Göttingen, 1972); T. Veijola, *Die ewige Dynastie* (Helsinki, 1975); ders., *Das Königtum in der Beurteilung der deuteronomistischen Historiographie* (Helsinki, 1977); E. Würthwein, *Die Bücher der Könige* (Göttingen, Bd. 1: 2. Aufl., 1985; Bd 2: 1984); G.H. Jones, *1 and 2 Kings* (Grand Rapids und London, 1984); M.A. O'Brien, *The Deuteronomistic History Hypothesis: A Reassessment* (Freiburg/Schweiz und Göttingen, 1989), auch L. Schmidt, "Deuteronomistisches Geschichtswerk", in H.J. Boecker – H.-J. Hermisson – J.M. Schmidt – L. Schmidt, *Altes Testament* (Neukirchen-Vluyn, 1983), S. 101–14, S. 105–10.

[19] Vgl. nur Dietrich, (Anm. 18), S. 42–6; Würthwein, *Könige* (Anm. 27), S. 396–97, und O'Brien (Anm. 18), S. 208–11.

Übernahme der "Satzungen der Völker" auf die spätdeuteronomistische Schicht zurückzuführen ist.

Bemerkenswert ist, daß auch bei der Reflexion über das zweite einschneidende negative Ereignis der israelitischen Königszeit eine ausführliche Stellungnahme dieses späten deuteronomistischen Bearbeiters erkennbar ist.[20] Die Trennung von Nordreich und Südreich ist zwar schon im älteren Deuteronomistischen Geschichtswerk als Strafe für den Götzendienst Salomos verstanden worden (1 Reg. xi 31, 33a, 34abα, 35, 37), doch leitet der spätdeuteronomistische Redaktor (xi 1–13*, 32, 33b, 34bβ, 36) diesen Götzendienst von einer der Tora widersprechenden Haltung gegenüber den Völkern ab. Nach dieser spätdeuteronomistischen Schicht zieht sich Israel die göttliche Strafe zu, weil es die Distanz zu den Völkern nicht einhält, die ihm Jahwe im sog. Kultischen Dekalog (Ex. xxxiv 15–16) und im Deuteronomium (Dtn. vii 1–5*) geboten hat. Von 1 Reg. xi 1–2 wird dieser Zusammenhang direkt formuliert: "König Salomo liebte viele ausländische Frauen . . .: Moabiterinnen, Ammoniterinnen, Edomiterinnen, Sidonierinnen, Hetiterinnen aus den Völkern, von denen Jahwe zu den Israeliten gesagt hatte: Ihr sollt euch nicht mit ihnen einlassen, . . . damit sie nicht euer Herz zu ihren Göttern hinlenken."

Die hier vorgenommene Aufzählung von Völkern erinnert dabei an ähnliche Listen im Josua—und im Richterbuch (Jos. iii 10, ix 1, xi 3, xii 8, xxiv 11 und Jdc. iii 5), bei denen ebenfalls heidnische Völker—jedoch jetzt der palästinischen Urbevölkerung—aufgezählt werden. Allerdings behandelt die Forschung diese Listen als mehr oder weniger zufällige Zusätze, hinter denen keine durchgängige redaktionelle Intention zu erkennen ist, wie dies zuletzt die Beurteilung dieser Listen durch Christoph Levin[21] als bloße "Glossen" beweist. Bei genauerer Beobachtung zeigt sich jedoch hinter der Einfügung dieser Listen durchaus eine redaktionelle Absicht. So macht zum Ende der Landnahmedarstellung in Jdc. i–iii* unser spätdeuteronomistischer Redaktor darauf aufmerksam, daß die Israeliten nach der Seßhaftwerdung "unter den Kanaanitern, Hetitern, Amoritern, Perisitern, Hiwitern und Jebusitern" lebten, sich mit ihnen verheirateten und ihren Göttern dienten (iii 5–6).[22] Während das ursprüngliche Deuteronomistische

[20] Vgl. Dietrich (Anm. 18), S. 15–20, und 68 Anm. 7; Würthwein (Anm. 18), S. 131–5, 139–44.

[21] *Der Jahwist* (Göttingen, 1993), S. 331.

[22] Zur Zuweisung von Jdc. ii 17, 20–1, 23, iii 5–6 an DtrN und damit an die oben vorausgesetzte spätdeuteronomistische Schicht vgl. Smend, *Mitte* (Anm. 13), S. 133–4, und (Anm. 9), S. 116.

Geschichtswerk damit rechnete, daß die Urbevölkerung Kanaans bei der Eroberung durch Israel ausgerottet wurde, will unser spätdeuteronomistischer Redaktor mit solchen Listen übriggebliebener Völker auf die Vielzahl der Völker verweisen, denen gegenüber Israel seine Identität wahren muß.[23]

Die Hauptfunktion dieser Listen der Urbevölkerung Kanaans[24] dürfte somit darin bestehen, Israel vor diesen Völkern und ihren Kulten zu warnen. Diese Funktion der Völkerliste ist jedoch nicht nur im Deuteronomistischen Geschichtswerk, sondern auch in Texten des Pentateuch zu erkennen. Am deutlichsten wird dies daran, daß in die drei zentralen alttestamentlichen Gesetzestexte aus Deuteronomium, Bundesbuch und dem sog. Kultischen Dekalog, die vor einem Bündnis mit den Völkern warnen, diese Völkerliste hineinkomponiert wurde (Dtn. vii 1;[25] Ex. xxiii 23,[26] xxxiv 11). Besonders deutlich wird diese warnende Funktion in dem zweiten Deuteronomiumtext, der diese Liste einfügt, nämlich in dem Kriegsgesetz von Dtn. xx, in dem es in *v*. 17–18 heißt: "... du sollst die Hetiter und Amoriter, Kanaaniter und Perisiter, Hiwiter und Jebusiter" der Vernichtung weihen, "... damit sie euch nicht lehren, alle Greuel nachzuahmen, die sie begingen, wenn sie ihren Göttern dienten".[27]

Die Warnung vor dem Götzendienst der Völker ist jedoch nur die eine Seite der mit diesen Völkerlisten verbundenen theologischen Aussagen. Ihre zweite theologische Intention wird auch wieder an den drei genannten Verboten des Bündnisses mit den Völkern besonders deutlich: Allen drei Verboten geht nämlich die Verheißung Jahwes voraus, daß er die Macht hat, diese Vielzahl von Völkern zu besiegen.

---

[23] Zum Verständnis der Völker in der deuteronomistischen (entspricht DtrH) und der spätdeuteronomistischen (entspricht DtrN) Schicht von Jos. i–Jdc. iii vgl. zusammenfassend Smend (Anm. 9), S. 114–16.

[24] Ein Überblick über diese im AT belegten Völkerlisten findet sich zuletzt bei R. Achenbach, *Israel zwischen Verheißung und Gebot* (Frankfurt a.M. u.a., 1991), S. 244. Vgl. auch T. Ishida, "The Structure and Historical Implications of the List of Pre-Israelite Nations", *Bib* 60 (1979), S. 461–90.

[25] Zur Einordnung der Völkerliste von Dtn. vii 1 in die spätdeuteronomistische Schicht (= die von Rose mit Schicht IV bezeichnete Schicht) vgl. M. Rose, *5. Mose* (Zürich, 1994), S. 337.

[26] Dafür, daß die Völkerlisten in Ex. xxiii 23 und in xxxii 11 auf eine (spät)deuteronomistische Redaktion zurückgehen, vgl. schon B. Baentsch, *Exodus – Leviticus – Numeri* (Göttingen, 1905), S. 210, 283. Ähnlich beurteilt W.H. Schmidt, *Exodus* 1 (Neukirchen-Vluyn, 1988), S. 140–2, die Völkerlisten von Ex. iii 8, 17. Zur Zuweisung der entsprechenden Stellen im Josuabuch (iii 10, ix 1, xi 3, xii 8, xxiv 11) an einen (spät)-deuteronomistischen Redaktor vgl. V. Fritz, *Das Buch Josua* (Tübingen, 1994), S. 50.

[27] Zum spätdeuteronomistischen Charakter von Dtn. xx 17f.* vgl. Rose (Anm. 25), S. 250–1.

Auch hinter der unterschiedlichen Zahl und Reihenfolge der Völker dürfte dabei eine redaktionelle Absicht stehen, die allerdings nur noch gelegentlich für uns durchschaubar ist. So will beispielsweise die Liste mit 7 Völkern unter Einschluß der Girgaschiter in besonderer Weise die Mächtigkeit dieser Jahwes Macht unterworfenen Völker herausstellen, wie vor allem Dtn. vii 1 zeigt (vgl. Jos. iii 10 und xxiv 11). Bemerkenswert ist auch, daß als Werkzeug dieser Macht Jahwes, die Völker zu vertreiben, in Ex. xxiii 23 und xxxiii 2 (vgl. auch Ex. xxiii 20, xxxii 34; Jdc. ii 1) der Engel Jahwes genannt ist. Erhard Blum ([Anm. 3] S. 365–77) hat daher ein Teilstück dieser spätdeuteronomistische Schicht zu Recht als *Mal'ak-Bearbeitung* bezeichnet. Außerdem wird, wie Ex. xxiii 23 im Zusammenhang mit xxiii 31[28] und ebenso Gen. xv 19–21[29] im Zusammenhang mit xv 18b zeigen, das Gebiet dieser Völker gleichgesetzt mit dem Gebiet vom Bach Ägyptens bis zum Euphrat, d.h. mit dem Umfang des Davidischen Großreiches. Bei dieser Ausdehnung des Gebietes Israels auf den Umfang des Davidischen Großreiches, die typisch ist für die spätdeuteronomistische Schicht des Deuteronomistischen Geschichtswerkes,[30] geht es ebenfalls darum, die Macht Jahwes zu betonen und dadurch zum "Glauben" an die Verheißung Jahwes zu ermutigen.

IV

Neben der "Völkerliste" gehört nun auch der Begriff des "Glaubens" zu den Vorstellungen, die Tetrateuch und Deuteronomistisches Geschichtswerk übergreifen. Daß das Thema des "Glaubens" (*hæ'ᵉmîn*) an die Wundermacht des Schöpfers Jahwe die Endgestalt des Tetrateuch bestimmt und dort an allen zentralen Stellen (Erzvätergeschichte: Gen. xv 6; Exodusgeschichte: Ex. iv 1ff., xiv 31; Sinaigeschichte: Ex. xix 9; Wüstenwanderungs- und Landnahmegeschichte: Num. xiv 11, xx 12)

---

[28] Daß der Epilog zum Bundesbuch Ex. xxiii 20–33 insgesamt einer spätdeuteronomistischen Schicht zuzuschreiben ist, hat zuletzt L. Schwienhorst-Schönberger, *Das Bundesbuch* (*Ex. xx 22–xxiii 33*) (Berlin und New York, 1990), S. 407–14, gezeigt.

[29] Zu Gen. xv 19–21 als Bestandteil einer späten deuteronomistischen Schicht vgl. zuletzt E. Blum, *Die Komposition der Vätergeschichte* (Neukirchen-Vluyn, 1984), S. 379.

[30] Die Vorstellung von einem Gebiet Israels, das dem Davidischen Großreich entspricht, findet sich ansonsten noch in den spätdeuteronomistischen Stellen Dtn. i 7, xi 24; Jos. i 4. Vgl. hierzu L. Perlitt, "Motive und Schichten der Landtheologie im Deuteronomium", in G. Strecker (Hrsg.), *Das Land Israel in biblischer Zeit* (Göttingen, 1983), S. 45–58, S. 51–3.

eine strukturgebende Funktion wahrnimmt, habe ich bereits in einem 1982 veröffentlichten Aufsatz[31] zu zeigen versucht. Wichtig ist allerdings, daß diese strukturierende Funktion der Glaubensthematik nicht auf die ersten vier Mosebücher beschränkt ist, sondern sich im Deuteronomistischen Geschichtswerk fortsetzt. Vor allem ist von Bedeutung, daß sowohl bei der die Glaubensthematik eröffnenden Abrahamverheißung von Gen. xv[32] als auch in der das Deuteronomistische Geschichtswerk abschließenden Reflexion über die Exilssituation Israels und Judas in 2 Reg. xvii[33] die Glaubensthematik mit dem soeben behandelten Thema des Verhältnisses zu den Völkern verbunden ist. Gen. xv 18–21 sprechen dabei von der Verheißung des Landes der Völker an die Nachkommen Abrahams und vom Glauben Abrahams an Jahwe, der in der Endgestalt von Gen. xv auch diese Verheißung umfaßt. In 2 Reg. xvii wird demgegenüber darauf hingewiesen, daß die Väter Israels deshalb die Völker nachgeahmt und Götzendienst getrieben haben, weil sie nicht an die Macht und die Verheißung Jahwes "geglaubt" (v. 14) haben. Wie im Pentateuch so ist auch in den Büchern Josua—Könige in dieser spätdeuteronomistischen Schicht somit das Thema des Verhältnisses zu den Völkern bereits mit dem Thema "Glaube an die Verheißung und Wundermacht Jahwes" verbunden (vgl. Schmitt [Anm. 31], S. 176).

Auch die beiden Belege für die "Glaubensthematik" im Deuteronomium (i 32 und ix 23) gehören in den Zusammenhang der Tetrateuch und Deuteronomistisches Geschichtswerk übergreifenden Schicht. So ist der Hinweis von Dtn. i 32, daß die Israeliten während der Wüstenwanderung Jahwe nicht geglaubt haben, Teil der spätdeuteronomistischen Ergänzungsschicht Dtn. i 20–45 (vgl. Rose [Anm. 25], S. 477–8). Für das Vorliegen dieser spätdeuteronomistischen Schicht spricht hier, daß als Gegenbild zu den ungläubigen Israeliten Kaleb (i 36) herausgestellt und mit dem Begriff "vollkommen in der Nachfolge Jahwes"[34] charakterisiert wird,[35] der auch im 1. Königsbuch in der

[31] H.-C. Schmitt, "Redaktion des Pentateuch im Geiste der Prophetie", *VT* 32 (1982), S. 170–89.

[32] Gen. xv 1–6 gehört mit Gen. xxii 15–18, xxvi 3b–5 zu der (spät)deuteronomistischen Bearbeitung des Pentateuch. Vgl. hierzu Blum (Anm. 29), S. 362–83. Zur Einheitlichkeit von Gen. xv vgl. gleichzeitig L. Perlitt, *Bundestheologie im Alten Testament* (Neukirchen-Vluyn, 1969), S. 55–77.

[33] Vgl. Würthwein (Anm. 18), S. 396–7, zur theologischen Aussage von 2 Reg. xvii 13–20.

[34] Vgl. zur Übersetzung von *millē' 'aḥărê yhwh* L. Perlitt, *Deuteronomium* Liefg. 2 (Neukirchen-Vluyn, 1991), S. 82, 117–18.

[35] Die gleiche Kaleb charakterisierende Wendung findet sich—ebenfalls spätdeuterono-

spätdeuteronomistischen Redaktionsschicht auf "David" angewandt wird (1 Reg. xi 6). Aber auch im Tetrateuch wird Kaleb bereits entsprechend bezeichnet: Vor allem zu nennen ist hier der Rückblick auf die Kundschaftererzählung von Num. xxxii 7–15 in der Darstellung der ostjordanischen Landnahme, der nach der communis opinio der neueren Pentateuchforschung nachpriesterlich anzusetzen ist und damit einen Hinweis auf die Entstehungszeit dieser Texte gibt, dem im letzten Teil unserer Ausführungen noch genauer nachzugehen sein wird.[36]

Die dritte die Glaubensthematik im Deuteronomistischen Geschichtswerk belegende Stelle Dtn. ix 23 gehört schließlich auch zu einem spätdeuteronomistischen Text, nämlich zu der spätdeuteronomistischen Reflexion[37] über die Sünde Israels in der Wüste ix 22–9, die an den Deuteronomium-Bericht vom Goldenen Kalb und von der Fürbitte des Mose angefügt ist. Dabei liegt hier die gleiche Vorstellung wie in der ebenfalls das Glaubensthema aufgreifenden Stelle Num. xiv 11ff.* vor,[38] nach der Israel nur durch die Fürbitte und das stellvertretende Leiden des Mose von den vernichtungbringenden Folgen des Unglaubens errettet wird. Eine ähnliche Aussage über die Bedeutung der Fürbitte des Mose findet sich schließlich in der Darstellung der Reaktion Jahwes auf die Sünde des Goldenen Kalbes in Ex. xxxii 7–14, die nach der Analyse von Erik Aurelius[39] auch als Teil einer von Genesis–2 Regum reichenden spätdeuteronomistischen Schicht zu verstehen ist.

Bemerkenswert ist, daß diese spätdeuteronomistische Darstellung der Erzählung vom Goldenen Kalb davon ausgeht, daß Israel sein Überleben der "Reue" Jahwes verdankt (Ex. xxxii 12, 14). Mit diesem Motiv der "Reue Jahwes" stoßen wir wieder auf eine Thematik, die sich

---

mistisch—in Jos. xiv 8, 14 (vgl. [Anm. 34], S. 117). Zur spätdeuteronomistischen Ansetzung von Jos. xiv 6–15* vgl. auch Fritz (Anm. 26), S. 152–3.

[36] Vgl. zuletzt J. Scharbert, *Numeri* (Würzburg, 1992), S. 126–7, der mit einer Entstehung des Stücks bei der Verbindung des Pentateuchs mit dem Deuteronomistischen Geschichtswerk rechnet. Eine nachpriesterschriftliche Entstehung nimmt auch L. Schmidt, *Studien zur Priesterschrift* (Berlin und New York, 1993), S. 81 an. Zur Abgrenzung Num. xxxii 7–15 vgl. Blum (Anm. 3), S. 112–14.

[37] Dtn. ix 7–x 11 ist nach Rose (Anm. 25), S. 307, insgesamt der spätdeuteronomistischen Schicht zuzuordnen. Allerdings dürften in Dtn. ix 20ff. mehrere Ergänzungen zu dieser Schicht vorliegen.

[38] Zur Einordnung von Num. xiv 11ff. in die die Glaubensthematik betonende nachpriesterschriftliche Endredaktionsschicht des Pentateuch vgl. Schmitt (Anm. 31), S. 179. Num. xiv 11ff. ist dabei, wie T. Römer, *Israels Väter* (Freiburg/Schweiz und Göttingen, 1990), S. 258–65, gezeigt hat, der gleichen Schicht wie Dtn. ix 22–9 zuzuweisen.

[39] *Der Fürbitter Israels* (Stockholm, 1988), S. 91–100.

sowohl in zentralen Texten des Tetrateuch als auch des Deuteronomistischen Geschichtswerks findet: Der Begriff liegt hier in der gleichen Verwendung vor wie in der—nachexilisch zu datierenden—deuteronomistischen Schicht von Jer. xviii, die von einer doppelten Reue Gottes spricht (Jer. xviii 8, 10):[40] Wenn ein Volk Jahwe nicht gehorcht, so wird er sich des Guten gereuen lassen, das er ihm verheißen hat. Andererseits läßt sich Jahwe aber auch des von ihm geplanten Unheils gereuen, wenn ein Volk zu ihm umkehrt (vgl. ähnlich Jer. xxvi 3, 13, 19, xlii 10).

Wie Jer. xviii 10 spricht der sog. jahwistische Prolog zur Sintfluterzählung Gen. vi 5–8 davon, daß Gott über die Schöpfung des Menschen Reue empfindet und daraufhin die Sintflut über die Menschheit bringt. Aufgrund der traditionsgeschichtlichen Beziehung zu dem nachexilischen Abschnitt von Jer. xviii 7–10 dürfte es sich hier nicht um einen aus der frühen Königszeit stammenden jahwistischen Text handeln.[41] Die gleiche Vorstellung von der Reue Jahwes über eine Heilstat ist nämlich auch im Deuteronomistischen Geschichtswerk belegt. Hier empfindet Jahwe in 1 Sam. xv 11, 35[42] Reue darüber, daß er Saul zum König gemacht hat. Da es sich nun auch bei 1 Sam. xv um einen nach- bzw. spätdeuteronomistischen Text handelt, wie bereits Herbert Donner[43] nachgewiesen hat, dürfte auch der sog. jahwistische Sintflutprolog dem nachexilischen Spätdeuteronomisten zuzuordnen sein.

Bestätigt wird dies dadurch, daß sich sowohl im Deuteronomistischen Geschichtswerk als auch im Tetrateuch nicht nur der negative Begriff der Reue Gottes—bei dem sich Gott eines zuvor beschlossenen Guten gereuen läßt—, sondern wie in Jer. xviii 8 auch der positive Begriff findet: So wird in den Stellen der Erzählung von Davids Volkszählung

---

[40] Zum spätdeuteronomistischen nachexilischen Charakter von Jer. xviii 7–10 vgl. G. Wanke, *Jeremia* 1 (Zürich, 1995), S. 173–4.

[41] Aufgrund der genannten Bezüge zur alttestamentlichen Schriftprophetie (vgl. auch Am. vii 3, 6) dürfte Gen. vi 6–7, entgegen der Auffassung von J. Jeremias, *Die Reue Gottes* (Neukirchen-Vluyn, 1975), S. 19–27, und L. Ruppert, *Genesis* I (Würzburg, 1992), S. 317–19, nicht von einem Jahwisten der frühen Königszeit stammen. Daß die Vorstellung von der Reue Jahwes durchaus in der spätnachexilischen Zeit bezeugt ist, zeigt Jona iii 1–10, iv 2.

[42] In 1 Sam. xv 11, 35 liegt die gleiche Vorstellung von der Reue Jahwes als der Zurücknahme einer Heilssetzung vor wie in Gen. vi 6–7. (vgl. H.J. Stoebe, *Das erste Buch Samuelis* [Gütersloh, 1973], S. 292, und Jeremias [Anm. 41] S. 36). Bemerkenswert ist, daß beide Texte—wie Jeremias gezeigt hat—auf eine neue Heilssetzung verweisen, die Jahwe nicht bereuen wird. Insofern liegt hier eine über Jer. xviii hinausgehende Reflexion über die Reue Jahwes vor.

[43] "Die Verwerfung des Königs Saul", in *Aufsätze zum Alten Testament* (Berlin und New York, 1994), S. 133–64, S. 145–54.

in 2 Sam. xxiv, die von der Erscheinung des Strafengels sprechen (2 Sam. xxiv 16–17),[44] berichtet, daß Gott sich der über David verhängten Strafe gereuen läßt, nachdem David seine Schuld bekannt hat. Die Vorstellung von einem Engel als Werkzeug Jahwes[45] entspricht dabei der Engelauffassung, die wir bereits im Zusammenhang der Völkerlisten[46] beobachtet hatten. Es spricht daher alles dafür, daß in den Texten, die von der Reue Jahwes sprechen, die gleiche spätdeuteronomistische Schicht vorliegt, auf die die oben behandelten Völkerlisten zurückgehen.[47] In ähnlicher Weise läßt im Tetrateuch, in der vorhin (vgl. oben bei Anm. 39) behandelten spätdeuteronomistischen Passage aus der Erzählung vom Goldenen Kalb, Gott sich der über Israel verhängten Strafe gereuen, nachdem Mose für es Fürbitte getan hat (Ex. xxxii 12, 14).[48]

Zusammenfassend läßt sich somit feststellen, daß sich in den Büchern Genesis–2 Könige eine Reihe von Tetrateuch und Deuteronomistisches Geschichtswerk übergreifende Vorstellungen finden, die sich am einfachsten durch die Annahme eines durch eine spätdeuteronomistische Redaktion geschaffenen Geschichtswerks von Gen. i–2 Reg. xxv erklären lassen.

V

John Van Seters[49] hat gegen die Annahme einer Deuteronomistisches Geschichtswerk und Tetrateuch übergreifenden deuteronomistischen

---

[44] Daß es sich bei 2 Sam. xxiv 16 um einen Einschub in die Erzählung von Davids Volkszählung (2 Sam. xxiv) handelt, hat Jeremias (Anm. 41), S. 66–9, gezeigt.

[45] Die Erwähnung des Strafengels dürfte ebenso wie in xxiv 16 auch in xxiv 17 auf diese spätdeuteronomistische Schicht zurückgehen.

[46] Vgl. zu dieser *Mal'ak*-Schicht in Ex. xxiii 20, 23, xxxii 34, xxxiii 2; Jdc. ii 1 oben bei Anm. 3, S. 365–77.

[47] Daß sich Jahwe hier "um Jerusalems willen" seine Strafe gereuen läßt, erinnert an die spätdeuteronomistische Vorstellung, daß Jahwe Juda nicht vernichtet "um seines Knechtes David" willen (2 Reg. xix 34; anders Jeremias, der mit einer Entstehung unseres Verses *vor* dieser spätdeuteronomistischen Auffassung rechnet). Auch in Jdc. ii 18b (ii 18a ist allerdings Dtr H!) könnte die "Reue Jahwes" auf die spätdeuteronomistische Schicht zurückgehen.

[48] Bemerkenswert ist, daß in Ex. xxxii 7–14; Num. xiv 11–25 und Dtn. ix 22–9 dieses Erbarmen Jahwes trotz der Sünde Israels wieder mit der Völkerthematik begründet wird. Die Völker sollen nicht sagen dürfen, Jahwe sei nicht in der Lage gewesen, sein Volk in das gelobte Land zu bringen (vgl. Ex. xxxii 12; Num. xiv 15–16; Dtn. ix 28).

[49] *Congress Volume* (oben Anm. 8), S. 58–77, und *Prologue* (Anm. 7), S. 227–45, besonders S. 242–3.

Redaktion eingewandt, daß in den Tetrateuchtexten ein von der Theologie des Deuteronomisten abweichendes Verständnis des Verhältnisses von Gesetz und Verheißung vorliege. Der Deuteronomist mache nämlich die Landzusage von der Bedingung des Gesetzesgehorsams abhängig, während in der Genesis und dann auch im übrigen Tetrateuch die Landverheißung bedingungslos ergehe. So wird dem Abraham in Gen. xv die Landverheißung in der Form eines Selbstverfluchungsritus übermittelt, der deutlich macht, daß es sich hier um eine einseitige Selbstverpflichtung Jahwes handelt.

Dabei kann Van Seters ([Anm. 7] S. 241–2) zeigen, daß dieses Kapitel nicht, wie Lothar Perlitt ([Anm. 32] S. 55–77) angenommen hatte, frühdeuteronomisch entstanden ist, sondern daß hier eine exilisch-nachexilische Theologie vorliegt. Auch die Tatsache, daß hier die vorexilische Vorstellung von der "Herausführung aus Ägypten" in eine "Herausführung aus Ur in Chaldäa" umgewandelt ist, spricht für eine exilisch-nachexilische und wohl auch für eine nachpriesterliche Enstehung des Stücks.[50] In die gleiche Schicht sind nach Van Seters ([Anm. 7] S. 223) die Verheißung im Anschluß an die Erzählung von Isaaks Opferung in Gen. xxii 16–18 und die Verheißungen zur Isaakgeschichte Gen. xxvi einzuordnen. Bemerkenswert ist, daß auch hier die Landverheißung unkonditional ergeht (S. 240–1). Zwar geschieht die Verheißung an die Nachkommen Abrahams "um Abrahams Gehorsam gegen die göttlichen Befehle und Gesetze willen" (vgl. Gen. xxvi 5: "darum, weil Abraham auf meine Stimme gehört hat und meine Ordnungen, meine Gebote, meine Satzungen und meine Gesetze gehalten hat").[51] Diese Begründung bedeutet jedoch nur, daß die Verheißung aufgrund von Abrahams Gehorsam geschieht, nicht jedoch, daß sie den Gehorsam von Abrahams Nachkommen voraussetzt. Van Seters hat somit recht, wenn er die hier vorliegenden Texte als Ausdruck einer bedingungslosen Verheißung interpretiert, die in Widerspruch zu der Tun-Ergehen-Theologie des Deuteronomistischen Geschichtswerks steht.

Allerdings übersieht Van Seters, daß es im Deuteronomistischen Geschichtswerk nicht nur die frühe deuteronomistische Schicht gibt, die mit einer bedingten Landzusage rechnet. Vielmehr muß hier—wie oben (bei Anm. 13) im Anschluß an Rudolf Smend gezeigt wurde—auch eine spätdeuteronomistische Schicht angenommen werden, in der

---

[50] Vgl. Van Seters (Anm. 7), S. 240, und schon Schmitt (Anm. 31), S. 182.
[51] Übersetzung nach R. Kilian, *Isaaks Opferung* (Stuttgart, 1970), S. 29.

sich ähnliche Vorstellungen wie in der Abrahamdarstellung finden. In der spätdeuteronomistischen Schicht der Königsbücher wird nämlich David in der gleichen Weise wie Abraham in der Genesis als exemplarischer Frommer dargestellt: Zwar wird hier nicht wie in Gen. xv 6 der Begriff "glauben" gebraucht, doch wird David in 1 Reg. xi 6 als "vollkommen in der Nachfolge Jahwes" bezeichnet,[52] mit einem Begriff, der—wie die bereits oben behandelte Kalebdarstellung in Dtn. i 20–45 (vgl. i 32 mit i 36) und Num. xiv 11–24 (vgl. xiv 11 mit xiv 24) zeigt[53]—in dieser spätdeuteronomistischen Schicht mit dem Glaubensbegriff parallelisiert wird. Gleichzeitig ergeht in diesen Texten der Königsbücher die Verheißung an die Nachkommen Davids, daß sie trotz ihrer Sünde einen Stamm behalten dürfen (1 Reg. xi 12–13, 32, 34bβ, 36, xv 4–5; 2 Reg. viii 19, xix 34, xx 6) "um Davids willen".[54] Dies entspricht genau der Verheißung in Gen. xxvi 24, in der davon gesprochen wird, daß die Verheißung an Abrahams Nachkommen "um Abrahams willen"[55] geschieht. Beide Textbereiche sind somit von der sonst im Alten Testament nur selten vertretenen Vorstellung des stellvertretenden Gehorsams eines vorbildlichen Frommen bestimmt. Entgegen der Meinung von Van Seters liegt somit in der spätdeuteronomistischen Schicht des Deuteronomistischen Geschichtswerks durchaus die gleiche Verhältnisbestimmung von Verheißung und Gesetz vor wie in der Endgestalt des Tetrateuch.

VI

Um die hier festgestellte spätdeuteronomistische Redaktion in die Schichtung des Pentateuch bzw. Enneateuch einzuordnen, müssen wir noch einmal auf die oben (bei Anm. 9) referierte Auffassung von Van

---

[52] Zur Zugehörigkeit von 1 Reg. xi 6 zur spätdeuteronomistischen Schicht vgl. Würthwein (Anm. 18), S. 131, der 1 Reg. xi 1–13 als ein "Gebilde von Dtr N-Kreisen" bezeichnet. Ähnlich I.W. Provan, *Hezekiah and the Books of Kings* (Berlin und New York, 1988), S. 68–9.

[53] Vgl. zu diesem Abschnitt oben bei Anm. 30 und bei Anm. 33.

[54] Zur Einordnung von 1 Reg. xi 12–13, 32, 34bβ, 36, xv 4–5; 2 Reg. viii 19; xix 34, xx 6 vgl. oben bei Anm. 19, 46, 51. Die Kritik von Provan (Anm. 52), S. 96–7, an der Zuordnung von 1 Reg. xi 36; xv 4 und 2 Reg. viii 19 an eine spätdeuteronomistische Schicht überzeugt nicht, da er die übrigen oben genannten Stellen auch seinem späten deuteronomistischen Ergänzer zuweist.

[55] Zur Zugehörigkeit von Gen. xxvi 24 zur gleichen Schicht wie Gen. xxii 15–18, xxvi 3–5* vgl. Van Seters (Anm. 7), S. 223, und auch L. Schmidt, "Pentateuch", in Boecker, u.a. (Anm. 18), S. 80–101, S. 98–9.

Seters, einige dieser spätdeuteronomistischen Texte gehörten zur priesterlichen Schicht, zurückkommen. Auch wenn wir diese Auffassung ablehnen mußten, so steht hinter der von Van Seters vorgenommenen Identifikation der spätdeuteronomistischen Schicht mit P eine sachgemäße Beobachtung, die für die Pentateuchforschung von entscheidender Bedeutung ist. Die in Num. xxxiii 50–6, Jos. xiii 2–6 und Jdc. i 1–ii 5 vorliegende Redaktion stellt nämlich eine Schicht dar, die—wie dies das oben angeführte Zitat von Norbert Lohfink ([Anm. 17] S. 307) bereits zum Ausdruck gebracht hat—einen "Priesterschriftliches und Deuteronomistisches mischenden Charakter" besitzt. Daß in Num. xxxiii 50–56 neben dem deuteronomistischen Gebot der Vertreibung der heidnischen Bevölkerung und der Vernichtung ihrer Kultobjekte priesterliches Gedankengut vorausgesetzt wird, zeigt die Lokalisierung des Abschnitts in den "Gefilden Moabs".[56] Ähnliche Feststellungen sind zu der ebenfalls spätdeuteronomistischen Perikope von der Engelerscheinung in Bochim Jdc. ii 1–5[57] zu machen. Auch hier werden priesterliche Vorstellungen vorausgesetzt: Wenn in Jdc. ii 1 Gott davon spricht, daß er *l^{e}ʿôlām* zu seiner *b^{e}rît* steht, so liegt hier deutlich eine Bezugnahme auf die P-Vorstellung von einer *b^{e}rît ʿôlām* vor.[58]

Schließlich ist auch noch einmal an die oben[59] bereits erwähnte Beobachtung zu erinnern, daß die für unsere spätdeuteronomistische Schicht typische Vorstellung von der "vollkommenen Nachfolge" Kalebs in Num. xxxii 7–15 in einem die Priesterschrift voraussetzenden Text vorkam. In gleicher Weise zeigt auch die Analyse der ostjordanischen Landnahmetexte von Num. xxxii, Jos. xiii und Jos. xxii, die die Erlanger Dissertation von Ulrike Schorn[60] vorgenommen hat, daß die spätdeuteronomistischen Texte von Num. xxxii und Jos. xiiiff. sich auf die—um spätpriesterliche Zusätze erweiterte—Priesterschrift[61] zurückbeziehen.

---

[56] Zu "Arbot Moab" als typisch für P vgl. Num. xxii 1 und dazu Baentsch (Anm. 26), S. 588. Vgl. auch die Bezeichnung der zu vernichtenden Götterbilder mit *maśkiyyôt*, die in ähnlicher Bedeutung sonst nur in Lev. xxvi 1 im Heiligkeitsgesetz bezeugt ist.

[57] Zur Einordnung von Jdc. ii 1–5 in P durch Van Seters vgl. oben bei Anm. 9.

[58] Vgl. hierzu H.-C. Schmitt, "Die Suche nach der Identität des Jahweglaubens im nachexilischen Israel", in J. Melhausen (Hrsg.) *Pluralismus und Identität* (Gütersloh, 1995), S. 259–78, S. 261 und Anm. 14.

[59] Vgl. ebd., S. 261.

[60] *Ruben* (Diss. Erlangen 1995/6), S. 206–325. Vgl. zu Jos. xiiiff. auch E. Cortese, *Josua 13–21* (Freiburg/Schweiz und Göttingen, 1990).

[61] Ebenso weist auch die spätdeuteronomistische Vorstellung, daß Israel aus den Völkern ausgesondert ist (*bdl mn hʿmym*), in 1 Reg. viii 53 eine enge Verwandtschaft mit späten

Daß auch die spätdeuteronomistischen Texte der Königsbücher nachpriesterschriftlich anzusetzen sind, wird durch einige Theologumena dieser Texte bestätigt, deren engste Parallelen sich in späten Schichten des Heiligkeitsgesetzes finden: So sieht die spätdeuteronomistische Reflexion über das Ende des Nordreiches in 2 Reg. xvii 7–20 die Schuld Israels darin, daß Israel "in den Satzungen (*ḥuqqôt*) der Völker" gewandelt ist (xvii 7–8), wie dies in gleicher Weise nur Lev. xviii (*v.* 3, 30) und Lev. xx (*v.* 23) tun.

Somit ist die Tetrateuch und Deuteronomistisches Geschichtswerk verbindende spätdeuteronomistische Schicht auf eine Redaktion zurückzuführen, die die Priesterschrift samt spätpriesterlicher Erweiterungen bereits voraussetzt. Sie stellt daher die letzte umfassende Bearbeitung des Pentateuch und auch des Enneateuch dar, die im wesentlichen die vorliegende Gestalt von Gen. i–2 Reg. xxv geschaffen hat.

VII

Julius Wellhausen[62] hat die Auffassung vertreten, daß der alttestamentliche Glaube in der Nachexilszeit nur dadurch überleben konnte, daß er sich in den Panzer theokratischer Institutionen zurückzog und daß sich das Volk Israel in eine Kultgemeinde verwandelte, die sich hermetisch nach außen abschottete. Die heutige Diskussion über die Entstehung des Pentateuch, in der in den unterschiedlichsten Modellen für den Abschluß der Pentateuchentstehung mit einer priesterlichen Redaktion oder Komposition gerechnet wird, zeigt, wie stark dieses Wellhausensche Bild der Nachexilszeit noch nachwirkt.[63]

Die hier vorgetragenen Beobachtungen zu Strukturen, die Pentateuch und Deuteronomistisches Geschichtswerk übergreifen, weisen in eine andere Richtung. Es war nicht die priesterliche Theokratie des Jerusalemer Tempelstaates, die der nachexilischen israelitischen Gemeinde Einheit und Identität gab, sondern es waren die schriftgelehrten deuteronomistischen Kreise, die angesichts der Konflikte zwischen theokra-

Bestandteilen des Heiligkeitsgesetzes in Lev. xx 24, 26 auf. Vgl. hierzu W. Thiel, "Erwägungen zum Alter des Heiligkeitsgesetzes", *ZAW* 81 (1969), S. 40–73, S. 70–2. Zum Zusammenhang des Heiligkeitsgesetzes mit der Endredaktion des Pentateuch vgl. auch E. Otto, *Theologische Ethik des ATs* (Stuttgart u.a., 1994), S. 233–43.

[62] Vgl. u.a. *Israelitische und jüdische Geschichte* (4. Aufl., Berlin, 1901), S. 178–90.

[63] Vgl. hierzu oben bei Anm. 12.

tischen und prophetischen Gruppen des nachexilischen Israel sich für eine Orientierung an dem Urpropheten Mose einsetzten und damit von einer ursprünglichen Zusammengehörigkeit von "Tora" und "Nebiim", von Gesetz und Propheten ausgingen. Die in der neueren Forschung—u.a. von Joseph Blenkinsopp[64] und Frank Crüsemann[65]—vertretene Auffassung, daß der Pentateuch unter antiprophetischer Zielsetzung kanonisiert worden sei, muß daher aufgegeben werden. Vielmehr will gerade die den Pentateuch abschließende Notiz von Dtn. xxiv 10–12, auf die sich Blenkinsopp und Crüsemann berufen, herausstellen, daß vom Erzpropheten Mose her die im Deuteronomistischen Geschichtswerk dargestellte Prophetie ihre Legitimation erhält.[66] Mark A. O'Brien hat daher Recht, wenn er Dtn. xxxiv 10–12 auf eine Redaktion zurückführt, in der Pentateuch und Deuteronomistisches Geschichtswerk miteinander verbunden sind ([Anm. 18] S. 66).

Diese Beobachtungen bestätigen somit die von Cees Houtman[67] vertretene These, daß der Pentateuch erst zusammen mit den Vorderen Propheten kanonischen Charakter erhalten hat. Die Sonderstellung des Pentateuch ist demgegenüber eine Entwicklung, die wohl erst für das Ende des 3. Jh.s. v. Chr. zu beobachten ist.[68] Tora und Propheten sind daher nicht als Gegensätze zu verstehen. Ihre kanonische Gestalt haben beide vielmehr nur in ihrem Bezogensein aufeinander erhalten.

---

[64] J. Blenkinsopp, *Prophecy and Canon* (London, 1977), S. 80–95.

[61] Vgl. zuletzt F. Crüsemann, *Die Tora* (München, 1992), S. 402. Vgl. dazu Schmitt, in *Pluralismus* (Anm. 58), S. 272.

[66] Vgl. hierzu Blum (Anm. 3), S. 194–7.

[67] *Der Pentateuch. Die Geschichte seiner Erforschung neben einer Auswertung* (Kampen, 1994), S. 441–6.

[68] Vgl. ebd. S. 444–5.

KONZEPTION UND VORGESCHICHTE DES STELLVERTRETUNGSGEDANKENS IM ALTEN TESTAMENT

von

HERMANN SPIECKERMANN
Hamburg

Im Jahre 1968 hielt W. Zimmerli auf dem VI. Congress of the International Organization for the Study of the Old Testament in Rom einen Vortrag mit dem Titel "Zur Vorgeschichte von Jes. liii".[1] Seine These lautete damals: Die Formulierung *nś' ʿwn* "Schuld (bzw. Sünde) tragen" wird im vierten Gottesknechtslied (Jes. lii 13–liii 12; im folgenden kurz: Jes. liii) in großer Freiheit variiert (vgl. Jes. liii 4–6, 11–12). Für ihre Verwendung sind zwei Traditionsvorgaben bestimmend: einmal die priesterlich geprägte Sühnung durch die stellvertretende Übernahme von Schuld und Strafe, wie sie in Lev. x 17 und xvi 22 bezeugt ist, zum anderen die zeichenhafte prophetische Darstellung der Schuldzeit des Volkes Israel, wie sie von Ezechiel berichtet wird (Ez. iv 4–8). Beide Traditionsvorgaben haben das vierte Gottesknechtslied entscheidend mitgeprägt. Zugleich ist der Unterschied zwischen dem Gottesknecht und Ezechiel unübersehbar. Das Schuldtragen Ezechiels hat für das Volk keinerlei sühnende Wirkung. Das stellvertretende Leiden "für die vielen" (vgl. liii 11–12) bleibt das Proprium des Gottesknechtes.

Die folgenden Überlegungen wollen an Zimmerlis These anknüpfen und sie im Lichte der neueren Forschung und eigener Einsichten modifizieren. Dazu soll zunächst die Konzeption des Stellvertretungsgedankens in Jes. liii näher betrachtet werden (I). Dann soll der Blick auf einige Texte gelenkt werden, deren Tradition das Profil des Stellvertretungsgedankens entscheidend mitgeprägt hat (II). Abschließend sollen der Ertrag und offene Fragen formuliert werden, die sich angesichts der Stellvertretung in Jes. liii ergeben (III).[2]

---

[1] In *Congress Volume: Rome 1968*, *SVT* 17 (Leiden, 1969), pp. 236–44 = ders., *Studien zur altttestamentlichen Theologie und Prophetie* (München 1974), pp. 213–21.

[2] Zum vierten Gottesknechtslied cf. W.A.M. Beuken, *Jesaja* II B (Nijkerk, 1983),

I

Ein wichtiges Resultat der neueren Forschung zu Jes. liii dürfte darin zu erkennen sein, daß der Terminus *ʾšm* in liii 10 nicht als "Schuldopfer", "Sühnopfer" oder "Bußleistung" zu verstehen ist, sondern als "Schuldverpflichtung" bzw. "Schuldtilgung". Er stammt aus dem eher rechtlich geprägten Kontext einer Schuldsituation mit der sich daraus ergebenden Verpflichtung zur Schuldableistung (cf. etwa Gen. xxvi 10; 1 Sam. vi 3–4, 8, 17).[3] Die Integration des Begriffes in die priesterliche Opfertora (Lev. iv–v, vii u.ö.) kann für Jes. liii nicht vorausgesetzt werden, da *ʾšm* in V. 10 überhaupt nicht kultisch konnotiert ist und die Einmaligkeit dieser Schuldtilgung dem auf Wiederholbarkeit angelegten Opfergedanken widerspricht.

Mit dem letztgenannten Argument ist auch schon die Problematik angesprochen, dem Terminus *nśʾ ʿwn* eine zentrale Funktion für das Verständnis von Jes. liii beizumessen. Zum einen kommt der Terminus in Jes. liii nicht vor, so daß man die Formulierungen in V. 4–5, 11–12 nur als freie Abwandlungen einer geprägten Sühnevorstellung verstehen könnte. Zum anderen ist es durchaus fraglich, ob eine derart fest geprägte Sühnevorstellung bei dem Begriff *nśʾ ʿwn* vorausgesetzt werden darf. Die beiden von Zimmerli angeführten Belege, Lev. x 17 und xvi 22, sind aller Wahrscheinlichkeit nach literarisch jünger als Jes. liii und verbinden ganz unterschiedliche Vorstellungen mit diesem Begriff. Während in Lev. x 17 die aaronidischen Priester durch das rite vollzogene Sündopfer als Mittler für die Gemeinde die Schuld wegtragen und dadurch Sühne bewirken,[4] geschieht in Lev. xvi 22

---

pp. 185–241; B. Janowski, "Er trug unsere Sünden. Jesaja 53 und die Dramatik der Stellvertretung" (1993), in ders., *Gottes Gegenwart in Israel* (Neukirchen-Vluyn 1993), pp. 303–26, 337 (dort weitere Literatur). Das Problem des Verhältnisses der vier Gottesknechtslieder zueinander und zum deuterojesajanischen Textkorpus kann und muß hier nicht erörtert werden. Man wird wohl stärker als bisher in Erwägung ziehen müssen, daß die Gottesknechtslieder ursprünglich keine selbständige literarische Sammlung waren, sondern daß sie von Anfang an zu den Wachstumsschichten des werdenden Deuterojesajabuches gehört haben. Zum Stand der Diskussion cf. H.-J. Hermisson, "Israel und der Gottesknecht bei Deuterojesaja", *ZThK* 79 (1982), pp. 1–24; H. Haag, *Der Gottesknecht bei Deuterojesaja* (Darmstadt, 1985); M. Sæbø, "Vom Individuellen zum Kollektiven", in *Schöpfung und Befreiung. FS C. Westermann* (Stuttgart, 1989), pp. 116–25; R.G. Kratz, *Kyros im Deuterojesaja-Buch* (Tübingen, 1991), pp. 128–47, 206–217; O.H. Steck, *Gottesknecht und Zion* (Tübingen, 1992), pp. 3–43, 149–72.

[3] Cf. R. Knierim, Art. *ʾšm*, *THAT* I (1971), col. 251–7 (umfassende Definition col. 254); A. Schenker, "Die Anlässe zum Schuldopfer Ascham", in ders. (ed.), *Studien zu Opfer und Kult im Alten Testament* (Tübingen, 1992), pp. 45–66 (weitere Literatur pp. 133–5); Janowski (n. 2), pp. 317–22.

[4] B. Janowski, *Sühne als Heilsgeschehen* (Neukirchen-Vluyn, 1982), p. 239 n. 272:

durch den Sündenbock eine rituelle Eliminierung des Unheils, welche weder für die priesterliche Opfertheologie repräsentativ ist noch den Stellvertretungsgedanken in Jes. liii anbahnt.[5]

Will man den Stellvertretungsgedanken in Jes. liii angemessen erfassen, hat es offenbar wenig Sinn, lediglich ein oder zwei in der Tradition geprägte wichtige Motive in den Blick zu nehmen und von daher das theologische Profil des ganzen Textes zu entschlüsseln. Demgegenüber soll hier der Versuch unternommen werden, die Kriterien für die Stellvertretungsvorstellung aus dem Text selbst möglichst vollständig zu entnehmen und sie auf ihren traditionsgeschichtlichen Hintergrund hin zu befragen.[6]

Fünf Kriterien scheinen für den Gedanken der Stellvertretung in Jes. liii zentral zu sein:

(a) *Einer tritt für die Sünden anderer ein.* Dieses Motiv wird in Jes. liii ausführlich entfaltet. Es muß zunächst rein deskriptiv verstanden werden, ohne nach dem Urheber oder den Urhebern des Stellvertretungshandelns zu fragen. In dem mittleren Teil des vierten Gottesknechtsliedes (liii 1–11aα) wird in V. 4a und 5 betont, daß es gerade der "Schmerzensmann" (liii 3) ist, der *unsere* Krankheiten und *unsere* Schmerzen getragen hat, und daß seine "Krankheit zum Tode" um *unserer* Sünden willen zu *unserem* Frieden und zu *unserer* Heilung

---

"Auch wenn man die Wendung *nś' 'wn* Lev. 10, 17b wörtlich versteht . . ., so ist doch nicht gemeint, daß dieses 'Tragen' (= Beseitigen) der Schuld durch das Essen der *ḥṭ't* geschieht, sondern vielmehr, daß die Priester aufgrund der ihnen von Gott gegebenen *ḥṭ't* . . . dazu bestellt sind, als *Mittler* für die Gemeinde Israel deren Schuld zu tragen, indem sie—so ist der das *nś' 'wn* explizierende Inf. cstr. *lkpr* zu verstehen . . .—für sie mit dem Sündopfer das Sühneritual vollziehen." Zu Lev. x 16–20 cf. K. Elliger, *Leviticus* (Tübingen, 1966), pp. 131–9; E.S. Gerstenberger, *Das 3. Buch Mose/Leviticus* (Göttingen, 1993), pp. 105–11.

[5] Cf. B. Janowski, "Azazel und der Sündenbock. Zur Religionsgeschichte von Leviticus 16,10.21f.", in ders., *Gottes Gegenwart in Israel* (Neukirchen-Vluyn, 1993), S. 285–302, 336–7; ders. und G. Wilhelm, "Der Bock, der die Sünden hinausträgt. Zur Religionsgeschichte des Azazel-Ritus Lev. 16, 10.21f.", in ders., K. Koch und G. Wilhelm (ed.), *Religionsgeschichtliche Beziehungen zwischen Kleinasien, Nordsyrien und dem Alten Testament* (Freiburg [Schweiz] und Göttingen, 1993), pp. 109–69.

[6] Die Bemühungen von Th.C. Vriezen gehen in dieselbe Richtung. Er urteilt im Blick auf Jes. liii: "Hier sind die prophetischen Erkenntnisse der Ausgangspunkt: das mediatorische Element (*reconciliatio*), das pädagogisch-rechtliche Element (Tragen der Strafe zur Rettung anderer) und die radikal ethische und glaubensbestimmte Sphäre der ganzen Verkündigung, während das kultische Element der *expiatio* im Hintergrund verbleibt, gleichsam bloß den äußerlichen Rahmen abgibt, in dem diese kerygmatische Fülle zusammengefaßt ist" (*Theologie des Alten Testaments in Grundzügen* [Wageningen und Neukirchen, 1956], p. 256). Obwohl dieses Urteil sehr differenziert ist und die dominierende Rolle der Prophetie in diesem Zusammenhang wohl zu Recht betont wird, scheinen die gewählten Distinktionen dem Text doch kaum angemessen zu sein. Hier muß größere Textnähe gesucht werden.

gedient hat. Er und wir werden gerade durch das Medium in ein Verhältnis der Stellvertretung gestellt, das vorher zwischen ihm und uns das Unverhältnis begründet hat: das Leiden des Knechtes, das ihm das Menschsein raubt (lii 14; liii 2–3). Es ist dieser leidende Knecht, von dem Gott im abschließenden Teil des Liedes (liii 11aβb–12) sagt, daß *er* (Aufnahme des betonten *hw*ʾ aus V. 4–5 in V. 11) durch seine Stellvertretung als ein Gerechter (*ṣdyq*) Gerechtigkeit für die vielen (*rbym*) erwirken werde (*ṣdq* hi.). Schon hier ist deutlich, daß das Verhältnis von Gott und Knecht für die Stellvertretung konstitutiv ist.

(b) *Der für die Sünden anderer Eintretende ist selber sündlos und gerecht.* Dieses Motiv ist im vierten Gottesknechtslied in liii 9 und 11 repräsentiert. Dabei wird in liii 9 kein direkter Zusammenhang zwischen der Sündlosigkeit des Knechtes und seinem Stellvertretungshandeln hergestellt. Gleichwohl wird sein für die Stellvertretung bedeutsames Gerechtsein in liii 11 mit seiner Sündlosigkeit in Verbindung stehen.[7]

(c) *Die Stellvertretung des einen geschieht einmalig und endgültig.* Dieses Kriterium wird nicht explizit benannt, ist aber in der Darstellung des Geschicks des Gottesknechtes zwingend vorausgesetzt. Der von ihm erlittene Tod kann nur einmal gestorben werden. Es gibt keine Textelemente, die die Adressaten zur Wiederholung des Geschehens aufforderten. Das ist zudem dadurch ausgeschlossen, daß in liii 10–12 diesem einen Todesgeschick auch für die Zukunft stellvertretende Kraft zugeschrieben wird. Was die vielen Völker einst sehen und verstehen werden, ist nicht die Erhöhung einer ganzen Reihe von Gottesknechten, sondern allein des einen Gottesknechtes, von dem Jes. liii spricht (cf. lii 13–15).

(d) *Einer tritt für die Sünden anderer aus eigenem Willen ein.* Prima vista scheint der eigene Entschluß des Gottesknechtes zur Stellvertretung kein Thema zu sein. Eindrücklich ist vor allem die Sprache des Passivs als die Sprache des Leidens, in welcher der Knecht präsentiert wird. Hier scheint es keinen Entscheidungsspielraum zu geben. Der Knecht ist "verachtet" und "bekannt" mit Krankheit (liii 3), von Gott qualvoll "berührt, gezeichnet, gedemütigt" (liii 4b), "verwundet" und "geschlagen" wegen unserer Sünden (liii 5), "bedrängt" und "gebeugt",

---

[7] Vielleicht soll der Zusammenhang der Sündlosigkeit mit dem Stellvertretungsgedanken auch durch liii 8bβ angedeutet werden. Der syntaktische Aufbau von liii 8–9 legt jedoch diese Verbindung nicht nahe. Die entgegensetzende Konjunktion zu Beginn des Nebensatzes liii 9b mit der Feststellung der Sündlosigkeit des Knechtes ist klar auf die recht- und ehrlose Behandlung des vermeintlich Schuldigen bezogen.

"zur Schlachtung gebracht" und "stumm" (liii 7). Das alles klingt nicht nach willentlicher Übernahme der Stellvertretung.

Und doch darf man sich nicht täuschen lassen. Dreimal wird im Text die Aussage variiert, daß der Knecht unsere Krankheiten und Sünden getragen habe (liii 4a, 11b, 12b). In V. 4b ist der Umschlag von der Sprache des Passivs im Kontext zur Sprache des Aktivs besonders deutlich. Erstmals durch betont gesetztes *hwʾ* wird der Knecht als handelndes Subjekt in den Mittelpunkt gerückt. In V. 4–5 macht dieser Knecht deutlich, daß das Auf-sich-nehmen des Leidens *sein* Handeln ist. Er stiftet dadurch Beziehung zu der Wir-Gruppe, die bis dahin nichts von ihm wissen wollte (liii 3b). "So werden seine Krankheiten an denen geheilt, die sie gar nicht getragen haben" (liii 5b).[8]

Bei der zweiten Variation des Auf-sich-nehmens der Sünden durch den Gottesknecht in V. 11 wird gesagt, daß seine einmalige Tat zum Tode auch in Zukunft ein stellvertretendes Tragen der Sünden bleibt. Als solches ist es die Grundlage für das, was der Knecht nach Gottes Urteil damit erreicht: daß er vielen als Gerechter zur Gerechtigkeit verhilft (liii 11aγ).

Die in V. 11 bereits zum Ausdruck gekommene Nähe zwischen dem Willen des Knechtes und Gottes Willen wird in der dritten Variation des Auf-sich-nehmens der Schuld in V. 12 nachgerade zu einer Vereinigung der Intentionen. Nachdem in V. 12aγ die Initiative des Knechtes vielleicht am deutlichsten zum Ausdruck gekommen ist (*ʿrh* hi. mit dem Knecht als Subjekt), wird in V. 12b daran bewußt eine komplexe Formulierung angeschlossen, die das vierte Gottesknechtslied zum Abschluß bringt. Gott urteilt über seinen Knecht, daß er für die Sünder eintreten wird. Die einmal geschehene Hingabe in den Tod wird in Zukunft für alle Sünder in Kraft bleiben. Das hier gebrauchte Verb, *pgʿ* hi. mit *l*,[9] verlangt an dieser Stelle die Übersetzung "eintreten für". Aber man darf dabei nicht aus dem Auge verlieren, daß dasselbe Verb (konstruiert mit *b*) in liii 6 bereits dazu gedient hat, Gottes Urheberschaft an der Stellvertretung zum Ausdruck zu bringen: "Jhwh hat ihn treffen lassen die Schuld von uns allen." So kommt in dem unterschiedlichen Gebrauch dieses einen Verbs bei Gott und dem Knecht die Willensgemeinschaft der beiden zum Vorschein.

---

[8] H.J. Stoebe, Art. *rpʾ*, *THAT* II (1976), col. 803–9, 809.

[9] Zu *pgʿ* cf. P. Maiberger, Art. *pgʿ*, *TWAT* VI (1989), col. 501–8; der semantische Zusammenhang von Jes. liii 6 und 12 ist dabei nicht angemessen berücksichtigt worden (cf. col. 505–6).

(e) *Gott führt die Stellvertretung des einen für die Sünden der anderen willentlich herbei.* Nur in Verbindung mit dem gerade behandelten Kriterium ist das letzte Kriterium richtig einzuordnen: *Gottes* Urheberschaft für die Stellvertretung des Knechtes. Schon der erste Teil des Liedes (lii 13–15) bringt Gottes Wirken durch die Verheißung der Erhöhung des Knechtes zur Geltung. Bewußt rahmen in lii 13 die Verbaladjektive der Erhöhung *rwm* und *gbh* das Partizip Nifal von *nś*ʾ. Dieses Partizip wird hier in seiner Grundbedeutung gehört werden müssen. Es meint das Getragen-werden des Knechtes durch Gott, der ihm das Tragen der Schuld der anderen auferlegt. Das ist die Erkenntnis, die den staunenden[10] Völkern verheißen wird (lii 15), gleichsam die konkrete Gestalt der "Hilfe unseres Gottes", die alle Enden der Welt sehen werden (cf. lii 10b).

Gottes Urheberschaft an der Stellvertretung des Knechtes wird erst explizit artikuliert, nachdem in liii 4a die aktive Leidensübernahme durch den Knecht festgestellt worden ist. Es sind vor allem zwei Stellen, die die Urheberschaft Gottes an der Stellvertretung thematisieren: liii 6 und 10. Formal ist die ähnliche Gestaltung wie bei den Stellen auffällig, die von der aktiven Leidensübernahme des Knechtes sprechen. Wird an ihnen das Personalpronomen *hw*ʾ pointiert gesetzt, so steht in liii 6 und 10 *wyhwh* betont voran. Da Konkurrenz um die Urheberschaft der Stellvertretung zwischen Gott und Knecht ausgeschlossen ist, kann auch dies nur auf die enge Willensgemeinschaft der beiden hinweisen.

Aufmerksamkeit verdienen die spezifischen theologischen Aussagen, die mit Gottes Urheberschaft der Stellvertretung verbunden werden. Auf die Verbindung, die in liii 6 durch den Gebrauch des Verbs *pg*ʿ zu liii 12 hergestellt wird, ist bereits hingewiesen worden. Ferner wird durch dieses Verb die von Gott gewollte Stellvertretung deutlich von dem unzureichenden Verständnis des Knechtes abgesetzt, das sich in den passivischen Formulierungen von liii 4b niederschlägt. Wo Gott den Knecht die Schuld "von uns allen" "treffen läßt", da ist die Dimension des Einzelschicksals (liii 4b) durchbrochen, ohne die Dimension des Einzelschicksals aufzugeben. Im Gegenteil: Es ist gerade das zu den anderen hin geöffnete Einzelschicksal, das im Zentrum der Stellvertretungsvorstellung steht. Das Urteil, daß diese anderen "wir

[10] Bei der Verbform *yzh* ist ohne die Hilfe der Septuaginta (θαυμάσονται) wohl kaum auszukommen.

alle" sind, wie zweimal in liii 6 betont wird, bedarf offensichtlich der Deckung durch Gottes Urheberschaft an der Stellvertretung.[11]

Von großem Gewicht ist die Formulierung der Initiative Gottes zur Stellvertretung in liii 10. Zweimal wird betont, daß Gott Gefallen an dem Leiden des Knechtes habe (*ḥpṣ* als Verb und als Nomen). Die Übersetzung dieses Wortes mit "planen" oder "Plan" ist nicht glücklich. Die innere Beteiligung Gottes am Geschick des Knechtes und an seinem Werk muß darin hörbar bleiben. Wo im Alten Testament von *ḥpṣ* die Rede ist, ist häufig genug Liebe im Spiel. So auch hier. Gottes Gefallen daran, den Knecht zu schlagen, ist kein Sadismus, sondern Manifestation seines liebenden Willens, durch das Leiden des Knechtes die Schuldtilgung (*ʾšm*) gelingen zu lassen.

Sollten die genannten fünf Kriterien den Inhalt des vierten Gottesknechtsliedes angemessen erfassen, ist deutlich, daß die enge Willensgemeinschaft zwischen Gott und Knecht mit der Intention der Schuldtilgung für die vielen im Mittelpunkt der Stellvertretungsvorstellung steht. Dann kann für die Vorgeschichte von Jes. liii aber nur eine Konstellation relevant sein, in der die personale Beziehung von Gott und bestimmten Menschen in Verbindung mit ihrer Funktion für andere von herausgehobener Bedeutung ist. Das ist bei Fürbitte und Leiden bestimmter Prophetengestalten der Fall. Hier werden die Wurzeln des Stellvertretungsgedankens von Jes. liii liegen.

II

Es ist kaum wahrscheinlich, "daß die Fürbitte zu den ursprünglichsten Aufgaben der Propheten" gehört hat.[12] Man darf sich über das Alter

---

[11] Man könnte die Aufweitung des Adressatenkreises durch das zweimal betonte *klnw* am Anfang und am Ende von liii 6 gleich wieder durch liii 8b eingeengt sehen. In liii 8bβ enthält MT in direkter Gottesrede—ein Stilbruch—die eigenartige Formulierung über Gottes Initiative zur Stellvertretung: "Wegen der Sünde meines Volkes (Q^a: seines Volkes) 'wurde er' für sie 'geschlagen'". Einmal die Integrität der Überlieferung dieses Satzes vorausgesetzt, ist der Beachtung wert, daß das nur hier erwähnte Volk als Verursacher der Schuld, nicht aber expressis verbis als Adressat der Stellvertretung genannt wird. Wer sich von dieser Argumentation nicht überzeugen lassen mag und die im Mittelteil des Liedes sprechende Wir-Gruppe mit Recht als eine Gruppe in Israel verstehen will ("wir alle" also allein auf Israel bezogen sein könnte), sei auf den größeren Deutehorizont hingewiesen, den im ersten Teil des Liedes die vielen Völker eröffnen und im letzten Teil des Liedes die vielen offenhalten.

[12] In Aufnahme eines Urteils von G. von Rad erneut bekräftigt von H. Graf Reventlow,

der Fürbitte im prophetischen Milieu nicht durch den Fürbitter par excellence, Mose, täuschen lassen. Ihm sind prophetische Züge erst in der deuteronomisch-deuteronomistischen Tradition zugewachsen.[13] Die häufigen Fürbitten des Mose für das Volk, auch die Kardinalstellen in Ex. xxxii 7–14 und 30–5, führen kaum in vordeuteronomische Zeit zurück.[14]

Auch durch die Fürbitte des Amos im Zusammenhang der ersten drei Visionen (Am. vii 1–8) läßt sich kein tragfähiger Grund für eine ältere prophetische Fürbittetradition gewinnen. Von den drei hintereinander geschalteten Visionen kann allenfalls die dritte Anspruch auf Authentizität erheben. Bei den ersten beiden Visionen (Heuschrecken und Feuer) liegt der Verdacht literarischer Topoi nahe, die eingesetzt zu sein scheinen, um Amos Gelegenheit zur Fürbitte zu geben.[15] Das tut er einmal erfolgreich mit dem Wort *slḥ*, das sonst in der vorexilischen

---

Gebet im Alten Testament (Stuttgart, 1986), p. 229, cf. pp. 228–64 (Literatur pp. 228–9); anders E.S. Gerstenberger. Art. *pll*, *TWAT* VI (1989), col. 606–17, 615.

[13] Cf. L. Perlitt, "Mose als Prophet" (1971) in ders., *Deuteronomium-Studien* (Tübingen, 1994), pp. 1–19.

[14] Zu Mose als Fürbitter cf. E. Aurelius, *Der Fürbitter Israels* (Stockholm, 1988); J. Van Seters, *The Life of Moses* (Kampen, 1994), pp. 77–103, 165–207, 220–44, 290–318. Ob, wie Van Seters meint, Mose über die Fürbitterrolle hinaus auch die Funktion eines "vicarious sufferer" für die Sünde des Volkes in Anbetracht von Dtn. i 37, iii 23–8, iv 21 hat (p. 462), ist sehr fraglich.

Zur Terminologie der prophetischen Fürbitte cf. S.E. Balentine, "The Prophet as Intercessor: A Reassessment", *JBL* 103 (1984), pp. 161–73; zur weithin plausiblen Auswertung der einschlägigen Belege cf. Van Seters, pp. 171–5.

[15] Anders V. Fritz, "Amosbuch, Amosschule und historischer Amos", in *Prophet und Prophetenbuch. FS O. Kaiser* (Berlin—New York, 1989), pp. 29–43; er schreibt über Amos: "Das Wesen seiner Prophetie bestand in der Schauung von Unheil und dessen Abwendung durch Fürbitte" (p. 42). Deshalb hält Fritz nur die beiden ersten Amos-Visionen für authentisch. Nach der hier vertretenen Ansicht dürfte gerade das Gegenteil zutreffen: Allenfalls die dritte und vierte Vision sind mit der Verkündigung des Propheten in Verbindung zu bringen, während Sprach- und Vorstellungsgehalt zumindest der ersten beiden Visionen in eine spätere Zeit verweisen.

Auch die in Anknüpfung an Vorgänger (A. Weiser, H.W. Wolff, H. Gese) von J. Jeremias profiliert vertretene These der kompositorischen Korrespondenz von Völkersprüchen und Visionsberichten im Amosbuch ist nicht unproblmatisch ("Völkersprüche und Visionsberichte im Amosbuch" in ibid. pp. 82–97). Die vorgeschlagene Disposition, die bei den Völkersprüchen einleuchtet, bereitet bei den Visionen Schwierigkeiten: die Zuordnung der ersten vier Visionen zu zwei Visionenpaaren. Darauf gründet die These: "Amos ist nicht freiwillig zum Unheilspropheten geworden, sondern erst, nachdem Jahwe ihm die Fürsprache für sein Volk untersagt hat" (p. 83, cf. p. 89). Sowenig von Freiwilligkeit zur Gerichtsverkündigung in irgendeinem Stadium der Überlieferung die Rede sein kann, dürfte doch wahrscheinlicher sein, daß das einzig faßbare kompositorische Stadium in der Zusammenordnung der ersten drei Visionen zu erkennen ist, und zwar im Sinne der scheiternden Fürbitte. Das dürfte kaum in der Zeit des Amos geschehen sein. Die Verkündigung des Propheten selbst dürfte immer noch am besten in der kompromißlosen Gerichtsbotschaft zu erkennen sein (cf. R. Smend, "Das Nein des Amos" [1963], in ders., *Die Mitte des Alten Testaments. Gesammelte Studien 1* [München, 1986], pp. 85–103).

Prophetie überhaupt nicht belegt ist, und ein zweites Mal mit dem Wort *ḥdl*, das nur hier in der Anrede an Gott gebraucht ist. Gott läßt sich des Unheils gereuen (*nḥm* ni. [mit *ʿl*], Am. vii 3, 6). *Alle* Belege dieser theologisch gewichtigen Vorstellung, auch Gen. vi 6–7, weisen frühestens in die Exilszeit (cf. Jer. xviii 8, 10; Joel ii 13; Jon. iv 2).[16] Besonders die Reue Gottes in Ex. xxxii 12, 14 führt in die Nähe der Reue Gottes bei Amos, weil sie beidemal eine Folge der Fürbitte ist. Doch diese Nähe hat sich nicht im achten Jahrhundert, sondern frühestens im sechsten Jahrhundert ergeben. Im achten Jahrhundert hingegen wird die Fürbitte für das Volk nicht in der Macht der Propheten, sondern in der des Königs gelegen haben. Jedenfalls weist die historisch glaubwürdige Nachricht über die Fürbitte des Hiskia in Jer. xxvi 19—obgleich deuteronomistisch formuliert wie Ex. xxxii 11, 14—in diese Richtung.

Von der spätvorexilischen Zeit ab ist die Fürbitte der Propheten fester Bestandteil des Prophetenbildes geworden. Danach sind es "Jhwhs Knechte, die Propheten", die wie Mose das Volk zur Umkehr ermahnen und zugleich durch ihre Fürbitte dafür sorgen, daß das Volk Gelegenheit zur Umkehr hat. Das Volk seinerseits erweist sich hingegen der Chance als unwürdig und setzt die Boten Gottes lebensbedrohender Verfolgung aus. Prophetische Fürbitte und prophetisches Leiden gehören deshalb unabdingbar zusammen.

Bei Jeremia, dessen Buch die Deuteronomisten zu ihrer theologischen Programmschrift gemacht haben, wird die Spannung zwischen prophetischer Fürbitte und prophetischem Leiden durch einen wichtigen theologischen Akzent verschärft. Es ist wohl auf die redaktionelle Gestaltgebung des Prophetenbuches zurückzuführen, daß die Vergeblichkeit der Umkehrforderung und die Bedrohung des Propheten darin gipfeln, daß bei Jeremia die Fürbitte nicht länger eine Option prophetischen Handelns ist. Bezeichnenderweise begegnet im Munde Jeremias die Fürbitte nur noch einmal in der Konfession Jer. xviii 18–23. Dort erinnert der klagende Prophet Gott an seine vergebliche Fürbitte für das Volk (xviii 20) in der Absicht, Gott von seinem eigenen Sühnehandeln abzubringen und zur Vollstreckung des beschlossenen Unheils zu bewegen.[17]

---

[16] Die zu den genannten Belegen notwendige exegetische Argumentation kann hier nicht erfolgen; zur Vorstellung der Reue Gottes cf. nach wie vor J. Jeremias, *Die Reue Gottes* (Neukirchen-Vluyn, 1975), allerdings mit zum Teil anderen literarhistorischen Einschätzungen; cf. außerdem E. Aurelius (n. 14), pp. 91–100.

[17] Der Gebrauch von *kpr* pi. in xviii 23 ist aller Beachtung wert: *Gott* wirkt Sühne, womöglich aufgrund prophetischer Fürbitte, dies jedoch offensichtlich ganz unkultisch,

Dem entspricht auf seiten Gottes das Verbot an Jeremia, Fürbitte für das Volk zu leisten. Dieses Verbot hat eine beachtliche Bedeutung im Umkreis der Texte, die Jeremias Leiden zur Konsequenz oder selbst zum Thema haben: Jer. vii 16, xi 14, xiv 11–12 (mit der vergeblichen Fürbitte in xiv 13–16), xv 1.[18]

Im Blick auf die Vorgeschichte der Stellvertretung ist das Verbot der Fürbitte in Jer. vii 16 von besonderem Interesse. Unter den fürbittenden Handlungen, die dem Propheten untersagt werden, ist auch eine, die durch *pgʿ* qal mit *b* ausgedrückt wird: "du sollst nicht in mich dringen".[19] Es ist dasselbe Verb, das in der kausativen Stammesmodifikation bei der Stellvertretungsvorstellung im vierten Gottesknechtslied von zentraler Bedeutung ist (Jes. liii 6, 12). Das Verb ist ein wichtiges Gelenk zwischen der verbotenen Fürbitte und dem neuen Stellvertretungsgedanken. Das komplexe personale Verhältnis zwischen Gott und Prophet, das für das Jeremia- und Ezechielbuch charakteristisch ist, hat sich beim Stellvertretungsgedanken zu einer besonderen Gemeinschaft zwischen Gott und Knecht vertieft. Aus einer seltenen Beziehung ist eine singuläre geworden. Und an die Stelle des Leidens am Volk und an Gott ist das Leiden für andere nach eigenem und nach Gottes Willen getreten.

Der Stellvertretungsgedanke hat seine Wurzeln jedoch nicht allein im Jeremiabuch, sondern auch im Ezechielbuch. Auch hier hat die Fürbitte keine Chance mehr. Wird sie auch nicht durch das explizite Verbot zurückgewiesen, so doch dadurch, daß die Fürbitte im praktischen Vollzug scheitert. Sucht noch in Ez. ix der Prophet durch seine Fürbitte (ix 8) die von Gott verhängte Vernichtung unter der Jerusalemer Bevölkerung zu verhindern, kann er gleichwohl keine Schonung mehr erwirken (ix 10). Bei der großen Abrechnung mit Jerusalem in Ez. xxii verhält es sich indessen bereits so, daß Gott nicht nur unter den Propheten (xxii 28), sondern überhaupt niemanden im Volk mehr findet,

---

ohne Opfer. Die Nähe dieser Sühnevorstellung zu der von Gottes Reue in Ex. xxxii und Am. vii bedürfte näherer Überprüfung. Ob auf diesem Hintergrund nicht auch noch weitere Erhellung des Gebrauchs von *ʾšm* in Jes. liii 10 möglich wäre?

[18] Der Text xiv 2–xv 4 ist redaktionell als eine große Klage- und Bittkomposition gestaltet worden, durch die nichts bewirkt werden kann, weil das Verbot der Fürbitte unumstößlich ist. Denkt man an die erfolgreiche (deuteronomistische) Fürbitte des Mose in Ex. xxxii 7–14 zurück, wo Gott sich des beschlossenen Unheils gereuen läßt (xxxii 14), klingt Jer. xv 6 fast wie eine nachgereichte Begründung zum Scheitern von Klage und Bitte des Volkes und zum Verbot der Fürbitte in xiv 2–xv 4: *nlʾyty hnḥm* "Ich bin (zu) erschöpft, (es) mich gereuen zu lassen" (cf. Jes. i 14).

[19] Ironisch gewendet wird dieses Verb noch einmal in Jer. xxvii 18 gebraucht; cf. ferner die textlich unsichere Stelle Jes. xlvii 3.

"der eine Mauer errichten und vor mir in die Bresche treten könnte für das Land, damit ich es nicht vernichte" (xxii 30; cf. xiii 5; Ps. cvi 23).

In der theologischen Programmatik des Ezechielbuches wird die Vorstellung der Fürbitte durch die starke Betonung der individuellen Vergeltung wirksam verdrängt. Hätten bei der Fürbitte Abrahams für Sodom noch zehn Gerechte ausgereicht, die Stadt zu retten (Gen. xviii 22b–33), und hätte nach Jer. v 1 einer, der Recht tut, für die Stadt Jerusalem Vergebung erwirken können, so sind nach Ez. xiv 12–20 nicht einmal die exemplarischen Gerechten Noah, Daniel und Hiob in der Lage, für irgendeinen anderen Menschen Rettung zu erwirken. Die eigene *sdqh* kann nur das eigene Leben retten.

Von dieser Überzeugung ist auch die große Darlegung über die individuelle Vergeltung in Ez. xviii geprägt. Übertragung der Schuld ist nicht einmal zwischen Vätern und Söhnen möglich. Damit wird die im deuteronomistischen Raum geschaffene Vergeltungslehre revoziert, die in Auslegung der Gnadenformel die Schuld der Väter bis ins dritte und vierte Glied wirksam sieht.[20] In Ez. xviii wird die Unmöglichkeit der Übertragung der Schuld eng mit der Unübertragbarkeit persönlich erworbener Gerechtigkeit verbunden. Was zwischen Vätern und Söhnen gilt, gilt generell: "Der Sohn soll nicht die Schuld des Vaters tragen, und der Vater soll nicht die Schuld des Sohnes tragen (*nś' bʿwn).* Die Gerechtigkeit des Gerechten liegt bei ihm, und die Gottlosigkeit des Gottlosen (*ršʿt ršʿ*) liegt bei ihm" (xviii 20b). Umkehr ist möglich und erwünscht. Aber auch die Zuwendung des Gerechten zur Gottlosigkeit wird bedacht, mit der Folge, daß dann nicht einmal die eigene Gerechtigkeit kompensatorische Kraft hat (xviii 21–32; cf. xxxiii 12–20).

Da im Ezechielbuch die individuelle Verantwortung so radikal gefaßt wird, verwundert es zunächst, daß der Gedanke des Schuld-Tragens Gegenstand einer prophetischen Symbolhandlung sein kann. Ezechiel soll nach iv 4–8 durch das zeitlich befristete Liegen auf der linken und auf der rechten Seite die Schuld von Israel und Juda tragen (*nś' ʿwn).* Da dies in gefesseltem Zustand geschehen soll, ist der Prophet ganz dem verhängten Leiden ausgeliefert, ohne daß sein Leiden stellvertretende

[20] Cf. H. Spieckermann, "Barmherzig und gnädig ist der Herr...", *ZAW* 102 (1990), pp. 1–18; es ist aber wichtig wahrzunehmen, daß auch im Deuteronomismus das Verhältnis von Väterschuld und eigener Schuld bereits intensiv bedacht worden ist. Die Textreihe Dtn. vii 9–10; Dtn. v 9–10 = Ex. xx 5–6; Ex. xxxiv 6–7 ist in dieser Hinsicht besonders aufschlußreich (cf. pp. 5–10).

Wirkung haben könnte. Der Prophet kann nur leidend versinnbildlichen, was das Volk als ganzes treffen wird. Individuelle Verantwortung und kollektive Schuld sind kein Widerspruch. Jene bringt diese allererst in ihrem ganzen Gewicht zum Vorschein.[21]

Zum prophetischen Leiden gehört bei Ezechiel auch sein gottgewolltes Verstummen (iii 26). Das Stummwerden Ezechiels wird ebenso mit *ʾlm* ni. formuliert wie das Stummsein des Gottesknechtes in Jes. liii 7. Doch auch dieser Aspekt von Ezechiels Leiden hat nicht wie im vierten Gottesknechtslied kompensatorische Kraft für andere, sondern die Funktion, das Volk ohne prophetische Warnung zu lassen. Kompositorisch bewußt folgt dieses Verstummen unmittelbar auf Ezechiels Einsetzung ins Wächteramt für das Haus Israel in iii 16–21 (cf. xxxiii 1–20). Dabei wird der Prophet mit einer nachgerade unerträglichen Verantwortung belastet. Er haftet mit seinem eigenen Leben für die zu verwarnenden Gerechten und Gottlosen, sofern er sein Wächteramt nicht auftragsgemäß wahrnimmt.

Sieht man diesen Auftrag, das Wächteramt, mit dem gottgewollten Verstummen des Propheten zusammen, steht seine Leidensexistenz in ihrer ganzen Spannung vor Augen. Was für einen Jeremia die Erschütterung seines Vertrauens in Gott wegen der mangelnden Deckung seines prophetischen Auftrages, verbunden mit dem Verbot der Fürbitte, bedeutet, das ist bei einem Ezechiel die Zerrissenheit zwischen Wächteramt und Verstummenmüssen, verbunden mit dem Scheitern der Fürbitte in actu. Das prophetische Leiden für Gott ist zu einem Leiden an Gott geworden. Unter dem Aspekt der verhinderten Fürbitte und des Leidens ist die Prophetie in eine Aporie geraten, in der als neuer theologischer Gegenentwurf der Stellvertretungsgedanke geboren worden sein könnte.

III

Blickt man von diesem prophetischen Hintergrund noch einmal auf das vierte Gottesknechtslied mit dem Stellvertretungsgedanken zurück,

[21] Zum Problem der individuellen Verantwortung im Ezechielbuch cf. P.M. Joyce, "Ezekiel and Individual Responsibility", in J. Lust (ed.), *Ezekiel and His Book* (Leuven, 1986), pp. 317–321. Joyce ist darin zuzustimmen, daß das Thema der individuellen Verantwortung im Ezechielbuch keine dominierende Rolle spielt. Über Joyce hinausgehend bedarf jedoch der Klärung, welchen spezifischen Stellenwert die unüberhörbare Betonung der individuellen Verantwortung angesichts der Gerichtsansage an das ganze Haus Israel hat.

wird die theologische Leistung der neuen Konzeption deutlich. Das prophetische Leiden erfährt eine neue Sinnstiftung. Es wird zum Leiden für die Schuld anderer, von Gott und dem Knecht gemeinsam gewollt. Zugleich wird das stellvertretende Leiden begrenzt und konzentriert auf das Geschick einer Person, deren Schuld ein für allemal schuldtilgende Kraft hat. Damit wird die Dimension prophetischen Leidens so entschieden transzendiert, daß es seine innere Konsequenz hat, daß der Gottesknecht nicht mehr als bestimmte prophetische Gestalt zu identifizieren ist. Der Gottesknecht ist im Raum der Prophetie gewissermaßen eine "u-topische" Gestalt, die namenlos bleiben muß, weil jede Identifizierung dem Stellvertretungsanspruch nicht genügen könnte.

Der Stellvertretungsgedanke überwindet außerdem die im Ezechielbuch radikal zugespitzte individuelle Vergeltungslehre. Sie ist das Spiegelbild der im Jeremiabuch explizit verbotenen und der im Ezechielbuch in actu scheiternden Fürbitte. Auch hier wagt das vierte Gottesknechtslied Neues (liii 11). Indem Gott den einen Knecht gerecht sein läßt, wird seine Gerechtigkeit Teil des stellvertretenden Handelns. Er macht die vielen gerecht und sprengt damit definitiv die Konzeption der individuellen Vergeltung und der prophetischen Fürbitte.

War im Jeremia- und Ezechielbuch die Thematik des prophetischen Leidens, der Fürbitte und der individuellen Vergeltung strikt auf Israel hin orientiert, so tut das vierte Gottesknechtslied in dieser Hinsicht einen letzten neuen Schritt. In Aufnahme der Aufgabenbestimmung des Gottesknechtes in den ersten beiden Gottesknechtsliedern kommt das Stellvertretungshandeln des Knechtes den vielen zugute (liii 11–12), welche in der vorliegenden Gestalt des Textes von den vielen Völkern in lii 15 kaum zu trennen sind. Die Völker werden nicht nur Zuschauer des "Heils unseres Gottes" sein, wie es sich in seiner Rückkehr zum Zion manifestieren wird (cf. lii 7–10), sondern sie werden selber Anteil an der Schuldtilgung des Gottesknechtes haben.

Steht die theologische Leistung der Stellvertretungsvorstellung außer Frage, ist zugleich unverkennbar, daß sie sich im vierten Gottesknechtslied noch in statu nascendi befindet. In Anknüpfung an die Einbeziehung der Völker in die Schuldtilgung des Gottesknechtes wäre darauf hinzuweisen, daß der Adressatenkreis für das Stellvertretungshandeln im Text unterschiedlich klar ins Auge gefaßt wird. Das Verhältnis der "vielen" zu den "vielen Völkern" und beider wiederum zur Wir-Gruppe, die in liii 6 pointiert von "uns allen" (*klnw*) spricht, aber auch einmal das Volk erwähnt (liii 8), läßt Fragen offen. Ob das vierte Gottesknechtslied noch etwas von der allmählichen Entwicklung der Geltung der Stellvertretung zu erkennen gibt: von der ursprünglichen Geltung allein für Israel hin zur Ausweitung auf die Völker?

Undeutlich bleibt auch, welcher Art die Gerechtigkeit des Gottesknechtes ist, durch die er für die vielen Gerechtigkeit erwirkt (liii 11). Gerade angesichts der strikten individuellen Vergeltungslehre im Ezechielbuch mit ihrer präzisen Vorstellung, wer ein Gerechter sein könne und wer nicht, bleibt in Jes. liii Klärungsbedarf zurück. Ist die Gerechtigkeit des Gottesknechtes tatsächlich nach ezechielischen Maßstäben zu verstehen, oder ist der Knecht von Gott selbst mit Gerechtigkeit begabt worden, damit er für die vielen Gerechtigkeit erwirken kann? Träfe die letztgenannte Alternative zu, welches theologische Profil würde dann die in Jes. liii 11 gemeinte Gerechtigkeit haben?

Auch die Namenlosigkeit des Gottesknechtes signalisiert ein Problem. Sosehr es gerade auf dem prophetischen Hintergrund verständlich ist, daß eine Identifizierung des Knechtes vermieden wird, sosehr kann die Namenlosigkeit des Gottesknechtes das Mißverständnis begünstigen, seine Aufgabe könne je und dann immer neu von bestimmten Personen übernommen werden. Mit Sicherheit entspricht eine solche Deutung nicht der ursprünglichen Intention des Textes. Es hat immerhin Erkenntniswert, daß das in nachexilischer Zeit gewiß bald einsetzende kollektive Verständnis auch des vierten Gottesknechtsliedes in ihm selbst keine redaktionellen Spuren verursacht hat. Aber ebensowenig ist das ursprüngliche individuelle Verständnis literarisch nachgezeichnet worden. Es wäre immerhin denkbar gewesen, daß Einmaligkeit und Endgültigkeit der Stellvertretung nachträglich stärker herausgearbeitet worden wären. Offensichtlich fehlten jedoch die Optionen für eine stärkere theologische Profilierung der Person des Gottesknechtes.

Für die Richtigkeit dieser Vermutung spricht die Folgenlosigkeit des vierten Gottesknechtsliedes im Alten Testament. Schon die einleitende Frage der Wir-Gruppe "Wer glaubt unserer Kunde?" (liii 1) hat einen skeptischen Unterton. Der Erfolg des Gottesknechtes wird in der Zukunft erwartet (lii 13) und Gott in den Mund gelegt, der offensichtlich die Glaubwürdigkeit schaffen soll, die die Wir-Gruppe erhofft, aber wohl nicht erreichen kann. Der literarische Erfolg des Stellvertretungsgedankens ist ausgeblieben. Selbst da, wo seine Rezeption und Weiterentwicklung am nächsten gelegen hätten, nämlich in den tritojesajanischen Wachstumsschichten, ist nichts zu finden, allenfalls eine Umdeutung oder gar implizite Absage an den Stellvertretungsgedanken. In Jes. lix 15–20 handelt Gott selbst, weil er feststellen muß, daß es keinen gibt, der stellvertretend eintritt (*'yn mpgy'*, lix 16). Man kann sich kaum vorstellen, daß hier absichtslos dasselbe seltene Verb wie in liii 12 gebraucht worden wäre. Eher wird es sich um eine Rückholung der Stellvertretungsvorstellung ins prophetisch Bekannte handeln, wonach Propheten und andere Menschen zwar eine Mittlerfunktion übernehmen können, Gott aber immer derjenige bleibt, der das Entscheidende selber tut.

So ist Jes. liii im Alten Testament ein singulärer Text geblieben. Er hat keine Nachgeschichte gehabt, und seine Vorgeschichte hat nichts "vorgebaut", sondern eine Aporie produziert, die die neue Konzeption der Stellvertretung lösen helfen sollte. In welchem Maße diese Konzeption in alttestamentlicher Zeit Erfolg gehabt hat, wissen wir nicht. Die literarisch dokumentierte Weiterführung ihrer theologischen Optionen ist jedenfalls erst außerhalb des Alten Testaments bezeugt.

FIGURATIVE POLICY, PROPAGANDA UND PROPHETIE[1]

von

CHRISTOPH UEHLINGER
Freiburg Schweiz

Daß die politische Propaganda der altorientalischen Großreiche des 1. Jts. vC in biblischen Texten ein vielfältiges Echo gefunden hat, ist hinlänglich bekannt: Ein summarischer Hinweis auf zahlreiche Arbeiten zur Verwandtschaft des Dtn bzw. seiner Teile mit neuassyrischen Loyalitätseiden,[2] auf das "Image" des Assyrerreiches im Jes.-Buch[3] oder auf die traditionsgeschichtlichen Beziehungen zwischen neuassyrischen und biblischen sog. Heilsorakeln[4] kann an dieser Stelle genügen. Ein Blick in die einschlägige Literatur läßt folgende Tendenzen und Desiderata erkennen:

– Studien zur Geschichte der Beziehungen zwischen den altorientalischen Großreichen und der palästinischen Kleinstaatenwelt haben

---

[1] Der folgende Text stellt eine leicht revidierte und um Anmerkungen erweiterte Fassung meines am 20. Juli 1995 in Cambridge gehaltenen Referates dar. Der Vortragscharakter wurde beibehalten, damit verbunden auch die weitgehend thetische Präsentation, die Illustrationen bleiben auf ein Minimum beschränkt. Ich hoffe, eine ausführlichere Diskussion der Problematik mit detaillierterer Argumentation von Einzelfragen gelegentlich in monographischer Form nachliefern zu können.

Frau Angelika Berlejung (Heidelberg), den Herren L. Dequeker (Leuven, s.u. Anm. 168), R.G. Kratz (Göttingen), M. Nissinen (Helsinki), D.L. Petersen (Denver, Colorado), A.J. Spalinger (Auckland) und wie immer O. Keel (Freiburg Schweiz) danke ich für Gespräche zur Sache und Hinweise auf weiterführende Literatur. A. Wolters (Ancaster, Ontario) stellte mir freundlicherweise sein noch unveröffentlichtes Manuskript eines unter dem Titel "Pasargadae and the Scene of Zechariah's First Vision" am SBL Annual Meeting in Washington, DC, gehaltenen Vortrags zur Verfügung (s.u. Anm. 160).

[2] Vgl. dazu jüngst P.E. Dion, "Deuteronomy 13: The Suppression of Alien Religious Propaganda in Israel during the Late Monarchical Era", in B. Halpern und D.W. Hobson (eds), *Law and Ideology in Monarchic Israel* (Sheffield, 1991), S. 147–216; H.U. Steymans, *Deuteronomium 28 und die* adê *zur Thronfolgeregelung Asarhaddons. Segen und Fluch im Alten Orient und in Israel* (Freiburg Schweiz und Göttingen, 1994).

[3] P. Machinist, "Assyria and its Image in the First Isaiah", *JAOS* 103 (1983), S. 719–37.

[4] M. Nissinen, "Die Relevanz der neuassyrischen Prophetie für die alttestamentliche Forschung", in M. Dietrich und O. Loretz (Hg.), *Mesopotamica—Ugaritica—Biblica* (FS K. Bergerhof) (Kevelaer und Neukirchen-Vluyn, 1993), S. 217–58; M. Weippert, "Die Herkunft des Heilsorakels für Israel bei Deuterojesaja", in D. Trobisch (Hg.), *In Dubio Pro Deo. Heidelberger Resonanzen auf den 50. Geburtstag von Gerd Theißen* (Heidelberg, 1993), S. 335–50.

sich lange Zeit weitgehend auf Probleme der politischen Ereignisgeschichte beschränkt. In jüngerer Zeit sind dazu wirtschafts- und sozialgeschichtliche Untersuchungen auf der Ebene der "histoire conjoncturelle" (F. Braudel)[5] getreten, die einen differenzierteren Einblick in Strukturen und Funktionsweisen altorientalischer Reiche erlauben. Die Neuorientierung der historischen Forschung in Richtung einer "archaeology of society"[6] ist zweifellos zu begrüßen. Die unübersehbare Zahl von altorientalischen Wirtschaftstexten—das quantitativ bei weitem überwiegende, von der Historiographie zu Unrecht vernachlässigte Textcorpus—zeigt freilich, daß die wirtschaftlichen Strukturen immer Teil eines umfassenderen Systems symbolischer Kommunikation waren und dieses Systems bedurften, um funktionieren zu können.[7] Altorientalische Großreiche können deshalb—zumal angesichts der kaum vorhandenen territorialen Kontrollmöglichkeiten und der geringen Penetration in "unterworfenen" Gebieten—als "networks of communication" (M. Liverani)[8] beschrieben und analysiert werden.

– Die politische Propaganda des neuassyrischen Reiches hat bisher viel mehr Aufmerksamkeit gefunden als die der neubabylonischen Könige oder der Achämeniden. Als Gründe dafür können (a) die intensivere Erforschung neuassyrischer Propaganda seitens der Assyriologie,[9] (b) die bessere Quellenlage mit teilweise direkten Bezugnahmen assy-

---

[5] "... une histoire lentement rythmée: on dirait volontiers si l'expression n'avait été détournée de son sens plein, une histoire sociale, celle des groupes et des groupements" (*La Méditerranée et le monde méditerranéen à l'époque de Philippe II* [Paris, 1949, [9]1990], bes. S. 13–14).

[6] Th.E. Levy (ed.), *The Archaeology of Society in the Holy Land* (London, 1995).

[7] Grundlegend immer noch A.L. Oppenheim, "Neo-Assyrian and Neo-Babylonian Empires", in H.D. Lasswell, D. Lerner und H. Speier (ed.), *Propaganda and Communication in World History* 1: *The Symbolic Instrument in Early Times* (Honolulu, 1979), pp. 111–44. Vgl. auch O. Thomson, *Mass Persuasion in History. An Historical Analysis of the Development of Propaganda Techniques* (Edinburgh, 1977).

[8] "The Growth of the Assyrian Empire in the Habur/Middle Euphrates Area: A New Paradigm", *SAAB* II,2 (1988), S. 81–98. Liverani beschreibt zwar nur die Situation einer bestimmten Region und will in der zweiten Hälfte des 9. Jhs. einen Übergang vom langsam und tief sich verwurzelnden "network-empire" zum schnell expandierenden "territorial empire" feststellen. Aber das Bild der territorialen Expansion des neuassyrischen Reiches, das moderne Karten entwerfen, ist ebenso trügerisch wie eine einseitige Erklärung der Expansion durch militärische Faktoren. Je schneller das Reich expandierte, desto größere Bedeutung bekamen Bürokratie und symbolische Kommunikation zwischen Zentrum und Peripherie.

[9] Vgl. neben dem in Anm. 7 genannten Aufsatz v.a. M.T. Larsen, *Power and Propaganda. A Symposium on Ancient Empires* (Copenhagen, 1979); F.M. Fales, *Assyrian Royal Inscriptions: New Horizons in literary, ideological, and historical analysis* (Roma, 1981); L. Canfora, M. Liverani und C. Zaccagnini, *I trattati nel mondo antico. Forma, ideologia, funzione* (Roma, 1990).

rischer Dokumente auf Israel[10] und Juda,[11] (c) die lange Vernachlässigung der Perserzeit und der persischen Dokumentation durch HistorikerInnen und AlttestamentlerInnen namhaft gemacht werden.[12]

– Die bisherige Forschung hat sich weitgehend darauf konzentriert, mittels punktueller Vergleiche von mesopotamischen mit biblischen Texten das *Daß* der genannten Beziehungen aufzuweisen. Weitgehend im Dunkeln blieb jedoch das *Wie* der Vermittlung, das genauso der Klärung bedarf, wenn von "Einflüssen" begründet geredet werden soll: Durch welche Kanäle floß die assyrische, babylonische und persische Propaganda? In welcher Gestalt erreichte sie die israelitische und judäische Gesellschaft, wurde sie von israelitisch-judäischen Schreibern rezipiert und weitertradiert?

– Mit der Frage nach der Gestalt ist auch die nach dem Medium verbunden. Altorientalische Propaganda operierte nicht nur im Medium von Texten, sondern auch vermittelt durch Architektur (sog. *public buildings*), Infrastrukturen—und Bilder (von Miniatur- bis Monumentalkunst).[13] In Anlehnung an Barbara N. Porters bahnbrechende Studie über die Baupolitik Esarhaddons in Babylonien[14] verwende ich für diesen Bereich königlichstaatlicher Tätigkeit den Begriff "figurative policy", der in prägnanter Weise die Aspekte Sichtbarkeit, Symbolik

[10] Im Blick auf die Propaganda-Problematik sei v.a. an den Schwarzen Obelisken Salmanassars III. erinnert; vgl. dazu O. Keel und Ch. Uehlinger, "Der Assyrerkönig Salmanassar III. und Jehu von Israel auf dem Schwarzen Obelisken", *ZKTh* 116 (1994), S. 391–420.

[11] In bezug auf politische Propaganda sind v.a. Sanheribs Palästina-Feldzug und die Rabschake-Episode 2 Kön. xviii–xix analysiert worden.

[12] Hier ist in jüngster Zeit eine klare Umorientierung der Forschung zu beobachten, wobei für die englischsprachige Forschung gegenwärtig die *Second Temple Studies*, für die französischsprachige Forschung die Gruppe *Transeuphratène* wegweisend sind. Zu letzterer vgl. die Programmschrift von Josette Elayi und J. Sapin, *Nouveaux regards sur la Transeuphratène* (Tournai, 1991) und jüngst E.-M. Laperrousaz und A. Lemaire (ed.), *La Palestine à l'époque perse* (Paris, 1994).

[13] Vgl. dazu bes. J. Reade, "Ideology and Propaganda in Assyrian Art", in *Power and Propaganda* (Anm. 9), S. 329–43; C. Nylander, "Achaemenid Imperial Art", ebd., S. 345–59; S. Moscati, *Il volto del potere: arte imperialistica nell'antichità* (Roma, 1978); E. Porada, "The Uses of Art to Convey Political Meanings in the Ancient Near East", in D. Castriota (ed.), *Artistic Strategy and the Rhetoric of Power. Political Uses of Art from Antiquity to the Present* (Carbondale und Edwardsville, 1986), S. 15–25, 188–9; sowie jüngst P. Matthiae, *Il sovrano e l'opera. Arte e potere nella Mesopotamia antica*, (Roma und Bari, 1994).

[14] *Images—Power—Politics. Figurative Aspects of Esarhaddon's Babylonian Policy* (Philadelphia, 1993); vgl. auch dies., "Conquest or *kudurru*'s. A note on peaceful strategies of Assyrian Government", in M.E. Cohen, D.C. Snell und D.B. Weisberg (ed.), *The Tablet and the Scroll. Near Eastern Studies in Honor of W.W. Hallo* (Bethesda, Maryland, 1993), S. 194–7.

und Öffentlichkeit integriert. In welcher sichtbaren Gestalt waren die altorientalischen Reiche in Israel und Juda präsent? Welchen Anteil hatten die verschiedenen Medien jeweils am Gesamtaufwand?

– Schließlich: Wie verhält sich die Selbstdarstellung der Reiche zu ihrer Wahrnehmung seitens der Untertanen?[15] Lassen sich in biblischen Texten Reflexe assyrischer, babylonischer und achämenidischer *figurative policy* und Propaganda erkennen, sei es im Blick auf die Inhalte, sei es in bezug auf die Überzeugungsstrategien?[16]

Der vorliegende Beitrag kann diesen und ähnlichen Problemen nur in sehr fragmentarischer Weise nachgehen, den einen oder anderen Aspekt etwas genauer beleuchten. Wir setzen ein bei der Frage nach Zeugnissen für assyrische *figurative policy* im Palästina des 7. Jhs., um an diesem Paradigma die politische und die religiöse Dimension figurativer Propaganda darzustellen (Abschnitt 1) und gleichzeitig das Hervortreten des Mondgottes von Harran nachzuzeichnen, dessen Heiligtum und Symbolik während zwei Jahrhunderten die Religionsgeschichte Syriens und Palästinas maßgeblich beeinflußt haben (Abschnitt 2).[17] Aus Raumgründen überspringen wir dann die Zeit babylonischer Vorherrschaft in Palästina[18] und wenden uns sogleich der figurativen Symbolik des frühen Achämenidenreiches zu (Abschnitt 3), um vor diesem Hintergrund den Visionszyklus des Sacharjabuches zu situieren (Abschnitt 4).

---

[15] Für eine frühere Skizze dieser Fragestellung vgl. Ch. Uehlinger, "Das Image der Großmächte. Altvorderasiatische Herrschaftsikonographie und Altes Testament. Assyrer, Perser, Israel", *Bibel und Kirche* 40 (1985), S. 165–72. Vgl. neben dem in Anm. 3 genannten Aufsatz von P. Machinist auch R. Liwak, "Die altorientalischen Großmächte in der Metaphorik der Prophetie", in ders. und S. Wagner (Hg.), *Prophetie und geschichtliche Wirklichkeit im alten Israel* (FS S. Herrmann) (Stuttgart u.a., 1991), S. 206–30.

[16] Vgl. dazu exemplarisch Irene J. Winter, "Art as Evidence for Interaction", in H.-J. Nissen und J. Renger (Hg.), *Mesopotamien und seine Nachbarn. Politische und kulturelle Wechselbeziehungen im alten Vorderasien vom 4.–1. Jahrtausend v. Chr.* (Berlin, 1982, ^{2}1987), S. 355–82; Michelle I. Marcus, "Centre, Province and Periphery: a New Paradigm from Iron Age Iran", *Art History* 13 (1990), S. 129–50.

[17] Erst nach Abschluß des Manuskripts wurde mir die unpublizierte Dissertation von S.W. Holloway zugänglich (*The Case for Assyrian Religious Influence in Israel and Judah: Inference and Evidence*, University of Chicago, 1992 [UMI order no. T-031910]), die zu den in Abschnitt 1 und 2 angesprochenen Problemen unbedingt zu vergleichen ist.

[18] Nur am Rande sei deshalb auf Ez. xxiii 14ff. hingewiesen, wo von bemalten Wandreliefs(?) chaldäischer Krieger die Rede ist, welche offenbar in Palästina—vermutlich in einem staatlichen Verwaltungsgebäude, vielleicht in Jerusalem—zu sehen waren. Vgl. dazu Silvia Schroer, *In Israel gab es Bilder. Nachrichten von darstellender Kunst im Alten Testament* (Freiburg Schweiz und Göttingen, 1987), S. 180–7. Zum Image der babylonischen Truppen als "Holzfäller" in einem ägyptischen Wald(!, Jer. xiv 22–3) vgl. neben Liwak (Anm. 15), S. 212, etwa Börker-Klähn (s.u. Anm. 29), Abb. 260.

Der Einsatz bei den Assyrern liegt darin begründet, daß die materielle Kultur, allem voran die Ikonographie, mit dem Übergang von der Eisenzeit II B (*ca.* 900–720/700) zur Eisenzeit II C (*ca.* 720/700–600) eine deutliche Umorientierung des Symbolsystems (von solarer zu astraler Symbolik)[19] dokumentiert, welche die assyrischen Eroberungen, in deren Gefolge sich neue interregionale Handelsbeziehungen v.a. zwischen Palästina und Nordsyrien entwickeln konnten, als eigentliche Epochenschwelle erscheinen läßt. Die Unterschiede zwischen assyrischer, babylonischer[20] und frühachämenidischer Kultur sind vergleichsweise geringer, zumal die ersten Achämeniden im Bereich der figurativen Symbolik durchaus bestrebt waren, an assyrobabylonische Vorbilder anzuknüpfen, um sich dadurch als legitime Erben jener Vorläufer auszuweisen (aber s.u. 3.1.).

1. *Aspekte assyrischer* "figurative policy" *in Palästina*

H. Donner hat eine sehr eindrückliche Schilderung der figurativvisuellen Präsenz assyrischer Symbole und ihres Einflusses auf die israelitisch-judäische Religion gegeben:

> Früher hatte Jahwe allein, über der Lade im Dunkel der Cella thronend, dem Tempel sakralen Nimbus und kultisches Gepräge gegeben. Der Blick des Israeliten, der durch das große Portal im Osten den Vorhof betrat, endete in gerader Verlängerung beim Allerheiligsten und erhielt durch die Gegenwart Jahwes Ziel und Richtung. Diese Richtungsgerade war jetzt, wenn nicht geradezu unterbrochen, so doch gestört. Zwischen dem Eintretenden und der Cella standen die Altäre und Embleme

[19] Vgl. im Überblick O. Keel und Ch. Uehlinger, *Göttinnen, Götter und Gottessymbole. Neue Erkenntnisse zur Religionsgeschichte Kanaans und Israels aufgrund bislang unerschlossener ikonographischer Quellen* (Freiburg i. Br. 1992, = ^{3}1995), Kap. VII und VIII (im folgenden abgekürzt als *GGG*).

[20] Archäologisch betrachtet markieren die assyrischen Eroberungen eine tiefere Zäsur als die von den biblischen Quellen stärker gewichteten babylonischen. Vgl. G. Barkay, in A. Ben-Tor (ed.), *The Archaeology of Ancient Israel* (New Haven, Conn., und London, 1992), S. 354–73. Hier werden das 7. und das 6. Jh. *zusammen* als Eisenzeit III bezeichnet. Zur Begründung vgl. ders., "The Redefining of Archaeological Periods: Does the Date 588/586 BCE. Indeed Mark the End of the Iron Age Culture?", in *Biblical Archaeology Today, 1990. Proceedings of the Second International Congress on Biblical Archaeology* (Jerusalem, 1993), S. 106–9. Daß die Kontinuität in die frühe Perserzeit hineinreicht, betont auch E. Stern," Notes on the Development of Stamp-Glyptic Art in Palestine during the Assyrian and Persian Periods", in L.M. Hopfe (ed.), *Uncovering Ancient Stones. Essays in Memory of H.N. Richardson* (Winona Lake, Indiana, 1994), S. 135–46.

> assyrischer Gottheiten und zogen den Blick mit der für Orientalen schwer widerstehlichen Kraft vordergründiger Anschauung auf sich. Jahwe geriet sozusagen in den Hintergrund. Es war angesichts der engen Verbindung sinnenfälliger Darstellung und geistiger Vorstellung nicht mehr als natürlich, daß Jahwe wie im Kultus so auch im religiösen Leben und Denken der Israeliten gewissermaßen nach hinten verschoben wurde.[21]

Hält man sich an die archäologischen,[22] textlichen[23] und ikonographischen Befunde, so ergeben diese ein weniger dramatisches Bild. Assyrische *figurative policy* in Palästina beschränkte sich weitgehend auf die folgenden Aspekte:

1. *Palast- und Verwaltungsbauten*[24] zeugen an einem runden Dutzend palästinischer Orte von der markanten architektonischen Präsenz der Reichsverwaltung jedenfalls in ihren wichtigsten Transmissionszentren.[25] Die Vorverlegung des Verwaltungs- bzw. Residenzbereichs von Str. IIIA/II in Megiddo ans Stadttor (Abb. 1)[26] wird nicht oder nicht nur das Ergebnis strategischer Überlegungen gewesen sein. Sie demonstriert, daß den Assyrern an der Kontrolle des Güterflusses gelegen war. Sie hat überdies figurative Bedeutung als symbolische

---

[21] *Geschichte des Volkes Israel und seiner Nachbarn in Grundzügen* 2: *Von der Königszeit bis zu Alexander dem Großen* (Göttingen, 1986), S. 337.

[22] Umfassendste Synthese bei Helga Weippert, *Palästina in vorhellenistischer Zeit* (München, 1988), S. 559–681.

[23] Einen knappen Überblick über in Palästina gefundene assyrische Texte gibt L.J. Ramafuthula, "All cuneiform materials excavated in ancient Palestine to date: Their contribution to the scientific discussion regarding Assyrian imperialism", *NGTT* 35 (1994), S. 24–31. Nachzutragen sind das auf dem Tell es-Sebaʿ gefundene Votivsiegel des Rimut-ilani (Y. Aharoni et al., *Beer Sheba I. Excavations at Tell Beer-Sheba, 1969–1971 Seasons* [Tel Aviv, 1973], S. 56–70), ein jüngst publiziertes Fragment eines Lamaštu-Amuletts (M. Cogan, "A Lamashtu Plaque from the Judaean Shephelah", *IEJ* 45 [1995], S. 155–61) und ein wohl aus babylonischer Zeit stammendes Ringblech vom Tell en-Naṣbe (Ch.Ch. McCown, *Tell en-Naṣbeh. Excavated under the Direction of the Late William Frederic Badè* 1: *Archaeological and Historical Results* [Berkeley und New Haven, Conn., 1947], S. 150–3). Zu Dokumenten aus dem Gebiet des einstigen Nordreichs Israel finden sich kompetente Bearbeitungen und mehr Informationen bei B. Becking, *The Fall of Samaria. An Historical and Archaeological Study* (Leiden, 1992), S. 105–18 (zu dem ebd., S. 112–13, genannten Wirtschaftstext vgl. nun Karen Radner, *N.A.B.U.* 1995/4: 90 no. 100).

[24] Vgl. Weippert (Anm. 22), S. 599–603; R. Reich, "Palaces and Residencies in the Iron Age", in ders. und A. Kempinski (ed.), *The Architecture of Ancient Israel. From the Prehistoric to the Persian Periods* (Jerusalem, 1992) (S. 202–22), S. 214–22.

[25] Eine Keilschrifttafel vom Tell Kēsān (M. Sigrist, "Une tablette cunéiforme de Tell Keisan", *IEJ* 32 [1982], S. 32–5) weist darauf hin, daß die assyrischen Verwaltungsstrukturen bis auf Kleinstadtebene hinuntergriffen. Zwei Tafeln aus Gezer (Becking [Anm. 23], S. 114–18) belegen, daß die assyrische Verwaltung dabei mit lokalen Notablen kooperierte. Eine Tafel aus Samaria bezeugt einen *rab ālāni* (ebd. S. 112–13).

[26] Reich (Anm. 24), S. 216–19. Vgl. auch J.-D. Macchi, "Megiddo à l'époque assyrienne. Remarques à propos du dossier archéologique", *Transeuphratène* 7 (1994), S. 9–34.

Zange, durch die die Stadtbewohner täglich mit dem Herrschaftsanspruch der Assyrer konfrontiert wurden.

Von bedeutenderen nordsyrischen Palästen wie denen von Til Barsip und Arslan Taš/Ḫadātu wissen wir, daß sie mit monumentalen Reliefs und/oder Wandmalereien ausgestattet waren und mit einem den lokalen Erfordernissen angepaßten Bildprogramm von der Macht der assyrischen Herrschaft zeugten. Ab dem letzten Drittel des 8. Jhs. wird dies die sichtbarste Gestalt assyrischer Herrschaft auch in Palästina gewesen sein. Allerdings sind hier vorderhand noch keine eindeutigen Zeugnisse für assyrische Monumentaldekoration bekannt geworden. Merkwürdige Kalksteintafelfragmente vom Tell eṣ-Ṣāfi[27] können dafür keinen Ersatz bieten, selbst wenn sie als Bildhauermodelle zu deuten sein sollten.[28]

2. Eine charakteristische Gestalt assyrischer *figurative policy* sind die zahlreichen *Stelen und Felsreliefs* (Abb. 2) mit Darstellungen des Königs, die assyrische Herrscher von Tiglatpileser I. bis Assurbanipal in vielen Teilen des Reiches anbringen ließen.[29] Für Palästina sind Felsreliefs der assyrischen Zeit bislang erst am Nahr el-Kelb (von Salmanassar III.[?] bis Asarhaddon, Abb. 3)[30] bezeugt. Ein jüngst in es-Selaʿ in Transjordanien lokalisiertes Felsrelief dürfte ersten Mitteilungen zufolge neubabylonisch sein.[31] Fragmente von Stelen sind in Samaria,[32] Ašdod[33] und in Qāqūn[34] gefunden worden, textlich auch

---

[27] F.J. Bliss und R.A.S. Macalister, *Excavations in Palestine During the Years 1898–1900* (London, 1902), S. 41 fig. 17.

[28] Die Deutung der Ritzzeichnungen von Ḫirbet Bēt Layy, die S. Mittmann gegeben hat ("A Confessional Inscription from the Year 701 B.C. Praising the Reign of Yahweh", *Acta Academica* [Bloemfontein] 21,3 [1989], S. 15–38, bes. 30–1), würde voraussetzen, daß die Zeichner nicht nur assyrische und phönizische Realia gesehen hat, sondern auch mit deren Darstellung in der assyrischen Monumentalkunst einigermaßen vertraut war.

[29] Vgl. im Überblick Jutta Börker-Klähn, *Altvorderasiatische Bildstelen und vergleichbare Felsreliefs* (Mainz am Rhein, 1982), S. 54–60, 69–71 und 177ff.; für Syrien und Palästina vgl. Holloway (Anm. 17), S. 541–2 (Table 3).

[30] Ebd. T 43_{151} und Nr. 211–16. Das Relief Salmanassars ist unmittelbar neben einem Felsrelief Ramses' II. angebracht worden, vgl. *AOB*, No. 146; *ANEP*, No. 335.

[31] Das rechteckige Bildfeld soll an einer senkrechten Felswand *ca.* 100m über dem Talgrund und 10m unterhalb der Klippe angebracht, mit einer 41–zeiligen Keilinschrift versehen sein und den König in charakteristisch neubabylonischer Gestalt mit konischer Mütze und langem Stab zeigen. Erste Hinweise verdanke ich A. Lemaire (Paris) und A.R. Millard (Liverpool).

[32] J.W. Crowfoot, G.M. Crowfoot und K.M. Kenyon, *The Objects from Samaria* (Samaria-Sebaste. Reports of the Work of the Joint Expedition in 1931–1933 and of the British Expedition in 1935, no. III) (London, 1957), S. 35, Pl. 4:2 (vermutlich Sargon II.).

[33] H. Tadmor in M. Dothan et al., *Ashdod II–III: The Second and Third Seasons of Excavations, 1963, 1965* (Jerusalem, 1971), S. 92–7 (Sargon II.).

[34] Vgl. *Ḥadašôt Arkeologiyôt* 51–2 (1974), S. 16; E. Stern,"Israel at the Close of

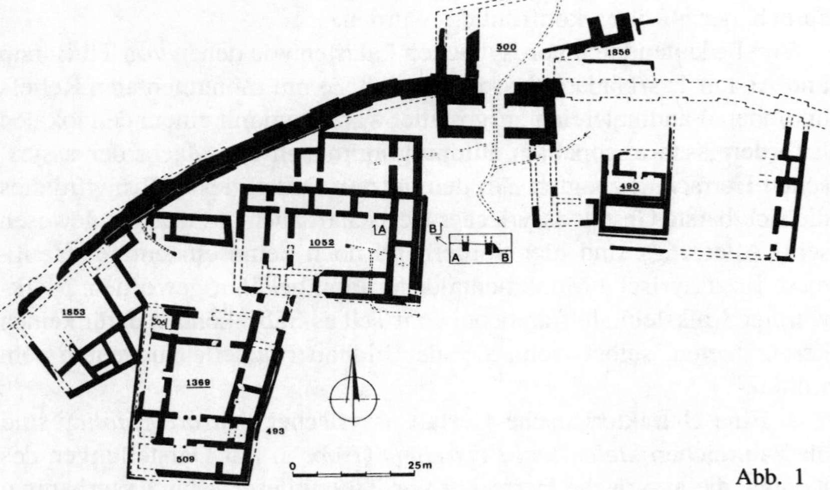

Abb. 1

Abb. 2

Abb. 3

Abb. 4

für Gaza und Naḫalmuṣur dokumentiert,[35] für weitere Orte wohl zu postulieren.

D. Morandi[36] hat gezeigt, daß die Errichtung von Felsreliefs und Stelen als "Hoheitszeichen" generell dazu diente, den assyrischen König dort gegenwärtig zu setzen, wo die Anerkennung seiner Herrschaft entweder besonders notwendig oder besonders ungesichert erschien. Für beide Bildgattungen ist bemerkenswert, daß sie den König nie als Krieger, sondern als "Priesterfürst Aššurs" (*iššak* ᵈ*Aššur*)[37] und loyalen Mandatar der in Form ihrer Symbole dargestellten assyrischen *ilāni rabûti* zeigen. Der König erscheint meist im rituellen Gestus "Fingerausstrecken" (*ubāna tarāṣu*,[38] so Abb. 2 und 4), der die Gunst der Großen Götter erwirken soll,[39] in der Spätzeit und seltener im Gestus "Nasestreichen" (*appa labānu*) mit einem Palmschößling (*libbi gišimmari*; so Abb. 3 und 5), bei dem der Lobpreis der Großen Götter im Vordergrund steht.[40] Die Felsreliefs an meist unzugänglicher Lage dienten weniger der direkten Propaganda als vielmehr der Schaffung königlicher Gegenwart und Ausdruck der Loyalität den Göttern gegenüber an Orten der Peripherie, an denen das assyrische Reich anderer als militärisch-administrativer Sicherung und in besonderem Maße des Schutzes Aššurs und der Großen Götter bedurfte. Anders die Stelen: Gut sichtbar und je nach anvisiertem Adressatenkreis in Palästen, in Toren (Abb. 4)[41] oder auf Plätzen aufgestellt, hatten sie dort eine eminente Propagandafunktion. Auch sie präsentieren die königliche

the Period of the Monarchy. An Archaeological Survey", *BA* 38 (1975) (S. 26–54), S. 28.—Da die Fragmente nach wie vor unpubliziert sind, ist eine Zuweisung an einen bestimmten König (evtl. Tiglatpileser III.?) nicht möglich.

[35] Börker-Klähn (Anm. 29), T 57_{172} (Tiglatpileser III.), und siehe im folgenden.

[36] "Stele e statue reali assire: localizzazione, diffusione e implicazioni ideologiche", *Mesopotamia* 23 (1988), S. 105–55.

[37] Vgl. dazu Ursula Magen, *Assyrische Königsdarstellungen—Aspekte der Herrschaft. Eine Typologie* (Mainz am Rhein, 1986), bes. S. 54; zum Gewand des Königs vgl. E.A. Braun-Holzinger, "Zum Schalgewand Nr. 2", in P. Calmeyer et al., *Beiträge zur Altorientalischen Archäologie und Altertumskunde* (FS B. Hrouda) (Wiesbaden, 1994), S. 31–41.

[38] Vgl. Magen (Anm. 37), S. 45–55.

[39] "In dem nach wichtigen Siegen jeweils errichteten *ṣalam šarrūtīja* wird der Erfolg gleichsam sofort öffentlich gemacht und den Göttern gemeldet. Damit erscheint der Sieg gesichert und sichtbar unter den Schutz der Götter gestellt" (Magen [Anm. 37], S. 54).

[40] Ebd., S. 55–64. In der Ersetzung von *ubāna tarāṣu* durch *appa labānu* (am Nahr el-Kelb anhand der Reliefs von Salmanassar III.[?] bis Asarhaddon augenfällig) äußert sich einerseits eine (behauptete) größere Sicherheit der Herrschaft, anderseits ihre noch stärkere kultische Einbindung.

[41] Vgl. zu dieser Darstellung Sargons II., die eine Stele Tiglatpilesers III. im Stadttor der medischen Stadt Tikrakka zeigt, Börker-Klähn (Anm. 29), Nr. 172.

Herrschaft als im Priesterdienst begründet, und umgekehrt: Herrschaft als Priesterdienst. Daß damit eine religiöse Propaganda für die assyrischen Gottheiten, besonders den Gott Aššur, beabsichtigt gewesen wäre, läßt sich den Quellen jedoch nicht entnehmen.

Das vielleicht deutlichste Beispiel für einen direkten judäischen *response* auf die figurative Propaganda von Königsstelen bietet Jes. xxxvii 28–29 (‖ 2 Kön. xix 28):

> Weil du gegen mich wütest und dein Lärm meine Ohren erreicht hat, ziehe ich dir einen Ring durch die Nase und lege dir einen Zaum ins Maul.
>
> Auf dem Weg, auf dem du kamst, treibe ich dich wieder zurück.

Entscheidend ist der Hinweis auf den demütigend durch Nase bzw. Kiefer gezogenen Zaumring. Von den Babyloniern und Persern sind solche Strafpraktiken nicht bezeugt. Sollte es sich in Jes. xxxvii um ein stereotypes Motiv handeln, so datiert dieses doch sicher in die Assyrerzeit. Zu den Epitheta Sargons II. gehört, daß er "den Rebellen der vier Himmelsrichtungen ein Leitseil (*ṣerretu*) anlegte".[42] Auch philistäische Fürsten hat er in dieser Weise gedemütigt.[43] Wahrscheinlicher ist aber ein Zusammenhang mit der Bildpropaganda *Asarhaddons*: Dieser hat sich nach der erfolgreichen Eroberung von Memphis 671 auf einer eigens in Auftrag gegebenen Stelenserie, von der drei Exemplare in Til Barsip und Zinçirli gefunden worden sind, auf ganz außergewöhnliche Weise darstellen lassen, wie er einen in die Knie gefallenen ägyptisch-nubischen Prinzen und einen phönizischen König (Abdimilkutti von Sidon)[44] an Zaumringen hält (Abb. 5) Die Inschrift der Stele von Zinçirli bezeichnet Asarhaddon u.a. als den "König der Könige von Ägypten, Patros und Kusch, (. . .) der Könige am Leitseil hält".[45] Der zitierte Jesaja-Text gehört in die Zeit Asarhaddons und ist am besten als *response* auf die Propaganda dieses Königs zu verstehen. Vielleicht ist auch der Hinweis auf die

---

[42] Zyl. 9; vgl. A. Fuchs, *Die Inschriften Sargons II. aus Khorsabad* (Göttingen, 1994), S. 33, 290.

[43] Vgl. P.E. Botta und E. Flandin, *Monument de Ninive* I–II (Paris 1849; Nachdr. Osnabrück, 1972), Pl. 83 und 118. Zur Deutung der letzteren Darstellung auf die Demütigung eines Philisters (Ḫanun von Gaza?) vgl. M. Wäfler, *Nicht-Assyrer neuassyrischer Darstellungen* (Kevelaer und Neukirchen-Vluyn, 1975), S. 34–7.

[44] R. Borger, *Die Inschriften Asarhaddons, Königs von Assyrien* (Graz, 1956), S. 101 (Mnm. B. Leiste, Z. 25); H.-U. Onasch, *Die assyrischen Eroberungen Ägyptens* II (Wiesbaden 1994), S. 14.

[45] Borger, ebd., S. 96–7 (Z. 24).

Abb. 5

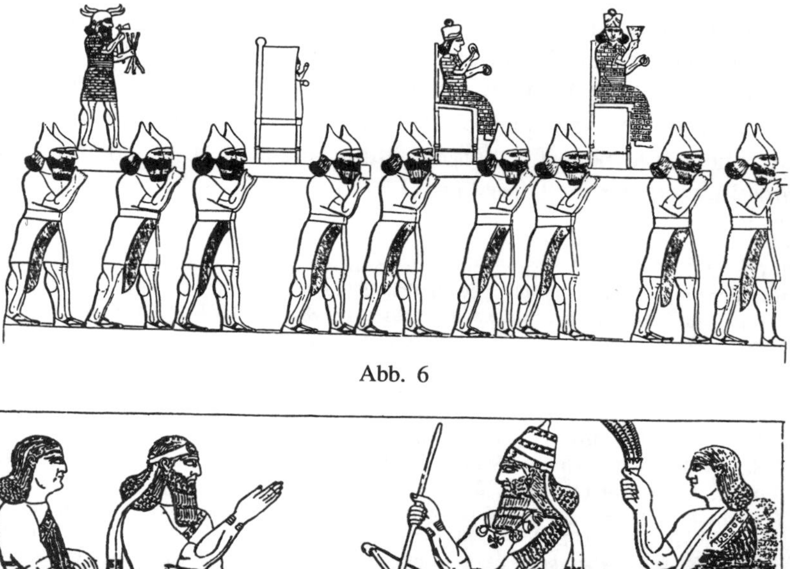

Abb. 6

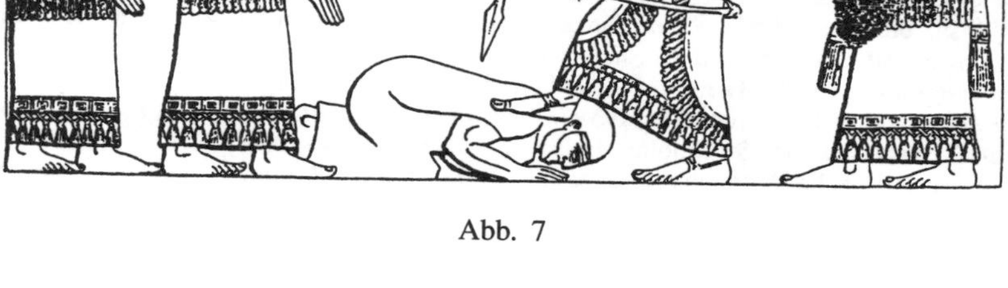

Abb. 7

unfreiwillige Rückkehr des Assyrers nicht nur durch den Kontext von 2 Kön. xviii–xix (Jes. xxxvi–xxxvii) bedingt, sondern ursprünglich mit dem gescheiterten dritten Ägyptenfeldzug von 669 zu verbinden, bei dem der kranke Asarhaddon den Tod fand.

3. Einen eher negativen—in Palästina freilich nie destruktiven[46] Aspekt assyrischer *figurative policy* stellt die *Deportation von Götterstatuen* dar,[47] wie sie in den Quellen im Blick auf Palästina für Gaza (Abb. 6, siehe gleich), Samaria, Aschdod (mit Gimtu/Gat? und Aschdod-Yam)[48] und Aschkelon bezeugt ist.[49] Von der Deportation der samarischen Götter unter Sargon II. wissen wir leider nur durch einen sehr summarischen Hinweis im Kalḫu-Prisma,[50] der für die Religionsgeschichte Israels immerhin insofern bedeutsam sein könnte, als er von einer Mehrzahl von Gottheiten der "Samarier"[51] spricht. Dabei handelt es sich m.E. nicht um einen Topos.[52] Der Kontext spricht von gleichzeitig erbeuteten Streitwagen ([2]*7280 nišē adi narkabāti u ilāni tiklīšun*), so daß die Nennung von "Gottheiten" zunächst an Kriegspalladien der Samarier (vielleicht Standarten)[53] denken läßt. Deren Mehrzahl gäbe kein zwingendes Argument für samarischen Polytheismus ab, so plausibel die Annahme eines solchen auch sein mag. Die Frage bedarf näherer Prüfung auch im Blick auf bildliche Darstellungen der Zeit Sargons II.

---

[46] Die in 2 Kön. xix 18 genannte *Zerstörung* von Götterbildern ist in assyrischen Textquellen nur für zwei ganz außergewöhnliche Situationen bezeugt (vgl. H. Spieckermann, *Juda unter Assur in der Sargonidenzeit* [Göttingen, 1982], S. 358–61). Im Bild wird diese seltene Praxis nie dargestellt. 2 Kön. xix 18 und das ganze Gebet Hiskijas sind nachexilisch und haben keine verläßliche Kenntnis assyrischer Religionspolitik.

[47] Vgl. dazu M. Cogan, *Imperialism and Religion. Assyria, Judah and Israel in the Eighth and Seventh Centuries B.C.E.* (Missoula, Montana, 1974), S. 22–41, 119–21; Spieckermann (Anm. 46), S. 347–54; Holloway (Anm. 17), S. 547–57 (Table 7).

[48] Sargon II., Götter der drei Städte; vgl. Fuchs (Anm. 42), S. 251 (326), 220 (348); R. Borger, *TUAT* I, 4 (1984), S. 380.

[49] Sanherib, Dynastiegötter Ṣidqas von Aschkelon; vgl. Spieckermann (Anm. 46), S. 350–1; R. Borger, *TUAT* I, 4 (1984), S. 388. Vgl. noch den Fall von Usû (Festland-Tyrus) zur Zeit Assurbanipals, dazu Josette Elayi, "Les cités phéniciennes et l'empire assyrien à l'époque d'Assurbanipal", *RA* 77 (1983), S. 45–58, hier 53–7.

[50] Spieckermann (Anm. 46), S. 349–50; Becking (Anm. 23), S. 30–1; R. Borger, *TUAT* I, 4 (1984), S. 382.

[51] Vgl. dazu I. Eph'al, "'The Samarian(s)' in the Assyrian Sources", in ders. und M. Cogan (ed.), *Ah, Assyria . . . Studies in Assyrian History and Ancient Near Eastern Historiography* (FS H. Tadmor) (Jerusalem, 1991), S. 36–45.

[52] So zuletzt T.N.D. Mettinger, *No Graven Image? Israelite Aniconism in Its Ancient Near Eastern Context* (Stockholm, 1995), S. 136 (vgl. 194–5).

[53] Vgl. zur Sache B. Pongratz-Leisten, K. Deller und E. Bleibtreu, "Götterstreitwagen und Götterstandarten: Götter auf dem Feldzug und ihr Kult im Feldlager", *BaghM* 23 (1992), S. 291–356.

Ein Ereignis, das bei der Diskussion um die assyrische Religionspolitik in den unterworfenen Gebieten immer wieder hervorgehoben worden ist, verdient auch hier besondere Erwähnung: die Deportation der Götter Ḫanuns von Gaza durch Tiglatpileser III. im Jahre 734. Die Episode ist in verschiedener Hinsicht außergewöhnlich: Historisch handelte es sich um den ersten Vorstoß eines assyrischen Königs bis in den äußersten Süden Palästinas. Ökonomisch wurde damit der Versuch gemacht, den arabischen Fernhandel, ja überhaupt den Landhandel mit Ägypten unter assyrische Kontrolle zu bringen. Religionsgeschichtlich ist die Episode interessant, weil sie uns einen Blick auf das Stadt- oder Dynastiepantheon von Gaza im 8. Jh. erlaubt und damit unsere überaus beschränkte Kenntnis der philistäischen Religion etwas befördern kann.[54] Schließlich ist sie für das vieldiskutierte Problem der assyrischen Religionspolitik in unterworfenen Gebieten[55] unmittelbar relevant.

Daß die Episode nicht nur aus dem Rückblick der Historiker, sondern bereits zu ihrer Zeit als besonders bedeutsam gegolten hat, läßt sich daran erkennen, daß sie von den Assyrern inschriftlich und im Bild festgehalten worden ist. Die drei erhaltenen *inschriftlichen* Versionen[56] stimmen in den wesentlichen Punkten ihrer Darstellung überein: (a) Die deportierten Gottheiten werden am Ende einer Liste des von Tiglatpileser erbeuteten Besitzes Ḫanuns als *ilānī*[*šu*] genannt, d.h. es dürfte sich um die Gottheiten der Dynastie bzw. des Palastes handeln. Sie wurden deportiert, nachdem der Stadtkönig aus Gaza geflohen war und sich damit dem Zugriff der Assyrer entzogen hatte. (b) Ḫanun hat sich Tiglatpileser schließlich dennoch unterworfen. Die assyrischen Inschriften nennen dafür keinen Grund: Auch dies ist außergewöhnlich. (c) Die Statuen wurden zur Beute gezählt, nicht zerstört. Von einer Rückgabe zu einem späteren Zeitpunkt hören wir nichts. Dennoch ist die Religion von Gaza, wie wir aus jüngeren Quellen

---

[54] Vgl. Ch. Uehlinger in O. Keel et al., *Studien zu den Stempelsiegeln aus Palästina/Israel III* (Freiburg Schweiz und Göttingen, 1990), S. 3–26; I. Singer, "Towards the Image of Dagon, the God of the Philistines", *Syria* 69 (1992), S. 431–50.

[55] Vgl. zuletzt M. Cogan, "Judah under Assyrian Hegemony: A Reexamination of *Imperialism and Religion*", *JBL* 112 (1993), S. 403–14; *GGG*, Kap. VIII (bes. S. 326–7).

[56] In Partitur bei Spieckermann (Anm. 46), S. 325–7, im Anschluß an die Texteditionen von M. Weippert, *Edom. Studien und Materialien zur Geschichte der Edomiter auf Grund schriftlicher und archäologischer Quellen* (unpubl. theol. Diss., Tübingen, 1971); jüngst auch bei H. Tadmor, *The Inscriptions of Tiglath-Pileser III, King of Assyria. Critical Edition, with Introductions, Translations and Commentary* (Jerusalem, 1994), S. 222–5 (Excursus 4).

wissen, nie assyrisch geworden. (d) Tiglatpileser ersetzte die deportierten Götter Ḫanuns von Gaza nicht durch assyrische Götterstatuen,wie in den meisten Übersetzungen der Episode[57] zu lesen ist. Im Text steht vielmehr:

> Ein Stelenbild (*ṣalam*, Sg.!) der {Großen} Gottheiten, meiner Herren, {und}[58] mein königliches Stelenbild (*ṣalam šarrūtīya*) fertigte ich in Gold an.
>
> Im Palast von Gaza stellte ich (es) auf (und) bestimmte (es/sie) zu ihren Göttern.

Die auf einem Textvertreter bezeugte Konjunktion *ù* "und" sowie die Tatsache, daß bei Stelensetzungen in der Regel von einer Darstellung der Gottheiten nicht die Rede ist, läßt hier zunächst an ein Nebeneinander von neu gefertigten Götterbild(ern) und Königsstele denken. Aber *ṣalam* steht zweimal im Singular, so daß wohl an eine Darstellung mehrerer Gottheiten zu denken ist. Die Materialangabe "in Gold" wird nur einmal gegeben. Nun ist eine monumentale Sammeldarstellung mehrerer assyrischer Gottheiten auf einem Relief in Gaza ebenso undenkbar wie ein goldenes Königsbild neben einem oder mehreren (neuen) Götterbildern aus billigerem Material. Gegen die Annahme, Asarhaddon habe in Gaza Statuen assyrischer Gottheiten anfertigen lassen, spricht auch die Tatsache, daß die Herstellung neuer Götterbilder ein nicht nur technisch, sondern auch rituell hochkomplizierter Vorgang und in Gaza kurzfristig ohnehin nicht zu realisieren war. Nicht einmal in Ägypten, wo Asarhaddon 671 regelmäßige Opfer für Aššur und die Großen Gottheiten festgesetzt hat,[59] hören wir etwas von neuen Kultbildern. Was Tiglatpileser in Gaza aufstellen ließ, waren demnach nicht Götterbilder im Sinne von Kultstatuen, sondern *eine* goldplattierte Stele mit einer Standarddarstellung des die Großen Götter im Gestus *ubāna tarāṣu* verehrenden Königs.[60] Die Emphase auf der

---

[57] Vgl. etwa A.L. Oppenheim, *ANET*, S. 283; R. Borger, *TGI*³ (1979), S. 56, 58, 59; ders., *TUAT* I, 4 (1984), S. 373, 376, 377; ebenso Spieckermann (Anm. 46), S. 326, u.v.a.

[58] Die Konjunktion *ù* ist in einem Textvertreter (IIIR 10 no. 2; Tadmors "Summ. 4") mit Sicherheit zu lesen (von Weippert [Anm. 56], S. 490, und Spieckermann [Anm. 46], S. 326, übersehen, vgl. aber Tadmor [Anm. 56], S. 138 und Pl. 49). Sie fehlt jedoch auf einem anderen Textvertreter (ND 400; Tadmors "Summ. 8"), während der dritte Text an dieser Stelle zerstört ist.

[59] Vgl. Borger (Anm. 44), S. 99, Z. 48–9; Onasch (Anm. 44), II, S. 24.

[60] Die Übersetzung von Tadmor trifft (m.W. erstmals) den Nagel auf den Kopf: "A (statue) bearing the image of the great gods my lords and my (own) royal image out of gold I fashioned" ([Anm. 56] S. 139/141, 177, 189; beachte S. 177, die Anm. zu Z. 16').

Darstellung der Gottheiten dürfte aus dem Kontrast zur vorangehenden Deportation der Gottheiten Ḫanuns zu erklären sein. (e) Die Stele Tiglatpilesers stand fortan *im Palast* von Gaza. An der künftigen Loyalität des nach seiner überraschenden Rückkehr wiedereingesetzten Stadtkönigs und der Stadtverwaltung war Tiglatpileser mehr gelegen als an der Religion der Stadtbevölkerung. (f) Daß die auf der Stele in ihren Symbolen dargestellten assyrischen Gottheiten fortan als "Gottheiten ihres Landes" (*ilāni mātīšunu*) gelten sollten, hängt mit dem besonderen Status von Gaza zusammen, das von Tiglatpileser als außerhalb des Provinzialsystems (vgl. Spieckermann [Anm. 46, S. 328) gelegene assyrische Zollstation (*bīt kāri*) in Richtung Ägypten genutzt wurde und deshalb nicht nur militärisch, sondern auch religiös entsprechend gesichert werden mußte.[61] Generalisierende Schlüsse in bezug auf die "religionspolitischen Auflagen der Assyrer" in unterworfenen Gebieten sind daraus nicht zu ziehen (zu Spieckermann [Anm. 46], S. 327).

Die *bildliche* Darstellung der Episode setzt ihre eigenen Akzente: Sie insistiert zunächst auf der Deportation der Gottheiten (Abb. 6), um dann die Wiedereinsetzung Ḫanuns durch Tiglatpileser darzustellen (Abb. 7).[62] Die religiöse Dimension der letzteren Zeremonie wird dadurch besonders expliziert, daß der assyrisch König mit einer Halskette dargestellt wird, welche die Symbole der Großen Götter aufreiht, er somit als "Priester" (*šangû*) handelt (vgl. Magen [Anm. 37], S. 54–5). Er vollzieht im Ritual eine "symbolische Tötung des Feindes" (ebd.), aber nur um diesem neues Leben unter der Herrschaft der assyrischen Gottheiten und ihres irdischen Mandatars zu verleihen. Die Stelensetzung wird im Bild übergangen.

Das zitierte Beispiel von Gaza bleibt hinsichtlich der in einer eroberten Stadt vorgenommenen Ersetzung lokaler Gottheiten durch assyrische Gottheiten ein *Ausnahmefall*, der wie gesagt durch die besondere Lage und Bedeutung Gazas, vielleicht auch durch die mit Ḫanuns Flucht und Rückkehr gegebenen besonderen Umstände erklärt werden muß. Die Assyrer zeigten ansonsten an der Religion der von

---

[61] Man wird aus der inschriftlichen Überlieferung zu dieser Episode sicher nicht schließen dürfen, daß der König eine Stele mit seinem Abbild "noch zu seinen Lebzeiten in den Rang eines Götterbildes erheben konnte" (Börker-Klähn [Anm. 29], S. 200), und daraus erst recht keine generelle Regel machen (ebd., S. 57).

[62] Die Interpretation der bekannten Darstellung bedarf ebenso wie ihre Deutung auf Gaza der ausführlichen Diskussion, weshalb ich mich an dieser Stelle kurz fasse. Vgl. einstweilen Keell und Uehlinger (Anm. 10), S. 412–13.

ihnen unterworfenen Städte und Staaten in Palästina kein Interesse. 2 Kön. xvii 25–8 ist aus nachexilischen Verhältnissen zu erklären.[63] Da den assyrischen Königen nie daran gelegen sein mußte, sich als König von Israel oder Juda, Ammon oder Moab und somit in Kategorien der entsprechenden nationalstaatlichen Symbolsysteme religiös zu legitimieren,[64] hatten sie auch keinen Anlaß, die lokalen Gottheiten besonders zu fördern oder überhaupt auf deren kultische Administration einzuwirken. Die Provinzen Du'ru, Magid(d)u, Gal'ad(d)a und Samerina (nicht Vassallenstaaten wie Juda, Ammon, Moab und Edom) werden sich am Unterhalt der *assyrischen* Reichsheiligtümer beteiligt haben müssen, aber von einer von offizieller Seite gesteuerten, ja auch nur aktiv geförderten assyrischen Überfremdung der palästinischen Lokalreligionen kann keine Rede sein.

Die Assyrer scheinen besonders die Kleinkunst in viel geringerem Maße zu dezidierten Propagandazwecken genutzt zu haben als etwa das ägyptische Neue Reich.[65] Ob dies damit zusammenhängt, daß siegelproduzierende Werkstätten in Assyrien und Nordsyrien über eine größere Autonomie gegenüber den Tempeln bzw. Tempelwerkstätten über größere Unabhängigkeit gegenüber dem Palast verfügten als in Ägypten, bleibt zu prüfen. Objekte mit politisch-militärischen Inhalten zirkulierten fast ausschließlich innerhalb der Kanäle der Verwaltung, und dasselbe gilt für die religiöse Propaganda.[66] Assyrische Gottheiten bzw. mit diesen verbundene Kultbräuche scheinen deshalb in Palästina kaum und wenn, dann dort aufgenommen worden zu sein, wo die traditionelle Religion ein Gefäß dafür bereithielt. So konnte die alte Aschera nun vermehrt Züge der assyrischen Himmelskönigin (Ištar),[67] der alte Drachenkämpfer solche des assyrischen Ninurta annehmen.[68] Historisch gesehen handelt es sich hierbei nicht um Überfremdungsphänomene, sondern um die Konsequenzen eines durch den Wegfall

---

[63] J.-D. Macchi "Les controverses théologiques dans le judaïsme de l'époque post-exilique. L'exemple de 2 *Rois* 17, 24–41", *Transeuphratène* 5 (1992), S. 85–93.

[64] Wie dies ganz anders für Babylonien gilt, vgl. Porter (Anm. 14).

[65] Zur Verbindung von Glyptik und Propaganda vgl. O. Keel, *Corpus der Stempelsiegel-Amulette aus Palästina/Israel von den Anfängen bis zur Perserzeit. Einleitung* (Freiburg Schweiz und Göttingen, 1995), § 721–4.

[66] Vgl. zur Frage der Penetration bereits *GGG*, S. 327ff.

[67] Vgl. neben *GGG* § 197 nun v.a. Ch. Frevel, *Aschera und der Ausschließlichkeitsanspruch YHWHs. Beiträge zu literarischen, religionsgeschichtlichen und ikonographischen Aspekten der Ascheradiskussion* (Weinheim, 1995), bes. S. 423–71; R. Jost, *Frauen, Männer und die Himmelskönigin. Exegetische Studien* (Gütersloh, 1995).

[68] Ch. Uehlinger, Art. "Nimrod", in K. van der Toorn, B. Becking und P.W. van der Horst (ed.), *Dictionary of Deities and Demons in the Bible* (Leiden, 1995), S. 1181–6.

bzw. die Lockerung der nationalstaatlichen Strukturen "internationaler" gewordenen Marktes. Die unverkennbaren Modifikationen im religiösen Symbolsystem Palästinas im 7. Jh. können nicht monokausal mit religionspolitischen Pressionen oder religiöser Propaganda der Assyrer erklärt werden. Zu Recht spricht M. Cogan von einer "new cultural and technological koine" und einer "cultural wave that inundated Judah *from all sides*".[69]

Erfolg und Macht des assyrischen Reiches müssen auf die Unterworfenen, besonders auf im Satellitenstatus verbliebene Vassallen wie Juda eine ungemeine Faszination ausgeübt und dadurch trendbildend gewirkt haben. Daß die assyrische Provinzverwaltung von den judäischen Vassallen teilweise kopiert wurde, legt die Übernahme des durch zwei Bullen des frühen 6. Jhs. bezeugten Beamtentitels "Stadtkommandant" (ass. *rab āli*, hebr. *śr hʿr*;[70] vgl. den in Samaria bezeugten Titel eines *rab ālāni*: s.o. Anm. 25) nahe. Ihr entspricht auf der "figurativen" Ebene wahrscheinlich die Ersetzung der *lmlk-* durch Rosettenstempel,[71] sicher aber die Anpassung hinsichtlich Haartracht und Kleidersitten (Abb. 8). Zef. i 8 kritisiert mit "fremdländisch gekleideten" (*lobəšîm malbûš nåkrî*) Jerusalemer Herren und "Königssöhnen" wohl solche in assyrischer Tracht, wie sie nach Ausweis der Ikonographie noch zur Zeit Jeremias Mode war (Abb. 9).[72] Auch die religiösen Veränderungen der Assyrerzeit sind (hierin ist Texten wie 2 Kön. xvi 10ff., 17–18, xxiii 5, 12 wohl Recht zu geben) auf der Ebene des "offiziellen" Staatskultes als konjunkturell bedingte Anpassungen der Untertanen an die mächtigen Vorbilder,[73] im Blick auf weitere Kreise wohl vorwiegend in Kategorien der Diffusion[74] (d.h.

---

69 Cogan (Anm. 55), S. 412–13 (meine Hervorhebung).

70 Vgl. N. Avigad, *Hebrew Bullae from the Time of Jeremiah. Remnants of a Burnt Archive* (Jerusalem, 1986), S. 32–3, no. 10.

71 Vgl. etwa J. Curtis et al., "British Museum excavations at Nimrud and Balawat in 1989", *Iraq* 55 (1993) (S. 1–38), S. 30 mit fig. 27; Curtis und E. Reed, *Art and Empire* (London, 1995), S. 106 no. 57; zu den judäischen Belegen nun Keel (Anm. 65), S. 122.

72 Vgl. zu Zef. i Ch. Uehlinger, "Astralkultpriester und Fremdgekleidete, Kanaanvolk und Silberwäger. Zur Verknüpfung von Kult- und Sozialkritik in Zef 1", in W. Dietrich und M. Schwantes (Hg.), *"Der Tag wird kommen". Ein interkontextuelles Gespräch über das Buch des Propheten Zefanja* (Stuttgart, 1996), S. 38–67.

73 Entsprechend bzw. erst recht gilt dies dann von den Gegenbewegungen (etwa im Rahmen der sog. "Reformen"). Vgl. Ch. Uehlinger, "Gab es eine joschijanische Kultreform? Plädoyer für ein begründetes Minimum", in W. Groß (Hg.), *Jeremia und die "deuteronomistische Bewegung"* (Frankfurt am Main, 1994), S. 57–89.

74 Vgl. G.W. Ahlström, "Diffusion in Iron Age Palestine: Some Aspects", *SJOT* (1, 1990), S. 81–105.

Abb. 8

Abb. 9

Abb. 10

Abb. 11

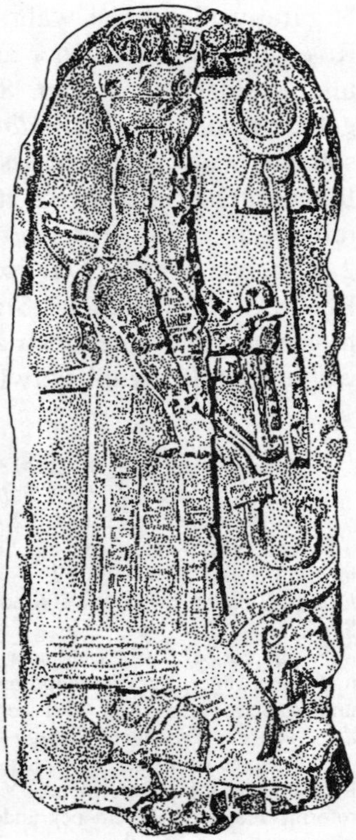

Abb. 12

einer weitgehend unkontrollierten Verbreitung neuer Vorstellungen und Praktiken) im Zuge der Neuorientierung der Handelsbeziehungen und eines damit verbundenen Plausibilitätswandels zu interpretieren.[75] Im Blick auf die Verehrung des Mondgottes von Harran sind diese generellen Feststellungen freilich zu präzisieren.[76]

2. *Der besondere Status des Mondgottes von Harran im 7. Jh.*

Der Kult des von den Assyrern mit Sîn identifizierten "Herrn von Harran" (*bʿl ḥrn, bēl Ḫarrāni*)[77] hat lange vor Nabonid[78]—der sich in seinen Inschriften wiederholt respektvoll auf Assurbanipal als seinen "großen Vorgänger", im Harran-Prolog von Nbn. 1 auch auf Salmanassar III. zurückbezieht[79]—bereits unter den Assyrern starke Förderung erfahren,[80] und dies ist nicht ohne Einfluß auf Palästina geblieben. Ein Rollsiegel aus Dothan, das einem assyrischen Beamten des ausgehenden 8. Jhs. gehört haben dürfte, mag dies mit seiner Verbindung von Königs- und Mondgott-Propaganda im gleichen Bild emblematisch verdeutlichen (Abb. 10). Schon Salmanassar III., der als erster assyrischer König des 1. Jts. den nordsyrischen Korridor fest im Griff hatte, hat am É.ḪUL.ḪUL von Harran gebaut. In Inschriften der Zeit Salmanassars IV., Šamši-ilu/Bar-Gayas und Assurniraris V.

---

[75] Auch die "kanaanäischen" *revivals* der EZ II C können auf diese Weise verstanden werden.

[76] Vgl. zum Folgenden O. Keel, "Das Mondemblem von Harran auf Stelen und Siegelamuletten und der Kult der nächtlichen Gestirne bei den Aramäern", in ders., *Studien zu den Stempelsiegeln aus Palästina/Israel IV* (Freiburg Schweiz und Göttingen, 1993), S. 135–202; E. Lipiński, "The Moon-God of Ḫarrān in Aramaean Cult and Onomastics", in ders., *Studies in Aramaic Inscriptions and Onomastics II* (Leuven, 1994), S. 171–92; St.W. Holloway, "Harran: Cultic Geography in the Neo-Assyrian Empire and its Implications for Sennacherib's 'Letter to Hezekiah' in 2 Kings", in ders. und L.K. Handy (ed.), *The Pitcher is Broken. Memorial Essays for G.W. Ahlström* (Sheffield, 1995), S. 276–314; zuletzt B.J. Schmidt, Art. "Moon", in *DDD* (Anm. 68), Sp. 1098–113. Zur Ikonographie des Mondgottes vgl. auch Dominique Collon, "The Near Eastern Moon God", in D.J.W. Meijer (ed.), *Natural Phenomena. Their Meaning, Depiction and Description in the Ancient Near East* (Amsterdam u.a., 1992), S. 19–37.

[77] Lipiński, S. 186–8.

[78] Vgl. zum Komplex Nabonid—Sîn, den wir hier übergehen, nun P.-A. Beaulieu, *The Reign of Nabonidus King of Babylon 556–539 B.C.* (New Haven, Conn., und London, 1989), bes. S. 43–65; F. D'Agostino, *Nabonedo, Adda-Guppi, il deserto e il dio Luna* (Pisa, 1994).

[79] Vgl. S. Langdon, *Die neubabylonischen Königsinschriften* (VAB 4) (Leipzig, 1912), S. 220–1, 224–5 (Nbn. 1 i 47–8, ii 3–4, 44–5), 286–7 (Nbn. 8 x 34–5), 290–1 (Nbn. 9 i 22).

[80] Vgl. im Überblick J.N. Postgate, Art. "Ḫarrān", *RLA* 4 (1972–5), S. 122–5.

erscheint [d]*Sîn* (*āšib Ḫarrāni*) in hervorragender Position neben dem Reichsgott Aššur, dem obersten Patron des Königs, als Garant von Grenzziehungen unter benachbarten Vassallen.[81] Im Zuge der sog. Aramaisierung Assyriens im Laufe des 8. Jhs. hat der Mondgott von Harran weiter an Prestige gewonnen: Sargon II. hat ihm in Dur-Šarrukin die größte Palastkapelle reserviert, gleichzeitig den Tempel von Harran mit königlichen Opfern versorgt und der Stadt *zakūtu* und *kidinnūtu* genannte Privilegien gewährt. Sanherib ließ ihn auf den Reliefs von Maltai und Faida[82] als vordersten Gott unmittelbar nach dem Spitzenpaar Aššur und Mullissu auftreten (Abb. 11).[83] Wie hier steht der Mondgott auch auf einer Stele aus Zinçirli (Abb. 12) auf einem geflügelten Löwendrachen,[84] und die Bewaffnung[85] macht zusätzlich klar, daß er Aspekte des Kriegsgottes Ninurta übernommen hat.[86] Andere Siegel des 8./7. Jhs. zeigen nicht den anthropomorphen Gott, sondern sein Kultsymbol, die Sichelmondstandarte, auf einem Löwendrachen.[87] Kein Zweifel: Die Sargoniden haben den Mondgott von Harran als den "Höchsten Gott" des Westens verstanden.[88] Das Rollsiegel von Abb. 13 bringt dies dadurch zum Ausdruck, daß es dem in Gestalt seines Kultsymbols in seinem Tempel dargestellten Gott die Symbole Marduks, Nabûs und Nuskus zuordnet.

Wie ein Brief des Haruspex Marduk-šumu-uṣur an Assurbanipal aus dem Jahr 667 mit einzigartiger Deutlichkeit dokumentiert,[89] galt

---

[81] V. Donbaz "Two Neo-Assyrian Stelae in the Antakya and Kahramanmaraş Museums", *ARRIM* 8 (1990), S. 5–24; *KAI* 222 (Sefire I A 9); *SAA* II 2 iv 4–7.

[82] Börker-Klähn (Anm. 29), Nr. 200–1, 207–10.

[83] Aus der Zeit Sanheribs dürfte eine Sîn-Stele von Açaği Yarimca stammen: Keel (Anm. 76), S. 139, Nr. 1 (vgl. 179, 199).

[84] Die Bezeichnung "Flügelstier" (Börker-Klähn [Anm. 29], S. 221) ist ebenso ungenau wie "Löwengreif mit Hörnern" (ebd., S. 211).

[85] Vgl. dazu auch das Rollsiegel bei Collon (Anm. 76), no. 21.

[86] Der Grund dafür liegt in der Tradition vom Kampf Ninurtas gegen den Anzû-Drachen, in dessen Gefolge Ninurta zum "Höchsten Gott" aufstieg, eine Tradition, die auch Marduk und Aššur beerbt haben. Vgl. zu diesem Komplex Ch. Uehlinger, "Drachen und Drachenkämpfe im alten Vorderen Orient und in der Bibel", in B. Schmelz und R. Vossen (Hg.), *Auf Drachenspuren* (Hamburg, 1995), S. 55–101.

[87] Vgl. etwa E. Porada, *Corpus of Ancient Near Eastern Cylinder Seals in North American Collections* I: *The Collection of the Pierpont Morgan Library* (Washington, DC, 1947), no. 712; Joyce G. Volk, *Habib Anavian Collection. Ancient Near Eastern Cylinder and Stamp Seals from the Early 6th Millennium* B.C. *to 651* A.D. (New York, 1979), no. 211.

[88] Man beachte, daß in der Sultantepe-Version des sog. Labbu-Mythos Sîn (nicht Aššur) den Vorsitz in der Götterversammlung einnimmt. Vgl. B. Foster, *Before the Muses. An Anthology of Akkadian Literature* I (Bethesda, Maryland, 1993), S. 488–9.

[89] *ABL* 923 = *LAS* 117 = *SAA* X 174. Vgl. den Kommentar von S. Parpola, *Letters from Assyrian Scholars to the Kings Esarhaddon and Assurbanipal*. II: *Commentary and Appendices* (Kevelaer und Neukirchen-Vluyn, 1983), S. 100–1.

der Gott von Harran den Assyrern im 7. Jh. als der eigentliche Patron der Westexpansion des Reiches:

> SAA X 174, Vs.
> 10 Als der Vater des Königs, meines Herrn (d.h. Asarhaddon), nach Ägypten ging,
> 11 wurde am Rand von Harran ein Zedernheiligtum gebaut.
> 12 Sîn "hockte" (*kammus*) auf einer Stange (^{giš}ŠIBIR),[90] zwei Kronen auf seinem Haupt,
> 13 und Nusku stand vor ihm. Der Vater des Königs, meines Herrn, trat ein,
> 14 setzte [die Krone$^{?}$] auf (sein) Haupt (und es wurde ihm gesagt): "Du wirst gehen und damit die Länder erobern."
> 15 [So gi]ng er und eroberte Ägypten. Den Rest der Länder,
> 16 [die] sich Aššur und Sîn(!) noch nicht unterworfen haben, wird der König, der Herr der Könige, erobern.

Sîn galt den Assyrern traditionell als *bēl agê* "Herr der Tiara".[91] Vor dem zweiten Ägyptenfeldzug Asarhaddons (671) soll er nun gar als Herr *zweier* Kronen aufgetreten sein und Asarhaddon, der sich eine der beiden Kronen aufsetzte, ausdrücklich zur Eroberung der "Länder" ermächtigt haben.[92] Die Zeremonie soll außerhalb der Stadt Harran stattgefunden haben. Es ist denkbar, daß es sich um eine visuell als Zeichenhandlung inszenierte Propagandaaktion[93] handelte.[94] Was mit

---

[90] Die Beschreibung ist wohl auf das Sichelmondemblem des Mondgottes von Harran zu beziehen, das sonst allerdings als *šurinnu* bezeichnet wird. Im Unterschied zu anderen Gottheiten ist die nicht-anthropomorphe Darstellung bei Sîn von Harran die Regel, wie Collon (Anm. 76) zu Recht betont.

[91] Vgl. K.L. Tallqvist, *Akkadische Götterepitheta* (Helsinki, 1938; repr. Hildesheim, 1974), S. 41 (vgl. S. 442–8).

[92] Man beachte, daß auch die kuschitischen Könige seit Šabaqo die Eroberung Ägyptens über eine spezifische Krone (die Zwei-Uräen-Krone) legitimiert haben. Zum Traum Tanutamanis in der Inschrift vom Ǧebel Barkal vgl. zuletzt Onasch (Anm. 44), I S. 132–3; zur Sache weiter A. Leavy, "Royal iconography and dynastic change, 750–525 BC: the blue and cap crowns", *JEA* 78 (1992), S. 223–40.

[93] "The ominousity of the incident (which may well have been prearranged) probably lay in the significance of the moment and in its deviation from the normal cultic routine" (Parpola [Anm. 89], S. 101).

[94] Ebenfalls in den Außenquartieren von Harran soll laut *ABI* 1217 im folgenden Jahr ein Nusku-Orakel ergangen sein, das eine Rebellion gegen Asarhaddon geschürt haben soll. Auf den einschlägigen Brief hat am Kongreß in Cambridge auch M. Nissinen (Helsinki) in seinem Vortrag "References to Prophecy in Neo-Assyrian Sources" hingewiesen. Vgl. einstweilen Parpola, S. 239 Anm. 412, 464 (App. N) no. 59; zu der Rebellion von Harran im Jahr Esh. 11' = 670, in die zahlreiche hohe Beamten verwickelt waren, ebd. 238ff.; weitere Hinweise bei Holloway (Anm. 76), S. 289 Anm. 53. In denselben Zusammenhang dürfte auch *ABL* 755+ = *SAA* X 179 gehören (freundlicher Hinweis von Angelika Berlejung, Heidelberg).

der zweiten Krone, die Asarhaddon sich aufgesetzt haben soll, genau gemeint ist, wissen wir leider nicht. Die Inschrift Asarhaddons vom Nahr el-Kelb scheint einen Hinweis darauf zu enthalten, daß die Eroberung Ägyptens mit einer Thronbesteigung in Memphis besiegelt wurde.[95] Die Anrede Asarhaddons als "Herr der (beiden?) Länder, Stelenbild des Sonnengottes" (EN.KUR.KUR *ṣalmu ša* [d]UTU) in einem Brief von 670 und die Umbenennung von Sais in *Kār-Bēl-mātāti* sind Indizien für die begrenzte Rezeption ägyptischer Königsideologie durch Asarhaddon,[96] und so ist denn auch die Übernahme einer ägyptischen Krone nicht auszuschließen.[97]

Wie dem auch sei: Der Kontext des oben zitierten Briefes läßt keinen Zweifel daran, daß der 671 erstmals erfolgreich vollzogenen Grenzüberschreitung nach Ägypten eine symbolische Ermächtigung durch den Mondgott von Harran voranging. In Erwiderung der göttlichen Gunst scheint Asarhaddon dann die Aufstellung von Stelen mit seinem und dem Bild seiner Söhne (vgl. Abb. 5) im Sîn-Tempel von Harran veranlaßt zu haben.[98]

Der Fund einer Mondsichelstandarte in der assyrischen Garnison von Tēl Śēraʿ (Abb. 14)[99] ist in diesem Zusammenhang kein Zufall. Auch sie dokumentiert die assyrische Westexpansion im 7. Jh. unter dem expliziten Patronat des Mondgottes von Harran. Der Erfolg der Assyrer—so kurzlebig er im historischen Rückblick erscheinen mag—hat überdies zur Prägung von eigenen Serien relativ billiger Zylindersiegel geführt, welche die Übermacht Assyriens über Ägypten dadurch zum Ausdruck bringen, daß sie die Sichelmondstandarte des Mondgottes von Harran vom ägyptischen Königsuräus verehrt, beschützt oder begleitet sein lassen (Abb. 15–18).[100] Von der Promotion des

---

[95] Borger (Anm. 44), S. 101, Z. 8; Onasch (Anm. 44), II, S. 9.

[96] Onasch, S. 135.

[97] A.J. Spalinger dachte bei den zwei Kronen Sîns ursprünglich an die ägyptische Doppelkrone ("An Egyptian Motif in an Assyrian Text", *BASOR* 223 [1976], S. 64–7), hat seine Meinung aber mittlerweile revidiert: "In restrospect, I would opt for the two horns of the (crescent) moon as a closer parallel. However, that is a result of my recent work on calendars and astronomy" (Brief vom 8.7.95). In der Tat ist *agû* "Tiara" im Blick auf Gestirne zunächst eine Kranzerscheinung (*AHw*, S. 116–17). Dennoch scheinen an dieser Stelle wirkliche Kronen gemeint zu sein (so auch Parpola, S. 101).

[98] Vgl. *ABL* 36 = *LAS* 7 = *SAA* X 13. Im Blick auf die Bildkonstellation von Abb. 32–5 und Sach. iv ist Rs. 3'–5' aufschlußreich: "Die großen Königsstelen/statuen sollen zur Rechten und zur Linken von Sîn aufgestellt werden; die Stelen/Statuen der Söhne sollen hinter und vor Sîn aufgestellt werden."

[99] Vgl. *GGG*, S. 339–40; Keel (Anm. 76), S. 144–5.

[100] Vgl. auch Barbara Parker, "Excavations at Nimrud, 1949–1953. Seals and Seal

Abb. 13

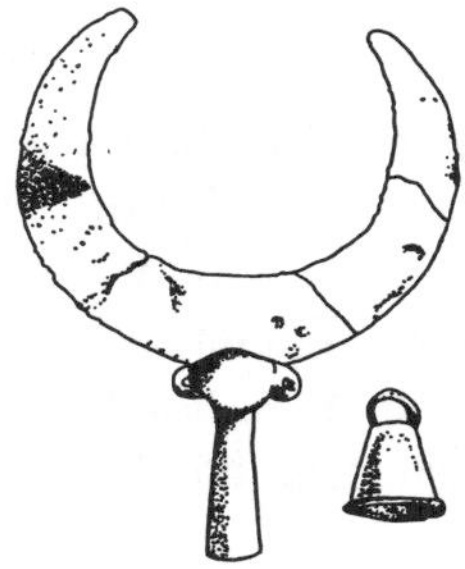

Abb. 14

Abb. 15

Abb. 16

Abb. 17

Abb. 18

Mondgottes von Harran im 7. Jh. dürfte übrigens auch der ägyptische Mondgott Chons betroffen gewesen sein, der im 7. Jh. auffällig oft auf in Palästina gefundenen Skarabäen bezeugt zu sein scheint (Hinweis von O. Keel).

Steven Holloway hat die weite Verbreitung des Mondgottes von Harran jüngst direkt mit der assyrischen Propaganda in Zusammenhang gebracht: "The spread of the moon-god cult of Harran was a self-conscious act of imperial statecraft, designed to foster the acceptance of a cult whose pantheon was understood as protecting and legitimating Assyrian interests in the West" ([Anm. 76] S. 307). Ist hier zweifellos Richtiges gesehen, so scheint mir freilich auch in diesem Fall Vorsicht vor einer monokausalen Erklärung geboten. Die Quellenlage ist zu komplex, die Bandbreite der Roll- und Stempelsiegel[101] mit Sichelmondemblem zu groß, als daß die Mondgott-Welle als ganze und in all ihren Verästelungen direkt auf assyrische Propaganda zurückgeführt werden könnte. Gleichwohl ist der Einfluß der assyrischen politischen Interessen und assyrischer *figurative policy* auf die palästinische Religionsgeschichte hier deutlicher erkennbar als irgendwo sonst.

Die Erhellung dieses zeitgeschichtlich-theologischen Hintergrunds hat Konsequenzen für die Deutung einiger biblischer Texte: Erstens wird deutlich, daß die Rede von generellen Astralisierungstendenzen unter assyrisch-aramäischem Einfluß bei aller Berechtigung der weiteren historischen Präzisierung und Konkretisierung bedarf. Zweitens könnten die geschilderten Zusammenhänge neues Licht auf die frühdtr Trias "Baal, Aschera und Himmelsheer" werfen (2 Kön. xxi 3, 5, xxiii 4–5; vgl. xvii 16, außerdem Zef. i 5; Jer. vii 17–18, xix 13, xliv 17). Angesichts des oben Vorgetragenen wird man bei dieser zunächst auf die Zeit von Manasse und Joschija zielenden Trias weder nur an autochthone "Kanaanaismen" denken[102] noch in bezug auf *bʿl* eine Engführung auf Aššur[103] oder einen phönizisch-israelitischen

Impressions", *Iraq* 17 (1955), S. 93–125, hier 106 mit Pl. 17:3; eine akkulturierte Variante (gehörnte Schlange) bei Ö. Tunca, *Catalogue des sceaux-cylindres du Musée régional d'Adana* (Malibu, 1979), S. 21 mit Pl. 9:87. Welche Bedeutung in unserem Zusammenhang einem *ca.* 10 cm, langen goldenen Uräus zukommt, der im Sommer 1995 im Palast des 7. Jhs. von Tēl Miqne/Ekron "near the dais of the king's throne, in a neo-Assyrian style chamber" (*Haaretz*, 21.7.95; vgl. nun *BAR* 22, 1 [1996], S. 28) gefunden worden ist, kann erst nach genauer Befundpublikation beurteilt werden.

[101] Zu letzteren vgl. *GGG*, S. 340ff.; Keel (Anm. 76), S. 154ff.

[102] J.W. McKay, *Religion in Judah under the Assyrians 732–609* BC (London 1973).

[103] Spieckermann (Anm. 46), S. 200–25; kritische Diskussion bei Frevel (Anm. 67), S. 451ff., 464ff.

bʿlšmm[104] vollziehen wollen. Vielmehr ist zumindest die Möglichkeit zu erwägen, daß mit *bʿl* der Mondgott von Harran, der "Höchste Gott" des Westens, gemeint sein kann, der in Nordsyrien ja schlicht "Baal von Harran" (*bʿl ḥrn, bēl Ḫarrāni*) hieß. Auf Rollsiegeln des späten 8./frühen 7. Jhs. erscheinen gelegentlich Ištar und Sîn miteinander, obwohl sie traditionell kein Paar bilden (Abb. 19–20). Ihr Nebeneinander ist dem biblischen von Baal und Aschera durchaus vergleichbar.

Schließlich wird man einen direkten Niederschlag der Harran-Tradition nicht erst in der nachexilischen Ur-Harran-*connection* der Genesis (xi 31–2, xii 4–5, xxvii 43, xxviii 10, xix 4) finden wollen. Spezifischer—und bislang offenbar unerkannt—läßt sich ein solcher vielleicht an der Entwicklung der Amos-Visionen ablesen: Die Visionen I, II und IV (Am. vii 1–3, 4–6, viii 1–2) bewegen sich ganz im Rahmen lokal-palästinischer Vorstellungen[105] und beschreiben überdies einen deutlich erkennbaren Progreß der Zerstörung auf der landwirtschaftlich-"natürlichen" Ebene (Heuschreckenplage, Trockenheit und Dürre,[106] Ernteausfall[107]). Vision III (vii 7–8)—wiewohl kompositorisch absolut parallel zu IV gestaltet[108]—durchbricht die Einheit der Bildebene ebenso wie den Progreß und formuliert zudem im Wortspiel gegenüber IV sichtlich schwerfälliger.[109] Ich habe Vision III vor einigen Jahren mit Hilfe einer altbabylonischen Terrakottaplakette zu interpretieren versucht,[110] dabei aber ein geographisch wie zeitlich näherliegendes Bild aus Til Barsip übersehen (Abb. 21).[111]

---

[104] H. Niehr, "JHWH in der Rolle des Baalšamem", in W. Dietrich und M.A. Klopfenstein (Hg.), *Ein Gott allein? JHWH-Verehrung und biblischer Monotheismus im Kontext der israelitischen und altorientalischen Religionsgeschichte* (Freiburg, Schweiz und Göttingen, 1994), S. 307–26.

[105] Vgl. Helga Weippert, "Amos. Seine Bilder und ihr Milieu", in K. Seybold et al., *Beiträge zur prophetischen Bildsprache in Israel und Assyrien* (Freiburg Schweiz und Göttingen, 1985) (S. 1–29), S. 23–4.

[106] Vision II (dazu jüngst S. Mittmann, "Der Rufende im Feuer [Amos 7:4]", *JNSL 20* [1994], S. 165–70) verbindet mit dem "Rufenden" offenbar die Vorstellung eines zerstörerischen Feuergottes (vgl. iv 11; Erra).

[107] Zum *leeren* Korb vgl. einleuchtend Weippert (Anm. 105), S. 24; H. Reimer, *Richtet auf das Recht! Studien zur Botschaft des Amos* (Stuttgart, 1992), S. 192–6.

[108] Vgl. J. Jeremias, "Völkersprüche und Visionsberichte im Amosbuch", in V. Fritz et al. (Hg.), *Prophet und Prophetenbuch* (FS O. Kaiser), *BZAW* 185 (Berlin, 1989), S. 82–97.

[109] Die letztere Beobachtung verdanke ich Ch. Levin (Gießen).

[110] "Der Herr auf der Zinnmauer. Zur dritten Amos-Vision (Am. vii 7–8)", *BN* 48 (1989), S. 89–104; vgl. Reimer (Anm. 107), S. 180–2.

[111] Die Oberseite befindet sich im Nationalmuseum von Aleppo (M. 4526; Anna Maria Bisi, "Un bassorilievo di Aleppo e l'iconografia del dio Sin", *OrAnt* 2 [1963], S. 215–21, tav. XL; Agnès Spycket, "Le culte du dieu-lune à Tell Keisan", *RB* 80 [1973],

Abb. 19

Abb. 20

Abb. 21

Der "Herr auf der Mauer" ist hier kein anderer als der über seinem Heiligtum bzw. seiner Kultstadt mit dem Szepter in der Hand (vgl. *ûbəyādô ʾănāk*) erscheinende Mondgott von Harran. Im Unterschied zur Erscheinung des Mondgottes auf dem Relief geschieht die Theophanie von Am. vii 7–8 freilich nicht zum Heil, sondern zur Schwächung, letztlich zum Untergang Israels.[112] Fassen wir das bislang Gesagte zusammen, so hat sich gezeigt, daß die *figurative policy* der Assyrer in Palästina relativ bescheiden war, sich nur in beschränktem Maße und wenn überhaupt, dann vorwiegend im Medium der Monumentalarchitektur und -kunst auf der politisch-administrativen Ebene äußerte. Was den spezifisch religiösen Bereich betrifft, so ist eine weitgehende Indifferenz der Assyrer gegenüber den palästinischen Lokalkulten festzustellen. Explizite Auseinandersetzungen sind nur in spezifischen Ausnahmesituationen (Gaza) dokumentiert. Der Penetrationsgrad der eigentlichen Propaganda scheint im großen Ganzen gering geblieben zu sein. Die bescheidene Investition der Assyrer spiegelt sich im entsprechend dünnen—wiewohl erkennbaren—Niederschlag in alttestamentlichen Texten. Er steht in keinem Verhältnis zu der viel stärkeren Rezeption *textlich* vermittelter assyrischer Herrschafts *rhetorik* (s.o. Anm. 2–4).

Eigenen Status und eigene Propaganda genoß nur der Mondgott von Harran, den man in Palästina mit eigenen Mondgottheiten ebenso identifiziert haben dürfte wie mit dem ägyptischen Mondgott Chonsu. Über den Fall des assyrischen Reiches hinaus blieb Harran bis in die Perserzeit das wichtigste Kultzentrum Nordsyriens. Von dieser Voraussetzung her verwundern weder die Kontinuität der einschlägigen Symbolik bis in die frühnachexilische Zeit noch die bekannte nachexilische Ur-Harran-Verbindung.

S. 384–95], S. 388–9, fig. 21; Börker-Klähn [Anm. 29], Nr. N 240). Der Unterteil ist 1935 bei den französischen Ausgrabungen auf Tell Aḥmar gefunden worden und wird heute im Louvre aufbewahrt (AO 26555; F. Thureau-Dangin und M. Dunand, *Til-Barsib, Texte* [Paris, 1936], S. 159 no. 9, pl. 14:5a–b; vgl. Pauline Albenda, *JANES* 21 [1992], S. 9–12, figs 5–6). Der Join ist gleichzeitig von K. Kohlmeyer (aufgrund der Originale "Drei Stelen mit Sin-Symbolen aus Nordsyrien", in B. Hrouda et al. (Hg.), *Von Uruk nach Tuttul* (FS E. Strommenger) (München, 1992), S. 91–100, hier 99–100, Taf. 40–1, und Ursula Seidl (aufgrund der isolierten Publikationen: "Kleine Stele aus Til Barsip", *N.A.B.U.* 1993/3: 72 no. 85) mitgeteilt worden. Vgl. auch Keel (Anm. 76), S. 143–4, Nr. 10, 184 Abb. 10.

[112] Die Vision erschöpft sich also nicht in einem Pastiche eines einzelnen assyrischen Bildes. Zum Zusammenhang von Stadt und Heiligtum wären entsprechende Siegelbilder und neuassyrische Städtehymnen zu vergleichen, zum Zusammenhang von Zinn, Feuerregen und Reinigung(!) u.a. eine assyrische Balag-Komposition (s.o. Anm. 1).

3. *Frühachämenidische* figurative policy

Damit können wir uns der *figurative policy* der Achämeniden zuwenden, die ich in drei Schritten behandeln möchte: Zunächst seien mit einem kurzen Blick auf die wichtigsten Motive der achämenidischen Groß- und Kleinkunst einige Charakteristika der Reichsideologie der Achämeniden skizziert. Danach soll nach der Existenz einer persischen *figurative policy* im Palästina des ausgehenden 6. Jhs. bzw.—angesichts des weitgehend negativen Ergebnisses—nach Formen lokal palästinischer *figurative policy* gefragt werden.

3.1 *Die Selbstdarstellung im Zentrum*

Die Reichsideologie der Achämeniden ist in neuerer Zeit wiederholt gerade auch im Blick auf Ikonographie und monumentale Bildprogramme untersucht worden.[113] Dabei ist deutlich geworden, daß das geläufige Bild vom gottgewollten Vielvökerreich im wesentlichen das Produkt der Regierung Darius' I. (521–486) ist. Zu seiner Zeit sind die meisten achämenidischen Bildprogramme geschaffen worden, einige haben in der Folgezeit geradezu normativ gewirkt. Die formale und ideologische Analyse der altpersischen Königsinschriften läßt ebenfalls die formative Bedeutung der Zeit Darius' I. erkennen.[114]

Die Zeit *vor* Darius läßt sich in zwei Perioden unterteilen: In der älteren, durch Kooperation bzw. Konfrontation mit den Medern geprägten Phase spielt das Reiter- und Stämmeethos eine große Rolle.[115] Mit der Beerbung des medischen Reiches und der raschen Expansion, die in der Eroberung Babylons 539 einen Höhepunkt fand, setzt eine zweite Phase ein, welche durch eine geradezu experimentelle Entdekkung der religiösen und ideologischen Implikationen der neu errungenen Herrschaft gekennzeichnet ist.

---

[113] B. Goldman, "Political Realia on Persepolitan Sculpture", *OLP* 5 (1974), S. 31–46; Nylander (Anm. 13); Margaret C. Root, *The King and Kingship in Achaemenid Art. Essays on the Creation of an Iconography of Empire* (Leiden, 1979; P. Frei und) K. Koch, *Reichsidee und Reichsorganisation im Perserreich* (Freiburg Schweiz und Göttingen, 1984), bes. S. 71–109; (^{2}1995), S. 159–205; Beiträge von M. Roaf, M.C. Root und D. Metzler in A.C. Gunter (ed.), *Investigating Artistic Environments in the Ancient Near East* (Washington, DC, 1990); M.C. Root, *Crowning Glories. Persian Kingship and the Power of Creative Continuity* (Ann Arbor, Michigan, 1990), u.v.a. Zusammenfassend jüngst M. Roaf, Art. "Art, Persian", in *ABD* 1 (1992), S. 440–7.

[114] Vgl. jüngst G. Ahn, *Religiöse Herrscherlegitimation im achämenidischen Iran. Die Voraussetzungen und die Struktur ihrer Argumentation* (Leiden und Louvain, 1992).

[115] Zum Ikonographischen vgl. Jutta Bollweg, "Protoachämenidische Siegelbilder", *AMI* 21 (1988), S. 53–61.

1. *Kyros* ist zunächst sehr pragmatisch vorgegangen: Was die Eroberung Babylons kultideologisch bedeutet, ließ er von babylonischen Priestern und Gelehrten formulieren.[116] Die biblische Entsprechung ist bekannt, es sind die Kyros-Texte im DtJes.-Buch,[117] die "ganz sicher in konzeptioneller Hinsicht zum Kern von Jes 40–48 gehören".[118] Nicht alle diese Texte datieren freilich in die Kyros-Zeit, wie R.G. Kratz gezeigt hat. M.E. lassen sich in Jes. xlff. drei Typen von Kyros-Aussagen unterscheiden, die drei Stadien der Textproduktion repräsentieren: (a) eine *Frühphase*, die—wohl noch vor 539 und entsprechenden Phänomenen in der Umgebung Nabonids vergleichbar[119]—die erstaunlichen Erfolge Kyros' in den Kategorien judäischer Mantik zu interpretieren versucht (z.B. xlviii 14–15) und—kurz nach 539?—die Richtigkeit der vorher offenbar nicht von allen geteilten Prognose hervorhebt (xl 1–5*, 21–29*; Stichwort: Kyros, ungenannt, als Völkerbezwinger); (b) eine Phase der eigentlichen *Herrscherlegitimation*, in der Kyros in durchaus propagandistischer Absicht und in dezidierter Aufnahme *spezifischer* Herrschaftsvorstellungen sein Königtum unter den Völkern proklamieren läßt (z.B. xlv 1ff. Kyros namentlich als "Gesalbter", vielleicht auch in xlii 1ff. als "Knecht" Yahwes), auf den sich entsprechend Erwartungen im Blick auf die Restauration Jerusalems richten (so xlv 13–14 mit der unterschwelligen Polemik gegen Lösegeld und Geschenke); (c) die länger andauernde Phase der *innerbiblischen Fortschreibung* des Kyros-Themas, in der das Bisherige aufgegriffen, teilweise auch wieder modifiziert und Kyros dann u.a. zum Initiator des Tempelneubaus in Jerusalem

[116] Grundlegend J. Harmatta, "Les modèles littéraires de l'édit babylonien de Cyrus", *Acta Iranica* 1 (1974), S. 29–44; R.J. van der Spek, "Did Cyrus the Great introduce a new policy towards subdued nations? Cyrus in Assyrian perspective", *Persica* 10 (1982), S. 278–83; Amélie Kuhrt, "The Cyrus Cylinder and Achaemenid Imperial Policy", *JSOT* 25 (1983), S. 83–97; dies., "Usurpation, conquest and ceremonial: from Babylonia to Persia", in D.A. Cannadine und S. Price (ed.), *Rituals of Royalty. Power and Ceremonial in Traditional Societies*, (Cambridge, 1987), S. 20–55; J. Wiesehöfer, "Kyros und die unterworfenen Völker. Ein Beitrag zur Entstehung von Geschichtsbewußtsein", *Quaderni di storia* xiii, 26 (1987) S. 107–26.

[117] Vgl. dazu bes. R.G. Kratz, *Kyros im Deuterojesaja-Buch. Redaktionsgeschichtliche Untersuchungen zu Entstehung und Theologie von Jes. 40–55* (Tübingen, 1991), mit ausführlicher Diskussion älterer Literatur.

[118] S. 14.

[119] W. von Soden, "Kyros und Nabonid. Propaganda und Gegenpropaganda", in H. Koch und D.N. Mackenzie (ed.), *Kunst, Kultur und Geschichte der Achämenidenzeit und ihr Fortleben* (Berlin, 1983), S. 61–8 = ders., *Aus Sprache, Geschichte und Religion Babyloniens. Gesammelte Aufsätze*, hg. von L. Cagni und H.-P. Müller (Napoli, 1989), S. 285–92.

erklärt wird (so als "Hirt" in xliv 28). Diese Texte dienen nicht mehr direkt der Legitimation, formulieren vielmehr ein "frühchronistisches"[120] Freilassungskonzept in Auseinandersetzung mit konkurrierenden Gruppen und Vorstellungen in Juda. In unserem Zusammenhang ist die zweite Phase, die der eigentlichen Legitimation des Kyros, besonders interessant, insofern sie einen judäisch-jahwistischen *response* auf achämenidische Propagandainteressen dokumentiert.

2. *Kambyses* hat das "herrschaftsideologische Experimentieren" des Kyros weitergeführt und sich auch in Ägypten von Gelehrten wie dem bekannten Udschahorresnet[121] beraten lassen, um den persischen Herrschaftsanspruch in einer dem lokalen Symbolsystem angemessenen Weise auszudrücken. Ein Monument wie die Apis-Stele (Root, *King* [Anm. 113], S. 124–5) zeugt von diesem authentischen Bemühen und verdient aus historischer Perspektive Vorzug vor den antiken Schauergeschichten über den wahnsinnigen Apis-Töter, gottlosen Heiligtumsschänder und Barbaren Kambyses.[122]

3. Mit den anschließenden Thronwirren und der Etablierung des Usurpators(?) *Darius*[123] hat die achämenidische Königsideologie ihre kritischste Phase durchlaufen, aus der sie stabilisiert und gegenüber der vorangehenden Experimentierphase leicht modifiziert hervorgegangen ist: Auch Darius griff auf lokale Spezialisten oder Kollaborateure zurück, er erhöhte aber gleichzeitig den Kontrollanspruch des Zentrums und machte auch nach außen unverkennbar deutlich, daß seine Herrschaft eine *persische* war und im Kern auf der Verläßlichkeit der persischen und der medischen Garden beruhte. Nur bei rein kultischen Darstellungen wie dem Naos von Hermopolis[124] oder im

---

[120] Von Soden, S. 84ff.

[121] A.B. Lloyd, "The Inscription of Udjaḥorresnet, a Collaborator's Testament", *JEA* 68 (1982), S. 166–80; Ursula Rößler-Köhler, "Zur Textkomposition der naophoren Statue des Udjahorresnet", *GM* 85 (1985), S. 43–54; J. Blenkinsopp, "The Mission of Udjahorresnet and Those of Ezra and Nehemiah", *JBL* 106 (1987), S. 409–21; T. Holm-Rasmussen, "Collaboration in Early Achaemenid Egypt", in *Studies in Ancient History and Numismatics* (FS R. Thomsen) (Aarhus, 1988), S. 29–38; neueste Übersetzung von Ursula Kaplony-Heckel, *TUAT* I, 6 (1985), S. 603–8.

[122] G. Burkard, "Literarische Tradition und historische Realität. Die persische Eroberung Ägyptens am Beispiel Elephantine", *ZÄS* 121 (1994), S. 93–106; 122 (1995), S. 31–7. Vgl. aber L. Depuydt, "Murder in Memphis: The Story of Cambyses' Mortal Wounding of the Apis Bull (ca. 523 B.C.E.)", *JNES* 54 (1995), S. 119–26.

[123] Vgl. nun P. Briant, *Darius, les Perses et l'empire* (Paris, 1992); Heidemarie Koch, *Es kündet Dareios der König . . . Vom Leben im persischen Großreich* (Mainz am Rhein, 1992).

[124] K. Myśliwiec, "Un naos de Darius—roi d'Egypte", in M. Mori et al., *Near Eastern Studies* (FS Prince T. Mikasa) (Wiesbaden, 1991), S. 221–46.

Tempel von Hibis (vgl. Root, *King* [Anm. 113], S. 125–8) ließ er sich ganz nach ägyptischem, also lokalem Kanon darstellen.[125] Bei öffentlichen Monumenten aber wie der Susa-Stele (Abb. 22) oder der Kanalstele nahmen die persischen Auftraggeber inhaltlich direkten Einfluß auf die Formulierung des Bildprogramms, so daß das dezidiert Persische dieser Herrschaft nun auch in Ägypten unverkennbar ist.[126]

Für das monumentale Bildprogramm des Darius gelten—in äußerster Kürze zusammengefaßt—folgende Prinzipien:

– Die *Legitimität der Thronbesteigung* wird in Bisotun in Anlehnung an ein lokales Vorbild dargestellt, freilich nicht im Sinne einer Kopie, sondern in eigenständiger Neuformulierung (Abb. 23) (Root, *King* [Anm. 113], S. 58–61, 182ff.).

– Die *Priorität des eigenen Zentrums*, der persischen und medischen Garden und der Aristokratie wird auf verschiedene Weise zum Ausdruck gebracht: Durch einfache Voranstellung von Persern und Medern auf der Susa-Stele (Abb. 22) oder bei den sog. Völkerthrondarstellungen (Abb. 24);[127] dadurch, daß am Aufgang zum Apadana[128] die Perser nicht unter den geschenkebringenden Völkern erscheinen, gleichzeitig persische und medische Aristokraten in trauter Verbundenheit(!) das Pendant zur Gesamtheit der Völker darstellen; durch den visuellen Kontrast von Völkergestell- und Gardenreliefs an den Türdurchgängen . . . Textlich heißt das: "Ich setzte das Volk auf den ihm gebührenden Platz, Persien und Medien und die anderen Länder" (DB § 14).

– Die *Universalität der Herrschaft über die Vielvölkerwelt* als gottgewollte (Schöpfungs)Ordnung durch die Reliefs in Palast und Grab,[129] welche das Throngestell von 28 (bzw. 28 + 2) loyalen Völkern getragen

---

[125] Ägyptische Tempelwerkstätten haben die im Thronnamen formulierte Legitimität des Königs auch wie üblich über die Kleinkunst propagiert, wie etwa ein unveröffentlichter Skarabäus aus Aschdod zeigt. Vgl. demnächst O. Keel (Anm. 65), I, s.v. Ašdod Nr. 52.

[126] Vgl. P. Calmeyer, "Ägyptischer Stil und reichsachaimenidische Inhalte auf dem Sockel der Dareios-Statue aus Susa/Heliopolis", in H. Sancisi-Weerdenburg und A. Kuhrt (ed.), *Achaemenid History VI. Asia Minor and Egypt: Old Cultures in a New Empire* (Leiden, 1991), S. 285–303.

[127] Root, *King* (Anm. 113), S. 131ff.; Koch (Anm. 113), S. 164ff.

[128] Root, S. 86ff., 227ff., Koch, S. 160ff. Diese Reliefs bedürften unbedingt einmal des Vergleichs bzw. der Kontrastierung mit Jes. lx, und sei es nur, um "intertextuell" die je verschiedenen Akzente profilieren zu können.

[129] Zu letzteren vgl. bes. Koch, S. 184ff. Die Throngestellreliefs des sog. Tripylons wurden früher Darius I. zugeschrieben. Heute denkt man eher an Artaxerxes I. Die Konzeption geht auf Darius I. zurück, wie sein Grabrelief in Naqš-i Rustam bezeugt. Vgl. neben Root, *King* (Anm. 113), S. 99–100 v.a. P. Calmeyer, "Zur Genese altiranischer Motive: V. Synarchie", *AMI* 9 (1976), S. 63–95, bes. 71–5.

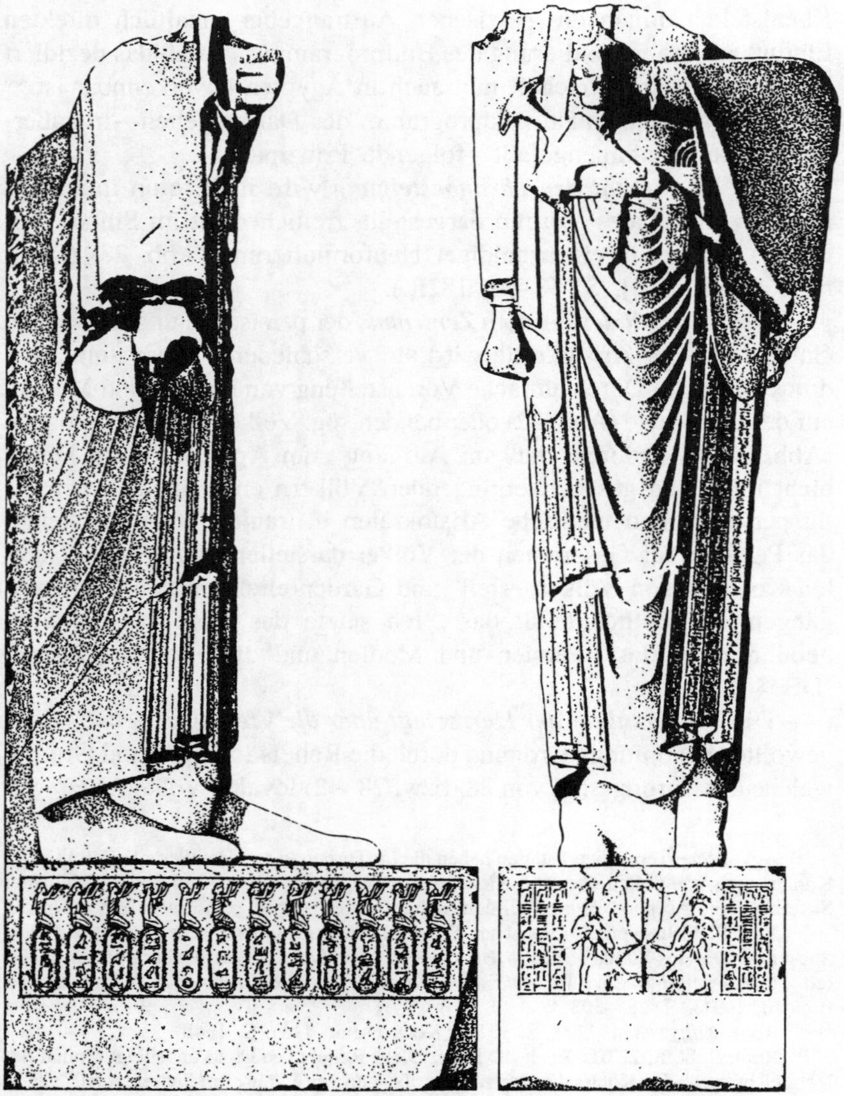

Abb. 22

Abb. 23

Abb. 24

sein lassen. Der Eindruck der Statik, der Loyalität und der Sicherheit dieser Macht sollte nicht trügen: Die das Throngestell tragenden Fremdvölker sind im Palast unbewaffnet—anders als die Fremdvölker-*fravašis*[130] auf den Grabreliefs. Die Apadana-Reliefs mit ihrer Gegenüberstellung von Fremdvölkern und Garden, wobei die letzteren auch den Wagen von König und Kronprinz mitführen, zeigen bei näherem Hinsehen durchaus, daß auch sie, wie P. Jamzadeh treffend formuliert hat, als "metaphor of conquest" zu verstehen sind.[131]

– *Aufruhr* gegen diese Weltordnung kann es—nachdem die Lüge des Gaumata beseitigt worden ist (Abb. 23)—im politischen Raum nicht mehr geben. Was sich jetzt noch dieser Ordnung entgegenstellt, hat metahistorisch-mythischen Charakter, gehört in den Raum des *Monströsen und Dämonischen* (Root, *King* [Anm. 113], S. 300–9). Es sind dies die Mächte des *drauga-*, der "Lüge" (Koch [Anm. 113], S. 153ff., 175), die der König bzw. ein königlicher Held (Abb. 25–26) eigenhändig bekämpft. Die sich seit Darius derart äußernde Herrschaftsideologie ist radikal *dualistischer* als die assyrische.

Auch auf beweglichen Bildträgern—die in Ägypten produzierten Skarabäen ausgenommen—lassen sich Darius und seine Nachfolger dezidiert in ihrem eigenen "ikonographischen Idiom" darstellen. Etliche auf Roll-[132] und Stempelsiegeln[133] und auf Münzen bezeugte emblematische Bildkonstellationen haben entweder keine Vorläufer in der mesopotamischen Glyptik (die Königsbüste im Weltkreis, der Bogenschütze im Knielauf auf den Dareiken u.ä. [Root, S. 116–18] oder modifizieren diese signifikant. Eine wichtige Ausnahme stellt das Motiv des Königs als Löwenkämpfer dar, das (von der anderen Kleidung abgesehen) bruchlos an sein Vorbild, das assyrische Königssiegel,[134] anschließt. Häufiger erscheint der König nicht als Löwenkämpfer, sondern als "Herr der Löwen" (Abb. 27) oder im Kampf

[130] Zu dieser Identifikation Koch (Anm. 113), S. 105–6.

[131] "The Apadana Stairway Reliefs and the Metaphor of Conquest", *Iranica Antiqua* 27 (1993), S. 125–47.

[132] Root, *King* (Anm. 113), S. 118–22; Paola D'Amore, "Glittica a cilindro achemenide: linee di uno sviluppo tematico-cronologico", *CMAO* 4 (1992), S. 187–272; M.B. Garrison, "Seals and the Elite at Persepolis: Some Observations on Early Achaemenid Persian Art", *Ars Orientalis* 21 (1992), S. 1–29; ders., "A Persepolis Fortification Seal on the Tablet MDP 11 308 (Louvre Sb 13078)", *JNES* 55 (1996), S. 15–35.

[133] H. Keel-Leu, *Vorderasiatische Stempelsiegel. Die Sammlung des Biblischen Instituts der Universität Freiburg Schweiz* (Freiburg Schweiz und Göttingen, 1991), Kap. XVI.

[134] A.R. Millard, Art. "Königssiegel", *RLA* 6 (1980–3), S. 135–40; Suzanne Herbordt, *Neuassyrische Glyptik des 8.–7. Jhs. v. Chr.* (Helsinki, 1992), S. 123–36.

Abb. 25

Abb. 26

Abb. 27

gegen gehörnte Mischwesen (Abb. 28–9)—d.h. in Rollen, die zuvor für Götter (Ninurta!) und Genien reserviert waren.[135]

Was das unter Darius in Gang gekommene achämenidische Münzwesen[136] betrifft, so beschränkte sich der *direkte* königliche Kontrollanspruch offenbar auf die Golddareiken und Silberschekel mit dem laufenden königlichen Bogenschützen. Nur sie sind als Reichswährungen auch direkte Propagandainstrumente gewesen. Alle anderen Prägungen—die griechischen Importe natürlich ausgenommen—wurden dagegen von lokalen Autoritäten vorgenommen, die bei der Wahl der Motive weitgehend freie Hand hatten,[137] was zum einen die große Beliebtheit der griechischen Vorbilder erklärt, wo wirtschaftlich ja der Hauptanziehungspunkt lag,[138] zum andern jene Prägungen besonders interessant erscheinen läßt, bei denen lokale Machthaber—wie etwa in Samarien oder Juda, allerdings erst im 5./4. Jh. erkennbar[139]—gleichwohl durch Reproduktion persischer Motive dezidiert ihre Loyalität gegenüber den Achämeniden bekundeten.

3.2 Figurative policy *im frühachämenidischen Juda?*

Waren die Achämeniden in Palästina im Sinne einer dezidierten *figurative policy* überhaupt gegenwärtig? Die Belege hierfür sind, soweit ich sehe, noch spärlicher als für die assyrische Zeit.[140]

Monumentale bzw. "öffentliche" Bauten[141] sind, wo nicht nur ältere Paläste der Assyrer oder Babylonier weiterverwendet wurden, nun meist

---

[135] Der Verschiebung entspricht reziprok die euhemeristische des Gottes Ninurta zum *König* Nimrod (Gen. x 8–12).

[136] Brillante Synthese jüngst bei L. Mildenberg, "Über das Münzwesen im Reich der Achämeniden", *AMI* 26 (1993), S. 55–79; vgl. auch U. Hübner, "Die Münzprägungen Palästinas in alttestamentlicher Zeit", *Trumah. Zeitschrift der Hochschule für Jüdische Studien Heidelberg* 4 (1994) (S. 119–45), S. 121–30.

[137] Hierin unterschied sich die Politik der Achämeniden charakteristisch von der des athenischen Münzmonopols.

[138] Zur doppelten Peripheriestellung Judas als "a colony of two competing world-systems—Persia and Greece" vgl. J.L. Berquist, *Judaism in Persia's Shadow. A Social and Historical Approach* (Minneapolis, 1995), S. 241–55.

[139] Vgl. etwa Mildenberg, in Weippert (Anm. 22), Taf. 22, 12–13 (*YHD*); ders. (Anm. 136), Taf. 7,28–30 (*ŠMRYN*); Y. Meshorer und Sh. Qedar, *The Coinage of Samaria in the Fourth Century* B.C.E. (Jerusalem, 1991), S. 45ff. no. 3, 16–19, 21–2, 31–3, 35–8, 41–2, 44–5, 48–52, 54, 56–7, 59–60 (beachte bes. die Prominenz der Kampfmotive im Hortfund von Samarien, ebd. Pl. 15–17, 37–41).

[140] Grundlegend nach wie vor E. Stern, *Material Culture of the Land of the Bible in the Persian Period 538–332* B.C. (Warminster und Jerusalem, 1982); im Überblick Weippert (Anm. 22), S. 682–728.

[141] Stern, S. 53–60; Weippert, S. 700–2.

Abb. 28

Abb. 29

Abb. 30 a

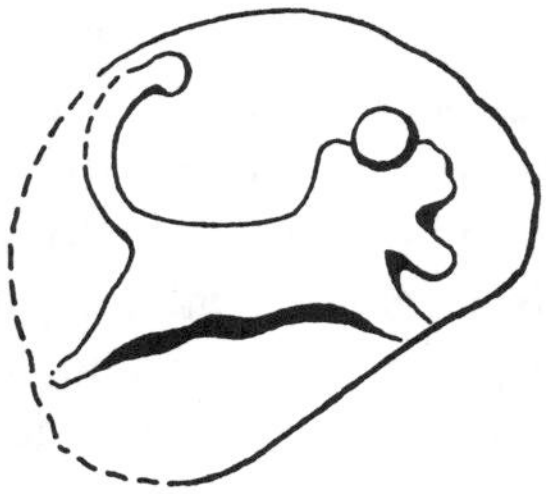

Abb. 30 b

Abb. 31

kleiner als jene, eine Zwischenform von Festung und Kleinpalast. Bei der bekannten Ausnahme, der Residenz von Lachisch, dürfte es sich um das Prestigeobjekt eines *lokalen*, von den Persern eingesetzten oder bestätigten Fürsten handeln. Eigentlich persische Präsenz scheint auf einige Festungen und *paradeisoi* (wie den in Neh. ii 8 erwähnten) beschränkt geblieben zu sein. Monumentale figurative Propaganda ist in Ägypten;[142] nicht aber in Palästina bezeugt. In der in Palästina gefundenen Glyptik[143] sind offizielle achämenidische Motive selten, im Münzwesen fehlen die Dareiken vorderhand ganz. Insgesamt ist unverkennbar, daß die Achämeniden jedenfalls in der frühen Perserzeit in Palästina noch weniger sichtbar waren als vor ihnen die Assyrer (und Babylonier).

Die im perserzeitlichen Palästina bezeugte Ikonographie dokumentiert vielmehr eine Vielfalt von nebeneinander herlaufenden regionalen und lokalen Bildprogrammen und spezialisierten Werkstätten: zyprisch-phönizische Steinskulpturen, phönizische, nordsyrische und griechische Siegel, phönizische und ägyptische Amulette, Kleinbronzen aus Ägypten, phönizische, zyprische und griechische Terrakotten—einen international gewordenen Markt also. Allerdings stammt das Gros der Dokumentation aus dem Küstenbereich. Für Juda ist, was Bilder und Bildprogramme angeht, im ausgehenden 6. und frühen 5. Jh. fast prinzipiell ein Fund *ausfall* zu vermelden. Auffälligstes und bestbezeugtes Bildmotiv sind hier die schreitenden, springenden oder aufgerichteten Löwen (Abb. 30 a–b), die funktional in der Nachfolge der *lmlk-* und Rosettenstempel stehen und eine Art offizielles Emblem der Provinz darstellen dürften (vgl. Gen. xlix 9).[144]

Die für die Achämeniden typische Berücksichtigung bzw. Toleranz lokaler Eigenart im administrativen und religiösen Bereich (im Unterschied zur assyrischen Indifferenz) und die unterschiedlichen ökonomischen Potentiale der verschiedenen lokalen politischen Größen sind Gründe dafür, daß sich innerhalb des palästinischen Raumes ab dem ausgehenden 6. Jh. auch im archäologischen Befund "deutliche kulturelle und kultische Grenzen" abzeichnen, "die mit den aus der histo-

---

142 Zusammenfassend Root, *King* (Anm. 113), S. 61ff., 123ff.

143 Stern (Anm. 140), S. 196–214; ders. (Anm. 20); M.G. Klingbeil, "Syro-Palestinian stamp seals from the Persian period: The iconographic evidence", *JNSL* 18 (1992), S. 95–124.

144 Vgl. *GGG*, S. 446–9; Keel (Anm. 65), § 312. Es sei darauf hingewiesen, daß E. Stern seine These der assyro-persischen Herkunft des Motivs des aufgerichteten Löwen leicht modifiziert hat (vgl. Stern [Anm. 140], S. 212 mit "Notes" [Anm. 20], S. 138). Die Bedeutung des Löwen ist freilich je nachdem, ob er von einem König gebändigt oder allein dargestellt wird, eine ganz andere (vgl. *GGG*, S. 448).

rischen Überlieferung bekannten politischen Grenzen übereinstimmen" (Weippert [Anm. 22], S. 718). Die weitgehende lokale Autonomie im Bereich der politischen wie religiösen Selbstorganisation hat die Formulierung *spezifischer* kultureller Identitäten, u.a. einer judäischen, gefördert. In Juda war freilich über politisch-institutionelle Machtverteilung und religiöse Organisationsformen noch längst nicht eindeutig entschieden, und so kann auch von einem homogenen Jahwismus[145] in der frühnachexilischen Zeit noch keine Rede sein. Von Kyros bis Artaxerxes I. bzw. von Scheschbazzar bis Nehemia stritten verschiedene konkurrierende Gruppen um die richtige politisch-religiöse Organisationsform in der Provinz Jehud. Dabei ging es historisch gesehen *nicht* um "Restauration", obwohl sich viele Texte jener Zeit dezidiert "traditionalistisch" geben, sondern, wie zunehmend deutlich wird, um eine Selbstorganisation unter ganz neuen Bedingungen, eben denen der Achämenidenherrschaft.[146]

Im folgenden soll, und zwar nach wie vor unter dem Gesichtspunkt der *figurative policy*, nach einer dieser Größen, nämlich der Gruppe um Serubbabel-*ṣemaḥ*,[147] gefragt werden. Letzterer konnte sich wohl durch davidische Herkunft legitimieren (1 Chr. iii 17–24) und war so für die Perser, die lokale Dynastien toleriert haben, ein naheliegender Kandidat für eine administrative Reorganisation in Jerusalem. Daß sein Anspruch bzw. der der Davididen überhaupt allerdings nicht unbestritten war, läßt sich u.a. aus den kontrastierenden Aussagen von Jer. xxii 24ff. und Hag. ii 20ff. über Yahwes "Siegelring" schließen:[148]

[145] Wir haben in *GGG* bereits in der babylonischen Zeit "Konturen einer neuen Orthodoxie" erkennen wollen und in einem summarischen Abschlußkapitel im Anschluß an E. Stern und H. Weippert bes. die Kultur*grenzen* betont. Ein erneuter Durchgang durch die Quellen könnte eine Herabdatierung der "Orthodoxie-Bewegung"—abgesehen davon, ob der Begriff den Befunden des 6. Jhs. wirklich angemessen ist—bzw. eine Komplexierung dieses Bildes im Blick auf die inneren Verhältnisse in Juda notwendig machen.

[146] Einen engen Zusammenhang zwischen achämenidischer und biblischer Restaurationsideologie betont E. Ben Zvi, "Inclusion in and Exclusion from Israel as Conveyed by the Use of the Term 'Israel' in Post-Monarchic Biblical Texts", in Holloway und Handy (Anm. 76), S. 95–149, bes. 145–8. Ich wurde leider zu spät auf den Artikel aufmerksam, um ihn hier noch organisch einarbeiten zu können. Es sei zu Ben Zvi jedoch bemerkt, daß Restaurationsmotive und Archaisierungstendenzen keine *spezifisch* achämenidischen Phänomene sind.

[147] Vgl. F. Bianchi, "Zorobabele re di Giuda", *Henoch* 13 (1991), S. 133–50; ders., "Le rôle de Zerobabel et de la dynastie davidique en Judée du VIe siècle au IIe siècle av. J.C.", *Transeuphratène* 7 (1994), S. 153–66. Daß *ṣemaḥ* in Sach. iii 8, vi 12–13 ein Personenname (vgl. Ostrakon Arad 49 iv 11), genauer der judäische Name Serubbabels sein dürfte, hat A. Lemaire am Kongreß in Cambridge in seinem Vortrag "Zorobabel et la Judée à la fin du VIe siècle av. notre ère" deutlich gemacht.

[148] Vgl. S. Japhet, "Sheshbazzar and Zerubbabel—Against the Background of the

Mit einzigartiger Deutlichkeit hat die JerG-Textform die jeremianische Behauptung der Verwerfung des Siegelrings "Konyahu" und seiner angeblichen Kinderlosigkeit bewahrt.[149] *Das Land* (fem.sg. rek., vgl. G) soll "diesen Mann" als kinderlos registrieren, denn "keinem aus seiner Nachkommenschaft wird es gelingen, sich auf den Thron Davids zu setzen" (V. 30d M = G!). Äußert sich hier Opposition gegen Serubbabel? Die proto-masoretische Textform repräsentiert eine jüngere Stufe der Fortschreibung. Sie historisiert (V. 25b: Nebukadrezzar), weiß um den Tod Konyahus und seiner Mutter in Babylon (V. 26), mildert freilich die Verwerfungsaussage, wenn sie von "diesem Mann (Konyahu, V. 28a, 30b) sagt, daß er "zu seinen Lebzeiten(!) kein Glück hatte" (V. 30c). Y. Goldman[150] hat die These vertreten, daß die protomasoretischen Erweiterungen zur Zeit Serubbabels entstanden seien und die Verwerfung auf Jojachin selber begrenzen wollten, sodaß spätere Nachkommen (zumal Serubbabel der dritten Generation) davon nicht mehr betroffen wären. V. 30d (G = M!) scheint gegen Goldmans These zu sprechen.[151] Aber vielleicht meint *zarʿô* nur Konyahus *direkte* Nachkommenschaft? Oder setzt V. 30d bereits den Abbruch der Davididenherrschaft zur Zeit Schelomits voraus?[152] Wie immer dem sei: Die Etablierung Serubbabels in Jerusalem wird nicht selbstverständlich gewesen sein,[153] sie bedurfte der propagandistischen Abstützung. Eine deutliche Antithese zu Jer. xxii 24ff. findet sich in Hag. ii 20ff., wo *Serubbabel* zum "Siegelring Yhwhs" erklärt wird. Sie setzt ihrerseits die Bestreitung auch dieses Anspruchs voraus.

Serubbabels Etablierung in Jerusalem ist offenbar mit einem prestige-

---

Historical and Religious Tendencies of Ezra-Nehemiah", *ZAW* 94 (1982) (S. 66–98), S. 77–8.

[149] Der Text ist sukzessive gewachsen: Am Anfang steht V. 24 (M = G), eine (wohl vor 598) auf unmittelbare Gegenwart gerichtete Unheilsdrohung des Propheten gegen den jungen König. V. 25–26b setzt die Deportation, V. 6c–27 das bleibende Exil trotz der Begnadigung (562) voraus. V. 28* ist als Frage *des Landes* (bzw. der im Land verbliebenen Bevölkerung), V. 29–30c* als die Antwort darauf zu verstehen.

[150] *Prophétie et royauté au retour de l'exil. Les origines littéraires de la forme massorétique du livre de Jérémie* (Fribourg und Göttingen, 1992), S. 231–5.

[151] Vgl. R.D. Wells, "Indications of Late Reinterpretation of the Jeremianic Tradition from the LXX of Jer. 21,1–23,8", *ZAW* 96 (1984), S. 405–20.

[152] Vgl. E.M. Meyers, "The Shelomith Seal and the Judean Restoration", *Eretz-Israel* 18 (1985), S. 33–8.

[153] Gehörten auch die Tradenten von DtJes., die mit ihrer Rede vom Messias Kyros den Anspruch der Davididen ja ebenfalls erloschen sehen, zu den Gegnern Serubbabels? Man beachte in diesem Zusammenhang die angesichts von 2 Chr. xxxvi 21–2 und zahlreicher Detailbeobachtungen einleuchtende These von R.G. Kratz, DtJes. habe ursprünglich den Abschluß der Jeremia-Rolle gebilde ("Der Anfang des Zweiten Jesaja in Jes. 40,1f. und das Jeremiabuch", *ZAW* 106 [1994], S. 243–61).

geladenen Bauprojekt verbunden gewesen: der Restauration des einstigen Dynastieheiligtums. Dieses Projekt wird man als das herausragendste Beispiel für judäische *figurative policy* in der frühen Perserzeit bezeichnen müssen. Zur prophetischen Propaganda, die das Bauprojekt, v.a. aber die politisch-religiöse Reorganisation in Jerusalem/Juda unter Serubbabel (und Joschua b. Jozadak) begleitete, gehört—als seinerseits figuratives Programm—der Zyklus der Sacharja-Visionen.[154]

4. *Prophetie und Propaganda: das Bildprogramm der Sacharja-Visionen*

Eine Klarstellung vorneweg: Die Programmatik der sacharjanischen Visionen[155] zielt nicht in erster Linie auf Tempelbaupropaganda.[156]

[154] Die vorausgehenden Bemerkungen und die folgenden Überlegungen zu den Sacharja-Visionen setzen *grosso modo* das herkömmliche Bild einer (begrenzten!) Rückwanderung um Serubbabel und Reorganisationsbemühungen zur Zeit Darius' I. voraus. Dieses Bild basiert wesentlich, wenn auch nicht ausschließlich, auf der Darstellung von Esr.-Neh. Ganz besonders gilt dies von der Chronologie. L. Dequeker ("Darius the Persian and the Reconstruction of the Jewish Temple in Jerusalem [Ezra 4, 24]", in J. Quaegebeur [ed.], *Ritual and Sacrifice in the Ancient Near East* [Leuven, 1993], S. 67–92) hat jüngst in sehr differenzierter Weise einige Grundaxiome des herkömmlichen Geschichtsbildes in Frage gestellt und die These vertreten, (a) der "Zweite Tempel" sei erst unter Darius II., d.h. nach dem Mauerbau durch Nehemia, fertiggestellt worden, (b) Serubbabels Rückkehr sei nicht in der Zeit des Kyros erfolgt, sondern zur Zeit Nehemias, und (c) Serubbabel sei *nach* Nehemia als dessen Nachfolger Gouverneur von Juda gewesen. Dequeker argumentiert primär mit redaktionsgeschichtlichen Überlegungen zu Esr.-Neh. bzw. Esdras α', die einer eingehenden Prüfung bedürfen. Da der Tempelbau in den Sacharja-Visionen keine direkte Rolle spielt, können wir (a) hier auf sich beruhen lassen. Wenig plausibel erscheint mir im Blick auf (b) und (c) aber Dequekers These, die genealogische Verknüpfung Serubbabels und Joschuas mit der Exilsgeneration (als b. Schealtiel bzw. b. Jozadak, vgl. Esr. iii 2, 8, v 2) sei die späte Konstruktion des Redaktors von Esra i–vi (S. 84–5). Schon Hag. i 1, 12, 14 und ii 2, 4, 23 (vgl. auch Sach. vi 11) bezeugen die Filiation. Dequeker scheint anzunehmen, daß auch Haggai und Sacharja erst unter Darius II. aufgetreten seien (S. 88), und in der Tat mag manch Sekundäres auf diese Weise zu erklären sein (zumal Sach. i 12ff., wo eine ganz andere visionäre Kommunikationssituation vorausgesetzt ist als im ursprünglichen Visionen-Zyklus). Eine Datierung z.B. von Sach. ii 5–9 (Grundschicht *und* erste Erweiterung, s.u. Anm. 182) *nach* Nehemias Mauerbau ist aber kaum denkbar.

[155] Vgl. nebst den Kommentaren v.a. H. Gese, "Anfang und Ende der Apokalyptik, dargestellt am Sacharjabuch", *ZThK* 70 (1973), S. 20–49 (= ders., *Vom Sinai zum Zion. Alttestamentliche Beiträge zur biblischen Theologie* [München, 1984], S. 202–30); K. Seybold, *Bilder zum Tempelbau. Die Visionen des Propheten Sacharja* (Stuttgart, 1974); Ch. Jeremias, *Die Nachtgesichte des Sacharja. Untersuchungen zu ihrer Stellung im Zusammenhang der Visionsberichte im Alten Testament und zu ihrem Bildmaterial* (Göttingen, 1977); Susan Niditch, *The Symbolic Vision in Biblical Tradition* (Chico, California, 1983), S. 73–176; H.-G. Schöttler, *Gott inmitten seines Volkes. Die Neuordnung des*

Diese ist im Buch Haggai viel deutlicher und direkter formuliert.[157] Der Bezug zum Tempelbau ist bei Sacharja ein indirekter, er wird erst durch die sekundäre Einfügung der nicht-visionären Orakel (bes. i 16, iv 7–10, vi 12–13) hergestellt. Die Visionen selber zielen auf eine umfassendere politische Konzeption. Sie wollen die (Re-)Organisation des judäisch-jerusalemischen Gemeinwesens durch Serubbabel (und Joschua) mantisch legitimieren und tun dies im Blick auf die mit Darius' Königsherrschaft gegebene besondere weltpolitische Konjunktur.[158]

Der Zyklus der Visionen ist ein gewachsener: Die literarkritische Methode erlaubt vielleicht nicht die Rekonstruktion der ursprünglichen Fassung, wohl aber den Rückgang auf zunächst fünf Visionen,[159] besser, eine fünfteilige Vision (Reiter, Hörner, Meßleine, Schriftrolle, Wagen), die bald um zwei weitere ergänzt (Leuchter, Efa), überar-

Gottesvolkes nach Sacharja 1–6 (Trier, 1987); F. Smyth, "L'espace d'un chandelier: *Zacharie* 1,8–6,15", in *Le livre de traverse. De l'exégèse biblique à l'anthropologie* (Paris, 1992), S. 281–9. Nicht zugänglich war mir R.J. Zanghi, *God's Program for Israel in Zechariah's Night Visions* (Diss., Dallas Theological Seminary, Dallas, 1986).

[156] So mit Recht (gegen Seybold, Halpern u.a.) P. Marinkovic, "Was wissen wir über den zweiten Tempel aus Sach 1–8?", in R. Bartelmus et al., *Konsequente Traditionsgeschichte* (FS K. Baltzer) (Freiburg Schweiz und Göttingen, 1993), S. 281–95 (= engl. in T.C. Eskenazi und K.H. Richards [ed.], *Second Temple Studies* 2: *Temple Community in the Persian Period* [Sheffield, 1994], S. 88–103).

[157] D.J.A. Clines, "Haggai's Temple Constructed, Deconstructed and Reconstructed", *SJOT* 7 (1993), S. 51–77 (= *Second Temple Studies* 2 [Anm. 156], S. 60–87); P.R. Bedford, "Discerning the Time: Haggai, Zechariah and the 'Delay' in the Rebuilding of the Jerusalem Temple", in Holloway und Hand (Anm. 76), S. 71–94. Zum weiteren Kontext vgl. D. Petersen, "The Temple in Persian Period Prophetic Texts", *BThB* 21 (1991), S. 88–96 (auch in P.R. Davies [ed.], *Second Temple Studies. 1. Persian Period* [Sheffield, 1991], S. 125–44).

[158] So schon K. Galling, *Studien zur Geschichte Israels in persischer Zeit* (Tübingen, 1964), bes. S. 109–48; vgl. Jeremias (Anm. 155), S. 13–36. Zum Jahr Darius 2' vgl. E.J. Bickerman, "La seconde année de Darius", *RB* 88 (1981), S. 23–8.

[159] Auch Schöttler (Anm. 155) rekonstruiert eine Grundschicht mit fünf Visionen: Reiter/Pferde, Meßschnur, Leuchter, Efa (ohne Frau!), Wagen. Eine detaillierte Auseinandersetzung mit seiner sehr informativen Arbeit ist an dieser Stelle nicht möglich. Daß ich eine der Grundthesen, wonach für die Deutung der Visionsbilder "altorientalische Parallelen nicht nötig und auch nicht hilfreich sind, das Bildmaterial . . . vielmehr aus der dem Jahweglauben eigenen Symbolik heraus verständlich ist (Tempelsymbolik und Paradiesmotivik)" (S. 10), nicht teilen kann, wird im folgenden zu Genüge deutlich. Es geht nicht an, die altorientalischen Hintergründe und Kontexte zur "Form", die innerbiblischen Bezüge zum "Inhalt" zu erklären (S. 265 mit Anm. 156 u.ö.) und damit die Tragweite der ersteren *a priori* entschärfen zu wollen. Auch der neuste Kommentar von R. Hanhart, *Sacharja* (Neukirchen-Vluyn, 1990), tendiert in diese Richtung ". . . so müssen analoge außeralttestamentliche religiöse bzw. mythologische Vorstellungen von vornherein (*sic*) so bestimmt werden, daß sie auch dann, wenn ihre bildhafte Ähnlichkeit größer scheint, als es bei alttestamentlichen Traditionen der Fall ist"—und das ist in der Tat die Regel!—"eine Bedeutung als Darstellungsmittel höchstens noch in dem Sinn haben können, daß

beitet und schließlich durch die Joschua-Vision vervollständigt wurde. Dies alles müßte und könnte *en détail* demonstriert werden. Im Rahmen dieses Vortrags liegt mir mehr an der Grundthese, daß sowohl die Fünfervision als auch noch der Siebner-Zyklus in ihrem Bildprogramm mit realgeschichtlichen Vorgängen, Realien *und* achämenidischer *figurative policy* unter Darius I. zusammenhängen. Dies ist wiederum kein Zufall: Wie wir gesehen haben, ist gerade unter diesem Achämeniden ein dezidierter Propagandaschub zu registrieren, ist seine Regierungszeit in dieser Hinsicht die produktivste Phase der Achämenidengeschichte gewesen.

1. Betrachten wir zunächst die Fünfersequenz und ihre *Motive*: Der Mann auf dem roten Pferd zwischen den Myrtenbäumen der *ersten Vision*[160] (i 8, 9a, 10*, 11*) weckt Theophanie-, geradezu Sonnengott-Erwartungen.[161] Die Farbe des Pferdes weist bei Vergleichung mit den Farben der letzten Vision (vi 2) nach Osten. Der Mann ist freilich kein Gott, sondern ein Reiter (Abb. 31).[162] Auffällig der—häufig übersehene[163]—Kontrast zwischen dem *einen* Reiter und den—je nach textkritischer Option[164]—*drei* (MT) oder *vier* (G) Pferde(gruppe)n. Wer 519
einen Reiter als Anführer von Pferden mit universaler Inspektions-

ihre außeralttestamentliche Herkunft nach der Intention des Zeugen selbst für ihr Verständnis nicht mehr vorausgesetzt ist" (S. 71). Das mag für eine Endgestalt von Sach. und die weitere Rezeption bis in moderne "Orthodoxien" gelten, im Blick auf die Entstehungsumstände des Visionszyklus sicher nicht.

[160] A. Wolters (Anm. 1) will in der Standortbeschreibung *bên hahădassîm ʾăšer bammǝṣillâ** eine Bezugnahme auf den von D. Stronach (*Pasargadae. A report on the excavations conducted by the British Institute of Persian Studies, from 1961 to 1963* [Oxford, 1978]; ders., "The Royal Garden at Pasargadae: Evolution and Legacy", in L. de Meyer und E. Haerinck [ed.], *Archaeologica Iranica et Orientalia* [FS L. Vanden Berghe] [Gent, 1989] I, S. 475–502) untersuchten Palastgarten von Pasargadae erkennen, der von Kyros erbaut und von Darius I. vollendet wurde. Ähnliche *parádeisoi* sind freilich auch für Persepolis und andere achämenidische Residenzen anzunehmen. Zum Gartencharakter der Szenerie vgl. bereits Seybold (Anm. 155), S. 70.

[161] Vgl. zu den mythologischen Konnotationen O. Keel, *Jahwe-Visionen und Siegelkunst. Eine neue Deutung der Majestätsschilderungen in Jes. 6, Ez 1 und 10 und Sach 4* (Stuttgart, 1977), S. 296–303; D.L. Petersen, *Haggai and Zechriah 1–8. A Commentary* (London und Philadelphia, 1984), S. 139–40. Zur Verbindung Pferde—Sonnengott (neben 2 Kön. xxiii 11) bereits H.G. May, "A Key to the Interpretation of Zechariah's Visions", *JBL* 57 (1938), S. 173–84.

[162] Reiter sind so typisch für die persische Ikonographie, daß die Kommentatoren die Pferde von Sach. i häufig zu Reitern machen. Vgl. Ann Farkas, "The Horse and Rider in Achaemenid Art", *Persica* 4 (1969), S. 57–76.

[163] Vgl. aber Schöttler (Anm. 155), S. 51.

[164] D. Barthélemy, *Critique textuelle de l'Ancien Testament* 3: *Ézéchiel, Daniel et les 12 Prophètes* (Fribourg und Göttingen, 1992), S. 935–6. Zu den Farben vgl. immer noch P. Fronzaroli", I cavalli del Proto-Zaccaria", *AANL.R* 26 (1971), S. 593–601.

kompetenz am östlichen Horizont sieht, dürfte an Darius selber denken, hat vielleicht gar dessen von Herodot (iii 88) genannte Statue in Babylon mit der Inschrift: "Dareios, Sohn des Hystaspes, hat durch seines Pferdes [und seines Stallmeisters][165] Verdienst den persischen Königsthron errungen")[166] oder eine ähnliche Darstellung[167] vor Augen. Was die rapportierenden Pferde generell betrifft, so überlagern sich hier wohl die in die Eisenzeit zurückreichende palästinische Tradition (Sonnenpferde, Himmelsheer?)[168] und neu der persische Nachrichtendienst.[169] Die Meldung "Die ganze Erde ist ruhig" (i 11b) entspricht vielleicht der realpolitischen Situation nach Februar 519, sicher aber der in Bisotun inschriftlich gesicherten Behauptung des Großkönigs, die beim Thronwechsel ausgebrochenen Revolten seien niedergeschlagen.

Die *zweite* Vision (ii 1, 2*, 4b)[170] nimmt mit der Charakterisierung der Mächte, die Juda zerstreut haben, als "Hörner" das für die Achämeniden-Ikonographie so typische Dämonisierungsmuster auf (vgl. Abb. 25, 28–29).[171] Die *dritte* Vision vom Mann mit der Meßleine (ii 5–6)[172] ist, so weit ich sehe, judäisches Eigengut, ohnehin

---

165 Ursprünglich oder abschätziger Einschub?

166 Root, *King* (Anm. 113), S. 129; J. Borchhardt, "Bildnisse achaimenidischer Herrscher", in Koch und Mackenzie (Anm. 119), S. 207–23, hier 208.

167 Zu einem freistehenden Siegesdenkmal in Babylon vgl. U. Seidl, "Ein Relief Dareios' I. in Babylon", *AMI* 9 (1976), S. 125–30; in Susa vgl. Root, *King* (Anm. 113), S. 110–14. Ich denke an mögliche ikonographische Vorbilder, ohne zu meinen, die Vision würde diese beschreiben. Wenn H. Graf Reventlow, *Die Propheten Haggai, Sacharja und Maleachi* (Göttingen, 1993), S. 41, im Blick auf i 8 von "einem unbeweglichen Standbild" spricht, meint auch er kein Monument, sondern—wie in der Sprache des Films—das unbewegte Visionsbild als "Momentaufnahme".

168 Vgl. dazu *GGG* § 198–200; vgl. jüngst wieder im Südfriedhof von Achzib: Eilat Mazar, "Akhziv", *ESI* 12, no. 99 (1993), S. 5–6, mit fig. 8 und pl. IX oben.

169 Vgl. E. Kornemann, Art. "Postwesen", *PRE* XXII,1 (1953), S. 988–1014; A.L. Oppenheim, "The Eyes of the Lord", *JAOS* 88 (1968), S. 173–80; vgl. Schöttler (Anm. 155), S. 225–7. Zur Sache bes. Herodot iii 126, viii 98; Est. viii 10,14. Analog vorgestellte himmlische Reiter sind im Avesta die "*fravaši* aller Länder" (Yašt 13, vgl. dazu Koch [Anm. 113], S. 194–6).

170 Die "Schmiede" oder "Handwerker" sind sekundär (Schöttler [Anm. 155], S. 60ff., bestimmt das Verhältnis gerade umgekehrt), in der Grundschicht dürfte sich das *wayyābo'û 'ēlleh* noch auf die zuvor vorgestellten und immer noch anwesenden "Pferde" beziehen. Die "Pferde" haben also ihre im AT generell gegebene kriegerische Funktion durchaus behalten.

171 Nicht zugänglich war mir die Arbeit von Margit L. Süring, *The Horn Motif in the Hebrew Bible and Related Ancient Near Eastern Literature and Iconography* (Berrien Springs, Michigan, 1980).

172 "Die Fortsetzung V. 8–9 setzt formal die Einführung des Deuteengels, inhaltlich Auseinandersetzungen um Bauprioritäten (Tempel oder Stadtmauer) voraus: gegenüber der eindeutigen Programmatik der Grundschicht eine kompliziertere Diskussionslage und Parteienbildung.

kein Ikonographem.[173] Bei der dann geschauten riesigen Schriftrolle[174] mit universalem Geltungsanspruch (v 1–3a[b?])[175] mußte ein mit der politischen Korrespondenz einigermaßen vertrauter Zeitgenosse sofort an die aramäischen Abschriften von Darius' Herrschaftsproklamation in Bisotun denken, zu deren propagandistischer Weitergabe der Großkönig ja ausdrücklich auffordert (§ 60–1) und die er nach eigener Aussage in alle Welt geschickt haben will (§ 70).[176] Diese Inschrift bzw. ihre Abschriften[177] bietet mit ihrem Insistieren darauf, daß nunmehr die "Lüge" besiegt sei, wohl auch den sachlichen Einsatzpunkt für die von v 3b statuierte Repression gegen Diebe und Meineidige. Deren Zusammenhang mit persischer Protektion verdeutlicht in eklatanter Weise Esra vi 8–12. Hier stehen realgesellschaftliche Konflikte in Juda im Hintergrund, die wir im einzelnen noch nicht genau fassen können.[178] Daß die Rolle nur Fluch, aber keinen Segen beinhaltet, zeigt, in welch konfliktgeladene, verhärtete Situation die Vision gehört.

Die *letzte* Vision[179] schließlich (vi 1–3* . . . 5*, 7–8) weiß, daß in der Achämenidenzeit die Wagen nicht mehr nur gefürchtete Kriegsgespanne sind, sondern ebenso und immer mehr von königlichen Beamten und Notablen als prestigiöse Transportmittel verwendet werden. So stellt

---

[173] Ein Bezug zur dritten Amos-Vision wird vielfach angenommen, allerdings meist aufgrund der (falschen) Annahme, dort sei von einem mit dem Senkblei hantierenden Maurer die Rede.

[174] Die Dimensionen der Schriftrolle bleiben auch dann rätselhaft, wenn die Entsprechung zu den Maßen des *ʾûlām* nach 1 Kön. vi beabsichtigt sein sollte (so Carol L. und E.M. Meyers, *Haggai, Zechariah 1–8. A New Translation with Introduction and Commentary* [Garden City, New York, 1987], S. 279–81, deren weitere Verbindung mit der Grundfläche des *dəbîr* jedoch abwegig ist und auf falschen Voraussetzungen beruht). Liegen sie in der "Doppelexistenz" der Darius-Inschrift von Bisotun als Monumentalinschrift und als Lederrolle (DB § 70) bzw. Papyrus (Elephantine) begründet?

[175] Vgl. Schöttler (Anm. 153), S. 127–31.

[176] R. Borger und W. Hinz, *TUAT* I, 4 (1984), S. 419ff.

[177] Fragmente der babylonischen Fassung wurden in Babylon, Fragmente einer aramäischen Übersetzung in Elephantine gefunden. Zu ersteren vgl. nun Florence Malbran-Labat, *La version akkadienne de l'inscription trilingue de Darius à Behistun* (Roma, 1994); zu letzteren J.C. Greenfield und B. Porten, *The Behistun Inscription of Darius the Great. Aramaic Version* (London, 1982). R. Borger rechnet mit einer aramäischen Urfassung, die mit der in Elephantine erhaltenen aber nicht identisch war: "Die Chronologie des Darius-Denkmals am Behistun-Felsen", *NAWG.PH* (1982), S. 103–32, bes. 111 und 130.

[178] Gese dachte an eine Gruppe von Menschen, die den Dekalog (vgl. zu Diebstahl und Meineid neben Sach. viii 16–17, bes. Ex. xx 15–17 || Dtn. v 19–21) nicht respektieren, "besonders die die Exulanten um ihr heimatliches Erbe bringen, indem sie ihre Grundstücke in Juda längst in Besitz genommen haben und auch trotz eines Gerichtsverfahrens nicht herausgeben" (Gese [Anm. 155], S. 212; vgl. Jeremias, [Anm. 155], S. 190–1).

[179] Vgl. dazu H. Graf Reventlow, "Tradition und Aktualisierung in Sacharjas siebentem Nachtgesicht Sach 6, 1–8", in J. Hausmann und H.-J. Zobel (Hg.), *Alttestamentlicher Glaube und Biblische Theologie* (FS H.D. Preuß) (Stuttgart, u.a., 1992), S. 180–90.

sie sich denn auch den Transport der für die Serubbabel'sche Reorganisation erforderlichen *rûah* in den "Norden", d.h. die Gola, in dieser Weise vor.

Summa summarum: ein Text, der hinsichtlich seiner figurativen Symbolik gezielt Bilder und politische Realia verwendet, die nach der Herrschaftsproklamation Darius' I. gerade im Kurs stehen. Das sich hier artikulierende "Jerusalem-Gemeinwesen-Konzept" will für seine Propaganda offenkundig die besondere Gunst der Stunde nutzen.

2. Im Unterschied zum eher linearen szenischen Nacheinander der Grundschicht ist der *Siebnerzyklus* dann—vielfach beobachtet—streng konzentrisch aufgebaut.[180] Die Konzentrik kann als ein "symbolic universe"[181] geradezu 'kosmographisch' interpretiert werden (vgl. das Schema): Die "Myrtenbäume in der Tiefe" der ersten Vision bezeichnen wohl ebenso wie die bronzenen Berge der letzten Vision ein Horizonttor;[182] die Pferde der ersten Vision erklären, die ganze Erde durchzogen und sie in Ruhe gefunden zu haben, die Wagen der letzten Vision stürmen wiederum in die ganze—befriedete!—Welt. Visionen II und III bzw. V und (neu) VI sind demgegenüber weniger "peripher": II und VI entsprechen sich dadurch, daß sie beidemale Juda von einer negativ qualifizierten Außenwelt unterscheiden (die der weggeschreckten Völker bzw. Sinear als einer Deponie für Sondermüll). III und V bilden einen inneren Kreis, III durch den Ortsnamen "Jerusalem" klar lokalisiert, wogegen v 3 *kål-hā'āreṣ* wie in v 6 schillert. Im Zentrum des Zyklus steht nun (neu) die Leuchtervision von Kap. iv*. Typisch altorientalisch und heiligtumsmythologisch gedacht kann der "Herr der ganzen Erde" einmal im Kultsymbol im Zentrum (iv 14), dann wieder (weil das Wirken seiner Gehilfen der Erscheinungsdynamik bedarf) hinter dem (östlichen) Horizont vorgestellt werden (vi 5).

3. Neu hinzugekommen sind im Siebnerzyklus die vierte und die

---

[180] A. Jepsen, "Kleine Beiträge zum Zwölfprophetenbuch III: 4. Sacharja", *ZAW* 61 (1945–48), S. 95–114; Jeremias (Anm. 155), S. 10–13; Hanhart (Anm. 159), S. 51–2. u.v.a. Von einem "Stufenschema" spricht Th. Lescow, "Sacharja 1–8: Verkündigung und Komposition", *BN* 68 (1993), S. 75–99, bes. 79ff. Der Ausdruck soll darauf hinweisen, daß der Zyklus zunächst *linear* gelesen wird und sich die konzentrische Struktur erst nach und nach erschließt, wobei ein Element auf der "absteigenden" Treppe jeweils die "Konkretion" des entsprechenden der aufsteigenden Treppe sein soll.

[181] P.D. Hanson, "In Defiance of Death: Zechariah's Symbolic Universe", in J.H. Marks und R.M. Good (ed.), *Love & Death in the Ancient Near East* (FS M.H. Pope) (Guilford, Conn., 1987), S. 173–9.

[182] Vgl. aber Anm. 160.

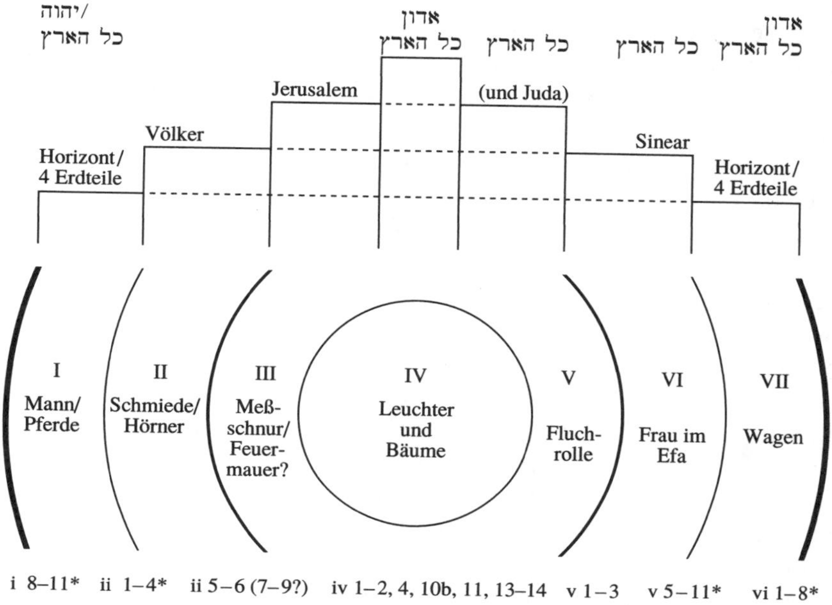

sechste Vision.[183] Die *vierte* Vision verarbeitet das Motiv des von zwei Männern, Bäumen oder Ähren flankierten Emblems des Mondgottes von Harran (vgl. Abb. 13), wie O. Keel wahrscheinlich gemacht hat ([Anm. 161], S. 274–320). In Ergänzung bzw. Korrektur der von Keel etablierten Verbindung ist allerdings darauf hinzuweisen, daß das emblematische Vorbild, die Sichelmondstandarte mit den beiden Bäumen, wie oben in Abschnitt 2 dargestellt seine Hochkonjunktur in der Assyrerzeit hatte. In der perserzeitlichen Glyptik ist das Motiv, so weit ich sehe, nicht mehr bezeugt. Davon abgesehen ist ein Sichelmond keine Schale (*gullâ*)[184] und haben die sieben Lampen (*nērôt*) im Bildsymbol der Glyptik ohnehin kein Äquivalent. Sacharja sieht und interpretiertdemnach *nicht* ein Symbol der ihm zeitgenössischen Glyptik, vielmehr ein Kultsymbol bzw. eben einen Leuchter, wie er 519 in Jerusalem(?) tatsächlich gestanden haben dürfte.[185] Daß dieser für den nächtlich verborgenen, also wohl lunar-epiphanisch gedachten

[183] M.E. gehören auch der Deuteengel und die stärkere Formalisierung der mantischen Kommunikation erst auf diese Stufe der Fortschreibung, doch kann diese Frage hier auf sich beruhen.

[184] Zu Recht eingewandt von Helga Weippert, "Siegel mit Mondsichelstandarten aus Palästina", *BN* 5 (1978), (S. 43–58), S. 53.

[185] Ob vorexilisch (J. Voß, *Die Menora. Gestalt und Funktion des Leuchters im Tempel*

Gott steht, bedarf gar keiner Interpretation durch den Deuteengel. Der Vision geht es vielmehr darum, *einzelne Elemente* der Bildkonstellation (die sieben Lampen als die "Augen Yhwhs" iv 4 . . . 10b, die beiden flankierenden "Ölbäume" iv 3, 11, 14, schließlich—tertiär—die "Ölbaumähren" iv 12) den veränderten religiösen und politischen Umständen entsprechend neu zu deuten.

Die Auflösung der Bäume als "Glanzölsöhne" (*bənê hayyiṣhār* iv 14) läßt an das Nebeneinander zweier königlicher Gestalten denken. Man zögert vor dem verwegenen Gedanken, hierin Darius und Serubbabel erkennen zu wollen. Im jetzigen Kontext sind die beiden "Ölsöhne" doch wohl Serubbabel und Joschua. Bild und Deutung perpetuieren jedenfalls die von Stelen wie Siegeln bekannte syrisch-palästinische, auch noch im 6. Jh. belegte Konstellation der ein Kultsymbol flankierenden Vertragspartner (Abb. 32–4),[186] wie sie ein vor kurzem in ʿEn Ḥaṣeva gefundenes Siegel (Abb. 35) erneut bezeugt. Der Sinn der Konstellation besteht darin, daß sie eine Art Dreiecksverhältnis gegenseitiger Loyalität skizziert: der Loyalität der "Ölsöhne" unter der Garantie des zentralen Symbols, hier eben des Leuchters bzw. des dadurch präsent gesetzten Gottes.[187]

4. Die *sechste* Vision thematisiert die Beseitigung des "Frevels" und seine Deponie in Sinear. Ihr möchte ich mich zum Schluß unter spezifisch religionsgeschichtlichem Gesichtspunkt zuwenden.[188]

Auch diese Vision hat ihre Geschichte. In ihrer älteren Gestalt (v 5–6, 8aα, 9) war wohl erst von der Ausschaffung des *ʿāwôn* (wozu ein Iranist altpersisch *drauga* assoziieren würde) in einem Efa-Gefäß die Rede gewesen. Traditionsgeschichtlich stehen dahinter Vorstellungen von Eliminationsriten.[189] Der *ʿāwôn* wird von numinosen Mischgestalten weggetragen, wie sie als geflügelte *ištarāti* auch ikon-

zu Jerusalem [Freiburg Schweiz und Göttingen], 1993, S. 47; Schöttler [Anm. 155], S. 113, 237: "salomonisch"), wissen wir nicht.

[186] Von Jeremias (Anm. 155), S. 180–8, unabhängig von Keel erkannt.

[187] Daß sich auf die "Glanzölsöhne" gleichzeitig Hoffnungen im Blick auf Segen und Fruchtbarkeit im Lande richten (so Schöttler [Anm. 155], S. 248ff., der nur an "ölreiche Ölbäume" denken und diese nicht im Sinne von Metaphern personal auflösen will), ist durchaus wahrscheinlich.

[188] Vgl. Ch. Uehlinger, "Die Frau im Efa (Sach 5,5–11): eine Programmvision von der Abschiebung der Göttin", *Bibel und Kirche* 49 (1994), 93–103; dazu Frevel (Anm. 67), S. 523–4, S. 529–31.

[189] M. Delcor, "La vision de la femme dans l'épha de Zach., 5, 5–11 à la lumière de la littérature hittite", *RHR* 187 (1975), S. 137–45; D.P. Wright, *The Disposal of Impurity. Elimination Rites in the Bible and in Hittite and Mesopotamian Literature* (Atlanta, Georgia, 1987), bes. S. 75–86; V. Haas, "Ein hurritischer Blutritus und die Deponierung der

ographisch bezeugt sind (Abb. 36–7), mit Beziehung zur Steppe bzw. Außenwelt.

In ihrer Endgestalt ist die Vision präzisiert geworden: Anstelle von *ʿāwôn* steht im masoretischen Text in V. 6–7 *ʿênām*, was ich als "ihr Anblick" verstehe (vgl. Uehlinger [Anm. 188], S. 95). Der Inhalt des Gefäßes heißt nun *riš‘â*. (V. 7b), und er hat eine Gestalt, nämlich einer *sitzenden Frau* (*ʾiššâ ʾaḥat yôšebet . . .*). Die Feststellung, daß dieser "Frau" in *Sinear* ein "*Haus*" gebaut (V. 11b) und sie dort auf einem *Podest* deponiert werde (V. 11c)—dies alles weist überdeutlich darauf hin, daß sich hinter der Frau eine Göttin verbirgt (ebenso zuletzt Frevel [Anm. 67], S. 524). Das Bild könnte an die Praxis anschließen, Kultfigurinen in Tonkrügen aufzubewahren bzw. auszurangieren.[190]

Die Vision inszeniert also die Beseitigung einer Göttin. Ist es eine *Hebrew Goddess*? Setzt man einmal voraus, daß da einer nicht einfach Hirngespinste niederschreibt, dann kommt eigentlich nur eine Göttin in Frage, die bislang in Palästina ebenso Heimatrecht hatte wie nun in Sinear, oder, näher am Text: zwischen deren palästinischer Gestalt und einer mesopotamischen Fama eine plausible Identität behauptet werden konnte. Die nächstliegende Kandidatin dafür ist m.E. die "Himmelskönigin", ištarisierte Form der alten Aschera, in der südlichen Küstenebene freilich längst auch von Isis überlagert und auf dem Weg zur großen Atargatis—die nach Jer. xliv von Frauen, Männern und Kindern umsorgte Göttin,[191] die weder nur in der Familienfrömmigkeit noch exklusiv im offiziellen Staatskult verehrt worden ist, sondern offenbar auf verschiedenen Ebenen gleichzeitig und in durchaus schillernder Gestalt. Für diese (*die*) Göttin, so das Programm der sechsten Vision, ist fortan in Juda kein Platz mehr. Die storchgeflügelten Frauen werden sie weit und zuverläßig[192] nach Sinear tragen und sie dort in einem neuen Haus deponieren.

Ritualrückstände nach hethitischen Quellen", in B. Janowski, K. Koch und G. Wilhelm (Hg.), *Religionsgeschichtliche Beziehungen zwischen Kleinasien, Nordsyrien und dem Alten Testament* (Freiburg Schweiz und Göttingen, 1993), S. 67–85.

[190] Vgl. zuletzt die 1990 in Aschkelon gefundene Stierstatuette: L.E. Stager, *Ashkelon Discovered. From Canaanites and Philistines to Romans and Moslems* (Washington, DC, 1991), S. 6–7.

[191] S.o. Anm. 67. Eine ganze (Klein-)Familie beim Kult vor der Himmelskönigin (bzw. der Ištar von Arbela im Strahlenkranz) zeigt ein neuassyrisches Rollsiegel, das sich heute im Besitz des Biblischen Instituts der Universität Freiburg Schweiz befindet: BIF VR 1993.11 = O. Keel und Ch. Uehlinger, *Altorientalische Miniaturkunst. Die ältesten visuellen Massenkommunikationsmittel. Ein Blick in die Sammlungen des Biblischen Instituts der Universität Freiburg Schweiz* (Erweiterte Neuauflage, Freiburg Schweiz, 1996), S. 154–5, mit Abb. 178.

[192] Zur Bedeutung der Storchenflügel vgl. Uehlinger (Anm. 188), S. 97.

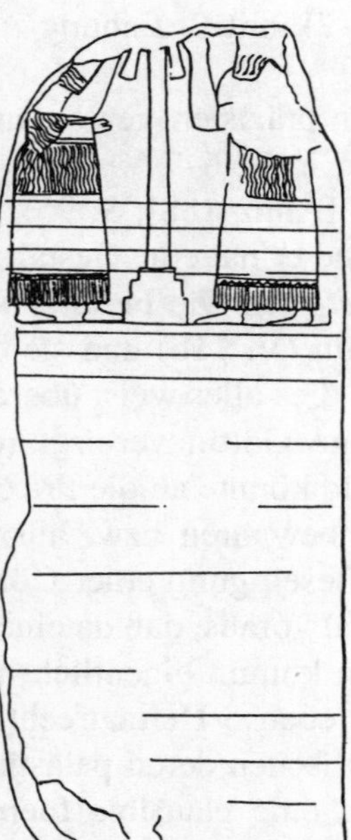

Abb. 32

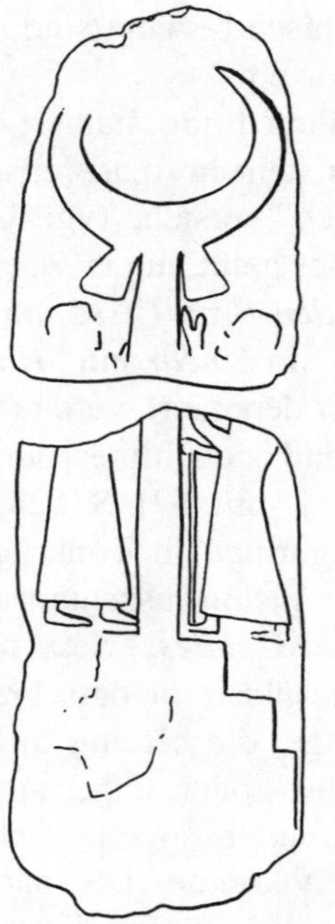

Abb. 33

Abb. 34

Abb. 35

Abb. 36

Abb. 37

Sinear, das ist Südmesopotamien, wo noch in der Perserzeit wichtige Göttinnentempel bestanden: das Eanna von Uruk,[193] der Inanna-Tempel von Nippur,[194] der Nanna/Ningal-Tempel von Ur,[195] jener Stadt, wo auch der Mondgott verehrt wurde und woher Abraham ausgewandert sein soll (Gen. i 31) . . . Ist es ein Zufall, daß am Nanna-Ningal-Tempel von Ur gerade in frühachämenidischer Zeit gebaut und dabei die Basis für das Kultbild verbreitert worden ist?[196] Oder haben wir hier das noch fehlende Korrelat zu Sach. v 11, wonach die sorgsam beseitigte "Frau" in Sinear in ihrem "Haus" auf einem Postament zur Ruhe kommen soll—und damit einen weiteren Hinweis auf die konkrete Pragmatik dieser Visionen?

Wir kommen zum Schluß: Alles weist darauf hin, daß in den Sacharja-Visionen ein Autor oder verschiedene Autoren am Werk sind, die in direktem Kontakt mit den persischen Autoritäten stehen; die wissen, was in der Propaganda Darius' I. in verschiedenen(!) Teilen des Reiches angesagt ist; Menschen, die von mesopotamischer Farbsymbolik gehört haben, Horizont- und Theophaniemetaphorik verstehen; Menschen, die wissen, daß man in Sinear gerade einen Göttinnentempel restauriert, und die ihrerseits ein konkretes Projekt für die Reorganisation von Juda haben. Menschen mit mesopotamisch gelehrtem bzw. informiertem Hintergrund, die nun aber in Juda sind, ihre Hoffnung angesichts dort angetroffener Widerstände freilich nach wie vor auf die Gola setzen, wie dies die letzte Vision festhält: Der Wagen eilt, Yahwes *rûaḥ* auf den Norden zu legen—nur so wird die Reorganisation gelingen können.

Sind damit die zu Beginn dieses Vortrags aufgeworfenen Fragen beantwortet? Nein. Wohl aber dürfte—im Sinne einer Forschungsoption—deutlich geworden sein, daß der Blick auf außerbiblisches Quellenmaterial, sei es textlicher, sei es ikonographischer Natur, für das Verständnis biblischer, zumal prophetischer Texte essentiell ist, weil er allein die Texte historisch, und d.h. sozio-politisch ebenso wie theologisch, ihrer ursprünglichen Pragmatik entsprechend zu situieren vermag. Die Fülle der verfügbaren Quellen—Archäologie,

---

[193] E. Heinrich, *Die Tempel und Heiligtümer im alten Mesopotamien. Typologie, Morphologie und Geschichte* (Berlin, 1982), S. 300, 326. Vgl. J. Blenkinsopp, "Temple and Society in Achaemenid Judah", in *Second Temple Studies 1* (Anm. 156), S. 22–53, hier 30–2; M.A. Dandamayev, "Was Eanna Destroyed by Darius I?", *AMI* 25 (1992), S. 169–72.

[194] Heinrich, S. 334–5.

[195] Ebd., S. 298–300, 325–6.

[196] Ebd., S. 326.

Ikonographie, Texte—in ihrer zugegeben oft beschwerlichen, aber auch faszinierenden Komplexität ist erforderlich, um das, was wir lesen, kontextuieren zu können und damit zu einer "dichtereren Beschreibung" (C. Geertz) biblischer Kultur, Ideologie—und Theologie zu gelangen.

Verzeichnis der Abbildungen

1 Reich, "Palaces" (Anm. 24), S. 216 fig. 13.
2 Börker-Klähn, *Bildstelen* (Anm. 29), Abb. 151 (Ausschnitt).
3 Ebd., Abb. 216.
4 Botta und Flandin, *Monument* (Anm. . . .), Pl. 64 (Ausschnitt).
5 Börker-Klähn, *Bildstelen* (Anm. 29), Abb. 219.
6 A.H. Layard, *The Monuments of Nineveh from Drawings made on the Spot* (London, 1849), Pl. 65 (vgl. *AOB*, no. 336; vgl. *ANEP*, no. 538).
7 Ebd., Pl. 82 Mitte.
8 *GGG*, Abb. 346 (Handel Jerusalem).
9 Ebd., Abb. 347 (Ramat Raḥel).
10 Ebd., Abb. 281 (Dothan).
11 *ANEP*, no. 537 (Ausschnitt).
12 Börker-Klähn, *Bildstelen* (Anm. 29), Abb. 240b.
13 E. Porada, in G. Markoe et al., *Ancient Bronzes, Ceramics and Seals. The Nasli M. Heerramaneck Collection of Ancient Near Eastern, Central Asiatic, and European Art* (Los Angeles, 1981), no. 1214 (Zeichnung H. Keel-Leu).
14 *GGG*, Abb. 295a (Tēl Śēraʿ).
15 Bisher unveröffentlicht; Handel (Libanon?), Kompositmaterial (Fritte), 27,4 x 12,2 mm, BIF Nr. VR 1991.68 (Zeichnung H. Keel-Leu).
16 Bisher unveröffentlicht; Handel Jerusalem, Kompositmaterial (Fritte), 27,5 x 10,3 mm, BIF Nr. VR 1995.19 (Zeichnung H. Keel-Leu).
17 Bisher unveröffentlicht; Handel Jerusalem, Kompositmaterial (Fritte), 23,2 x 12,2 mm, BIF Nr. VR 1995.20 (Zeichnung H. Keel-Leu).
18 *GGG*, Abb. 295b (Tell Ğemme).
19 Bisher unveröffentlicht; Handel (Libanon?), hellbeiger, grau und dunkelbeige melierter Stein, 31,5 x 14 mm, BIF Nr. VR 1991. 57.
20 Sotheby's, *Western Asiatic Cylinder Seals and Antiquities from the Erlenmeyer Collection (Part I)* (London 9.7.1992), no. 212; heute BIF VR 1992.17 (Zeichnung H. Keel-Leu).
21 Keel, *Studien IV* (Anm. 76), S. 184 Abb. 10.
22 D. Stronach, "La statue de Darius le Grand découvert à Suse", *CahDAFI* 4 (1974) S. 204–5, Fig. 20–21.
23 Koch, *Es kündet Dareios* (Anm. 123), S. 17 Abb. 7.
24 Koch, *Reichsidee*² (Anm. 113), S. 176 Abb. 10.
25 F. Lajard, *Introduction à l'étude du culte public et des mystères de Mithra en Orient et en Occident* (Paris, 1847), Pl. 14.
26 Ebd. Pl. 21.
27 E. Porada, *Alt-Iran. Die Kunst in vorislamischer Zeit* (Baden-Baden, ²1979), S. 172 Fig. 85.
28 *GGG*, Abb. 361a (Gezer).
29 Ebd., Abb. 360b (Tell Kēsān).

30a Ebd., Abb. 381c (Ramat Raḥel).
30b Ebd., 382b (Ramat Raḥel).
31 Uehlinger, "Frau" (Anm. 188), S. 99 Abb. 3 (Tēl Ērānī).
32 Keel, *Studien IV* (Anm. 76), S. 182, Abb. 7.
33 Ebd., Abb. 8.
34 *GGG*, Abb. 303.
35 R. Cohen und Y. Yisrael, *On the Road to Edom. Discoveries from 'En Ḥaṣeva*, (The Israel Museum, catalogue no. 370 (Jerusalem, 1995), S. 24.
36 U. Winter, *Frau und Göttin. Exegetische und ikonographische Studien zum weiblichen Gottesbild im Alten Israel und in dessen Umwelt* (Freiburg Schweiz und Göttingen, [2]1987). Abb. 174.
37 Ebd., Abb. 181.

JEZREEL, SAMARIA AND MEGIDDO: ROYAL CENTRES OF OMRI AND AHAB

by

DAVID USSISHKIN
Tel Aviv

The biblical text informs us that Omri built Samaria as the capital of the northern kingdom of Israel. On the other hand, the events related in 1 Kings xxi and 2 Kings ix–x indicate that Jezreel was also a royal centre of the Omride dynasty. This leads to the question of the role of Jezreel *vis à vis* Samaria in the kingdom of Israel. A number of possible explanations—based primarily on geographical, historical and biblical considerations—have been proposed. Morgenstern (1941, pp. 286, 288, 303) and others who followed him suggested that Samaria was the summer capital, while the royal winter palace was located in Jezreel. Alt (1959) believed that the kingdom of Israel had two capitals, one for the Canaanite and one for the Israelite population. Yadin (1978) suggested that Samaria served as the capital but that the temple of Baʿal was built on Mount Carmel rather than Samaria, not far from Jezreel. Finally, Olivier (1987) believed that Samaria was the capital while Jezreel was a kind of "gateway city", controlling the access from the east to the Valley of Jezreel and the hilly, central regions of the kingdom.

The discussion about Samaria and Jezreel should also include Megiddo. This large and central city is located *ca.* 15 km. from Megiddo as the crow flies, and eye contact exists between the two places. It needs to be explained, therefore, why a new centre had to be built in Jezreel, situated so near to Megiddo.

A fresh evaluation of these problems is now possible in view of the data retrieved in the recent archaeological excavations at Tel Jezreel. Intensive excavations have been carried out at this site for six seasons, between 1990 and 1996, by the British School of Archaeology in Jerusalem and the Institute of Archaeology of Tel Aviv University under the direction of John Woodhead and myself (see Ussishkin and Woodhead 1992; 1994; forthcoming). The excavations provided us with a clear picture of the settlement at the time of the Omride dynasty, which will form the starting-point of our discussion.

The fortified enclosure at Jezreel

Tel Jezreel is located on a ridge extending along the southern edge of the Valley of Jezreel. Situated on a prominent summit, it dominates the valley below, where the highway from Megiddo to Beth-shan extended in ancient times. In addition to its strategic position, Tel Jezreel commands a breathtaking view of the valley below and of Mount Gilboa to the east. The climate here is mild: in summer it is not as hot as in the valley below, and a breeze often blows from north and north-west. There is ample water; a spring, ʿEn Jezreel, is situated in the valley below, and the site contains many rock-cut cisterns used to collect rainwater. The roughly rectangular site is *ca.* 60 dunams (*ca.* 14 acres) in size.

On the basis of evidence of unstratified pottery, it is clear that Tel Jezreel had been settled in the Early Bronze Age and the Late Bronze Age as well as during Iron Age I immediately before the Omride enclosure to be discussed below was built, that is, in the 10th century B.C. In the periods following the Iron Age, Jezreel has continuously been settled till present times. A large settlement extended over the site in the Byzantine period. A medieval village from the period of the Crusades is situated in the western part of the site, where the remains of a church and a tower still stand; later the Arab village of Zerʿin was built here.

The settlement relevant to us is that dating to the 9th century B.C. A large rectangular fortified enclosure, symmetrical in plan, was built here (Fig. 1). On its northern side[1] the enclosure bordered on the steep slope of the site facing the Valley of Jezreel. A casemate wall was built around the enclosure. Squarely shaped, projecting towers were built in the corners. The wall and the towers were supported on the outside by a ramp. The lower, interior part of the ramp was made of layers of brown soil, and its upper, exterior part was made of limestone chips and gravel. A rock-cut moat surrounded the enclosure on three sides, except for the northern side where the wall and the ramp extended along the edge of the steep slope. The rock-cut moat, which is 8 to 12 m. wide, is at present mostly filled with later-in-date debris; its

[1] As can be seen in Fig. 1, the sides of the enclosure are, in fact, oriented to the north-north-east, east-south-east, south-south-west and north-north-west. For the sake of simplicity, the sides of the enclosure are referred to here as if they are oriented to the north, east, south and west respectively.

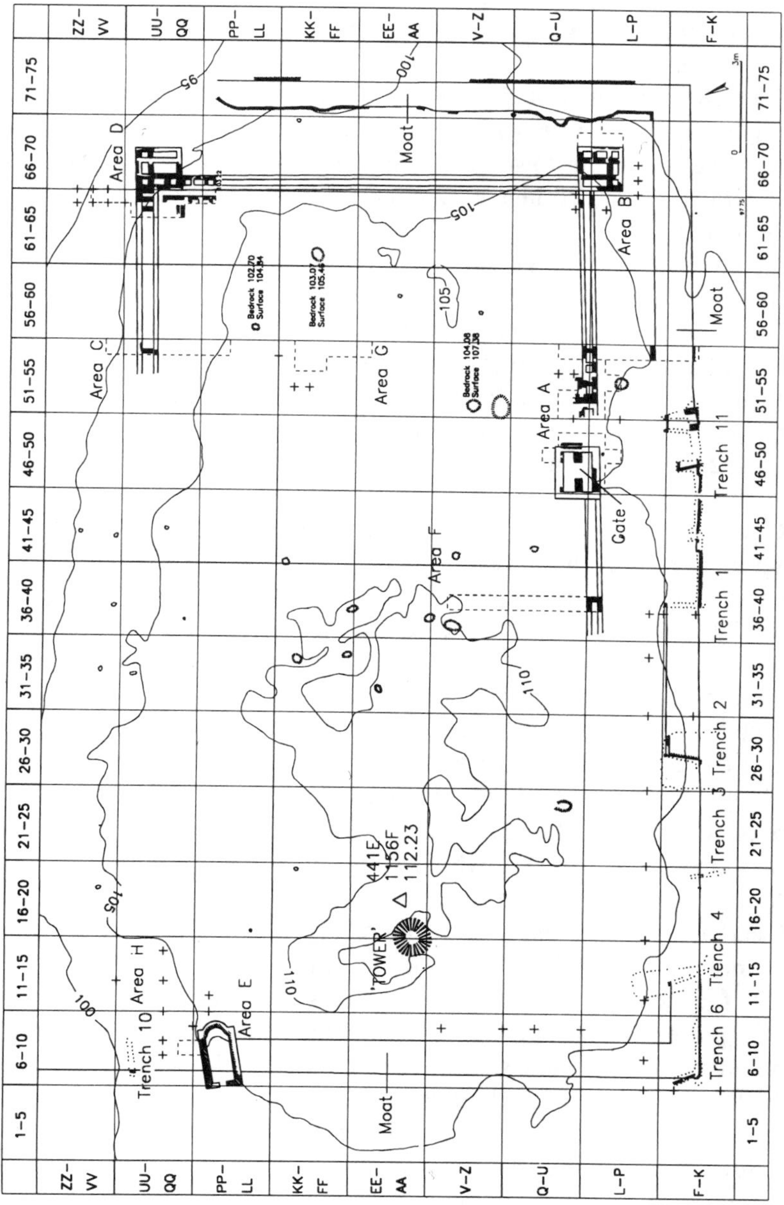

Fig. 1. Plan of Tel Jezreel.

bottom was exposed by us at one point, being *ca.* 6.5 m. beneath the surface. Significantly, the impressive moat is an unusual feature in Iron Age Palestine, indicating the special importance and strength of the fortifications.

The gate is located at the southern side, but not in the centre of the enclosure. It is a three-entry type gatehouse, apparently also square in plan like the corner towers. The moat extended in front of the gate, and a bridge or a drawbridge was probably erected here to enable access to the enclosure.

The enclosure was large and much effort was invested in constructing it. Along the line of the wall the enclosure was 289 m. long and 157 m. wide, and the area enclosed within the walls was *ca.* 45 dunams (*ca.* 11 acres). The overall length of the moat along three sides of the enclosure was *ca.* 670 m. It was roughly estimated that building the moat had involved the hewing of *ca.* 26800 cubic metres of stone, and *ca.* 23300 cubic metres of soil and gravel had been dumped to form the ramp.

Regarding the inside of the enclosure, relatively little is known at present, as most of the excavations took place near the corner towers and the gate area. In the central parts of the enclosure bedrock is relatively high. It seems that much work was invested in levelling the surface of the enclosure, in order to create a kind of podium here: fills made of brown, natural soil brought here from the vicinity of the site were dumped along the upper edge of the slopes around the site; in the gate area also debris taken from the Late Bronze Age and Iron Age I settlements was used. Remains of two public buildings were uncovered near the gate and the north-east tower, but no monumental structures or walls, which could have belonged to a palatial building, have so far been discerned. In the rooms of the casemate wall and adjacent to them were found relatively poor domestic remains. The finds consist mainly of domestic pottery.

The fortifications, including the towers and the gatehouse, were mostly preserved at foundation level. The walls are generally built of boulders laid in courses, with smaller stones filling the spaces between them. The size of the boulders varies, and sometimes large blocks were incorporated in the bottom of the foundations. At least the superstructure of the south-east corner tower was built of sun-dried bricks. The use of ashlars is very limited; sometimes ashlar stones were incorporated in the walls, and several corners were built of ashlars. An exceptionally well-built corner was uncovered in the foundations of the south-east corner tower.

No structural changes or phases have been discerned in the enclosure, and it apparently fell into disuse a relatively short period of time after its construction. The south-east corner tower was destroyed by fire, but it cannot be established whether the destruction that occurred was due to a "local" cause and was limited to the tower, or whether it marks a wilful destruction of the entire enclosure. In any case, above the disused enclosure and its walls, from which many stones had been robbed for reuse, extend domestic remains dating to the later Iron Age.

The dating of the enclosure is based primarily on the biblical evidence. We assume that it was built after the ascent to the throne of Omri in 882 B.C.,[2] and came to end during Jehu's revolt in 842 B.C.—altogether a short period of forty years. If indeed the enclosure was destroyed by fire during Jehu's revolt—and this seems to me a plausible theory—this destruction could be associated with the bloody events at Jezreel hinted at in 2 Kings x 11 and Hosea i 4.

If we turn to discuss the function of the enclosure, the archaeological evidence can be summarized as follows: (a) the enclosure was built at one time according to an overall plan; it served for a relatively short period of time. (b) The enclosure was built on a summit, located in a dominating position above the Valley of Jezreel. (c) Emphasis in construction was put on strong fortifications. (d) In the fortifications the rock-cut moat is perhaps the most prominent feature. (e) The quality of construction is relatively poor; and the characteristic elements of contemporary Israelite monumental architecture—in particular, consistent construction with ashlar masonry—hardly appear here. (f) In the enclosure an effort was made to level the surface by laying fills in order to create a kind of podium. (g) It seems reasonable to assume that a central building had been built here, but nothing associated with it has so far been found; also, no indications of a palace or any other monumental building were encountered. (h) Poor domestic remains were uncovered in association with the wall and the towers.

On the basis of the above data both John Woodhead and I believe that Jezreel was not a royal capital, but that it was built and served as a military base, possibly the military centre of the kings of the House of Omri. It seems that Jezreel served as a central base for the cavalry and chariotry units of the Israelite army. The strength and size of these units in Ahab's army are emphasized in the description of the battle of Karkar in 853 B.C. found in the annals of Shalmaneser III.

---

[2] The dates used in this article are after H. Tadmor, "Chronology", *Enclopaedia Biblica* (Hebrew) IV (Jerusalem, 1962), cols 245–310.

Significantly, it seems that barley—an important component in the diet of war horses—was cultivated in the eastern part of the Valley of Jezreel (see Har-el 1994).

An interesting point recently raised by Williamson (1996) should be mentioned here. The size and imposing nature of the fortifications clearly served the purposes of propaganda. They express the interest and need to show the strength and position of the royal dynasty of Omri, and to use these grandiose public works as a means of social control and as a means of overawing the local population.

Finally, as already hinted by Williamson (1991, p. 82), it seems possible that structures of the enclosure are referred to in the biblical account of Jehu's conquest of Jezreel in 2 Kings ix–x. "The tower in Jezreel" (ix 17), on which stood the watchman who first noticed the rebellious army approaching Jezreel from the direction of the Gilead hills, should be identified with the north-east corner tower of the enclosure. The gate used by Jehu to enter Jezreel immediately before being challenged by Jezebel (ix 31), apparently the same gate in front of which Jehu later exhibited the seventy heads of "Ahab's sons" sent to him from Samaria (x 8), is almost certainly the gatehouse located on the southern side of the enclosure.

Samaria: the capital of the Northern Kingdom of Israel

Turning to discuss Samaria we have at our disposal the data uncovered in the systematic excavations of Harvard University directed by Reisner between 1908 and 1910 (Reisner et al. 1924), and of the Joint Expedition directed by Crowfoot, between 1931 and 1935 (Crowfoot et al. 1942).

Analysis of the data from Samaria leads to two observations. First, all the data indicate that Samaria was the royal capital. It was a large and important city, characterized by monumental architecture. Second, regarding concepts of architecture and building style, a strong resemblance to contemporary Jezreel can be discerned. We can conclude, therefore, that the planners and builders of Samaria and Jezreel belonged to the same architectural school although concurrently they built two centres whose functions were different.

Samaria was built on a summit of a hill and on its slopes (Fig. 2). As in Jezreel, the site dominated its surroundings, bedrock was relatively high on the summit, and a 10th-century B.C. settlement existed

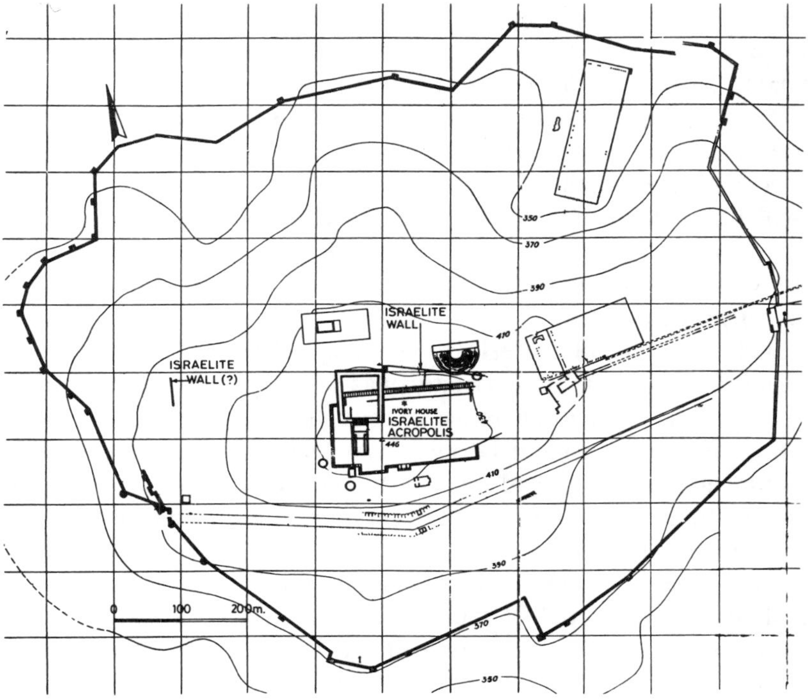

Fig. 2. Plan of Samaria.

here, its debris used for the constructional fills of the Omride structures (on this settlement, see recently Stager 1990).

The Israelite acropolis was located on the summit, while the city extended over the surrounding slopes. The gates to the city and the acropolis were probably built on the unexcavated eastern side, where the slope is mild and a modern Arab village is now situated. As in Jezreel, the acropolis was a rectangular enclosure surrounded by a casemate wall, but it was much smaller in size. The acropolis at Samaria, *ca.* 220 m. long and *ca.* 120 m. wide, enclosed an area of *ca.* 26 dunams (*ca.* 6 acres), as compared to 45 dunams (11 acres) at Jezreel. However, at Jezreel the enclosure formed the entire settlement while in Samaria it formed only the acropolis.

Very little is known about the city of Samaria which surrounded the acropolis. Reisner uncovered several segments of massive revetment walls, obviously parts of the city's fortifications, on the northern, western and southern slopes. For lack of data it is difficult to estimate the size of the city accurately, but I assume it reached 100 to 120 dunams (*ca.* 23 to 28 acres), including the acropolis.

The acropolis contained various royal buildings situated between large open courtyards. As in Jezreel, the acropolis walls are based on bedrock and extend along the upper edge of the slope. Constructional fills, which include debris of the earlier settlement, were laid to support the walls and to level the surface, thus turning the summit into a kind of podium. The floors of the structures were laid upon the constructional fills.

Unlike the case of Jezreel, the buildings of Samaria are of monumental character. Ashlar masonry was lavishly used in the various structures, and in particular the construction of the casemate walls with ashlar stones should be noted. At least some entrances to the monumental buildings had been decorated with stone-carved Proto-Ionic capitals mounted on pillars or pilasters, and several such capitals were uncovered in the excavations.

Finally, the rich finds also indicate the importance of Samaria and its status as the capital of the kingdom. Numerous Hebrew ostraca of administrative character—part of the royal administration—were uncovered in one of the buildings. A group of beautiful Phoenician ivory carvings were also found (Crowfoot and Crowfoot 1938). Ivory carvings of this kind were usually kept in royal collections, or decorated furniture in royal palaces, and this group may well have been associated with Ahab's "ivory house which he made" (1 Kings xxii 39).

Megiddo: the central city guarding the Via Maris

Ancient Megiddo was strategically located in the western part of the Valley of Jezreel, at the point where the coastal highway—the *via maris*—turned into the valley after crossing Mount Carmel. Hence the special importance of Megiddo in antiquity, including the period relevant to us. Very intensive excavations took place in Megiddo, first by a German expedition directed by Schumacher between 1903 and 1905 (Schumacher 1908), then by the Chicago Oriental Institute between 1927 and 1939 (for the Iron Age see Lamon and Shipton 1939), and finally by Yigael Yadin of the Hebrew University of Jerusalem in 1960 and later (Yadin 1970). Systematic excavations have recently been renewed at Tel Megiddo by Tel Aviv University under the direction of Israel Finkelstein and myself.

The city levels relevant to us were also extensively excavated (see the summary in Davies 1986). However, the function of the excavated structures, their stratigraphy and date, are subjects of different and often contradictory scholarly interpretations. It would seem that there is no unanimous agreement about the interpretation of most of the data associated with Megiddo of the 10th and 9th centuries B.C. I cannot present here all the interpretations, and the discussion below will be based in the main on my own views.

The starting point for our discussion is the city level labelled Stratum VA-IVB (Fig. 3). Stratigraphically, it includes all the structures immediately beneath City Wall 325—the fortification wall of the later Iron Age city (Stratum IVA). This means that all the structures of Stratum VA-IVB predate the city wall in question, but they were not necessarily all constructed at the same time: some of them could have been erected at a slightly earlier date and others at a slightly later date.

Stratum VA-IVB was an unfortified city, possibly protected by a row of adjoining buildings situated around the upper periphery of the site. This city was characterized by several monumental palatial buildings built of ashlar masonry. Noticeable among them was the southern palace (No. 1723), situated in a large compound, with a huge annexed building erected nearby (No. 1482). The Stratum VA-IVB city must have been a provincial royal city and an administrative centre for the entire region.

It seems that the city of Stratum VA-IVB (or at least a large part of it) was constructed during the reign of Solomon (965–928 B.C.). This attribution is primarily based on the statement in 1 Kings ix 15 that Solomon built Hazor, Megiddo and Gezer, and it relies on the historicity of this source. It is also based on the interpretation of this verse that public monumental buildings are referred to here. On purely archaeological grounds this stratum and its monumental buildings could be later, and date to the period of the Divided Monarchy.

Three data seem to indicate that the city of Stratum VA-IVB lasted well into the 9th century B.C.

First, Pharaoh Shoshenq I erected a stele in Megiddo during his campaign in Israel and Judah in *ca.* 923 B.C. Assuming that he would have erected a monumental stele in an existing city to mark its conquest and domination rather than on a ruined site, we have to conclude that

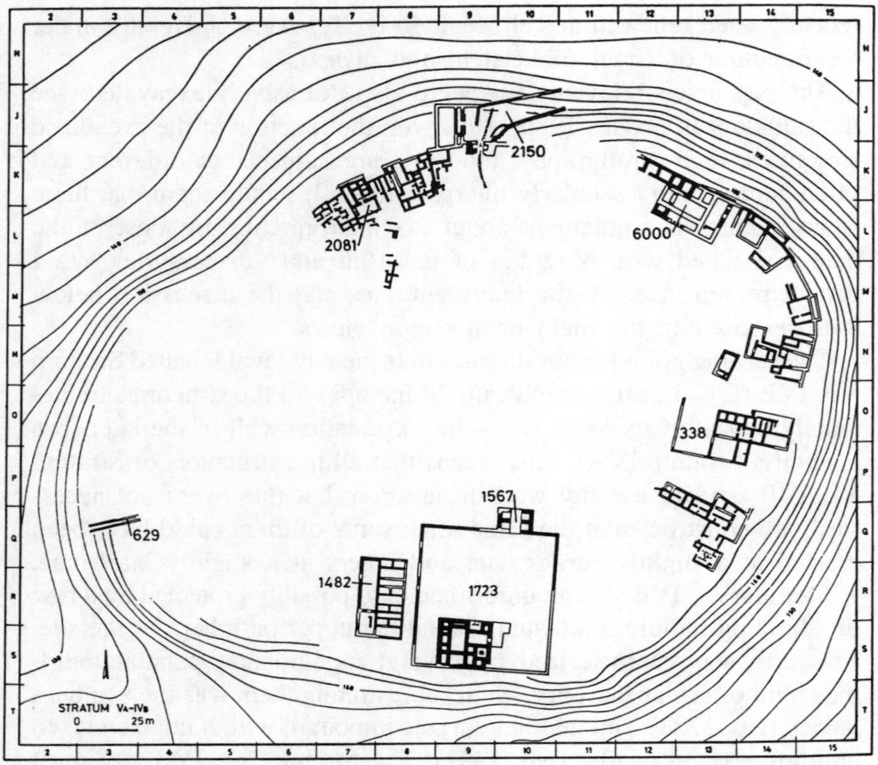

Fig. 3. Plan of Megiddo, Stratum VA-IVB.

Shoshenq I did not destroy Megiddo (Davies 1986, p. 96; Ussishkin 1990, pp. 71–4). Hence the conclusion that the Stratum VA-IVB lasted till after Shoshenq I's campaign.

Second, the seal of "Shema, Servant of Jeroboam" was found apparently in association with the gatehouse (No. 1567) to the southern palatial compound of Stratum VA-IVB (Fig. 3). In following Yeivin (1960) and Ahlström (1993), it seems that Jeroboam should be identified with Jeroboam I rather than with Jeroboam II, hence an indication that Stratum VA-IVB existed during the reign of Jeroboam I (928–907 B.C.) (Ussishkin 1994).

Third, the pottery assemblage associated with the enclosure of Jezreel dates to the short period of use of the enclosure, that is, to the period of the Omride dynasty (882–842 B.C.) (or even later if the enclosure was destroyed at a later date). The Jezreel pottery assemblage has been studied by Zimhoni (1992); it portrays close affinities with the pottery assemblage of Megiddo Strata VA-IVB and IVA. Hence the indication that the latter stratum still existed at the first half of the 9th century B.C.

The above indications are in line with the conclusions of Crowfoot (1940), Kenyon (1957) and recently Whitman (1990), who dated the monumental structures of this stratum and their pottery to the 9th century B.C., on the basis of their resemblance to the monumental buildings in the acropolis of Samaria and its pottery.

In our second report of the excavations at Tel Jezreel (Ussishkin and Woodhead 1994, p. 47) we assumed that Megiddo Stratum VA-IVB had been destroyed prior to the construction of the Omride enclosure at Jezreel and that Megiddo Stratum IVA had been built not before the later part of the 9th century B.C. However, with the above data and considerations in mind it seems more plausible that the Jezreel enclosure was built when the Stratum VA-IVB city still existed. At this stage of the discussion we have to turn to 2 Kings ix 27. This verse informs us that Ahaziah king of Judah fled to Megiddo during Jehu's revolt, where he was caught and killed by the rebels. If we assume that Ahaziah took refuge in an existing rather than a desolate city, this event supports the supposition that the Stratum VA-IVB city still existed at that time.

Numerous structures in Stratum VA-IVB, such as the gate (No. 1567) to the southern palace compound and the northern palace (No. 6000), were destroyed by fire, indicating that this city level met its end by a wilful destruction. Is it possible that the destruction is associated with Jehu's revolt in 842 B.C. and with the flight of the king of Judah to this Omride stronghold?

Summary and conclusions

The archaeological data—as dated and interpreted on the basis of the biblical evidence—are summarized below. They seem to support the following reconstruction of the history of Jezreel, Samaria and Megiddo in the period after the division of the United Monarchy in 928 B.C.

Megiddo was a central city controlling a major highway before and after the division of the United Monarchy. The city at that time Stratum VA-IVB—was not fortified and included several palatial buildings and public structures. It was conquered and shortly held by the Egyptian army of Shoshenq I in 923 B.C. Megiddo and then served as an administrative provincial centre during the reigns of Jeroboam I and the kings that followed him. In 882 B.C. Omri ascended the throne by force, and introduced vast changes to the administration of the kingdom. Megiddo continued to be an important provincial centre, but probably lost some of its special importance.

Following his ascent to the throne Omri founded a new capital, Samaria, in the heart of the hilly regions of the kingdom. A monumental fortified acropolis, containing the royal palace and various annexed buildings was erected on the summit of the site with the city proper extending over the surrounding slopes. Samaria continued to serve as the capital of the northern kingdom of Israel till its conquest by Sargon II in 720 B.C.

Omri and Ahab developed the army, turning it into a large and strong military force which included substantial units of cavalry and chariotry. A large, fortified military centre had to be built, to serve, first and foremost, as a central base for the enlarged army, also as a strong fort of the newly-established ruling dynasty. Samaria was the capital, and also located in the hills—thus not suitable for garrisoning chariotry units. On the other hand, Megiddo, an unfortified administrative centre characterized by monumental buildings, was also unsuitable for the purpose. Therefore it was decided to found a new centre at Jezreel. It seems that several considerations were in mind when choosing this particular site: (1) it was located in a central part of the kingdom, not far from Samaria and Megiddo, near the roads leading to these cities, and near the road leading to Beth-shan and further eastwards. (2) It was located near the valley rather than in a hilly region. (3) Barley and chaff needed for feeding the war horses were available in the valley nearby. (4) It was located on a topographically dominating summit. (5) Water was available here.

The enclosure of Jezreel was thus built, probably concurrently with Samaria. The planners and architects of both sites came from the same "school". In Jezreel emphasis was placed on the strength of the fortifications rather than on the quality of architecture. Various buildings were probably built inside the large levelled podium. They certainly included a central building—possibly a royal residence. In any case, at least shortly before Jehu's revolt, King Jehoram and the dowager Queen Jezebel were in residence in Jezreel.

Following Jehu's *coup d'état* in 842 B.C. the enclosure was destroyed or abandoned, and quite possibly the destruction of Megiddo Stratum

VA-IVB is also associated with the same event. The Jezreel enclosure was not rebuilt, and later settlements, in the later Iron Age and the following periods, continuously reused the stones robbed from its walls. The military centre of the northern kingdom of Israel was now transferred to Megiddo. The ruins of the Stratum VA-IVB city were largely demolished, their stones removed for reuse in the construction of the new Stratum IVA city. The newly-built city drastically differed from the previous one, befitting its new role as a military centre. It was surrounded by a strong city wall which included a massive city gate (wrongly widely labelled as the "Solomonic" city gate). Two large complexes of stables for horses and a huge silo for keeping chaff were built. A huge water system to enable access to the spring from inside the fortified city was also constructed. The Stratum IVA city remained as a central royal stronghold till the conquest and annexation of northern Israel by Tiglath-pileser III in 733–732 B.C.

REFERENCES

G.W. Ahlström, "The Seal of Shema", *SJOT* 7 (1993), pp. 208–215.
A. Alt, "Der Stadstaat Samaria", reproduced in *Kleine Schriften zur Geschichte des Volkes Israel* III (Munich, 1959), pp. 258–302.
J.W. Crowfoot, "Megiddo—A Review", *PEQ* 1940, pp. 132–147.
J.W Crowfoot, and G.M. Crowfoot, *Samaria-Sebaste II: Early Ivories from Samaria* (London, 1938).
J.W. Crowfoot, K.M. Kenyon and E.L. Sukenik, *Samaria-Sebaste I: The Buildings at Samaria* (London, 1942).
G.I. Davies, *Megiddo* (Cambridge, 1986).
M. Har-el, "'The Chariots of Israel and the Horsemen Thereof!' (2 Kings 2:12)", in *Judea and Samaria Research Studies, Proceedings of the Third Annual Meeting of the College of Judea and Samaria* (1994) (Hebrew).
K.M. Kenyon, "The Evidence of the Samaria Pottery and its Bearing on Finds at Other Sites", in J.W. Crowfoot, G.M. Crowfoot and K.M. Kenyon, *Samaria-Sebaste III: The Objects from Samaria* (London, 1957), pp. 198–209.
R.S. Lamon and G.M. Shipton, *Megiddo I: Strata I–V* (Chicago, 1939).
J. Morgenstern, *Amos Studies* I (Cincinnati, 1941).
H. Olivier, "A Tale of Two Cities: Reconsidering Alt's Hypothesis of Two Capitals for the Northern Kingdom", *Ned. Geref. Teologiese Tydskrif* 28 (1987), pp. 2–19.
G.A. Reisner, C.S. Fisher and D.G. Lyon, *Harvard Excavations at Samaria 1908–1910* I–II (Cambridge, Mass., 1924).
G. Schumacher, *Tell el-Mutesellim I: Fundbericht* (Leipzig, 1908).
L.E. Stager, "Shemer's Estate", *BASOR* 277/8 (1990), pp. 93–107.
D. Ussishkin, "Notes on Megiddo, Gezer, Ashdod, and Tel Batash in the Tenth to Ninth Centuries B.C.", *BASOR* 277/8 (1990), pp. 71–91.
———, "Gate 1567 at Megiddo and the Seal of Shema, Servant of Jeroboam", in M.D. Coogan, J.C. Exum and L.E. Stager, *Scripture and Other Artifacts* (Louisville, 1994), pp. 410–28.
D. Ussishkin and J. Woodhead, "Excavations at Tel Jezreel 1990–1991: Preliminary Report", *Tel Aviv* 19 (1992), pp. 3–56.

———, "Excavations at Tel Jezreel 1992–1993: Second Preliminary Report", *Levant* 26 (1994), pp. 1–48.

———, "Excavations at Tel Jezreel 1994–1995: Third Preliminary Report", *Tel Aviv*, forthcoming.

H.J. Wightman, "The Myth of Solomon", *BASOR* 277/8 (1990), pp. 5–22.

H.G.M. Williamson, "Jezreel in the Biblical Texts", *Tel Aviv* 18 (1991), pp. 72–92.

———, "Tel Jezreel and the Dynasty of Omri", *PEQ* 1996, pp. 41–51.

Y. Yadin, "Megiddo of the Kings of Israel", *BA* 33 (1970), pp. 66–96.

———, "The House of Baal of Ahab and Jezabel in Samaria, in R. Moorey and P. Parr, (ed.), *Archaeology in the Levant: Essays for Kathleen Kenyon* (Warminster, 1978), pp. 127–35.

S. Yeivin, "The Date of the Seal 'Belonging to Shema (the) Servant (of) Jeroboam'", *JNES* 19 (1960), pp. 205–12.

O. Zimhoni, "The Iron Age Pottery from Tel Jezreel—An Interim Report", *Tel Aviv* 19 (1992), pp. 57–70.

LE RÉCIT DE LA MER (EXODE XIII 17–XIV 31) REFLÈTE-T-IL UNE RÉDACTION DE TYPE DEUTÉRONOMIQUE? QUELQUES REMARQUES SUR LE PROBLÈME DE L'IDENTIFICATION DES ÉLÉMENTS DEUTÉRONOMIQUES CONTENUS DANS LE TÉTRATEUQUE

par

MARC VERVENNE
Leuven

Le présent essai est conçu comme un cheminement entre deux titres. En 1983 J.L. Ska publiait un article intitulé "Exode xiv contient-il un récit de 'guerre sainte' de style deutéronomiste?"[1] Le titre que j'ai choisi pour ma contribution fait allusion à cette étude. Le cheminement veut se déployer au cours de l'exposé, qui vise surtout à une réflexion sur le problème de l'identification et de la détermination des éléments deutéronomiques dans le Tétrateuque.

C'est enfoncer une porte ouverte, à présent, d'affirmer que nous nous trouvons devant un bouleversement dans les recherches sur le Pentateuque.[2] Les sources classiques sont contestées de manière tout à fait radicale. Dans un grand nombre de travaux de critique biblique, l'une ou l'autre de ces sources est remplacée, déplacée, déconstruite, voire éliminée. Au début des années soixante-dix, M. Weinfeld, dans son ouvrage magistral *Deuteronomy and the Deuteronomic School*,[3] pouvait encore affirmer l'existence de quatre sources bien distinctes:

> In Pentateuchal literature we meet with two schools of crystallized theological thought: that found in the Priestly strand and that reflected in the book of Deuteronomy. These schools were, to be sure, antedated by the Jahwist and Elohist documents. But J and E are merely narrative

[1] *VT* 33 (1983), pp. 454–67.

[2] Cf. A. de Pury, Th. Römer, "Le Pentateuque en question: position du problème et brève histoire de la recherche", dans A. de Pury (éd.), *Le Pentateuque en question. Les origines et la composition des cinq premiers livres de la Bible à la lumière des recherches récentes* (Genève, 1989), p. 9; C. Houtman, *Der Pentateuch. Die Geschichte seiner Erforschung neben einer Auswertung* (Kampen, 1994), pp. 365–419.

[3] (Oxford, 1972).

> sources in which no uniform outlook and concrete ideology can as yet be discerned, and thus contrast strongly with P and deuteronomic literature, each of which embodies a complex and consistent theology which we may search for in vain in the earlier sources (p. 179).

A l'heure actuelle, le consensus classique, qui se reflète dans la proposition de Weinfeld, est sérieusement remis en question. L'attribution documentaire habituelle ne s'impose plus, surtout pour ce qui est des traditions anciennes J et E. Cependant, le refus d'attribuer un texte ou un passage à J ou E ne "signifie pas pour autant", note J. Briend, "que l'on ait comme unique solution de qualifier le texte de deutéronomique, ce qui est malheureusement trop souvent le cas dans les recherches actuelles".[4] Ce jugement nous amène à l'objet de la présente contribution.

I

Les théories de M. Noth sur l'Histoire deutéronomiste ont introduit une séparation nette entre le Tétrateuque et le Deutéronome. L'une des quatre sources de la théorie documentaire classique a été ainsi détachée des trois autres. L'étude critique du Deutéronome, et surtout celle de l'Histoire deutéronomiste, s'est intensifiée énormément dans les dernières décennies. La publication, depuis 1961, d'une documentation considérable dans la *Theologische Rundschau*—et l'on ne pourrait pas se passer des contributions de H. Weippert (1985) et de H.D. Preuß (1993)—témoigne de l'importance de l'examen des textes deutéronomiques (le Deutéronome) et deutéronomistes (Histoire Dtr et Jér-Dtr) contenus dans l'Ancien Testament.[5] Du même coup, le problème de la présence d'éléments deutéronomiques dans la Genese, l'Exode et les Nombres, ainsi que de parties deutéronomistes dans

[4] "Lecture du Pentateuque et hypothèse documentaire", dans P. Haudebert (éd.), *Le Pentateuque. Débats et recherches. XIVe congrès de l'ACFEB* (*Angers, 1991*) (Paris, 1992), p. 27.

[5] Voir E. Jenni, "Zwei Jahrzehnte Forschung an den Büchern Josua bis Könige", *ThRu* NF 27 (1961), pp. 97–146; A.N. Radjawane, "Das deuteronomistische Geschichtswerk. Ein Forschungsbericht", *ThRu* NF 38 (1974), pp. 177–216; H. Weippert, "Das deuteronomistische Geschichtswerk. Sein Ziel und Ende in der neueren Forschung", *ThRu* NF 50 (1985), pp. 213–49; H.D. Preuß, "Zum deuteronomistischen Geschichtswerk", *ThRu* NF 58 (1993), pp. 229–64, 341–95. J'ajoute aussi l'importante contribution de W. Baumgartner, "Der Kampf um das Deuteronomium", *ThRu* NF 1 (1929), pp. 7–25.

certains livres prophétiques (par ex. Amos) a dû être posé d'une manière plus nette.

Le débat sur la nature et l'origine de ces éléments dans le Tétrateuque s'est longtemps limité à l'étude de quelques cas plus ou moins typiques (Gen. xv; Ex. xii 24–27a, xiii 3–16, et xxxii–xxxiv). Aujourd'hui, cependant, le nombre d'éléments deutéronomiques que la critique littéraire croit pouvoir discerner a augmenté, et le problème doit être posé en termes nouveaux. Cela a suscité—et suscite toujour— un vif intérêt, et par conséquent la critique vétérotestamentaire continue à produire tant des articles affirmant le caractère dt/dtr de telle ou telle péricope ou composition déterminée dans la Genèse, l'Exode et les Nombres[6] que des monographies étudiant la question de la présence d'éléments deutéronomiques dans le Tétrateuque d'une manière plus générale.[7] Mais, chose remarquable que nous signale N. Lohfink, ceux qui se consacrent au problème du Pentateuque en général et à la question des éléments deutéronomiques en particulier ne tiennent guère—ou si peu—compte des problèmes qui sont inhérents au Deutéronome et à l'Histoire Dtr, et qui surgissent aussi bien dans l'examen diachronique que dans l'approche synchronique.[8]

---

[6] Voir, par exemple: C. Begg, "The Destruction of the Calf (Exod. 32,20 / Dt. 9,21)", dans N. Lohfink (éd.), *Das Deuteronomium. Entstehung, Gestalt und Botschaft* (Leuven, 1985), pp. 208–251.—W. Johnstone, "The Decalogue and the Redaction of the Sinai Pericope in Exodus", *ZAW* 100 (1988), pp. 361–85; "The Two Theological Versions of the Passover Pericope in Exodus", dans R.P. Caroll et al. (éd.), *Text as Pretext. Essays in Honour of Robert Davidson*, (Sheffield, 1992), pp. 160–78; "The Deuteronomistic Cycles of 'Signs' and 'Wonders' in Exodus 1–13", dans A.G. Auld (éd.), *Understanding Poets and Prophets. Essays in Honour of George Wishart Anderson* (Sheffield, 1993), pp. 166–85.—H. Lamberty-Zielinski, *Das "Schilfmeer". Herkunft, Bedeutung und Funktion eines alttestamentlichen Exodusbegriffs* (Frankfurt am Main, 1993).—J. Vermeylen, "L'affaire du veau d'or (Ex. 32–34). Une clé pour la 'question deutéronomiste'?", *ZAW* 97 (1985), pp. 1–22; "Les sections narratives de Deut. 5–11 et leur relation à Ex. 19–34", dans N. Lohfink (éd.), *Das Deuteronomium*, pp. 174–207.

[7] Voir, par exemple: E. Blum, *Studien zur Komposition des Pentateuch, BZAW* 189 (Berlin/New York, 1990), pp. 219–360—W. Johnstone, *Exodus* (Sheffield, 1990).—C. Levin, *Der Jahwist* (Göttingen, 1993).—R. Rendtorff, *Das überlieferungsgeschichtliche Problem des Pentateuch, BZAW* 147 (Berlin/New York, 1977).—M. Rose, *Deuteronomist und Jahwist. Untersuchungen zu den Berührungspunkten beider Literaturwerke* (Zürich, 1981).—H.H. Schmid, *Der sogenannte Jahwist. Beobachtungen und Fragen zur Pentateuchforschung* (Zürich, 1976).—J. Van Seters, *Abraham in History and Tradition* (New Haven, Conn., and London, 1975); *Der Jahwist als Historiker* (Zürich, 1987); *Prologue to History. The Yahwist as Historian in Genesis* (Louisville/Zürich, 1992); *The Life of Moses. The Yahwist as Historian in Exodus-Numbers* (Kampen, 1994).

[8] Cf. N. Lohfink, "Deutéronome et Pentateuque. État de la question", dans Haudebert (éd.) (n. 4), p. 37. Voir aussi Th. Römer, "The Book of Deuteronomy", dans S.L. McKenzie, et M.P. Graham (éd.), *The History of Israel's Traditions. The Heritage of Martin Noth* (Sheffield, 1994), pp. 1178–212, spéc. pp. 208–9.

C'est dans le cadre de la problématique renouvelée des éléments dits deutéronomiques, dans le sens large du mot, que je voudrais me concentrer sur quelques difficultés relatives à cette question, qui est fondamentale dans le débat actuel sur la naissance de la collection Genèse à 2 Rois. Je traiterai, avant tout, la question de la méthodologie et cela, à partir de mes études sur une unité compositionelle bien déterminée, à savoir le récit de la Mer (Ex. xiii 17–xiv 31), qui est sans aucun doute une *crux interpretum* dans la critique du Pentateuque.

Je m'appuie sur deux travaux antérieurs. Tout d'abord, une étude que j'ai faite des éléments sacerdotaux mis en évidence dans la péricope en question, en vue d'examiner la nature de la partie P.[9] La conclusion en était que la narration sacerdotale présente les caractéristiques d'une rédaction "théologique" plutôt que celles d'un récit indépendant. Un rédacteur sacerdotal s'est servi d'une narration déjà existante, son texte-source donc, que je désigne par le sigle conventionnel "JE". Je tends à penser que ce récit pré-sacerdotal présente des caractéristiques qu'on pourrait qualifier de "proto-deutéronomiques".[10] P aurait remanié cette narration à la façon de l'école sacerdotale pour en faire une composition aux idées nouvelles. Mais je me hâte de souligner que cette conclusion concerne le récit de la Mer uniquement, et qu'elle ne peut en aucun cas être élargie à la totalité de la tradition sacer-dotale dans le Pentateuque sans que soient examinés d'autres textes appartenant à cette tradition.[11] Cette relativisation n'est pas sans importance, à ce qu'il me semble, pour l'étude des éléments deutéronomiques présents dans le Tétrateuque. La même péricope peut, en effet, contenir aussi bien des éléments proto-dt que dt/dtr, voire post-

[9] "The 'P' Tradition in the Pentateuch: Document and/or Redaction? The 'Sea Narrative' (Exodus 13,17–14,31) as a Testcase", dans C. Brekelmans, et J. Lust (éd.), *Pentateuchal Studies and Deuteronomistic History* (Leuven, 1990), pp. 67–90. Le problème de l'origine et de la nature de P a été étudié plus récemment dans L. Schmidt, *Studien zur Priesterschrift, BZAW* 214 (Berlin/New York, 1993), et T. Pola, *Die ursprüngliche Priesterschrift. Beobachtungen zur Literarkritik und Traditionsgeschichte von* P^g (Neukirchen-Vluyn, 1995). Voir aussi J.L. Ska, "De la relative indépendance de l'écrit sacerdotal", *Biblica* 76 (1995), pp. 396–415.

[10] Cf. M. Vervenne, "The Sea Narrative Revisited", *Biblica* 75 (1994), p. 85.

[11] J'ai exprimé cette réserve de la façon suivante: "However, this does not mean that the Priestly tradition in the Pentateuch as a whole should everywhere be conceived as a mere redactional expansion. The study of other compositions evidences that the P redactors might also have disposed of existing Priestly material, which they paralleled with the JE traditions. In my view, however, scholars must seriously reckon with the marked redactional character of 'P', yet without slipping back in seemingly dogmatic statements" (Vervenne [n. 9], p. 88). Voir aussi Ska, pp. 402–5.

dtr; en outre, des éléments authentiquement dt ou dtr peuvent figurer à côté de composants empruntés à des auteurs non-dt/dtr ou calqués sur le mode d'expression dt/dtr.

En second lieu, mon exposé est surtout conçu comme ajustement et complément d'un article publié dans les Mélanges offerts à C.J. Labuschagne en 1994.[12] Dans cette contribution, j'ai exposé l'état de la question quant à la présence d'éléments deutéronomiques dans la couche dite "JE" du récit de la Mer, ainsi que les diverses approches méthodologiques relatives à la nature et à l'origine de tels éléments dans le Tétrateuque.

La question essentielle à reprendre ici est celle de l'identification précise et de l'appréciation de ces composants deutéronomiques: est-ce qu'ils doivent être situés à l'aube (proto-dt), au zénith (dt/dtr) ou au crépuscule (dtr tardif) de ce qu'on appelle le "deutéronomisme"?[13] Ou encore: avons-nous affaire à la formation d'un langage et d'une pensée typiquement deutéronomique à partir d'une tradition plus ancienne (pré-dt), ou s'agit-il plutôt de l'imitation d'un vocabulaire deutéronomiste établi (post-dtr)? Je pourrais adapter le titre de ma contribution comme suit: "Ex. xiii 17–xiv 31, *quel type* de rédaction deutéronomique ce passage reflète-t-il?"

Il est clair que la critique actuelle a besoin de clarté méthodologique ainsi que de profondeur dans son argumentation. Sans nier la nécessité et l'importance des contributions de R. Rendtorff, J. Van Seters et E. Blum—pour ne mentionner que ces noms—il faut quand même reconnaître que leur approche de la naissance du Pentateuque sous son aspect général risque de généraliser, voire de proposer des résultats qui ressemblent à des solutions définitives pour le problème de la présence d'éléments deutéronomiques dans le Tétrateuque, alors que tout le monde sait qu'on se trouve dans un "brouillard d'incertitude" (*cloud of unknowing*) et que les solutions proposées par la critique sont, pour la plus grande partie, le résultat d'un jeu de devinettes.

J'ai souvent le sentiment que la forêt cache les arbres, si l'on me

---

[12] M. Vervenne, "The Question of 'Deuteronomic' Elements in Genesis to Numbers", dans F. García Martínez, A. Hilhorst, J.T.A.G.M. van Ruiten et A.S. van der Woude (éd.), *Studies in Deuteronomy. In Honour of C.J. Labuschagne on the Occasion of his 65th Birthday, SVT* 53 (Leiden/New York/Köln, 1994), pp. 243–68.

[13] Pour une réflexion critique du terme "deutéronomisme" voir l'article récent de R. Coggins, "What Does 'Deuteronomistic' Mean?", dans J. Davies, G. Harvey et W.G.E. Watson (éd.), *Words Remembered, Texts Renewed. Essays in Honour of John F.A. Sawyer* (Sheffield, 1995), pp. 135–48. Voir aussi la note suivante.

permet cette audacieuse inversion. Pourtant, il y a des questions que l'on ne peut éviter. Un texte écrit, c'était quoi dans l'Antiquité, et plus particulièrement dans la société israélite que représentait-il au juste? Comment les textes ont-ils été produits et répandus? Pendant combien de temps a-t-on travaillé avec une seule copie du texte? Qui étaient les destinataires de ces textes? Qui était capable de les lire? Comment peut-on se représenter la naissance de mouvements politiques, spirituels et religieux dans l'Antiquité? Quelle influence excerçaient-ils sur la vie sociale et religieuse? Et comment s'imaginer les conditions et les circonstances dans lesquelles la production littéraire a vu le jour au cœur de ces mouvements? En fin de compte, la présence d'un vocable ou d'une idée de tendance dt ou dtr dans un texte signifie-t-elle que ce texte est incontestablement authentique, c'est-à-dire d'origine dt ou dtr? Ou faut-il tenir compte de cette éventualité que l'auteur du texte aurait simplement imité le langage dt/dtr? Dans cet ordre d'idées, j'aimerais porter à l'attention des chercheurs une contribution remarquable que N. Lohfink a publiée en 1995 dans un recueil traitant du livre de Jérémie et du "mouvement deutéronomiste".[14] Il me semble que cette étude ouvre de nouvelles perspectives pour l'examen des éléments deutéronomiques dans le Tétrateuque.[15]

Dans ce qui suit, je complèterai d'abord ce que j'ai dit à une autre occasion concernant l'occurrence d'éléments deutéronomiques dans Genèse-Nombres. Je prêterai tout particulièrement attention aux critères d'identification de ces éléments. Ensuite, je me concentrerai sur le problème de l'identification d'éléments deutéronomiques dans le récit de la Mer.

II

Les opinions courantes à propos de l'origine des éléments deutéronomiques contenus dans le Tétrateuque étaient déjà formées dès avant la fin du 19ᵉ siècle. Il y avait trois modèles d'explication:[16]

---

[14] "Gab es eine deuteronomistische Bewegung?", dans W. Groß (éd.), *Jeremia und die deuteronomistische Bewegung* (Weinheim, 1995), pp. 313–82.

[15] Voir aussi la contribution de Coggins, plus haut la note 13.

[16] Cf. Vervenne (n. 12), pp. 246–51. Je note, en passant, ce que Lohfink a écrit en 1992: "En domaine scientifique, les hypothèses peuvent faire objet de mouvements circulaires." Voir Lohfink (n. 8), p. 35.

(1) L'auteur du Deutéronome a utilisé les traditions de la Genèse, de l'Exode et des Nombres, qui lui servaient en quelque sorte de "banque de données", véritable réservoir à partir duquel il s'est élaboré un langage typique pour exprimer ses idées à lui. [W.M.L. de Wette]

(2) Au 6ᵉ siècle, l'auteur du Deutéronome a lié sa composition à un ouvrage existant (Genèse-Nombres), qu'il a légèrement retouché afin de l'adapter au Deutéronome. [F. Bleek]

(3) Beaucoup de textes d'origine R^{JE} sont proches du vocable, du style et de la théologie deutéronomiques, de sorte qu'ils seraient "presque-deutéronomiques", tandis d'autres textes sont clairement post-dt. [J. Wellhausen, A. Kuenen]

L'approche nuancée des fondateurs de la critique du Pentateuque se fige au cours du 20ᵉ siècle, pour faire place à la conviction qu'il est inimaginable que l'auteur du Deutéronome ait emprunté des idées et des formes d'expression aux traditions pré-deutéronomiques du Tétrateuque. Par conséquent, on conclut que les éléments ou passages deutéronomiques décelés dans la Genèse, l'Exode et les Nombres proviennent d'une révision dtr de ces livres.

La redécouverte de l'importance du phénomène deutéronomique dans le Tétrateuque revient avant tout à L. Perlitt, qui a posé clairement le problème. Avant la parution de son ouvrage, intitulé *Bundestheologie im Alten Testament* (Neukirchrn-Vluyn, 1969), C. Brekelmans et N. Lohfink (1963) avaient donné une première impulsion à l'étude plus systématique de ces éléments, de sorte que la problématique—qui reste toujours ouverte—avait déjà été portée à l'attention de l'exégèse contemporaine.[17]

Aujourd'hui, l'état de la question quant aux modèles permettant d'expliquer la présence de composants deutéronomiques dans la Genèse, l'Exode et les Nombres est vite fait. Il est bien établi que nous sommes en présence de trois types d'explication (et la ressemblance avec l'état de la question telle qu'elle se présentait vers la fin du 19ᵉ siècle est frappante):

(1) Ces éléments peuvent résulter d'une sorte de remaniement proto-deutéronomique des vieilles traditions du Pentateuque, et ce travail

[17] C.H.W. Brekelmans, "Éléments deutéronomiques dans le Pentateuque", *Recherches Bibliques* 8 (Louvain, 1967), pp. 77–91 (conférence donnée lors des Journées Bibliques de Louvain en 1963); id., "Die sogenannten deuteronomischen Elemente in Genesis bis Numeri", *SVT* 15 (Leiden, 1966), pp. 90–6; N. Lohfink, *Das Hauptgebot. Eine Untersuchung literarischer Einleitungsfragen zu Dtn. 5–11* (Rome, 1963), pp. 121–4.

de retouche annonce le début d'une "école" dite deutéronomique.[18]

(2) Les éléments deutéronomiques dans le Tétrateuque proviennent d'un remaniement deutéronomiste des traditions existantes qui seront à la base du Pentateuque. Dans ce cas, l'Histoire Dtr aurait déjà existé au moment où l'on fit les retouches dtr.[19]

(3) Les éléments deutéronomiques sont (en partie) des composants post-dtr, qui s'expliquent comme étant des "traces" deutéronomistes provenant soit d'un Yahwiste post-dtr qui a bien connu l'Histoire Dtr,[20] soit des rédacteurs post-exiliques, qui dans leur volonté de faire concorder les traditions dominantes (P et Histoire Dtr), ont imité, pour ainsi dire, le langage et le style dtr.[21]

J. Van Seters affirme, non sans raison, qu'une telle divergence d'opinions et de solutions nous amène à nous poser la question de savoir comment faire avancer et progresser le débat.[22] C'est précisément dans le cadre de cette constatation que se pose le problème de la méthodologie, et tout particulièrement celui des critères nous permettant d'identifier des éléments deutéronomiques dans le Tétrateuque.

Dans ma contribution aux Mélanges Labuschagne,[23] je suis parti d'une remarque faite par Van Seters, qui affirme qu'il est "methodologically dubious to use the language and terminology of Dtn/Dtr to identify a group of texts as 'proto-Dtn' simply because they are embedded within that part of the Pentateuch that has been considered by the documentary hypothesis as earlier than Dtn."[24] Dans une note en bas de page, j'avais réagi un peu audacieusement en inversant les termes de sa remarque.[25] Aujourd'hui, je voudrais souligner que je ne me trouve pas en complet désaccord avec Van Seters concernant sa

[18] Voir, par exemple, Begg (n. 6), Brekelmans (n. 17), Lamberty-Zielinski (n. 6), Lohfink (n. 17); D.E. Skweres, *Die Rückverweise im Buch Deuteronomium* (Rome, 1979).

[19] Voir, par exemple, Blum (n. 7), Johnstone (n. 6 et 7), Rendtorff (n. 7), Vermeylen (n. 6).

[20] Voir, par exemple, Levin (n. 7), Rose (n. 7), Van Seters (n. 7).

[21] Voir, par exemple, Lohfink (n. 14) et E. Otto, "Kritik der Pentateuchkomposition", *ThRu* NF 60 (1995), pp. 163–91; id., "Die nachpriesterschriftliche Pentateuchredaktion im Buch Exodus", dans M. Vervenne (éd.), *The Book of Exodus* (Leuven, 1996) (sous presse).

[22] "The So-Called Deuteronomistic Redaction of the Pentateuch", dans J.A. Emerton (éd.), *Congress Volume: Leuven 1989, SVT* 43 (Leiden, 1991), p. 58.

[23] Voir plus haut la note 12.

[24] (n. 22), p. 59.

[25] Vervenne (n. 12), p. 251, n. 24: "To this one could remark that it is 'methodologically dubious to use the language and terminology of Dtn/Dtr to identify a group of texts as' *post-Dtr* 'simply because they are embedded within that part of the Pentateuch that has been considered by the documentary hypothesis as' J which is now regarded by several scholars as a late, post-exilic literary composition."

remarque de nature méthodologique. Ce que je veux dire, c'est qu'un examen fondamental du problème des éléments deutéronomiques présents dans le Tétrateuque doit s'effectuer sur la base d'une analyse approfondie de la forme (vocable, style, co-texte) et du contenu (les tendances ou, si l'on veut, la théologie) du texte concerné, *sans tenir compte de l'attribution reconnue et traditionnelle de ce texte à une source ou une tradition ou une rédaction, qui seraient typiques, selon l'une ou l'autre hypothèse établie ou selon une théorie novatrice.*

En ce qui concerne les éléments dits deutéronomiques dans le Tétrateuque, si un texte figurant dans ce corpus littéraire contient des constituants qui *paraissent* être dt ou dtr, il s'agit de les mettre en rapport avec le système linguistique, littéraire et théologique du corpus identifié comme étant d'origine dt/dtr, c'est-à-dire le Deutéronome, l'Histoire Dtr et Jér-Dtr. Cependant, il est clair qu'on doit tenir compte des développements survenus dans ce corpus même et donc, que la *Redaktionsgeschichte* des textes dt/dtr (dt, proto-dtr, dtr, dtr tardif) entre aussi en jeu.[26] Une telle étude comparée aboutira à la détermination—plus ou moins hypothétique, plus ou moins certaine—du caractère deutéronomique d'un texte. Dès lors, ce texte pourra être défini soit comme dt/dtr dans le sens plein des termes (texte d'origine dt/dtr), soit comme proto-dt (débuts ou essor du "deutéronomisme") ou dtr tardif (seconde floraison), soit comme pré-dt (texte-source, ou concordance accidentelle) ou post-dtr (imitation, ou concordance accidentelle). Il s'ensuit que l'on devra apporter des arguments sérieux pour démontrer qu'un texte ou passage du Tétrateuque, montrant les marques des tournures dt/dtr, est effectivement d'origine dt ou dtr.

Quels sont les critères qui nous permettent d'identifier un texte comme dt/dtr? N. Lohfink a consacré quelques pages remarquables à ce problème d'identification.[27] Les critères qu'il a avancés m'ont aidé, pour ma part, à rectifier et compléter ma propre critériologie.[28] C'est avec deux critères de base que je propose de travailler pour

---

[26] Voir une remarque de N. Lohfink, "Bundestheologie im Alten Testament. Zum gleichnamigen Buch von Lothar Perlitt", dans N. Lohfink, *Studien zum Deuteronomium und zur deuteronomistischen Literatur I* (Stuttgart, 1990), p. 360: "Im dtr Bereich wiederum scheint P. [= Perlitt] nicht genügend zwischen verschiedenen Schichten differenziert zu haben. Außerdem ist er im dtr Bereich dem Wort *bryt* semantisch wohl nicht gerecht geworden." Voir aussi Römer (n. 8), pp. 210–12.

[27] Lohfink (n. 14), pp. 323–33. Voir aussi W.H. Schmidt, "Elementare Erwägungen zur Quellenscheidung im Pentateuch", dans Emerton (éd.) (n. 22), pp. 31, 37–8, 45.

[28] Cf. Vervenne (n. 12), pp. 251–4.

juger du caractère dt/dtr (ou non-dt/non-dtr) d'un texte non sacerdotal dans le Tétrateuque:

(1) Le critère portant sur la *forme* du texte, c'est-à-dire:
- le critère linguistique:[29] le dénombrement statistique des occurrences de mots, d'expressions et de phrases,[30] l'analyse linguistique de ces données et la contre-épreuve à l'aide d'un corpus témoin (par ex. le Pentateuque, la collection Josué-Rois);
- le critère du style;
- le critère de la structure compositionelle.

(2) Le critère portant sur le *contenu* du texte, c'est-à-dire: les thèmes et conceptions théologiques.

L'application de ces critères—qui sont complémentaires—peut nous renseigner sur le caractère dt/dtr ou non-dt/non-dtr du texte. Si un texte ou un élément du texte ne présente ni la forme pleine ni le contenu établi du langage et de la théologie dt/dtr, mais uniquement un accord partiel et fragmentaire, alors ce texte ou cet élément ne peut pas être considéré comme un témoin direct et authentique de la tradition dt/dtr. Tout ce que l'on peut dire, c'est qu'il est en relation indirecte avec cette tradition. Dès lors, il faudra qualifier de tels composants d'éléments de source (pré-dt), d'essor (proto-dt), de seconde floraison (dtr tardif), ou d'imitation (post-dtr).

III

A propos du récit de la Mer figurant dans le livre de l'Exode, l'histoire de la recherche montre que l'inventaire des éléments deutéronomiques ne cessait d'augmenter depuis la fin du 19e siècle.[31] J.L. Ska constate qu' "il est devenu presque un lieu commun d'affirmer que le récit J d'Ex. xiv est coulé dans le moule des récits de "guerre sainte", qui serait "un concept propre à l'école deutéronomique ou deutéronomistique".[32]

---

[29] Voir aussi E. Talstra, *Solomon's Prayer. Synchrony and Diachrony in the Composition of I Kings 8, 14–61* (Kampen, 1993), pp. 9–86.

[30] Voir surtout les listes exposant la phraséologie dt/dtr dans Weinfeld (n. 3), pp. 320–65. Lohfink se réfère à bon droit à cet instrument de travail indispensable, auquel il ajoute l'utilisation d'instruments électroniques.

[31] Cf. Vervenne (n. 12), pp. 260–3.

[32] Ska (n. 1), pp. 454–5. Référence est faite à F. Stolz, *Jahwes und Israels Kriege* (Zürich, 1972), et H.H. Schmid, *Der sogenannte Jahwist. Beobachtungen und Fragen zur Pentateuchforschung* (Zürich, 1976).

Par conséquent, la couche dite Yahwiste remonterait à une époque plus tardive que l'opinion courante, en général, ne l'admet.

La critique récente se concentre, entre autres, sur les sections Ex. xiv 13–14, 24b, 25b, 28b, 30–1. A celles-ci l'on peut aussi ajouter l'ouverture du récit en Ex. xiii 17–22. Le bilan de l'étude critique de Ska est clair: "Ex. xiv . . . se rapproche davantage d'un récit de théophanie que d'un récit de combat. Son vocabulaire est en général indépendant de celui des textes dt/dtr, et plutôt antérieur" (p. 466).

Il me semble que l'analyse minutieuse de Ska montre à suffisance qu'il n'y a pas d'arguments sérieux, ni formels, ni sur le plan du contenu, pour soutenir la thèse d'un substrat dt/dtr, au sens strict des termes, en Ex. xiii 17–xiv 31. Cependant, on ne peut nier le fait que le texte du récit porte l'empreinte d'une tradition présentant des formes et des idées qui ont des points communs avec des textes dt/dtr. Une discussion plus élaborée nous ferait sortir du cadre que l'on s'était fixé pour la présente contribution. Toutefois, je me pencherai sur deux cas frappants, à savoir les formules (*yhwh*) *hlk lpny* (Ex. xiii 21 et xiv 19) et *yhwh nlḥm l* (Ex. xiv 14, 25),[33] qui montrent une relation formelle avec Dt. i 30–33.

L'opinion classique concernant le rapport entre Dt. i et les textes du Tétrateuque est bien représentée dans le commentaire qu'a fait M. Weinfeld de Dt. i 33. Selon lui, l'auteur de ce verset se serait servi des passages Ex. xiii 21; Nb. x 33 et xiv 14, qu'il aurait légèrement remaniés.[34] Cependant, des études récentes ont souligné le fait que ces textes sont issus d'une tradition deutéronomique commune. Pour certains exégètes, Ex. xiv, ainsi que Nb. xiv, reflèterait une étape préparatoire dans le processus de développement de la littérature dt/dtr établie,[35] tandis que pour d'autres il faudrait supposer une origine dtr,[36] et même post-dtr.[37] Cependant, ce qui manque particulièrement dans la plupart des études, c'est une analyse approfondie de la phraséologie des textes qui montrent des liens formels.[38]

---

[33] Voir déjà Vervenne (n. 12), pp. 263–7.

[34] *Deuteronomy 1–11: A New Translation with Introduction and Commentary* (New York, 1991), p. 149. Voir aussi Weinfeld (n. 3), p. 208.

[35] Voir Lamberty-Zielinski (n. 6), pp. 106–10; Vervenne (n. 10), pp. 84–5.

[36] P. Weimar, *Die Meerwundererzählung. Eine redaktionskritische Analyse von Ex. 13, 17–14, 31* (Wiesbaden, 1985), pp. 151–6.

[37] Blum (n. 7), pp. 175–6; Van Seters, *Life of Moses* (n. 7), pp. 128–39.

[38] Blum, par exemple, en se référant à une série de textes appartenant au corpus dt/dtr, prétend que la phrase "voir ce que Yhwh a fait" (*r'h 't 'šr 'śh yhwh*) est une expression

1. La formule (*yhwh*) *hlk lpny* est caractéristique des textes qui parlent de la marche des Israélites vers Canaan (Ex. xiii 21, xiv 19, xxiii 23, xxxii 1, 23, 34; Nb. xiv 14; Dt. i 30, 33, xxxi 8) ou se réfèrent à cet événement (Isa. xl 2, xlii 12, xlviii 8). On peut en dire autant de l'expression au Hifil *yhwh hwlyk*, qui figure en Dt. vii 2, 15, xxix 4; Jos. xxiv 3; Am. ii 10; Hos. ii 16; Isa. xlii 16, xlviii 21, lxiii 12, 13; Jér. ii 6, xxx 8, 9. En outre, la phrase (*yhwh*) *hlk lpny* est liée à plusieurs reprises à un motif de théophanie (Ex. xiii 21, xiv 19, xxiii 23, xxx 34; Nb. xiv 14; Dt. i 33). La formule (*yhwh*) *hlk lpny* est régulièrement construite au *qōtēl*. La forme participiale est utilisée en tant que prédicat en Ex. xiii 21; Nb. xiv 14; Isa. lii 12, et comme attribut en Ex. xiv 19; Dt. i 30, 33, xxxii 8. Les phrases en Ex. xxiii 23, xxxii 1, 23, 34 et Isa. xlv 2 usent d'un *yiqtōl*.

En ce qui concerne la relation entre Ex. xiii 21 et xiv 19, d'une part, et Dt. i 33, d'autre part, J. Van Seters pense que Dt. i 30–3 est une addition tardive,[39] mais son argumentation, qui suggère une origine post-dtr pour Ex. xiii–xiv, ne couvre que quelques lignes.[40] On trouve une analyse plus détaillée chez Ska.[41] Selon lui, il semble difficile d'admettre une dépendance d'Ex. xiii 21–2 (et xiv 19) vis-à-vis des textes dt/dtr. Il attire l'attention sur le fait que l'expression *ky yhwh ʾlhykm hhlk ʿmkm lhlḥm lkm* en Dt. xx 4 dépend de textes provenant en partie de la tradition la plus ancienne de l'Exode. Dt. xx 4, un texte qui est aussi mentionné par Van Seters, aurait "thématisé en une phrase ce qui était simplement juxtaposé dans le récit de l'Exode" (p. 460). Ska conclut que ce réflexe conscient, dans le Dt., laisse supposer qu'il est postérieur au récit de l'Exode (p. 461). Dt. i 33 reprend donc la formule d'Ex. xiii 21–2 en lui donnant une interprétation propre.[42]

---

typique du deutéronomiste. Toutefois, il omet de bien distinguer les différentes formules qui n'appartiennent pas uniquement aux traditions dt/dtr établies. En fait, il y a quatre types de formules, comme je l'ai expliqué ailleurs. Voir Vervenne (n. 12), p. 266.

39 *Life of Moses* (n. 7), p. 332, n. 42.

40 Ibid., pp. 371–2: "A similar example of such a retrospective extension of a speech of Moses is found in Deut. 11:4–7, which is clearly a post-Dtr addition and which also contains items from J's history (. . .) thus vs. 30b–33 at least should be considered as a post-DtrH addition." Voir aussi p. 376.

41 Voir plus haut la note 1.

42 Voir surtout N. Lohfink, "Darstellungskunst und Theologie in Dtn. 1,6–3,29", *Biblica* 41 (1960), pp. 105–34, et W.L. Moran, "The End of the Unholy War and the Anti-Exodus", *Biblica* 44 (1963), pp. 333–42. Voir cependant Römer (n. 8), pp. 208–9.

2. Outre Ex. xiv 14, 25, la formule *yhwh nlḥm* (Nifal) se trouve en Dt. i 30, iii 22, xx 4, Jos. x 14, 42, xxiii 3, 10; Isa. xxx 32, lxiii 10; Jér. xxi 5; Zach. xiv 3; 2 Chr. xx 29, xxxii 8; Néh. iv 14. L'expression est parfois combinée avec la préposition *l* (*dativus commodi*: Yhwh favorise les Israélites);[43] la mention des adversaires est introduite par les prépositions *b*, *ʿm* ou *ʾt*.[44]

En ce qui concerne la forme du verbe *lḥm*, il faut faire la distinction entre les *yiqṭōl, qāṭāl, qōṭēl et qĕṭōl* (inf.). La formule au *yiqṭōl* est utilisée en Ex. xiv 14; Dt. i 30; Néh. iv 14. La structure et l'ordre des mots sont les mêmes dans les constructions courtes en Ex. xiv 14 et Néh. iv 14. La formule en Dt. i 30 est—pour sa part—une construction longue, qui lie la phrase *yhwh nlḥm l* à *yhwh hlk lpny* (voir plus haut et comparez aussi avec Dt. xx 14). La formule au *qāṭāl* figure en Isa. xxx 32, lxiii 10; Jér. xxi 5; Zach. xiv 3; 2 Chr. xx 29. La forme *qōṭēl* est utilisée en Ex. xiv 25; Jos. x 14, 42 (*nlḥm*), et en Dt. iii 22; Jos. xxiii 3, 10 (*hwʾ hnlḥm*). Les formules en Dt. iii 22; Jos. x 42, xxiii 3, 10 sont longues, tandis que la phrase en Ex. xiv 25 est plus proche de celle de Jos. x 14. Enfin, l'expression en Dt. x 4 est à la forme *qĕṭōl* (inf.).

La formule *yhwh nlḥm* en Ex. xiv 14, 25 a une structure assez stéréotypée, qui se rapproche de celle des expressions en Deutéronome, Josué, Zacharie et Néhémie. L'ordre des mots est le suivant: sujet (Yhwh) et verbe (*nlḥm*). Néanmoins, il faut souligner que les formules en Dt. et Jos. sont plus amples.[45] L'expression *yhwh nlḥm* est utilisée quelques fois dans un discours prononcé avant d'entrer en guerre (Ex. xiv 14; Dt. i 30, iii 22, xx 4; Néh. iv 14; 2 Chr. xxxii 8).[46] D'autre part, *yhwh nlḥm* se trouve aussi comme simple constatation ou dans un contexte de confession (Ex. xiv 25; Jos. x 14, 42, xxiii 3, 10; Isa. xxx 32, lxiii 10; Jér. xxi 5; Zach. xiv 3; 2 Chr. xx 29). Tout comme Ex. xiv, la plupart des textes parlent d'un combat d'Israël. Il est frappant qu'en Ex. xiv 13–14, la formule *yhwh nlḥm* ne fonctionne pas comme motivation en vue de mobiliser les Israélites pour la bataille contre

---

[43] Ex. xiv 14, 25; Dt. i 30; iii 22, xx 4; Jos. x 14, 42, xxiii 3, 10; Néh. iv 14.

[44] Avec *b*: Ex. xiv 25; Isa. xxx 32, lxiii 10; Zach. xiv 3.—Avec *ʿm*: Dt. xx 4; 2 Chr. xx 29.—Avec *ʾt*: Jér. xxi 5.

[45] Voir Ska, p. 460, et P. Weimar, E. Zenger, *Exodus. Geschichte und Geschichten der Befreiung Israels* (Stuttgart, 1975), pp. 61–2.

[46] Weimar, Zenger, p. 59 ("Kriegsansprache"), et Rose (n. 7), p. 198 ("Ermutigungsorakel vor dem Kampf").

les Égyptiens. Au contraire, le discours de Moïse est un procédé de style qui a la fonction d'une exhortation "anti-guerre" (*Anti-Kriegsansprache*).[47] L'action de Yhwh, dont les Israélites ne sont que les spectateurs, est étroitement liée au thème de la foi (*hʾmyn*), thème qui se trouve aussi en Isa. vii 9; 2 Chr. xx 20, et, sous forme négative, en Dt. i 32 (*lʾ hʾmyn*). En outre, la formule *yhwh nlḥm* en Ex. xiv 13–14 explique le sens de l'expression *yhwh yšʿ* (v. 13: construction nominale). La combinaison des deux formules, qui associe guerre et salut, se trouve aussi en Dt. xx 4; Isa. lxiii 8–9; 2 Chr. xx 9, xxxii 22.

3. La question qui se présente à l'esprit est celle de savoir si Ex. xiii 21–2 et xiv 19, d'une part, et xiv 14, 25, d'autre part, sont des éléments de source, et donc pré-dt, comme Ska et d'autres savants le suggèrent, ou bien des éléments d'essor, qui, par suite, pourraient être qualifiés de proto-dt. Par ailleurs, le fait que le récit qu'on appelle JE semble être antérieur à la rédaction sacerdotale du récit de la Mer[48] ne signifie pas qu'il faille exclure *a fortiori* l'hypothèse que les composants de caractère deutéronomique puissent être des éléments de floraison tardive (dtr tardif) ou d'imitation (post-dtr). Il me paraît, par exemple, que le passage Ex. xiii 21–2 porte les traces d'une rédaction, ou d'une retouche, tardive, dans le sens qu'un éditeur post-dtr, et même post-sacerdotal aurait retouché le texte. J'ai suggéré cette intervention à propos d'une différence remarquable entre la forme textuelle de la Septante (texte court) et celle du TM (texte long).[49] Je ne vais pas reprendre les détails de l'analyse, mais en résumé: Ex. xiii 21 LXX = Dt. i 33 TM, et Ex. xiii 21 TM = Néh. ix 12, 19. Ex. xiii 21 pourrait donc refléter un remaniement tardif en vue de faire concorder les textes d'Ex. xiii 21 et de Néh. ix 12, 19.

Le fait même que les formules (*yhwh*) *hlk lpny* et *yhwh nḥm* se trouvent dans quelques textes qui datent d'une époque tardive n'est pas forcément preuve d'une origine dtr ou post-dtr d'Ex. xii 21–2, xiv 14, 19, 25. Et c'est une base trop étroite pour construire l'hypothèse d'une tradition proto-dt, qui aurait annoncé les débuts d'une école dt/dtr. Le caractère deutéronomique des quelques passages du récit de la Mer—qu'on ne pouvait traiter d'ailleurs, dans le cadre de la présente

---

[47] Weimar, Zenger, p. 63. Voir aussi Rose, pp. 60 sqq., et P. Weimar, "Die Jahwekriegserzählungen in Exodus 14, Josua 10, Richter 4 und 1 Samuel 7", *Biblica* 57 (1976), pp. 40–1.

[48] Voir plus haut, ainsi que la note 9.

[49] Voir Vervenne (n. 12), p. 267.

contribution, que de manière trop sommaire—doit provisoirement être déterminé comme pré-dt, dans ce sens que "l'école" deutéronomique/ deutéronomiste a probablement emprunté des matériaux à des textes existant dans le corpus que nous appelons le Tétrateuque (relation source-rédaction). Il est évident que d'autres textes, comme ceux d'Ex. xiii 3–16, xxiii 20–33 et xxxii–xxxiv, doivent être examinés pour conclure à l'existence d'une couche proto-dt (aspect essor).[50]

IV

"Ex. xiv contient-il un récit de 'guerre sainte' de style deutéronomiste?" Il m'a paru qu'il fallait poser la question d'une manière différente: le récit de la Mer reflète-t-il une *rédaction* de *type deutéronomique*? Les trois termes—"rédaction", "type" et "deutéronomique"—sont importants: le mot "rédaction" suggère une approche qui tient compte de la complexité du processus d'élaboration des textes du Tétrateuque; le mot "type" inclut tant la forme que le contenu des éléments textuels; le mot "deutéronomique", qui est modifié par le terme "type", embrasse toutes les "identités" des éléments textuels ou rédactionnels, c'est-à-dire pré-dt, proto-dt, dt, dtr, dtr tardif, et post-dtr.

Reste la question essentielle, celle de l'identification et de la détermination précises de l'origine de "cette rédaction de type deutéronomique": le "JE" (ou R^{JE}, si l'on veut) du récit de la Mer doit-il être situé à l'aube, au zénith ou au crépuscule du "deutéronomisme'? La réflexion que j'ai faite à ce sujet a abouti, me semble-t-il, à un élargissement et à un apport de nuances. Il est clair qu'Ex. xiii 17–xiv 31 contient des éléments de type deutéronomique. Il est très vraisemblable que ces éléments relèvent d'une rédaction qui est aussi à l'œuvre dans d'autres textes du Pentateuque (ou faut-il dire: de l'Hexateuque?). Mais je me hâte de rappeler qu'il faut encore faire une étude approfondie des composants deutéronomiques dans le récit de la Mer, en rapport avec les autres textes de l'Exode qui présentent des caractéristiques deutéronomiques.

---

[50] En ce qui concerne Ex. xxiii 20–33, voir H. Ausloos, "Deuteronomic and Deuteronomistic: What Do These Terms Mean? Some Methodological Remarks Based on the Study of Ex. 23, 20–33", dans M. Vervenne (éd.), *Studies in the Book of Exodus* (Leuven, 1996) pp. 481–500.

La conclusion à laquelle j'arrive, en fin de compte, est que l'examen de la naissance d'un texte du Tétratauque doit faire entrer beaucoup d'aspects en ligne de compte. Cependant, il n'est pas toujours possible de les embrasser tous à l'aide des hypothèses classiques. Il me semble que jusqu'à ce jour, nous sommes restés trop soumis à l'application des modèles établis dans la deuxième moitié du 19e siècle et au début du 20e siècle. Toutefois, il y a de nouvelles perspectives qui s'ouvrent. Je pense notamment à quatre approches qui sont en train de se développer graduellement:

(1) L'étude des retouches faites par des "rédacteurs" ou des "éditeurs" tardifs qui voulaient mettre en harmonie les textes existants (Dt, Histoire Dtr, P).[51]

(2) L'étude de la "zone" entre formation littéraire et production textuelle.[52]

(3) L'étude de la relation entre la Bible dite canonique et les textes de provenance non canonique (ou pseudépigraphiques). Il y a, en effet, des éléments textuels "canoniques" qui semblent provenir d'une source "non canonique" ou pseudépigraphique.[53]

(4) L'étude de la relation entres les textes bibliques et les traditions juives anciennes.[54]

---

[51] Les idées de Lohfink (voir plus haut la note 14) et E. Otto (voir plus haut la note 21) sont novatrices à ce sujet.

[52] Voir la contribution d'A. van der Kooij dans le présent volume.

[53] Voir, par exemple, M. Vervenne, "All They Need is Love: Once More Genesis 6.1–4", dans J. Davies et al. (ed.) (n. 13), pp. 19–40.

[54] Voir la contribution d'A. Rofé dans le présent volume.

HEBREW AND SYRIAC TEXTS OF THE BOOK OF JOB

by

MICHAEL WEITZMAN
London

The extant Hebrew and Syriac texts of any biblical book share a common origin. Yet the semantic correspondence between the Hebrew of the MT and the Syriac of the extant manuscripts of the Peshiṭta (P)[1] is often elusive, even with due allowance for the diversity of modern views on the sense of the Hebrew; and sometimes it breaks down altogether. These problems are particularly acute in the difficult book of Job. This paper is concerned with serious discrepancies, rather than cases where P has understood the Hebrew in a manner acceptable to modern scholarship but adjusted it for the benefit of readers, e.g. by removing a metaphor[2] or anomaly.[3]

In principle, there are three reasons for semantic discrepancy between P and the MT. First, the Hebrew *Vorlage* before the translator may have differed from the MT. Second, the translator may have modified the sense. Third, the text of the Syriac translation may have suffered change in transmission.

Each of these explanations has its limits. A different Hebrew *Vorlage* must bear a credible relationship to the MT in palaeographic terms: the putative Hebrew variant in the *Vorlage* may be the source of the MT reading, or a development thereof, or both may be separate developments from some supposed earlier reading. As to inner-Syriac change, the putative original Syriac text must relate better to the MT than does the existing Syriac text; moreover, the existing text must be explicable as a development thereof, through accidental or deliberate change.

---

[1] Although Peshiṭta Job seems to offer no internal evidence, a date in the 2nd century AD seems likely, as proposed for Genesis by S.P. Brock in "A Palestinian Targum Fragment in Syriac", *JJS* 46 (1995), pp. 271–282, esp. p. 275, and for Isaiah by A. van der Kooij, *Die alten Textzeugen des Jesajabuches* (Göttingen, 1981), p. 295.

[2] E.g. iii 21: MT *wayyaḥpĕrūhū* "and they dig for it", P *wbāʿēn leh* "... seek it".

[3] E.g. at xlii 11 in the MT, all Job's relatives and friends came to eat with him in his house "and they grieved for him (*wayyānūdū lō*) and comforted him". P instead writes that they came to his house "where they had grieved for him ..." *(d'akrī(w) (h)waw ʿlaw(hy))*, so that they do not grieve after his restoration.

Finally, translation technique has to be both rational and coherent. Any semantic discrepancy ascribed to this cause must have arisen through some logical procedure. When all such passages are taken together, moreover, the overall impression of the translation technique in the whole book[4] must show a measure of consistency.

Thus no one of the three possible explanations suffices in itself to explain all the semantic discrepancies. On the other hand, these limitations are not stringent enough to identify in each case of semantic discrepancy in the book of Job which of the three factors is responsible. However, where all else is equal, an explanation through translation technique is to be preferred. The transmission of the Hebrew text, as well as of the Syriac, was in principle intended to be faithful and mechanical.[5] A Hebrew variant in the *Vorlage*, or an inner-Syriac change, will (at least as a rule) imply failure somewhere in the transmission of a sacred text, while an explanation in terms of translation technique entails the more probable eventualities of either creative interpretation or sheer puzzlement on the part of the translator.

We need, then, to build up a picture of translation technique in the book of Job, particularly in relation to difficult Hebrew passages. Whether the translator understood the text well or not, he had to produce a translation. To discharge that duty, he must have allowed himself certain devices. The aim here is to identify those devices, as specifically and as economically as possible. Obviously, it is impossible to discuss every semantic discrepancy between the Hebrew and Syriac texts of Job; but the devices identified here should be capable of explaining every one of those discrepancies, apart from those arising from inner-Hebrew or inner-Syriac textual differences.

The procedure will be inductive and in some measure subjective. This is inevitable, given that we are trying to reconstruct the translator's reasoning. A wholly objective analysis, by contrast, would have to confine itself to formal features which were not the translator's prime concern, and so could not explain fully the many discrepancies in meaning.[6]

---

[4] Or rather, in the translation unit (i.e. the work of a single translator); but there is no evidence of more than one translator. Note, however, the alternation between *ḥasinā*ʾ and ʾ*alāhā*ʾ to render Heb. *šadday*, as pointed out by G. Rignell, *The Peshiṭta to the Book of Job Critically Investigated with Introduction, Translation, Commentary and Summary* (Stockholm, 1994), p. 365. This book was posthumously edited by the author's brother, Dr K.E. Rignell.

[5] On the Hebrew side this is an oversimplication to the extent that exegetical need can produce variants in the text, as for example in biblical texts and commentaries from Qumran.

[6] An analysis based primarily on formal linguistic features is H.M. Szpek, *Translation*

The primary intention, then, is not to take a position on any individual passage, but rather to explain the whole phenomenon of semantic discrepancy. Should any example chosen to illustrate a particular device appear unsatisfactory, it should be possible to substitute another and to rė-classify the disputed example—if the devices have been properly defined. Paramount here are the devices themselves, and the implied classification for the semantic discrepancies between the MT and P.

Cases where the translator worked within the constraints of the consonantal text

In this broad category fall those cases of discrepancy in sense where a semantic path can nevertheless be traced from the MT to P. Here the translator had room for manoeuvre in three respects. First, he may have had a selection of lexical items to which he could attribute a given Hebrew form, given that the *Vorlage* was unvocalised and that he could if necessary set aside any tradition of vocalisation. Second, once a lexical item was identified, its sense could be stretched. Third, the grammatical framework of the lexical items could be freely changed.

These three devices are all illustrated in xl 2a:

MT *hărōb ʿim-šadday yissōr*
P *sagiʾin ʾenon melkaw[hy] dʾalāhāʾ*
"many are the counsels of God"

Here the lexical item *rab* "many" rather than *roôb* "quarrel" is identified, the sense of *ysr* is extended from "chastise" to "counsel", the preposition *ʿim* is ignored and the word order changed.

Further notes on these three devices:

(a) Unusual identifications of lexical items may run in a series, for example at xxviii 4a:

MT *pāraṣ naḥal mēʿim-gār*
P *turʿtā īret(w) men ʿammāʾ giyorāʾ*
"they inherited the pass from a foreign people"

Here P finds the Hebrew lexical items *pereṣ* "breach", *nāḥal* "inherit", *ʿam* "people" and *gēr* "stranger". In all of these, P differs from the

---

Technique in the Peshiṭta to Job: A Model for Evaluating a Text with Documentation from the Peshiṭta to Job (Atlanta, 1992).

construal of the text in the MT or in modern interpretations, yet the result well fits the context of a mysterious place where precious metals are mined.

A special possibility open to this translator was to understand the Hebrew word in its Syriac sense, e.g.:

vi 9 MT *wīdakkĕʾēnī*, P *wanĕdakkēn(y)* "let him cleanse me"

In a few such cases, however, it can be argued that the Syriac points to the true Hebrew sense and thus that there is no semantic discrepancy, e.g.

xxii 25 MT *wĕkesep tōʿāpōt*, P *waksep ḥušbānin*

P has connected *tōʿāpōt* with Syr. *ʾap* "double, multiply",[7] and has stretched that to "reckoning, calculation". The *Revised English Bible* agrees with P as to the lexical item present in the Hebrew and renders: "silver in double measure".

(b) Special extensions of the sense may arise from the ambiguity of the Syriac equivalent, e.g.:

xi 4 MT *zak liqḥī* P *kēnāʾīt ʾetdabret* "rightly was I treated"

In the simple stem, Syriac *dbr* means "take" and is a common equivalent of Hebrew *lqḥ*, with a personal object. The translator has however utilised the equivalence in order to take *dbr* in the different sense "treat", which lies well beyond the range of the Hebrew word.

(c) An extreme case of grammatical modification is addition or omission of a negative, e.g. iv 4a "your words will *not* raise the sick".[8] This recurs at iv 16b, vii 3b (unless corrupt), ix 15a, xii 3c, 6c, xiii 21a, xiv 16a, xvi 5b, xvii 4b, xviii 5b, xxxiv 36b.

Doublets are frequent in Peshiṭta Job,[9] and some may be due to hesitation between alternative treatments allowed by these devices. For example, xx 4b is rendered twice, with the opening word *minnī* taken first as "since" and then as the interrogative "who?" (Syr. *mannū*).

---

[7] The latter appears, for example, in a discourse ascribed to Ephrem: the fragrance of the ointment (Luke vii 38) that came upon Christ was multiplied one-hundredfold (*ḥad bm(ʾ)ā ʿap (h)wā rēḥeh*). See T.J. Lamy (ed.), *Sancti Ephraem Syri Hymni et Sermones* 1 (Mechliniae, 1882), p. 367, lines 12, 14.

[8] This device recurs in other books of P, and in the Targums, as noted by M.L. Klein, "Converse translation: a targumic technique", *Biblica* 57 (1976), pp. 515–37. Here P did not recognize the Hebrew imperfect usage.

[9] These are listed by E.P. Dhorme, *Le livre de Job* (Paris, 1926), p. clxxiv.

Manipulation of the Hebrew consonantal text

Here we may classify passages where the translator could apparently construct nothing meaningful from the lexical items which he found in the consonantal text, and so deliberately misread the text itself. Thus Heb. *rahab* at ix 13, xxxvi 12 was treated as "many" (*rab*). At xxiv 11, the obscure *yaṣhīrū* is rendered *maghĕnin* "they lie down"; perhaps the translator misread the Hebrew as *yighărū*, rendered with the root *ghn* by P thrice in Kings. Again, at xv 27–

MT *wayyaʿaś pīmāh ʿălē-kāsel*
P *waʿbad kimāʾ lʿel men ʿyutāʾ*

P has treated Heb. *pīmāh* as if it were *kīmāh*, reaching the sense: "he [the wicked] places Pleiades above Aldebaran",[10] or in other words is arrogant enough to rearrange the heavens.

The word misread may then be taken in a Syriac sense, as at xvii 6–

MT *tōpet lĕpānīm*
P *taḥpitāʾ ʿal ʾappayhon*

The translator treated the first Hebrew word as if it had an extra consonant: *tḥpt*.

It may be objected that in such cases we should rather assume that the translator had a different Hebrew text in black and white. Against this, however, we find a number of doublets where each rendering implies a different reading of the Hebrew. Thus xxxiii 14b is rendered twice, with the first Hebrew word read alternatively as *ūbištayim* and *ūbiśĕpātayim*. Further examples:

(i) xxxv 15:

MT *wĕlōʾ-yādaʿ bappaš mĕʾōd*
P *wlāʾ mabʾeš lnapšeh* "and he does not harm himself"

Although the consonants of the third word are *bpš* in the MT, P suggests two alternative readings: *byš* and *npš*. The translator apparently felt unable to render the remaining Hebrew words without marring the sense.

[10] This is one possible identification of the star called *ʿyūta* in Syriac; see C. Brockelmann, *Lexicon Syriacum* (2nd edn, Halle, 1928), col 523b.

(ii) xxxix 18:

MT *tamrī* P *tettrīm 'a(y)k deqlā'* "will rise like a date-palm"

Here P has read the Hebrew alternatively as *tāmār* and *tārīm*.

In passages of this sort, the two alternative readings of the Hebrew could hardly both have stood in the *Vorlage*. At least one must therefore result from deliberate manipulation, which was thus one of the translator's devices.[11]

Such misreading recalls the rabbinic Al-Tiqre.[12] While this device usually varies vowels or vowel letters only, it occasionally exchanges consonants that are phonetically distant, or introduces or omits a whole letter, e.g.

	MT	read as:	
Gen. xx 16	*kĕsūt*	*kēhūt*	(B. Meg. 28a)
Deut. xxxii 17	*śĕʿārūm*	*šāʿūm*	(Sifre ad loc.)
Ezek. xvi 7	*baʿădī ʿdāyīm*	*bĕʿedrē ʿădārīm*	(B. Sot. 11b)
Qoh. viii 10	*qĕbūrīm*	*qĕbūṣīm*	(B. Git. 56b)

In P, however, the scale of the phenomenon is altogether larger.

Manipulation of the Syriac equivalent

Occasionally, it may be that the translator began with a Syriac equivalent of a Hebrew word and deliberately misread that, e.g. at xv 11a–

MT *hamĕʿaṭ mimmĕkā tanḥūmōt 'ēl*
P *'azgar mennāk luḥāmaw(y) dʾalāhā'*
"withhold from yourself the rebukes of God"

There is no semantic link between the MT and P, but *'azgar* looks much like *zʿōr*, which is a common equivalent of Heb. *mĕʿaṭ*, while *luḥāmaw(y)* bears an obvious resemblance to *nuḥāmaw(y)*, which would be obtained by rendering Heb. *tanḥūmōt* in the Syriac sense. This first seems a case of inner-Syriac corruption. If we restore the obvious

---

[11] Some 200 instances of this phenomenon in Psalms were assembled by A. Vogel, "Studien zum Pešiṭta-Psalter", *Biblica* 32 (1951), pp. 32–56, 198–231, 336–63, 481–502; see pp. 208–13.

[12] A. Rosenzweig, "Die Al-Tiqri-Deutungen", in M. Brann and I. Elbogen (ed.), *Festschrift zu Israel Lewy's siebzigstem Geburtstag* (Breslau, 1911), pp. 204–53.

Syriac equivalents, however, the English equivalent will be: "little for you is the resurrections of God" (with discord of number between subject and predicate). This hardly makes enough sense to be the translator's finished work. It is rather as if he first wrote a provisional Syriac translation on a "scratchpad" and then adjusted the consonants until satisfactory sense was reached. That *ʾazgar* goes back to the translator seems confirmed by the second half of the verse, which likewise has an imperative verb:

wmallel banyāḥ lwāt napšāk

Similarly at xli 1a–

MT *tōḥaltō nikzābāh*
P *šaryāʾ raglāk*
"your foot is loosened"

Semantically, P utterly differs from the MT, but the Syriac words resemble *šurāyāʾ* "beginning" and *dgl* "deceive", which are normal renderings of the Hebrew words (the first being re-vocalised *tĕḥillātō*). Yet the latter Syriac words, if restored, hardly yield acceptable sense, especially in context: "the beginning deceived you". The change to the present text seems due to the translator himself.

Rignell ([n. 1] pp. 5, 367) found this phenomenon so widespread that he inferred two stages in the translation process. In the first, annotations showing the Syriac equivalents of individual Hebrew words were added to a Hebrew text between the lines or in the margin. Next, a continuous Syriac translation was obtained from those annotations, which were sometimes misread. The "scratchpad" theory proposes instead that such manipulation of the Syriac equivalents was confined to isolated passages. If the phenomenon is denied altogether, the original translation must have contained some well-nigh unintelligibly literal readings.

Guesswork

In all the cases yet considered, the translator has in some way accommodated every word of the Hebrew text, albeit after modifying the sense or the Hebrew text or its primary Syriac equivalent. Sometimes, however, these devices were insufficient. The translator was then forced to set aside a difficult Hebrew word altogether, and instead to guess a meaning that would fit the context.

Guesswork may be identified by the following criteria. First, P may use vague wording, e.g.

(a) vi 16

MT *(ʿālēmō) yitʿallem-šāleg*
P *sgī talgāʾ* "snow was much"

(b) xi 20

MT *ūmānōs ʾābad minhem*
P *wtuqphon nēʾbad menhon*

Words for "strength" (from roots *tqp, ʿšn)* are frequent in P, as in the Targums, to render Hebrew words of unknown sense.[13]

(ii) P's wording, though specific, could easily be inferred from the context. Here two possibilities cannot always be distinguished: the translator may not have recognized the Hebrew word at all, or he may have known its normal meaning but rejected it as unsuited to the context. Examples:

(a) xxxix 15a

MT *regel tĕzūrehā*
P *regleʾ dṭayrāʾ ʾīt lāh*
"she has bird's feet"

P did not recognize *tĕzūreha* but knew that this section concerned a bird.

(b) xxxi 10

MT *tiṭḥan lĕʾaḥēr ʾištī wĕʿālehā yikrĕʿūn ʾăḥērīn*
P *ʾelāʾ ṭeḥnat lʾaḥrēnin ʾa(n)tat(y) wʾepat bdukāʾ ʾḥrēnyāʾ*

Here P innocently took "grind" in the first line as part of the process of making bread. He was thus baffled by *yikrĕʿūn in* the second half, and so guessed a suitable sense: "and she baked in another place".

Where the text seemed incomplete, guesswork could result in addition rather than substitution. Thus xxvii 10 in the MT begins with *ʾim*, introducing a question: "Will he . . . call upon God at every time?"

---

[13] R.P. Gordon, "The Citation of the Targums in Recent English Translations" (RSV, JB, NEB)", *JJS* 36 (1975), pp. 50–66. On p. 51 he traces this tendency back to the Aramaic translation of Job from Qumran.

P however took *ʾim* as "if", and, finding no apodosis, added: "God will answer him and hear him".

Influence from outside the text

Where the Syriac cannot be credibly traced back to the Hebrew, and no rational basis for guesswork can be identified, two possibilities remain. Either the translator had in mind something external to the text being rendered—i.e. another text or some theological doctrine—or else the Syriac text has been damaged in transmission. Cases where P has thought of a different text fall into the following categories:

(a) P draws on a neighbouring passage, e.g. vi 10

MT *waʾăsallĕdāh*, P *wʾeštamleʾ*

Here P thought of the previous verse, where Heb. *wībaṣṣĕʿēnī* "and may he finish me" was rendered *wanšalmayn(y).*

This device of borrowing from closely neighbouring verses will at least lend coherence to the translation, if not accuracy.

(b) P looked farther afield in Job, e.g. x 10–

MT *keḥālāb tattīkēnī*
P *wʾa(y)k ḥalbāʾ rabbaytān(y)*
"and as with milk you reared me".

The association of this verb with milk seems to derive from iii 12: "why did knees rear me (MT *qiddemūnī*, P *rabbyan*(*y*)), and from breasts why did I suck?"

(c) P examined another occurrence of the problematic word in a different biblical book, and—at least in some cases—borrowed the Syriac equivalent. Because of the relevance of such cases to possible relationships among the different Syriac translators, this phenomenon is treated more fully below.

(d) P consulted a text outside the Hebrew Bible, as, arguably, at xx 22–

MT *bimĕlōʾt sipqō yēṣer lō*
P *bakyāltāʾ dʾakīl netpraʿ*
"with the measure that he measured he will be punished"

Although the doctrine of "measure for measure" is biblical, the first occurrences of the expression are in post-biblical texts such as Mishnah

Sota I 7 and Mark iv 24.[14] There is a partial parallel in the Targum, which will be discussed below:

> *titmĕlēʾ saʾteh yitpĕraʿ mineh*
>
> his seah shall be filled; he shall be punished from it

Another case where the translator may have thought of an extra-biblical text is xxii 15–16. The opening phrase in both P and MT runs: "Do you observe the everlasting (i.e. ancient) path . . .?", but P continues:

> . . . which the people (*ʿammāʾ*) of falsehood trod not at their (right) time; and on the other side of the river they were checked (*ʾetklī*(*w*)), and they did not remember (*wlāʾ ʿehad*(*w*)) the one who set their foundations.

The relevant words in the MT are:

> *ʾăšer dārĕkū mĕtē-ʾāwen: ʾăšer-qummĕṭū wĕlōʾ-ʿēt nāhār yūṣaq yĕsōdām*

Apparently, the translator first omitted *qummĕṭū*, and added "on the other side" before *nāhār*. He then went back to *qummĕṭū* which he rendered correctly—since Syriac has the related root *qmṭ* "grasp"—and translated the following words afresh. This time, however, the consonants *ʿ[tn]hr* were interpreted as *ʿhd* "remember", by deliberate misreading and by ascribing a Syriac sense to the resulting form. This would explain why the root *ʿhd* occurs here only in Peshiṭta Job; elsewhere, the root for "remember" is *dkr*. Finally, *yūṣaq w*as taken as active (*yōṣēq*).

This combination of devices suggests that the translator was aiming for a specific overall meaning. Perhaps he thought of the Ephraimites, who, according to rabbinic tradition, "ignored the stipulated term" (*ʿābĕrū ʿal haqqēṣ*) and so left Egypt for Canaan prematurely, only to be killed by the Philistines at Gath.[15] The proof-text adduced by the rabbis is Ps. lxxviii 9; according to neighbouring verses, the Ephraimites were "evil and rebellious" (lxxviii 7) and "forgot" the works of God (lxxviii 11). P's references to falsehood and to not remembering God may confirm that P had this tradition in mind. P's phrase "the other side of the river" is compatible, since the Ephraimites

[14] Though the rabbis (e.g. at B. Shab. 105b) read it into *bĕsa(ʾ)ssĕʾāh* at Isa. xxvii 8, which they interpreted as *bĕ-* plus *sĕʾāh* (a measure) repeated.

[15] So Mekilta Beshallaḥ 1, and other sources cited by R.P. Gordon, "ΚΑΙ ΤΟ ΤΕΛΟΣ ΚΥΡΙΟΥ ΕΙΔΕΤΕ (Jas. V. 11)", *JTS*, N.S. 26 (1975), pp. 91–5.

must have crossed the "river of Egypt", south of Gaza; P's addition "other side" speaks against the alternative possibility that Pharaoh at the Red Sea was intended.

(e) An external theological doctrine, namely life after death, e.g. vii 7b

MT *lōʾ-tāšūb ʿēnī lirʾōt ṭōb*
P *wtehpok ʿayn(y) lmeḥzāʾ ṭābtāʾ*

Converse translation turns denial of immortality to affirmation.

xxx 23

MT *kī-yādaʿtī māwet tĕšībēnī ūbēt mōʿēd lĕkol-ḥāy*
P *mekēl yādaʿnā dmen mawtāʾ tahpkan(y) lbayt waʿdāʾ dkulhon ḥayye*
"for I know that from death you will return me to the gathering place of all the living"

Here again grammatical elements were treated freely to yield the desired sense.

xlii 6a

MT *ʾemʾas wĕniḥamtī*
P *ʾeštoq wʾetnaḥam*

The normal sense of Syriac *nḥm* suggests that the last word be rendered: "I shall be resurrected", especially as this verse is the last uttered by Job. Such an intepretation existed before P, possibly in Aramaic, because the addition at the end of Job in the LXX states that Job will be resurrected and that it is interpreted thus (reading οὕτως for οὗτος) ἐκ τῆς Συριακῆς βίβλου. One must note, however, that although this meaning for *nḥm* is well attested in later Syriac, there is no parallel in the Old Testament.

(f) For completeness, we must consider whether P in Job was influenced by other biblical versions. There is no evidence that the translator consulted the LXX, despite the difficulty of the Hebrew;[16] he may have been deterred by the many lacunae which make the LXX about one-sixth shorter than the MT in Job, as Origen noted (PG xiii 1293 f).

In Baumann's view, P in Job is influenced by the Targum, or rather by a putative earlier form of the existing medieval text. However,

---

[16] So E. Baumann, *ZAW* 19 (1899), p. 19, and Rignell, p. 328.

Baumann's lengthy list of parallels between P and the Targum in Job contains hardly any not readily attributable to polygenesis.[17] Thus, no relationship between P and the Targum can be inferred when both translate literally, or fill in an elliptic Hebrew phrase,[18] or make an obvious guess at an obscure Hebrew word.[19] Only in two places does the similarity seem significant. The first is the reference to "measure for measure" at xx 22. The other is in one of two alternative versions of the Targum at xxxvi 20–

MT *ʾal-tišʾap hallāylāh*
P *wmen duḥāqāʾ dablelyāʾ*
"and (you will not be afflicted) by the pressing in the night"

Tg *lāʾ tidḥōq bĕlelyāʾ* "do not press in the night"

This is an unusual lexical identification: Heb. *šʾp* is taken as *šwp* "press, bruise" (as in Gen. iii 15), which is equated with Aramaic *dḥq*. The roots *šʾp* and *dḥq* are also equated in a Midrash on Job v 5.[20]

In either passage, the shared material is better integrated in P than in the Targum, and this suggests that any influence may have originated from P. There is no external evidence of the existing Targums on the Writings (other than Esther) until the 10th century CE. During the Islamic period, P was consulted by Jewish scholars, and this is a likely background for the borrowing of P as the basis of the Targum on Proverbs. Jewish regard for the P version of Job specifically is attested in the biblical commentary of Rabbi Joseph ben Nissim Masnut of Aleppo (13th century): in four verses from Job, the citations which he ascribes to the Targum in fact come from P.[21]

Abdication of translation role

Relatively seldom did obscurity in the Hebrew force the translator to abdicate his role altogether, either by leaving an obscure translation or by omitting words. An example of the former is xi 17–

---

[17] *ZAW* 19 (1899), pp. 64–5; 20 (1900), pp. 286–91.

[18] E.g. xl 18a "his bones are *as strong as* (tubes of) bronze".

[19] E.g. *rahab* taken as "many" (*rab*) at ix 13.

[20] Leviticus Rabba 28 and parallels. The verse is applied to various heroes, and the last line (*wĕšāʾap ṣammīm ḥēlām*) taken to mean that their followers (*mĕṣummātīm*) pushed away (*dāḥaq*) the wealth of their adversaries.

[21] M.P. Weitzman, "Peshiṭta, Septuagint and Targum", *OCA* 247 (1992) (pp. 51–84), 81–3.

MT *ūmiṣṣohŏrayim yāqūm ḥāled*
P *wmen ṭahrā' nqum ḥeprā'*
"and from noon, digging will arise"

Evidently *ḥāled* was understood on the basis of *ḥōled* "mole", but readers must have been puzzled.

Odd words that the translator could not accommodate might be omitted, e.g. "thither" at i 21. Omission on a larger scale is mostly confined to particularly intractable passages (xxix 6, xxx 3–4, xxxviii 25a, xli 21a, 22–24a); note also the compression of xxxix 3–4 to about half their length. On the other hand, the omission of xl 16, which is not especially difficult, perhaps suggests physical damage to the *Vorlage*.

Links between Job and other biblical books in P

The following are examples of renderings which P in Job has borrowed from other biblical books.

(i) i 10

MT *śaktā baʿădō*
P *'aggent īdāk ʿlaw(hy)*

The reference to the hand may have been introduced from Exod. xxxiii 22, where the MT has *wĕśakkōtī kappī* and P *'aggen īd(y)*.

(ii) x 17a

MT *tĕhaddēš ʿēdekā negdī*
P *wamahre' 'a(n)t zaynāk luqbal(y)*
"and you rouse your weaponry against me"

The verb *maḥre'* is probably, as G.H. Bernstein supposed, a corruption of *mḥadet* "(you) renew".[22] Whence, however, the noun *zaynāk*? It seems that the translator understood the Hebrew as if vocalized *ʿedyĕkā*, and consulted Exod. xxxiii 5–6, where Heb. *ʿădī* is rendered *zaynā'*, as in the Targums.

(iii) xx 2

[22] "Syrische Studien I. Beiträge zur Berechtigung einzelner Stellen und Wörter in den bisher gedruckten syrischen Werken", *ZDMG* 3 (1849), pp. 385–428, 392.

MT *lākēn śĕʿippay yĕšībūnī ūbaʿăbūr ḥūšī bī*
P *meṭṭul helkāt(y) ʾatibun(y) wmeṭulāt(y) kattar(w) lī*
"for the sake of my steps, answer me; and for my sake, wait for me"

To render *śĕʿippay*, P found the related word *śarʿappay* at Ps. cxxxix 23, which is likewise rendered *helkāt(y)*, on the basis of the LXX τὰς τρίβους μου. Likewise, the rendering of Heb. *ḥūš* "hasten" by its near-opposite *kattar* is also characteristic of P in Psalms, notably but not exclusively at lv 9, where the LXX again agrees: προσεδεχόμην.

(iv) xx 10b

MT *wĕyādā(y)w tāšēbnāh ʾōnō*
P *wīdaw(hy) nawšṭān ʿal yaldeh*
"and his hands will stretch out against his offspring"

The equivalence in the last word echoes Deut. xxi 17, where *rēʾšīt ʾōnō* is rendered *rēš yaldeh.*

(v) Job xxxi 34c

MT *wāʾeddōm lōʾ-ʾēṣēʾ pātaḥ*
P *wabmamllāʾ dsepwātāʾ lāʾ rnīt*
"and on the speech of lips I did not meditate"

The rendering of the first Hebrew word suggests that the translator of Job consulted Ps. iv 5, where *wĕdōmmū* is rendered *warnaw*. This equivalence seems due originally to the translator of Psalms, who guessed on the basis of the neighbouring phrase: "speak in your hearts". In Job, the translator then apparently took *petaḥ* as the organs of speech (cf. Mic. vii 5 *pitḥē pīkā*), and selected an expression from a similar context in Psalms: the protestation of innocence at xvii 14. P's uncertainty led him to add an alternative rendering (where the first Hebrew word is instead read *wĕʾādām*) beforehand:

wbarnāšāʾ lāʾ ʾahpĕkēt btarʿāʾ

"and I turned back no man in the gate"

(vi) Job xxxi 35b

MT *hen-tāwī šadday yaʿănēnī*
P *gurāgaw(hy) dʾalāhāʾ makkun(y)*

The rendering of *tāwī* goes back to Ps. lxxviii 41, where the MT has *hitwū* and P *gareg(w)*, again with the LXX παρώξυναν. A little later, P adds an alternative translation:

> *ʾen ʾītaw(hy) ʾalāhāʾ naʿnēn(y)*

Here *tāwī* has instead been rearranged and taken in a Syriac sense.

Job vii 6a may fall into the same category:

MT *yāmay qallū minnī-ʾāreg*
P *yawmay qal(w) men gdād qawīn*

Now the Hebrew root *ʾrg* occurs again at Isa. xxxviii 12–

MT *qippadtī kāʾōrēg ḥayyay middallāh yĕbaṣṣĕʿēnī*
P *ʾetqped(w) ʾa(y)k sīres ḥayay wʾa(y)k nawlāʾ dqarib lmetgaddādu* "my life was shortened like threads and like a web close to being cut off"

It is hardly a coincidence that the root *gdd* occurs in both passages. It may be that *gdād* in Job has been borrowed from Isaiah, and thus means "cutting off". Thus P would mean: "my days are swifter than the snapping-off of threads". This would yield a sentiment similar to ix 25, which in P begins with the same two words.[23]

An explicit reference to another biblical passage occurs in the list of precious materials surpassed by wisdom (xxviii 15–19). P's final phrase is: "the stones of the ephod are not equal to her". Apparently, the translator was puzzled by many items in the list, and thought of Exod. xxviii 12–21 (which in fact describes the breastplate) because both mention the stones *sappīr* and *šōham*. Note, however, that P's guesses in these verses owe less to Exodus than to some conventional listing of precious materials.[24]

It may seem surprising that the P translator of Job should have been ignorant of the meaning of a word which he was nevertheless capable of tracking down in another book. However, to track down a parallel form requires nothing more than hard work, which in principle is

---

[23] H.M. Szpek, "The Peshitta on Job 7:6: 'My Days are Swifter (?) than an *ʾrg*'", *JBL* 113 (1994), pp. 287–90, instead suggests that the sense of P—and indeed of the MT—is: "my days are more trifling than the thrum of looms".

[24] Here occur, for example, all items in line 83 of the Hymn of the Soul: *dahbāʾ, bruleʾ, qarqedneʾ, ptawtkeʾ*.

always in supply. In any case, the effort need not have been prodigious, because the different translators may have conferred. To recognize a word, by contrast, requires knowledge of the meaning, which, once lost in a given community, cannot be recovered—except through the unusual possibilities of successful guesswork or recourse to a different community. Hence we must beware of judging the ancient translators by the standards of our own knowledge, which has been drawn from many different circles of tradition, including the different versions as well as rabbinic and patristic exegesis. The knowledge available in any one circle in antiquity would have been far more restricted.

The drive for continuous sense

The translator's choice among the various devices at his disposal was often shaped by the desire to give coherent sense for an extended passage, as may be illustrated through xxxvi 16–20a.

The preceding verse (xxxvi 15) describes the salvation awaiting the righteous. In the MT, xxxvi 16 changes tack: the righteous are now warned not to be misled or bribed into adopting wicked ways. However, P still thinks of the happiness of the righteous, as well as the punishment of the wicked, and so guesses as necessary to achieve that understanding. P's rendering of these verses may be translated as follows:

> (16) And he will save you from the mouth of the oppressor, and (grant) relief instead of oppression, and set up a table filled with fatness. (17) And he will judge the wicked fully in judgement, and in judgement they will be caught. (18) In the fierceness of war he will not disturb you, and he will not let you lack for abundance of salvation. (19) He will be mighty over you to save you, and you will not be afflicted by all those mighty in strength (20) or by the pressing that is in the night; and he will give peoples in exchange for you and nations in exchange for yourself.

Here we encounter:

(16b) free treatment of grammatical elements: ignoring a negative
(17a) replacing second by third person
(17b) stretching of the sense of Hebrew words: *yitmōkū* "they grasp" rendered *nettaḥdūn* "they will be caught"

We also find unusual identification of lexical items in 20a (discussed above) and 19a: *šūʿăkā* derived from *yšʿ* "save".

Guesswork too is in evidence:

(16a) Heb. *hăsītĕkā* "he [the wicked] misleads you"; P *nšawzbāk* "he [God] will save you", inspired by *neštawzab* (for Heb. *yĕḥallēṣ*) in the previous verse.

(18b/19a) Heb. *ʾal-yaṭṭekkā: hăyaʿărōk*; P *netqap ʿlayk*

The overall interpretation is reinforced by borrowings from outside passages. Thus (20bc) in P evidently derives from Isa. xliii 4; the MT in Job has only *laʿălōt ʿammīm taḥtām*. Moreover, in (18) the addition of war in P attempts to clarify Heb. *ḥēmāh* through v 20b, where Eliphaz, in a similar vein to P here, promises the righteous man deliverance "in war from the sword". Through all these devices, P has achieved continuous sense, though accuracy is another matter.

Inner-Syriac corruption

Inner-Syriac corruption may be suspected where the existing text cannot be explained as an interpretation of the Hebrew, nor through any of the other factors yet considered. A few conjectures were proposed by Bernstein (pp. 391–2), including x 17 above, and many more by Baumann.[25]

Many of these conjectures deserve acceptance. However, it must not be forgotten that any restoration must relate well to the MT. The emendation proposed by Bernstein at iv 19 neglects this principle. Here both texts mention "those who dwell in houses of clay" and continue:

MT *ʾăšer ʿāpār yĕsōdām*
P *dabʿaprāʾ mšaklĕlin*

The usual meaning of Syr. *šaklel* is "complete", which makes poor sense. Bernstein (p. 392) emended to *mkalšin*, meaning: "which are plastered in earth (or dust)", on the basis of *mukallasat* in the Arabic daughter-version. However, the emended text cannot be linked with the MT. In fact no emendation is needed, because *šaklel* can also mean

[25] (1899), pp. 32–48.

"found", as elsewhere in P, e.g. at 1 Kgs v 31 and (in 9a1) at 1 Kgs vi 37, and also in the Targums (e.g. at Exod. ix 18).[26] Thus P as it stands agrees with the Hebrew, though the Arabic translator missed the ancient sense of *šaklel* and tacitly emended it.

The long list of conjectures by Baumann presupposes that Peshiṭta Job was a literal translation, and some would be superfluous on the basis of the more varied translation technique proposed here. Thus xxxvi 14b in the MT states that the wicked will die *baqqĕdēšīm* "as male prostitutes". In P, they instead die of hunger (*bkapnā'*). Baumann emends P to *bnakpe'* "among the chaste", to create some link with the Hebrew root *qdš*. More probably, however, the male prostitutes were either not recognized or deliberately excluded, and P instead guessed a common cause of death.

On the other hand, some conjectures could be added. A possible example occurs at iv 6a–

MT *hălō' yir'ātĕkā kislāteka*
P *hā' deḥltāk (h)ī ʿedlāyāk*
"behold your fear is your blame"

P makes little sense, nor is there any semantic path between the MT and P. The noun *ʿedlāyā'* apparently does not recur in the Old Testament Peshiṭta. Perhaps the last word in P was originally *ʿyutāk* "your star". The related Hebrew form *kesel* is rendered *ʿyutā'* at xv 23 (where the translator thought that the star *kĕsīl* was meant). Moreover, it gives fair sense, viz. that Job's fear (of God) was his emblem, or his guiding light.

Vorlage *different from the MT*

The Hebrew text obtained by retroversion of P is sometimes attractive. Thus at xli 24b, in the MT, the crocodile reckons the depths like "white hair" (*śybh*). P instead has "dry land", which seems easier and corresponds to Hebrew *ybšh*. However, if the above picture of P's translation technique is right, it is doubtful whether *ybšh* existed in P's *Vorlage*, rather than his mind.

[26] For further discussion see M.P. Weitzman, "The Originality of Unique Readings in Peshiṭta MS 9a1", in P.B. Dirksen and M.J. Mulder (ed.), *The Peshiṭta: its Early Text and History* (Leiden, 1988), pp. 225–58: see pp. 229–30.

It is safer to posit a different *Vorlage* where corroborating evidence exists, e.g.

x 8 MT *yḥd*, P (with the LXX) "afterwards", implying *ʾḥr*
xxix 7 MT *ʾkyn*, P *bāyšāʾ* "poor", implying *ʾby(w)n* (with a Hebrew manuscript)

Seldom, however, can the MT be corrected confidently on the basis of P. P is valuable rather as a record of interpretation, showing how—and how well—the Hebrew text was understood.

MICHAL UND DIE ANFÄNGE DES KÖNIGTUMS IN ISRAEL

von

INA WILLI-PLEIN
Hamburg

In der älteren israelitischen Geschichtsschreibung[1] kommt den Frauen um David[2] eine Schlüsselfunktion für die Anfänge des Königtums zu. Dabei geht es auch wesentlich um die Frage des Verhältnisses zwischen israelitischem Königtum, das erstmals von Saul als Stammeskönigtum[3] realisiert und nach der uns vorliegenden Darstellung von den Repräsentanten der zehn Stämme David in Ḥebron angetragen wurde, und Königtum in Juda.[4] Die für David bezeugte Personalunion zwischen beiden war von Anfang an gefährdet[5] und zerbrach bereits in der zweiten Generation. Der Bericht über die Verhandlungen zwischen den Stämmevertretern und Davids Enkel Rehabeam (1 Kön. xii 1–19) läßt erkennen, daß nach Meinung des Verfassers die jüngere Generation der Hofkreise in Jerusalem nicht mehr durchschaute, worum es eigentlich ging bzw. daß zumindest der Theorie nach der König über Israel ein *primus inter pares* war, dem allein der Konsens der

---

[1] Darunter verstehe ich vordtr. Geschichtsschreibung, die nach wie vor in der Einarbeitung ins dtr. Geschichtswerk zu finden ist, gegen z.B. J. Van Seters, *In Search of History. Historiography in the Ancient World and the Origins of Biblical History* (New Haven, Conn./London, 1983), dessen Darlegungen zur antiken Historiographie und zur Unterscheidung von "traditio-historical method" und "form critical analysis" allerdings unbedingt Beachtung finden sollten, um zu "give new impetus to the literary appreciation of the prose authors in the Bible especially in the understanding of the structure and unity of their work" (p. 17). Seiner These der Abhängigkeit der "court history" vom dtr. Geschichtswerk liegt die Annahme zugrunde, Dtr.H. könne die Davidsgeschichte (i.F. DHG) nicht in sein Werk aufgenommen haben, weil sein Anliegen gewesen sei, David als idealen König hinzustellen. Wäre denn die gegenteilige Tendenz nachdtr. denkbar?

[2] Vgl. I. Willi-Plein, "Frauen um David: Beobachtungen zur Davidshausgeschichte", in S. Timm und M. Weippert (eds), *Meilenstein. Festgabe für Herbert Donner* (Wiesbaden, 1995), pp. 349–61, deren methodische Erwägungen (v.a., pp. 350–1) und Ergebnisse hier vorausgesetzt werden.

[3] Über maximal 10 Stämme, vielleicht aber auch nur Benjamin

[4] Juda ist dabei eine primär territorial definierte Größe, vgl. dazu W. Zwickel, "Die Landnahme in Juda", *UF* 25 (1993), pp. 473–91.

[5] Vgl. dazu den in n. 2 genannten Aufsatz; ganz deutlich wird dies an den Aufständen Absaloms und Schebas, 2 Sam. xv–xx.

Stammesvertreter[6] seine Autorität sicherte. Die sogenannte Thronnachfolgeerzählung (TNE), deren Leitsatz die Frage ist, "wer sitzen wird auf dem Thron von euer Majestät"(1 Kön. i 20), schildert tatsächlich den Weg des Königtums von Israel über Juda nach Jerusalem und den allmählichen Verlust der israelitischen Komponente, der schließlich den endgültigen Dualismus von Nord- und Südreich bekräftigte.

Der Anfang der TNE bzw. der hier angenommenen Davidshausgeschichte (DHG)[7] ist offen.Teile der sogenannten Aufstiegsgeschichte Davids (AGD) gehören wesentlich dazu, und zwar sind dies die Teile, in denen Frauen um David thematisiert werden—ein Thema, das einerseits in der weiteren dtr. Geschichtsdarstellung nicht fortgeführt wird und andererseits zu deutlichen Konkurrenzerzählungen in der AGD geführt hat. V.a. die Rettung Davids vor dem depressiven Saul durch den Saulsohn Jonatan bildet eine Konkurrenzerzählung zur Rettung Davids durch die Saultochter Michal. Ist letztere durch die aus späterer Sicht theologisch empörende Kritik Michals am Ladetanz belastet, so ist die Beziehung zu Jonatan für den antiken Leser gewissermaßen makelloser Nachweis des gottgefälligen Übergangs des israelitischen Königtums von Saul auf David: Der "Kronprinz" selbst hatte ja mit dem (bereits, falls die proph. Erzählschicht nicht jünger ist, prophetisch designierten?) Hoffnungsträger (*nāgîd*) einen Bund geschlossen und darüber hinaus ihm mit den Freundschaftsgaben (1 Sam. xviii 4) gewissermaßen die Insignien künftiger Würde in einem inoffiziellen Investiturakt übertragen.

Diese Darstellung der durch keinen Fehler getrübten Freundschaft zweier junger Männer, die je für sich ohne Tadel sind, ist wohl vor allem aus Davids Leichenlied auf Saul und Jonatan herausgesponnen (2 Sam. i 23).

Beiden Erzählungen liegt das Motiv der engen Verbindung Davids zur Familie Sauls zugrunde, in der David wesentlich mehr Rückhalt zu haben scheint als in seiner eigenen Sippe. Daß aber diese Verbindung primär an Michal geknüpft ist und somit auch Michal ganz entscheidend in die Reihe der Frauen um David gehört, die die Grunderzählung der Davidshausgeschichte[8] strukturiert, wird durch

[6] Vielleicht auch der Ältesten des einzelnen Stammes, wird doch Saul überwiegend in benjaminitischem Umfeld gezeichnet, und das gilt noch mehr für seinen Sohn Ischbaal.

[7] S.o. n. 2. Auseinandersetzung mit anderen Forschungsmeinungen (Lit.) im dort genannten Aufsatz.

[8] Vorausgreifend sei deren Bestand in bezug auf den Teil, innerhalb dessen die Michal-

verschiedene Einzelbeobachtungen deutlich, die sich anders und v.a. durch die Annahme sekundärer Einfügung der Michalnachrichten in den vorliterarischen oder literarischen Überlieferungsprozeß nicht erklären lassen.[9] In bezug auf David ergeben sich folgende Erzählzusammenhänge: David wird als Saitenspieler für den schwermütigen König angestellt (1 Sam. xvi 14–23): Zu diesem Erzählstrang vom bösen Geist über Saul bzw. Sauls Depression gehört (1 Sam. xviii 10–15) der Lanzenanschlag auf David und (1 Sam. xx 24ff.) ganz ähnlich auf Jonatan. Hiermit wiederum hängt der gesamte Jonatan-Komplex zusammen, und zwar 1 Sam. xx und als Vorgeschichte xix 1–7 sowie xviii 1, 3, 4 mit der Verbündung zwischen David und Jonatan. Dadurch wird deutlich, daß die Rettung durch Jonatan eine Konkurrenzerzählung zur Rettung durch Michal ist. Die Jonatan-Erzählung setzt aber David als Spielmann Sauls und als bekannte Persönlichkeit voraus; sie ist aus 2 Sam. i 17–27 herausgesponnen (und Werk eines dtr Historiographen?).

Ein Saul *unbekannter* David wird von Saul in 1 Sam. xviii 2 in Dienst genommen. Dazu gehört 1 Sam. xvii 55–8: Im jetzigen Zusammenhang ist "der Philister", dem David entgegengeht, Goliat. Doch setzt die ganze Goliatgeschichte ihrerseits einen weiteren Erzählstrang voraus: Dort bewaffnet ja Saul zunächst den jungen David; es wäre sonderbar, wenn er ihn hinterher nach seiner Familie befragte, die doch zum Erzählinventar von 1 Sam. xvii gehört. M.a.W., *die Goliatgeschichte gehört ebensowenig wie die Jonatangeschichte zu dem ältesten Erzählstrang, in dessen Verlauf Michal David rettet.* Andererseits könnten Davids Salbung (1 Sam. xvi), evtl. auch xv, und cap. xvii in die Jonatan-Erzähllinie gehören.

Nach Abzug aller Konkurrenzlinien bleibt für die Einführung von

---

Verbindung—immer in der Grundschicht!—thematisiert wird, hier grob, d.h. ohne detaillierte Unterteilungen der Einzelverse, umrissen mit 1 Sam. xiv 47–52, 55–8, xviii 2, 5–9, 16–30, xix 8–17, xxi 2–6, 9–16, xxii 1–2 . . . (?)–23, xxv, Teile von xxvi*, xxvii 1–4, xxviii 1–2, xxix, 1–6 . . . 8 . . . 11, xxx ? . . ., xxx 1–13; 2 Sam. i 1–4 . . . 11, 17–27, ii, 2–4, 8–9, 12–32, iii, iv 1–v 3, (v 4–9)*, v 17–18 . . ., vi 10 12b–14, 16–23, vii 1–3 15–18; also Davids Dienst bei Saul, Geschichte der Eheschließung mit Michal, Flucht vor Saul mit Michals Hilfe, David im Untergrund und im Philisterdienst, Ansammlung seiner Kampfgruppe, Heirat mit Abigail, Asyl bei Achisch von Gat, Ziklag, Sauls Tod u. Beklagung, Abner und das isr. Nachfolgekönigtum, Königtum in Juda und Auseinandersetzungen zwischen Sauls und Davids Gefolgschaft; Abners Seitenwechsel und Ermordung durch Joab; Königtum von Israel, Einnahme Jerusalems, Auseinandersetzungen mit Philistern, Ladeeinholung und Etablierung des Davidshauses in Jerusalem.

[9] Gegen z.B. O. Kaiser, "Beobachtungen zur sogenannten Thronnachfolgeerzählung Davids", *EThL* 64 (1988) pp. 5–20, der insgesamt zu anderen Annahmen kommt.

1 Sam. xvii 55–8 + xviii 2, 5–9, 14–15 nur 1 Sam. xiv 47. Dieser Satz thematisiert das Königtum (*mlwkh*) über Israel und führt dann das ganze von Sauls Seite für den Aufstieg Davids relevante Personal vor: Sauls Söhne (wegen der Nachfolgefrage) und Töchter (*v*. 49) sowie seine Frau,[10] seinen Vater und seinen Feldherrn. Warum aber werden hier Sauls Töchter genannt, obwohl im Gegenstück 2 Sam. iii 1ff. nicht von Davids Töchtern die Rede ist?

Wenn wir nicht annehmen wollen, daß David überhaupt nur Söhne hatte, so spielten *seine* Töchter offenbar keine Rolle, und das heißt umgekehrt, daß die Frage nach der besonderen Rolle, die der vordtr. Historiker den Saultöchtern und speziell Michal zuschrieb, berechtigt ist.

Michal taucht an enscheidenden Übergängen auf—bei Davids Trennung von Saul bzw. seiner Flucht vor ihm, bei Davids Verhandlungen mit Abner (und Ischbaal), die sein Königtum über Israel in die Wege leiten, sowie bei der Einholung der Lade nach Jerusalem, also der entscheidenden Maßnahme, mit der David Jerusalem zum religiösen und politischen Zentrum eines stämmeübergreifenden Königtums macht. Sobald aber Davids Königtum in Jerusalem wirklich etabliert ist, ist Michal aus dem Blickfeld des Erzählers verschwunden. Dabei handelt es sich um ein gewissermaßen ausdrückliches Verschwinden, das vom Erzähler mit dem Vorgriff[11] auf Michals Kinderlosigkeit bis zu ihrem Tode (2 Sam. vi 23) zur Sprache gebracht wird.

Dieser und andere Hinweise der Erzählung drängen die von ihr ins Auge gefaßten Adressaten und mithin auch uns zu der Frage, wie und warum die Ereignisse um die Anfänge des Königtums mit der Person der Michal verbunden werden. Diese Frage ist nicht zu verwechseln mit jener, welche Rolle die historische Michal "in Wirklichkeit" gespielt haben mag. Allerdings kann zum *Ergebnis* der Betrachtung des literarischen Werkes DHG auch Aufschluß über die Bedingungen, unter denen die Erzählung konzipiert wurde, gehören. *Wir fragen also nicht nach Michals historischer Rolle für die Entstehung des oder eines Königtums in der nachmaligen Größe Israel, sondern nach der Bedeutung,*

---

[10] Ein judäisch geprägter Gesichtspunkt, der auch für die David betreffenden Ereignisse der DHG später wichtig ist, 1 Sam. ii 2.

[11] "Eine Vorblende ist ein Ausdruck erzählerischer Ungeduld" (U. Eco, *Im Wald der Fiktionen. Sechs Streifzüge durch die Literatur. Harvard-Vorlesungen, Norton Lectures,* 1992–3 [a.d. Italienischen von B. Kroeber, München/Wien, 1994], p. 44, mit A.6 und der dort genannten Literatur zur Erzählforschung). Da es sich hier um das Ende des Michal-Erzählstranges handelt, muß die die Prolepse motivierende "Ungeduld" des Erzählers (und seines Modell-Lesers!) einem anderen Thema als dem persönlichen Ergehen Michals gelten. Das verborgene Thema ist die Thronfolge Davids.

die Michal für die literarische Darstellung der Anfänge des Königtums in der angenommenen Texteinheit hat.[12] Warum führte der Verfasser überhaupt Michal ein? Und warum läßt er sie gerade so sprechen und handeln, wie er es tut?

Aus dieser Hauptfrage ergibt sich eine Reihe weiterer Fragen:

– Welche Bedeutung hat die wechselvolle Braut- und Ehegeschichte für die Konzeption der DHG?

– Was ist der Sinn der Terafimepisode 1 Sam. xix?

– Sind die Verwirrungen um Michals zweite Ehe, Davids Rückforderung an Ischbaal und/oder Abner und das Beweinen Michals durch Paltiel Resultat literarkritisch zu behebender Konfusion oder durchdachtes Erzählungselement?

– Warum wird den Lesern mitgeteilt, daß David von Michal[13] keine Kinder hatte?

– Was spielt sich in der *erzählten* Geschichte von 2 Sam. vi ab?

Daß Michal überhaupt thematisiert wurde, dürfte zwei Gründe haben: Ihr Name und damit sie selbst war in der Tradition vorgegeben, und der Verfasser der DHG hielt die Darstellung ihrer Beziehung zu David für ein geeignetes literarisches Mittel seiner historiographischen Konzeption. In ihr gewährleisten durch Frauen wahrgenommene Familienbeziehungen das Gleichgewicht der Kräfte in der Gesellschaft des vorexilischen Königtums. Der Verfasser hatte also nicht ein unerklärliches Interesse an Davids Privatleben,[14] sondern er beschreibt Vorgänge in einer durch genealogische bzw. konnubiale Beziehungen strukturierten Gesellschaft.

Offensichtlich ist die zur Konsolidierung des Davidshauses als

[12] Zu dieser Unterscheidung vgl. auch die Erwägungen von C. Hardmeier, *Prophetie im Streit vor dem Untergang Judas. Erzählkommunikative Studien zur Entstehungssituation der Jesaja- und Jeremiaerzählungen in II Reg 18–20 und Jer. 37–40, BZAW* 187 (Berlin, 1989), bes. pp. 23–86 über "Erzähltextanalytische Grundlagen", und dort p. 32: "Im Blick auf den Quellenwert insbesondere von Erzählungen, die historische Ereignisse zum Inhalt haben, muß hervorgehoben werden, daß sie in erster Linie Dokumente und Zeugnisse der Erzählzeit sind . . . Erst wenn die Darstellungsabsicht des Autors . . . geklärt [ist]. . ., kann auch der Quellenwert des Dargestellten genauer beurteilt werden."

[13] Und umgekehrt; ungeachtet der Frage, ob die 2 Sam. xxi 8 erwähnten fünf Kinder Michal oder Merab zuzuschreiben sind.

[14] H. Schnabl, *Die "Thronfolgeerzählung David's". Untersuchungen zur literarischen Eigenständigkeit, literarkritischen Abgrenzung und Intention von 2Sam. 21,1–14; 9–28; 1Kön. 1–2*, (Regensburg, 1988), meint, daß die einzelnen, jedoch nicht voneinander zu trennenden Episoden der TNE "sich fast ausschließlich auf das Privatleben der Königlichen Familie" konzentrieren, ohne daß ein übergeordnetes Thema erkennbar wäre (p. 141). Aber das Beziehungssystem, um das es geht, ist eben in der Gesellschaft, in der die DHG verfaßt wurde, nicht "privat", sondern von allgemeinem politischem Interesse.

Jerusalemer Dynastie führende Entwicklung vor allem deshalb erstaunlich, weil Davids Familie im Gegensatz zu jener Sauls unbedeutend, wenn nicht unbekannt war. Diese sicher allgemein bekannte (und später, z.B. in Mi. v 1, geradezu topisierte) Tatsache wird in der Erzählung wiederholt v.a. in den David selbst zugeschriebenen wörtlichen Reden ausgesprochen; sie ist ein Problem, das durch die Darstellung der Ereignisse einer Lösung zugeführt wird.

1 Sam. xiv 47*–52 bildet die Exposition dieses literarischen Erzählzusammenhanges: Saul nahm das Königtum (*mlwkh*) über Israel ein, führte Krieg ringsum und baute (*v*. 48) eine entsprechende Truppe auf (*v*. 48, 52). In diese Maßnahmen ist die Nennung der Familie und des Heerführers Sauls eingebettet, d.h. die dargestellten Familienverhältnisse hängen nach Meinung des Verfassers unmittelbar mit Sauls militärischen Maßnahmen zusammen: Abner ist ein Verwandter Sauls,[15] und auch Sauls Vater und Ehefrau werden genannt, um das Beziehungsgeflecht anzudeuten, auf das Saul sich verlassen konnte: Seine Macht war nicht offiziell institutionalisiert, sondern durch persönliche Verpflichtungen gesichert.

Zusätzlich zu dieser Hausmacht sammelt Saul aber "tapfere Männer" um sich, ob als Söldner oder als freiwillig Verpflichtete, bleibt zunächst offen und ist vielleicht auch nicht immer klar zu unterscheiden. In diese Konstellation tritt David als *homo novus* ein. Er wird als anhangloser *naʿar*[16] und *ʿælæm* von Saul gesehen (xvii 55ff.) und angeworben (xvii 58 + xviii 2). Zugleich wird seine mindere Abstammung thematisiert.

David ist ein Niemand gegenüber Saul und tritt insofern in dessen *familia* ein, als er nicht mehr ins Vaterhaus zurückkehrt (xviii 2). In faktischer, aber freiwilliger Abhängigkeit von Saul beginnt Davids Karriere. Sein persönlicher Erfolg und seine Popularität rufen Sauls Argwohn hervor. Der Siegesgesang der Frauen (1 Sam. xviii 7, xxi 12, xxix 5) strukturiert als Leitmotiv die Darstellung des Ablösungsprozesses Davids von Saul. In diese Entwicklung gehört die Ehegeschichte Michals, die von Saul in die Wege geleitet wird, um David loszuwerden. Saul bietet dem erfolgreichen Soldaten, der zu diesem Zeitpunkt weniger als ein Emporkömmling ist, seine älteste Tochter an. Hierbei kann es sich nach Lage der Dinge nicht um eine Verhandlung von Familie zu Familie handeln. 1 Sam. xviii 17 bedeutet

[15] Ganz vergleichbar dem Verhältnis zwischen David und Joab.

[16] D.h. als ein (junger) Mann, der selbst (noch) nicht patriarchales Familienoberhaupt ist.

ein Vasallitätsangebot, das übrigens auch Sauls Mittellosigkeit[17] erkennen läßt. David entzieht sich ihm, indem er es als Brautverhandlung mißdeutet und selbst das familiäre Mißverhältnis darstellt (xviii 18). Damit ist die Sache erledigt (xviii 19).

Michals Liebe (xviii 20) gibt Saul eine neue Chance: Diesmal aber läßt er durch seine Knechte verhandeln (*v.* 22), d.h. die Sache ist als Familienehe deutbar, aber, wie das Folgende zeigt, von Saul nicht so gemeint. David beharrt (*v.* 23) auf seiner Sicht. Daraufhin fällt in *v.* 25 das entscheidende Wort *mōhar*, "Brautsumme".[18] Dies erscheint David "billig" (*v.* 26). Es "ist ihm recht", sich "mit dem König zu verschwägern". So wird Michal Davids Frau (*v.* 27).

---

[17] Er kann sich aus eigenem Vermögen—und nur dieses kommt offenbar für diesen Zweck in Frage—nicht genug zu eigenverantwortlichen Einsätzen fähige Soldaten leisten. Daneben—und dies könnte ein Topos sein—will er David auf ähnliche Weise loswerden wie jener später den Uria (2 Sam. xi 15).

[18] Nicht "Brautpreis", weil der Mann die Frau nicht kauft, sondern ihre Familie für den Verlust ihrer Arbeitskraft entschädigt, vgl. E. Lipínski, "Brautpreis", *NBL* I,2 (1989), col. 324–5. Zu Eheformen und -Konzeptionen im alttestamentlichen Israel und seiner Umgebung: B. Lang, "Ehe (I) AT", in *NBL* I, 3 (1990) cols 475–8; zur Darstellung der verschiedenen (auch hypothetischen) Eheformen: J. Scharbert, "Ehe etc. II. Altes Testament", *TRE* 9 (1982), pp. 311–13; für mesopotamische Verhältnisse E. Ebeling (pp. 280–6) und V. Korošec (pp. 286–98), "Ehe", *RLA* 2 (1938), pp. 281–98; für Ägypten S. Allam, "Ehe", *LÄ* 1 (1975), col. 1162–82. Die hier vertretene Auffassung der "Vasallenehe" (Scharbert, p. 312) wird von F. Horst, "II. Ehe im AT", *RGG*³ II (1958), col. 316–18, hierzu 316, als "Abart" der errēbu-Ehe angesehen und ohne Begründung als Belehnung gedeutet. Zur Relativierung der Sonderform einer "errēbu-Ehe" und Ablehnung ihrer Geltung in at.lichen Zusammenhängen vgl. jetzt Irmtraud Fischer, *Die Erzeltern Israels, BZAW* 222 (Berlin/New York, 1994), bes. p. 105, n. 118, mit Berufung auf J. Van Seters, *HThR* 62 (1969), pp. 377–95. Statt "Vasallenehe" wäre vielleicht die Bezeichnung "Dienstehe" vorzuziehen. Sie ist auch in Gen. xxviii–xxix vorausgesetzt und läßt sich mit Eheformen des Sklavenrechts (Ex. xxi 2–6) vereinbaren. Dabei stellt der Hausherr seinem *ʿbd* eine Ehefrau zur Verfügung, die jedoch zusammen mit den von ihr geborenen Kindern im Besitz des Dienstherrn bleibt. Ein Sonderfall dieses Sklavenrechts liegt in 1 Chr. ii 34–41 vor, wo ein Israelit ohne männliche Nachkommen seine Tochter einem ägyptischen Sklaven gibt, damit seine Linie fortgeführt wird. Der Fall und sein juristischer und soziologischer Hintergrund ist ausführlich erörtert worden bei S. Japhet, "The Israelite Legal and Social Reality as Reflected in Chronicles: A Case Study", in M. Fishbane and E. Tov (ed.), *Shaʿarei Talmon. Studies in the Bible, Qumran, and the Ancient Near East Presented to Shemaryahu Talmon* (Winona Lake, Indiana, 1992), pp. 79–91. Diese Form der Dienstehe, deren Kinder als Nachkommen des Vaters der Braut (der zugleich Dienstherr des Bräutigams ist) gelten, erfüllt eine ähnliche Funktion wie die in Israel nicht praktizierte Adoption und wird dadurch ermöglicht, daß der Bräutigam nicht selber eine Vatersfamilie in Israel hat. Eine Brautsumme muß dabei nicht gezahlt werden, weil die Braut ihrer Familie als Produktionskraft erhalten bleibt. Die Familie des Mannes spielt keine Rolle. All dies scheint auch für Davids Ehe mit Sauls Tochter zuzutreffen. In bezug auf Jakobs Ehe macht zwar Fischer, p. 87, mit Recht darauf aufmerksam, daß Jakob als "mittelloser Flüchtling" geschildert wird, der aber dennoch "freier Israelit ist und in seine eigene Verwandtschaft kommt." Dem Erzähler der DHG konnte aber David durchaus als *ʿbd* des Königs Saul gelten, vgl. U. Rüterswörden, "*ʿāḇaḏ* III.5", *ThWAT* 5 (1986), col. 997–9.

Daß aber der Saul dieser Erzählung die Sache anders sieht als David, ergibt sich aus der Terafimepisode 1 Sam. xix 8, 11–17. Sie wird eingeleitet durch die Ur-Lanzenszene *v.* 8, 10, aus der die sekundäre Jonatangeschichte herausgesponnen sein könnte.[19]

Die Erzählung ist als solche vollkommen stimmig, wenn man sich von der Erwartung löst, eine einlinige Aufzählung von Fakten vor sich zu haben. Sie spielt sich auf drei Ebenen ab. Die erste schildert Sauls Handlungen: Er versucht im Affekt, David zu töten. David entkommt, und nun entschließt sich Saul zu einem offiziellen Schritt: Er schickt Abgesandte, um David vor seinem Haus zu erwarten und vorzuladen. Eine zweite Delegation wird mit einem direkten Haftbefehl hinterhergeschickt (*v.* 14) und von Michal unter dem Vorwand von Davids Krankheit abgewiesen. Erst die dritte Botengruppe (*v.* 15) bekommt den Befehl, David notfalls mitsamt seinem Bett zu Saul zu bringen. Es ist also durchaus nicht unglaubwürdig, daß die erste Delegation nicht bemerkt hat, daß David durch das Fenster floh.[20] Das Fenster der Erzählung befindet sich nicht in der gleichen Hauswand wie die Haustür, ohne daß deshalb an ein Fenster über einer Stadtmauer zu denken wäre.[21] Die Wache ist vielmehr vor der wohl in einen Innenhof führenden Haustür oder innerhalb desselben postiert und hat keinen weiteren Auftrag, als David zu erwarten. Der Befehl zur Hausdurchsuchung ergeht erst an die zweite Delegation. Es sind also Konven-

---

Von den Konnotationen des Übersetzungswortes "Sklave" wird man sich ohnehin lösen müssen; immerhin wird aber auf diesem Hintergrund das Problem der Entstehung eines "Davidshauses" als solches deutlich.

[19] David "spielt" oder gibt eine Melodie (einen Rhythmus?) an (*mngn*) "mit der Hand". Vielleicht sollte man nicht vorschnell an ein Saitenspiel denken, sondern eher an ein Spiel der Finger, an das auch beim Ladetanz gedacht werden könnte, vgl. P. Kyle McCarter, *II Samuel* (Garden City, 1984), p. 171, zu 2 Sam. vi 14, mit Verweis auf Ugarit (Lit).

[20] Dieser Ausdruck wird in 2 Sam. vi bei der entscheidenden Zerwürfnisszene wiederholt.

[21] Das Szenario ist nicht das gleiche wie in Jos. ii, wo die Stadtmauer gebraucht wird, um das unbemerkte Entkommen der Kundschafter zu bewerkstelligen. Andererseits sind die Kundschafter gewissermaßen zu dem einzigen Erzählzweck im Haus der Rahab, um von ihr über die Stimmung der Landesbewohner informiert zu werden und mit ihrer Familie die Sondervereinbarung schließen zu können. David dagegen ist mit Michal in dem Haus, das z.Zt. der Erzählung seine Wohnung ist. Er braucht keine Stadtmauer, um zu entkommen, weil er sich nicht eingeschlossen in einer fremden Stadt befindet, sondern unter Arrest in seinem eigenen Hause. Es reicht völlig, wenn plausibel berichtet werden kann, daß er sich von den Posten unbemerkt aus dem Haus entfernen konnte. Wenn man überhaupt ein literarisches Abhängigkeitsverhältnis zwischen beiden Erzählungen annehmen will, so ist Jos. ii von 1 Sam. xix abhängig. Damit dürfte allerdings noch kein Urteil über das hohe Alter der DHG gefällt sein, weil die Erzählungen in der ersten Hälfte des Josuabuches entgegen den Thesen der älteren Forschung ohnehin von der Erzähltechnik her den Verdacht später Entstehung erwecken.

tionen vorausgesetzt, die es Fremden—auch Boten—normalerweise verbieten, in ein Privathaus oder jedenfalls dessen der eigentlichen Privatsphäre vorbehaltenen Teil[22] einzudringen. David kann ohne weiteres im Schutze der Dunkelheit entkommen, vielleicht sogar über die Dächer. Vorausgesetzt sind eher städtische Wohnverhältnisse, aber keine bestimmte Stadt: Der Erzähler erzählt mit dem ihm zur Verfügung stehenden Vorstellungsrepertoire eine in sich plausible Handlung. Er nimmt an, daß David als Sauls Vasall in einem Stadthaus wohnte, d.h. er entstammt selber städtischen Verhältnissen.

Die zweite Handlungsebene ist die erzählte Erlebnisebene Michals. Sie rechnet damit, daß ihr Vater früher oder später David verhaften lassen wird. Sie kann aber offenbar auch mit normalen Anstandsregeln rechnen, die Besucher vom Betreten der innersten Kammer des Hauses abhalten werden. Ihre Terafiminstallation täuscht ein Heilungsritual

---

[22] Zu der üblichen Hausaufteilung vgl. H. Weippert, *Palästina in vorhellenistischer Zeit* (München, 1988), pp. 393ff., zu Dorfhäusern, v.a. pp. 437ff., zu Stadthäusern der Eisen IIA-Zeit (*ca.* 1000–900 v.Chr.), zu Wohnhäusern der städtischen Architektur der Eisen IIB-Zeit (*ca.* 925/900–850 v.Chr.), pp. 530ff. Mit dem Heranziehen dieser Informationen ist keine Vorentscheidung über die Datierung des Textes verbunden, weil der Vierraumhaustyp mit seinen Variationen (zum praktischen Vorgang der Variation von architektonischen Grundmodellen vgl. Kenneth W. Schaar, "An Architectural Theory for the Origin of the Four-Room House", *Scandinavian Journal of the OT* 2 [1991], pp. 75–98) lange erhalten und die für das immanente Textverständnis wichtigen Einzelheiten die gleichen blieben. Vorausgesetzt ist also eine gemeinsame Häusereingangsfront bzw. eine Hausrückseite, die wegen Zusammenbaus der Häuser oder aus anderen Gründen nicht von der Eingangsseite her einsehbar ist, d.h. städtische Wohnverhältnisse, und ein "Fenster", durch das ein Mensch nach außen gelangen kann, obwohl dies als ungewöhnlich vorausgesetzt ist. Da Fenster in den archäologisch erschlossenen Hausanlagen nicht nachweisbar sind, gab es sie entweder überhaupt nicht (so V. Fritz, *Die Stadt im alten Israel* [München, 1990]), der vom eigentlichen Wohnraum des von ihm geschilderten eingeschossigen israelitischen Normalhauses annimmt (p. 117): "Licht und Luft erhielt er allein durch die Tür"), oder sie spielten nicht die gleiche Rolle wie in modernen Häusern. Räume mit nur einer Türöffnung dürften klimatisch bedingt ungünstig gewesen sein, so daß wohl mit einem "Fenster" zur Gewährleistung der Luftzirkulation sowie als zumindest indirekter Lichtquelle in der Höhe eines Oberlichtes zu rechnen ist; so auch A. Kempinski – R. Reich (ed.), *The Architecture of Ancient Israel. From the Prehistoric to the Persion Period* (Jerusalem, 1992), bes. p. 322, s.v. "Window": "Opening in the wall, usually located at a high level, made to let air and light into a room . . ." Die gleichen Autoren rechnen ibid., pp. 191ff., für (städtische) Wohnhäuser mit einem die ganze Grundfläche bedeckenden Obergeschoß, zu dem nicht nur äußere Treppen, sondern auch eine innere Leiter durch ein ebenfalls als *ḥlwn* zu bezeichnendes "opening in the ceiling" geführt hätte, so daß David durch diesen Ausstieg über die Dächer hätte fliehen können.

Daß ein Wohnraum in einer in die (Kasematten-)Stadtmauer eingearbeiteten Hausanlage zur Außenseite der Mauer hin ein mannsbreites Fenster aufgewiesen haben sollte, ist so lange unwahrscheinlich, wie die Mauer eine Verteidigungsaufgabe hat. Das Fenster der Rahab setzt eine Stadtanlage voraus, die grundsätzlich nicht der Verteidigung bedarf. Umgekehrt ist in 1 Sam. xix nicht mit der Lage des Hauses an der Stadtmauer zu rechnen.

am Krankenbett vor.[23] Bei Wahrung der üblichen Diskretion können von außen in den Raum Blickende im dunklen Zimmer keine Einzelheiten erkennen, sondern werden einfach feststellen, daß sie ein Krankenzimmer vor sich haben. Michal bestärkt den erwarteten Augenschein mit ihrer knappen Auskunft, "er ist krank" (*v.* 14). Als ihr Vater sie nach der Täuschung zur Rede stellt, gebraucht sie eine Ausrede: David habe sie an Leib und Leben bedroht und somit zur Fluchthilfe gezwungen (*v.* 17). Bemerkenswert hieran ist, daß Michal gerade zu dieser Ausrede greift: Indem sie damit ihre Unschuld an Davids Entkommen nachzuweisen trachtet, bestätigt sie die Berechtigung von Sauls Vorwurf. Wieso aber erwartet er Loyalität gegenüber dem Vater, die die Loyalität gegenüber dem Ehemann hintansetzt?

Mit dieser Frage begeben wir uns auf die dritte Ebene—die des Erzählers bzw. der von ihm intendierten Leserinnen oder Hörer. Aus dem Ineinander der v.a. aus ihren Reden zu erschließenden erzählten Erlebnisebenen der Akteure kann ein Gesamtbild der Sicht des "allwissenden Erzählers"[24] gewonnen werden. Zu diesem Gesamtbild gehört das Problem der widerstreitenden Verpflichtungen Michals, und d.h. das Problem der Doppeldeutigkeit dieser Ehe. Die Michal der Erzäh-

---

[23] Diese Erzählung setzt eindeutig eine Verwendbarkeit des Terafim—zur Diskussion seiner Bedeutung und Funktionen I. Willi-Plein, *Opfer und Kult im alttestamentlichen Israel. Textbefragungen und Zwischenergebnisse* (Stuttgart, 1993). U. Hübner, *Spiele und Spielzeug im antiken Palästina* (Fribourg/Göttingen, 1992), nimmt (p. 93) zu 1 Sam. xix 8–17 an, daß Michal "das häusliche Götterbild" zur Täuschung verwende und damit wiederhole, "was sie als Mädchen oft gespielt hat, wenn sie ihre Puppe(n) schlafen legte". Er illustriert damit seine These, daß Götterbild und Spielzeug austauschbar sein können. Daß "eine so schöne, täuschend echte Puppe", wie sie s.E. der Terafim war, "der Traum eines jeden palästinischen Mädchens gewesen" sei, ist allerdings nicht anzunehmen. Eine lebensgroße Puppe, zumal in Erwachsenengröße, wird von Kindern beiderlei Geschlechts nicht zum Spielen akzeptiert. Das Material des Terafim könnte auch nur Holz sein (eine lebensgroße Lumpenpuppe kann es nicht geben, und Keramik wäre viel zu zerbrechlich) und wäre zu schwer. Vielleicht muß man sich von der Vorstellung lösen, als hätte die Terafimfigur Davids Körper vorgetäuscht. Tatsächlich kann der Text (*'l!*) am besten so verstanden werden, daß Michal ein auch als Bettdecke dienendes Kleidungsstück mit "dem" (dafür in Frage kommenden) Ziegenfell auf der Liegefläche drapiert und den Terafim daran oder dagegen legt oder lehnt. Er könnte demnach die Form eines Brettidols gehabt haben, möglicherweise mit einer Standstütze für eine Sitzfigur. Diese Position des Terafim auf dem Bett läßt offenbar eindeutig den Schluß zu bzw. bekräftigt die Aussage, daß der (angeblich) darunter Liegende krank ist. Die Erzählung setzt also bei ihren Adressaten einvernehmliches Wissen um ein entsprechendes Heilungsritual voraus, das als gängig gilt, hat doch Michal ohne weiteres "den" (mithin dafür in Frage kommenden) Terafim nehmen können.

[24] Vgl. F.K. Stanzel, *Theorie des Erzählens* (Göttingen, ^{5}1991). Die Außenperspektive des im Idealfall allwissenden Erzählers wird der auktorialen Erzählsituation zugeordnet, die (neben der Ich-Erzählsituation) die typische Erzählsituation aller vormodernen Literatur ist.

lung weiß, daß ihr Vater ihre Ehe mit David als Dienstehe ansieht und insofern annehmen wird, daß seine Tochter weiter im Sinne ihres Vaters, der nun zugleich Dienstherr ihres Mannes ist, handeln wird. Andererseits verhält sie sich aber wie eine normale Ehefrau und bestätigt so ihre Liebe (2 Sam. xviii 20) und Davids Einschätzung der Ehe als einer von gleich zu gleich geschlossenen Verbindung. Am Ende der Terafimepisode ist also weiter offen, für welche Möglichkeit sich der Erzähler selbst entscheidet, welche er also als die zutreffende darstellen will. Aus dieser Spannung lebt der Bericht über die Verhandlungen mit und durch Abner (2 Sam. iii 12–20). Man würde die literarische Konzeption mit Füßen treten, wenn man hier literarkritisch im Sinne einer Alternative zwischen Abner und Ischbaal als Davids Verhandlungspartner operieren wollte.

Nach Davids Besuch beim Priester Ebjatar in Nob (1 Sam. xxi 2–6 + 9–11), der die Ausrottung der Priesterschaft von Nob durch Saul bzw. Ebjatars Gefolgschaft gegenüber David begründet (xxii 6(?)–23), nach Davids Dienst bei Achisch von Gat (xxi 13–16) und seinem Aufenthalt in der Wüste Sif (xxiii 14–15) wird ausführlich Davids Begegnung mit Abigail als ein erster entscheidender Schritt zur Konsolidierung seiner Position in Juda geschildert.[25] Danach ist David mit der vermögenden Judäerin Abigail verheiratet, und Michal wird von Saul anderweitig verheiratet (xxv 44). Was aber hat es zu bedeuten, daß (2 Sam. iii 1) "der Krieg lang wurde zwischen dem Hause Sauls und dem Haus Davids"[26] und dabei das Haus Davids immer mehr zunahm, Sauls "Haus" aber an Bedeutung verlor? War David nicht ein hergelaufener Emporkömmling?

Diese Frage müssen sich nach Ansicht des Erzählers die Israeliten, die sich Sauls Königtum einst unterstellt hatten, vorgelegt haben. Wenn sich Abner aus sehr persönlichen Gründen entschließt, David "ganz Israel" (und zumindest Benjamin) zuzuführen, so wird dieses Israel Sauls nicht leicht zu gewinnen sein. Deshalb stellt der David der Erzählung seinerseits eine Bedingung für die Aufnahme der von Abner vorgeschlagenen Verhandlungen. Natürlich muß er diese Bedingung Abner stellen, aber ebenso natürlich ist sie als Verlangen an den Saulsohn (und -Nachfolger) Ischbaal formuliert, das Abner nur als Unterhändler weiterleiten soll.

David verlangt die Rückgfabe Michals als "meiner Frau, die ich

[25] Vgl. den oben n. 2 genannten Aufsatz, v.a. p. 5.
[26] Hier steht zum erstenmal ausdrücklich Haus gegen Haus!

mir anverlobt habe", d.h. er suggeriert, daß es sich nicht um eine Dienstehe, sondern wirklich um eine echte Verschwägerung handelt und er also mit dem Sauliden von gleich zu gleich verhandeln kann. Damit, daß dieser, durch Abner inoffiziell vorbereitet, Davids Antrag als solchen behandelt, ist die Sache endgültig entschieden: Die Leser werden nun die Ansicht des Erzählers übernehmen, daß keine Dienst- oder Vasallenehe vorlag, sondern David rechtmäßiger König und Begründer eines den Sauliden ebenbürtigen "Hauses" war. So kam also David zum Königtum über Israel.

Wie wird sich nun dieses Königtum weiterentwickeln? Welche Linie wird weitergeführt werden—das in Hebron begründete Königtum in Juda oder das gewissermaßen von Saul auf David übergegangene Königtum über Israel?—Endgültig entscheidet sich dies erst in der Nachfolge Davids, und darum ist von diesem Punkt an die Frage, welcher Sohn die Nachfolge antreten wird, die entscheidende. Damit ist untrennbar und für den politischen Bestand des künftigen Königtums sehr wesentlich die Frage verbunden, welche Frau das[27] Amt der Königinmutter[28] antreten wird. Der Erzähler führt uns zu der Frage, wieso es nicht Michal geworden ist, und erzählt die Schlüsselszene 2 Sam. vi, in der in der Person Michals das nordisraelitische Königtum mit der höfischen Kultur Jerusalems konfrontiert wird.

Die zum "Michal-Zusammenhang" gehörenden Partien von 2 Sam. vi sind *v*. 1, 10, (12aα?,) 12b–14, 16–20, 21b, 22–3. Der im dtr. Text geschilderte erste, gescheiterte Versuch der Ladeeinholung ist deutlich ein sekundäres Element, das vom Dtr aus dem vorhandenen älteren Material herausgesponnen wurde. Der Grund hierfür war wohl vor allem die merkwürdige Feststellung, daß David "nicht im Sinn hatte, die Lade JHWHs zu sich in die Davidsstadt zu transportieren"(2 Sam. vi 10). Hierfür mußte der dtr. Historiker aufgrund seines eigenen Davidsbildes einen Grund finden: Irgendetwas war schiefgegangen. Traditionsbruchstücke und eine Ortsnamenaetiologie werden mit Elementen der älteren Erzählung zu einer ersten Ladeepisode verarbeitet, in der die Lade anders als in der ursprünglichen Erzählung (aber wie in 1 Sam. vi) gefahren wird (*v*. 3) und in der nicht nur David, sondern

[27] Faktisch vielleicht erst später, in Jerusalem aufgekommene oder übernommene.

[28] Grundlegend ist dazu zu konsultieren H. Donner, "Art und Herkunft des Amtes der Königinmutter im Alten Testament" (1958), in *FS Johannes Friedrich 65* (Heidelberg, 1959), pp. 105–45, jetzt auch in: H. Donner, *Aufsätze zum Alten Testament aus vier Jahrzehnten. BZAW* 224 (Berlin/New York, 1994), pp. 1–24.

er "und das ganze *Haus* Israel" (*v.* 5) vor der Lade herziehen und sie mit "Freudenbekundungen"[29] begleiten. Offenbar verstand Dtr. Davids Darbeitung nicht (nur) als Tanz, sondern als musikalische Aufführung und zählte darum die zu seiner Zeit üblichen Instrumente auf (*v.* 5). Dazu gehören auch Fingerinstrumente. Erst durch diese dtr. Erweiterung wird also der Anschein einer gemeinschaftlichen musikbegleiteten Prozession[30] vor der Lade her erweckt. Davon ist im älteren Bericht nicht die Rede; in ihm produziert sich der König allein.

Nach dem *dtr. Erzählzusammenhang* unterbricht David die Prozession nach dem Unfall. Sein *zeitweiliges* Desinteresse an einer Einbringung der Lade hat nun einen auch theologisch einwandfreien Grund. *V.* 15 deutet an, daß beim zweiten Versuch die große Prozession des ersten Anlaufs wiederholt bzw. fortgesetzt wird. Michals Mißbilligung einer vom ganzen "Haus Israel" durchgeführten Prozession wirkt so skandalös. Davids Antwort ist denn auch in *v.* 21a eindeutig dtr. überarbeitet. Zur alten Erzählung aber dürfte nur *v.* 21b, "ich habe Spaß gemacht vor JHWH",[31] gehören, worauf unmittelbar die persönliche Absichtserklärung, sich auch künftig ähnlich zu verhalten, folgt (*v.* 22). David informiert Michal über den JHWH-Bezug seiner Darbietung.

Angesichts des so eingegrenzten Erzählzusammenhanges ergeben sich folgende Fragen:

– Welche Funktion haben die in *v.* 13 und 18 erwähnten Opfer?
– Welche Rolle spielt David?
– Warum nimmt Michal Anstoß an Davids Auftreten?
– Warum wird Michals Kinderlosigkeit mitgeteilt?

Wieder sollen diese Fragen textimmanent beantwortet werden, d.h. noch ohne Rückfrage danach, was sich "wirklich" ereignet hat oder was für Traditionen dem Erzähler vorlagen.

---

[29] *śḥq* Pi., entnommen aus *v.* 21!

[30] Die dann zu Vergleichen mit assyrischen Prozessionen einlädt und auch so beeinflußt sein kann, vgl. McCarter (s.o. n. 19), p. 181: "It can be compared, therefore, to other ancient Near Eastern accounts of the introduction of a national god to a new royal city. The several Assyrian examples exhibit a similar and more or less fixed pattern." All dies paßt zur dtr. Konzeption der Ereignisse, aber nicht zum hier angenommenen älteren Kern.

[31] Vielleicht erst in der dtr. Überarbeitung als perf. cons. *śḥq* pi. ist Unterhaltungskunst (Ri. xvi 25), wird aber für Dtr. gewissermaßen durch David geadelt und als musikalisch begleiteter Prozessionstanz gedeutet. Noch weiter geht 1 Chr. xv 27, wonach David zum Tanz Efod und Mantel trägt. Seine Darbietung besteht in Drehbewegungen (*v.* 27), s.o. n. 19 den Verweis auf McCarter, p. 171, zu 2 Sam. vi 14, und die neueren Lexika zu *krkr*.

Die in *v.* 13 und *v.* 18 erwähnten Opfer unterscheiden sich wesentlich voneinander. In *v.* 13 schlachtet man,[32] nachdem die Ladeträger die ersten sechs Schritte getan haben,[33] einen Stier und ein Masttier. Diese Schlachtung markiert den Beginn eines Weges, an dessen Ziel die Brandopfer und Schelamimopfer durch David dargebracht werden. David tritt dabei als königlicher Opferherr auf.

Das Brandopfer ist eine junge Opferform für das alttestamentliche Israel,[34] aber kaum in Jerusalem. Der Eindruck drängt sich vielmehr auf, daß David in ein Jerusalemer Priesterkönigtum eintritt. Als königlicher Opferherr verteilt er anschließend Speisen an die Bevölkerung, wohl nicht nur im Sinne einer Verproviantierung, sondern als Bestandteil eines mit dem Verteilen von Speiseanteilen verbundenen Rituals.[35] Daß er dies alles bei der Einholung der Lade tat, mag auf Israeliten befremdend gewirkt haben. Es könnte sein, daß der Erzähler Michals Empfindungen mitteilt, um auszudrücken, was eigentlich jeder Israelit bzw. Nicht-Jerusalemer empfinden würde. Vielleicht ist der Verfasser selbst nicht-jerusalemischer Herkunft.

Allerdings ist in der Forschung immer angenommen worden, daß Michals moralisches Empfinden beleidigt war, daß also der beanstandeten "Entblößung" auch eine sexuelle Färbung zugehörte. Dies legt sich zwar bei ungewohntem Kleiderverzicht immer nahe, doch wird eine obszöne Aufführung weder angedeutet, noch ließe sich ein Sinn für sie im Zusammenhang der Ladeprozession finden.

Zwar erwähnt Michal die "Mägde", denen Davids Auftreten nicht nur gefallen werde, sondern vor denen er sich damit "wichtig machen" wolle. Die Mägde wissen nach Meinung des Erzählers gerade das zu schätzen, was Michal mißfallen hat, Davids Solotanz, der vielleicht durch Fingerinstrumente oder Pantomime[36] begleitet war—offenbar eine kraftvolle Körperbewegung, die das Ablegen des Obergewandes oder positiv das Anlegen des Leinenefods nötig machte. Dies findet Michal

[32] Ob David selbst schlachtet, wird nicht deutlich.

[33] Das in der Exegese immer wieder erwogene iterative Verständnis, als wäre jeweils nach 6 Schritten geopfert worden, ist nicht nur aus sachlichen Gründen ganz unwahrscheinlich, sondern wird sich auch schwerlich grammatisch plausibel machen lassen.

[34] Dazu Willi-Plein (s.o. n. 23), bes. pp. 85–90.

[35] Der Gedanke an die Rolle Melchisedeks in den älteren Partien von Gen. xiv drängt sich auf.

[36] *mkrkr v.* 14 (s.o. n. 31) ist eher kein Ausdruck für Tanz (mit den Füßen), sondern für eine Betätigung mit den Fingern oder eine Kraft erfordernde (kreisende) Bewegung, vielleicht ein kunstvolles "Verrenken", der Hände oder Arme. Die entsprechende Fußbewegung—vielleicht Trippeln—oder doch eher Stampfen?—wird in *v.* 16 mit *pzz // krkr* genannt.

peinlich. Die Begründung (*v.* 20) ist sachlich und sprachlich schwer zu erfassen. "Der König hat sich enthüllt in bezug auf die Augen der Mägde seiner Dienstmänner wie ein Enthüllen von Enthüllten eines der Leeren".

Das größte Problem an diesem Vers ist die Infinitivhäufung: Auf den mit der Präposition *k*^{e} präfigierten Inf. cstr. Nif. von *glh* folgt mit *nglwt* entweder ein unregelmäßig gebildeter Inf. abs. Nif. oder—von der Bildung auf *-ôt* her eigentlich wahrscheinlicher—ein weiterer, allerdings dann irregulär gebildeter Inf. cstr. Nif., oder—formal einwandfrei—eine Form des Part. fem. pl. Nif. von *glh.*

Die Annahme eines Inf. abs. wird zwar in den Kommentaren, wenn auch offensichtlich als Verlegenheitslösung, durchgehend befürwortet, sie ist aber, auch abgesehen von der ungewöhnlichen Form, aus syntaktischen Gründen ganz unwahrscheinlich. Der nachgestellte Inf. abs. würde dann ja die Genetivverbindung zwischen dem vorangehenden Inf. cstr. und seinem nomen rectum *ʾḥd hrqym* sprengen. Nachgestellter inf. abs. der gleichen Wurzel wäre auch ganz ungewöhnlich und ergäbe keinen Sinn, bezeichnet er doch die begleitenden Handlungen zu einem vorhergehenden Verb, z.B. im gleichen literarischen Zusammenhang in 2 Sam. iii 16: "Und da ging ihr Mann mit ihr, *indem* er [die ganze Zeit] hinter ihr her ging und weinte". Diese Möglichkeit entfällt aber hier; gedacht wird vielmehr an den die Aussageintention eines finiten Verbs verstärkenden *vorangestellten* Inf. abs. der gleichen Wurzel (*figura etymologica*). Doch auch diese Möglichkeit liegt hier nicht vor, weil der inf. abs. hier gerade nicht zu einem finiten Verb träte und auch nicht vorangestellt wäre. Mit anderen Worten, ein Inf. abs. kann nicht angenommen werden.

Da die grammatische Schwierigkeit des Textverständnisses die Annahme sekundärer Texterweiterung nicht nahelegt, bleiben nur zwei Erklärungsversuche möglich:

(1) *nglwt* ist eine (ältere?) Variantform des Inf. cstr. Nif. und wurde durch Beifügung der Normalform ersetzt bzw. erläutert. Zu übersetzen ist dann einfach: ". . . wie sich einer der 'Leeren' enthüllt."

(2) *nglwt* ist Ptc. fem. plur. Nif., und es ist zu übersetzen: ". . . wie sich die 'Enthüllten' (fem.) eines der 'Leeren' enthüllen".—In diesem Fall würde Michal Davids Tanz mit den Darbietungen *femininer* "Enthüllter/sich Enthüllender", also spärlich bekleideter Tänzerinnen eines der "Leeren" vergleichen. Die *rqym* wären dann eine Menschengruppe, die sich als Lustbarkeit Vorführungen von Tänzerinnen leisten kann, also im historischen Kontext der Erzählung "Snobs" oder

Exponenten höfischer, d.h. im Jerusalem der Königszeit, ägyptisierender Kultur.

Michal nimmt Anstoß an einer Kultur, in die sie selbst nicht passen will, und zwar im Gegensatz zu den Mägden. Sie spricht als Saulstochter, Benjaminitin, Israelitin: Der König hat sich enthüllt, wie sich "einer der Leeren" enthüllt.—Er hat "sich selbst entlarvt".

In Michals Rede geht es um den Zusammenstoß zweier Gesellschaftsformen, um nicht zu sagen, zweier Welten. Wie sich "der König Israels" zu benehmen hat, weiß die Tochter Sauls. Ihrer Meinung nach weiß David es nicht und hat sich damit "selbst bloßgestellt".[37] Am Tag der Ladeeinholung hat dieser König Israels die Maske fallengelassen und sich als einer entpuppt, der nichts Anderes ist als das Gesindel, mit dem er sich nach 1 Sam. xxii 2, xxv 10 umgeben hat.[38]

Der Riß geht mitten durch die Festversammlung und mitten durch das Haus Davids. Die Erzählung supponiert einen Gegensatz zwischen Michal und den "Mägden", die ihrerseits durch die "Dienstleute" (*ʿbdym*) Davids als solche bestimmt sind: Es geht um die nichtisraelitische Jerusalemer Hofgesellschaft, die von David abhängigen, nicht eigene Familien in Israel bildenden Hofbeamten[39] und deren Frauen.[40]

Es muß also nicht unbedingt Davids (künftiger) Harem sein, auf den sich Michals Bemerkung bezieht. Davids Antwort eröffnet allerdings mit *v*. 22 die Aussicht auch auf diese Möglichkeit,[41] die im Folgenden und nicht zuletzt durch die Beziehung mit Batscheba, der

---

[37] Auch das Deutsche kennt diese Metapher; zum hebr. *glh* Nif. für "sich zeigen/offenbaren" vgl. 1 Sam. xiv 8, 11 bzw. "aus der Deckung herausgehen" 1 Sam. ii 27, iii 21 (Gegstz. *ksh*).

[38] Vgl. *HAL* s.v. *ryq*, die *ʾnšym rqym* von Ri. ix 4, xi 3; 2 Chr. xiii 7, sowie akk. *rīqu(m), rāqu(m), AHW*, pp. 987–8, "leer", d.h. "unbeschäftigt". Zur Interpretation des hebr. Ausdrucks für "Ledige, Haltlose, Bindungslose" im Sinne eines "sozialen Status" als "besitzlose und aufrührerische Elemente, vergleichbar mit den Habiru . . ." vgl. B. Kedar-Kopfstein, *Art. ryq ThWAT* VIII,3–5 (1990), col. 501–7, das Zitat 505.

[39] Möglicherweise in dieser Form auch erst in der Wirklichkeit des Erzählers vorkommend.

[40] A. Jepsen, "Ama^h und Schiphcha^h", *VT* 8 (1958), pp. 293–7, mit dem Nachtrag (Verweis auf B. Jacob) ebd, p. 426, nimmt an, die *ʾāmâ* sei die "unfreie Frau, sowohl die Nebenfrau des Mannes, wie die unfreie Frau eines unfreien Mannes, eines Sklaven", die *šipḥâ* aber "das noch unberührte, unfreie Mädchen, v.a. im Dienst der Frau des Hauses", wobei wohl im Blick auf 2 Sam. xxv 41 die Unberührtheit in bezug auf den für das in Rede stehende Eheverhältnis in Frage kommenden Mann einzuschränken wäre. Dazu auch: C. Cohen, "Studies in Extra-Biblical Hebrew Inscriptions 1, The Semantic Range and Usage of the Terms *ʾmh* and *špḥh*", *Shnaton* 5–6 (1978–9), pp. XXV–LXIV.

[41] In 1 Chr. xv 29 wird denn auch der Dialog zwischen David und Michal fortgelassen und die Geschichte und ihre Folgen nur mit Michals Verachtung für David angedeutet.

Frau von Davids nichtisraelitischem Dienstmann Uria, entfaltet wird, während sich im gleichen Atemzug[42] die endgültige Trennung zwischen David und Michal vollzieht. Michal ist nicht die künftige Königinmutter,[43] wenngleich noch lange offen bleiben wird, wer sonst die Gebira sein wird.

Mit *v*. 23 schließt der Verfasser die Akten der Michal, aber durch den Vorausblick eröffnet er zugleich eine neue Spannungslinie, die erst am Schluß mit der Krönung des Jerusalemers Salomo und der Etablierung der Jerusalemerin Batscheba als Königinmutter gelöst werden wird. Die Lösung dieser Spannung ist zugleich die Auflösung der Frage, wer nach David auf dem Thron sitzen wird, und somit der Abschluß des ganzen Erzählgefüges, das in 2 Sam. vi allerdings einen entscheidenden Wendepunkt erreicht hat.

Daß hier eine Weichenstellung erfolgt, ist durch die Abfolge der Kapitel vi und vii bzw. durch die Hinführung auf die sogenannte Natanweissagung gesichert. Wie auch immer man den älteren Kern in bezug auf spätere und v.a. dtr. Ausweitungen oder überhaupt erst Formulierungen der "Natanweissagung" im engeren Sinne bestimmen mag, so ist doch sicher anzunehmen, daß ein solcher Kern in cap. vii zu suchen ist.[44] Ein Hinweis darauf dürfte schon allein der im jetzigen Kontext merkwürdige Widerruf Natans in bezug auf Davids Tempelbaupläne sein: Der ursprüngliche Zusammenhang sprach nicht vom Tempelbau, sondern allenfalls vom Gegensatz zwischen Davids gemauerter Residenz und der provisorisch[45] anmutenden Unterbringung der Lade. Im Hinblick hierauf beruhigt Natan den König, vielleicht sagte er ihm aber ursprünglich auch bedingungslos zu,[46] "alles,

---

[42] Syntaktisch eindeutig als Gegenüberstellung durch die Form we-x-qatal ausgedrückt in *v*. 23.

[43] S.o. n. 28.

[44] So auch L. Rost, "Die Überlieferung von der Thronnachfolge Davids" (1926), in L. Rost, *Das kleine Credo und andere Studien zum Alten Testament* (Heidelberg, 1965), pp. 119–253, hierzu pp. 160–83, allerdings mit umfangreicherer Textbestimmung.

[45] Aus späterer Sicht; falls aber die Lade wirklich ursprünglich ein transportables Kultobjekt war, kann auch die Unterbringung in einem Zelt in Ordnung gewesen sein. Auf Eigenart und Funktion (nach Art der neuassyrischen Götterbildstandarten, die in den Krieg mitgeführt werden, vgl. L. Schwienhorst, *Die Eroberung Jerichos. Exegetische Untersuchung zu Josua 6* [Stuttgart, 1986], pp. 76–7) der Lade aus den Erzählungen des Josuabuches (Jos. iii 15, iv 11, vi 11) schließen zu wollen, empfiehlt sich nicht, da die Bestimmung von vordtr. Elementen dort sehr unsicher ist.

[46] Auch hier—wie sicher am Anfang von cap. vi, wo er den zweimaligen Versuch der Ladeeinholung aus dem übernommenen, nicht ersetzten, sondern durch eigene Quellenauswertung ergänzten älteren Text herausspann—zeigt sich der behutsame Umgang des/der dtr. Historiker mit den älteren Erzählungen.

was in deinem Sinn ist, geh, tue es; denn JHWH ist mit dir", um darauf fortzufahren (*v*. 16): "Und vertrauenswürdig ist dein Haus, dein Thron aber[47] wird beständig sein auf unabsehbare Zeit." Davids Haus ist etabliert—anders als das Haus Sauls es war, und ohne Michal; sein Thron soll beständig sein—wer aber als Nächster darauf sitzen wird, ist noch lange offen.

Die vordtr. DHG ist das Werk eines Verfassers der frühen Köngiszeit, der selber in städtischen Verhältnissen lebte, aber nicht von stadtjerusalemischer Herkunft war. Er schildert politische Entwicklungen mit Hilfe der Darstellung ihres gesellschaftlichen Hintergrundes, wie er sich in den Frauen um David und deren Familienbeziehungen manifestiert.

Michal steht am Anfang des Aufstiegs Davids und am Ende einer genuin israelitischen Sicht des Königtums Israels oder jedenfalls dessen, was sich der judäische Verfasser der DHG als Wesen "des Königs Israels", wie ihn die Ältesten Israels gewollt hatten, vorstellte. Saul ist tot, seine Söhne gefallen und ausgerottet, Michal von David getrennt,[48] die Hoffnung auf einen Thronerben aus israelitischem Geist begraben; Jerusalem hat gesiegt.

Nach Ansicht des Erzählers siegte Jerusalem in dem Moment, als David mit der Lade den Gott Israels nach Jerusalem holte, aber das Erbe Sauls ausschlug, indem er nicht Vergangenes erneuerte, sondern Neues begann. Allerdings war all dies neu nur für Israel, nicht für die alteingesessenen vorisraelitischen Bevölkerungselemente. Zu Anfang der Prozession sichert der König den begonnenen Umzug mit einem vielleicht noch genuin israelitisch interpretierbaren Schlachtopfer (vi 13). Den feierlichen Abschluß am Bestimmungsort aber bildet (vi 17) eine Kombination von Brand- und Schelamimopfer, wie sie in der kanaanäischen Umwelt, namentlich in Ugarit[49] üblich waren.

---

[47] Invertierter Verbalsatz.

[48] Ihre 2 Sam. xxi 8 erwähnten, von David den Gibeoniten ausgelieferten Kinder könnten durchaus zur alten Überlieferung gehören und danach der Ehe mit Paltiel (es wäre dann der Name des Vaters, nicht der der Mutter verwechselt) entstammen; dazu würde das Verhalten Paltiels bei Michals Fortführung passen: Er betrauert seine Frau wie eine Tote, sieht also selbst seine Ehe als gewaltsam, aber nicht durch Scheidung seinerseits beendet an.

[49] B. Janowski, "Erwägungen zur Vorgeschichte des israelitischen *šᵉlamîm*-Opfers", *UF* 12 (1980), pp. 231–59, erwägt (p. 251) Übernahme von den Mykenern. Jedenfalls geht es bei dieser Kombination von Ganzopfer und Mahlopfer mit Teilverbrennung, die als Holokautoma + Thysia auch in die griechische Kultpraxis übernommen wurde, um ein in der zweiten Hälfte des 2. Jtsd. v.Chr. in den östlichen Mittelmeer- bzw. den westlichen Bereich des Vorderen Orients gelangtes Ritual, das in Ugarit v.a. den Kontext von Totenmahl und Ahnenverehrung hatte.

So ist in einem ugaritischen Text[50] im Zusammenhang von Riten zum Einzug von Götterstatuen in den Königspalast das Schelamimopfer erwähnt. Die Beschreibung der von David veranstalteten Opfer könnte also für die Primäradressaten durchaus mehr Hintergrundinformationen über die Richtung, die er bezüglich seiner Kultpolitik und damit auch seiner Königtumskonzeption einschlug, enthalten als für moderne Leserinnen.[51]

Michal paßte nicht ans Fenster eines Jerusalemer Frauenhauses, nicht einmal in das Erscheinungsfenster einer palästinischen Stadtfürstin[52] und wahrscheinlich auch in keinen Palast. Vielleicht blickte sie nach dem ursprünglichen Verständnis der Erzählung nur verstohlen durch die Lichtluke eines Wohnhauses, während die "Mägde", als die sie die Damen der Stadtaristokratie bezeichnet, am Fest teilnahmen.

Durch das Fenster ihres Hauses hatte sie David einst den Häschern Sauls entkommen lassen, und damit hatten sich ihre Wege im Grunde schon endgültig getrennt. Der Mann, der im leinenen Priesterschurz[53] einen kultischen Solotanz aufführte und anschließend mit Brand- und Schelamimopfer und Speisenverteilung ein Kultfest kanaanäischer Stadtkultur beging, war nicht mehr ihr Mann—und er war, nach ihrer und somit nach der Ansicht des durch sie sprechenden Erzählers, auch nicht mehr in dem Sinne, in dem Saul es gewesen war, der König von Israel.

---

[50] *KTU* 1.43, zitiert bei Janowski, *UF* 12, p. 234.

[51] In 1 Chr. xvi 1 wird das Problem umgangen, indem 3. pl. m. steht: "Sie", und d.h. in diesem Zusammenhang, die Priester "opferten", David aber "schließt" nur (*v.* 2) das Opfer mit Segen und Speiseverteilung "ab".

[52] Bei der aus dem Fenster blickenden Michal—einem sehr allgemeinen Topos!—an Kultprostitution, die Göttin am Fenster oder heilige Hochzeit zu denken, zeugt von nicht primär textbezogenen Assoziationen. Wenn man unbedingt in dem Fenster mehr sehen will als einen geeigneten Ort, um Davids Tanzplatz zu überblicken, so liegt jedenfalls die Reminiszenz an das Fenster, durch das David sie einst verließ, um sich auf ihr Betreiben und mit ihrer Hilfe vor ihrem Vater zu retten, sicher näher, dazu s.o. n. 22.

[53] Das Efod läßt sich (mit M. Görg, Art. *Efod*, *NBL* I, 3 [1990], pp. 472–3) an allen at.lichen Belegstellen als "Götter- oder Priesterkleid", d.h. ein für sakrale Zwecke verwendbares Kleidungsstück verstehen. Nach *LÄ* IV, p. 1105, ist als ägyptische Priestertracht erst in der Spätzeit die altertümliche Schurztracht üblich. Ihr Gebrauch im Jerusalem der frühen Königszeit oder gar im vorisraelitischen Jerusalem ist sehr gut möglich. Es ist dann (vgl. A. Erman – H. Grapow, *Wörterbuch der Äg. Sprache . . . I* [Leipzig, 1926]. p. 71, s.v. *ἰfd*) an ein Leinenviereck zu denken, das als Schurz getragen wurde. In den P-Texten wird es im hohepriesterlichen Ornat durch Schürzenbänder bzw. Träger in der richtigen Position fixiert. Die Annahme, das Efod sei auch in Ugarit belegt, kann nach M. Dietrich – O. Loretz, "Der Tod Baals als Rache Mots für die Vernichtung Leviathans in *KTU* 1.5 I 1–8", *UF* 12 (1981), pp. 404–7, bes. p. 407, mit Diskussion der Forschungslage, nicht sicher aufrechterhalten werden.

SUPPLEMENTS TO VETUS TESTAMENTUM

2. Pope, M.H. *El in the Ugaritic texts.* 1955. ISBN 90 04 04000 5
3. *Wisdom in Israel and in the Ancient Near East.* Presented to Harold Henry Rowley by the Editorial Board of Vetus Testamentum in celebration of his 65th birthday, 24 March 1955. Edited by M. Noth and D. Winton Thomas. 2nd reprint of the first (1955) ed. 1969. ISBN 90 04 02326 7
4. *Volume du Congrès* [International pour l'étude de l'Ancien Testament]. Strasbourg 1956. 1957. ISBN 90 04 02327 5
8. Bernhardt, K.-H. *Das Problem der alt-orientalischen Königsideologie im Alten Testament.* Unter besonderer Berücksichtigung der Geschichte der Psalmenexegese dargestellt und kritisch gewürdigt. 1961. ISBN 90 04 02331 3
9. *Congress Volume,* Bonn 1962. 1963. ISBN 90 04 02332 1
11. Donner, H. *Israel unter den Völkern.* Die Stellung der klassischen Propheten des 8. Jahrhunderts v. Chr. zur Aussenpolitik der Könige von Israel und Juda. 1964. ISBN 90 04 02334 8
12. Reider, J. *An Index to Aquila.* Completed and revised by N. Turner. 1966. ISBN 90 04 02335 6
13. Roth, W.M.W. *Numerical sayings in the Old Testament.* A form-critical study. 1965. ISBN 90 04 02336 4
14. Orlinsky, H.M. *Studies on the second part of the Book of Isaiah.* — The so-called 'Servant of the Lord' and 'Suffering Servant' in Second Isaiah. — Snaith, N.H. Isaiah 40-66. A study of the teaching of the Second Isaiah and its consequences. Repr. with additions and corrections. 1977. ISBN 90 04 05437 5
15. *Volume du Congrès* [International pour l'étude de l'Ancien Testament]. Genève 1965. 1966. ISBN 90 04 02337 2
17. *Congress Volume,* Rome 1968. 1969. ISBN 90 04 02339 9
19. Thompson, R.J. *Moses and the Law in a century of criticism since Graf.* 1970. ISBN 90 04 02341 0
20. Redford, D.B. *A study of the biblical story of Joseph.* 1970. ISBN 90 04 02342 9
21. Ahlström, G.W. *Joel and the temple cult of Jerusalem.* 1971. ISBN 90 04 02620 7
22. *Congress Volume,* Uppsala 1971. 1972. ISBN 90 04 03521 4
23. *Studies in the religion of ancient Israel.* 1972. ISBN 90 04 03525 7
24. Schoors, A. *I am God your Saviour.* A form-critical study of the main genres in Is. xl-lv. 1973. ISBN 90 04 03792 2
25. Allen, L.C. *The Greek Chronicles.* The relation of the Septuagint I and II Chronicles to the Massoretic text. Part 1. The translator's craft. 1974. ISBN 90 04 03913 9
26. *Studies on prophecy.* A collection of twelve papers. 1974. ISBN 90 04 03877 9
27. Allen, L.C. *The Greek Chronicles.* Part 2. Textual criticism. 1974. ISBN 90 04 03933 3
28. *Congress Volume,* Edinburgh 1974. 1975. ISBN 90 04 04321 7
29. *Congress Volume,* Göttingen 1977. 1978. ISBN 90 04 05835 4
30. Emerton, J.A. (ed.). *Studies in the historical books of the Old Testament.* 1979. ISBN 90 04 06017 0
31. Meredino, R.P. *Der Erste und der Letzte.* Eine Untersuchung von Jes 40-48. 1981. ISBN 90 04 06199 1
32. Emerton, J.A. (ed.). *Congress Vienna* 1980. 1981. ISBN 90 04 06514 8
33. Koenig, J. *L'herméneutique analogique du Judaïsme antique d'après les témoins textuels d'Isaïe.* 1982. ISBN 90 04 06762 0

34. Barstad, H.M. *The religious polemics of Amos.* Studies in the preachings of Amos ii 7B-8, iv 1-13, v 1-27, vi 4-7, viii 14. 1984. ISBN 90 04 07017 6
35. Krašovec, J. *Antithetic structure in Biblical Hebrew poetry.* 1984. ISBN 90 04 07244 6
36. Emerton, J.A. (ed.). *Congress Volume,* Salamanca 1983. 1985. ISBN 90 04 07281 0
37. Lemche, N.P. *Early Israel.* Anthropological and historical studies on the Israelite society before the monarchy. 1985. ISBN 90 04 07853 3
38. Nielsen, K. *Incense in Ancient Israel.* 1986. ISBN 90 04 07702 2
39. Pardee, D. *Ugaritic and Hebrew poetic parallelism.* A trial cut. 1988. ISBN 90 04 08368 5
40. Emerton, J.A. (ed.). *Congress Volume,* Jerusalem 1986. 1988. ISBN 90 04 08499 1
41. Emerton, J.A. (ed.). *Studies in the Pentateuch.* 1990. ISBN 90 04 09195 5
42. McKenzie, S.L. *The trouble with Kings.* The composition of the Book of Kings in the Deuteronomistic History. 1991. ISBN 90 04 09402 4
43. Emerton, J.A. (ed.). *Congress Volume,* Leuven 1989. 1991. ISBN 90 04 09398 2
44. Haak, R.D. *Habakkuk.* 1992. ISBN 90 04 09506 3
45. Beyerlin, W. *Im Licht der Traditionen.* Psalm LXVII und CXV. Ein Entwicklungszusammenhang. 1992. ISBN 90 04 09635 3
46. Meier, S.A. *Speaking of Speaking.* Marking direct discourse in the Hebrew Bible. 1992. ISBN 90 04 09602 7
47. Kessler, R. *Staat und Gesellschaft im vorexilischen Juda.* Vom 8. Jahrhundert bis zum Exil. 1992. ISBN 90 04 09646 9
48. Auffret, P. *Voyez de vos yeux.* Étude structurelle de vingt psaumes, dont le psaume 119. 1993. ISBN 90 04 09707 4
49. García Martínez, F., A. Hilhorst and C.J. Labuschagne (eds.). *The Scriptures and the Scrolls.* Studies in honour of A.S. van der Woude on the occasion of his 65th birthday. 1992. ISBN 90 04 09746 5
50. Lemaire, A. and B. Otzen (eds.). *History and Traditions of Early Israel.* Studies presented to Eduard Nielsen, May 8th, 1993. 1993. ISBN 90 04 09851 8
51. Gordon, R.P. *Studies in the Targum to the Twelve Prophets.* From Nahum to Malachi. 1994. ISBN 90 04 09987 5
52. Hugenberger, G.P. *Marriage as a Covenant.* A Study of Biblical Law and Ethics Governing Marriage Developed from the Perspective of Malachi. 1994. ISBN 90 04 09977 8
53. García Martínez, F., A. Hilhorst, J.T.A.G.M. van Ruiten, A.S. van der Woude. *Studies in Deuteronomy.* In Honour of C.J. Labuschagne on the Occasion of His 65th Birthday. 1994. ISBN 90 04 10052 0
54. Fernandéz Marcos, N. *Septuagint and Old Latin in the Book of Kings.* 1994. ISBN 90 04 10043 1
55. Smith, M.S. *The Ugaritic Baal Cycle. Volume 1.* Introduction with text, translation and commentary of KTU 1.1-1.2. 1994. ISBN 90 04 09995 6
56. Duguid, I.M. *Ezekiel and the Leaders of Israel.* 1994. ISBN 90 04 10074 1
57. Marx, A. *Les offrandes végétales dans l'Ancien Testament.* Du tribut d'hommage au repas eschatologique. 1994. ISBN 90 04 10136 5
58. Schäfer-Lichtenberger, C. *Josua und Salomo.* Eine Studie zu Autorität und Legitimität des Nachfolgers im Alten Testament. 1995. ISBN 90 04 10064 4
59. Lasserre, G. *Synopse des lois du Pentateuque.* 1994. ISBN 90 04 10202 7
60. Dogniez, C. *Bibliography of the Septuagint – Bibliographie de la Septante (1970-1993).* Avec une préface de Pierre-Maurice Bogaert. 1995. ISBN 90 04 10192 6
61. Emerton, J.A. (ed.). *Congress Volume,* Paris 1992. 1995. ISBN 90 04 10259 0

62. Smith, P.A. *Rhetoric and Redaction in Trito-Isaiah.* The Structure, Growth and Authorship of Isaiah 56-66. 1995. ISBN 90 04 10306 6
63. O'Connell, R.H. *The Rhetoric of the Book of Judges.* 1996. ISBN 90 04 10104 7
64. Harland, P.J. *The Value of Human Life.* A Study of the Story of the Flood (Genesis 6-9). 1996. ISBN 90 04 10534 4
65. Roland Page Jr., H. *The Myth of Cosmic Rebellion.* A Study of its Reflexes in Ugaritic and Biblical Literature. 1996. ISBN 90 04 10563 8
66. Emerton, J.A. (ed.). *Congress Volume.* Cambridge 1995. 1997. ISBN 90 04 106871
67. Joosten, J. *People and Land in the Holiness Code.* An Exegetical Study of the Ideational Framework of the Law in Leviticus 17–26. 1996. ISBN 90 04 10557 3
68. Beentjes, P.C. *The Book of Ben Sira in Hebrew.* A Text Edition of all Extant Hebrew Manuscripts and a Synopsis of all Parallel Hebrew Ben Sira Texts. 1997. ISBN 90 04 10767 3
69. Cook, J. *The Septuagint of Proverbs – Jewish and/or Hellenistic Proverbs?* Concerning the Hellenistic Colouring of LXX Proverbs. 1997. ISBN 90 04 10879 3
70. I. Broyles, G. and C. Evans (eds.). *Writing and Reading the Scroll of Isaiah.* Studies of an Interpretive Tradition. 1997. ISBN 90 04 10936 6 (*Vol.* I); ISBN 90 04 11027 5 (*Set*)
70. II. Broyles, G. and C. Evans (eds.). *Writing and Reading the Scroll of Isaiah.* Studies of an Interpretive Tradition. 1997. ISBN 90 04 11026 7 (*Vol.* II); ISBN 90 04 11027 5 (*Set*)